NARRATIVE STRUCTURE
AND
DISCOURSE CONSTELLATIONS

HARVARD SEMITIC MUSEUM PUBLICATIONS

Lawrence E. Stager, General Editor
Michael D. Coogan, Director of Publications

HARVARD SEMITIC STUDIES

Jo Ann Hackett and John Huehnergard, editors

NARRATIVE STRUCTURE
AND
DISCOURSE CONSTELLATIONS

*An Analysis of Clause Function
in Biblical Hebrew Prose*

by

Roy L. Heller

EISENBRAUNS
Winona Lake, Indiana
2004

NARRATIVE STRUCTURE AND DISCOURSE CONSTELLATIONS
An Analysis of Clause Function in Biblical Hebrew Prose

by
Roy L. Heller

Printed in the United States of America

Library of Congress Cataloging-in-Publication Data

Heller, Roy L., 1963
    Narrative structure and discourse constellations : an analysis of clause
function in biblical Hebrew prose / by Roy L. Heller.
      p.   cm. — (Harvard Semitic studies ; no. 55)
    Includes bibliographic references and index.
    ISBN 1-57506-918-0 (cloth)
    1. Hebrew language—Syntax. 2. Hebrew language—Clauses. 3. Bible.
O.T. Genesis XXXVII–XLVII—Criticism, Narrative. 4. Bible. O.T. Samuel,
2nd, IX–XX—Criticism, Narrative. 5. Narration in the Bible. 6. Hebrew
language—Discourse analysis. 7. Hebrew prose literature. I. Title.
II. Series.
PJ4717.H45   2004
492.4′5—dc22

                           2003025470

Dedication

To the memory of my grandfather, Roy Harvey, who taught me that
without passion, all study is worthless;

To my grandmother, Minnie Harvey, who taught me that
without goodness, all study is worthless;

To my parents, Louis and Velma Heller, who taught me that
without discipline, all study is worthless;

To my wife, Amy, who continually teaches me that
without love, all study is worthless; and

To my children, Noah and Anne, who, every day, teach me that
there are some things in life more important than study,

This book is dedicated.

Contents

Acknowledgments

While a study such as this seems to claim to be the final fruition of the work of a single scholar, no study is such. It is based upon innumerable sources, countless hours of conversation among colleagues and numerous opportunities for probing and questioning of and from many advisors, both informal and official. While the flowering of the research appears as a single work, its roots are multitude. I want, here, to thank several persons and organizations that have helped this work to continue on its way to this point.

I must express my gratitude to Yale University who provided me with both Graduate Fellowships and a Dissertation Fellowship. Without its generous financial support, I could have never begun a graduate program, much less completed one. I also would like to thank Christ Church Parish, New Haven, for their support—both financial and personal—during the final two years of the writing of the dissertation upon which this work is based.

During the extended time that I was editing this work, I have been extremely grateful to the administration of Perkins School of Theology for their financial assistance, and to the community of St. Michael and All Angels Episcopal Church, for their emotional and spiritual support during these, often harrowing, last three years.

My mentor, Robert R. Wilson, has been a constant source of encouragement and insight in this process. His willingness to allow his students the freedom to explore while simultaneously holding them to strict standards of professionalism and scholarship has been an example of graduate education that I hope to continue in my own career.

I also want to thank Mark S. Smith who, in a graduate seminar on "Advanced Hebrew Grammar" in the Fall of 1991, made the off-hand comment, while working through Waltke and O'Connor's *Biblical Hebrew Syntax*, that verbal function in narrative seemed to be very different from verbal function in direct discourse. Because of that small seed planted in my head and heart, this study has come to be.

I am extremely grateful for the encouragement and dedication of my editors, Michael Coogan, Jo Ann Hackett, and John Huehnergard. Thanks to them, this book is far better than it once was.

And, finally, I thank my wife, Amy, for her unwavering faith and unrelenting emotional support in the midst of all the chaos that has occurred during the past decade. Because of her love and dedication, I find within myself the hope and confidence to continue both my studies and writing.

For what is true and positive in this work, I must thank my colleagues and mentors. Any errors that remain are, of course, my own responsibility.

Roy L. Heller, Dallas, 2003

List of Abbreviations

Abbreviations are those used by the Society of Biblical Literature.
Quotations are sometimes drawn from the RSV and NRSV; where there is no
notation, the translations are those of the author.

AB	Anchor Bible
ABD	*Anchor Bible Dictionary* (ed. D. N. Freedman; Garden City: Doubleday, 1992)
BDB	Francis Brown, S. R. Driver, and C. A. Briggs, *A Hebrew and English Lexicon of the Old Testament* (Oxford: Clarendon, 1971)
BHS	*Biblia Hebraica Stuttgartensia*
BSO(A)S	*Bulletin of the School of Oriental (and African) Studies*
BWANT	Beiträge zur Wissenschaft vom Alten und Neuen Testament
BZ	*Biblische Zeitschrift*
BZAW	Beihefte zur *Zeitschrift für die altestamentliche Wissenschaft*
CBQ	*Catholic Biblical Quarterly*
CBQMS	Catholic Biblical Quarterly Monograph Series
CILT	Centre for Information on Language Teaching and Research
CJT	*Canadian Journal of Theology*
CN	Narrative of David's Court (2 Sam 9:1-20:26; 1 Kgs 1:1-2:46)
Coh.	Cohortative
ED	Expository Discourse
FOTL	Forms of the Old Testament Literature
HD	Hortatory Discourse
HSS	Harvard Semitic Studies
ID	Interrogative Discourse
ICC	International Critical Commentary
Impv.	Imperative
JAAR	*Journal of the American Academy of Religion*
JBL	*Journal of Biblical Literature*
JBLMS	Journal of Biblical Literature Monograph Series
JN	Joseph Novella (Gen 37:1-36; 39:1–46:8a; 46:26–47:27)
JNES	*Journal of Near Eastern Studies*
JNSL	*Journal of Northwest Semitic Languages*
JSOT	*Journal for the Study of the Old Testament*
JSOTSupp	Journal for the Study of the Old Testament Supplements
Juss.	Jussive
KHCAT	Kurzer Hand-Commentar zum Alten Testament
LXX	Septuagint
MT	Massoretic Text (as represented in *BHS*)
ND	Narrative Discourse
NRSV	New Revised Standard Version
Q	Qere

PD	Predictive Discourse
RSV	Revised Standard Version
SBL	Society of Biblical Literature
SS	Syntax and Semantics
SSU	Studia Semitica Upsaliensa
TANAKH	*TANAKH: The Holy Scriptures* (New York: The Jewish Publication Society of America, 1985)
TSK	*Theologische Studien und Kritiken*
UF	*Ugarit-Forschungen*
VT	*Vetus Testamentum*
VTSupp	Vetus Testamentum Supplements
ZAW	*Zeitschrift für die altestamentliche Wissenschaft*
ZDMG	*Zeitschrift der deutschen morgenländische Gesellschaft*
ZDMG Supp	*Zeitschrift der deutschen morgenländische Gesellschaft Supplementband*
ZP	*Zeitschrift für Phonetik*
†	Quotation within a speech
††	Quotation within a quotation within a speech
//	Precedes a reference to an original speech that is quoted or paraphrased
. . .	Paragraph/speech continues before or after a quotation
( )	Enclosure of Inner-Paragraph Comment
- - - - - - - - - -	Enclosure before and after Extra-Paragraph Comment

Chapter One
The Structure of Biblical Narrative and the
Functions of Biblical Discourse:
An Introduction to the Problem

In his *Introduction to Biblical Hebrew,* Thomas O. Lambdin points out a characteristic of the structuring function of clauses in biblical Hebrew:

> One of the most striking features of Hebrew prose syntax is the relative rarity of subordinating conjunctions marking adverbial clauses as such. Instead, one finds almost interminable sequences of clauses connected only by a form of the conjunction wə- (and). A closer inspection of these sequences, however, has shown us that there is a great deal of differentiation in clause function signalled, not by variation of the conjunction, but by a variation of the word order within the clause or by a variation of the verbal form used immediately after the conjunction.[1]

Lambdin notes that all clauses in biblical Hebrew may be divided into two main categories:

1) *conjunctive-sequential,* in which the second clause is temporally or logically posterior or consequent to the first, and
2) *disjunctive,* in which the second clause may be in various relations, all nonsequential, with the first.

The basic signal that differentiates between conjunctive and disjunctive clauses, Lambdin notes, is the type of word that stands immediately after the wə- :

wə- (or wa-) + verb is conjunctive
wə- + non-verb is disjunctive.[2]

---

[1] Thomas O. Lambdin, *Introduction to Biblical Hebrew* (New York: Charles Scribner's Sons, 1971), 162.
[2] Lambdin, *Introduction,* 162.

The following outline shows the possible conjunctive clauses that, according to Lambdin, may occur within narrative sequences or in imperative sequences:

  (1) the narrative sequences:
      (a) punctual past tense: perfect + *wa* + (short) imperfect
      (b) punctual future or punctual habitual: imperfect + *wə* + perfect
      (c) immediate future: non-verbal clause + *wə* + perfect
  (2) the imperative sequences:
      (a) explicit consecution: imperative + *wə* + perfect
      (b) purpose or result: imperative + *wə* + imperfect.[3]

Lambdin notes that, among the range of possible disjunctive clause types, most function in one of four basic ways in biblical Hebrew prose:

a) *contrastive*, by which the disjunctive clause is contrasted to the immediately preceding clause;
b) *circumstantial*, by which the disjunctive clause is seen as preceding or as synchronous with the preceding clause;
c) *explanatory* or *parenthetical*, by which the disjunctive clause provides information not temporally related to the preceding clause; and
d) *terminative* or *initial*, by which the disjunctive clause signals the end or beginning of an episode within a larger storyline.[4]

By means of these categories of conjunctive and disjunctive clause types, Lambdin suggests, the whole of biblical Hebrew prose provides the deep texture and narratological variations that have been recognized by biblical interpreters.

Lambdin's discussion, standing as it does within an introductory grammar, is, of course, limited. His examples are few and any objective criterion by which one may distinguish between the various functions of disjunctive clauses is lacking. While Lambdin's explanation is very suggestive, a more thorough and uniform treatment of the various functions of clauses in biblical Hebrew prose is needed—a treatment that is consistent and textually based.

Lambdin's categories are essentially functional or pragmatic; that is, rather than trying to explain the various verbal forms in terms of inherent meaning, Lambdin instead notes that the various clauses perform certain tasks in their structuring of biblical Hebrew prose. Within the past decade, Lambdin's insights have paralleled the work of discourse linguists, who take their basic stance toward language by asking "What does this verbal form/word/clause do?" instead of asking "What does this verbal form/word/clause mean?"[5]

---

[3]Lambdin, *Introduction,* 163.
[4]Lambdin, *Introduction,* 163-64.
[5]For a full discussion of the aims and methods of discourse-linguistics, see the treatment later in this chapter.

This examination, based upon these suggestive comments by Lambdin and taking its methodological bearings from the work of discourse linguistics, will provide a functional/pragmatic treatment of the various clause types within Biblical Hebrew prose. In the remainder of this introductory chapter, I will survey four basic treatments of the problem of the Hebrew verb and clause types in the history of biblical scholarship: tense-based approaches, historical-comparative approaches, aspect-based approaches, and, most recently, discourse-linguistic approaches. These four general (but not necessarily mutually exclusive) methods all attempt to explain how the grammar and syntax of classical and biblical Hebrew produce the fullness and intricacy of expression that the language, almost self-evidently, has.[6] After a survey of these approaches, the chapter will conclude with an outline of the basic method and objectives of this study.

A Historical Survey of Approaches

Tense-Based Approaches

The earliest Jewish grammarians, probably under the influence of their native Arabic, saw the verbal system of biblical Hebrew as based upon tense.[7] They noted that the foundational two conjugations, *QATAL* and *YIQTOL,* referred, respectively, to past tense and future tense.[8] The addition of the *waw* onto *QATAL*

---

[6]Throughout this study, the distinction between "biblical" and "classical" Hebrew will be an important one. While the two terms are often used interchangeably, in this work "biblical" Hebrew will refer to the written Hebrew language found in the Bible. Most often, the specific text meant when the phrase "biblical Hebrew" is used will be the *Biblia Hebraica Stuttgartensia* (ed. K. Elliger and W. Rudolph; Stuttgart: Deutsche Bibelgesellschaft, 1984) edition of the Masoretic Text of the Hebrew Bible. "Classical" Hebrew refers to the language spoken during the first millennium BCE and preserved through writing, not only in the Hebrew Bible, but also in epigraphical artifacts and also in extended corpora, such as the Qumran scrolls. The primary interest in this study will be the system of the verb in, specifically, "biblical" Hebrew.

[7]The historical surveys of the tense-based approaches and early aspect-based approaches are gleaned from Leslie McFall, *The Enigma of the Hebrew Verbal System: Solutions from Ewald to the Present Day* (Sheffield: Almond, 1982), and from Bruce Waltke and M. O'Connor, *An Introduction to Biblical Hebrew Syntax* (Winona Lake: Eisenbrauns, 1990), in particular pp. 455-66.

[8]In order not to prejudge the function or meaning of the various verbal or clausal forms in biblical Hebrew, this study will use the following descriptive terms:

QATAL = "suffix conjugation" or "perfect(ive) form"
WĕQATAL = "conjunctive *waw* + suffix conjugation/perfect"
YIQTOL = "prefix conjugation" or "imperfect(ive) form"
WĕYIQTOL = "conjunctive *waw* + prefix conjugation/imperfect"
WAYYIQTOL = "*waw*-consecutive + (short) prefix conjugation"

could, furthermore, "convert" the tense of the verb to its opposite; thus *WēQAṬAL* signified a future tense. Likewise, the addition of the *waw* onto *YIQṬOL* could "convert" its future tense meaning into past; thus *WAYYIQṬOL* signified a past tense. The prefixed *waw* that changes or converts the meaning of the basic tense of the basic verbal form was called by many names. The famous medieval grammarian David Qimḥi (1160-1235) called it *waw haššārût*, "waw of service." It was, however, Elijah Levita (1468-1549) who coined what was to become its well-known, standard nomenclature: *waw hippûk*, "waw conversive."[9]

Until the seventeenth century, the tense-oriented explanation was universal. The medieval Jewish grammarians' designations of the three representations of tense, *QAṬAL/WAYYIQṬOL* (past), *QŌṬĒL* (the participial form, present), and *YIQṬOL/WeYIQṬOL/WēQAṬAL* (future) were taken over into the studies of the earliest Christian scholars of Hebrew.[10] Yet, near the end of the eighteenth century, some scholars became bewildered and frustrated with the simple tense based approach. C. Bayley, in 1782, remarked what was clearly true yet almost universally denied: "The Tenses are often used promiscuously especially in the poetic and prophetic books."[11] While it is true that *usually WAYYIQṬOL* signifies the past tense, it does not always do so. The other conjugations are even more varied in their meanings.[12] Because of these weaknesses, the view that the Hebrew verbal

---

[9]Waltke and O'Connor, *Syntax*, 459. The technical term "conversive *waw*" is generally used by scholars who hold to a basic temporal view of the Hebrew verbal system. Additional names are often given by those who hold differing views; for example, the term "consecutive *waw*" or "*waw*-consecutive" is generally used to those holding to an aspectual perspective. In many recent works (including this study) the descriptive terms, "*WAYYIQṬOL*" or "*wayyqtl*" are most often used. This descriptive term for the form is an attempt not to unduly skew the meaning or function of the form at the outset.

[10]The *waw* that seemed, according to Levita, to "overturn" the meaning of the base verbal form, the *waw hippûk*, was called by the Christian Hebraists the *waw conversivum*; the simple waw, called by Levita the *waw ḥibbûr* (*waw* of joining) was called the *waw conjunctivum*. See Waltke and O'Connor, *Syntax*, 459.

[11]Cornelius Bayley, *An entrance into the sacred language containing the necessary rules of Hebrew Grammar in English* (London: n.p., 1782), 22.

[12]McFall (*Enigma*, 18-21) has noted the English tense used by the translators of the *Revised Standard Version* of the Bible for occurrences of *YIQṬOL*. Throughout the Bible, it is rendered as a past tense 774 times, a present tense 3,376 times, a future tense 5,451 times, a non-past modal 1,200 times, a past modal 423 times, an imperative 2,133 times, a jussive/cohortative 789 times, and non-verbally 153 times. In the book of Job, the *QAṬAL* conjugation is rendered as a past tense 252 times, as a present tense 244 times; *WēQAṬAL* is rendered as a past 12 times, a present 23 times, and a future 14 times. Job is, of course, mostly a poetic book, rather than a prose narrative.

system is *grammatically* marked for tense has not been generally held since the mid-nineteenth century.[13]

In 1821 Philip Gell, however, offered a solution to the seeming capricious nature of the verbal forms. In his view, the meaning of a verb in a clause should be seen syntactically in combination with the previous clause, rather than as a separate entity:

> When two or more Verbs are connected in Hebrew, the leading or Governing Verb expresses the absolute and General Time to be understood throughout the Series; and the subordinate Verbs are, in this respect, elliptical: they have the temporal power of the Governing Verb, by an ideal communication, implied in them.[14]

Gell's theory was revolutionary in that he saw that the meaning of verbs is not simply inherent in the morphology of the verb itself, but is also conditioned upon the wider context of the clause in which the verb is found.[15]

There were problems, however. The meaning and function of *WěQAṬAL*, did not work well with Gell's theory, as he himself acknowledged. Moreover, Gell could not sufficiently answer the question of which verbs in a series should be seen as "governing" and which are "subordinate." The work of Gell, however, was a proleptic venture into an area investigated further in the late twentieth century by scholars holding the discourse-linguistic approach to understanding texts, to which I will turn in a moment.

The inherent weaknesses of the simple tense approach to explain the meaning of the biblical text itself finally caused the internal collapse of the approach as a whole and made way for the development of two separate perspectives on the Hebrew verbal forms, one nuancing the tense-based theory with comparative work in other ancient Near Eastern languages and one completely abandoning the tense-based system for one based upon verbal aspects. Both theories have strong supporters down to the present day.

---

[13]This statement does not mean that tense is not represented in the written language. The theory, however, that a single grammatical verbal form (e.g., *QAṬAL* or *YIQṬOL*) is a consistent marker for a specific tense (e.g., past tense or future tense) collapsed in the early 1800s purely out of the tremendous number of exceptions being made to the rule.

[14]Philip Gell, *Observations on the Idiom of the Hebrew Language, Respecting the Powers Peculiar to the Different Tenses* (2d ed.; London: Richard Watts, 1821), 8.

[15]The thirteen original editions (1813-1842) of the grammar by W. Gesenius all held to the basic temporal view of the Hebrew verbal system including the "conversive" nature of the *waw* in *WAYYIQṬOL* verbal forms and of the double-clause syntactical theory, based, mostly, upon the views of Gell (Waltke and O'Connor, *Syntax*, 459).

Historical-Comparative Approaches

While other Semitic languages, in particular Aramaic, Arabic and Ethiopic, had long been used by scholars to explain the biblical Hebrew verbal system, it was not until the successful decipherment of Akkadian in 1857 that significant comparative work was performed. The 1889 thesis of J. A. Knudtzon, *Om det saakaldte Perfectum og Imperfectum i Hebraisk* (*On the So-Called Perfect and Imperfect in Hebrew*) stated that the *QAṬAL* form of the verb was not essentially a past tense form but rather a present tense form, based upon the permansive-perfect in Akkadian.[16] The sense of the active *QAṬAL* form found in biblical Hebrew developed, according to Knudtzon, very naturally from this "present at hand" meaning, "since 'he is old' easily changes to 'he has become old'; 'he is clothed' to 'he has clothed himself'; 'he is a murderer' to 'he has murdered'."[17] While Knudtzon's theory has not held up under closer scrutiny, his comparative work paved the way for other studies, many studying the reflexes of the *WAYYIQṬOL* form in Northwest Semitic.

H. Bauer, both in a seminal article published in 1910 and in his historical grammar of Hebrew first published in 1922, set the stage for the historical understanding of the past tense meaning of the *WAYYIQṬOL* form.[18] According to Bauer, in proto-Semitic the prefix conjugation (*YIQṬOL*), which he called the "aorist," functioned as a perfect participle and the suffix

---

[16]For the permansive-perfect in Akkadian, see the seminal work of J. Barth, "Das semitische Perfect im Assyrischen," *Zeitschrift für Assyriologie* 2 (1887), 375-86; see also, more recently, M. B. Rowton, "The Use of the Permansive in Classic Babylonian," *JNES* 21 (1962), 233-303; Jussi Aro, "Parallels to the Akkadian Stative in West Semitic Languages," in *Studies in Honor of Benno Landsberger on His Seventy-Fifth Birthday, April 21, 1965*, ed. H. Güterbock and T. Jacobsen (Chicago: Chicago University, 1965), 407-415; Giorgio Buccellati, "An Interpretation of the Akkadian Stative as a Nominal Sentence," *JNES* 27 (1968), 1-12; and "The State of the 'Stative'," In *Fucus: A Semitic/Afrasian Gathering in Remembrance of Albert Ehrman*, (ed. Yoël L. Arbeitman; CILT 58; New York: Benjamins, 1988), 153-89; Burkhart Kienast, "Der sogenannte 'Stativ' des Akkadischen," *ZDMG* Supp 4 (1980), 84-86; F. R. Kraus, *Nominalsätze in Altbabylonische Briefen und der Stativ* (Amsterdam: Noord-hollandsche Uitgevers Maatschappij, 1984); John Huehnergard, "'Stative,' Predicative Form, Pseudo-Verb," *JNES* 46 (1987), 215-32; N. J. C. Kouwenberg, "Nouns as Verbs: The Verbal Nature of the Akkadian Stative," *Orientalia* 69 (2000), 21-71.

[17]McFall, *Engima*, 89.

[18]H. Bauer, "Die Tempora im Semitischen," *Beiträge zur Assyriologie und semitischen Sprachwissenschaft* 81 (1910), 1-53; H. Bauer and P. Leander, *Historische Grammatik der hebräischen Sprache des Alten Testaments* (Halle: Niemeyer, 1922). Note also the survey in McFall, *Engima*, 93-115.

conjugation (*QATAL*), which he called the "nominal," functioned as a present participle. On the basis of the Akkadian preterite *iprus* conjugation, Bauer believed that in proto-Semitic, an original preterite-jussive *yaqtul* "short form" conjugation developed diachron-ically into a future *yaqtula* "long form" conjugation. The original preterite *yaqtul* form can still be seen, according to Bauer, in poetry or, in narrative, in "fixed-word combinations" of אָז, (בְּ)טֶרֶם) or עַד־ with *yaqtul*.[19]

The discovery in 1928 of the Ugaritic tablets at Ras Shamra in Syria propelled the comparative method of study in Semitics to unprecedented lengths. In the study of verbal morphology, grammar, and syntax, however, the Ugaritic evidence did not lend itself easily to finding solutions because of its unvocalized nature. In some cases, nevertheless, it seemed to support a version of Bauer's view of the dual temporal nature of the *YIQTOL* conjugation. In this matter the work of W. L. Moran and Anson F. Rainey has shown that there were probably several distinct conjugations in the verbal system of proto-Semitic: a punctual *qatala*, a durative *yaqtulu*, a jussive or preterite *yaqtul*, and an "emphatic" jussive *yaqtula*.[20] When final short vowels were dropped from nouns and verbs

---

[19]The grammar of G. Bergsträsser (*Hebräische Grammatik* [vol. 2; Leipzig: J. C. Hinrichs, 1929]) was built fully upon the Bauer theory of the dual temporal nature (i.e., future/jussive and preterite) of the *YIQTOL* form. See also: Anson F. Rainey, "The Ancient Hebrew Prefix Conjugation in the Light of Amarnah Canaanite," *Hebrew Studies* 27 (1986), 4-19; J. A. Hughes, "Another Look at the Hebrew Tenses," *JNES* 29 (1970), 12-24; Douglas M. Gropp, "Progress and Cohesion in Biblical Hebrew Narrative: The Function of kĕ/bĕ + the Infinitive Construct," in *Discourse Analysis of Biblical Literature*, (Walter R. Bodine, ed; Atlanta: Scholars, 1995) 183-212. Note also the comprehensive summary of the problem of the *WAYYIQTOL* form in Mark S. Smith, *The Origins and Development of the Waw-Consecutive: Northwest Semitic Evidence from Ugarit and Qumran* (HSS 39; Atlanta: Scholars, 1991).

[20]Moran's work has mainly concentrated on the Amarna correspondence; Rainey's, on the Ras Shamra tablets. W. L. Moran, "A Syntactical Study of the Dialect of Byblos as Reflected in the Amarna Tablets" (Ph.D. diss.; Johns Hopkins University, 1950); "Early Canaanite *yaqtula*," *Orientalia* 29 (1960), 1-19; "The Hebrew Language in Its Northwest Semitic Background," in *The Bible and the Ancient Near East: Essays in Honor of William Foxwell Albright* (ed. G. E. Wright; Garden City: Doubleday, 1961), 54-66, esp. 63-66; *Amarna Studies: Collected Writings* (ed. John Huehnergard and Shlomo Isre'el; Winona Lake: Eisenbrauns, 2003). See also Anson F. Rainey, "Reflections of the Suffix Conjugation in West Semitized Amarna Tablets," *UF* 5 (1973), 235-62; "Morphology and the Prefix-Tenses of West Semitized El Amarna Tablets," *UF* 7 (1975), 395-426; "Further Remarks on the Hebrew Verbal System," *Hebrew Studies* 29 (1988), 35-42; "The Prefix Conjugation Patterns of Early Northwest Semitic," in *Lingering over Words: Studies in Ancient Near Eastern Literature in Honor of William L. Moran* (ed. T. Abusch, J. Huehnergard and P. Steinkeller; HSS 37; Atlanta: Scholars, 1990), 407-20.

in early Hebrew, around 1100 BCE, the durative, preterite, and jussive forms coalesced and thus produced the uneven nature of the Hebrew verbal system preserved in the Bible and in epigraphic artifacts.

This historical-comparative approach, like Gell's theory before it, was revolutionary. It has served well in explaining, diachronically, how the Hebrew verbal system developed. It, furthermore, accounts for what had been seen as the "capricious" nature of the Hebrew verbal system as a whole and goes far in explaining the biblical text as we have it. The few weaknesses that it does have are well known and need not be belabored here. There are those who point out that the "shortened form of the imperfect" (*yaqtul*) is not present in the very places where it is expected (e.g., Exod 15:1).[21] Moreover, the explanatory power of the historical-comparative, diachronic approach has been criticized when it is used to describe the meaning of actual verbal forms as they function synchronically within the text of the Bible. Ziony Zevit has noted: "Etymological explanations that purport to describe the origins of the Hebrew verbal system are inadequate as descriptions of how this system works in fact."[22] Eward Greenstein has further propounded the methodological formula: "Sense is determined not on the basis of forms [alone] but on the basis of the contrast or opposition of forms."[23] While the historical-comparative approaches have illuminated much in the development of the language, their diachronic explanations of the development of morphological forms should not be uncritically used to explain synchronic grammatical and syntactical problems.

Aspect-Based Approaches

The view that the syntax of the Hebrew verb is marked not for tense, but for aspect originates in the early nineteenth century with the work of Heinrich Ewald (1803-1875). In his 1827 Hebrew grammar, Ewald proposed that:

> The first aorist [or *QAṬAL*] conveys a completed (perfectam) thing, whether present, preterite, or future. . . . The second aorist [or

---

[21]J. Huehnergard, "The Early Hebrew Prefix-Conjugations," *Hebrew Studies* 29 (1988), 19-23; Ziony Zevit, "Talking Funny in Biblical Henglish and Solving a Problem of the Yaqtúl Past Tense," *Hebrew Studies* 29 (1988), 25-33.

[22]Zevit, "Yaqtúl Past Tense," 27.

[23]E. Greenstein, "On the Prefixed Preterite in Biblical Hebrew," *Hebrew Studies* 29 (1988), 7-17; quotation from 14. Note also Rainey's response in the same issue, "Further Remarks," 35-42.

YIQṬOL] conveys a non-completed (imperfectam) thing, whether present, preterite, or future.[24]

These two poles, the "perfect" and "imperfect," are, as Ewald continues, "the two grand and opposite aspects under which every conceivable action may be regarded." Regarding the perfect, McFall outlines Ewald's view: "It is used of actions which the speaker from his *present* regards as actually past and therefore complete. It is used of actions which are regarded as finished but which reach right into the present." Regarding the imperfect, McFall further summarizes: "From the basic idea of Incompleteness there arise two distinct meanings which are very widely different from one another. Firstly, what is stated absolutely to be incomplete refers to time and is therefore a mere time-form or tense. Secondly, what is stated to be dependent on something else is set forth as in a particular '*kind* of being, which hence becomes more a *mood* than a *tense.*'"[25]

In the minds of many, Ewald's view of the verbal system of biblical Hebrew more accurately described the data than did the defunct grammatical tense theories of the Jewish grammarians and Gell. One such scholar was S. R. Driver, who took Ewald's views and popularized them to such an extent that "perfect" and "imperfect" are still used as the names of the two basic verbal forms, even among those who do not have an aspectual view of the Hebrew verb.[26] For Driver, as for Ewald, the polar opposites were basically not marked for tense:

> It is . . . of the utmost consequence to understand and bear constantly
> in mind the fundamental and primary facts . . . : (1) that the Hebrew
> verb notifies the character without fixing the date of an action, and
> (2) that, of its two forms . . . , one is calculated to describe an action
> as *nascent* and so as imperfect; the other to describe it as *completed*
> and so as perfect.[27]

---

[24]G. H. A. von Ewald, *Kritische Grammatik der hebräischen Sprache* (Leipzig: J. C. Hinrichs, 1827), 524, §277.

[25]McFall, *Enigma*, 45-46. The quotation is from Ewald's *Ausführliches Lehrbuch der hebräischen Sprache des alten Bundes* (Leipzig: J. C. Hinrichs, 1870), 7. The eighth edition of this work (1870) was translated into English by J. Kennedy: *The Syntax of the Hebrew Language* (Edinburgh: T. & T. Clark, 1879).

[26]Credit should also be given to E. Rödiger, who took over the editing and updating of Gesenius' comprehensive grammar with the fourteenth edition and "immediately adopted Ewald's grammatical terms, Perfect and Imperfect" (McFall, *Enigma*, 15).

[27]Samuel R. Driver, *A Treatise on the Use of the Tenses in Hebrew and Some Other Syntactical Questions* (3d ed.; Oxford: Clarendon, 1892), 3. Hereafter the second edition of this work (1881) will be used and abbreviated as *Tenses*.

Driver's severing the tense from the verbal forms produced two irregularities in his theory, however. In order to explain the ubiquitous *QAṬAL* form present in prophecies throughout the Bible, Driver had to accept and develop an earlier view of Ewald—the prophetic perfect: "[With] ease and rapidity [the prophet] *changes his standpoint*, at one moment speaking of a scene as though still in the remote future, at another moment describing it as though present to his gaze."[28] The switching of verbal forms in biblical poetry is, therefore, dependent upon the mental or spiritual perspective of the seer at the moment of inspiration. This view has not held up well under closer scrutiny because it is as impossible to refute as it is impossible to prove.

The other problematic element in Driver's understanding is the sense of the *WAYYIQṬOL* form. Since, in Driver's conception, verbal forms are not marked for tense, the concept of a temporally "conversive-*waw*" was untenable for Driver's system. Driver proposed that the form, based as it was upon the imperfect, represented a "becoming" and "incomplete" activity, but relatively rather than absolutely. In a similar fashion to Gell's earlier temporal "double-clause" theory, Driver believed that in clauses governed by *WAYYIQṬOL*, or, as he named it, the "consecutive-" or "consequential-*waw*," the aspect of the clause is subordinate in relationship to the preceding verbal expression.[29] In his later work, however, Driver had to abandon this view of the "consecutive-*waw*" as unsupported textually.[30] With these two exceptions, within English-speaking biblical scholarship, the legacy of Driver is prevalent and persistent even to the present day.[31]

In the mid-twentieth century objections began to be raised against Ewald's and Driver's understanding of the Hebrew verbal system. The perfect/imperfect aspectual view began to be seen as simplistic and reductionistic and, moreover, not accurately representing the verbal forms found in prose as well as prophecy.[32] In his 1960 study of the conjugations in the Psalter, Diethelm Michel roundly criticized all contemporary approaches to the study of the Hebrew verbal system

---

[28]Driver, *Tenses,* 5 (emphasis mine).

[29]Driver, *Tenses,* 98.

[30]Driver, *Tenses* (3rd ed.; 1892), 94: "The use of the *waw*-consecutive in the historical books . . . renders it inconceivable that it should have suggested anything except the idea of a *fact done.*"

[31]The syntaxes of J. Wash Watts (*A Survey of Syntax in the Hebrew Old Testament* [Grand Rapids: Eerdmans, 1964]) and Ronald J. Williams (*Hebrew Syntax: An Outline* [2d ed.; Toronto: University of Toronto Press, 1976]) both establish their analyses of the verb upon aspectual bases.

[32]Note the criticisms of Waltke and O'Connor, *Syntax,* 464, 470.

and called for a fresh reappraisal of the material.[33] His criticism of the older temporal views, which in some quarters still had advocates, focuses on the *WAYYIQTOL* and *QATAL* forms:

> It appears unexpected and odd, to say the least, that a *tempus* should be turned around into its opposite by the mere prefixing of ‏ו‎. And if one further considers that this same form ‏ו‎ plus perfectum is said to be used on one occasion as a "perfectum copulativum," like the customary perfectum, and on another occasion as "perfectum consecutivum," like the customary imperfectum, the questions become unbearably loud.[34]

In criticizing the earlier aspectual views, Michel writes:

> Suddenly in poetry there is an "archaic narrative imperfectum with past meaning"; in poetry one must accept a "prophetic perfectum" and apply psychology in order to explain its existence; in poetry there is in direct address a "perfectum of execution," also called "declarative perfectum," which accompanies an action and therefore designates an uncompleted, present action.[35]

He also criticizes the historical-comparative methods:

> We do not take over . . . the results of comparative linguistic studies concerning the meaning of the Semitic verb forms. Where one can end up, if he takes his starting point here, Brockelmann has now shown very beautifully with the help of Bauer's theories. Comparative linguistics is only possible if the languages to be compared are understood on their own.[36]

Having thus rejected aspectual and temporal theories and comparative approaches to the verbal system, Michel investigates the function of the verb forms in the Psalms with an empirical and inductive method.

---

[33]Diethelm Michel, *Tempora und Satzstellung in den Psalmen* (Bonn: Bouvier, 1960); hereafter *Tempora*.

[34]Michel, *Tempora*, 12.

[35]Michel, *Tempora*, 11.

[36]Michel, *Tempora*, 14. Michel's criticisms here seem to imply that the study of ancient Near Eastern languages and their comparative use form a circular argument: one "fills in the gaps" in one language by employing data from another language and then uses the similar data in doing comparative work. Such a criticism is, however, unfounded in most contemporary comparative studies.

Michel begins his study with the *WAYYIQTOL* form, where the relation with the preceding verb form (*QATAL, YIQTOL, WAYYIQTOL*, nominal clause, participle, and infinitive) is taken into consideration. From his lengthy analysis he draws the conclusion that *WAYYIQTOL* always denotes *consequence* or *dependence*, regardless of time. Moreover, he states that "there is no difference between both 'tenses' [i.e., *YIQTOL* and *WAYYIQTOL*] with regard to their meaning as verbal forms. The impf.cs. [*WAYYIQTOL*] simply expresses a closer relationship with the preceding clause."[37] He, therefore, calls the *WAYYIQTOL* form the "*waw*-consequential."[38]

Michel next turns his attention to the *QATAL* form, observing that this verbal form can refer to any time period and is often used in constructions which append explanatory fact to something pictured earlier. According to Michel, the *QATAL* "perfectum" does not refer to a period of time but rather "reports an event which stands in no dependent relationship but which is important in itself."[39] This, he argues, functions in three ways in the book of Psalms:

1. If a perfectum stands in isolation or at the beginning of a clause it expresses a fact. . . .
2. If a perfectum follows syndetically or asyndetically on an imperfectum or a participle, it does not advance them but rather sets an explicating fact alongside of them. . . .
3. If several perfecta stand unconnected alongside of one another, they do not advance the action, but itemize equally important facts. . . . Of the imperfectum it can be said right at the start that it does not do this; it reports an action that stands in a relationship.[40]

Furthermore, Michel attempts to describe the significance of the conjugations in relation to the acting subject. By means of an in-depth investigation of Psalm 1, he theorizes that the "perfectum" and "imperfectum" have an "accidental" and "substantial" character, respectively:

> The typical actions expressed by the perfecta designate facts, which a person does but can also theoretically not do. The actions could be called typical to the extent that the person who does them manifests his belonging to a certain type of individual. If the person acted otherwise, he would exhibit himself as belonging to another type of

---

[37]Michel, *Tempora*, 51.
[38]Michel, *Tempora*, 41.
[39]Michel, *Tempora*, 98.
[40]Michel, *Tempora*, 98-99.

individual. Accordingly, the actions are not reported under the point of view that they proceed from a definite kind of person, but that they make this kind of being first manifest. In short: the actions designated by the perfectum with regard to the acting person have an accidental character.

On the other hand, the kind of tree in [Psalm 1:]3 is established from what precedes: it is a matter of a tree planted by streams of water. That this tree brings fruit in its season, that its leaves do not wither are not actions which it can or cannot do; rather they result with necessity from the character [*Wesen*] of the tree. In short: the actions designated by the imperfectum with regard to the acting subject have a substantial character.[41]

The choice of verb form, therefore, "does not lie in the action itself (period of time, *Aktionsart,* etc.), but in the relationship which the speaker wishes to see expressed."[42]

Michel also studies the *YIQTOL* "imperfectum" form similarly. After a lengthy investigation, he concludes that "between the imperfectum and imperfectum consecutivum no distinction exists with regard to their meaning. . . . The two conjugations are distinguished only by the fact that with the so-called imperfectum consecutivum a closer connection is effected by the prefixed *ן."[43] Thus, Michel denies the idea that an archaic "short form" of the prefixed-preterite *yaqtul* is anywhere preserved in the Psalter. Furthermore, he demonstrates that even the modal and iterative uses of the *YIQTOL* imperfectum form can also be explained through his "substantial" theory.[44]

The later work of Péter Kustár parallels the work of Michel.[45] Where Michel, however, wrote of *QATAL* and *YIQTOL* as reflecting "independent/substantial" and "dependent/accidental" actions, Kustár refers to them as expressing "determining" and "determined" aspects:

> The basic law of the use of the aspect categories is the following: the speaker, through the use of *qtl* and *yqtl* aspect categories, distinguishes the actions, according to which some are to be considered in the immediate relationship of the actions to one another as determining ("determinierend") and some as determined ("determiniert"), that is, the speaker wants to point to some actions as the originating point, the

---

[41]Michel, *Tempora,* 110.

[42]Michel, *Tempora,* 127.

[43]Michel, *Tempora,* 132.

[44]See the extended discussion of Michel's explanation of this in Waltke and O'Connor, *Syntax,* 472-73.

[45]Péter Kustár, *Aspekt im Hebräischen* (Basel: Reinhardt, 1972); hereafter *Aspekt.*

basis, the determining moment, the purpose, result, or concluding point of the other actions, and to other actions as having their basis, purpose, or moment determined. The determining actions are designated through the *qtl* forms, the determined actions by the *yqtl* forms.[46]

Thus, according to Kustár, *QAṬAL* expresses a determining action ("determinierend"), while *YIQṬOL* (in all its forms) expresses a determined action ("determiniert").[47]

Frithiof Rundgren's 1961 study approached the problem of the verbal system deductively, nuancing the "polar opposite" method of Michel and Kustár.[48] Taking a basic principle of phonology from the Prague school of linguistics and applying it to his investigation of syntax, Rundgren introduces the "primitive opposition": "marked" versus "unmarked".[49] The marked term has a positive value, whereas the unmarked term always has two values: a negative and a neutral value.[50]

---

[46]Kustár, *Aspekt*, 55.

[47]See the list of criticisms of both Michel and Kustár noted in Waltke and O'Connor, *Syntax*, 473-75. Of particular importance is the reductionistic bipolar basis of the whole method: "Michel . . . fails . . . when he alleges that the prefix conjugation must be the precise opposite of the suffix conjugation. An unmarked grammatical form is not necessarily the (logical) opposite of a marked form. . . . Michel has also fallen into the same trap as researchers before him, the trap of reductionism through abstraction. A form does not necessarily have just one meaning; *it may cover several meanings which speaker and audience distinguish by context*" [emphasis mine]. The criticism is sound (and taken into consideration by F. Rundgren and his students) but, for their own part, Waltke and O'Connor do not attempt in their *Syntax* to establish the "contexts" which would lead "speaker and audience" to distinguish between the several meanings that they recognize a single verbal form may have. Moreover, their criticisms of some finer points of Michel's theory are inconsistent, their examples being taken from narrative prose instead of the psalmic poetry explicitly set forth by Michel as his textual database.

[48]Frithiof Rundgren, *Das althebräische Verbum: Abriss der Aspektlehre* (Stockholm: Almqvist & Wiksell, 1961); hereafter *Verbum*.

[49]Cf. J. Kurylowicz, "Verbal Aspect in Semitic," *Orientalia* 42 (1973), 114-20. For the approach of the Prague school, see R. Jakobson, "On Linguistic Aspects of Translation" in *On Translation* (ed. R. A. Brower; Cambridge: Harvard University Press, 1959), 232-39; *Russian and Slavic Grammar: Studies, 1931-1981* (ed. L. R. Waugh and M. Halle; Berlin: Mouton, 1984). Note also the recent insightful dissertation of Paul Dmytro Korchin, *Markedness and Semitic Morphology*, Ph.D. diss., Harvard University, 2001.

[50]Rundgren, *Verbum*, 35-37.

According to Rundgren, the verbal system of classical Hebrew is based upon a series of aspectual dichotomies. The first aspectual opposition is *stativ* versus *fiens*, "stativity versus action." This aspectual opposition is realized in the morphological opposition *QATAL* versus *YIQTOL*. The *stativ* verb form (*QATAL*) represents the marked positive term expressing "terminality," in which the expressed verbal content is viewed as a state. On the other hand, the *fiens* verb form (*YIQTOL*) represents the unmarked negative term, and has a further dichotomous character with a negative and a neutral value.

The *YIQTOL* verb form with a negative value signifies "non-terminality" or a "cursive" (imperfective) aspect, where the verb is viewed as an action. The *YIQTOL* verb form with a neutral value does not signify any stativity, "terminal" or "non-terminal," and is called "constative". This aspectual opposition "cursive" versus "constative" is realized in the diachronic, morphological opposition *yaqtulu* ("long form") versus *yaqtul* ("short form").

The "constative" value has, further, a negative and a neutral value. The opposition within the "constative" value, "punctual" versus "neutral," is expressed in the morphological opposition *WAYYIQTOL* versus jussive.[51] This view of the verbal system is represented in the following schema:[52]

$$Stativ \,:\, Fiens$$
$$\downarrow$$
$$Kursiv \,:\, Konstativ$$
$$\downarrow$$
$$Punktuell \,:\, Neutral$$

Rundgren's approach has been adopted and expanded by two of his students, Bo Isaksson and Mats Eskhult.[53] Isaksson, in particular, has taken the aspectual opposition scheme and explained it by metaphors. For him, the *QATAL* form expresses a "resting fact" ("ruhenden Faktums") which is "seen from the outside" and is "standing still, punctual, and momentary." The *YIQTOL* form expresses an "action" ("Handlung der im Substantiv wirkenden Energie") which is "seen from the inside" and is "cursive." He illustrates the opposition as follows: "The perfect

---

[51]Rundgren, *Verbum*, 94-97.

[52]Rundgren, *Verbum*, 72

[53]Bo Isaksson, *Studies in the Language of Qoheleth, with Special Emphasis on the Verbal System* (SSU 10; Uppsala: Uppsala University Press, 1987); Mats Eskhult, *Studies in Verbal Aspect and Narrative Technique in Biblical Hebrew Prose* (SSU 12; Uppsala: Uppsala University Press, 1990). Note also the work of Bo Johnson, *Hebräisches Perfekt und Imperfekt mit vorangehendem w^e* (Lund: CWK Gleerup, 1979).

is a slide projection (Lichtbild), and the imperfect is a motion picture (Film)."[54] Both *WěYIQṬOL* and *WěQAṬAL* retain the same functions that they have without *waw*. In the case of *WAYYIQṬOL*, however, Isaksson admits that it functions very similarly to *QAṬAL*. However, according to Isaksson, "*WěQAṬAL* is not used in narrative, since *WAYYIQṬOL* is already dominant, appearing only in clause initial position."[55]

The most recent application of the aspectual opposition method of understanding the Hebrew verbal system is the work of Beat Zuber, who attempts to explain the system by "modality" while also taking into account temporal considerations.[56] His basic opposition is one of "recto (direct)" versus "obliquo (indirect)." Recto verbal forms refer directly to reality and consist of *QAṬAL*, *WěQAṬAL*, and *WAYYIQṬOL* (sometimes, however, without the *waw*). These forms are used in "indicative" utterances. Obliquo verbal forms refer indirectly to reality and consist of *YIQṬOL, WěYIQṬOL, WěQAṬAL* (here with a *conversive waw*). Any utterance that provides information concerning the speaker's attitude is marked with the obliquo forms. Thus, future, present, and subjunctive utterances are all governed by obliquo verbal forms.[57] In order to have the same verbal form play both opposing roles (e.g., *WěQAṬAL* as functioning as both "future" and "past" form; *YIQṬOL* without *waw* as a "future" and "subjunctive" form, and with *waw*—as *WAYYIQṬOL*—as a "past" form), Zuber goes back and reclaims the medieval Jewish grammarians' original understanding and designation of the initial *waw* as the *waw*-conversive, *waw hippûk*, form.[58]

While both the early and more contemporary exemplars of aspectual approaches have many advocates in recent scholarship, the method as a whole is often criticized on two fronts. On the one hand, whether it is couched in terms of Driver's psychologically motivated "prophetic perfect" or in Michel's view that the meanings of the verbal forms "lie in the relationship which the *speaker wishes* to see expressed" or in Zuber's seeing the "modality" of the verb having "something to do with the *speaker's attitude*" [emphases mine], the aspectual

---

[54]Isaksson, *Studies,* 30-31.

[55]The quotation is from Yoshinobu Endo, *The Verbal System of Classical Hebrew in the Joseph Story: An Approach from Discourse Analysis* (SSN 32; Assen: Van Gorcum, 1996), 8; hereafter *Verbal System.* The fact is, however, that *WěQAṬAL does* appear in narrative. Note, in my data sample, Gen 37, 39–47 and 2 Sam–1 Kgs 2, the following instances: Gen 37:3; 47:22; 2 Sam 12:16 (three times), 31; 13:18; 14:26 (three times); 15:2, 5 (four times), 30; 16:5, 13; 17:17 (three times); and 19:18, 19.

[56]Beat Zuber, *Das Tempussystem des biblischen Hebräisch: Eine Untersuchung am Text* (BZAW 164; Berlin: Walter de Gruyter, 1986).

[57]Zuber, *Tempussystem,* 29, 78-90.

[58]Zuber, *Tempussystem,* 143-46.

approaches can quickly devolve into *ad hoc* arguments based upon a projected psychological perspective of the "speaker." As such, they often appear irrefutable, while at the same time they are, in fact, not provable.

On the other hand, the aspectual approaches have been criticized for their extreme complexity and general unhelpfulness when they attempt to explain long sections of biblical material. Furthermore, as with all methods, the general schema often overrides the data and the interpreter must make statements that are clearly wrong.

Yet the aspectual approaches have also done much to illuminate the fact that, in Hebrew, verbal forms *are* often opposed to one another, one form appearing almost always in certain narrative or poetic contexts while almost never appearing in others. The various aspectual approaches (especially Michel) have also led the way into noting that "genre effects" may preempt certain constructions: poetry will not obey the same syntactical rules as prose; the verbal constructions in legal material are highly stylized in a way that they may not be in narrative. On the basis of this particular insight of the aspectual approaches, we turn now to a discussion of discourse-linguistic approaches, which note that, in describing the use and function of the verbal forms in Hebrew, context is everything.

Discourse-Linguistic Approaches

While the specific methods of the tense- and aspect-based approaches and the historical-comparative approach are different, they all share a common presupposition: the workings of the Hebrew verbal system are understood on the basis of "sentence grammar." Sentence grammar theoretically restricts the study of language to relationships within the boundaries of single sentences. Leonard Bloomfield, a twentieth-century pioneer in contemporary syntactical studies within linguistics, unequivocally defined "sentence" as "an independent linguistic form, not included by virtue of any grammatical construction in any larger linguistic form."[59] J. Lyons, another linguist, restated Bloomfield's view in the dictum, "The sentence is the largest unit of grammatical description."[60] It is from this theoretical presupposition that practically all biblical Hebrew grammatical and syntactic study of has proceeded in the past.

An illustration of this perspective within biblical studies is the layout of the monumental *Introduction to Biblical Hebrew Syntax* by Bruce Waltke and

---

[59]Leonard Bloomfield, *Language* (New York: Henry Holt, 1933), 170; see also, more recently, J. E. Grimes, *The Thread of Discourse* (The Hague: Mouton, 1975), 1-5.

[60]J. Lyons, *Introduction to Theoretical Linguistics* (Cambridge: Cambridge University Press, 1968), 172.

M. O'Connor.[61] The fundamental approach to Hebrew syntax in this work is aspectually based, situated largely upon the work of Driver and others, with considerations of tense also included. In the explication of the *YIQTOL* ("Non-Perfective") Conjugation, they present "a historical view," outlining the diachronic derivations from Canaanite *yaqtul* and *yaqtulu*. They then provide "a working view," derived mostly from aspectual studies, proposing that the "prefix conjugation has two major values: to signify either an imperfective situation in past and present time, or a dependent situation. In the latter use, the situation may be dependent on the speaker, the subject, or another situation."[62] When, however, they proceed to describe pragmatically the meanings the "non-perfective" conjugation has, they must simply list out the various options with no discernable criteria by which to adjudicate what a particular form might mean in a particular clause. Among the possible meanings for *YIQTOL*, Waltke and O'Connor include:[63]

> 1)   a customary non-perfective,
> 2)   an incipient past non-perfective,
> 3)   a progressive non-perfective,
> 4)   a stative non-perfective,
> 5)   an incipient present non-perfective,
> 6)   a habitual non-perfective,

---

[61]While they clearly know about the advantages of a discourse-linguistic approach, Waltke and O'Connor prefer, instead, to rely on the older approaches: "We have resisted the strong claims of discourse grammarians in part for the theoretical and practical reasons mentioned earlier: most syntax can be and has been described on the basis of the phrase, clause, and sentence. Further, it is evident that the grammatical analysis of Hebrew discourse is in its infancy. As an infant, it offers little help for the many problems of grammar which have not been well understood. Most translators, we think it fair to say, fly by the seat of their pants in interpreting the Hebrew conjugations. . . . For our purposes, therefore, we are content to stay with more traditional bases than those of discourse grammar" (55). And yet they also note that "if we seek to systematize our understanding of textual organization, we need to introduce the notion of different levels and types of organization. Not every verse, for example, works in the same way in itself and in relation to the verses around it. We may recognize a class of major textual markers or macrosyntactic signs, by which we mean conjunctions and other expressions that *bind together the sentences constituting a larger span of text*. . . . Like the Masoretic accent system, this method of analyzing textual organization requires independent study. A simpler approach may be offered" (634) [emphasis mine]. Yet the approach they offer is not simpler or more lucid, but instead focuses on particulars rather than patterns.

[62]Waltke and O'Connor, *Syntax*, 502.

[63]Waltke and O'Connor, *Syntax*, 502-514.

7) a non-perfective of capability,
8) a non-perfective of permission,
9) a non-perfective of possibility,
10) a non-perfective of deliberation,
11) a non-perfective of obligation,
12) a non-perfective of desire,
13) a non-perfective of injunction,
14) a non-perfective of instruction,
15) a non-perfective of prohibition,
16) a non-perfective expressing contingency,
17) a non-perfective of a consequential real situation, and
18) a non-perfective of a specific future.

In all cases, the explanation of the use follows the same formula: a statement that the prefix conjugation "may" or "can" have the stated usage, followed by single clauses from the Hebrew Bible, translated in light of the stated usage.[64] Waltke and O'Connor provide no consistent criterion by which one can easily adjudicate between the 18 listed uses of the form. And, indeed, there cannot be any criterion if the study of Hebrew grammar is restricted to the level of the clause and sentence. The same form appears in all 91 illustrative examples of Hebrew clauses in their chapter on the "non-perfective conjugation"; on the basis of sentence grammar, one can only list the various options of meanings of the form.

Because of situations such as this in languages, "discourse grammar" or "discourse linguistics" or "Textlinguistik"/"text-linguistics" was developed in general linguistics, starting with a study of Zellig Harris in 1952.[65] While it is

---

[64]It is very telling that often translations of a specific clause will differ significantly when it is presented in different sections of the *Syntax*. Note, e.g., 2 Sam 14:20: "My lord is wise" p. 434 / "My lord has wisdom" p. 607; 2 Sam 14:10: "As for the one who speaks to you" p. 536 / "Whoever speaks to you" p. 621.

[65]Zellig S. Harris, "Discourse Analysis," *Language* 28 (1952), 1-30. The differing nomenclatures for the approach are due to the relative newness of it and to the emphases that different scholars see as important within its various facets. "Text-linguistics" is the name applied to the study of written texts from a structural linguistic perspective. See Walter R. Bodine ("Discourse Analysis of Biblical Literature: What It Is and What It Offers," in *Discourse Analysis of Biblical Literature* [ed. Walter Bodine; Atlanta: Scholars, 1995], 1-20) for a lucid introduction to the discipline as a whole and its application in biblical studies.

true, as Walter R. Bodine has noted, that this discipline is "a relatively new endeavor to linguists, it is not new to those who have studied texts as texts."[66]

The underlying two presuppositions of "discourse-linguistics" are: 1) that the "meaning" of any particular verbal form arises *only* out of the "use" and "function" of that verbal form within its context (i.e., "form" follows "function"),[67] and 2) that relationships between sentences are often the same as those we find between elements of a single sentence.[68] For example, the statement "He'll be here in a moment" presupposes "the previous occurrence of some masculine noun or noun-phrase to which the pronoun *he* refers."[69] This clause is, therefore, a *derived utterance* where a noun has been replaced with an understood pronoun. Another example is: "John's, if he gets here in time." In this case, on the level of sentence grammar, the utterance is completely unexplainable because the utterance is not a sentence at all but a fragment or an "incomplete clause." It is, of course, completely understandable if it is seen in relationship with a previous utterance, "Whose car are we going in?"[70]

Since the early 1970s, many Hebrew grammarians have seen much explanatory value in this approach to the Hebrew textual clausal system. The pioneering work of F. I. Andersen, *The Sentence in Biblical Hebrew,* showed conclusively that narrative prose follows regular verbal patterns, which tie the narrated events together into a "chain."[71] When, according to Andersen, the narrative chain is broken by a negated clause (e.g., *wĕlōʾ* + *QAṬAL*), the clause interrupts the sequence of events and "generally reports an event contemporaneous, concomitant, or 'circumstantial' to the main stream."[72] This

---

[66]Walter R. Bodine, "Linguistics and Philology in the Study of Ancient Near Eastern Languages," in *Working with No Data: Semitic and Egyptian Studies Presented to Thomas O. Lambdin* (ed. D. M. Golomb; Winona Lake: Eisenbrauns, 1987), 39-54; quotation from 53.

[67]Thus, discourse grammarians do not, in general, see any specific, particular, inherent meaning of a *YIQTOL* or *QAṬAL* verbal form. The meaning of the form is dependent upon the function is has within the context in which it is found, either in prose/poetry, narrative/comment, or story line/discourse.

[68]Thus, for discourse grammarians, there is an unbroken continuum of "universal syntactic structures" which are found in all languages and include, from the smallest building block to the largest: MORPHEME-WORD-PHRASE-CLAUSE-SENTENCE-PARAGRAPH-TEXT. Note the discussion in David A. Dawson, *Text-Linguistics and Biblical Hebrew* (JSOTSupp 177; Sheffield: JSOT, 1994), 21.

[69]Lyons, *Introduction,* 173.

[70]Lyons, *Introduction,* 174-75.

[71]Francis I. Andersen, *The Sentence in Biblical Hebrew* (The Hague: Mouton, 1974), especially 77-91.

[72]Andersen, *Sentence,* 77-78; quotation is from Endo, *Verbal System,* 21.

"circumstantial clause" is usually structurally marginal to a narrative episode; that is, it often appears as a "signal either of episode onset, or of episode interruption, or of episode close-out."[73] Thus, what would have simply been a negated "perfective" conjugation when viewed from sentence grammar is shown to have an overarching narrative structural purpose when looked at from discourse linguistics.

The use of a discourse-linguistic or discourse-grammatical perspective does not necessarily define a particular method. Another approach employing discourse grammar is based on the "foregrounding-backgrounding" hypothesis, explained by P. J. Hopper:

> It is evidently a universal of narrative discourse that in any extended text an overt distinction is made between the language of the actual storyline and the language of supportive material which does not itself narrate the main events. I refer to the former—the parts of the narrative which relate events belonging to the skeletal structure of the discourse—as FOREGROUND and the latter as BACKGROUND. . . . One finds . . . a tendency for punctual verbs to have perfective aspect (i.e., to occur in foregrounded sentences) and conversely for verbs of the durative/stative/iterative types to occur in imperfective, i.e., backgrounded clauses. . . . Strictly speaking, only foregrounded clauses are actually NARRATED. Backgrounded clauses do not themselves narrate, but instead they support, amplify, or COMMENT on the narration. . . . Discourse grammarians are coming to recognize more and more that in the telling of a story in any language, one particular tense is favored as the carrier of the backbone or storyline of the story

---

[73]Endo, *Verbal System,* 21-22; Andersen, *Sentence,* 80. Note also, in this context, Lambdin's category of "Initial or Terminative" in his *Introduction,* 164. An analogous example of the structural significance of syntactical verbal changes in English narrative literature is provided by Dawson, *Text-Linguistics,* 44-45. He notes that in Mary Shelley's *Frankenstein,* the following clause distribution is found between chapters two and three:
   —a long string of 'simple past' clauses;
   —a string of 11 clauses built on the verb 'to be';
   —a long series of clauses with 'past perfect' forms, and the occasional 'modal clause' and 'stative clause';
   —then, another long string of 'simple past' clauses.
The chapter break occurs after the 11 "to be" clauses. The interruption of the "simple past" story line with "to be" and "past perfect" verbal forms *syntactically* signals a break in the narrative.

> while other tenses serve to present the background, supportive, and
> depictive material in the story.[74]

This basic "foregrounding-backgrounding" perspective has been developed
for biblical Hebrew by Alviero Niccacci in his *The Syntax of the Verb in Classical Hebrew Prose.*[75] Niccacci, in his analysis, divides clauses found in prose into
two sets, "discourse" and "narrative": "Narrative concerns persons or events
which are not present or current in the relationship involving writer-reader and
so the third person is used. In discourse, on the other hand, the speaker addresses
the listener directly (dialogue, sermon, prayer)."[76]

Moreover, Niccacci divides "discourse" into two further categories: "discourse (proper)" and "comment." The latter term is used "when the writer holds
up the story in order to relate his reflection on the events narrated or to define
them in some way" within a narrative.[77] In all cases, Niccacci attempts to show
that Hebrew syntax is different for "narrative" and for "discourse." According to
Niccacci, in discourse, *YIQTOL* is the main, dominant form, both *QATAL* and
WeQATAL being secondary, while in narrative *WAYYIQTOL* is the main form, and
QATAL is secondary.

The approach of Robert Longacre is similar to that of Niccacci and other
discourse grammarians.[78] He, however, refines two of the insights of Hopper and
Niccacci to account for the highly nuanced texture of biblical storytelling. Longacre notes that while "narrative" performs the same basic purpose

---

[74]P. J. Hopper, "Aspect and Foregrounding in Discourse," in *Discourse and Syntax,*
ed. T. Givón (New York: Academic, 1979), 213-241, quotation from 213-15.

[75]Alviero Niccacci, *The Syntax of the Verb in Classical Hebrew Prose,* trans. W. G.
E. Watson (JOSTSupp. 86; Sheffield: Sheffield Academic, 1990), especially 17-34. Note
the author's original study in Italian: *Sintassi del verbo ebraico nella prosa biblica
classica* (Jerusalem: Franciscan, 1986).

[76]Niccacci, *Syntax,* 29.

[77]Niccacci, *Syntax,* 33-34.

[78]The work of Longacre concerning the method and application of discourse-
linguistics is extensive. Among the general introductions to his theory of discourse
grammar and its application to biblical interpretation, see "The Discourse Structure of the
Flood Narrative," *JAAR* 47, Suppl. B (1979), 89-133; *The Grammar of Discourse* (New
York: Plenum, 1983); "Who Sold Joseph into Egypt?" in *Interpretation and History:
Essays in Honour of Allan A. MacRae* (ed. R. L. Harris, S.-H. Quek and J. R. Vannoy;
Singapore: Christian Life, 1986), 75-92; *Joseph: A Story of Divine Providence: A Text
Theoretical and Textlinguistic Analysis of Genesis 37 and 39-48* (Winona Lake: Eisen-
brauns, 1989); and "Discourse Perspective on the Hebrew Verb: Affirmation and
Restatement," in *Linguistics and Biblical Hebrew* (ed. Walter R. Bodine; Winona Lake:
Eisenbrauns, 1992), 177-189.

regardless of where it may be found (i.e., to report a series of events in the form of a story), there is no such overarching purpose that can be applied to "discourse" as Niccacci proposes. Instead, Longacre differentiates between four basic functions of speech:[79]

1) Narrative Discourse, in which a character reports an event or series of events that have occurred;
2) Predictive Discourse, in which a character proposes or plans for events that have not occurred;
3) Expository Discourse, in which a character explains or describes a fact or situation; and
4) Hortatory Discourse, in which a character attempts to elicit a response from another character or other characters.

Longacre, moreover, clearly shows that each of these "text-types" of discourse has its own "constellation" of verbal forms that constitute it.[80] This fact will become clearer within the textual analyses in the next chapter of this book.

The second element that Longacre nuances in the general discussion of Hebrew prose is the use of *QATAL* in narrative. Whereas Niccacci saw all instances of *QATAL* as basically parallel with the *WAYYIQTOL* form in narrative, Longacre notes two important exceptions to this rule.

First, he notes the peculiar nature of the verb "to be" in all languages, and the verb *hāyâ* in Hebrew in particular:

> It is immediately necessary, however, to qualify the above hypothesis in one important particular. The verb *hāyâ*, 'be', even in its form *wayhî*, 'and it happened', does not function on the storyline of a narrative. In this respect, the behavior of Hebrew is similar to that of a great many contemporary languages around the world. For example, English uses its past tense to encode the storyline of a story, but the verb *be* (and some other stative verbs)—even when in the past tense (for example, forms such as *was*, *were*)—is typically descriptive and depictive and does not figure on the backbone of a story. This is simply a peculiarity of the verb *be* in many languages past and present.[81]

---

[79]Longacre, *Joseph*, 80-136.

[80]The technical term "constellation" for the group of possible verbal forms for a particular discourse text-type is used by Longacre (*Joseph*, 59-60). While Longacre notes the verbal constellations for the text-types that he proposes, he does not deal with the limited tense and aspect possibilities for the particular verbal forms in the various verbal constellations.

[81]Longacre, *Joseph*, 66.

Thus, according to Longacre, when any verbal form of *hāyâ* appears in a clause in a narrative, the clause does not cause the narrative to progress, but rather the clause is explanatory because of the nature of the verb.

The second exception to Niccacci's view of *QAṬAL* involves the nature of the construction *lōʾ* + *QAṬAL*. Hopper noted that the negated *QAṬAL* verb automatically causes the clause as a whole to become a backgrounded statement, and thus, by definition, it does not cause the narrative to progress.[82] Longacre, however, notes a few instances in which the negating of the action itself actually *does* cause the action of the narrative chain to progress. While usually a negated *QAṬAL* clause does provide a summary or contrast as a backgrounded or "off-line" comment, occasionally an instance of "momentous negation" will further the narrative along in the same way that a *WAYYIQṬOL* verbal form would.[83]

General Remarks

While all the approaches noted in this introduction have strengths and weaknesses, it seems obvious that "these different views show that no clear consensus of opinion exists at the moment on the function of the verb in Biblical Hebrew."[84] Moreover, these differing views are in no way mutually exclusive, nor is it required that one approach should be wholeheartedly accepted and all others absolutely rejected. Those holding to a primarily tense- or aspect-based or discourse-linguistic approach—all of which are synchronic studies of the verbal system—can certainly accept the diachronic and comparative views of the historical approach with no reservations whatsoever. Furthermore, those holding to a discourse-linguistic approach can certainly appreciate the concerns of the early proponents of tense-based systems as well as the insights into the dichotomous nature of the *QAṬAL/YIQṬOL* opposition within modern aspectual approaches.

---

[82]Hopper, "Aspect," 213.

[83]Longacre (*Joseph,* 85) provides the example of the failure of the dove to return to the ark in the Flood Story (Gen 8:12) as an instance of "momentous negation." While this example is noteworthy, perhaps better examples are the refusal of Joseph to heed Potiphar's wife's advances (Gen 39:10) and Amnon's refusal to listen to the pleadings of Tamar (2 Sam 13:14,16). In each of these cases, the negation of the verb implies an activity ("did not [i.e., refused to] take heed") by the character, and it is this implied activity of refusal that propels the narrative forward.

[84]F. C. Fensham, "The Use of the Suffix Conjugation and the Prefix Conjugation in a Few Old Poems," *JNSL* 6 (1978), 9-18, quotation from 14.

What discourse grammarians *cannot* support, however, is the basic approach of "sentence grammar" held by the other three approaches. It seems clear, even among those holding to tense- and aspect-based approaches, that the existence of "tense" within biblical Hebrew is a discourse phenomenon; that is, it can only be analyzed and observed on the linguistic level beyond that of the sentence.[85] If the maximum level of analysis is that of the "sentence," the representation of both tense and aspect will continue to appear to be random and capricious.

This awareness that the meaning and function of clauses in biblical Hebrew is based upon the wider narrative context was the basis of Lambdin's explication of the structural function of disjunctive clauses in Hebrew. In Lambdin's view, disjunctive clauses in the narrative chain of biblical Hebrew prose mark either clauses that provide additional, nonsequential information (contrastive, circumstantial, or explanatory clauses) or they mark defined boundaries of smaller narrative episodes (terminative or initial).

This study will provide an in-depth investigation into the function of verbal and non-verbal clauses in biblical Hebrew prose. It will be based upon a basic methodological differentiation between two primary types of material found in prose: narrative and direct discourse. It seems clear in all the approaches (including historical-comparative methods) that the same verbal form (e.g., *QAṬAL*) or clause type (e.g., participial clause) often has very different functions or meanings depending upon whether it occurs within the story line or within speeches by characters. This study will, therefore, make a distinction between narrative and direct discourse within two extended portions of biblical prose and, in turn, investigate the presence and pragmatic function of the various types of clauses both in narrative and in direct discourse. Its analysis of biblical Hebrew narrative will be based upon the insights of Lambdin, but will incorporate other concepts noted within contemporary discourse linguistics.

Its analysis of direct discourse will be based upon the work of Robert Longacre. Longacre's insight that, within direct discourse, the function of any specific example of speech in prose is determined by its conforming to one of the four discourse text-types is a key to understanding the consistency within which the limited Hebrew verbal system functions. Longacre's differentiation of four verbal text-types, however, will be expanded to five in this book. In addition to Narrative Discourse (ND), Predictive Discourse (PD), Expository Discourse (ED), and Hortatory Discourse (HD), this study will also include Interrogative Discourse (ID), in which a character attempts to elicit a verbal

---

[85]Note, for example, the admitted need to "introduce the notion of *different levels and types of organization*" into the study of Hebrew verbal conjugations by Waltke and O'Connor, *Syntax*, 634 (emphasis mine).

response from the hearer(s). The five text-types, therefore, are differentiated into two general areas:

1) Discourses based upon the relaying of information:
   A) Narrative Discourse, in which a character relates events that happened in the past (from the perspective of the speech act);
   B) Predictive Discourse, in which a character proposes or plans for events that will occur or may occur in the future; and
   C) Expository Discourse, in which a character explains or describes general or present facts or actions.
2) Discourses based upon the expressing of the speaker's volition:
   A) Interrogative Discourse, in which a character attempts to elicit a verbal response from the hearer(s); [86] and
   B) Hortatory Discourse, in which a character attempts to elicit an active or attitudinal response from the hearer(s).

This study will attempt to make explicit the various verbal constellations that comprise the text-type (and, therefore, the function) of any particular speech sample within biblical Hebrew prose.

This study has four goals:

1) After an initial recognition that the basic narrative story line of a text is based upon chains of *WAYYIQTOL* clauses, I will show that when any of the three additional verbal clauses (those governed by *QATAL, YIQTOL,* or *WĕQATAL*) or three non-verbal clauses (participial, verbless, or incomplete) appear in the *narrative story line of a text,* these verbal and non-verbal clauses provide either nonsequential, "background" information or mark episode boundaries. Building upon Lambdin's analysis, however, I will also provide objective criteria by which one may differentiate between the providing of non-sequential information or the marking of episode boundaries. I will further note that the type of information expressed in nonsequential, background comments is not of a single sort but can be differentiated between information closely related to the story line and information more remotely related to the story line.

---

[86]Interrogative Discourse occasionally questions the hearer for a non-verbal response. Such is the case with "rhetorical questions" or "leading questions," which *functionally* are much closer to Hortatory Discourse than straightforward Interrogative Discourse. The syntactical *form* of rhetorical or leading questions are, of course, patterned after Interrogative Discourse. It is, therefore, into this category that such questions are classified in this study.

2) I will show that in *direct discourse,* there are five predominant types of speech, or "text-types," each defined by a limited set of possible verbal/clausal combinations, or "discourse constellations."

3) I will show that *within each of these defined text-types,* the verbal forms used (*QATAL, YIQTOL, WĕQATAL, WĕYIQTOL,* and *WAYYIQTOL*), as well as participial, verbless, incomplete and hortatory (imperative, cohortative, and jussive) verbal clauses, are consistent in their meaning.

4) And finally, by the means of this contextual discourse analysis of both narrative and direct discourse, this study will provide an easily accessible and straightforwardly functional approach to the system of verbal and verbless clauses in biblical Hebrew prose.

Methodological Overview

In order to investigate the function of the various clauses within Hebrew narrative and discourse, this study will analyze two coherent, extended biblical narratives: the Joseph Novella (Gen. 37, 39-47) and The Narrative of David's Court (2 Sam. 9-20; 1 Kings 1-2). In both cases, it will analyze each independent, main clause within the texts in order to determine the significance and function of each clause within itself and within its wider immediate context. Each of the following chapter analyses is divided into four sections:

Textual Layout of the Narrative by Chapters

For each biblical chapter of the two blocks of material, a presentation of the text of the chapter appears in a specialized format; this format clarifies the immediate context of each clause in the subsequent analyses.[87] The text is arranged according to individual main clauses, which are then numbered sequentially. The number of the individual clause consists of three parts, each divided by a period: the chapter and verse in which the clause appears and the sequential number of the clause within the text as a whole. Thus, clause 100 of the Joseph Novella, which stands in Genesis 37:28, appears in this text as:

37.28.100 וַיִּמְכְּרוּ אֶת־יוֹסֵף לַיִּשְׁמְעֵאלִים בְּעֶשְׂרִים כָּסֶף

37.28.100 And they sold Joseph to the Ishmaelites for twenty silver (pieces).

---

[87]The (medieval) chapter divisions are used as a matter of convention and convenience. Occasionally, as will be illustrated, these divisions inaccurately represent a break in a coherent story line.

Subordinate or dependent clauses (most notably those initiated with כִּי or אֲשֶׁר) within each sentence are set off separately and indented. This indentation helps indicate the main clause of each sentence and, therefore, of the primary governing verb in each main clause.[88] For highly complex sentences in which there are nonsequential dependent clauses, or for sentences in which there are dependent clauses occurring before the main clause, the subordinate clauses are labeled with the number of their governing clause along with a Greek letter, depending upon their placement. This is occasionally complex, since the main clause and the dependent clause are often separated by several intervening, independent sentences. For example, in Genesis 37:22, Reuben attempts to persuade his brothers not to kill Joseph but rather to throw him into a nearby pit in the desert. After the speech, the narrator provides a dependent purpose clause explaining Reuben's intentions in his proposed plan. While the grammatical connection of this final purpose clause is difficult to place in the text as it appears in the MT, in this textual layout its connection to the original narrative clause is made clear, in spite of Reuben's intervening Hortatory Discourse:

37.22.075 וַיֹּאמֶר אֲלֵהֶם רְאוּבֵן

HD

37.22.076 אַל־תִּשְׁפְּכוּ־דָם
37.22.077 הַשְׁלִיכוּ אֹתוֹ אֶל־הַבּוֹר הַזֶּה
אֲשֶׁר בַּמִּדְבָּר
37.22.078 וְיָד אַל־תִּשְׁלְחוּ־בוֹ
075α לְמַעַן הַצִּיל אֹתוֹ מִיָּדָם לַהֲשִׁיבוֹ אֶל־אָבִיו:

37.22.075 And Reuben said to them,
(Hortatory Discourse:)
37.22.076 "Do not spill blood!
37.22.077 Throw him into this cistern
which is in the desert!
37.22.078 But don't stretch out a hand against him!"
075α in order to rescue him from their power, to return him to his father.

Sentences that are too long to be conveniently scanned will be divided into two lines with an open bracket (]) before the second line of the sentence.

---

[88]It should be noted that this examination of the function of clauses in biblical Hebrew prose concentrates only upon main, independent clauses. The meaning of verbal forms in subordinate clauses will occasionally arise, but will not be the primary focus of attention.

The sentences of the Hebrew text will, as in the example given above, be divided into separate columns, that on the right containing the narrative and that on the left containing the direct discourse of the characters. For instances of quotation within direct discourse—that is, when a character recites a separate speech within his or her own discourse (i.e. a "quote within a quote")—each line of such quotations will be preceded by a dagger (†). Instances of double quotations—when a character quotes a quotation—are preceded by double daggers (††).

Finally, each instance of direct discourse will be headed by an abbreviation according to its text-type, that is, according to its particular rhetorical function. The speech by Reuben above urges his brothers to perform (or, in this case, not to perform) certain actions or have certain dispositions; it attempts to elicit an active or attitudinal response from its hearers. It is, therefore, Hortatory Discourse and is headed by the abbreviation "HD". Any particular example of an act of speech may consist of a single text-type (as above) or, if the speech has numerous functions, it may consist of multiple text-types. In such cases, when a text-type changes within a speech, each new text-type is headed by its abbreviation. For example, in Genesis 37:32, after the brothers sell Joseph, dip his special coat in blood, and bring it to Jacob, their speech contains three simple clauses each having its own text-type:

37.32.114 וַיֹּאמְרוּ

ND
37.32.115 זֹאת מָצָאנוּ
HD
37.32.116 הַכֶּר־נָא
ID
37.32.117 הַכְּתֹנֶת בִּנְךָ הִוא אִם־לֹא:

37.32.114 And they said,

                        (Narrative Discourse:)
            37.32.115 We found this.
                        (Hortatory Discourse:)
            37.32.116 Recognize (it)!
                        (Interrogative Discourse:)
            37.32.117 Is this the coat of your son, or not?

Clause 115 recounts an event that occurred in the past; it is, therefore, Narrative Discourse (ND). Clause 116 attempts to elicit an active or attitudinal response from the hearer; it is, therefore, Hortatory Discourse (HD). Clause 117 questions the hearer for a verbal response; it is, therefore, Interrogative Discourse (ID).[89] In addition to these three discourse text-types, this study will also note the occurrences of speeches that predict, foretell, or plan for the future, Predictive Discourses (PD), and speeches which relate facts concerning the present state of affairs, Expository Discourses (ED).

Chart of Governing Verbal Forms/Sentence Types

Following the text of the chapter, a chart provides a synopsis of the verbal forms found within the chapter, labeling each clause according to its clausal type (for participial, verbless, or incomplete clauses) or governing verbal form.

A sample of the table is presented here:

	Narrative: 003,006,010,036,131	5	38.5%
QATAL	ND: 017,018,028,057,†069,115,121,122	8	61.5%
	PD:		
Total Clauses:	ED:		
13	ID:		
	HD:		

The column on the left labels the specific verb form or clause type and the number of independent clauses governed by the specified verbal form or clause type within the chapter. The central column of the chart categorizes the clauses of the chapter according to whether they appear in the narrative story line or, for clauses in direct speech, its text-type. The two columns on the right provide the total number of clauses within the narrative or each of the discourse text-types and the percent of each total for all instances of that specific verbal form or sentence type.

Critical Analysis of the Narrative Prose and Discourse Text-Types

The third section will provide an analysis of the various verb forms found in the various contexts, whether, on the one hand, in narrative or, on the other, in

---

[89] The unusual form of the interrogative particle הֲ in Clause 117 (הַכְּתֹנֶת) should be noted. The usual form of the ה-interrogative before a *shewa* is a *pataḥ* (e.g., Gen 17:38; 18:17; 29:5; 30:15; 34:31). In about ten passages, however, the following consonant contains a dagesh and the ה-interrogative appears identical to the definite article (Gen 17:17; 18:21; 37:32; Num 13:19; Ezek 20:30; Job 23:6). The dagesh also occasionally appears even in ר (1 Sam 10:24; 17:25; 2 Kgs 6:32). No consistent reason can be given for the forms containing the dagesh.

discourse text-types. The analysis will first investigate the general layout of the syntactical structure of the chapter's narrative prose, noting the general "back-bone" of *WAYYIQTOL*-chains and where that narrative spine is broken with divergent verbal forms. These breaks, it will be shown, consist of major disjunctions (verbal forms or constructions which separate blocks of narrative from each other) and minor disjunctions (verbal forms or constructions which simply comment on the narrative in progress with an "off-line" exposition).

After the examination of the narrative structure of the chapter, the analysis will investigate the examples of direct discourse. The five discourse text-types (Narrative, Predictive, Expository, Interrogative, and Hortatory Discourses) will be analyzed separately. In each case, the analysis will highlight which verbal forms appear most regularly in each text-type, whether there are any consistent non-verbal markers which are used in conjunction with the verb in order to mark a specific text-type, difficult or divergent verbal forms within the chapter, and what functions the many verbal forms perform within each text-type.

The Discourse Constellation Chart

The final section of each chapter analysis will be a chart providing a clear means of accounting for the verbal/clause combinations in four of the discourse text-types, Narrative, Predictive, Expository, and Hortatory Discourses.[90] The chart will note the text-types accounted for in the chapter, will list the various combinations of verbal or non-verbal clauses within each text-type, and will note how many speeches within the chapter fall within each combination. Thus, for example in Genesis 37, there are four cases in which a single speech employs only *QATAL* clauses, one case in which a speech employs *QATAL* clauses and participial or verbless clauses, and one case in which a speech employs *QATAL* clauses, *WAYYIQTOL* clauses, participial or verbless clauses, and a *YIQTOL* clause. The various combinations of verbal or non-verbal clauses for a particular text type are the verbal "constellations" which are possible for each discourse text type. The verbal constellation chart at the end of the analysis of Genesis 37 will, thus, tally the data for Narrative Discourse in the following manner:

---

[90]Since Interrogative Discourse, as will be shown, is defined as a text-type by the presence of interrogative particles (e.g., הֲ, מָה, אֵיךְ) and not by verbal constellations, its accounting in the Verbal Constellation Chart is unnecessary.

Chapter   Total

		Chapter	Total
	QATAL	4	4
	QATAL, WAYYIQTOL		
	QATAL, (Ptc./Vbl.)	1	1
ND	*QATAL, WAYYIQTOL, (Ptc./Vbl.)*		
	QATAL, WAYYIQTOL, (Ptc./ Vbl.), YIQTOL	1	1
	Vbl/Ptc. (Dream Report)		
	Inc. (Answer)		

The chart will, of course, also keep the totals for Predictive Discourses, Expository Discourses, and Hortatory Discourses. The first column on the right of the chart provides the number of times each constellation appears within the present chapter; the second column will keep the total for the entire narrative from the beginning through the present chapter.

After all the chapters of the Joseph Novella and the Narrative of David's Court have been analyzed in this way, the final chapter will attempt to assess and discuss the main points of the chapter analyses. It will review the various means by which biblical Hebrew narrative organizes its main story line and its off-line comments. It will also look at the constituent features of the dialogue portions of the text. By accounting the totals for all constellations in all text-types in all the chapters, this study will show that the various verbal/clausal constellations or combinations are completely regular for each distinct discourse text-type and, further, that the meanings and functions of the various verbal conjugations are regular within each distinct text type.

Chapter Two
The Joseph Novella: A Discourse-Linguistic Analysis

Formal Considerations:
Limits of the Joseph Novella

The Beginning of the Novella

For numerous reasons Genesis 37 constitutes the beginning, not only of the final "movement" of the biblical book of Genesis, chapters 37–50, but also of a more defined collection of stories which have come to be referred to as "The Joseph Novella."[1] In 37:2, the opening of a new section in the epic of the

---

[1]The definition of the cycle of stories surrounding the character of Joseph as a "novella" is, actually, not a recent development. The pioneering work of Gunkel and of his student Gressmann illustrates the unique literary form of the Joseph story. While the characters in the story have already been introduced in the earlier parts of Genesis and the main character, Joseph, is mentioned in Exod 1:8 and, later, in Josh 24:32, there do seem to be broad formal grounds which justify a study of Genesis 37–47 as a unit to itself. Gunkel noted that large parts of the Joseph story could not be accurately labeled according to traditional source-critical divisions propounded by Wellhausen (*Die Composition des Hexateuchs und der historischen Bücher des Alten Testaments* [Berlin: Walter de Gruyter, 1876-77; reprint ed. 1963], 50-61), in spite of many continued attempts to do so (e.g., Skinner, *A Critical and Exegetical Commentary on Genesis* [ICC 1; New York: Charles Scribner's Sons, 1910]). Gunkel, furthermore, noted that much of the material dealing with Joseph could not be placed into the categories of "legend" or "saga" which characterized the Abraham and Jacob cycles. Unlike these earlier collections, the legends surrounding Joseph are "very cunningly blended into a whole." Gunkel described the Joseph story as a "Romance," while Gressmann, his student, designated it, not as a *Sagenkranz*, but as a *Novelle*. See H. Gunkel, *The Legends of Genesis: The Biblical Saga and History* (New York: Schocken, 1964), 77-117; "Die Komposition der Joseph-Geschichten," *ZDMG* 76 (1922), 55-71; and H. Gressmann, "Ursprung und Entwicklung der Joseph-Sage," *Forschungen zur Religion und Literatur des Alten und Neuen Testaments* 36 (1923) 1-55. The designation "novella" by Gressmann has continued to the present day, and the "novella-like" character of the story of Joseph has been recognized by many scholars, including Gerhard von Rad ("The Joseph Narrative and Ancient Wisdom," in *The Problem of the Hexateuch and Other Essays* [New York: McGraw-Hill, 1966], 292-300; *Genesis: A Commentary* [London: SCM, 1972], 347-48); Robert Davidson (*Genesis 12–50* [New York: Cambridge University Press, 1979], 211-14); and, recently, W. Lee Humphreys (*Joseph and His Family* [Columbia: University of South Carolina Press, 1988], 15-31). Moreover, some modern interpreters attempt to combine

ancestors appears as a formulaic *toledot* notice: אֵלֶּה תֹּלְדוֹת יַעֲקֹב. Moreover, this verse signals a change in narrative focus. In most of the previous *toledot* notices in Genesis, the subject of the notice is also the subject of the subsequent story cycle, which begins with the character's name. This juxtaposition of the proper name is regularly found throughout Genesis:

Genesis 6:9	אֵלֶּה תּוֹלְדֹת נֹחַ נֹחַ אִישׁ צַדִּיק תָּמִים
Genesis 11:10	אֵלֶּה תּוֹלְדֹת שֵׁם שֵׁם בֶּן־מְאַת שָׁנָה
Genesis 11:27	וְאֵלֶּה תּוֹלְדֹת תֶּרַח תֶּרַח הוֹלִיד אֶת־אַבְרָם
Genesis 36:1-2	וְאֵלֶּה תֹּלְדוֹת עֵשָׂו . . . עֵשָׂו לָקַח אֶת־נָשָׁיו

Even in Genesis 25:19-20, the subject of the *toledot* notice and the subject of the following story are the same, but the proper name that is immediately doubled is that of another character:

וְאֵלֶּה תּוֹלְדֹת יִצְחָק בֶּן־אַבְרָהָם אַבְרָהָם הוֹלִיד אֶת־יִצְחָק:
וַיְהִי יִצְחָק בֶּן־אַרְבָּעִים שָׁנָה בְּקַחְתּוֹ אֶת־רִבְקָה בַּת־בְּתוּאֵל הָאֲרַמִּי מִפַּדַּן אֲרָם
אֲחוֹת לָבָן הָאֲרַמִּי לוֹ לְאִשָּׁה:

It is clear in these examples, that the usual form of *toledot* notices occurring before narratives consists of: (1) the introductory phrase תּוֹלְדֹת אֵלֶּה(וְ), (2) the doubling of a proper name after the phrase, and (3) the following story, commencing with the second of the doubled names.[2]

---

the source-critical and form-critical approaches; e.g., Norman Gottwald, *The Hebrew Bible—A Socio-Literary Introduction* (Philadelphia: Fortress, 1985), 150.

[2]The remaining *toledot* notices (Gen 2:4; 5:1; 10:1; 25:12) do not follow this pattern. Their form, however, seems to be constrained by the fact that they do not precede narratives. They either occur at the end of their subject's narrative (2:4a; note the reversal of אֶרֶץ וְשָׁמָיִם in v.4b) or they precede genealogies (5:1; 10:1; 25:12). See Joseph Blenkinsopp, *The Pentateuch: An Introduction to the First Five Books of the Bible* (New York: Doubleday, 1992), 58-133, for a recent exposition of the *toledot* series in Genesis. On the *toledot* in general, see Karl Budde, "Ellä Toledoth," *ZAW* 34 (1914), 241-53; "Noch einmal 'Ellä Toledoth'," *ZAW* 36 (1916), 1-7; O. Eissfeldt, "Toledot," *Texte und Untersuchungen* 77 (1961), 1-8; J. Scharbert, "Der Sinn der Toledot-Formel in der Priesterschrift," in *Wort-Gebot-Glaube: Walther Eichrodt zum 80. Geburtstag* (Zurich: Zwingli Verlag, 1970), 45-56; Frank Moore Cross, *Canaanite Myth and Hebrew Epic*, (Cambridge: Harvard Univeristy Press, 1973), 301-8; P. Weimar, "Die Toledot-Formel in der priester-schriftlichen Geschichtsdarstellung," *BZ* (1974), 65-93; S. Tengström, *Die Toledotformel und die literarische Struktur der priesterlichen Erweiterungsschicht im Pentateuch* (Lund: Gleerup, 1981); T. L. Thompson, *The Origin Tradition of Ancient Israel* (Sheffield: JSOT, 1987), 61-131.

In Genesis 37:2, however, this pattern is broken. Although the *toledot* notice introduces a long and complex narrative, the proper name is not doubled nor is it the same as that of the main character of the subsequent narrative:

אֵלֶּה תֹּלְדוֹת יַעֲקֹב יוֹסֵף בֶּן־שְׁבַע־עֶשְׂרֵה שָׁנָה הָיָה רֹעֶה אֶת־אֶחָיו בַּצֹּאן

This break from the usual syntactical form of the Genesis *toledot* series signals a new beginning which demarcates the following narrative, not just from the preceding narrative cycle, but also from the rest of the book as a whole.

The role played by Genesis 37:1 in defining the present limits of the Joseph Novella should likewise be noted. The placement of the verse,

וַיֵּשֶׁב יַעֲקֹב בְּאֶרֶץ מְגוּרֵי אָבִיו בְּאֶרֶץ כְּנָעַן

is unusual, however, since the immediately preceding section (36:9-42) is clearly a *toledot* list of tribal chiefs of Edom, while the immediately following verse is the formal *toledot* marker for the beginning of the Joseph narrative block.[3] The verse, in its present location, appears isolated, without context. It probably originally followed 36:8 and formed the end of the JE Jacob cycle. Seen in this context, it provides a contrast between the final dwelling places of, on the one hand, Esau (וַיֵּשֶׁב עֵשָׂו בְּהַר שֵׂעִיר עֵשָׂו הוּא אֱדוֹם) and, on the other hand, Jacob (וַיֵּשֶׁב יַעֲקֹב בְּאֶרֶץ מְגוּרֵי אָבִיו בְּאֶרֶץ כְּנָעַן).[4] In its present context, however, Genesis 37:1 forms a tight inclusio with the final verse of the Joseph Novella, Genesis 47:27: וַיֵּשֶׁב יִשְׂרָאֵל בְּאֶרֶץ מִצְרַיִם בְּאֶרֶץ גֹּשֶׁן. The significance of this inclusio for the present state of the Joseph Novella will be argued in the next section.[5]

Finally, the story of Genesis 37 as a whole provides the backdrop against which the remainder of the narrative will be told. The narratological and structural movement of the novella as a whole is one of "descent" or "going down,"

---

[3] For the genealogical form of the name list found in Genesis 36, see Robert R. Wilson, *Genealogy and History in the Biblical World* (New Haven: Yale University Press, 1977), 168-83.

[4] See Skinner, *Genesis*, 430, 443; Lothar Ruppert, *Die Josephserzählung der Genesis: Ein Beitrag zur Theologie der Pentateuchquellen* (Munich: Kösel-Verlag, 1965), 30-31. E. A. Speiser (*Genesis: Introduction, Translation, and Notes* [AB; New York: Doubleday, 1964], 280) tries to undo the problem of the *toledot* formula in 37:2a by attempting to see the notice as a colophon, ending the Jacob cycle as a whole. In light of the above discussion of the *toledot*, his attempt seems to raise more problems than it solves.

[5] A third option–that the clause forms an inclusio with a much later clause in Gen 50:22–will be discussed and critiqued later.

first of Joseph, then of Jacob/Israel. The root יָרַד, in various verbal forms, occurs 25 times throughout the narrative.[6] In Chapter 37, this double movement of Joseph on the one hand, and Jacob on the other is intimated by verses 25 and 35:

37:25 וַיִּרְאוּ וְהִנֵּה אֹרְחַת יִשְׁמְעֵאלִים בָּאָה מִגִּלְעָד
וּגְמַלֵּיהֶם נֹשְׂאִים נְכֹאת וּצְרִי וָלֹט הוֹלְכִים לְהוֹרִיד מִצְרָיְמָה׃
37:35 וַיֹּאמֶר כִּי־אֵרֵד אֶל־בְּנִי אָבֵל שְׁאֹלָה

Even as the Ishmaelite caravan's camels bring down spices to Egypt, so will they bring down Joseph, also (Gen 39:1). In like manner, Jacob himself knows that he too will descend to his son. The ultimate irony of the story is, however, that Israel ends his journey going down to his son in a fertile land (Gen 46:3), rather than the sterile underworld.

For these reasons, the beginning of the Joseph Novella is clearly delineated in the opening verses of Genesis 37. Formally, canonically, and narratively, the turn that occurs at this point in the book of Genesis signals a new beginning to the story of the ancestors.

The Ending of the Novella

While the *toledot* notice in 37:2a is generally accepted by most scholars to indicate the beginning of the Joseph Novella, there is little consensus about where the narrative ends. Most scholars, taking their orientation from the book of Genesis as a whole, posit the Joseph Novella as encompassing chapters 37 through 50, inclusive. The rationale behind this view seems to rest more on assumptions than on clearly set out formal analysis. It is claimed that seeing Genesis 37–50, inclusive, as the Joseph Novella has several warrants.

Some scholars have argued that having the Joseph Novella continue through Genesis 50 causes the overall structure of Genesis to fall into four discrete sections:

> A. Primeval History (chs. 1–11)
> B. Ancestral Histories (chs. 12–50)
>   1. Abraham Cycle (chs. 12:1-25:18)
>   2. Jacob Cycle (chs. 25:19-37:1)
>   3. Joseph Novella (chs. 37:2-50:26)

All 50 chapters, therefore, have their place in the overall scheme of Genesis.[7]

---

[6]Gen 37:25, 35; 39:1; 42:23, 38 (bis); 43:4, 5, 7, 11, 15, 20 (bis), 22; 44:11, 21, 23, 26 (bis), 29, 31; 45:9, 13; 46:3, 4.

[7]Speiser, *Genesis*, lviii-lx.

It is also often claimed that, because Joseph appears as a major character throughout Genesis 37–50, the Novella must be all-inclusive, tracing the life of Joseph into his final years. It is only in chapter 50, at the end of Genesis, that the death of Joseph is recorded. Some have argued, therefore, that the Joseph Novella cannot end before the story of Joseph as a whole ends.[8]

Finally, some have interpreted the notice in 50:22, "So Joseph dwelt in Egypt," as a concluding narrative bracket parallel to 37:1, "Jacob dwelt in the land of his father's sojourning, in the land of Canaan." It is claimed that the two notices, standing at the beginning and ending of the Joseph story, tie the novella as a whole together.[9]

When looked at more carefully, however, these explanations for the inclusive nature of the Joseph story, while compelling on a certain general level, do not address specifically the nature and extent of the Joseph Novella as a definable literary unit having an integrity of its own.

While the positing of an overall outline of Genesis provides context for the various individual sections of the book, such an outline does not answer the question of the beginning and ending of smaller definable sections within the scheme. For example, the Jacob-Laban stories have long been seen as a definable unit within the structure of Genesis.[10] Yet, simply because the Jacob-Laban tales have a definable beginning and ending and a coherent plot does not mean that they necessarily must comprise the *whole* of the Jacob Cycle. Indeed, they are a part of the larger cycle while simultaneously having an integrity all their own. While it is certainly true that the *story* of Joseph (and, therefore, the final "movement" of the Ancestral Histories) continues in Genesis until his death in 50:26, this does not necessarily imply that the Novella which began in the opening verses of Genesis 37 could not have reached its coherent end *before* chapter 50, with the final verses or chapters of Genesis having a different specific subject and serving a different purpose from that of the Novella.

Furthermore, while Joseph does appear as a major character in the final chapters of Genesis, he by no means appears as the central determining figure in these chapters as he does in the majority of the scenes following Genesis 37. In Genesis 48, the central determining character is Jacob/Israel, not Joseph:

> in verses 1-7, Jacob describes the theophany at Bethel/Luz (cf. 35:9-15; 28:10-17);
>
> in verses 8-16, Jacob blesses Ephraim and Manasseh;
>
> in verses 17-20, Jacob reprimands Joseph for wanting to switch the order of blessing and Jacob reiterates the blessing over Ephraim and Manasseh;

---

[8]Speiser, *Genesis*, 378.

[9]Humphreys, *Family*, 55.

[10]Among various treatments, see Gottwald, *Hebrew Bible*, 150-51.

in verses 21-22, Israel (Jacob) predicts his death and the return of Joseph to Canaan and grants Joseph a parcel of land.

In Genesis 49, Jacob's blessing on the twelve sons dominates the chapter. Although the length of Joseph's blessing (19 cola, vv. 22-26) is rivaled only by that of Judah (17 cola, vv. 8-12), the *character* of Joseph does not appear in the chapter, but is simply included in the general addressees, שִׁבְטֵי יִשְׂרָאֵל שְׁנֵים עָשָׂר, the Twelve Tribes of Israel (v. 28).

In Genesis 50, while the character of Joseph does appear, he does not propel the movement of the plot as in the earlier chapters. Verses 1-14 outline his return of Jacob's body to the cave of Machpelah in Canaan, as Jacob had caused him to promise earlier (47:29-31). In verses 15-21, Joseph responds to the fears of his brothers, with much of the story paralleling scenes occurring before chapter 47. In the conclusion of the book, verses 22-26, a notice is given concerning Joseph's life span; Joseph predicts his death and the eventual exodus from Egypt; and the notice is given concerning Joseph's death.

In chapters 48–50, therefore, the figure of Joseph, while still present, either appears as a foil to his father Jacob, stands silently along with the eleven other "tribes," or reacts to his father's death and brothers' fears. In these concluding chapters in Genesis, he does not appear as the central figure who propels the narrative, as he was in chapters 37 and 39–47. Narratively, these chapters, therefore, should not be considered part of the Novella that begins in chapter 37.

Finally, while the death of Joseph in 50:26 does mark the end of the book of Genesis as a whole, it need not necessarily mark the end of the more restricted Novella. Even as the birth of Joseph (30:22-24) occurs before 37:2, and even as the Novella begins in Joseph's seventeenth year, even so the Novella itself need not end with his death, but may end before. The genre of the Joseph story is not "Biography," but rather "Novella"; its purpose is to tell a story about a central character, rather than to provide a list of events in the patriarch's life.

While the notice in 50:22 does form a parallel with the notice in 37:1, the forms do not correspond closely:

37:1 וַיֵּשֶׁב יַעֲקֹב בְּאֶרֶץ מְגוּרֵי אָבִיו בְּאֶרֶץ כְּנָעַן:
50:22 וַיֵּשֶׁב יוֹסֵף בְּמִצְרַיִם הוּא וּבֵית אָבִיו

The only similarities between the two sentences are the *WAYYIQTOL* form of ישׁב, the preposition בְּ prefixed to a geographical name, and (coincidentally) the presence of the word אָבִיו. A much closer parallel with Genesis 37:1 is, in fact, found in 47:27:

37:1 וַיֵּשֶׁב יַעֲקֹב בְּאֶרֶץ מְגוּרֵי אָבִיו בְּאֶרֶץ כְּנָעַן:
47:27 וַיֵּשֶׁב יִשְׂרָאֵל בְּאֶרֶץ מִצְרַיִם בְּאֶרֶץ גֹּשֶׁן

Here, the parallelism of the two statements comes closer to forming a tight *inclusio*, marking the beginning and ending of the novella. The parallels between the two sentences are many: the *WAYYIQTOL* form of יֵשֶׁב; the same character as the subject of both sentences (while the specific designation is shifted from "Jacob" to "Israel"); a double prepositional phrase in apposition, both parts marked with the preposition בְּ prefixed to the noun אֶרֶץ; the objects of both phrases are geographical designations; the final prepositional phrases include a proper geographical name (גֹּשֶׁן, כְּנָעַן).

Seeing 47:27 as the formal end of the Joseph Novella, therefore, solves several narratological problems, including the relative absence or passivity of Joseph in the final three chapters of Genesis, the lack of consistent narratological organization in the final three chapters, and the bringing of the Novella to an appropriate conclusion, with the nation of Israel as a whole occupying the best land in Egypt (47:6) and multiplying in its fertility (47:27), while the Egyptians as a whole are bought as slaves for Pharaoh (47:20-21). The rise of Joseph (and, figuratively, of Israel) reaches its climax in 47:27. Therefore, on both formal and narratological grounds, it is appropriate to see the end of the Joseph Novella in Genesis 47:27.

Internal Considerations

Having determined the beginning and end of the novella, it is now necessary to consider whether there are passages within it that should be excluded from the syntactical analysis. Two such passages require particular attention. The first of these, the story of Judah and Tamar (Gen 38), has recently received much scholarly attention. The narrative has long been seen by critical scholars to be a secondary "intrusion" or, less polemically, an "interlude" in the Joseph story.[11] Within recent years, however, an attempt has been made to view the chapter in light of its function within the novella (and, more widely, within the book) that surrounds it. Robert Alter and Brevard Childs have both argued persuasively that, because of similar themes and intentions between the Judah and Tamar story and the larger story of Joseph, by seeing chapter 38 in its present final form within Genesis, one gains a more unified view of the perspective of Genesis as a whole. Since the *toledot* notice in 37:2 was concerned with the whole *tôlĕdôt ya'ăqōb* the whole "family of Jacob," then chapter 38 fulfills this

---

[11]For different critical approaches to Gen 38, see, in particular, Skinner, *Genesis,* 449-56; H. Holzinger, *Genesis* (Freiburg: J. C. B. Mohr, 1898), 227-30; Speiser, *Genesis,* 295-300. Note also the insightful article by Judah Goldin, "The Youngest Son or Where does Genesis 38 Belong," *JBL* 96 (1977): 27-44.

title by reporting a tale concerning another son of Jacob.[12] Indeed, Robert Longacre notes that the story of Jacob involves "the three *J*s: Jacob, Joseph, and Judah," and that Judah also plays a major role in the resolution of the novella as a whole.[13]

There is no argument that Genesis 38 does not belong within the book of Genesis nor is there a denial that its themes of deception, revelation, and blessing parallel those found, not only in the Joseph Novella, but also within Genesis as a whole. In reading the final form of Genesis, chapter 38 does indeed provide a story that complements and witnesses to the larger perspectives of the book.

This study, however, will not include Genesis 38 in its analysis of the narrative and discourse function of verbal forms and clausal types. The purpose of this study is not to provide and argue for an interpretation of the Joseph Novella, much less the book of Genesis as a whole. It is, rather, to investigate a specific phenomenon concerning the significance of the verbal and clausal forms found within the text of the Joseph Novella. As such, a conservative stance should be employed. Since Genesis 38 does not *directly* involve the descent of Joseph and Israel into Egypt, or treat the rise of Joseph and Israel while in Egypt, and since the story of Joseph, his brothers, and his father can be read with integrity without Genesis 38, it need not be considered *essential* to the text chosen for this study of verbal and clausal syntax.[14]

---

[12]Note the careful insights of Brevard Childs, *Introduction to the Old Testament as Scripture* (Philadelphia: Fortress, 1979), 155-57. For a literary perspective, note the work of Robert Alter, *The Art of Biblical Narrative* (New York: Basic Books, 1981), 3-11.

[13]Robert E. Longacre, *Joseph—A Story of Divine Providence: A Text and Text-linguistic Analysis of Genesis 37 and 39–48* (Winona Lake: Eisenbrauns, 1989), 26. Longacre here also passes on a private communication from Doris Myers, in which she suggests three main areas of parallelism between chapter 38 and the larger Joseph Novella: "(a) [Tamar] suffers injustice from her brothers-in-law and father-in-law, even as Joseph suffered from his own family; (b) the problem is solved through her concealing her identity, degradation (and threatened death), and revelation; and (c) her sons cross-up at birth in a way reminiscent of Jacob and Esau, and Manasseh and Ephraim (Jacob's crossed hands)."

[14]This concept of the "necessity of scenes" as integral to the characterization of the genre of "novella" is well described by von Rad: "We begin with a brief word about the literary quality of the Joseph story as a whole. It is distinct from all previous narratives because of its unusual length, for it considerably exceeds the length of the longest of the patriarchal stories, the one about Eliezer's suit of Rebekah (ch. 24). Further, it has not attained this length by means of a gradual comprehensive composition of individual narrative units. It does not belong to an 'epic cycle,' but it is from beginning to end an organically constructed narrative, no single segment of which can have existed independently as a separate element of tradition" (*Genesis,* 347). The ability to interpret the story

A second passage that will not be included in this syntactical analysis is Genesis 46:8-25, the Genealogical Name List of the Descendants of Jacob. Here, the exclusion of the passage is due to the genre of the passage itself. Being a list, it is not prose and contains neither substantial narrative nor discourse.[15] It, therefore, is not conducive to the type of analysis used in this study.

Texts Used in this Study

In consideration of the formal markers of the beginning and ending of the Joseph Novella, as well as the exclusion of Genesis 38 (on form-critical and narratological grounds) and Genesis 46:8-25 (on grounds of genre), the text of the Joseph Novella which this study will use as a database is the following: Genesis 37:1-36; 39:1–46:8a; 46:26–47:27.

---

of Judah and Tamar (Gen 38) as a discreet, self-cohesive story hints, therefore, that it has a secondary (although supportive) role to play within the Novella.

[15]The few narrative sentences in the list are so scattered and fragmentary as to be essentially incapable of syntactical study. The only complete fientic sentences in the passage are v. 12b: וַתֵּלֶד אֶת־אֵלֶּה לְיַעֲקֹב, v.18b: וַיָּמָת עֵר וְאוֹנָן בְּאֶרֶץ כְּנַעַן, and 20a: וַיִּוָּלֵד לְיוֹסֵף בְּאֶרֶץ מִצְרַיִם . . . אֶת־מְנַשֶּׁה וְאֶת־אֶפְרָיִם. All other sentences in the list are consistently verbless clauses (vv. 9, 10, 11, 12a, 13, 14, 15b, 16, 17, 19), some of which employ relative clauses using inflected verbs: 46:8a, 15a. For the form of the genealogical name-list, see Wilson, *Genealogy*, 188-89.

Genesis 37 – Joseph, His Dreams, and His Brothers – Clauses 1-131

Text in Syntactical/Paragraph Units

Initial Narrative Boundary

37.01.001	וַיֵּשֶׁב יַעֲקֹב בְּאֶרֶץ מְגוּרֵי אָבִיו בְּאֶרֶץ כְּנָעַן׃

Toledot Notice

37.02.002	אֵלֶּה תֹּלְדוֹת יַעֲקֹב

Introductory Setting (Comment)

37.02.003	יוֹסֵף בֶּן־שְׁבַע־עֶשְׂרֵה שָׁנָה הָיָה רֹעֶה אֶת־אֶחָיו בַּצֹּאן
37.02.004	וְהוּא נַעַר אֶת־בְּנֵי בִלְהָה וְאֶת־בְּנֵי זִלְפָּה נְשֵׁי אָבִיו
37.02.005	וַיָּבֵא יוֹסֵף אֶת־דִּבָּתָם רָעָה אֶל־אֲבִיהֶם׃
37.03.006	וְיִשְׂרָאֵל אָהַב אֶת־יוֹסֵף מִכָּל־בָּנָיו כִּי־בֶן־זְקֻנִים הוּא לוֹ
37.03.007	וְעָשָׂה לוֹ כְּתֹנֶת פַּסִּים׃
37.04.008	וַיִּרְאוּ אֶחָיו כִּי־אֹתוֹ אָהַב אֲבִיהֶם מִכָּל־אֶחָיו
37.04.009	וַיִּשְׂנְאוּ אֹתוֹ
37.04.010	וְלֹא יָכְלוּ דַּבְּרוֹ לְשָׁלֹם׃

Joseph Has Two Dreams

37.05.011	וַיַּחֲלֹם יוֹסֵף חֲלוֹם
37.05.012	וַיַּגֵּד לְאֶחָיו

37.05.013 וַיּוֹסִפוּ עוֹד שְׂנֹא אֹתוֹ
37.06.014 וַיֹּאמֶר אֲלֵיהֶם

37.08.021 וַיּוֹסִפוּ עוֹד שְׂנֹא אֹתוֹ

37.08.024 וַיּוֹסִפוּ עוֹד שְׂנֹא אֹתוֹ עַל חֲלֹמֹתָיו וְעַל דְּבָרָיו׃
37.09.025 וַיַּחֲלֹם עוֹד חֲלוֹם אַחֵר
37.09.026 וַיְסַפֵּר אֹתוֹ לְאֶחָיו
37.09.027 וַיֹּאמֶר

37.06.015 HD
שִׁמְעוּ נָא הַחֲלוֹם הַזֶּה
אֲשֶׁר חָלָמְתִּי׃
ND (Dream Report)
37.07.016 וְהִנֵּה אֲנַחְנוּ מְאַלְּמִים אֲלֻמִּים בְּתוֹךְ הַשָּׂדֶה
וְהִנֵּה
37.07.017 קָמָה אֲלֻמָּתִי
וְגַם נִצָּבָה
37.07.018 וְהִנֵּה תְסֻבֶּינָה אֲלֻמֹּתֵיכֶם
וַתִּשְׁתַּחֲוֶיןָ לַאֲלֻמָּתִי׃
37.07.019
37.07.020

37.08.022 ID
הֲמָלֹךְ תִּמְלֹךְ עָלֵינוּ
אִם מָשׁוֹל תִּמְשֹׁל בָּנוּ
37.08.023

ND (Dream Report)
37.09.028 וְהִנֵּה הַשֶּׁמֶשׁ וְהַיָּרֵחַ וְאַחַד עָשָׂר כּוֹכָבִים
וְהִנֵּה
37.09.029 חָלַמְתִּי חֲלוֹם עוֹד
וְהִנֵּה

וַיֹּאמְרוּ לוֹ 37.10.030
וַיִּגְעַר־בּוֹ אָבִיו 37.10.031
וַיֹּאמֶר לוֹ 37.10.032

מָה הַחֲלוֹם הַזֶּה 37.10.033
הֲבוֹא נָבוֹא אֲנִי וְאִמְּךָ וְאַחֶיךָ 37.10.034
לְהִשְׁתַּחֲוֺת לְךָ אָרְצָה:

וַיְקַנְאוּ־בוֹ אֶחָיו 37.11.035
וְאָבִיו שָׁמַר אֶת־הַדָּבָר 37.11.036

Joseph Searches for His Brothers

וַיֵּלְכוּ אֶחָיו לִרְעוֹת אֶת־צֹאן אֲבִיהֶם בִּשְׁכֶם: 37.12.037
וַיֹּאמֶר יִשְׂרָאֵל אֶל־יוֹסֵף 37.13.038

ID
הֲלוֹא אַחֶיךָ רֹעִים בִּשְׁכֶם 37.13.039
HD
לְכָה 37.13.040
וְאֶשְׁלָחֲךָ אֲלֵיהֶם 37.13.041

וַיֹּאמֶר לוֹ 37.13.042

הִנֵּנִי:

וַיֹּאמֶר לוֹ 37.14.043

HD
לֶךְ־נָא 37.14.044
רְאֵה אֶת־שְׁלוֹם אַחֶיךָ וְאֶת־שְׁלוֹם הַצֹּאן 37.14.045
וַהֲשִׁבֵנִי דָּבָר 37.14.046

37.14.047	וַיִּשְׁלָחֵהוּ מֵעֵמֶק חֶבְרוֹן				
37.14.048	וַיָּבֹא שְׁכֶמָה:				
37.15.049	וַיִּמְצָאֵהוּ אִישׁ				
	(וְהִנֵּה)				
37.15.050	תֹעֶה בַּשָּׂדֶה				
37.15.051	וַיִּשְׁאָלֵהוּ הָאִישׁ				
	לֵאמֹר				
		ID	מַה־תְּבַקֵּשׁ:	37.15.052	
37.16.053	וַיֹּאמֶר				
		ED	אֶת־אַחַי אָנֹכִי מְבַקֵּשׁ	37.16.054	
		HD	הַגִּידָה־נָּא לִי אֵיפֹה הֵם רֹעִים:	37.16.055	
37.17.056	וַיֹּאמֶר הָאִישׁ				
		ND	נָסְעוּ מִזֶּה	37.17.057	
			כִּי שָׁמַעְתִּי אֹמְרִים		
			†HD נֵלְכָה דֹתָיְנָה	37.17.058	
37.17.059	וַיֵּלֶךְ יוֹסֵף אַחַר אֶחָיו				
37.17.060	וַיִּמְצָאֵם בְּדֹתָן:				
37.18.061	וַיִּרְאוּ אֹתוֹ מֵרָחֹק				

The Brothers Plot to Kill Joseph

062α	וּבְטֶרֶם יִקְרַב אֲלֵיהֶם
37.18.062	וַיִּתְנַכְּלוּ אֹתוֹ לַהֲמִיתוֹ:
37.19.063	וַיֹּאמְרוּ אִישׁ אֶל־אָחִיו

ED

וַיֹּאמְרוּ

37.19.064   אִישׁ אֶל־אָחִיו הִנֵּה בַּעַל הַחֲלֹמוֹת הַלָּזֶה בָּא׃

HD

37.20.065   לְכוּ

37.20.066   וְנַהַרְגֵהוּ

37.20.067   וְנַשְׁלִכֵהוּ בְּאַחַד הַבֹּרוֹת

37.20.068   וְאָמַרְנוּ חַיָּה רָעָה אֲכָלָתְהוּ

†ND

37.20.069   וְנִרְאֶה מַה־יִּהְיוּ חֲלֹמֹתָיו׃

37.20.070   וַיִּשְׁמַע רְאוּבֵן וַיַּצִּלֵהוּ מִיָּדָם

37.21.071   וַיֹּאמֶר

37.21.072   אֲלֵהֶם רְאוּבֵן

37.21.073   אַל־תִּשְׁפְּכוּ־דָם

PD

37.21.074   לֹא נַכֶּנּוּ נָפֶשׁ׃

37.22.075   וַיֹּאמֶר אֲלֵהֶם רְאוּבֵן

075α   אַל־תִּשְׁפְּכוּ־דָם הַשְׁלִיכוּ אֹתוֹ אֶל־הַבּוֹר הַזֶּה אֲשֶׁר בַּמִּדְבָּר׃

HD

37.22.076   הַשְׁלִיכוּ אֹתוֹ אֶל־הַבּוֹר

37.22.077   וְיָד אַל־תִּשְׁלְחוּ־בוֹ לְמַעַן הַצִּיל אֹתוֹ מִיָּדָם

37.22.078   לַהֲשִׁיבוֹ אֶל־אָבִיו׃

The Brothers Execute the Plot to "Kill" Joseph

37.23.079	וַיְהִי כַּאֲשֶׁר־בָּא יוֹסֵף אֶל־אֶחָיו
37.23.080	וַיַּפְשִׁיטוּ אֶת־יוֹסֵף אֶת־כֻּתָּנְתּוֹ אֶת־כְּתֹנֶת הַפַּסִּים אֲשֶׁר עָלָיו
37.24.081	וַיִּקָּחֻהוּ
37.24.082	וַיַּשְׁלִכוּ אֹתוֹ הַבֹּרָה
37.24.083	(וְהַבּוֹר רֵק)
37.24.084	אֵין בּוֹ מָיִם
37.25.085	וַיֵּשְׁבוּ לֶאֱכָל־לֶחֶם
37.25.086	וַיִּשְׂאוּ עֵינֵיהֶם
37.25.087	וַיִּרְאוּ
37.25.088	וְהִנֵּה אֹרְחַת יִשְׁמְעֵאלִים בָּאָה מִגִּלְעָד
37.25.089	וּגְמַלֵּיהֶם נֹשְׂאִים נְכֹאת וּצְרִי וָלֹט הוֹלְכִים
37.25.090	(לְהוֹרִיד מִצְרָיְמָה)
37.26.091	וַיֹּאמֶר יְהוּדָה אֶל־אֶחָיו

ID

37.26.092	מַה־בֶּצַע

HD

37.27.093	כִּי נַהֲרֹג אֶת־אָחִינוּ
37.27.094	וְכִסִּינוּ אֶת־דָּמוֹ
37.27.095	לְכוּ וְנִמְכְּרֶנּוּ לַיִּשְׁמְעֵאלִים
37.27.096	וְיָדֵנוּ אַל־תְּהִי־בוֹ
37.28.097	כִּי־אָחִינוּ בְשָׂרֵנוּ הוּא
37.28.098	וַיִּשְׁמְעוּ אֶחָיו

37.28.099   וַיֵּלֶךְ רְאוּבֵן אֶל־הַבּוֹר

37.28.100   וְהִנֵּה אֵין־יוֹסֵף בַּבּוֹר

37.28.101   וַיִּקְרַע אֶת־בְּגָדָיו׃

37.29.102   וַיָּשָׁב אֶל־אֶחָיו וַיֹּאמַר

37.29.103   הַיֶּלֶד אֵינֶנּוּ

37.29.104   וַאֲנִי אָנָה אֲנִי־בָא׃

    (וַיִּקְחוּ)

37.30.105   וַיִּקְחוּ

37.30.106   אֶת־כְּתֹנֶת יוֹסֵף

ED   וַיִּשְׁחֲטוּ שְׂעִיר עִזִּים   37.30.107

ID   וַיִּטְבְּלוּ אֶת־הַכֻּתֹּנֶת בַּדָּם׃   37.30.108

37.31.109   וַיְשַׁלְּחוּ אֶת־כְּתֹנֶת הַפַּסִּים

37.31.110   וַיָּבִיאוּ אֶל־אֲבִיהֶם

37.31.111   וַיֹּאמְרוּ

37.32.112   זֹאת מָצָאנוּ

37.32.113   הַכֶּר־נָא

37.32.114   הַכְּתֹנֶת בִּנְךָ הִוא אִם־לֹא׃

ND   וַיַּכִּירָהּ וַיֹּאמֶר   37.32.115

HD   כְּתֹנֶת בְּנִי   37.32.116

ID   חַיָּה רָעָה אֲכָלָתְהוּ   37.32.117

    טָרֹף טֹרַף יוֹסֵף׃

37.33.118   וַיַּכִּירָהּ

37.33.119   וַיֹּאמֶר

ED

37.33.120	וַיַּכִּירָהּ וַיֹּאמֶר כְּתֹנֶת בְּנִי

ND

37.33.121	חַיָּה רָעָה אֲכָלָתְהוּ
37.33.122	טָרֹף טֹרַף יוֹסֵף׃

PD

37.35.129	כִּי־אֵרֵד אֶל־בְּנִי אָבֵל שְׁאֹלָה

37.34.123	וַיִּקְרַע יַעֲקֹב שִׂמְלֹתָיו
37.34.124	וַיָּשֶׂם שַׂק בְּמָתְנָיו
37.34.125	וַיִּתְאַבֵּל עַל־בְּנוֹ יָמִים רַבִּים
37.35.126	וַיָּקֻמוּ כָל־בָּנָיו וְכָל־בְּנֹתָיו לְנַחֲמוֹ
37.35.127	וַיְמָאֵן לְהִתְנַחֵם
37.35.128	וַיֹּאמֶר
37.35.130	וַיֵּבְךְּ אֹתוֹ אָבִיו׃
37.36.131	וְהַמְּדָנִים מָכְרוּ אֹתוֹ אֶל־מִצְרָיִם

Table of Independent Clause Types in Genesis 37

Clause Type	Clause Distribution	Total	Percent
QAṬAL Total Clauses: 13	Narrative: 003,006,010,036,131	5	38.5%
	ND: 017,018,028,057,†069,115,121,122 PD: ED: ID: HD:	8	61.5%
WeQAṬAL Total Clauses: 2	Narrative: 007	1	50.0%
	ND: PD: ED: ID: HD: 068	1	50.0%
YIQṬOL Total Clauses: 10	Narrative:	0	0
	ND: 019	1	10.0%
	PD: 074,129	2	20.0%
	ED:		
	ID: 022,023,034,052	4	40.0%
	HD: 041,076,078	3	30.0%
WeYIQṬOL Total Clauses: 1	Narrative:	0	0
	ND: PD: ED: ID: HD: 066,067,070,094	4	100%
WAYYIQṬOL Total Clauses: 70	Narrative: 001,005,008,009,011,012,013,014,021, 024,025,026,027,030,031,032,035,037,038,042,043, 047,048,049,051,053,056,059,060,061,062,063,071, 072,073,075,079,080,081,082,085,086,087,091,096, 097,098,099,100,101,102,104,105,106,109,110,111, 112,113,114,118,119,123,124,125,126,127,128,130	69	98.6%
	ND: 020 PD: ED: ID: HD:	1	1.4%

Participle Total Clauses: 10	Narrative: 050,088,089,090	4	40.0%
	ND: 016,029	2	20.0%
	PD:		
	ED: 054,064	2	20.0%
	ID: 039,108	2	20.0%
	HD:		
Verbless Total Clauses: 9	Narrative: 002,004,083,084,103	5	55.6%
	ND:		
	PD:		
	ED: 107	1	11.1%
	ID: 033,092,117	3	33.3%
	HD:		
Incomplete Total Clauses: 1	Narrative:	0	0
	ND:		
	PD:		
	ED: 120	1	100%
	ID:		
	HD:		
Imperative Total Clauses: 10	Narrative:	0	0
	HD: 015,040,044,045,046,055,065,077,093,116	10	100%
Cohortative Total Clauses: 1	Narrative:	0	0
	HD: †058	1	100%
Jussive Total Clauses: 1	Narrative:	0	0
	HD: 095	1	100%

Analysis of the Narrative Structure and
Discourse Text-Types in Genesis 37

Narrative Structural Analysis

The degree to which the *WAYYIQTOL* verbal form dominates the narrative portion of Genesis 37 is overwhelming.[16] The 69 clauses governed by *WAYYIQTOL* verbal forms outnumber any other clause type, either in narrative or, even, in direct speech. The syntactical structure of the chapter is built upon a number of *WAYYIQTOL* chains—groups of three or more subsequent clauses all with a consistent, initial *WAYYIQTOL* verbal form:

> Clauses 011-035
> Clauses 037-049
> Clauses 051-061
> Clauses 062-082
> Clauses 085-087
> Clauses 091-102
> Clauses 104-130

Besides these *WAYYIQTOL* chains, there also appear clauses not governed by *WAYYIQTOL* verbs:

A. *QATAL* clauses: 003, 006, 010, 036, 131
B. *WeQATAL* clause: 007
C. Participial clauses: 050, 088, 089, 090
D. Verbless clauses: 002, 004, 083, 084, 103

These four clause types all share one fundamental characteristic. In light of the basic feature of *WAYYIQTOL* as the primary narrative verb form—that is, *WAYYIQTOL* by its nature causes the action of a narrative to progress—the four non-*WAYYIQTOL* verb forms all share the quality of providing information *off* the basic story line. None of these verb forms cause the narrative to proceed in the same way as the *WAYYIQTOL* forms do.[17]

---

[16]For historical appraisals of the purpose and development of the *WAYYIQTOL* verbal form, note in particular the studies by Leslie McFall, *The Enigma of the Hebrew Verbal System* (Sheffield: Almond, 1982), especially 1-149, and Mark S. Smith, *The Origins and Development of the Waw-Consecutive* (Atlanta: Scholars, 1991).

[17]This is generally recognized for *QATAL* as well. *QATAL* is no longer seen, as it once was, as the basic narrative verbal form. "In broad terms *QATAL* can be described as a verb form functioning retrospectively. . . . Generally, it is not a narrative form, in spite

In addition to these four disjunctive verbal forms, one should note the function of the verbal root היה, found twice in the chapter (clauses 003, 079):

37.02.003 יוֹסֵף בֶּן־שְׁבַע־עֶשְׂרֵה שָׁנָה הָיָה רֹעֶה אֶת־אֶחָיו בַּצֹּאן

37.23.079 וַיְהִי כַּאֲשֶׁר־בָּא יוֹסֵף אֶל־אֶחָיו

In clause 003, היה plays a full verbal role. Here, it denotes the existence of Joseph, a shepherd, among his brothers.[18] In Clause 079, the verb, in the *WAYYIQTOL* form, introduces a temporal phrase, and is closely tied (narratively, if not explicitly syntactically) to the following clause. In neither of these cases (or, incidentally, in no other cases) does the verb היה *advance the action of the narrative*.[19] By its very semantic nature, היה always governs clauses whose function is to comment upon some aspect of the narrative, rather than to advance the narrative. Thus, in addition to the four disjunctive verbal forms noted above should be added two others:

E. Clauses employing היה as a full verbal form, denoting existence.[20]

---

of what most grammars say, unlike *WAYYIQTOL*, precisely because instead of being used to convey information concerning the 'degree zero' (i.e., the tense of the narrative), it conveys recovered information (an antecedent event or flashback) or even a comment on the main events (background)," from Alviero Niccacci, *The Syntax of the Verb in Classical Hebrew Prose* (Sheffield: Sheffield, 1990), 35. Note also the placement of the "perfect" verbal form in Robert E. Longacre's verbal rank scheme for Narrative Discourse in his analysis, *Joseph—A Story of Divine Providence* (Winona Lake: Eisenbrauns, 1989), 81.

[18]The somewhat common construction of *hāyâ* + participle often denotes a continuous action in the past, a concept usually conveyed by the presence of the participle either alone (e.g., clause 050) or with an explicit subject (e.g., clauses 088-089). Structurally, it is significant that the presence of היה with the participle does not affect the basic role played by the participle of providing off-line commentary, either within paragraphs or between them. Both clausal types, participial and היה verbal clauses, perform identical roles, one describing off-line actions and the other describing off-line states (see next footnote). In the case of clause 003, the status of Joseph as "shepherding" is conveyed without advancing the narrative proper.

[19]This point is noted by Longacre, *Joseph,* 66. See also David A. Dawson, *Text-Lingusitics and Biblical Hebrew* (Sheffield: JSOT, 1994), 62-65. *Hāyâ* clauses, therefore, share this characteristic with the previous four disjunctive clauses mentioned above.

[20]It is important to note that a *WAYYIQTOL* clause may employ היה as a verbal form. The resultant clause initially appears to be a וַיְהִי temporal clause, but the verb is used either as a copulative or as denoting existence. Note the examples of this in the next

F. Clauses introduced by וַיְהִי and functioning as a temporal introductory construction.

These six clause types all stand in opposition to the *WAYYIQTOL* clauses in the chapter. Whereas the *WAYYIQTOL* clauses provide a "chain" or "backbone" upon which the different events of the story are sequentially joined, the six disjunctive clause types outlined above all break the sequential progression of the narrative.

Although their foundational effect upon the narrative is similar, however, the narrative and structural *functions* of these six disjunctive clauses are not completely uniform. The basic functions of the non-*WAYYIQTOL* clauses within the narrative portion of the chapter are as follows:

1. To divide the longer text into smaller, cohesive blocks (i.e., paragraphs) of narrative.
2. To provide commentary off the sequence of the story line about some aspect of the narrative (e.g., subsequent events, previously undisclosed information about characters or settings, eventual outcomes of actions, etc.).

The kinds of information provided by means of the commentary function of the non-*WAYYIQTOL* disjunctive clauses are further divided into two differing types:

1. "Inner-paragraph comments," short off-line comments inserted *within* a narrative *WAYYIQTOL* chain and providing information directly related to the paragraph in which they occur, and
2. "Extra-paragraph comments," longer off-line comments inserted between larger blocks of narrative (or "paragraphs") and providing information further removed from the basic story line of the narrative.

To these various functions I will now turn, showing how the story line of Genesis 37 is divided into smaller discrete blocks of narrative and how the narrator provides different types of off-line commentary within the story line.

---

chapter, Gen 39:2, where the three clauses are all היה verbal clauses and also *WAYYIQTOL* clauses. Clause 134 employs היה as a copulative; clauses 135 and 136 employ היה as denoting existence.

The Paragraph-Boundary Function of non-WAYYIQṬOL Clauses

The non-*WAYYIQṬOL* clauses in the narrative portion of this chapter consistently do not advance the story line; their function, therefore, is not the same as the *WAYYIQṬOL* chain of clauses. Yet, it is also clear that the functions of all non-*WAYYIQṬOL* clauses are not identical. Some, such as וַיְהִי temporal clauses, serve as introductory markers for a following narrative chain. Their presence severs the *WAYYIQṬOL* chain which precedes each disjunction from the *WAYYIQṬOL* chain following it:

> ...*WAYYIQṬOL*
> *WAYYIQṬOL*
> *WAYYIQṬOL*
>   <break>
> וַיְהִי Temporal Clause
> *WAYYIQṬOL*
> *WAYYIQṬOL*...

These two types of clauses–וַיְהִי temporal clauses and *WAYYIQṬOL* clauses–essentially divide the narrative into "paragraph" blocks.[21]

This paragraph delineation within Hebrew narrative prose is also accomplished by clauses governed by *isolated, independent QAṬAL forms.*[22] An example of this is found in Genesis 37:11. After Joseph has related his two sets of dreams to his brothers and to his father, all the brothers and Jacob express disbelief (in the form of rhetorical questions, clauses 022-023; 033-034) and the narrator notes:

> 37.11.035 וַיְקַנְאוּ־בוֹ אֶחָיו
> 37.11.036 וְאָבִיו שָׁמַר אֶת־הַדָּבָר׃

The purpose of the *QAṬAL* form in clause 036 is twofold. The verb here stands in opposition to the verb in the preceding clause and the divergent verbal form

---

[21]Note Gesenius, *Grammar,* §111g: "This loose connexion (*sic*) by means of ויהי is especially common, when the narrative or a new section of it begins with any expression of time." Note also the more recent treatment by Douglas M. Gropp, "Progress and Cohesion in Biblical Hebrew Narrative: The Function of *kĕ/bĕ* + the Infinitive Construct" in *Discourse Analysis of Biblical Literature* (ed. Walter R. Bodine; Atlanta: Scholars, 1995), 183-212.

[22]When, on the other hand, multiple *QAṬAL* clauses occur together or multiple clauses governed by non-*WAYYIQṬOL* verbal forms occur together, they constitute an extra-paragraph comment. Note an illustration of this below.

performs a semantic disjunction: "His brothers were JEALOUS of him, BUT his father KEPT the matter (in mind)."[23] In a broader context, however, the *QAṬAL* clause 036 also divides the narrative of Joseph's dream reports (clauses 011-036) from the narrative of Joseph's search for his brothers (clauses 037-061). This division is signaled by the *QAṬAL* in clause 036.[24]

In this way, also, clause 131 concludes the paragraph of "The Brothers Execute the Plot to 'Kill' Joseph" by its background notice that the Midianites sold Joseph to the Egyptians:

$$\text{וְהַמְּדָנִים מָכְרוּ אֹתוֹ אֶל־מִצְרָיִם} \quad 37.36.131$$
$$\text{וְלְפוֹטִיפַר סְרִיס פַּרְעֹה שַׂר הַטַּבָּחִים:}$$

This background reiteration of clause 101 (וַיָּבִיאוּ אֶת־יוֹסֵף מִצְרָיְמָה) emphasizes that through all the trials endured by Joseph in clauses 079-101, and the ignorance of Jacob in clauses 102-130, Joseph remains safe at the end of the story. As will be shown throughout this study, isolated and independent *QAṬAL* clauses consistently mark paragraph boundaries, either initially or terminally, as clauses 036 and 131 do here in Genesis 37.

The Hebrew narrative prose in Genesis 37 is, therefore, composed of a basic "backbone" sequence of clauses governed by *WAYYIQṬOL* verbs which is divided into major constituent blocks by two different non-*WAYYIQṬOL* clauses:

1. Clauses introduced by וַיְהִי and functioning as a temporal introductory construction.
2. Isolated, independent *QAṬAL* clauses.

---

[23]This type of semantic disjunction is noted by Lambdin, *Introduction*, 279-81. Lambdin also notes that *QAṬAL* clauses occasionally indicate the completion or one episode or beginning of another (*Introduction*, 164-65). As noted in the first chapter of this study, he does not, however, provide criteria by which to determine when such "disjunctive" clauses are used as "explanatory or parenthetical" statements or as "terminative or initial" markers.

[24]Isolated *QAṬAL* clauses may mark not only the conclusion of a paragraph, but occasionally occur at the beginning of a paragraph (see clauses 667, 801, 867, 893). Thus a paragraph break may occur either before or after a *QAṬAL* clause. Where the break occurs depends upon whether the subject and setting of the *QAṬAL* clause is similar or different from the preceding *WAYYIQṬOL* chain. *QAṬAL* clauses which stand outside a *WAYYIQṬOL* chain (and thus cannot begin or end a paragraph) are part of extra-paragraph comments, which provide substantial commentary upon the narrative. Note explanation below.

By means of these two disjunctive clauses, the narrative is divided and grouped into discrete sections or paragraphs.

The Commentary Functions of non-WAYYIQTOL Clauses

The remaining four non-*WAYYIQTOL* disjunctive clauses noted at the beginning of this chapter (*WeQATAL*, participial, and verbless clauses, and clauses employing היה as a full verbal form) do not begin or conclude blocks of narrative but are, rather, "comments" or "asides" provided by the narrator which explain some aspect of the narrative.[25] These clauses never propel the narrative forward; rather, they provide antecedent, circumstantial, or proleptic information off the basic narrative story line.[26] They may be classified as either "inner-paragraph comments" or "extra-paragraph comments". Inner-paragraph comments occur when:

> Participial and/or verbless and/or verbal היה clauses stand within a *WAYYIQTOL* chain of at least three clauses.

Inner-paragraph comments occur *within* a paragraph and provide background information about some single element of the narrative at hand.

Extra-paragraph comments, on the other hand, occur *between* defined paragraphs. Since extra-paragraph comments stand outside paragraphs formed by *WAYYIQTOL* chains within the narrative, any type of clause may serve in this function as long as it occurs outside a formal paragraph. Extra-paragraph comments may even employ *WAYYIQTOL* clauses, as long as they are not combined into a chain of three or more members. Thus, extra-paragraph comments within narrative occur in:

---

[25]The basic concept of "off-line comment" in narrative prose is outlined by Niccacci, *Syntax,* 71. Niccacci is, however, in my opinion, off the mark when he states that *all* non-*WAYYIQTOL* "tenses" perform the same "background" function.

[26]A limited exception to this rule occurs when a negated verb (thus, not a *WAYYIQTOL* form), by its nature as not performed, does propel the narrative forward. Longacre calls this type of clause a "momentous negation" and promotes a clause that would otherwise be "non-real" ("X did not occur") into the state of "backgrounded actions", which, for Longacre, are practically on the primary "preterite story line" (Longacre, *Joseph,* 81). In almost all cases in the textual databases used in this study, momentous negation occurs only with the negated verbs אָבָה (2 Sam 13:14, 16, 25; 14:29[bis]) and יָכֹל (Gen 45:1), both of which imply a type of activity (often, a struggle) in their being negated, i.e., "he was unwilling . . ." and "he was unable . . .". The negations of these verbs in Gen 37:4 and 2 Sam 12:17 both occur in inner-paragraph comments and are, therefore, off the main narrative story line.

A combination of multiple *QAṬAL*, *WeQAṬAL*, or *YIQṬOL* clauses (and accompanying participial and verbless clauses and isolated, unchained *WAYYIQṬOL* clauses) that stands *outside* a *WAYYIQṬOL* chain of at least three clauses.

Extra-paragraph comments provide extensive information related to the story line, but outside of any single element in the narrative at hand. This combination of inner- and extra-commentary, along with the paragraph boundary markers noted above, provides the depth and texture of all Hebrew narrative prose.

A. Inner-Paragraph Comments

Instances of inner-paragraph comments in Genesis 37 are listed here.[27]

1. Participial clauses:

37.15.049	וַיִּמְצָאֵהוּ אִישׁ (וְהִנֵּה
37.15.050	תֹעֶה בַּשָּׂדֶה)
37.15.051	וַיִּשְׁאָלֵהוּ הָאִישׁ

While Joseph is searching for his brothers in Shechem, a man finds him and the man asks him what he is looking for. Here, the information provided in clause 050 is not actually on the sequential story line of the narrative; the "wandering of Joseph" occurs before and during the "man's finding him" in clause 049, not subsequent to it.[28] The aimlessness of Joseph here seems to belie his status as a shepherd (cf. clause 003); not only is he not with his brothers and the sheep, he cannot even find them when told to.

---

[27]No example of a הָיָה verbal clause being used as an inner-paragraph comment occurs in Gen 37. See the analysis of the next chapter, however, for an excellent example of this. Moreover, while in Gen 37 participial clauses and verbless clauses are used separately in inner-paragraph comments, they may, of course, be used together (e.g., in the Court Narrative, clauses 046-051), although this is rare in the textual databases used in this study.

[28]The absence here of the subject of the participle is unusual. In contexts immediately following הִנֵּה, however, the subject is sometimes dropped (Waltke and O'Connor, *Syntax,* 625-26). Here and in clauses 103-104, the function of הִנֵּה in the narrative seems to introduce an inner-paragraph comment whose content forms the basis for the immediately subsequent action (D. J. McCarthy, "The Uses of *wᵉhinneh* in Biblical Hebrew," *Biblica* 61 [1980], 330-42).

In a similar way, the threefold participial notice of the Midianite caravan in clauses 088-090 (also highlighted by וְהִנֵּה) is off the direct story line (in that they did not simply arrive subsequent to the brothers' sight of them, but were, rather, in transit from Gilead to Egypt before, during, and after the sighting), yet the information provided in the background comment deals directly with the sight of the brothers in clauses 086-087.

2. Verbless clauses:

37.24.082 וַיַּשְׁלִכוּ אֹתוֹ הַבֹּרָה
37.24.083 (וְהַבּוֹר רֵק
37.24.084 אֵין בּוֹ מָיִם:)

37.29.102 וַיָּשָׁב רְאוּבֵן אֶל־הַבּוֹר
(וְהִנֵּה
37.29.103 אֵין־יוֹסֵף בַּבּוֹר)

The verbless clauses here, like all verbless clauses in biblical narrative prose, provide information off the story line since they, by their nature, do not represent any action but only static description. Unlike the participial clauses noted above, which relate non-sequential *actions* occurring off the story line, verbless clauses in narrative provide information that is static and adjectival, rather than fientic or active.[29] In both cases, however, the information provided by the inner-paragraph comment, whether active or static, is closely tied to its immediate narrative context.

B. Extra-Paragraph Comments

In addition to these inner-paragraph comments, there is also a long example of an extra-paragraph comment at the beginning of the Novella in clauses 001-010. Since, canonically, the end of Genesis 36 is composed of a different genre (genealogy) and no *WAYYIQTOL* chain occurs either before the first clause of Genesis 37 or anywhere in the first ten clauses of the novella, the clauses beginning the story of Joseph are extra-paragraph commentary. This extra-paragraph

---

[29]In this instance, the information provided in the double verbless clauses seems to be ironic. The term בּוֹר (var. בְּאֵר) most often implies a "spring, well, or cistern," i.e. "a source or repository for water" (BDB, *s.v.*). It is, therefore, ironic that the brothers, after being dissuaded by Reuben from killing Joseph directly (clauses 074, 076-078), are not able to kill Joseph even passively. The boy seems indestructible.

comment here is composed of a wide selection of non-*WAYYIQṬOL* and isolated *WAYYIQṬOL* clauses, none of which provide progressive sequential narrative, but rather a general descriptive introduction to Joseph and his family. The various types of clauses present in the comment are listed here.

1. היה Verbal Clause

37.02.003 יוֹסֵף בֶּן־שְׁבַע־עֶשְׂרֵה שָׁנָה הָיָה רֹעֶה אֶת־אֶחָיו בַּצֹּאן

2. Verbless Clause

37.02.004 וְהוּא נַעַר אֶת־בְּנֵי בִלְהָה וְאֶת־בְּנֵי זִלְפָּה נְשֵׁי אָבִיו

3. *WeQAṬAL* Clause[30]

37.03.007 וְעָשָׂה לוֹ כְּתֹנֶת פַּסִּים:[31]

---

[30]In the history of scholarship concerning the forms of the Hebrew verb, the *WeQAṬAL* form has been particularly distressing. G. J. Spurrel (*Notes on the Book of Genesis* [Oxford: Clarendon, 1896], 304) suggests that in a case of the "perfect with a simple waw," the verb often takes on a frequentive sense, and considers this to be an instance of such a meaning. Spurrel's parallels with Gen 29:3 and 1 Sam 2:19 are, however, not conclusive, since the narrative context of Gen 29:3 is explicitly repetitive and the context of 1 Sam 2:19 explicitly covers an extended span of time (מִיָּמִים יָמִימָה). G. R. Driver (*Problems of the Hebrew Verbal System* [Edinburgh: T. & T. Clark, 1897], 93), Gesenius (*Grammar*, §112h), and, more recently, Waltke and O'Connor (*Syntax*, 530-34) all seem to see the frequentive sense as the only possible meaning of a *WeQAṬAL* in this context, in spite of the narratological difficulty of continually making (or remaking?) a coat. The difficulty of the verbal form is seen in its altered form in the Samaritan Pentateuch (ויעש), which renders it simply as a *WAYYIQṬOL* form. It appears, from a discourse-linguistic perspective, that the *WeQAṬAL* form marks the clause as providing information about an action off-line in the extra-paragraph comment. If the form had been a *WAYYIQṬOL* form, as the Samaritan Pentateuch suggests, a *WAYYIQṬOL* chain would be formed (clauses 007-009) and the narrative of the novella would begin in clause 007 rather than later in clause 011.

[31]The translation of כְּתֹנֶת פַּסִּים has long been disputed. It seems probable that the term refers to a coat "distinguished from the usual ones by its length, and the length of its sleeves; it was a luxury which only those who did not have to work could think of having" (Von Rad, *Genesis*, 351). The term also appears in 2 Sam 13:18, where it refers to a garment of a royal princess. Its significance in the Joseph Novella seems dependent upon the information given just previously in Genesis 37:2. The narrator has related that Joseph is, in fact, a shepherd and a *na'ar*, neither term denoting high standing. Yet, here he wears a royal robe. Already, the narrator prepares the reader not to take surface appearances for granted. The one who looks like a prince may actually be only a shepherd

4. Isolated *WAYYIQTOL* Clauses

37.02.005 וַיָּבֵא יוֹסֵף אֶת־דִּבָּתָם רָעָה אֶל־אֲבִיהֶם:

37.04.008 וַיִּרְאוּ אֶחָיו
כִּי־אֹתוֹ אָהַב אֲבִיהֶם מִכָּל־אֶחָיו
37.04.009 וַיִּשְׂנְאוּ אֹתוֹ

5. *QATAL* Clauses

37.03.006 וְיִשְׂרָאֵל אָהַב אֶת־יוֹסֵף מִכָּל־בָּנָיו
כִּי־בֶן־זְקֻנִים הוּא לוֹ

37.04.010 וְלֹא יָכְלוּ דַּבְּרוֹ לְשָׁלֹם:

While they do not occur in this example, extra-paragraph comments may also contain:

6. Initial וַיְהִי temporal clauses (Gen 39:10; clause 161).
7. *YIQTOL* clauses (2 Sam 12:31; clause 353)
8. Participial clauses (2 Sam 17:17; clause 908)
9. Verbless clauses (2 Sam 14:26; clause 616)

In all cases, the combination of these disjunctive clauses provides substantial off-line commentary between paragraphs. The content of these extra-paragraph comments is further removed from the basic story line and may provide a general introduction (as here), may describe continual or repeated actions that occur between paragraphs, or may relate the eventual outcome of the actions portrayed in a previous paragraph.

Having seen the particular examples of disjunctive narrative clauses–both in marking paragraph boundaries and within inner- and extra-paragraph commentary–a short analysis of the long extra-paragraph comment (clauses 003-010, along with clauses 001 and 002) that begins the story would be in order before turning to the analysis of the discourse text-types in the chapter. In light of the long *WAYYIQTOL* chain of Clauses 011-035 and the concluding *QATAL* sentence of Clause 036, the preceding ten clauses are unique in the narrative prose of the Joseph Novella in their sustained absence of any *WAYYIQTOL* chain.[32] The four clauses which *are* governed by *WAYYIQTOL* verbs (001, 005, 008, 009) in the

---

servant. On the other hand, one who is presented as a shepherd servant may actually be destined to be a prince!

[32]A "*WAYYIQTOL* chain" is, as defined earlier, a series of at least three continuous, uninterrupted clauses, each of which is governed by a (non-היה) *WAYYIQTOL* verb.

comment provide instances of punctilliar past action; they do not, however, provide enough narrative "momentum" to signal the initiation of the explicit narrative of the novella. One need only compare clauses 008 and 009 to the narrative proper beginning in clause 011 to see the evident difference.

The sustained absence of any *WAYYIQTOL* chain in these initial ten clauses indicates that these clauses perform an introductory function, providing all the necessary background information against which the narrative beginning in clause 011 should be understood. The material provided in the introduction consists of three types of information.

First, clauses 001 and 002 provide the placement of the novella within the larger book of Genesis. By means of clause 001, the narrator proleptically signals the ultimate change that will occur within the novella. Clause 001 parallels the final clause 967, and this *inclusio* ties the novella together as a unit. By means of clause 002, the reader is invited to see the subsequent novella in light of the larger themes contained in the preceding *toledot* formulas in the book. Clause 002 is an example of the meta-narrative structuring elements in the biblical text upon which many modern literary or canonical approaches are securely founded.[33] Thus the first two clauses of the novella provide anticipatory and recollected perspectives for the wider interpretation of the Joseph Novella.

Second, by means of verbless clauses and היה verbal clauses, the introduction provides background facts concerning the characters of Joseph and the brothers. In clauses 003 and 004, the narrator provides two facts about Joseph: he is a shepherd with (just like?) his brothers, and he is a boy with (just like?) the sons of his father's concubines.[34] In neither case is his state described as exalted or special.

Third, by means of *QATAL*, *WeQATAL*, and isolated *WAYYIQTOL* clauses, the introduction provides backgrounded actions concerning the characters of Jacob/Israel. Because all the clauses describing actions in this introduction are non-narrative and preliminary, the clauses employing *WAYYIQTOL* forms (005, 008, 009) are separated from each other by those governed by *QATAL* (006, 010) or *WeQATAL* (007) verbs. The lack of *WAYYIQTOL* chains from this comment allows them to describe actions as backgrounded information without being the narrative itself. Thus the actions present in the clauses before clause 011 are not the story line itself but are backgrounded and, therefore, highlighted as essential for an understanding of the subsequent narrative.

---

[33]See the "Formal Considerations" section above for further analyses of clauses 001 and 002 in their canonical shape and placement.

[34]For this particular meaning of את, note BDB, 85, and see Lev 26:39; Jer 23:28 and especially Isa 45:9.

In the remaining narrative analyses of each chapter, the three structural types of organization (paragraph boundaries, inner-paragraph comments, and extra-paragraph comments) will provide the format for the analysis. Because each clause of each chapter is represented in the chart following the chapter text, the analyses will, of course, not provide specific commentary upon each verbal form. The analyses will highlight only especially paradigmatic or divergent or additional clause types.

Discourse Function Analysis

Narrative Discourse

Twelve clauses comprising six cases of Narrative Discourse occur in Genesis 37.

> Clauses 016-020: Joseph's "Sheaf Dream" Report
> Clauses 028-029: Joseph's "Star/Sun/Moon Dream" Report
> Clause 057: The Shechemite's Report
> Clause †068: The Brothers' Planned Report of Joseph's Death
> Clause 115: The Brothers' Actual Report of Joseph's Coat
> Clauses 121-122: Jacob's Imagined Recounting of Joseph's Death

Excluding for the moment the first two cases of Narrative Discourse, all clauses in the remaining four cases are governed by *QATAL* verbs. *QATAL* verbs appear in every clause belonging to the final four cases of Narrative Discourse.

The first two cases are both dream reports, which, as will be shown clearly in the analyses of Genesis 40 and 41, are constrained syntactically to a certain form and, therefore, do not behave as consistently as other historical reports. Here, it will be sufficient to note a few similarities that the dream reports share which are not patterned in the other narrative reports.

In both dream reports, the first sentence of each report is prefaced by וְהִנֵּה (clauses 016, 028). Moreover, the first sentence of each report is governed by an active participle (מִשְׁתַּחֲוִים, מְאַלְּמִים), the subject of which is explicitly named (הַשֶּׁמֶשׁ וְהַיָּרֵחַ וְאַחַד עָשָׂר כּוֹכָבִים, אֲנַחְנוּ). Because of the brief nature of the second dream report, further similarities are unavailable. Yet, in the first dream report, note should also be made that the particle וְהִנֵּה marks turning points in the dream narrative and that, like the participle which heads the report, the *QATAL* clauses (017, 018) are also accompanied by a *YIQTOL* clause (019) and a *WAYYIQTOL* clause (020).

In the majority of cases, the use of *QATAL* in Narrative Discourse seems to function in the same role as *WAYYIQTOL* clauses do in narrative prose. Just as *WAYYIQTOL* chains provide the "backbone" to narrative prose, when characters describe real or imagined events that occurred before their speech act, they use primarily the *QAṬAL* verbal form to govern the clauses of their discourse. When actions are specifically described as occurring sequentially, however, *WAYYIQṬOL* chains may occur in Narrative Discourse in a way similar to that in narrative prose.

Predictive Discourse

The two cases of Predictive Discourse occurring in Genesis 37 contain only a single clause each.

> Clause 074: Reuben's Plan Not to Kill Joseph Directly
> Clause 129: Jacob's Prediction of His Own Wretched Death

Reuben's original plan not to kill Joseph actively, stated as a simple clause of Predictive Discourse (074) has already been commented on above. The use of the *YIQṬOL* form in Clause 129 is, likewise, indicative of the text-type of Predictive Discourse. The sentence serves as a simple predictive statement concerning Jacob's eventual descent to Joseph in death, "I shall go down to my son, mourning, to Sheol." The *YIQṬOL* clause, appearing in direct discourse and having no other clauses before or after it in the speech, refers to the future in a simple indicative manner. The irony of the prediction is, of course, found in its being overturned in the conclusion of the novella: Jacob does, indeed, descend to Joseph, his son. His descent, however, is with hope and joy (clause 838) rather than pain and mourning.

Expository Discourse

Four cases of Expository Discourse occur in Genesis 37, all being single clause speeches.

> Clause 054: Joseph's Answer to the Shechemite's Question
> Clause 064: The Brothers' Notice of Joseph's Approach
> Clause 107: Reuben's Notice of Joseph's Absence
> Clause 120: Jacob's Answer to his Sons' Question

All cases of Expository Discourse describe, explain, or respond to some immediate fact. The immediacy of the subject is usually conveyed by the use of participial (054, 064) or verbless (either true verbless, 107, or incomplete, 120) clauses. When the participle is used, the discourse tells or explains an action:

37.16.054 אֶת־אַחַי אָנֹכִי מְבַקֵּשׁ

and

הִנֵּה
37.19.064 בַּעַל הַחֲלֹמוֹת הַלָּזֶה בָּא:[35]

On the other hand, when a verbless clause is used, the discourse states a fact:

37.30.107 הַיֶּלֶד אֵינֶנּוּ

This quality of verbless clauses also holds true for incomplete clauses, which are often a response to a question (Interrogative Discourse) concerning a fact (rather than a question concerning an action).[36] In response to his sons' question concerning the identification of the bloody robe (clauses 052-054), Jacob responds with a two word incomplete clause:

37.22.120 כְּתֹנֶת בְּנִי

In all cases, whether the Expository Discourse is one of action or one of fact, the sense of all clauses is immediate and present.[37]

Interrogative Discourse

Genesis 37 contains seven examples of Interrogative Discourse.

Clauses 022-023: The Brothers' Rhetorical Questions to Joseph
Clauses 033-034: The Father's Rhetorical Questions to Joseph
Clause 039: Israel's Rhetorical Question to Joseph
Clause 052: The Shechemite's Question to Joseph
Clause 092: Judah's Rhetorical Question to the Brothers
Clause 108: Reuben's Rhetorical Question to the Brothers
Clause 117: The Brothers' Question to Their Father

---

[35]The question of whether the verb in clause 064 (בָּא) is a participle or *QATAL* is, of course, dubious on purely morphological considerations. The case is usually decided on two grounds: the presence of הנה immediately before the clause, and the fact that, narratively, Joseph had not yet completely "come" (clause 062). See McCarthy, "*w^ehinneh*," 330-42.

[36]However, incomplete clauses *are* rarely used to provide a response to a question concerning an action: note Gen 42:7; clause 433. The fact that the brothers here employ an incomplete clause rather than a *QATAL* clause insinuates that they are commenting upon their (stative) origin rather than their (past-active) journey.

[37]Expository Discourse may also employ היה verbal clauses, usually as *QATAL*, but occasionally as *YIQTOL*.

Among these, five of the questions are "rhetorical" questions, that is, questions to which no answer is given because the answer to the question is generally well known to the hearer and "unconditionally admitted by him."[38] The general *functions* of the rhetorical question differ from those of natural questions. Natural questions elicit a response, usually verbal, of information that is unknown to the speaker but known to the hearer. Rhetorical questions, on the other hand, may seek to elicit an action from the hearer (as hortatory statements), may be used instead of a negative assertion or refusal (as expository statements), or may serve as "rhetorical" introductions or conclusions to other forms of discourse. The form of the rhetorical question is, however, syntactically indistinguishable from that of the natural question, its nature being dependent upon narrative contextual circumstances. Because of this similarity of basic form, rhetorical questions and natural questions are here treated together.

Unlike other types of speech, Interrogative Discourse is usually explicitly marked by interrogative particles.[39] For this reason, the verbal forms used within clauses contained in Interrogative Discourse are not determinative of this discourse text-type as they are, for instance, in statements of Predictive or Expository Discourse, which do not have specific "predictive particles" or "expository markers".[40] Thus, in Genesis 37, the verbal forms used in Interrogative Discourse encompass *YIQTOL* (022,023,034,052), participial (039, 108), and verbless (033,092,117) clauses.

---

[38]Gesenius, *Grammar,* §150e. Also note the recent work on rhetorical questions by Lenart J. de Regt, "Functions and Implications of Rhetorical Questions in the Book of Job" in *Biblical Hebrew and Discourse Linguistics* (ed. Robert D. Bergen; Dallas: Summer Institute of Linguistics, 1994), 361-73.

[39]The use of interrogative particles is not, however, a universal marker of interrogative discourse. The number of such "unmarked" interrogative statements is rather low (according to H. G. Mitchell, "The omission of the interrogative particle," in *Old Testament and Semitic Studies in Memory of W. R. Harper* [Chicago: The University of Chicago Press, 1907], 113, the total is less than 39) and most occur in poetic/prophetic genres. When unmarked interrogative clauses do occur in narrative, they always occur in interrogative contexts, in which the clause immediately before (or sometimes after) is explicitly marked with an interrogative particle. The entire discourse is, therefore, marked as interrogative and the sense of the unmarked clause is understood as a question. See Gesenius, *Grammar,* §150a.

[40]The significance of verbal form in Interrogative Discourse will be fully treated in the final chapter of this study.

Hortatory Discourse

There are ten examples of Hortatory Discourse in Genesis 37, more than any other text-type in the chapter.

> Clause 015: Joseph's Introduction to his First Dream
> Clauses 040-041: Israel's Initial Sending of Jacob to His Brothers
> Clauses 044-046: Israel's Detailed Sending of Joseph to His Brothers
> Clause 055: Joseph to the Shechemite Man.
> Clause †058: The Report of the Brothers leaving for Dothan
> Clauses 065-070: The Brothers' Plotting Joseph's Death
> Clauses 076-078: Reuben's Detailed Refusal to Kill Joseph
> Clauses 093-095: Judah's Plan to Sell Joseph
> Clause 116: The Brothers' Request for Jacob's Recognition

The verbal forms present in Hortatory Discourse are widespread: *WeQATAL, YIQTOL, WeYIQTOL*, Imperative, Cohortative, and Jussive, the final three occurring *only* in Hortatory Discourse.[41] The historical developments of the *YIQTOL* verbal form and or the jussive verbal form have been outlined elsewhere.[42] The ambiguity of the *YIQTOL* verbal form in Hortatory Discourse, should be recognized, since the *YIQTOL* clause is, itself, the primary means by which a character signals Predictive Discourse in a speech act (see above). The instances of true ambiguity are, however, rare, because of the common presence of parallel commands set as imperatives or cohortatives or of attached hortatory particles (e.g., הַ ־ , נָא־) marking the *YIQTOL* clause as hortatory (note the examples from Genesis 37 below).[43]

---

[41]Only forms which are *explicitly* marked as jussive and cohortative are accounted in those categories in this study. The notorious ambiguity between the *YIQTOL* and the volitive forms is, in light of this study, not so much a confusion of forms, as it is a confusion of text-types. The high number of *YIQTOL*s which perform volitive functions when they appear in hortatory contexts points to the fact that the function of the clause is connected more to its text-typical context than to any inherent meaning of the governing verbal form.

[42]Here, note the works of William Moran and Anson Rainey in the discussion of the "Historical-Comparative Approaches" in Chapter One of this study. Also note the basic treatments in Waltke and O'Connor, *Syntax*, 566-67; and Leslie McFall, *Enigma*, 54-55.

[43]One should note that the treatment of "Jussive and Cohortative after Imperative" in Waltke and O'Connor (*Syntax*, 577), while correct insofar as it goes, does not fully appreciate the complexity of Hortatory Discourse: "After an imperative a verbal form not preceded by its subject or a negative particle is normally either a jussive or a cohortative. Where a non-perfective is not morphologically marked in such a context, it may be taken as having jussive or cohortative force." What is missing from this analysis is the fact that

Most instances of Hortatory Discourse in the Joseph Novella contain clauses that are governed by imperative, cohortative, or jussive verbal forms and are, therefore, explicitly marked as hortatory. In cases in which the Hortatory Discourse is the only discourse in the speech, the included volitive verbal form (imperative, cohortative, or jussive) will signal the hortatory nature of the speech, even if subsequent verbal forms in the speech are not explicitly volitive (*WeQATAL*, *YIQTOL*, or *WeYIQTOL*). Thus, for example, when Jacob sends Joseph in search for his brothers in Shechem, he employs an initial imperative, followed by another imperative, followed in turn by a *WeQATAL* clause:

37.14.044 לֶךְ־נָא
37.14.045 רְאֵה אֶת־שְׁלוֹם אַחֶיךָ וְאֶת־שְׁלוֹם הַצֹּאן
37.14.046 וַהֲשִׁבֵנִי דָּבָר

The final *WeQATAL* clause, although not explicitly a hortatory clausal form (since it also occurs in both narrative prose and in Predictive Discourse), functions in this particular context the same as an imperative clause due to the hortatory context of its text-type.

Furthermore, in cases of a single speech act when the Hortatory Discourse occurs immediately after another text-type, the presence of the explicitly volitive form often marks the boundary of the following Hortatory Discourse and, thus, differentiates it from the preceding text-type. For example, when Judah attempts to dissuade his brothers from simply leaving Joseph in the cistern to die, he urges them with a rhetorical question followed immediately by a hortatory sequence initiated by an unambiguous imperative:

ID
37.26.092 מַה־בֶּצַע
כִּי נַהֲרֹג אֶת־אָחִינוּ
וְכִסִּינוּ אֶת־דָּמוֹ:

HD
37.27.093 לְכוּ
37.27.094 וְנִמְכְּרֶנּוּ לַיִּשְׁמְעֵאלִים
37.27.095 וְיָדֵנוּ אַל־תְּהִי־בוֹ
כִּי־אָחִינוּ בְשָׂרֵנוּ הוּא

Note that the transitional clause 093 provides the base upon which the volitive function of the following clauses proceed, even if (as with clause 094) the verbal

---

often an ambiguous *YIQTOL* ("non-perfective") form *precedes* the clear volitive form. One must look, not only at the preceding verbal form, but also at *the entire constellation of clausal types within the discourse* in order to determine its function and the meaning of the verbal forms and clauses within it.

form is not *explicitly* a volitive form. As such, Hortatory Discourses are often explicitly marked either by the presence of simple unambiguous volitive verbal forms (clauses 058, 093), by the extension of the imperative with the ה ָ ־ suffix (clause 040), or by the particle of entreaty נָא־ (clauses 015, 044, 055, and 116).

When the Hortatory Discourse is a negative request or demand, however, the volitive forms may not stand in the discourse. In such cases (clause 076), the hortatory function of the verb and the hortatory nature of the discourse as a whole is marked by the negative particle אַל.[44]

---

[44]The seminal work on the negative in Semitic languages is Dean A. Walker, *The Semitic Negative: With Special Reference to the Negative in Hebrew* (Chicago: The University of Chicago Press, 1896).

Table of Discourse Constellations for Genesis 37

		Present Ch.	Total in JN
ND	*QATAL*	4	4
	QATAL, WAYYIQTOL		0
	QATAL, (Ptc./Vbl.)	4	4
	QATAL, WAYYIQTOL, (Ptc./Vbl.)		0
	QATAL, WAYYIQTOL, (Ptc./Vbl.), *YIQTOL*	1	1
	QATAL, YIQTOL (w/ past adverb)		0
	WAYYIQTOL, (Ptc./Vbl.)		0
	Vbl/Ptc/Inc (Dream Report)		0
PD	*YIQTOL*	2	2
	YIQTOL, WeQATAL		0
	YIQTOL, WeQATAL, (Ptc./Vbl../Inc.)		0
	YIQTOL, (Ptc./Vbl../Inc.)		0
	WeQATAL		0
	WeYIQTOL		0
ED	Ptc./Vbl.	3	3
	Ptc./ Vbl., Inc.		0
	Inc.		0
	Ptc./Vbl., *QATAL/YIQTOL* of היה		0
	Ptc./Vbl., *QATAL/YIQTOL* of היה, Front. Obj.+ *QATAL/YIQTOL*		0
	QATAL/YIQTOL of היה		0
HD	Impv./Coh./Juss.	5	5
	Impv./Coh./Juss., *WeYIQTOL/YIQTOL*	1	1
	Impv./Coh./Juss., *WeQATAL*		0
	Impv./Coh./Juss., *WeYIQTOL/YIQTOL, WeQATAL*	1	1
	Impv./Coh./Juss., *QATAL*		0
	Impv./Coh./Juss., *WeYIQTOL/YIQTOL,* (We)*QATAL*		0
	Impv./Coh./Juss., ʾal-*YIQTOL*	1	1
	Impv./Coh./Juss., *WeQATAL,* ʾal-*YIQTOL*	1	1
	ʾal-*YIQTOL*		0
	ʾal-*YIQTOL, WeQATAL/YIQTOL*		0
	(We)*YIQTOL-nāʾ,* (*WeQATAL/*[We]*YIQTOL*)		0
	QATAL, YIQTOL/WeQATAL		0

Genesis 39 — Joseph, Potiphar's Wife, and Prison Life — Clauses 132-200

Text in Syntactical/Paragraph Units

Joseph is Appointed over Potiphar's House

39.01.132	וַיּוֹסֵף הוּרַד מִצְרָיְמָה
39.01.133	וַיִּקְנֵהוּ פּוֹטִיפַר סְרִיס פַּרְעֹה שַׂר הַטַּבָּחִים אִישׁ מִצְרִי
	מִיַּד הַיִּשְׁמְעֵאלִים
39.02.134	וַיְהִי יְהוָה אֶת־יוֹסֵף
39.02.135	וַיְהִי אִישׁ מַצְלִיחַ
39.02.136	וַיְהִי בְּבֵית אֲדֹנָיו הַמִּצְרִי׃
39.03.137	וַיַּרְא אֲדֹנָיו
39.04.138	כִּי יְהוָה אִתּוֹ
39.04.139	וְכֹל אֲשֶׁר־הוּא עֹשֶׂה
39.04.140	יְהוָה מַצְלִיחַ בְּיָדוֹ
39.04.141	וַיִּמְצָא יוֹסֵף חֵן בְּעֵינָיו
	וַיְשָׁרֶת אֹתוֹ

YHWH Blesses Potiphar's House

39.05.142	וַיַּפְקִדֵהוּ עַל־בֵּיתוֹ
39.05.143	וְכָל־יֶשׁ־לוֹ נָתַן בְּיָדוֹ׃
39.05.144	וַיְהִי מֵאָז הִפְקִיד אֹתוֹ בְּבֵיתוֹ
39.05.145	וְעַל כָּל־אֲשֶׁר יֶשׁ־לוֹ

39.06.146   וַיַּעֲזֹב כָּל־אֲשֶׁר־לוֹ בְּיַד־יוֹסֵף

39.06.147   וְלֹא־יָדַע אִתּוֹ מְאוּמָה כִּי אִם־הַלֶּחֶם אֲשֶׁר־הוּא אוֹכֵל

39.06.148   (וַיְהִי) יוֹסֵף יְפֵה־תֹאַר וִיפֵה מַרְאֶה׃

Potiphar's Wife Tempts and Joseph Rejects: I

39.07.149   וַיְהִי אַחַר הַדְּבָרִים הָאֵלֶּה

39.07.150   וַתִּשָּׂא אֵשֶׁת־אֲדֹנָיו אֶת־עֵינֶיהָ אֶל־יוֹסֵף

39.07.151   וַתֹּאמֶר

39.07.152   שִׁכְבָה עִמִּי׃   **HD**

39.08.153   וַיְמָאֵן

39.08.154   וַיֹּאמֶר אֶל־אֵשֶׁת אֲדֹנָיו

39.08.155   הֵן אֲדֹנִי לֹא־יָדַע אִתִּי מַה־בַּבָּיִת   **ND**

39.08.156   וְכֹל אֲשֶׁר־יֶשׁ־לוֹ נָתַן בְּיָדִי

39.09.157   אֵינֶנּוּ גָדוֹל בַּבַּיִת הַזֶּה מִמֶּנִּי

39.09.158   וְלֹא־חָשַׂךְ מִמֶּנִּי מְאוּמָה כִּי אִם־אוֹתָךְ בַּאֲשֶׁר אַתְּ־אִשְׁתּוֹ

39.09.159   וְאֵיךְ אֶעֱשֶׂה הָרָעָה הַגְּדֹלָה הַזֹּאת   **ID**

39.09.160   וְחָטָאתִי לֵאלֹהִים

Potiphar's Wife's Subsequent Proposals/Rejections (Comment)

וַיְהִי כְּדַבְּרָהּ אֶל־יוֹסֵף יוֹם וֹ יוֹם	39.10.161
וְלֹא־שָׁמַע אֵלֶיהָ לִשְׁכַּב אֶצְלָהּ לִהְיוֹת עִמָּהּ	39.10.162

Potiphar's Wife Tempts and Joseph Rejects: II

וַיְהִי כְּהַיּוֹם הַזֶּה	39.11.163
וַיָּבֹא הַבַּיְתָה לַעֲשׂוֹת מְלַאכְתּוֹ	39.11.164
וְאֵין אִישׁ מֵאַנְשֵׁי הַבַּיִת שָׁם בַּבָּיִת׃	39.11.165
וַתִּתְפְּשֵׂהוּ בְּבִגְדוֹ לֵאמֹר	39.12.166

HD
שִׁכְבָה עִמִּי 39.12.167

וַיַּעֲזֹב בִּגְדוֹ בְּיָדָהּ	39.12.168
וַיָּנָס	39.12.169
וַיֵּצֵא הַחוּצָה׃	39.12.170

Potiphar's Wife Reports an Attempted Rape

וַיְהִי כִּרְאוֹתָהּ	39.13.171
כִּי־עָזַב בִּגְדוֹ בְּיָדָהּ	
וַיָּנָס הַחוּצָה׃	
וַתִּקְרָא לְאַנְשֵׁי בֵיתָהּ	39.14.172
וַתֹּאמֶר לָהֶם	39.14.173
לֵאמֹר	

HD
רְאוּ 39.14.174

39.16.182 לַאמֹר

39.17.183 וַתְּדַבֵּר אֵלָיו כַּדְּבָרִים הָאֵלֶּה לַאמֹר

בָּא־אֵלַי הָעֶבֶד הָעִבְרִי אֲשֶׁר־הֵבֵאתָ לָּנוּ לְצַחֶק בִּי׃

Joseph is Appointed over the Round House

וַיֹּאמֶר אֲדֹנֵי יוֹסֵף אֶת־דְּבָרָיו 39.19.188

39.19.188 אֲשֶׁר דִּבְּרָה אֵלָיו לַאמֹר

כַּדְּבָרִים הָאֵלֶּה עָשָׂה לִי עַבְדֶּךָ

39.14.175 ND

39.14.176 וַתִּקְרָא לְאַנְשֵׁי בֵיתָהּ

39.14.177 וַתֹּאמֶר לָהֶם לֵאמֹר

39.15.178 רְאוּ הֵבִיא לָנוּ אִישׁ עִבְרִי לְצַחֶק בָּנוּ

בָּא אֵלַי לִשְׁכַּב עִמִּי

וָאֶקְרָא בְּקוֹל גָּדוֹל׃

39.15.179 וַיְהִי כְשָׁמְעוֹ

39.15.180 כִּי־הֲרִימֹתִי

39.15.181 וָאֶקְרָא

וַיַּעֲזֹב בִּגְדוֹ אֶצְלִי

וַיָּנָס

וַיֵּצֵא הַחוּצָה׃

39.17.184 ND

כַּדְּבָרִים הָאֵלֶּה עָשָׂה לִי עַבְדֶּךָ׃

39.18.185 וַיְהִי כַּהֲרִימִי קוֹלִי

וָאֶקְרָא

39.18.186 וַיַּעֲזֹב בִּגְדוֹ אֶצְלִי

39.18.187 וַיָּנָס הַחוּצָה׃

39.19.189 ND

וַיִּחַר אַפּוֹ׃ וַיִּקַּח אֲדֹנֵי יוֹסֵף אֹתוֹ

39.33.200

39.33.199

39.22.198

39.22.197

39.21.196

39.21.195

39.21.194

39.20.193

39.20.192

39.20.191

39.19.190

Table of Independent Clause Types in Genesis 39

Clause Type	Clause Distribution	Total	Percent
QAṬAL Total Clauses: 13	Narrative: 132,141,143,147,162,198	6	46.2%
	ND: 155,156,158,175,176,184,189 PD: ED: ID: HD:	7	53.8%
WeQAṬAL Total Clauses: 0	Narrative:	0	0
	ND: PD: ED: ID: HD:	0	0
YIQṬOL Total Clauses: 1	Narrative:	0	0
	ND: PD: ED: ID: 159 HD:	1	100%
WeYIQṬOL Total Clauses: 1	Narrative: 0	0	0
	ND: PD: ED: ID: 160 HD:	1	100%
WAYYIQṬOL Total Clauses: 46	Narrative: 133,134,135,136,137,138,139,140,142, 144,145,146,148,149,150,151,153,154,161,163,164, 168,169,170,171,172,173,182,183,188,190,191,192, 193,194,195,196,197	38	82.6%
	ND: 177,178,179,180,181,185,186,187 PD: ED: ID: HD:	8	17.4%

	Narrative: 200	1	100%
Participle Total Clauses: 1	ND: PD: ED: ID: HD:	0	0
	Narrative: 165,166,199	3	75.0%
Verbless Total Clauses: 4	ND: 157 PD: ED: ID: HD:	1	25.0%
	Narrative:	0	0
Incomplete Total Clauses: 0	ND: PD: ED: ID: HD:	0	0
Imperative	Narrative:	0	0
Total Clauses: 3	HD: 152,167,174	3	100%
Cohortative	Narrative:	0	0
Total Clauses: 0	HD:	0	0
Jussive	Narrative:	0	0
Total Clauses: 0	HD:	0	0

Analysis of the Narrative Structure and
Discourse Text-Types in Genesis 39

Narrative Structural Analysis

Narrative/Paragraph Structure

Genesis 39, the story of "Joseph, Potiphar's Wife, and Prison Life" is composed of six main paragraphs, all explicitly marked either at their beginning, their ending, or both.

> Clauses 132-141: Joseph is Appointed over Potiphar's House
> Clauses 142-147: YHWH Blesses Potiphar's House
> Clauses 149-154: Potiphar's Wife Tempts and Joseph Rejects: I
> Clauses 163-170: Potiphar's Wife Tempts and Joseph Rejects: II
> Clauses 171-183: Potiphar's Wife Reports an Attempted Rape
> Clauses 188-200: Joseph is Appointed over the Round House

The first paragraph, clauses 132-141, begins and concludes with *QATAL* clauses. All other paragraphs in this chapter are initially marked with clauses introduced by וַיְהִי and followed by an infinitive construct, the entire clause functioning as a temporal introductory construction (clauses 142, 149, 163, 171, and 188). In addition to these initial paragraph markers, the second paragraph in the chapter, clauses 142-147, is terminally marked with a *QATAL* clause.

Extra-Paragraph Comments

Between the third and fourth paragraphs, a comment occurs whose content is not closely tied to the narrative sequences of the paragraphs surrounding it. This extra-paragraph comment (Clauses 161-162) allows the reader to see an elapsed period of time during which the narrative does not actually progress (in that the same event which happened in the third paragraph happens again and again), and during which Joseph's honor and righteousness are highlighted:

> 39.10.161 וַיְהִי כְּדַבְּרָהּ אֶל־יוֹסֵף יוֹם יוֹם
> 39.10.162 וְלֹא־שָׁמַע אֵלֶיהָ לִשְׁכַּב אֶצְלָהּ לִהְיוֹת עִמָּהּ׃

The form of this extra-paragraph comment is unusual in that it appears, at first glance, to be the beginning of a new paragraph, complete with the וַיְהִי introductory temporal marker. Yet, no *WAYYIQTOL* picks up the story line. Instead, a negated *QATAL* clause comments that during all this time (יוֹם יוֹם), Joseph did not heed Potiphar's Wife's suggestions and seductions. Then, in Clause 163ff,

the narrative does start again with a וַיְהִי temporal clause 163 continued by the
WAYYIQTOL clause 164.

Inner-Paragraph Comments

There are twelve comments set into the six main paragraphs of Genesis 39.
Of these twelve, eight comments are comprised of clauses employing היה as a
full verbal form used as a copula or as denoting existence. Three occur within
the first paragraph of the chapter:

39.02.134 וַיְהִי יְהוָה אֶת־יוֹסֵף
39.02.135 וַיְהִי אִישׁ מַצְלִיחַ
39.02.136 וַיְהִי בְּבֵית אֲדֹנָיו הַמִּצְרִי׃

One occurs within the second paragraph:

39.05.145 וַיְהִי בִרְכַּת יְהוָה בְּכָל־אֲשֶׁר יֶשׁ־לוֹ בַּבַּיִת וּבַשָּׂדֶה׃

One stands at the end of the second paragraph:

39.06.148 וַיְהִי יוֹסֵף יְפֵה־תֹאַר וִיפֵה מַרְאֶה׃

Three occur within the final paragraph:

39.20.193 וַיְהִי־שָׁם בְּבֵית הַסֹּהַר׃
39.21.194 וַיְהִי יְהוָה אֶת־יוֹסֵף

and

23.22.198 וְאֵת כָּל־אֲשֶׁר עֹשִׂים שָׁם הוּא הָיָה עֹשֶׂה׃

In all of these comments, the presence of YHWH or the placement or status of
Joseph does not, in fact advance the narrative any, but the information granted
by these היה verbal commentary clauses performs three services. When they
apply to Joseph, the information either helps situate the reader in relationship to
the focus of the narrative (clauses 135,136,193) or provides a piece of information which aids in interpreting a following paragraph (clause 148).[45] They

---

[45]Note that the final inner-paragraph comment in the second paragraph (clause 148)
stands *after* the *QATAL* paragraph boundary marker in clause 147. Since היה verbal
clauses do not advance the narrative, such inner-paragraph comments may occasionally
stand after a paragraph boundary but still be considered a part of the paragraph.

answer the question: Where is the action taking place now? Additionally, when the clauses apply to YHWH, they provide the theological underpinning that will come to the fore during Joseph's revelation of himself in Chapter 45.

In addition to these inner-paragraph comment clauses providing existential information, there are also two comment clauses which inform the reader that something or someone did not exist, one in the fourth paragraph of the chapter:

39.11.165 וְאֵין אִישׁ מֵאַנְשֵׁי הַבַּיִת שָׁם בַּבָּיִת׃

and one in the final paragraph of the chapter:

39.23.199 אֵין שַׂר בֵּית־הַסֹּהַר רֹאֶה אֶת־כָּל־מְאוּמָה בְּיָדוֹ בַּאֲשֶׁר יְהוָה אִתּוֹ

Both comments are verbless clauses employing אֵין (וְ).

One comment occurs in the final paragraph that informs the reader of some action that takes place during the course of the narrative. In this case, the governing verb of the comment is a participle:

39.23.200 וַאֲשֶׁר־הוּא עֹשֶׂה יְהוָה מַצְלִיחַ׃

The action related in this clause *does not advance the story line.* The presence of the participle informs the reader that the action represented in this clause ("was making successful") does not transpire sequentially after a previous clause, or, even, sequentially before the following *WAYYIQTOL* chain. The action, rather, is to be thought of as informing the story line, rather than advancing it.

There is one final inner-paragraph comment that occurs at the beginning of the second paragraph of the chapter. The first three clauses of that paragraph are reproduced here:

39.05.142 וַיְהִי מֵאָז
39.05.143 הִפְקִיד אֹתוֹ בְּבֵיתוֹ וְעַל כָּל־אֲשֶׁר יֶשׁ־לוֹ
39.05.144 וַיְבָרֶךְ יְהוָה אֶת־בֵּית הַמִּצְרִי בִּגְלַל יוֹסֵף

The sense of clause 143 is complex. Most commentators see the *QAṬAL* form as simply part of the temporal clause before it. Thus, relying on a parallel construction in Ezekiel 40:1, Waltke and O'Connor translate the three clauses as "*And from the time that* he (the master) had set him (Joseph) over his house . . . YHWH blessed the Egyptian's house." This translation is possible because of the fact that the narrative temporal introduction in clause 142 is undoubtedly picked up by the *WAYYIQTOL* of clause 144. Consistently within this chapter and throughout the Joseph Novella and Genesis in general, temporal clauses composed of וַיְהִי and a prepositional phrase or an infinitive construct are resolved by a clause with a *WAYYIQTOL* as the governing verb. In the translation presented above, however, the second clause is represented as a relative, dependent clause.[46] The original Hebrew sentences are, however, independent, with no relative pronoun introducing the second clause.

The paragraph opening could have stood as well without the intervening clause 143. The presence of that clause, in fact, does not advance the narrative since the information that it provides (i.e., that the master appointed Joseph over his house and over everything that he had) had already been given by *WAYYIQTOL* clauses in the preceding paragraph (clauses 140-141). Therefore, an argument can be made that the setting of clause 143 immediately after the introductory temporal construction in clause 142, constitutes an inner-paragraph comment, in spite of the fact that the governing verb of the clause is a *QATAL*.[47]

Discourse Function Analysis

Narrative Discourse

In Genesis 39, there are four examples of Narrative Discourse; the first is Joseph's rehearsal of the past goodness of his master; the remaining three are all from the mouth of Potiphar's Wife, all concerning Joseph's alleged sexual assault of her, and all (from the perspective of the reader) blatantly false:

> Clauses 155-158: Joseph's Reasons for Rejecting Potiphar's Wife
> Clauses: 175-181: Potiphar's Wife's First Rape Report
> Clauses: 184-187: Potiphar's Wife's Second Rape Report
> Clause 189: Potiphar's Wife's Third Rape Report (Truncated)

In the first example, Joseph retells the privileges that his master had extended to him, illustrating the complete trust that the master has in Joseph.

---

[46]Here, the supposed parallel between Gen 39:5 and Ezek 40:1 is misleading. First, the two verses come from different genres: narrative and prophecy. Second, the temporal clause in Ezekiel is composed of (a series of) prepositional phrases without an introductory וַיְהִי. Third, the reference from Ezekiel 40 occurs in the midst of a long, extended relative clause: בְּעֶשְׂרִים וְחָמֵשׁ שָׁנָה לְגָלוּתֵנוּ בְּרֹאשׁ הַשָּׁנָה בֶּעָשׂוֹר לַחֹדֶשׁ בְּאַרְבַּע עֶשְׂרֵה שָׁנָה אַחַר אֲשֶׁר הֻכְּתָה הָעִיר בְּעֶצֶם הַיּוֹם הַזֶּה הָיְתָה עָלַי יַד־יְהוָה וַיָּבֵא אֹתִי שָׁמָּה. And fourth, in the verse from Ezekiel, the phrase in question is introduced explicitly with the relative pronoun אֲשֶׁר. The two clauses should not, therefore, be considered parallel and informative one for the other.

[47]Clause 143 may also be seen as a dependent clause following the prepositional phrase מֵאָז. The sense of the clause would, however, be very similar, if not identical, to seeing clause 143 as an inner paragraph comment. This clause will be discussed more fully in the final chapter of this study.

39.08.155 אֲדֹנִי לֹא־יָדַע אִתִּי מַה־בַּבָּיִת
39.08.156 וְכֹל אֲשֶׁר־יֶשׁ־לוֹ נָתַן בְּיָדִי:
39.09.157 אֵינֶנּוּ גָדוֹל בַּבַּיִת הַזֶּה מִמֶּנִּי
39.09.158 וְלֹא־חָשַׂךְ מִמֶּנִּי מְאוּמָה
כִּי אִם־אוֹתָךְ
בַּאֲשֶׁר אַתְּ־אִשְׁתּוֹ

The rehearsal is composed of simple *QATAL* clauses, either positive (156) or negated (155, 158), and a verbless clause (157). As such, the discourse conforms closely to Narrative Discourse and is highly regular.

Unlike the examples of Narrative Discourse in the preceding chapter, the use of *WAYYIQTOL* chains in the following two examples noted above link these reports much more closely to the syntactical environment of narrative prose, with its on-line/off-line distinctions with respect to verbal forms. One should not, however, jump to the conclusion that narrative prose and Narrative Discourse are syntactically identical.[48] As seen from the examples in the previous chapter and in the preceding example, the predominant verbal form in Narrative Discourse is *QATAL*. The *QATAL* verbal form is the basic backbone upon which characters build their accounts of past events in their speeches. In the cases where *WAYYIQTOL* rises and takes over the role of *QATAL*, the subject of the discourse will consistently be paralleled with a preceding account of the subject in the narrative prose section of the story.

For example, in the second and third cases of Narrative Discourse above, the *WAYYIQTOL* form (present here in *WAYYIQTOL* chains) signals the parallel Potiphar's Wife's report has with the preceding narrative prose account (Clauses 163-172). The similarity between the two syntactically and lexically is surely not coincidence, as can be seen in the chart below:

---

[48]This seems to be the running assumption in most text-linguistic approaches of biblical prose. Note, for examples, the treatments in Longacre, *Joseph*, 64-106; Dawson, *Text-Linguistics*, 63-65; Niccacci, *Syntax*, 102-9; Yoshinobu Endo, *The Verbal System of Classical Hebrew in the Joseph Story: An Approach from Discourse Analysis* (SSN 32; Assen: Van Gorcum, 1996), 232-76.

Genesis 39:14b-15		Genesis 39:11-14a	
הֵבִיא לָנוּ אִישׁ עִבְרִי לְצַחֶק בָּנוּ	I. Introductory Clause	וַיְהִי כְּהַיּוֹם הַזֶּה	I. Introductory Phrase
בָּא אֵלַי [וְלִשְׁכַּב עִמִּי	II. Entrance	וַיָּבֹא הַבַּיְתָה לַעֲשׂוֹת מְלַאכְתּוֹ	II. Entrance
	III. Offline Statement	וְאֵין אִישׁ מֵאַנְשֵׁי הַבַּיִת שָׁם בַּבָּיִת:	III. Offline Statement
נָבֹא אֵלַי לִשְׁכַּב עִמִּי	IV. Sexual Reference	וַתִּתְפְּשֵׂהוּ בְּבִגְדוֹ לֵאמֹר שִׁכְבָה עִמִּי	IV. Sexual Reference
וָאֶקְרָא בְּקוֹל גָּדוֹל:	V. Call/Scream	וַיַּעֲזֹב בִּגְדוֹ בְּיָדָהּ וַיָּנָס וַיֵּצֵא הַחוּצָה:	V. Exit
וַיְהִי כְשָׁמְעוֹ כִּי־הֲרִימֹתִי קוֹלִי וָאֶקְרָא	VI. Realization	וַיְהִי כִּרְאוֹתָהּ כִּי־עָזַב בִּגְדוֹ בְּיָדָהּ וַיָּנָס הַחוּצָה:	VI. Realization
וַיַּעֲזֹב בִּגְדוֹ אֶצְלִי וַיָּנָס וַיֵּצֵא הַחוּצָה:	VII. Exit	וַתִּקְרָא לְאַנְשֵׁי בֵיתָהּ	VII. Call/Scream

By means of *WAYYIQTOL* chains within the Narrative Discourse of Potiphar's Wife, the reader is lead to compare her account of the "rape" with that of the narrator. By means of the comparison, the reader recognizes her account as weighed in the balances and found wanting. Her lie highlights Joseph's innocence and the injustice of his imprisonment in the denouement of the story.

Predictive Discourse

No examples of Predictive Discourse occur in Genesis 39.

Expository Discourse

No examples of Expository Discourse occur in Genesis 39.

Interrogative Discourse

One example of Interrogative Discourse occurs in Genesis 39, containing two clauses:

Clauses 159-160: Joseph's Question to Potiphar's Wife

Clause 159 is unambiguously marked as a question by the Interrogative Particle אֵיךְ(וְ). The second clause is semantically related to the first and thus remains unmarked:

39.09.159 וְאֵיךְ אֶעֱשֶׂה הָרָעָה הַגְּדֹלָה הַזֹּאת
39.09.160 וְחָטָאתִי לֵאלֹהִים:

The question stands as a rhetorical statement of Joseph's refusal to participate in "this great sin."

Hortatory Discourse

There are three examples of Hortatory Discourse in Genesis 39, each of which is composed of a single clause:

> Clause 152: Potiphar's Wife's Request to Joseph for Sex
> Clause 167: Potiphar's Wife's Request to Joseph Again for Sex
> Clause 174: Potiphar's Wife's Call to Her Servants (Rhetorical
>   Introduction)

In her initial and final attempts to seduce Joseph, Potiphar's Wife employs the identical imperative clause:

39.07.152 שִׁכְבָה עִמִּי

and

39.12.167 שִׁכְבָה עִמִּי

The discourses are, of course, marked in both cases by the imperative verbal form, extended by means of the הָ ־ suffix.

The third case is actually a simple rhetorical introduction to a Narrative Discourse. When Potiphar's Wife reports her false account of the rape to her servants she begins with a simple imperative clause, "See!":

HD

39.14.174 רְאוּ

ND

39.14.175 הֵבִיא לָנוּ אִישׁ עִבְרִי לְצַחֶק בָּנוּ

39.14.176 בָּא אֵלַי לִשְׁכַּב עִמִּי

In this case, the function of the discourse actually amounts to little more than that performed by the deictic particle הִנֵּה.

Table of Discourse Constellations for Genesis 39

		Present Ch.	Prev. Ch.	Total in JN
	QATAL	1	4	5
	QATAL, WAYYIQTOL	2	0	2
	QATAL, (Ptc./Vbl.)	1	4	5
ND	QATAL, WAYYIQTOL, (Ptc./Vbl.)		0	0
	QATAL, WAYYIQTOL, (Ptc./Vbl.), YIQTOL	1	1	2
	QATAL, YIQTOL (w/ past adverb)		0	0
	WAYYIQTOL, (Ptc./Vbl.)		0	0
	Vbl/Ptc/Inc (Dream Report)		0	0
	YIQTOL		2	2
	YIQTOL, WeQATAL		0	0
PD	YIQTOL, WeQATAL, (Ptc./Vbl../Inc.)		0	0
	YIQTOL, (Ptc./Vbl../Inc.)		0	0
	WeQATAL		0	0
	WeYIQTOL		0	0
	Ptc./Vbl.		3	3
	Ptc./ Vbl., Inc.		0	0
	Inc.		0	0
ED	Ptc./Vbl., QATAL/YIQTOL of היה		0	0
	Ptc./Vbl., QATAL/YIQTOL of היה, Front. Obj.+ QATAL/YIQTOL		0	0
	QATAL/YIQTOL of היה		0	0
	Impv./Coh./Juss.	3	5	8
	Impv./Coh./Juss., WeYIQTOL/YIQTOL		1	1
	Impv./Coh./Juss., WeQATAL		0	0
	Impv./Coh./Juss., WeYIQTOL/YIQTOL, WeQATAL		1	1
	Impv./Coh./Juss., QATAL		0	0
HD	Impv./Coh./Juss., WeYIQTOL/YIQTOL, (We)QATAL		0	0
	Impv./Coh./Juss., ʾal-YIQTOL		1	1
	Impv./Coh./Juss., WeQATAL, ʾal-YIQTOL		1	1
	ʾal-YIQTOL		0	0
	ʾal-YIQTOL, WeQATAL/YIQTOL		0	0
	(We)YIQTOL-nāʾ, (WeQATAL/[We]YIQTOL)		0	0
	QATAL, YIQTOL/WeQATAL		0	0

Genesis 40 – Joseph, the Butler, and the Baker – Clauses 201-261

Text in Syntactical/Paragraph Units

The Butler and Baker Dream and Joseph Interprets

40.01.201	וַיְהִי אַחַר הַדְּבָרִים הָאֵלֶּה
40.01.202	חָטְאוּ מַשְׁקֵה מֶלֶךְ־מִצְרַיִם וְהָאֹפֶה
40.06.211	(לַאֲדֹנֵיהֶם:)
40.07.212	וַיִּקְצֹף
40.02.203	וַיִּקְצֹף פַּרְעֹה עַל שְׁנֵי סָרִיסָיו עַל שַׂר הַמַּשְׁקִים וְעַל שַׂר הָאוֹפִים:
40.03.204	וַיִּתֵּן אֹתָם בְּמִשְׁמַר בֵּית שַׂר הַטַּבָּחִים אֶל בֵּית הַסֹּהַר
40.04.205	מְקוֹם אֲשֶׁר יוֹסֵף אָסוּר שָׁם:
40.04.206	וַיִּפְקֹד שַׂר הַטַּבָּחִים אֶת יוֹסֵף אִתָּם
40.04.207	וַיְשָׁרֶת אֹתָם
40.05.208	וַיִּהְיוּ יָמִים בְּמִשְׁמָר:
40.06.209	וַיַּחַלְמוּ חֲלוֹם שְׁנֵיהֶם אִישׁ חֲלֹמוֹ בְּלַיְלָה אֶחָד אִישׁ כְּפִתְרוֹן חֲלֹמוֹ
40.06.210	הַמַּשְׁקֶה וְהָאֹפֶה אֲשֶׁר לְמֶלֶךְ מִצְרַיִם אֲשֶׁר אֲסוּרִים בְּבֵית הַסֹּהַר:

לֵאמֹר

40.07.213 ID וַיִּשְׁאַל אֶת־סְרִיסֵי פַרְעֹה אֲשֶׁר אִתּוֹ בְמִשְׁמַר בֵּית אֲדֹנָיו לֵאמֹר מַדּוּעַ פְּנֵיכֶם רָעִים הַיּוֹם׃

40.08.214 וַיֹּאמְרוּ אֵלָיו

40.08.215 ND חֲלוֹם חָלָמְנוּ
40.08.216 וּפֹתֵר אֵין אֹתוֹ

40.08.217 וַיֹּאמֶר אֲלֵהֶם יוֹסֵף

40.08.218 ID הֲלוֹא לֵאלֹהִים פִּתְרֹנִים
40.08.219 HD סַפְּרוּ־נָא לִי׃

40.09.220 וַיְסַפֵּר שַׂר־הַמַּשְׁקִים אֶת־חֲלֹמוֹ לְיוֹסֵף
40.09.221 וַיֹּאמֶר לוֹ

ND (Dream Report)
40.09.222 בַּחֲלוֹמִי
40.09.223 וְהִנֵּה־גֶפֶן לְפָנָי
40.10.224 וּבַגֶּפֶן שְׁלֹשָׁה שָׂרִיגִם
40.10.225 וְהִיא כְפֹרַחַת עָלְתָה נִצָּהּ
40.10.226 הִבְשִׁילוּ אַשְׁכְּלֹתֶיהָ עֲנָבִים
40.11.227 וְכוֹס פַּרְעֹה בְּיָדִי
40.11.228 וָאֶקַּח אֶת־הָעֲנָבִים
40.11.229 וָאֶשְׂחַט אֹתָם אֶל־כּוֹס פַּרְעֹה
40.11.230 וָאֶתֵּן אֶת־הַכּוֹס עַל־כַּף פַּרְעֹה

40.12.231 וַיֹּאמֶר לוֹ יוֹסֵף

ED
40.12.232 זֶה פִּתְרֹנוֹ
40.12.233 שְׁלֹשֶׁת הַשָּׂרִגִים שְׁלֹשֶׁת יָמִים הֵם׃

40.16.241 וַיֹּאמֶר אַף־אֲנִי בַּחֲלוֹמִי

40.16.242 וְהִנֵּה שְׁלֹשָׁה סַלֵּי חֹרִי עַל־רֹאשִׁי

40.18.247 וַיַּעַן יוֹסֵף וַיֹּאמֶר

40.18.248

40.13.234 PD
בְּעוֹד שְׁלֹשֶׁת יָמִים יִשָּׂא פַרְעֹה אֶת־רֹאשֶׁךָ

40.13.235 וַהֲשִׁיבְךָ עַל־כַּנֶּךָ

40.13.236 וְנָתַתָּ כוֹס־פַּרְעֹה בְּיָדוֹ כַּמִּשְׁפָּט הָרִאשׁוֹן אֲשֶׁר הָיִיתָ מַשְׁקֵהוּ

40.14.237 HD
כִּי אִם־זְכַרְתַּנִי אִתְּךָ

40.14.238 כַּאֲשֶׁר יִיטַב לָךְ

40.14.239 וְעָשִׂיתָ־נָּא עִמָּדִי חָסֶד

40.14.240 וְהִזְכַּרְתַּנִי אֶל־פַּרְעֹה

[40.15] וְהוֹצֵאתַנִי מִן־הַבַּיִת הַזֶּה

40.16.243 ND (Dream Report)
וַיַּרְא שַׂר־הָאֹפִים כִּי טוֹב פָּתָר

40.16.244 וַיֹּאמֶר אֶל־יוֹסֵף אַף־אֲנִי בַּחֲלוֹמִי

40.17.245 וּבַסַּל הָעֶלְיוֹן מִכֹּל מַאֲכַל פַּרְעֹה מַעֲשֵׂה אֹפֶה

40.17.246 וְהָעוֹף אֹכֵל אֹתָם מִן־הַסַּל מֵעַל רֹאשִׁי

40.18.249 ED
זֶה פִּתְרֹנוֹ

Joseph's Predictions are Fulfilled

וַיְהִי | בַּיּוֹם הַשְּׁלִישִׁי יוֹם הֻלֶּדֶת אֶת־פַּרְעֹה 40.20.254

וַיַּעַשׂ מִשְׁתֶּה לְכָל־עֲבָדָיו 40.20.255

וַיִּשָּׂא אֶת־רֹאשׁ | שַׂר הַמַּשְׁקִים וְאֶת־רֹאשׁ שַׂר הָאֹפִים בְּתוֹךְ עֲבָדָיו: 40.20.256

וַיָּשֶׁב אֶת־שַׂר הַמַּשְׁקִים עַל־מַשְׁקֵהוּ 40.21.257

וַיִּתֵּן הַכּוֹס עַל־כַּף פַּרְעֹה: 40.21.258

וְאֵת שַׂר הָאֹפִים תָּלָה כַּאֲשֶׁר פָּתַר לָהֶם יוֹסֵף: 40.22.259

The Final Outcome (Comment)

וְלֹא־זָכַר שַׂר־הַמַּשְׁקִים אֶת־יוֹסֵף 40.23.260

וַיִּשְׁכָּחֵהוּ: פ 40.23.261

וַיְהִי בַיּוֹם הַשְּׁלִישִׁי וַיֵּרָא 40.18.250
PD

אֵלֶיךָ נֹשֵׂא פַרְעֹה אֶת־רֹאשְׁךָ | מֵעָלֶיךָ 40.19.251

וְתָלָה אוֹתְךָ עַל־עֵץ 40.19.252

וְאָכַל הָעוֹף אֶת־בְּשָׂרְךָ מֵעָלֶיךָ: 40.19.253

Table of Independent Clause Types in Genesis 40

Clause Type	Clause Distribution	Total	Percent
QAṬAL Total Clauses: 7	Narrative: 202,259,260	3	42.9%
	ND: 215,225,226 PD: ED: ID:	3	42.9%
	HD: 237	1	14.2%
WeQAṬAL Total Clauses: 7	Narrative:	0	0
	ND: PD: 235,236,252,253 ED: ID:	4	57.1%
	HD: 238,239,240	3	42.9%
YIQṬOL Total Clauses: 2	Narrative:	0	0
	ND: PD: 234,251 ED: ID: HD:	2	100%
WeYIQṬOL Total Clauses: 0	Narrative:	0	0
	ND: PD: ED: ID: HD:	0	0
WAYYIQṬOL Total Clauses: 70	Narrative: 201,203,204,205,206,207,208,209,210, 212,214,217,220,221,231,241,242,247,248,254,255, 256,257,258,261	25	89.3%
	ND: 228,229,230 PD: ED: ID: HD:	3	10.7%

	Narrative: 211	1	50.0%
Participle	ND: 246	1	50.0%
	PD:		
Total Clauses:	ED:		
2	ID:		
	HD:		
	Narrative:	0	0
Verbless	ND: 216,223,224,227,244,245	6	50.0%
	PD:		
Total Clauses:	ED: 232,233,249,250	4	33.3%
12	ID: 213,218	2	16.7%
	HD:		
	Narrative:	0	0
Incomplete	ND: 222,243	2	100%
	PD:		
Total Clauses:	ED:		
2	ID:		
	HD:		
Imperative	Narrative:	0	0
Total Clauses: 1	HD: 219	1	100%
Cohortative	Narrative:	0	0
Total Clauses: 0	HD:	0	0
Jussive	Narrative:	0	0
Total Clauses: 0	HD:	0	0

Analysis of the Narrative Structure and Discourse Text-Types in Genesis 40

Narrative Analysis

Narrative/Paragraph Structure

Genesis 40, the story of "Joseph, the Butler, and the Baker," is composed of two main paragraphs, both explicitly marked.

> Clauses 201-248: The Butler and Baker Dream and Joseph Interprets
> Clauses 254-261: Joseph's Predictions are Fulfilled

Both paragraphs are initially marked with וַיְהִי temporal clauses (201, 254). The second paragraph is terminally marked with a *QATAL* clause (259).

Extra-Paragraph Comments

There is only one instance of an extra-paragraph comment in Genesis 40. After the final paragraph of the chapter (clauses 260-261), the narrator provides an aside concerning the final outcome of the story:

40.23.260 וְלֹא־זָכַר שַׂר־הַמַּשְׁקִים אֶת־יוֹסֵף
40.23.261 וַיִּשְׁכָּחֵהוּ:

This notice, consisting of a negated *QATAL* clause and an independent, un-chained *WAYYIQTOL* clause, occurs after the final *QATAL* clause (259) of the previous paragraph and before the initial וַיְהִי temporal clause (262) of the next paragraph. In contrast with Joseph's request that the Butler remember Joseph when the promised good fortune occurs (clauses 237-240; see Discourse Function Analysis below), the final notice of the chapter relates, off the story line, that Joseph is forgotten in prison, kept safe there until the momentous dreams of the next chapter.

Inner-Paragraph Comments

There are three inner-paragraph comments in Genesis 40, all of which occur in the first paragraph. One provides a comment about the Butler and Baker's existence in custody over many days:

40.04.207 וַיִּהְיוּ יָמִים בְּמִשְׁמָר:

This internal comment about the state of a character employs a true וַיְהִי verbal clause, denoting existence.

A second inner-paragraph comment concerns the actions of the Butler and Baker after their fateful dreams:

40.06.211 וְהִנָּם זֹעֲפִים:

This comment upon non-narrative actions employs a participle, introduced by a form of וְהִנֵּה.

The third inner-paragraph comment is the most complex and is the first to occur in the chapter. Clause 202 concerns the retrospective actions of the Butler and Baker, relative to the focus of the main story line. The וַיְהִי temporal clause (201) which introduces the chapter is resolved with the *WAYYIQTOL* clause following it (203):

40.01.201 וַיְהִי אַחַר הַדְּבָרִים הָאֵלֶּה
40.01.202 חָטְאוּ מַשְׁקֵה מֶלֶךְ־מִצְרַיִם וְהָאֹפֶה לַאֲדֹנֵיהֶם לְמֶלֶךְ מִצְרָיִם:
40.02.203 וַיִּקְצֹף פַּרְעֹה עַל שְׁנֵי סָרִיסָיו עַל שַׂר הַמַּשְׁקִים וְעַל שַׂר הָאוֹפִים:

Thus the primary narrative sense of these clauses is that "(201) After these events, . . . (203) Pharaoh became angry against his two officers, the head of the butlers and the head of the bakers." Clause 202 is inserted before this resolution to provide an off-line explanation for the action of clause 203: "After these events, (the Butler of the King of Egypt and the Baker having wronged the King of Egypt), Pharaoh became angry against his two officers." While the construction does not translate well into standard English prose, it is a clear and simple statement of retrospective action in the Hebrew text.[49]

Discourse Function Analysis

Narrative Discourse

Three examples of Narrative Discourse stand in Genesis 40, and encompass fifteen clauses.

    Clauses 215-216: The Butler and the Baker's Statement about Their
                         Dreams
    Clauses 222-230: The Butler's Dream Report
    Clauses 243-246: The Baker's Dream Report

---

[49]Its usage here is consistent with the backgrounded information given in the previous chapter about Potiphar's installment of Joseph over his house (clauses 142-144).

Of these three cases, one is a simple relating of a past event (clauses 215-216), and two are dream reports (clauses 222-230; 243-246). The first case is a combination of a *QATAL* clause and a verbless clause, denoting nonexistence:

40.08.215 חֲלוֹם חָלַמְנוּ

40.08.216 וּפֹתֵר אֵין אֹתוֹ

There is no disjunction, such as וְהִנֵּה, between the two clauses; the second, therefore, should probably be seen as a continuation of the Narrative Discourse begun in clause 215, rather than a statement of Expository Discourse.[50]

The syntax of the dream reports of the Butler and the Baker is in line with those seen earlier in Chapter 37. Both dream reports are introduced by incomplete clauses (222, 243) composed primarily of the single phrase בַּחֲלוֹמִי.[51] Furthermore, the word וְהִנֵּה marks crucial turning points in the dreams.[52] And finally, a large percentage of participial and verbless clauses make up the report in addition to the usual *QATAL* and *WAYYIQTOL* clauses usually found in Narrative Discourse.

Predictive Discourse

In Genesis 40, the first extended examples of Predictive Discourse occur in the Joseph Novella. Whereas in Chapter 37, Joseph's Brothers and Jacob cast their forward-looking interpretations of Joseph's dreams in Interrogative Discourse (clauses 022-023, 033-034), and Jacob himself plans his own expected painful death in a single clause (clause 129), in this chapter Joseph twice envisions the future and foretells the events he sees. Two examples of Predictive Discourse occur in Genesis 40, each containing three clauses.

Clauses 234-236: Joseph's Prediction to the Butler
Clauses 251-253: Joseph's Prediction to the Baker

---

[50]The sense of the speech is, therefore, "We had a dream and there was no interpreter of it," rather than "We have had a dream and there is no one to interpret it." The RSV not only switches the discourse for no explainable reason but also pluralizes the dream: "We have had *dreams* . . . no one to interpret *them*." Even the Butler and Baker recognize the close similarity of the single dream that they both have had.

[51]Compare this to the introductory clause of Pharaoh's dream report in Chapter 41 (41.17.313 בַּחֲלוֹמִי).

[52]Compare the use of וְהִנֵּה in Joseph's dream reports (clauses 016, 017, 019, 029) and Pharaoh's dream report (clauses 314, 315, 317, 325, 326).

Throughout the Novella, Predictive Discourse plays a major part in the story. Its syntactical structure parallels that of Narrative Discourse. Tense inflections and on-line/off-line perspectives are present in both types of discourse:

Narrative Discourse	Predictive Discourse
On-line Clauses:	
QATAL	*YIQTOL*
WAYYIQTOL	*WeQATAL*
Off-line Clauses:	
Verbless	*Verbless*
Participial	*Participial*

Even as in Narrative Discourse, where *QATAL* usually performs the role of direct, on-line reporting of the narrative with *WAYYIQTOL* often enabling the continuation of the narrative, in Predictive Discourse *YIQTOL* performs the role of direct, on-line reporting of the future events with *WeQATAL* often enabling the continuation of the prediction.[53] When off-line comments are made concerning the existence or quality of some element, verbless clauses are used; if the comment deals with some action, participial clauses are used.

Joseph's predictions based upon the dreams of the Butler and Baker are text-book cases, each beginning with a *YIQTOL* and continued with *WeQATALs*:

40.13.234 בְּעוֹד שְׁלֹשֶׁת יָמִים יִשָּׂא פַרְעֹה אֶת־רֹאשֶׁךָ
40.13.235 וַהֲשִׁיבְךָ עַל־כַּנֶּךָ
40.13.236 וְנָתַתָּ כוֹס־פַּרְעֹה בְּיָדוֹ כַּמִּשְׁפָּט הָרִאשׁוֹן
אֲשֶׁר הָיִיתָ מַשְׁקֵהוּ:

40.19.251 בְּעוֹד שְׁלֹשֶׁת יָמִים יִשָּׂא פַרְעֹה אֶת־רֹאשְׁךָ מֵעָלֶיךָ
40.19.252 וְתָלָה אוֹתְךָ עַל־עֵץ
40.19.253 וְאָכַל הָעוֹף אֶת־בְּשָׂרְךָ מֵעָלֶיךָ:

In addition to the *YIQTOL* clauses which head each prediction, the meta-syntactical adverbial particle בְּעוֹד also aids in distinguishing each example of

---

[53]Note the distinct roles played by *WeQATAL* in Predictive Discourse and in Narrative Prose. In Predictive Discourse, *WeQATAL* plays an on-line role and directly continues the progression of the prediction. In narrative prose (see the Analyses concerning clause 007 in Chapter 37, and clause 952 in Chapter 47), *WeQATAL* plays an off-line role and directly prohibits the narrative from progressing. *WeQATAL* does not appear in any instance of Narrative Discourse found in this chapter.

Predictive Discourse from the examples of Expository Discourse immediately preceding each case.

Expository Discourse

Two examples of Expository Discourse stand within Genesis 40, each example composed of two clauses.

> Clauses 232-233: Joseph's Explanation of the Butler's Dream
> Clauses 249-250: Joseph's Explanation of the Baker's Dream

All four clauses provide Joseph's basic hermeneutical key for his interpretation of the respective dreams. They equate certain elements of the dream with certain elements of time; as such, they consistently employ verbless clauses:

40.12.232 זֶה פִּתְרֹנוֹ

40.12.233 שְׁלֹשֶׁת הַשָּׂרִגִים שְׁלֹשֶׁת יָמִים הֵם:

and

40.18.249 זֶה פִּתְרֹנוֹ

40.18.250 שְׁלֹשֶׁת הַסַּלִים שְׁלֹשֶׁת יָמִים הֵם:

On the basis of this basic static equation of elements, Joseph uses these examples of Expository Discourse to introduce his predictions for both the Butler and the Baker (see above).

Interrogative Discourse

Genesis 40 contains two examples of Interrogative Discourse, one a true question and one a rhetorical question, each containing a single clause.

> Clause 213: Joseph's Question to the Butler and the Baker (True)
> Clause 218: Joseph's Question to the Butler and the Baker (Rhetorical)

Both clauses are unambiguously marked as Interrogative Discourse by their respective prefixed Interrogative Particles, מַדּוּעַ and הֲלוֹא:

40.07.213 מַדּוּעַ פְּנֵיכֶם רָעִים הַיּוֹם:

40.8.218 הֲלוֹא לֵאלֹהִים פִּתְרֹנִים

The second Interrogative Discourse, being introduced by הֲלוֹא, stands as a rhe-torical declaration affirming the certainty of the statement.[54]

Hortatory Discourse

Genesis 40 contains only two examples of Hortatory Discourse.

Clause 219: Joseph's Request to the Butler and the Baker
Clauses 237-240: Joseph's Urging of the Butler to Remember Him

The first example contains only a single clause and is Joseph's invitation to the Butler and the Baker to tell him the content of their dreams:

40.08.219 סַפְּרוּ־נָא לִי:

The hortatory nature of the discourse is marked, not only by the imperative ver-bal form which governs the clause, but also by the particle of entreaty, ־נָא.

The second example of Hortatory Discourse in Genesis 40 has caused much scholarly discussion, in particular because the introductory clause of the dis-course does not conform to the general means for expressing commands or requests.[55] After Joseph relates the positive future which the Butler will enjoy after being released from prison, Joseph requests him to remember him and bring him out from his incarceration. Joseph's entire speech is given here:

40.12.231 וַיֹּאמֶר לוֹ יוֹסֵף

---

[54]Note Moshe Held, "Rhetorical Questions in Ugaritic and Biblical Hebrew," *Eretz-Israel* 9 (1969), 71-79; and M. L. Brown, "'Is It Not?' or 'Indeed!': HL in Northwest Semitic," *Maarav* 4 (1987) 201-19. Within the textual databases used in this study, inter-rogative clauses introduced with הֲלוֹא are almost always rhetorical. Only a single example of a true question governed by הֲלוֹא stands in the textual database, clause 366 in the Court Narrative.

[55]Gesenius (§106, n. 2) considers the *QATAL* verbal form זְכַרְתַּנִי a "perfect of con-fidentiae." The *QATAL* form in hortatory contexts is usually defined as "Koinzi-denzfall," "performative utterance/perfect," "instantaneous perfective" or "precative per-fect." See Waltke and O'Connor, *Syntax*, 488-89; Delbert Hillers, "Some Performative Utterances in the Bible," in *Pomegranates and Golden Bells: Studies in Biblical, Jewish, and Near Eastern Ritual, Law, and Literature in Honor of Jacob Milgrom*, 757-69 (ed. David P. Wright, David Noel Freedman, and Avi Hurvitz; Winona Lake: Eisenbrauns, 1995). The view that זְכַרְתַּנִי is a "performative utterance" is taken by Endo, *Verbal Sys-tem*, 215-19, who translates the clause, however, not as a precative perfect, but as an imperative: "Only keep me in mind (pf.) when it goes well (impf.) with you."

ED

40.12.232 זֶה פִּתְרֹנוֹ

40.12.233 שְׁלֹשֶׁת הַשָּׂרִגִים שְׁלֹשֶׁת יָמִים הֵם׃

PD

40.13.234 בְּעוֹד שְׁלֹשֶׁת יָמִים יִשָּׂא פַרְעֹה אֶת־רֹאשֶׁךָ

40.13.235 וַהֲשִׁיבְךָ עַל־כַּנֶּךָ

40.13.236 וְנָתַתָּ כוֹס־פַּרְעֹה בְּיָדוֹ כַּמִּשְׁפָּט הָרִאשׁוֹן

אֲשֶׁר הָיִיתָ מַשְׁקֵהוּ׃

HD

40.14.237 כִּי אִם־זְכַרְתַּנִי אִתְּךָ

כַּאֲשֶׁר יִיטַב לָךְ

40.14.238 וְעָשִׂיתָ־נָּא עִמָּדִי חָסֶד

40.14.239 וְהִזְכַּרְתַּנִי אֶל־פַּרְעֹה

40.14.240 וְהוֹצֵאתַנִי מִן־הַבַּיִת הַזֶּה׃

[40.15] כִּי־גֻנֹּב גֻּנַּבְתִּי מֵאֶרֶץ הָעִבְרִים

וְגַם־פֹּה לֹא־עָשִׂיתִי מְאוּמָה

כִּי־שָׂמוּ אֹתִי בַּבּוֹר׃

The *QAṬAL* verbal form governing clause 237 cannot be a part of the preceding Predictive Discourse, nor does it appear possible to interpret it as beginning a Narrative Discourse, which is usually initiated by a *QAṬAL* clause. It appears to be closely tied to the following clause 238, which is unambiguously marked as Hortatory Discourse by the particle of entreaty following its governing *WeQAṬAL* verbal form, וְעָשִׂיתָ־נָּא.

The unusual presence of a *QAṬAL* in Hortatory Discourse almost always functions as a performative utterance. While it is true that in most cases, performative utterances occur in first person singular forms, this is by no means true in all cases.[56] The second person *QAṬAL* verbal form in clause 237 functions as a volitional form since it clearly stands within a Hortatory Discourse. The use of the prepositional phrase אִתְּךָ along with the verb זכר in most instances implies a volitional reminding of oneself.[57] The sense of Joseph's entreaty in this episode therefore means, "You are hereby reminded (or, you hereby remind yourself) when it goes well with you: You must be faithful to me and remind Pharaoh of me and bring me out from this prisonhouse!"

---

[56]For examples of first-person performative utterances in the textual databases used in this study, note in the Joseph Novella clause 367, and in the Court Narrative clauses 595, 793, and 1187. For an example of a second-person performative utterance in the Joseph Novella, note clause 814.

[57]See BDB, p. 86c.

Table of Discourse Constellations for Genesis 40

		Present Ch.	Prev. Chs.	Total in JN
ND	QATAL		5	5
	QATAL, WAYYIQTOL		2	2
	QATAL, (Ptc./Vbl.)	1	5	6
	QATAL, WAYYIQTOL, (Ptc./Vbl.)	1	0	1
	QATAL, WAYYIQTOL, (Ptc./Vbl.), YIQTOL		2	2
	QATAL, YIQTOL (w/ past adverb)		0	0
	WAYYIQTOL, (Ptc./Vbl.)		0	0
	Vbl/Ptc/Inc (Dream Report)	1	0	1
PD	YIQTOL		2	2
	YIQTOL, WeQATAL	2	0	2
	YIQTOL, WeQATAL, (Ptc./Vbl../Inc.)		0	0
	YIQTOL, (Ptc./Vbl../Inc.)		0	0
	WeQATAL		0	0
	WeYIQTOL		0	0
ED	Ptc./Vbl.	2	3	5
	Ptc./ Vbl., Inc.		0	0
	Inc.		0	0
	Ptc./Vbl., QATAL/YIQTOL of היה		0	0
	Ptc./Vbl., QATAL/YIQTOL of היה, Front. Obj.+ QATAL/YIQTOL		0	0
	QATAL/YIQTOL of היה		0	0
HD	Impv./Coh./Juss.	1	8	9
	Impv./Coh./Juss., WeYIQTOL/YIQTOL		1	1
	Impv./Coh./Juss., WeQATAL		0	0
	Impv./Coh./Juss., WeYIQTOL/YIQTOL, WeQATAL		1	1
	Impv./Coh./Juss., QATAL		0	0
	Impv./Coh./Juss., WeYIQTOL/YIQTOL, (We)QATAL		0	0
	Impv./Coh./Juss., ʾal-YIQTOL		1	1
	Impv./Coh./Juss., WeQATAL, ʾal-YIQTOL		1	1
	ʾal-YIQTOL		0	0
	ʾal-YIQTOL, WeQATAL/YIQTOL		0	0
	(We)YIQTOL-nāʾ, (WeQATAL/[We]YIQTOL)		0	0
	QATAL, YIQTOL/WeQATAL	1	0	1

Genesis 41 – Pharaoh's Dreams and Joseph's Interpretaion – Clauses 262-408

Text in Syntactical/Paragraph Units

Pharaoh Has Two Dreams

41.01.262	וַיְהִי מִקֵּץ שְׁנָתַיִם יָמִים
41.01.263	וּפַרְעֹה חֹלֵם
41.01.264	וְהִנֵּה עֹמֵד עַל־הַיְאֹר׃
41.02.265	וְהִנֵּה מִן־הַיְאֹר עֹלֹת שֶׁבַע פָּרוֹת יְפוֹת מַרְאֶה וּבְרִיאֹת בָּשָׂר
41.02.266	וַתִּרְעֶינָה בָּאָחוּ׃
41.03.267	וְהִנֵּה שֶׁבַע פָּרוֹת אֲחֵרוֹת עֹלוֹת אַחֲרֵיהֶן מִן־הַיְאֹר רָעוֹת מַרְאֶה וְדַקּוֹת בָּשָׂר
41.03.268	וַתַּעֲמֹדְנָה אֵצֶל הַפָּרוֹת עַל־שְׂפַת הַיְאֹר׃
41.04.269	וַתֹּאכַלְנָה הַפָּרוֹת רָעוֹת הַמַּרְאֶה וְדַקֹּת הַבָּשָׂר אֵת שֶׁבַע הַפָּרוֹת יְפֹת הַמַּרְאֶה וְהַבְּרִיאֹת
41.04.270	וַיִּיקַץ פַּרְעֹה׃
41.05.271	וַיִּישָׁן
41.05.272	וַיַּחֲלֹם שֵׁנִית
41.05.273	וְהִנֵּה שֶׁבַע שִׁבֳּלִים עֹלוֹת בְּקָנֶה אֶחָד בְּרִיאוֹת וְטֹבוֹת׃
41.06.274	וְהִנֵּה שֶׁבַע שִׁבֳּלִים דַּקּוֹת וּשְׁדוּפֹת קָדִים צֹמְחוֹת אַחֲרֵיהֶן׃
41.07.275	וַתִּבְלַעְנָה הַשִּׁבֳּלִים הַדַּקּוֹת אֵת שֶׁבַע הַשִּׁבֳּלִים הַבְּרִיאוֹת וְהַמְּלֵאוֹת וַיִּיקַץ פַּרְעֹה וְהִנֵּה חֲלוֹם׃

41.07.276	[וַתִּבְלַעְנָה הַשִׁבֳּלִים הַדַּקּוֹת]
41.07.277	אֵת שֶׁבַע הַשִׁבֳּלִים הַבְּרִיאוֹת וְהַמְּלֵאוֹת וַיִּיקַץ פַּרְעֹה וְהִנֵּה חֲלוֹם:

Joseph Interprets the Dreams and Is Placed over Egypt

41.08.278	וַיְהִי בַבֹּקֶר וַתִּפָּעֶם רוּחוֹ
41.08.279	וַיִּשְׁלַח וַיִּקְרָא
41.08.280	אֶת כָּל חַרְטֻמֵּי מִצְרַיִם וְאֶת כָּל חֲכָמֶיהָ
41.08.281	וַיְסַפֵּר פַּרְעֹה לָהֶם אֶת חֲלֹמוֹ
41.08.282	וְאֵין פּוֹתֵר אוֹתָם לְפַרְעֹה:
41.08.283	(וַיְדַבֵּר שַׂר הַמַּשְׁקִים אֶת פַּרְעֹה לֵאמֹר:)
41.09.284	לֵאמֹר

ED	41.09.285	אֶת חֲטָאַי אֲנִי מַזְכִּיר הַיּוֹם:
ND		
	41.10.286	פַּרְעֹה קָצַף עַל עֲבָדָיו
	41.10.287	וַיִּתֵּן אֹתִי בְּמִשְׁמַר בֵּית שַׂר הַטַּבָּחִים אֹתִי וְאֵת שַׂר הָאֹפִים:
	41.11.288	וַנַּחַלְמָה חֲלוֹם בְּלַיְלָה אֶחָד אֲנִי וָהוּא
	41.11.289	אִישׁ כְּפִתְרוֹן חֲלֹמוֹ חָלָמְנוּ:
	41.12.290	וְשָׁם אִתָּנוּ נַעַר עִבְרִי עֶבֶד לְשַׂר הַטַּבָּחִים
	41.12.291	וַנְּסַפֶּר לוֹ
	41.12.292	וַיִּפְתָּר לָנוּ אֶת חֲלֹמֹתֵינוּ אִישׁ כַּחֲלֹמוֹ פָּתָר:
	41.12.293	
	41.13.294	וַיְהִי כַּאֲשֶׁר פָּתַר לָנוּ כֵּן הָיָה אֹתִי הֵשִׁיב עַל כַּנִּי וְאֹתוֹ תָלָה:

41.14.298 וַיֹּאמֶר פַּרְעֹה אֶל־יוֹסֵף
41.14.299 וַיִּשְׁלַח פַּרְעֹה
41.14.300 וַיִּקְרָא אֶת־יוֹסֵף
41.14.301 וַיְרִיצֻהוּ
41.14.302 מִן־הַבּוֹר
41.14.303 וַיְגַלַּח
41.15.304 וַיְחַלֵּף שִׂמְלֹתָיו

41.16.309 וַיַּעַן יוֹסֵף אֶת־פַּרְעֹה לֵאמֹר

41.17.312 וַיְדַבֵּר פַּרְעֹה אֶל־יוֹסֵף

41.13.295 כֵּן הָיָה
41.13.296 אֹתִי הֵשִׁיב עַל־כַּנִּי
41.13.297 וְאֹתוֹ תָלָה

ND
41.15.305 חֲלוֹם חָלַמְתִּי
41.15.306 וּפֹתֵר אֵין אֹתוֹ
41.15.307 וַאֲנִי שָׁמַעְתִּי עָלֶיךָ

PD
41.15.308 תִּשְׁמַע חֲלוֹם לִפְתֹּר אֹתוֹ

PD
41.16.310 בִּלְעָדָי
41.16.311 אֱלֹהִים יַעֲנֶה אֶת־שְׁלוֹם פַּרְעֹה

ND (Dream Report)
41.17.313 בַּחֲלֹמִי

41.17.314 הִנְנִי עֹמֵד עַל־שְׂפַת הַיְאֹר

41.25.330	וַיֹּאמֶר יוֹסֵף אֶל־פַּרְעֹה
41.25.331	חֲלוֹם פַּרְעֹה אֶחָד הוּא ED

41.18.315	וְהִנֵּה מִן־הַיְאֹר עֹלֹת שֶׁבַע פָּרוֹת
41.18.316	בְּרִיאוֹת בָּשָׂר וִיפֹת תֹּאַר
41.19.317	וַתִּרְעֶינָה בָּאָחוּ
41.19.318	וְהִנֵּה שֶׁבַע־פָּרוֹת אֲחֵרוֹת עֹלוֹת אַחֲרֵיהֶן דַּלּוֹת וְרָעוֹת תֹּאַר מְאֹד וְרַקּוֹת בָּשָׂר
41.20.319	לֹא־רָאִיתִי כָהֵנָּה בְּכָל־אֶרֶץ מִצְרַיִם לָרֹעַ:
41.21.320	וַתֹּאכַלְנָה הַפָּרוֹת הָרַקּוֹת וְהָרָעוֹת
41.21.321	אֵת שֶׁבַע הַפָּרוֹת הָרִאשֹׁנוֹת הַבְּרִיאֹת:
41.21.322	וַתָּבֹאנָה אֶל־קִרְבֶּנָה
41.21.323	וְלֹא נוֹדַע כִּי־בָאוּ אֶל־קִרְבֶּנָה
41.22.324	וּמַרְאֵיהֶן רַע כַּאֲשֶׁר בַּתְּחִלָּה וָאִיקָץ:
41.22.325	וָאֵרֶא בַּחֲלֹמִי
41.23.326	וְהִנֵּה שֶׁבַע שִׁבֳּלִים עֹלֹת בְּקָנֶה אֶחָד מְלֵאֹת וְטֹבוֹת:
41.24.327	וְהִנֵּה שֶׁבַע שִׁבֳּלִים צְנֻמוֹת דַּקּוֹת שְׁדֻפוֹת קָדִים צֹמְחוֹת אַחֲרֵיהֶם:
41.24.328	וַתִּבְלַעְןָ הַשִּׁבֳּלִים הַדַּקֹּת
41.24.329	אֵת שֶׁבַע הַשִּׁבֳּלִים הַטֹּבוֹת

HD

41.32.346 (לָהֶם) וַיִּפְתֹּר

ED

41.31.345

41.30.344

41.30.343

41.30.342

41.29.341

41.29.340

PD

41.28.339

41.28.338

41.27.337

41.27.336

41.26.335

41.26.334

41.26.333

41.25.332 אֶת

41.41.365

41.39.360

41.37.357
41.38.358

41.33.347
41.33.348
41.34.349
41.34.350
41.34.351
41.35.352
41.35.353
41.35.354
41.36.355

PD

41.36.356

ID

41.38.359

ED

361α

41.39.361

PD

41.40.362
41.40.363
41.40.364

HD

41.41.366 וַיֹּאמֶר פַּרְעֹה אֶל־יוֹסֵף
41.41.367 רְאֵה נָתַתִּי אֹתְךָ עַל כָּל־אֶרֶץ מִצְרָיִם:

41.42.368 וַיָּסַר פַּרְעֹה אֶת־טַבַּעְתּוֹ מֵעַל יָדוֹ
41.42.369 וַיִּתֵּן אֹתָהּ עַל־יַד יוֹסֵף
41.42.370 וַיַּלְבֵּשׁ אֹתוֹ בִּגְדֵי־שֵׁשׁ
41.42.371 וַיָּשֶׂם רְבִד הַזָּהָב עַל־צַוָּארוֹ
41.43.372 וַיַּרְכֵּב אֹתוֹ בְּמִרְכֶּבֶת הַמִּשְׁנֶה אֲשֶׁר־לוֹ
41.43.373 וַיִּקְרְאוּ לְפָנָיו

ED (Exclamation)

41.43.374 אַבְרֵךְ

41.43.375 וְנָתוֹן אֹתוֹ עַל כָּל־אֶרֶץ מִצְרָיִם:

Joseph Gathers Grain in the Years of Plenty

41.44.376 וַיֹּאמֶר פַּרְעֹה אֶל־יוֹסֵף

ED

41.44.377 אֲנִי פַרְעֹה

PD

41.44.378 וּבִלְעָדֶיךָ לֹא־יָרִים אִישׁ אֶת־יָדוֹ וְאֶת־רַגְלוֹ בְּכָל־אֶרֶץ מִצְרָיִם:

41.45.379 וַיִּקְרָא פַרְעֹה שֵׁם־יוֹסֵף צָפְנַת פַּעְנֵחַ
41.45.380 וַיִּתֶּן־לוֹ אֶת־אָסְנַת בַּת־פּוֹטִי פֶרַע כֹּהֵן אֹן לְאִשָּׁה
41.45.381 וַיֵּצֵא יוֹסֵף עַל־אֶרֶץ מִצְרָיִם:
41.46.382 (וְיוֹסֵף בֶּן־שְׁלֹשִׁים שָׁנָה בְּעָמְדוֹ לִפְנֵי פַּרְעֹה מֶלֶךְ־מִצְרָיִם)
41.46.383 וַיֵּצֵא יוֹסֵף מִלִּפְנֵי פַרְעֹה
41.46.384 וַיַּעֲבֹר בְּכָל־אֶרֶץ מִצְרָיִם:

41.47.385 וַתַּעַשׂ הָאָרֶץ בְּשֶׁבַע שְׁנֵי הַשָּׂבָע לִקְמָצִים׃

41.48.386 וַיִּקְבֹּץ אֶת־כָּל־אֹכֶל שֶׁבַע שָׁנִים אֲשֶׁר הָיוּ בְּאֶרֶץ מִצְרַיִם

41.48.387 וַיִּתֶּן־אֹכֶל בֶּעָרִים אֹכֶל שְׂדֵה־הָעִיר אֲשֶׁר סְבִיבֹתֶיהָ נָתַן בְּתוֹכָהּ׃

The Source and Amount of Grain (Comment)

41.48.388 ————

41.49.389 וַיִּצְבֹּר יוֹסֵף בָּר כְּחוֹל הַיָּם הַרְבֵּה מְאֹד עַד כִּי־חָדַל לִסְפֹּר כִּי־אֵין מִסְפָּר׃

The Birth and Naming of the Sons of Joseph (Comment)

41.50.390 ———— וּלְיוֹסֵף יֻלַּד שְׁנֵי בָנִים בְּטֶרֶם תָּבוֹא שְׁנַת הָרָעָב אֲשֶׁר יָלְדָה־לּוֹ אָסְנַת בַּת־פּוֹטִי פֶרַע כֹּהֵן אוֹן׃

41.51.391 וַיִּקְרָא יוֹסֵף אֶת־שֵׁם הַבְּכוֹר מְנַשֶּׁה

391α

41.51.392 ND כִּי־נַשַּׁנִי אֱלֹהִים אֶת־כָּל־עֲמָלִי וְאֵת כָּל־בֵּית אָבִי׃

41.52.393 וְאֵת שֵׁם הַשֵּׁנִי קָרָא אֶפְרָיִם

393α

41.52.394 ND כִּי־הִפְרַנִי אֱלֹהִים בְּאֶרֶץ עָנְיִי׃

Joseph Distributes Grain in the Years of Drought

41.53.395	וַתִּכְלֶינָה שֶׁבַע שְׁנֵי הַשָּׂבָע אֲשֶׁר הָיָה בְּאֶרֶץ מִצְרָיִם
41.54.396	וַתְּחִלֶּינָה שֶׁבַע שְׁנֵי הָרָעָב לָבוֹא כַּאֲשֶׁר אָמַר יוֹסֵף
41.54.397	(וַיְהִי רָעָב בְּכָל־הָאֲרָצוֹת)
41.54.398	וּבְכָל־אֶרֶץ מִצְרַיִם הָיָה לָחֶם
41.55.399	וַתִּרְעַב כָּל־אֶרֶץ מִצְרַיִם
41.55.400	וַיִּצְעַק הָעָם אֶל־פַּרְעֹה לַלָּחֶם
41.55.401	וַיֹּאמֶר פַּרְעֹה לְכָל־מִצְרַיִם
41.56.404	וְהָרָעָב הָיָה עַל כָּל־פְּנֵי הָאָרֶץ
41.56.405	וַיִּפְתַּח יוֹסֵף אֶת־כָּל־אֲשֶׁר בָּהֶם
41.56.406	וַיִּשְׁבֹּר לְמִצְרַיִם
41.56.407	וַיֶּחֱזַק הָרָעָב בְּאֶרֶץ מִצְרָיִם
41.57.408	(וְכָל־הָאָרֶץ בָּאוּ מִצְרַיְמָה לִשְׁבֹּר אֶל־יוֹסֵף כִּי־חָזַק הָרָעָב בְּכָל־הָאָרֶץ)

HD

41.55.402	לְכוּ אֶל־יוֹסֵף
403α	אֲשֶׁר־יֹאמַר לָכֶם
41.55.403	תַּעֲשׂוּ

Table of Independent Clause Types in Genesis 41

Clause Type	Clause Distribution	Total	Percent
QAṬAL Total Clauses: 22	Narrative: 388,390,393,398,404,408	6	28.6%
	ND: 286,289,293,295,296,297,305,307,318,321,332, 339,392,394	14	66.7%
	PD:		
	ED:		
	ID:		
	HD: 367		1
WeQAṬAL Total Clauses: 7	Narrative: 375*	1	14.3%
	ND:		
	PD: 342,343,344,355	4	57.1%
	ED:		
	ID:		
	HD: 351,354	2	28.6%
YIQṬOL Total Clauses: 12	Narrative:	0	0
	ND:		
	PD: 308,311,345,356,362,363,364,378	8	66.7%
	ED: 337	1	8.3%
	ID: 359	1	8.3%
	HD: 349,403	2	16.7%
WeYIQṬOL Total Clauses: 3	Narrative:	0	0
	ND:		
	PD:		
	ED:		
	ID:		
	HD: 348,352,353	3	100%
WAYYIQṬOL Total Clauses: 67	Narrative: 262,266,268,269,270,271,272,275,276, 278,279,280,281,282,284,298,299,300,301,302,303, 304,309,312,330,357,358,360,365,368,369,370,371, 372,373,376,379,380,381,383,384,385,386,387,389, 391,395,396,397,399,400,401,405,406,407	55	82.0%
	ND: 287,288,291,292,294,316,319,320,323,324, 327,328	12	18.0%
	PD:		
	ED:		
	ID:		
	HD:		

*Clause 375 is a rare instance of an infinitive absolute standing in the place of a finite conjugation (QAṬAL or WeQAṬAL). See below for discussion.

Participle Total Clauses: 13	Narrative: 263,264,265,267,273,274	6	46.1%
	ND: 314,315,317,325,326	5	38.5%
	PD: 340	1	7.7%
	ED: 285	1	7.7%
	ID:		
	HD:		
Verbless Total Clauses: 15	Narrative: 283,382	2	13.3%
	ND: 290,306,322,329	4	26.7%
	PD: 341	1	6.7%
	ED: 331,333,334,335,336,338,361,377	8	53.3%
	ID:		
	HD:		
Incomplete Total Clauses: 5	Narrative: 277	1	20.0%
	ND: 313	1	20.0%
	PD:		
	ED: 310,346,374	3	60.0%
	ID:		
	HD:		
Imperative	Narrative:	0	0
Total Clauses: 2	HD: 366,402	2	100%
Cohortative	Narrative:	0	0
Total Clauses: 0	HD:	0	0
Jussive	Narrative:	0	0
Total Clauses: 2	HD: 347,350	2	100%

Analysis of the Narrative Structure and Discourse Text-Types in Genesis 41

Narrative Analysis

Narrative/Paragraph Structure

Genesis 41, the story of "Pharaoh's Dreams and Joseph's Interpretation," is composed of four main paragraphs.

> Clauses 262-277: Pharaoh Has Two Dreams
> Clauses 278-375: Joseph Interprets the Dreams and Is Placed over Egypt
> Clauses 376-387: Joseph Gathers Grain in the Years of Plenty
> Clauses 395-408: Joseph Distributes Grain in the Years of Drought

Setting aside for the moment the first paragraph (clauses 262-277), only the second paragraph has an explicit initial marker, a וַיְהִי temporal clause followed by a *WAYYIQTOL* clause as its resolution (clauses 278-279). The final two paragraphs are headed by *WAYYIQTOL* clauses (clauses 376, 395) which lead into *WAYYIQTOL* chains and are initially marked by the non-*WAYYIQTOL* clauses immediately before them (clauses 375, 394). Thus, while the beginnings of these two paragraphs are not formally marked, they are explicitly set apart by the clauses immediately preceding them.

The second and fourth paragraphs of the chapter also have concluding markers. The *QATAL* in clause 408 marks the end of the final paragraph in the chapter. The infinitive absolute used as the governing verb of clause 375, in the second paragraph, is, however, unusual. The use of the infinitive absolute as a finite verb occurs over 88 times in the Hebrew Bible. The construction, however, only occurs 16 times in narrative:[58]

---

[58]The genres of most of the remaining occurrences are:

Poetry/Prophecy: 2 Kgs 19:29; Ps 17:5; Isa 14:31; 21:5; 22:13; 59:4; Jer 2:2; 3:1; 7:9-10 (6x); 8:15; 14:5, 19; 19:13; 31:2; 32;33; Ezek 21:31; 23:30, 46; Hos 4:2; 10:4; Amos 4:4; Hab 2:15; Hag 1:6; Zec 7:5;

Legal Materials: Exod 13:3; 20:8; Lev 2:6; 6:7; 25:14; Num 4:2; 6:5; 15:35; 25:17; 30:3; Deut 1:16; 5:2,12;

Gnomic Materials: Job 15:35; 40:2; Pro 17:12; and

Direct Discourse: Gen 17:10; Exod 12:48; Deut 14:21; Josh 1:13; 9:20; 1 Sam 2:28; 2 Kgs 3:16; 4:43; 5:10; 11:15; 1 Chr 5:20; 21:24; 2 Chr 28:19; 31:10; Ezra 7:14; Neh 9:8, 13; Est 2:3; 6:9; Eccl 4:2; Isa 7:4; 37:19, 30; 38:5; Jer 32:44; Dan 9:5; Zech 3:4. The categorization of the instances in prophetic books to either direct discourse or po- etry/prophecy is based upon the presence of *WAYYIQTOL* narrative chains in the immediate context. For standard treatments of the finite use of the infinitive absolute,

Genesis 41:43
Exodus 8:11; 36:7
Judges 7:19
1 Kings 9:25
1 Chronicles 5:20; 16:36
2 Chronicles 7:3; 28:19
Esther 3:13; 9:1,6,16,18
Nehemiah 8:8
Jeremiah 36:23; 37:21

Consistently in all these cases, the infinitive absolute never simply takes the place of a WAYYIQTOL form in the unfolding of the narrative. The infinitive absolute construction as a finite verb is used either as a concluding marker for a narrative WAYYIQTOL chain or in a series of extra-paragraph comments between separate sections of narrative.[59]

In Genesis 41, the infinitive absolute which is present in clause 375 marks the end of the paragraph describing the appointment of Joseph over Egypt and distinguishes it from the following paragraph which outlines Joseph's activities during the seven years of plentiful harvests, including his marriage to Asenath (clause 380) and his agrarian policy (clauses 385-387). Therefore, the waw + infinitive absolute construction, when it is used as a finite verbal form in narrative prose, should be added to the list of the disjunctive clauses which define the limits of paragraphs in narrative prose and also to the list of disjunctive clauses which may comprise extra-paragraph comments. When a clause governed by an infinitive absolute stands independently as a paragraph marker, it will consistently stand at the end of paragraphs, even as the וַיְהִי temporal clause consistently stands at the beginning of paragraphs.

The first paragraph of Genesis 41 is very unusual syntactically. While the paragraph is marked initially by a regular וַיְהִי temporal clause (262), the end of the paragraph contains the only incomplete clause in the narrative portion of the Joseph Novella (277; וְהִנֵּה חֲלוֹם).[60] Furthermore, while a WAYYIQTOL chain

---

note especially the thorough examination in Gesenius, *Grammar*, §113y, z, and Waltke and O'Connor, *Syntax*, 594-97.

[59] As a terminal paragraph marker, the waw + infinitive absolute is used in Exod 8:11; 36:7; 1 Chr 5:20; 16:36; 2 Chr 7:3; 28:19; Neh 8:8; Jer 37:21; and possibly Judg 7:19. The construction is present in inner-paragraph comments in Est 3:13; 9:16, 16, 18; and Jer 36:23. Its function parallels that of WeQATAL which also serves as a paragraph terminal marker when it is independent and as an element in extra-paragraph comments when it occurs along with other non-WAYYIQTOL clauses.

[60] The end of the paragraph is, of course, also marked by the וַיְהִי temporal clause at the head of the following paragraph (clause 278). Therefore, clause 277 must stand as the terminal clause of the first paragraph. As opposed to the preceding discussion of infinitive

may be reconstructed throughout the paragraph (clauses 266, 268-272, 275-276), its function here does not parallel that found elsewhere in the novella. The resolution of the initial וַיְהִי temporal clause (262) cannot be seen in the following *WAYYIQṬOL* clause (266) as is usual. Such a reading would produce the clearly absurd meaning: "At the end of two full years, . . . they grazed among the reeds"! The initial וַיְהִי temporal clause is clearly resolved in the following participial clause (263): "At the end of two full years, Pharaoh dreamed/was dreaming." Moreover, the participial clauses found throughout the paragraph (clauses 263-265, 267, 273-274) do not perform their usual function of providing inner-paragraph commentary, but rather, in this context they, along with the *WAYYIQṬOL* clauses noted above, provide the narrative movement within the story line itself.

The unusual nature of the narrative syntax of clauses 262-277, it seems clear, is related to their subject matter, the description of dreams. Throughout this paragraph, the participial and *WAYYIQṬOL* clauses work together in order to produce a schema of setting vs. climax, as opposed to the more usual narrative schema of story line vs. comment. Thus, during the dream sequences of clauses 264-269 and 273-275 there are two primary types of clauses:

1. Participial clauses introduced by וְהִנֵּה, which focus the narrative on certain actions of characters, and,
2. *WAYYIQṬOL* clauses, which signal the climax and resolution to scenes within the dream sequence.

Thus, Pharaoh's "Dream of the Fat and Lean Cows" divides into two primary parts, each with its own scenes and its own resolution. The final resolution, however, also provides the climax of the dream itself. This can be illustrated as below:

Dream A: Part 1: Fat Cows
   Scene 1: Pharaoh

וְהִנֵּה

41.01.264 עֹמֵד עַל־הַיְאֹר:

   Scene 2: Fat Cows

וְהִנֵּה

41.02.265 מִן־הַיְאֹר עֹלֹת שֶׁבַע פָּרוֹת יְפוֹת מַרְאֶה וּבְרִיאֹת בָּשָׂר

---

absolute clauses as paragraph markers, the presence of incomplete clauses in narrative is very sparse. Furthermore, because of the other unusual features found in clauses 262-277, the context deprives the final clause of the paragraph of much narratological significance. This study will not, therefore, argue that incomplete clauses in narrative are used, like infinitive absolute clauses, as paragraph markers.

Resolution --

41.02.266 וַתִּרְעֶינָה בָּאָחוּ

Dream A: Part 2: Lean Cows
   Scene 1: Lean Cows

41.03.267 וְהִנֵּה שֶׁבַע פָּרוֹת אֲחֵרוֹת עֹלוֹת אַחֲרֵיהֶן
[מִן־הַיְאֹר רָעוֹת מַרְאֶה וְדַקּוֹת בָּשָׂר

Resolution and Climax --

41.03.268 וַתַּעֲמֹדְנָה אֵצֶל הַפָּרוֹת עַל־שְׂפַת הַיְאֹר:
41.04.269 וַתֹּאכַלְנָה הַפָּרוֹת רָעוֹת הַמַּרְאֶה וְדַקֹּת הַבָּשָׂר
[אֵת שֶׁבַע הַפָּרוֹת יְפֹת הַמַּרְאֶה וְהַבְּרִיאֹת

Likewise, Pharaoh's "Dream of the Robust and Withered Ears of Corn" is
divided into separate scenes with a single resolution and climax:

Dream B:
   Scene 1: Robust Corn

וְהִנֵּה
41.05.273 שֶׁבַע שִׁבֳּלִים עֹלוֹת בְּקָנֶה אֶחָד בְּרִיאוֹת וְטֹבוֹת:

   Scene 2: Withered Corn

וְהִנֵּה
41.06.274 שֶׁבַע שִׁבֳּלִים דַּקּוֹת וּשְׁדוּפֹת קָדִים צֹמְחוֹת אַחֲרֵיהֶן:

Resolution and Climax --

41.07.275 וַתִּבְלַעְנָה הַשִּׁבֳּלִים הַדַּקּוֹת אֵת שֶׁבַע הַשִּׁבֳּלִים הַבְּרִיאוֹת וְהַמְּלֵאוֹת

This unusual syntactical pattern is not paralleled anywhere else in the narrative
portions of the Joseph Novella. It does, however, find a close parallel with certain dialogical text-types, especially those particular instances of Narrative
Discourse whose subject matter is, again, the reporting of dreams.[61] In these
dream reports, participial clauses, verbless clauses, *QATAL* clauses, and
YIQTOL clauses all play a role in the flow of the narrative of the dream, as opposed to their commentary function elsewhere. The high use of, in particular,
participial and *YIQTOL* clauses reflects the "unreal" or "ephemeral" quality of
the dreams. The events that occurred in the dreams, while clearly happening
before the report, were not events that actually occurred in reality. This is,

---

[61]Note the discourse analyses in Chapter 37 (clauses 016-020; 029), Chapter 40
(clauses 222-230; 243-246), and Chapter 41, below (clauses 313-327).

perhaps, a specialized dialogical form and may have provided the foundation for the irregular syntactical construction seen here.[62]

Extra-Paragraph Comments

Between the third and fourth paragraphs of the chapter an extra-paragraph comment is inserted, consisting of a participial clause, two *WAYYIQTOL* clauses, and two *QATAL* clauses. The subject of the comment is twofold: the source and amount of grain that Joseph gathers (clauses 388-389) and the birth of Joseph's two sons, Manasseh and Ephraim (390-394). In the formatted text preceding this analysis, the two comments are presented as separate. This layout is based only upon the subject matter of the comments rather than the syntactical nature of the disjunctive comments contained in them.

Inner-Paragraph Comments

There are only four inner-paragraph comments found in the chapter. All four comments describe the state or existence of some element in the narrative. In the third paragraph, the author notes, by means of a verbless clause, Joseph's age when he interpreted Pharaoh's dream:

41.46.382 וְיוֹסֵף בֶּן־שְׁלֹשִׁים שָׁנָה בְּעָמְדוֹ לִפְנֵי פַּרְעֹה מֶלֶךְ־מִצְרָיִם

This notice informs the reader that approximately twelve or thirteen years have elapsed since the beginning of the novella, when Joseph was seventeen years old (clause 003).

The remaining comments all employ היה verbal clauses:

41.54.397 וַיְהִי רָעָב בְּכָל־הָאֲרָצוֹת
41.54.398 וּבְכָל־אֶרֶץ מִצְרַיִם הָיָה לָחֶם:

and

41.56.404 וְהָרָעָב הָיָה עַל כָּל־פְּנֵי הָאָרֶץ

---

[62]The beginning of the dream of Jacob at Bethel (Gen 28:10-13a) is the only example in the Hebrew Bible outside the Joseph Novella of an account of a dream in which action takes place within the dream (as opposed to a simple speech or verbal interaction, e.g., 1 Kings 3:5-15). In this example, like those in the Joseph Novella, the particle הִנֵּה and participial clauses take over the usual sequential role of *WAYYIQTOL* in the narrative portion of the dream (נִצָּב, מַגִּיעַ, יֹרְדִים, and מָצָב).

Discourse Function Analysis

Narrative Discourse

There are five examples of Narrative Discourse in Genesis 41.

> Clauses 286-297: The Butler's Report to Pharaoh
> Clauses 305-307: Pharaoh's Statement about His Dream
> Clauses 313-329: Pharaoh's Dream Report
> Clause 392: Joseph's Naming of Manasseh
> Clause 394: Joseph's Naming of Ephraim

The first two examples are straightforward retellings of past events and, there-fore, use *QATAL* clauses as the basis of their narratives. Even the occasional use of *WAYYIQTOL* clauses in the Butler's Report to Pharaoh does not parallel the frequent and nuanced usage of *WAYYIQTOL* clauses in narrative prose.

Moreover, the Dream Report of Pharaoh conforms to what has been shown to be a special narrative form, employing incomplete, verbless, participial, and *WAYYIQTOL* clauses along with the usual *QATAL* clauses found in Narrative Discourse.[63] This Dream Report form, furthermore, is so influential that even the narrator, in describing the dream as Pharaoh sees it, reverts to the form in the narrative prose at the beginning of the chapter in the original description of the dream (clauses 263-277; see Narrative Analysis above).

The final two cases of Narrative Discourse in the chapter are used as etio-logical etymologies of the names of Joseph's two sons. Being Narrative Discourse, they both employ *QATAL* forms as their governing verbs. The *QATAL* clauses stand here, in spite of the fact that, in the case of the etymology of "Manasseh," the participial verbal form would have been closer to the origi-nal name (מְנַשֶּׁה) rather than the *QATAL* verbal form (*נשׁה), which was, in fact, used (clause 392).

Predictive Discourse

Four examples of Predictive Discourse occur in Genesis 41, containing in all twelve clauses.

> Clause 308: Pharaoh's Hope for Joseph to Hear the Dream
> Clauses 310-311: Joseph's Hope for Pharaoh's Goodwill
> Clauses 340-345: Joseph's Prediction for Pharaoh
> Clauses 355-356: Joseph's Plan for the Deposited Grain
> Clauses 362-364: Pharaoh's Plans for Joseph

---

[63]Note the treatments of Joseph's dream reports in Gen 37 and the Butler and Baker's dream reports in Gen 40, above.

The first two examples are comprised of *YIQTOL* clauses (308, 311), the second also containing an incomplete clause (310). The presence of *YIQTOL* clauses in Predictive Discourse is, of course, completely regular and causes no problems in these two particular cases.

In the next example, after a lengthy explanation of Pharaoh's dream (clauses 331-339, see below), Joseph's prediction is initially marked by הִנֵּה followed by a participial clause. This construction, the *futuram instans* participle, is often used when the events foretold are certainly and immediately to occur:[64]

הִנֵּה

41.29.340 שֶׁבַע שָׁנִים בָּאוֹת

41.29.341 שָׂבָע גָּדוֹל בְּכָל־אֶרֶץ מִצְרָיִם:

41.30.342 וְקָמוּ שֶׁבַע שְׁנֵי רָעָב אַחֲרֵיהֶן

41.30.343 וְנִשְׁכַּח כָּל־הַשָּׂבָע בְּאֶרֶץ מִצְרָיִם

41.30.344 וְכִלָּה הָרָעָב אֶת־הָאָרֶץ:

41.31.345 וְלֹא־יִוָּדַע הַשָּׂבָע בָּאָרֶץ מִפְּנֵי הָרָעָב הַהוּא אַחֲרֵי־כֵן
כִּי־כָבֵד הוּא מְאֹד:

Clause 341, like 340, is an off-line comment concerning the seven years of plenty. The prediction itself does not wholly begin until the foretelling of woe with the *WeQATAL* verbal forms in clauses 342-344 and the negated *YIQTOL* clause in 345. The interesting syntactical construction of the prediction highlights the seven years of drought, with the seven years of plenty given only two, off-line comments.

After Joseph's advice concerning the future, Pharaoh himself explains his plans for his new overseer, Joseph, introduced with an Expository Discourse describing Joseph's uniqueness:

ED

361α [אַחֲרֵי הוֹדִיעַ אֱלֹהִים אוֹתְךָ אֶת־כָּל־זֹאת

41.39.361 אֵין־נָבוֹן וְחָכָם כָּמוֹךָ:

PD

41.40.362 אַתָּה תִּהְיֶה עַל־בֵּיתִי

41.40.363 וְעַל־פִּיךָ יִשַּׁק כָּל־עַמִּי

41.40.364 רַק הַכִּסֵּא אֶגְדַּל מִמֶּךָּ:

The *YIQTOL* clause which heads this discourse contains a pleonastic pronoun, pointing again to Joseph's importance in Pharaoh's future plans.[65]

---

[64]For examples of the *futuram instans*, see Waltke and O'Connor, *Syntax*, 627-28.

[65]The discourse of clauses 362-364 could be seen as Hortatory. However, several factors argue against such a reading. 1) No unambiguous volitive form occurs anywhere

Expository Discourse

There are five instances of Expository Discourse in Genesis 41, composed of thirteen clauses.

> Clause 285: The Butler's Admission of his Mistake to Pharaoh
> Clauses 331-339: Joseph's Explanation of Pharaoh's Dream
> Clause 346: Joseph's Explanation of the Double Nature of the Dream
> Clause 361: Pharaoh's Praise of Joseph
> Clause 374: Exclamation of the People concerning Joseph

Of these five instances, one is a simple verbless clause (361) and one is a simple participial clause (285), both being highly regular for Expository Discourse and needing no further comment.

Likewise, the three examples in this chapter of incomplete clauses standing as Expository Discourse point to the explanatory or informative nature of the phrases. Clause 346 appears as an example of anacoluthon, in which the primary verb was elided from the explanation of the reason for the double nature of the dream. Clause 310, likewise, appears as a reaction to Pharaoh's statement that Joseph has the ability to interpret dreams (תִּשְׁמַע חֲלוֹם לִפְתֹּר אֹתוֹ 41.15.308, see above). Clause 374 has received much study and is generally acknowledged to be an interjection pronounced during Joseph's procession through Egypt.[66] Such interjections, including לֹא when it stands syntactically alone, are considered examples of Expository Discourse, since by their nature they make a statement about contemporary events or statements.

During Joseph's extended explanation of Pharaoh's dream, clauses 331-339, a series of verbless, היה temporal, Object + *QATAL,* and *YIQTOL* clauses is arranged in such a manner as to emphasize the explanatory nature of the speech, rather than the relating of actions as in Narrative Discourse:

41.26.331　חֲלוֹם פַּרְעֹה אֶחָד הוּא

41.26.332　אֵת (אֲשֶׁר הָאֱלֹהִים עֹשֶׂה) הִגִּיד לְפַרְעֹה׃

41.26.333　שֶׁבַע פָּרֹת הַטֹּבֹת שֶׁבַע שָׁנִים הֵנָּה

41.26.334　וְשֶׁבַע הַשִּׁבֳּלִים הַטֹּבֹת שֶׁבַע שָׁנִים הֵנָּה

41.26.335　חֲלוֹם אֶחָד הוּא׃

41.27.336　וְשֶׁבַע הַפָּרוֹת הָרַקּוֹת וְהָרָעֹת הָעֹלֹת אַחֲרֵיהֶן שֶׁבַע שָׁנִים הֵנָּה

---

in the discourse. 2) No hortatory particle appears in the discourse. 3) Clause 364, with its introductory exceptive adverb, is syntactically difficult if seen in a hortatory fashion. 4) The actual hortatory granting of power to Joseph is unambiguously present later in clauses 366-367. 5) The discourse is understandable as Predictive, both in its syntax and in its general meaning and function.

[66]The actual meaning of the word אַבְרֵךְ is, however, disputed.

41.27.337 וְשֶׁבַע הַשִׁבֳּלִים הָרֵקוֹת שְׁדֻפוֹת הַקָּדִים יִהְיוּ שֶׁבַע שְׁנֵי רָעָב:
41.28.338 הוּא הַדָּבָר
אֲשֶׁר דִּבַּרְתִּי אֶל־פַּרְעֹה
41.28.339 אֲשֶׁר הָאֱלֹהִים עֹשֶׂה הֶרְאָה אֶת־פַּרְעֹה:

The clauses employing *QATAL* verbal forms consistently place the object of the verb first in the clause (clauses 332, 339). The היה verbal clause stands as a paralleled substitute for a verbless clause (clause 337; note the parallel with clause 336).

Interrogative Discourse

Only one clause of Interrogative Discourse occurs in Genesis 41 and consists of Pharaoh's response to Joseph's Interpretation of his dream.

Clause 359: Pharaoh's Rhetorical Question to his Servants

The clause governed by a *YIQTOL* verbal form is unambiguously marked as a question by the prefixed interrogative particle הֲ and, therefore, stands as a rhetorical statement about Joseph's uniqueness:

41.28.359 הֲנִמְצָא כָזֶה אִישׁ
אֲשֶׁר רוּחַ אֱלֹהִים בּוֹ:

Hortatory Discourse

Five examples of Hortatory Discourse occur in Genesis 41, encompassing sixteen clauses in all.

> Clauses 347-354: Joseph's Instructions for Pharaoh
> Clauses 366-367: Pharaoh's Instructions for Joseph
> Clauses 377-378: Pharaoh's Instruction for Joseph
> Clauses 402-403: Pharaoh's Orders for the People

The final instance of Hortatory Discourse in the chapter provides an excellent example of how, in the context of volitive verbal force, non-volitive verbal forms may take on volitive functions. Pharaoh sends the people of Egypt to Joseph for grain, heading his speech with an unambiguous imperative clause and employing a *YIQTOL* clause in the place of a second imperative clause:

41.55.402 לְכוּ אֶל־יוֹסֵף
403α [וַאֲשֶׁר־יֹאמַר לָכֶם
41.55.403 תַּעֲשׂוּ:

In terms of text-types, it is clear that Pharaoh does not switch to a Predictive Discourse in the second clause. The *YIQTOL* verbal form standing there is accounted as if it were another imperative because it stands in a Hortatory context.

The example from clauses 366-367 also shows this tendency to incorporate non-volitive forms into hortatory functions. The *QATAL* clause 367 reflects Pharaoh's desire and willingness to grant the oversight of Egypt into Joseph's power:

41.41.366 רְאֵה

41.41.367 נָתַתִּי אֹתְךָ עַל כָּל־אֶרֶץ מִצְרָיִם:

Because it stands as a first person *QATAL* form in a hortatory context, most contemporary Hebrew grammarians would designate נָתַתִּי as a "precative perfect" or a "performative utterance" and translate it as "I, hereby, do give."[67]

Clauses 377-378 constitute Pharaoh's granting Joseph power over the Egyptian populace. Although the main *YIQTOL* clause 378 does not contain an unambiguous volitive form, the discourse should probably be seen as Hortatory nonetheless because of its introduction by the verbless clause of self-identification (377), a form which often precedes Hortatory Discourse:[68]

41.44.377 אֲנִי פַרְעֹה

41.44.378 וּבִלְעָדֶיךָ לֹא־יָרִים אִישׁ אֶת־יָדוֹ וְאֶת־רַגְלוֹ בְּכָל־אֶרֶץ מִצְרָיִם:

The introductory self-designation provides the basis upon which the following statement should be performed. The speech is, therefore, hortatory in its force: "I am Pharaoh! (Therefore,) without you, let no one raise his hand or his foot in all the land of Egypt!"

Finally, Joseph's Instructions for Pharaoh (clauses 347-354) provide an excellent example of how the hortatory nature of a speech is carried forward, in spite of its containing only a few unambiguous volitive verbal forms. In the ten clauses which comprise the discourse, only two are clearly volitive (clauses 347 and 350), five are ambiguous (*WeQATAL*: 351 and 354; *WeYIQTOL* forms which may be jussive: 348, 352, and 353), and three are clearly not volitive forms, but are treated as such in the discourse (*WeQATAL* clause 355; *lō-YIQTOL* clause 356; *YIQTOL* form, not jussive: clause 349):

---

[67]Note the discussion in the previous chapter on "performative perfect" forms and also these references: Waltke and O'Connor, *Syntax,* 488-89; C. Brockelmann,. *Grundriss der vergleichenden Grammatik der semitischen Sprachen,* (Berlin: Reuter & Reichard, 1913), 40; Hillers, "Performative Utterances," 757-66.

[68]Clauses 775, 853.

וְעַתָּה
41.33.347 יֵרֶא פַרְעֹה אִישׁ נָבוֹן וְחָכָם
41.33.348 וִישִׁיתֵהוּ עַל־אֶרֶץ מִצְרָיִם:
41.34.349 יַעֲשֶׂה פַרְעֹה
41.34.350 וְיַפְקֵד פְּקִדִים עַל־הָאָרֶץ
41.34.351 וְחִמֵּשׁ אֶת־אֶרֶץ מִצְרַיִם בְּשֶׁבַע שְׁנֵי הַשָּׂבָע:
41.35.352 וְיִקְבְּצוּ אֶת־כָּל־אֹכֶל הַשָּׁנִים הַטֹּבֹת הַבָּאֹת הָאֵלֶּה
41.35.353 וְיִצְבְּרוּ־בָר תַּחַת יַד־פַּרְעֹה אֹכֶל בֶּעָרִים
41.35.354 וְשָׁמָרוּ:
41.36.355 וְהָיָה הָאֹכֶל לְפִקָּדוֹן לָאָרֶץ לְשֶׁבַע שְׁנֵי הָרָעָב
אֲשֶׁר תִּהְיֶיןָ בְּאֶרֶץ מִצְרָיִם
41.36.356 וְלֹא־תִכָּרֵת הָאָרֶץ בָּרָעָב:

Clause 349, in particular, has caused much scholarly commentary since it is clearly not a jussive clause, yet it performs a jussive function in the discourse.[69] The sense and significance of the clause is rendered correctly by Longacre: "Let Pharaoh act (vigorously)!"[70]

---

[69]The Samaritan Pentateuch actually has a jussive: ויעש—a datum paralleled by the LXX and Targum translations. While the commentators consistently translate the YIQTOL verb as a jussive, they also note that the form is unusual. See, e.g., Skinner, *Genesis,* 468; Spurrel, *Notes,* 330.

[70]Longacre, *Joseph,* 251. Longacre, however, does not comment upon the non-volitive form of the verb in this hortatory context.

Table of Discourse Constellations for Genesis 41

		Present Ch.	Prev. Chs.	Total in JN
ND	*QATAL*	2	5	7
	QATAL, WAYYIQTOL		2	2
	QATAL, (Ptc./Vbl.)	1	6	7
	QATAL, WAYYIQTOL, (Ptc./Vbl.)	1	1	2
	QATAL, WAYYIQTOL, (Ptc./Vbl.), *YIQTOL*		2	2
	QATAL, YIQTOL (w/ past adverb)		0	0
	WAYYIQTOL, (Ptc./Vbl.)		0	0
	Vbl/Ptc/Inc (Dream Report)		1	1
PD	*YIQTOL*	3	2	5
	YIQTOL, WeQATAL	1	2	3
	YIQTOL, WeQATAL, (Ptc./Vbl../Inc.)	1	0	1
	YIQTOL, (Ptc./Vbl../Inc.)	1	0	1
	WeQATAL		0	0
	WeYIQTOL		0	0
ED	Ptc./Vbl.	1	5	6
	Ptc./ Vbl., Inc.		0	0
	Inc.	2	0	2
	Ptc./Vbl., *QATAL/YIQTOL* of היה		0	0
	Ptc./Vbl., *QATAL/YIQTOL* of היה, Front. Obj.+ *QATAL/YIQTOL*	1	0	1
	QATAL/YIQTOL of היה		0	0
HD	Impv./Coh./Juss.		9	9
	Impv./Coh./Juss., *WeYIQTOL/YIQTOL*	1	1	2
	Impv./Coh./Juss., *WeQATAL*		0	0
	Impv./Coh./Juss., *WeYIQTOL/YIQTOL, WeQATAL*	1	1	2
	Impv./Coh./Juss., *QATAL*	1	0	1
	Impv./Coh./Juss., *WeYIQTOL/YIQTOL*, (*We*)*QATAL*		0	0
	Impv./Coh./Juss., *ʾal-YIQTOL*		1	1
	Impv./Coh./Juss., *WeQATAL, ʾal-YIQTOL*		1	1
	ʾal-YIQTOL	1	0	1
	ʾal-YIQTOL, WeQATAL/YIQTOL		0	0
	(*We*)*YIQTOL-nāʾ*, (*WeQATAL*/[*We*]*YIQTOL*)		0	0
	QATAL, YIQTOL/WeQATAL		1	1

Genesis 42— Joseph Meets and Tests His Brothers — Clauses 409-542

Text in Syntactical/Paragraph Units

Jacob Sends the Ten Brothers to Egypt

42.01.409	וַיַּרְא יַעֲקֹב	
42.01.410	כִּי יֶשׁ־שֶׁבֶר בְּמִצְרָיִם וַיֹּאמֶר יַעֲקֹב לְבָנָיו	
42.01.411	ID	לָמָּה תִּתְרָאוּ׃
42.02.412	וַיֹּאמֶר	
42.02.413	ND	הִנֵּה שָׁמַעְתִּי
42.02.414	HD	כִּי יֶשׁ־שֶׁבֶר בְּמִצְרָיִם רְדוּ־שָׁמָּה
42.02.415		וְשִׁבְרוּ־לָנוּ מִשָּׁם
42.02.416		וְנִחְיֶה
42.02.417		וְלֹא נָמוּת׃
42.03.418	וַיֵּרְדוּ אֲחֵי־יוֹסֵף עֲשָׂרָה לִשְׁבֹּר בָּר מִמִּצְרָיִם׃	
42.04.419	וְאֶת־בִּנְיָמִין אֲחִי יוֹסֵף לֹא־שָׁלַח יַעֲקֹב אֶת־אֶחָיו כִּי אָמַר	
42.04.420	ED	פֶּן־יִקְרָאֶנּוּ אָסוֹן׃

Joseph Encounters the Ten Brothers

42.05.421	וַיָּבֹאוּ בְּנֵי יִשְׂרָאֵל לִשְׁבֹּר בְּתוֹךְ הַבָּאִים כִּי־הָיָה הָרָעָב בְּאֶרֶץ כְּנָעַן׃	

42.06.422 וְיוֹסֵף הוּא הַשַּׁלִּיט עַל־הָאָרֶץ הוּא הַמַּשְׁבִּיר לְכָל־עַם הָאָרֶץ (וַיָּבֹאוּ אֲחֵי יוֹסֵף וַיִּשְׁתַּחֲווּ־לוֹ אַפַּיִם אָרְצָה)

42.06.423 וַיַּרְא יוֹסֵף אֶת־אֶחָיו

42.06.424 וַיַּכִּרֵם

42.06.425 וַיִּתְנַכֵּר אֲלֵיהֶם

42.07.426 וַיְדַבֵּר אִתָּם קָשׁוֹת

42.07.427 וַיֹּאמֶר

42.07.428 אֲלֵהֶם

42.07.429 מֵאַיִן בָּאתֶם

42.07.430 וַיֹּאמְרוּ

ID

42.07.431 מֵאַיִן בָּאתֶם

42.07.432 וַיֹּאמְרוּ

ND (Incomplete)

42.07.433 מֵאֶרֶץ כְּנַעַן לִשְׁבָּר־אֹכֶל:

42.08.434 וַיַּכֵּר יוֹסֵף אֶת־אֶחָיו

42.08.435 וְהֵם לֹא הִכִּרֻהוּ:

Joseph Accuses and Tests the Ten Brothers

42.09.436 וַיִּזְכֹּר יוֹסֵף אֵת הַחֲלֹמוֹת אֲשֶׁר חָלַם לָהֶם

42.09.437 וַיֹּאמֶר אֲלֵהֶם

ED

42.09.438 מְרַגְּלִים אַתֶּם

42.09.439 לִרְאוֹת אֶת־עֶרְוַת הָאָרֶץ בָּאתֶם:

42.10.440 וַיֹּאמְרוּ אֵלָיו

ND

42.10.441 לֹא אֲדֹנִי

42.10.442 וַעֲבָדֶיךָ בָּאוּ לִשְׁבָּר־אֹכֶל:

וַיֹּאמֶר אֲלֵהֶם	42.12.446
וַיֹּאמְרוּ	42.13.449
וַיֹּאמֶר אֲלֵהֶם יוֹסֵף	42.14.454

ED	...	42.11.443
		42.11.444
		42.11.445
ED (Interjection)		
ND	לֹא	42.12.447
	448α	
		42.12.448
ED		42.13.450
		42.13.451
		42.13.452
		42.13.453
ED		42.14.455
†ED		42.14.456
PD		
	בְּמִרְמָה הַזֹּאת	42.15.457
ED (Oath)	חֵי פַרְעֹה	42.15.458

42.17.465 וַיֶּאֱסֹף אֹתָם אֶל־מִשְׁמָר שְׁלֹשֶׁת יָמִים׃
42.18.466 וַיֹּאמֶר אֲלֵהֶם יוֹסֵף בַּיּוֹם הַשְּׁלִישִׁי זֹאת עֲשׂוּ וִחְיוּ אֶת־הָאֱלֹהִים אֲנִי יָרֵא׃

42.20.476 וַתַּעֲשׂוּ־כֵן׃

HD
42.16.459 שִׁלְחוּ מִכֶּם אֶחָד וְיִקַּח
42.16.460 אֶת־אֲחִיכֶם וְאַתֶּם
42.16.461 הֵאָסְרוּ וְיִבָּחֲנוּ
42.16.462 דִּבְרֵיכֶם הַאֱמֶת אִתְּכֶם
ID
42.16.463 וְאִם־לֹא חֵי פַרְעֹה
ED (Oath)
464α אִם־לֹא
42.16.464 כִּי מְרַגְּלִים אַתֶּם׃
464β

HD
42.18.467 וַיֹּאמֶר אֲלֵהֶם
42.18.468 יוֹסֵף
ED
42.18.469 אֶת־הָאֱלֹהִים אֲנִי יָרֵא׃
HD
470α אִם־כֵּנִים אַתֶּם
42.19.470 אֲחִיכֶם אֶחָד יֵאָסֵר
42.19.471 בְּבֵית מִשְׁמַרְכֶם
42.19.472 וְאַתֶּם לְכוּ
42.20.473 הָבִיאוּ שֶׁבֶר רַעֲבוֹן בָּתֵּיכֶם׃
42.20.474 וְאֶת־אֲחִיכֶם הַקָּטֹן תָּבִיאוּ אֵלַי
42.20.475 וְיֵאָמְנוּ דִבְרֵיכֶם וְלֹא תָמוּתוּ

וַיֹּאמְרוּ אִישׁ אֶל־אָחִיו 42.21.477

וַיַּעַן רְאוּבֵן אֹתָם לֵאמֹר 42.22.481
לֵאמֹר

לוֹא דִבַּרְתִּי 42.23.486
אֲלֵיכֶם לֵאמֹר
אַל־תֶּחֶטְאוּ בַיֶּלֶד:

Joseph's Trick Is Discovered by One

וְהֵם לֹא יָדְעוּ 42.24.487
כִּי 42.24.488
שֹׁמֵעַ יוֹסֵף 42.24.489
כִּי הַמֵּלִיץ 42.24.490
וַיִּסֹּב מֵעֲלֵיהֶם וַיֵּבְךְּ 42.24.491

ND

וַיֵּשְׁבוּ לֶאֱכָל־לֶחֶם וַיִּשְׂאוּ עֵינֵיהֶם 42.21.478

וַיִּרְאוּ וְהִנֵּה אֹרְחַת יִשְׁמְעֵאלִים בָּאָה מִגִּלְעָד 42.21.479

וּגְמַלֵּיהֶם נֹשְׂאִים נְכֹאת וּצְרִי וָלֹט 42.21.480
הוֹלְכִים לְהוֹרִיד מִצְרָיְמָה:

ID (Rhetorical Question)
וַיֹּאמֶר יְהוּדָה אֶל־אֶחָיו 42.22.482
לֵאמֹר

†HD
מַה־בֶּצַע כִּי נַהֲרֹג אֶת־אָחִינוּ 42.22.483
וְכִסִּינוּ אֶת־דָּמוֹ:

ED
לְכוּ וְנִמְכְּרֶנּוּ לַיִּשְׁמְעֵאלִים 42.22.484
וְיָדֵנוּ אַל־תְּהִי־בוֹ 42.22.485
כִּי־אָחִינוּ בְשָׂרֵנוּ הוּא:

42.24.492 וַיִּקַּח מֵאִתָּם אֶת־שִׁמְעֹן

42.25.493 וַיְצַו יוֹסֵף

493α וַיְמַלְאוּ אֶת־כְּלֵיהֶם בָּר

493β וּלְהָשִׁיב כַּסְפֵּיהֶם אִישׁ אֶל־שַׂקּוֹ

493γ וְלָתֵת לָהֶם צֵדָה לַדָּרֶךְ

42.25.494 וַיַּעַשׂ לָהֶם כֵּן:

42.26.495 וַיִּשְׂאוּ אֶת־שִׁבְרָם עַל־חֲמֹרֵיהֶם

42.26.496 וַיֵּלְכוּ מִשָּׁם:

42.27.497 וַיִּפְתַּח הָאֶחָד אֶת־שַׂקּוֹ

42.27.498 לָתֵת מִסְפּוֹא לַחֲמֹרוֹ בַּמָּלוֹן

42.27.499 וַיַּרְא אֶת־כַּסְפּוֹ

42.28.500 וְהִנֵּה־הוּא בְּפִי אַמְתַּחְתּוֹ:

(וַיֹּאמֶר—)

ND
42.28.501 הוּשַׁב כַּסְפִּי
ED וְגַם

42.28.502 הִנֵּה בְאַמְתַּחְתִּי

ID
42.28.505 אֶל־אֶחָיו לֵאמֹר:

42.28.503 אֶל־אֶחָיו

42.28.504 מַה־זֹּאת עָשָׂה אֱלֹהִים לָנוּ:

42.29.506 וַיָּבֹאוּ אֶל־יַעֲקֹב אֲבִיהֶם אַרְצָה כְּנָעַן

42.29.507 וַיַּגִּידוּ לוֹ אֵת כָּל־הַקֹּרֹת אֹתָם לֵאמֹר

לֵאמֹר׃

ND	
דִּבֶּר הָאִישׁ אֲדֹנֵי הָאָרֶץ אִתָּנוּ קָשׁוֹת	42.30.508
וַיִּתֵּן אֹתָנוּ כִּמְרַגְּלִים אֶת־הָאָרֶץ׃	42.30.509
וַנֹּאמֶר אֵלָיו	42.31.510
†ED	
כֵּנִים אֲנָחְנוּ	42.31.511
לֹא הָיִינוּ מְרַגְּלִים׃	42.31.512
שְׁנֵים־עָשָׂר אֲנַחְנוּ אַחִים בְּנֵי אָבִינוּ	42.32.513
הָאֶחָד אֵינֶנּוּ	42.32.514
וְהַקָּטֹן הַיּוֹם אֶת־אָבִינוּ בְּאֶרֶץ כְּנָעַן׃	42.33.515
†PD	
וַיֹּאמֶר אֵלֵינוּ	42.33.516
†HD	
הָאִישׁ אֲדֹנֵי הָאָרֶץ בְּזֹאת אֵדַע	42.33.517
כִּי כֵנִים אַתֶּם אֲחִיכֶם הָאֶחָד הַנִּיחוּ	42.33.518
אִתִּי	42.33.519
וְאֶת־רַעֲבוֹן בָּתֵּיכֶם קְחוּ	42.34.520
וָלֵכוּ׃	42.34.521
וְהָבִיאוּ אֶת־אֲחִיכֶם הַקָּטֹן אֵלַי	42.34.522
וְאֵדְעָה כִּי לֹא מְרַגְּלִים אַתֶּם	42.34.523

Joseph's Trick Is Discovered by All

42.35.524		וַיְהִי הֵם מְרִיקִים שַׂקֵּיהֶם
42.35.525		וְהִנֵּה־אִישׁ צְרוֹר־כַּסְפּוֹ בְּשַׂקּוֹ
42.35.526		וַיִּרְאוּ אֶת־צְרֹרוֹת כַּסְפֵּיהֶם הֵמָּה וַאֲבִיהֶם
42.35.527		וַיִּירָאוּ׃
42.36.528		וַיֹּאמֶר אֲלֵהֶם יַעֲקֹב אֲבִיהֶם
42.36.529	ED	אֹתִי שִׁכַּלְתֶּם
42.36.530		יוֹסֵף אֵינֶנּוּ
42.36.531		וְשִׁמְעוֹן אֵינֶנּוּ
42.36.532		וְאֶת־בִּנְיָמִן תִּקָּחוּ
42.36.533		עָלַי הָיוּ כֻלָּנָה׃
42.37.534		וַיֹּאמֶר רְאוּבֵן אֶל־אָבִיו לֵאמֹר
42.37.535	HD	אֶת־שְׁנֵי בָנַי תָּמִית
42.37.536		אִם־לֹא אֲבִיאֶנּוּ אֵלֶיךָ
42.37.537		תְּנָה אֹתוֹ עַל־יָדִי וַאֲנִי אֲשִׁיבֶנּוּ אֵלֶיךָ׃
42.38.538		וַיֹּאמֶר
42.38.539	PD	לֹא־יֵרֵד בְּנִי עִמָּכֶם
42.38.540	ED	(כִּי־אָחִיו מֵת)
42.38.541	PD	וְהוּא לְבַדּוֹ נִשְׁאָר וּקְרָאָהוּ אָסוֹן בַּדֶּרֶךְ אֲשֶׁר תֵּלְכוּ־בָהּ
42.38.542		וְהוֹרַדְתֶּם אֶת־שֵׂיבָתִי בְּיָגוֹן שְׁאוֹלָה׃

Table of Independent Clause Types in Genesis 42

Clause Type	Clause Distribution	Total	Percent
QAṬAL Total Clauses: 18	Narrative: 419,435,486	3	16.6%
	ND: 413,439,442,448,479,480,501,508,529 PD:	9	50.0%
	ED: 445,†512,533	3	16.7%
	ID: 431,482,484 HD:	3	16.7%
WeQAṬAL Total Clauses: 2	Narrative:	0	0
	ND: PD: 541,542 ED: ID: HD:	2	100%
YIQṬOL Total Clauses: 13	Narrative:	0	0
	ND: PD: 457,516,522,523,539	5	38.4%
	ED: 532	1	7.7%
	ID: 411	1	7.7%
	HD: 417,470,473,†483,535,537	6	46.2%
WeYIQṬOL Total Clauses: 4	Narrative:	0	0
	ND: PD: ED: ID: HD: 460,462,474,475	4	100%
WAYYIQṬOL Total Clauses: 51	Narrative: 409,410,412,418,421,424,425,426,427, 428,429,430,432,434,436,437,440,446,449,454,465, 466,476,477,481,487,488,489,490,491,492,493,494, 495,496,497,498,500,503,504,506,507,524,526,527, 528,534,538	48	94.1%
	ND: 509,510,515 PD: ED: ID: HD:	3	5.9%

	Narrative:	0	0
Participle	ND:		
	PD:		
Total Clauses:	ED: 469,478,485,540	4	100%
4	ID:		
	HD:		
	Narrative: 422,423,499,525	4	20.0%
Verbless	ND:		
	PD:		
Total Clauses:	ED: 438,443,444,450,451,452,453,455,†456,†511,	14	70.0%
20	†513,†514,530,531		
	ID: 463,505	2	10.0%
	HD:		
	Narrative:	0	0
Incomplete	ND:		
	PD:		
Total Clauses:	ED: 420,433,441,447,458,464,502	7	100%
7	ID:		
	HD:		
Imperative	Narrative:	0	0
Total Clauses:	HD: 414,415,459,461,467,468,471,472,†517,518,	13	100%
13	519,520,536		
Cohortative	Narrative:	0	0
Total Clauses:	HD: 416,521	2	100%
2			
Jussive	Narrative:	0	0
Total Clauses:	HD:	0	0
0			

Analysis of the Narrative Structure and Discourse Text-Types in Genesis 42

Narrative Analysis

Narrative/Paragraph Structure

Genesis 42, the story of "Joseph Meets and Tests His Brothers," is composed of five main paragraphs.

> Clauses 409-419: Jacob Sends the Ten Brothers to Egypt
> Clauses 421-435: Joseph Encounters the Ten Brothers
> Clauses 436-486: Joseph Accuses and Tests the Ten Brothers
> Clauses 487-507: Joseph's Trick Is Discovered by One
> Clauses 524-538 (543): Joseph's Trick Is Discovered by All.[71]

Of the five paragraphs of this chapter, only the final paragraph is initially marked by a וַיְהִי temporal clause, here comprised of the word וַיְהִי followed by a participial phrase:

42.35.524 וַיְהִי הֵם מְרִיקִים שַׂקֵּיהֶם

The construction is slightly unusual, but the temporal nature of the phrase is unmistakable. The beginnings of the remaining paragraphs are marked by the concluding *QATAL* clauses of each preceding paragraph (clauses 408, 419, 435, 486) and are, therefore, headed by simple *WAYYIQTOL* clauses.

The final paragraph is also terminally marked at the beginning of Chapter 43 by the *QATAL* notice that the drought was severe in the land of Canaan:

43.01.543 וְהָרָעָב כָּבֵד בָּאָרֶץ׃

This concluding sentence, of course, raises the stakes of the paragraph as a whole. Jacob says that the brothers cannot take Benjamin with them to get Reuben (clause 539); therefore, Reuben will die in Egypt. If, however, the brothers *do* take Benjamin, according to Jacob, Benjamin will die on the way and Jacob will, himself, die of a broken heart (clauses 541-542). The narrator, however, in the concluding clause of the paragraph informs the reader that, unless something is done, everyone will die—Reuben in his Egyptian exile and Jacob and his sons by hunger.

---

[71]Although Genesis 42 ends with the *WAYYIQTOL* in clause 538, the paragraph clearly extends until Genesis 43:1, the *WAYYIQTOL* chain not being broken until the governing *QATAL* in clause 543.

Extra-Paragraph Comments

There are no extra-paragraph comments in Genesis 42.

Inner-Paragraph Comments

There are four inner-paragraph comments in Genesis 42. They all inform the reader of the existence of elements in the narrative or describe the state of a character. Therefore, they all employ verbless clauses:

42.06.422 וְיוֹסֵף הוּא הַשַּׁלִּיט עַל־הָאָרֶץ
42.06.423 הוּא הַמַּשְׁבִּיר לְכָל־עַם הָאָרֶץ

These two clauses describe the office held by Joseph in Egypt.

וְהִנֵּה־
42.27.499 הוּא בְּפִי אַמְתַּחְתּוֹ:

This clause tells of the presence of the money of one of the brothers in the opening of his travel bag. The fourth inner-paragraph comment is based upon clause 499 but broadens the subject to include all the brother's money.

42.35.524 וַיְהִי הֵם מְרִיקִים שַׂקֵּיהֶם
וְהִנֵּה־
42.35.525 אִישׁ צְרוֹר־כַּסְפּוֹ בְּשַׂקּוֹ
42.35.526 וַיִּרְאוּ אֶת־צְרֹרוֹת כַּסְפֵּיהֶם הֵמָּה וַאֲבִיהֶם
42.35.527 וַיִּירָאוּ:

The parenthetical notice does not resolve the temporal introduction of clause 524. The resolution of the ויהי temporal clause is the *WAYYIQTOL* form governing clause 526. The inner-paragraph comment of clause 525 is to remind the reader of the presence of the pouches of each of the brothers in each of their sacks. The brothers, however, do not discover the pouches until the resolution in clause 526. Their subsequent response in clause 527 ("They were afraid") is quite understandable. Thus, the sense of clauses 524–527 is:

When they were emptying their sacks
(each one's pouch of money being in his sack!),
they and their father saw their pouches of money
and they were afraid.

Discourse Function Analysis

Narrative Discourse

Nineteen clauses encompassing ten instances of Narrative Discourse acts occur in Genesis 42.

> Clause 413: Jacob's Report about Grain in Egypt
> Clause 439: Joseph's First Account of the Brothers' Coming
> Clause 442: The Ten Brothers' Repeated Report to Joseph
> Clause 448: Joseph's Second Account of the Brothers' Coming
> Clauses 478-480: The Brothers' Confession of their Guiltiness
> Clause 484: Reuben's Account of the Killing of Joseph
> Clause 501: A Brother's Report about the Return of the Money
> Clauses 508-515: The Brothers' Report to Jacob
> Clause 529: Jacob's Accusation of the Brothers' Bereaving Him

Most of these instances require no comment, being governed by the expected *QATAL* verbal form (clauses 413, 439, 442, 448, 479 and 484 with לֹא, 480, 501, and 529) and thus are extremely regular for Narrative Discourse.

Clauses 508-515, The Brothers' Initial Report to Jacob concerning their activities in Egypt, while headed by a *QATAL* clause, also contains a *WAYYIQTOL* chain (clauses 509, 510, 515). As seen previously, the *WAYYIQTOL* chain, while standard in narrative prose, is not common in Narrative Discourse. Its presence in discourse usually signals that a close comparison exists between what is said in the Narrative Discourse and what has been reported directly by the narrator in a preceding example of narrative prose. This comparison may highlight a close parallel between the two, thus attributing truthfulness and trustworthiness to the speaker (as with Pharaoh's Report of His Dream, clauses 313-329, above) or the comparison highlights deception and the duplicity of the speaker (as with Potiphar's Wife's Reports, clauses 175-181 and 184-187, above).

Here, in the initial report of the Brothers to Jacob, their account of the events in Egypt closely parallels the events that the reader has seen occur in clauses 437-475 in the narrative prose. While their account is a conflation of two separate encounters between the unrecognized Joseph and the Brothers, the discussion which they recount parallels elements that actually transpired. This initial trustworthiness of the Brothers will begin to deteriorate in Genesis 43, during further accounts of what actually happened in Egypt between them and "the man, the lord of the land" (clause 508).

Predictive Discourse

Genesis 42 contains five clauses of Predictive Discourse arranged into four speeches, the last two closely related.

Clause 457: Joseph's Proposed Test of the Brothers
Clause †516: The Brothers' Paraphrase of Joseph's Proposed Test
(// Clause 457)
Clause 539: Jacob's Plan for Benjamin to Remain
Clauses 541-542: Jacob's Concern about Benjamin's Death

In clause 457 and in its paraphrase in the mouths of the brothers before Jacob in clause †516, Joseph plans for the brothers to be tested. In both cases, the free-standing *YIQTOL* clause signals that Joseph is speaking about future events:[72]

42.15.457 בְּזֹאת תִּבָּחֵנוּ

42.33.516 בְּזֹאת אֵדַע כִּי כֵנִים אַתֶּם

In the final speech of the chapter, Jacob notes that Benjamin will not accompany the Brothers on their return trip to Egypt:

PD

42.38.539 לֹא־יֵרֵד בְּנִי עִמָּכֶם
כִּי־אָחִיו מֵת

ED

42.38.540 וְהוּא לְבַדּוֹ נִשְׁאָר

PD

42.38.541 וּקְרָאָהוּ אָסוֹן בַּדֶּרֶךְ
אֲשֶׁר תֵּלְכוּ־בָהּ

42.38.542 וְהוֹרַדְתֶּם אֶת־שֵׂיבָתִי בְּיָגוֹן שְׁאֹלָה:

The *YIQTOL* in the initial clause 539 and the *WeQATAL* clauses 541 and 542 clearly show that this is an example of Predictive Discourse. The function of the intervening participial clause 540 is, however, ambiguous. Its governing verbal form may be seen as either a parenthetical example of Expository Discourse (as is represented in the formatted text) or as an off-line comment within the Predictive Discourse of clauses 539-542. The former seems closer to the sense of the

---

[72]The clauses could be interpreted as Hortatory Discourse, since *YIQTOL* clauses often appear in that text-type. The sense in these cases would be "In this way may you be tested" and "In this way let me know." (Note, however, that the cohortative is not used here, but *is* present in the hortatory clause 521.) In the majority of cases, however, Hortatory Discourse is signaled by other, less ambiguous verbal forms, or by meta-syntactical particles (e.g., וְעַתָּה). Since in both these cases the *YIQTOL* clauses stand alone, clearly distinguished from immediately preceding and following text-types, the clauses should be seen as simply Predictive in their sense: "In this way you will be tested" and "In this way I shall know."

text; clause 540, although independent, is tied to the sense of the present tense of the subordinate clause in clause 539, כִּי־אָחִיו מֵת. The case is, however, unclear.

Expository Discourse

Genesis 42 contains the largest number of cases of Expository Discourse in the Novella. Seventeen examples of Expository Discourse encompass 29 clauses.

> Clause 420: Jacob's Reason for Keeping Benjamin at Home
> Clause 433: The Ten Brothers' Answer to Joseph
> Clauses 438: Joseph's Accusation of the Ten Brothers
> Clauses 441: The Brothers' Denial of Joseph's Accusation
> Clauses 443-445: The Brothers' Explanation of Their Identity
> Clause 447: Joseph's Denial of the Brothers' Explanation
> Clauses 450-453: The Brothers' Repeated Explanation of Their Identity
> Clause 455: Joseph's Repeated Denial (with Internal Quote)
> Clause †456: Joseph's Quote of the Original Accusation (// Clause 438)
> Clause 458: Joseph's Oath by the Life of Pharaoh
> Clause 464: Joseph's Repeated Oath by the Life of Pharaoh
> Clause 469: Joseph's Remark concerning His Fear of God
> Clause 485: Reuben's Remark of Joseph's Bloodguilt
> Clause 502: A Brother's Report of the Presence of the Money
> Clauses †511-†514: The Brothers' Paraphrase of Their Speech to
>   Joseph (// Clauses 443-445, 450-453)
> Clauses 530-533: Jacob's Accusation of the Brothers' Bereaving Him
> Clause 540: Jacob's Remark concerning Benjamin

The clause type that occurs most in Expository Discourse is verbless, totaling fourteen (see chart). In combination with three participial clauses (469, 485, and 540) and six incomplete clauses (including לֹא used alone: 441, 447; pronouncement of an oath: 458, 464; and explanatory result clauses: 420, 502), the verbless clauses provide the backbone upon which most of the examples of Expository Discourse stand. In addition, one incomplete clause stands alone as an answer to a preceding question (clause 433).

Of the remaining forms, the three *QAṬAL* clauses all employ the verb היה (445, †512, 533). The use of the *YIQṬOL* clause 532 in an instance of Expository Discourse is not uncommon. Its function here and elsewhere seems to imply an incipient action.

42.36.530 יוֹסֵף אֵינֶנּוּ
42.36.531 וְשִׁמְעוֹן אֵינֶנּוּ
42.36.532 וְאֶת־בִּנְיָמִן תִּקָּחוּ
42.36.533 עָלַי הָיוּ כֻלָּנָה:

If a participial clause (the usual means of expressing action in Expository Discourse) had been used in clause 532, the meaning of the sentence would have been, "You are (even as I speak) taking Benjamin." The use of the *YIQTOL* verbal form here implies the incipient nature of the action whose initiation is in the present: "You are going to take Benjamin."

In clause 433, the Brothers answer Joseph's question (clause 431) concerning their point of origin (מֵאַיִן בָּאתֶם). Their answer is an incomplete clause, a usual form for answers to questions:

42.07.433 מֵאֶרֶץ כְּנַעַן לִשְׁבָּר־אֹכֶל:

The elliptical nature of their answer is only understandable by its juxtaposition to the preceding question.[73]

Interrogative Discourse

Five cases of Interrogative Discourse occur in Genesis 42, each unambiguously marked with an interrogative particle and each consisting of a single clause.

> Clause 411: Jacob's Rhetorical Question to His Sons
> Clause 431: Joseph's Question to the Ten Brothers about Their Origin
> Clause 463: Joseph's Question to the Ten Brothers about Their Honesty
> Clause 482: Reuben's Rhetorical Question to the Brothers
> Clause 505: The Brothers' Question to Each Other about God

The interrogative particles used here encompass both those prefixed to true questions (לָמָּה, clause 411; [מֵאַיִן] , clause 431; מָה, clause 505) as well as those used in rhetorical questions (הֲלוֹא, clause 482). The form of the prefixed particle in clause 463 is regular, followed by an example of an alternative interrogative וְאִם, standing as a subordinate clause:[74]

42.16.463 הַאֱמֶת אִתְּכֶם
463α וְאִם־לֹא

---

[73]The clause by itself, of course, cannot be analyzed according to sentence grammar. None of the classical grammars or syntaxes (e.g., Gesenius, Davidson, Driver) or modern treatments (Waltke and O'Connor, *Syntax*) make any statement about this clause. Note Lyons's remark that derived or contingent clauses can never be explained on the basis of sentence grammar but only from the perspective of discourse grammar (*Introduction*, 174-75).

[74]Gesenius, *Grammar*, §100m. On the alternative וְאִם in prose see §150; Waltke and O'Connor, *Syntax*, 684-85.

The entire clause seems to be performing the role of an aside in the midst of Joseph's planned test of the Brothers.

Hortatory Discourse

Seven examples of Hortatory Discourse occur in Genesis 42, composed of twenty-seven total clauses.

Clauses 414-417: Jacob's Order to His Sons to Buy Grain
Clauses 459-462: Joseph's Test of the Brothers I
Clauses 467-468: Joseph's Test of the Brothers II (Intro)
Clauses 470-475: Joseph's Test of the Brothers II
Clauses †483: Reuben's Paraphrase of His Earlier Prohibition
(// Clause 074)
Clauses †517-†523: The Brothers' Paraphrase of Joseph's Command to the Brothers (// Clauses 470-475)
Clauses 535-537: Reuben's Order for Jacob to Kill His Sons

All seven cases of Hortatory Discourse have unambiguous volitive forms either in the first (441, 459, 467, 517) or second (471, 563) clause of the discourse, or either have a volitive particle marking the speech as hortatory (אַל־, clause †483). No unusual clauses occur in the examples of Hortatory Discourses in this chapter.

Table of Discourse Constellations for Genesis 42

		Present Ch.	Prev. Chs.	Total in JN
	QATAL	6	7	13
	QATAL, WAYYIQTOL	1	2	3
	QATAL, (Ptc./Vbl.)	1	7	8
ND	*QATAL, WAYYIQTOL*, (Ptc./Vbl.)		2	2
	QATAL, WAYYIQTOL, (Ptc./Vbl.), *YIQTOL*		2	2
	QATAL, YIQTOL (w/ past adverb)		0	0
	WAYYIQTOL, (Ptc./Vbl.)		0	0
	Vbl/Ptc/Inc (Dream Report)		1	1
	YIQTOL	3	5	8
	YIQTOL, WeQATAL		3	3
PD	*YIQTOL, WeQATAL*, (Ptc./Vbl../Inc.)		1	1
	YIQTOL, (Ptc./Vbl../Inc.)		1	1
	WeQATAL	1	0	1
	WeYIQTOL		0	0
	Ptc./Vbl.	7	6	13
	Ptc./ Vbl., Inc.		0	0
	Inc.	3	2	5
ED	Ptc./Vbl., *QATAL/YIQTOL* of היה	2	0	2
	Ptc./Vbl., *QATAL/YIQTOL* of היה, Front. Obj.+ *QATAL/YIQTOL*	1	1	2
	QATAL/YIQTOL of היה		0	0
	Impv./Coh./Juss.	1	9	10
	Impv./Coh./Juss., *WeYIQTOL/YIQTOL*	4	2	6
	Impv./Coh./Juss., *WeQATAL*		0	0
	Impv./Coh./Juss., *WeYIQTOL/YIQTOL, WeQATAL*	1	2	3
	Impv./Coh./Juss., *QATAL*		1	1
HD	Impv./Coh./Juss., *WeYIQTOL/YIQTOL*, (We)*QATAL*		0	0
	Impv./Coh./Juss., *ʾal-YIQTOL*		1	1
	Impv./Coh./Juss., *WeQATAL, ʾal-YIQTOL*		1	1
	ʾal-YIQTOL	1	1	2
	ʾal-YIQTOL, WeQATAL/YIQTOL		0	0
	(We)*YIQTOL-nāʾ*, (We*QATAL*/[We]*YIQTOL*)		0	0
	QATAL, YIQTOL/WeQATAL		1	1

Genesis 43 – Joseph's Brothers Return and Are Welcomed – Clauses 543-657

Text in Syntactical/Paragraph Units

Joseph's Trick is Discovered by All (Cont.)

43.01.543 וְהָרָעָב כָּבֵד בָּאָרֶץ׃

Jacob Sends the Brothers and Benjamin to Egypt in a Famine

43.02.544 וַיְהִי כַּאֲשֶׁר כִּלּוּ לֶאֱכֹל אֶת־הַשֶּׁבֶר

43.02.545 אֲשֶׁר הֵבִיאוּ מִמִּצְרָיִם

43.02.546 HD וַיֹּאמֶר

43.02.547 אֲלֵיהֶם אֲבִיהֶם שֻׁבוּ שִׁבְרוּ־לָנוּ מְעַט־אֹכֶל׃

43.03.548 וַיֹּאמֶר אֵלָיו יְהוּדָה לֵאמֹר

43.03.549 ND הָעֵד הֵעִד בָּנוּ הָאִישׁ לֵאמֹר

43.03.550 †PD לֹא־תִרְאוּ פָנַי בִּלְתִּי אֲחִיכֶם אִתְּכֶם׃

43.04.551 HD אִם־יֶשְׁךָ מְשַׁלֵּחַ אֶת־אָחִינוּ אִתָּנוּ

551α נֵרְדָה

43.04.552 וְנִשְׁבְּרָה לְךָ אֹכֶל׃

553α וְאִם־אֵינְךָ מְשַׁלֵּחַ

43.05.553 לֹא נֵרֵד

43.06.555 וַיֹּאמֶר, אֲלֵהֶם

43.07.557 וַיֹּאמְרוּ

43.08.564 וַיֹּאמֶר יְהוּדָה אֶל־יִשְׂרָאֵל אָבִיו

בְּאִלְהֵי אָבִי אֲלֵהֶם

†PD
43.05.554 אֵלַי הַאַרְגָּזֶת
לֵאמֹר הַעוֹד אֲבִיכֶם חָי:

ID
43.06.556 לָכֶם לְהַגִּיד לָאִישׁ הַעוֹד לָכֶם אָח:

ND
43.07.558 שָׁאוֹל שָׁאַל־הָאִישׁ לָנוּ וּלְמוֹלַדְתֵּנוּ
לֵאמֹר

†ID
43.07.559 הַעוֹד אֲבִיכֶם חַי
43.07.560 הֲיֵשׁ לָכֶם אָח

ID
43.07.561 וַנַּגֶּד־לוֹ עַל־פִּי הַדְּבָרִים הָאֵלֶּה
43.07.562 הֲיָדוֹעַ נֵדַע
כִּי יֹאמַר

†HD
43.07.563 הוֹרִידוּ אֶת־אֲחִיכֶם:

HD
43.08.565 שִׁלְחָה הַנַּעַר אִתִּי
43.08.566 וְנָקוּמָה וְנֵלֵכָה
43.08.567 וְנִחְיֶה
43.08.568 וְלֹא נָמוּת
43.08.569 גַּם־אֲנַחְנוּ גַם־אַתָּה גַּם־טַפֵּנוּ:
43.09.570 אָנֹכִי אֶעֶרְבֶנּוּ
43.09.571 מִיָּדִי תְּבַקְשֶׁנּוּ

43.15.586

43.15.587

43.11.573

43.11.574

43.11.575

43.11.576

43.12.577

43.12.578

HD

43.12.579

ED

HD

43.13.580

43.13.581

43.13.582

43.14.583

43.14.584

43.14.585

| 574α |

43.09.572

572α

572β

[43.10]

**Joseph Welcomes the Brothers and Benjamin to Egypt
with a Feast and Another Test**

43.15.588	וַיָּקֻמוּ
43.15.589	וַיֵּרְדוּ מִצְרַיְמָה
43.15.590	וַיַּעַמְדוּ לִפְנֵי יוֹסֵף
43.16.591	וַיַּרְא יוֹסֵף אִתָּם אֶת־בִּנְיָמִין
43.16.592	וַיֹּאמֶר לַאֲשֶׁר עַל־בֵּיתוֹ

HD

43.16.593	הָבֵא אֶת־הָאֲנָשִׁים הַבָּיְתָה
43.16.594	וּטְבֹחַ טֶבַח
43.16.595	וְהָכֵן כִּי אִתִּי יֹאכְלוּ הָאֲנָשִׁים בַּצָּהֳרָיִם

43.17.596	וַיַּעַשׂ הָאִישׁ
43.17.597	כַּאֲשֶׁר אָמַר יוֹסֵף
43.18.598	וַיָּבֵא הָאִישׁ אֶת־הָאֲנָשִׁים בֵּיתָה יוֹסֵף
43.18.599	וַיִּירְאוּ הָאֲנָשִׁים

ED

43.18.600	כִּי הוּבְאוּ בֵּית יוֹסֵף וַיֹּאמְרוּ עַל־דְּבַר הַכֶּסֶף הַשָּׁב בְּאַמְתְּחֹתֵינוּ בַּתְּחִלָּה אֲנַחְנוּ מוּבָאִים

43.19.601	וַיִּגְּשׁוּ אֶל־הָאִישׁ אֲשֶׁר עַל־בֵּית יוֹסֵף

43.19.602	וַיֹּאמֶר אֲלֵהֶם מָה הַדָּבָר הַזֶּה
43.20.603	וַיֹּאמְרוּ

43.23.613 וַיֹּאמֶר

43.23.618	
43.24.619	
43.24.620	
43.24.621	
43.24.622	
43.25.623	

43.20.604	ND
43.20.605	
43.21.606	
43.21.607	
43.21.608	
43.21.609	
43.21.610	
43.22.611	
43.22.612	
43.23.614	HD
43.23.615	
43.23.616	ND
43.23.617	

43.26.624　וַיָּבֹא יוֹסֵף

43.26.625　הַבַּיְתָה

43.26.626　וַיָּבִיאוּ לוֹ אֶת־הַמִּנְחָה

43.27.627　אֲשֶׁר־בְּיָדָם הַבָּיְתָה

43.27.628　וַיִּשְׁתַּחֲווּ־לוֹ אָרְצָה:

43.27.629　ID　וַיִּשְׁאַל לָהֶם לְשָׁלוֹם

43.27.630　ID　וַיֹּאמֶר הֲשָׁלוֹם אֲבִיכֶם הַזָּקֵן

43.28.631　וַיֹּאמְרוּ

43.28.632　ED　שָׁלוֹם לְעַבְדְּךָ לְאָבִינוּ

43.28.633　ED　עוֹדֶנּוּ חָי

43.28.634　וַיֹּאמַר

43.28.635　וַיִּקְּדוּ [וַיִּשְׁתַּחוּ]:

43.29.636　וַיִּשָּׂא עֵינָיו

43.29.637　וַיַּרְא אֶת־בִּנְיָמִין אָחִיו בֶּן־אִמּוֹ

43.29.638　וַיֹּאמֶר

43.29.639　ID　הֲזֶה אֲחִיכֶם הַקָּטֹן

43.29.640　וַיֹּאמַר

43.29.641　HD　אֱלֹהִים יָחְנְךָ בְּנִי:

43.30.642　וַיְמַהֵר יוֹסֵף

43.30.643　כִּי־נִכְמְרוּ רַחֲמָיו אֶל־אָחִיו

43.30.644	וַיֹּ֫אמֶר יִשְׂרָאֵ֫ל
43.30.645	אָבִ֫יהֶם
43.31.646	עֲשׂ֣וּ זֹ֔את
43.31.647	וָחְי֑וּ
43.31.648	וְנֵצֵ֑אָה
43.31.649	וַיֹּ֫אמֶר אֲלֵהֶ֫ם

43.31.650 יְהוּדָ֖ה לֵאמֹ֑ר HD

43.32.651	הָעֵ֣ד הֵעִד֩ בָּ֨נוּ הָאִ֜ישׁ לֵאמֹ֗ר
43.33.652	וַיֹּ֣אמֶר אֲלֵהֶ֗ם יִשְׂרָאֵ֤ל אֲבִיהֶם֙
43.33.653	לֵאמֹ֔ר
43.34.654	לָ֤מָּה הֲרֵעֹתֶם֙ לִ֔י
43.34.655	לְהַגִּ֣יד לָאִ֔ישׁ
43.34.656	הַע֥וֹד לָכֶ֖ם אָֽח
43.34.657	וַיֹּ֫אמְר֫וּ

Table of Independent Clause Types in Genesis 43

Clause Type	Clause Distribution	Total	Percent
QAṬAL Total Clauses: 10	Narrative: 587	1	10.0%
	ND: 549,558,605,611,612,616,617 PD: ED:	7	70.0%
	ID: 556	1	10.0%
	HD: 585	1	10.0%
WeQAṬAL Total Clauses: 2	Narrative:	0	0
	ND: PD: ED: ID:		
	HD: 572,584	2	100%
YIQṬOL Total Clauses: 11	Narrative:	0	0
	ND: PD: †550,†554	2	18.2%
	ED:		
	ID: 562	1	9.1%
	HD: 553,569,570,571,578,583,615,641	8	72.7%
WeYIQṬOL Total Clauses: 0	Narrative:	0	0
	ND: PD: ED: ID: HD:	0	0
WAYYIQṬOL Total Clauses: 61	Narrative: 544,545,548,555,557,564,573,586, 588,589,590,591,592,596,597,598,599,601,602,603, 613,618,619,620,621,622,623,624,625,626,627,628, 631,634,635,636,637,638,640,642,643,644,645,646, 647,648,649,651,652,653,654,655,656,657	57	93.4%
	ND: 561,606,607,610 PD: ED: ID: HD:	4	6.6%

Participle Total Clauses: 1	Narrative:	0	0
	ND: PD: ED: 600 ID: HD:	1	100%
Verbless Total Clauses: 12	Narrative: 543	1	8.3%
	ND: 608,609	2	16.7%
	PD:		
	ED: 579,632,633	3	25.0%
	ID: †559,560,629,630,639	5	41.7%
	HD: 614	1	8.3%
Incomplete Total Clauses: 1	Narrative:	0	0
	ND: 604 PD: ED: ID: HD:	1	100%
Imperative Total Clauses: 15	Narrative:	0	0
	HD: 546,547,†563,565,574,575,576,577,580,581, 582,593,594,595,650	15	100%
Cohortative Total Clauses: 5	Narrative:	0	0
	HD: 551,552,566,567,568	5	100%
Jussive Total Clauses: 0	Narrative:	0	0
	HD:	0	0

Analysis of the Narrative Structure and
Discourse Text-Types in Genesis 43

Narrative Structural Analysis

Narrative/Paragraph Structure

Genesis 43, the story of "Joseph's Brothers Return and Are Welcomed," is composed of two main paragraphs, the first of which is initially and terminally marked.

> Clauses 544-587: Jacob Sends the Brothers and Benjamin to Egypt in a Famine
>
> Clauses 588-657 (662): Joseph Welcomes the Brothers and Benjamin to Egypt with a Feast and Another Test[75]

The first paragraph of the chapter, clauses 544-587, is headed by a וַיְהִי temporal clause which is resolved by the immediate *WAYYIQTOL* clause following it:

43.02.544 וַיְהִי כַּאֲשֶׁר כִּלּוּ לֶאֱכֹל אֶת־הַשֶּׁבֶר
אֲשֶׁר הֵבִיאוּ מִמִּצְרָיִם
43.02.545 וַיֹּאמֶר אֲלֵיהֶם אֲבִיהֶם

It is, likewise, terminally marked by a *QATAL* clause:

43.15.587 וּמִשְׁנֶה־כֶּסֶף לָקְחוּ בְיָדָם וְאֶת־בִּנְיָמִן

The second paragraph, clauses 588-664, is not marked initially, the initial clause being a simple *WAYYIQTOL* verb, וַיָּקֻמוּ. The paragraph is, however, marked terminally by the inner-paragraph comment following it (see Narrative Analysis of Chapter 44). This paragraph contains one of the longest uninterrupted *WAYYIQTOL* chains found in the Joseph Novella, including forty-five unbroken, sequential clauses.

Extra-Paragraph Comments

No extra-paragraph comments occur in Genesis 43.

---

[75]Although Genesis 43 ends with the *WAYYIQTOL* in clause 567, the paragraph clearly extends to the beginning of Genesis 44:3f. The *WAYYIQTOL* chain remains unbroken until the extra-paragraph comment composed of the series of four *QATAL* clauses beginning with clause 663 and extending to clause 666.

Inner-Paragraph Comments

No inner-paragraph comments occur in Genesis 43

Discourse Function Analysis

Narrative Discourse

Fourteen clauses constitute four separate instances of Narrative Discourse in Genesis 43:

> Clause 549: The Brothers' Recounting Joseph's Ultimatum
> Clauses 558-561: The Brothers' False Account of the Conversation
>   with Joseph (cf. Clauses 450-453)
> Clauses 604-612: The Brothers' Account of Their Trip
> Clauses 616-617: Joseph's Account of the Returned Money

In all these cases, *QATAL* remains the predominant governing verbal form. While *WAYYIQTOL* clauses are present in four places (clauses 561, 606, 607, 610), they never create a chain which carries the narrative as the form does in narrative prose. Moreover, in the third example above, clauses 604-612, the Brothers relate their finding the money in their sacks to Joseph and employ several verbless clauses as well as an introductory incomplete clause (604):

43.20.604 בִּי אֲדֹנִי
43.20.605 יָרֹד יָרַדְנוּ בַּתְּחִלָּה לִשְׁבָּר־אֹכֶל:
43.21.606 וַיְהִי
          כִּי־בָאנוּ אֶל־הַמָּלוֹן
43.21.607 וַנִּפְתְּחָה אֶת־אַמְתְּחֹתֵינוּ
          וְהִנֵּה
43.21.608 כֶסֶף־אִישׁ בְּפִי אַמְתַּחְתּוֹ
43.21.609 כַּסְפֵּנוּ בְּמִשְׁקָלוֹ
43.21.610 וַנָּשֶׁב אֹתוֹ בְּיָדֵנוּ:
43.22.611 וְכֶסֶף אַחֵר הוֹרַדְנוּ בְיָדֵנוּ לִשְׁבָּר־אֹכֶל
43.22.612 לֹא יָדַעְנוּ מִי־שָׂם כַּסְפֵּנוּ בְּאַמְתְּחֹתֵינוּ:

This passage reveals the usual manner by which characters report consecutive events that occurred before the speech. Although the events and actions occur one after the other, true *WAYYIQTOL* clauses constitute only clauses 607 and 610. Clause 606 seems to perform a temporal function; the syntax of the clause, however, is unlike the usual וַיְהִי temporal clause found in narrative prose. The passage is primarily "held together" by the *QATAL* clauses found throughout it.

Predictive Discourse

The two instances of Predictive Discourse which occur in chapter 43 each are composed of the same clause.

> Clause †550: The Brothers' False Paraphrase of Joseph's Plan for Their Return (No Parallel)
> Clause †554: The Brothers' False Paraphrase of Joseph's Plan for Their Return (No Parallel).

In both cases the simple negated *YIQTOL* verb, לֹא־תִרְאוּ, provides the brothers' understanding of Joseph's original plan for their bringing back of Benjamin. This line does not occur in any discourse, Predictive or Hortatory, of Joseph.

Expository Discourse

Three cases of Expository Discourse occur in Genesis 43, composed of four clauses.

> Clause 579: Jacob to the Brothers concerning the Returned Money
> Clause 600: The Brothers' Supposition
> Clauses 632-633: The Brothers' Answer concerning Jacob

Of these four examples of Expository Discourse, three are governed by verbless clauses explaining a present set of circumstances (clauses 579, 632, 633) and one by a participial clause, explaining a present action (clause 600).

Interrogative Discourse

Seven clauses make up the five examples of Interrogative Discourse found in Genesis 43.

> Clause 556: Jacob's Question to the Brothers
> Clauses †559-†560: The Brothers' False Paraphrase of the Questions of Joseph (No Parallel)
> Clause 562: The Brothers' Rhetorical Question about Joseph
> Clauses 629-630: Joseph's Questions about Jacob
> Clause 639: Joseph's Question about Benjamin

All the clauses are unambiguously marked by prefixed interrogative particles. The first clause is headed by לָמָה; the remaining six clauses are all headed by the polar question particle הֲ. In clause 562, the brothers ask Jacob if they truly could know that Joseph would tell them to bring Benjamin back to Egypt:

43.07.562   הֲיָדוֹעַ נֵדַע
כִּי יֹאמַר
†HD
43.07.563   †הוֹרִידוּ אֶת־אֲחִיכֶם:

The question is asked with an Interrogative הֲ with the infinitive absolute and the *YIQTOL* form of the verb. This combination lends the question the sense of a negative rhetorical question in the same way as הֲלוֹא signals a positive rhetorical question. For this reason, it is unanswered by Jacob in the text.

Hortatory Discourse

Ten examples of Hortatory Discourse occur in Genesis 43, encompassing in all thirty-two discrete clauses.

> Clauses 546-547: Jacob's Order for the Brothers to Return
> Clauses 551-553: The Brothers' Urging for Jacob to Release Benjamin
> Clause †563: The Brothers' Paraphrase of Joseph's Order concerning
>   Benjamin (// Clause 473)
> Clauses 565-572: Judah's Urging for Jacob to Release Benjamin
> Clauses 574-578: Jacob's Orders to the Brothers
> Clauses 580-585: Jacob's Orders to the Brothers
> Clauses 593-595: Joseph's Orders concerning the Brothers
> Clauses 614-615: Joseph's Welcome to the Brothers
> Clause 641: Joseph's Welcome of Benjamin
> Clause 650: Joseph's Order for Food

In most cases, imperative clauses dominate multi-clausal examples of Hortatory Discourse in this chapter. A single example will suffice to show this phenomenon. When Jacob finally relents and decides to send Benjamin along with his Brothers back to Egypt, he provides a list of commands for the Brothers to perform:

43.13.580   וְאֶת־אֲחִיכֶם קָחוּ
43.13.581   וְקוּמוּ
43.13.582   שׁוּבוּ אֶל־הָאִישׁ:
43.14.583   וְאֵל שַׁדַּי יִתֵּן לָכֶם רַחֲמִים לִפְנֵי הָאִישׁ
43.14.584   וְשִׁלַּח לָכֶם אֶת־אֲחִיכֶם אַחֵר וְאֶת־בִּנְיָמִין
43.14.585   וַאֲנִי כַּאֲשֶׁר שָׁכֹלְתִּי שָׁכָלְתִּי:

Because of the initial string of three imperative clauses, the final clauses also take on a hortatory function. This phenomenon has been seen and commented upon in previous chapters. The *YIQTOL* clause 583 and the *WeQATAL* clause

584 both take on jussive functions. Even the final *QATAL* clause also takes on hortatory force, here as a performative utterance.[76] The sense of this final climactic sentence by Jacob is best rendered: "And as for me, just as I was bereaved, I am hereby (by the sending off of Benjamin) bereaved."[77]

In the two cases of welcoming found within this chapter, while the clausal types are not strictly volitive, the hortatory force of the clauses is evident because of the specific genre and function of the speech acts themselves. Thus, when Joseph greets the Brothers generally, he pronounces a two-clause speech. The first clause is verbless, the second is governed by a *YIQTOL* whose hortatory purpose is marked by the negative particle אַל־:

> 43.23.614 שָׁלוֹם לָכֶם
>
> 43.23.615 אַל־תִּירָאוּ

While verbless clauses are not commonly used in Hortatory Discourse, in the specific narrative context of greeting they may appear in such speeches. Likewise, when Joseph welcomes Benjamin, his solitary *YIQTOL* clause takes on jussive force even though, morphologically, it is ambiguous:[78]

> 43.29.641 אֱלֹהִים יָחְנְךָ בְּנִי:

---

[76] The possibility of a *QATAL* clause taking on hortatory force when appearing in a Hortatory Discourse was discussed in the Analysis of Genesis 40.

[77] Both Longacre (*Joseph,* 277) and Endo (*Verbal System,* 214), in their analyses, seem to miss the fact that the *QATAL* in the dependent clause, כַּאֲשֶׁר שָׁכֹלְתִּי, refers to the past event of Jacob's bereavement over Joseph, which he has already paralleled with his expected bereavement over Benjamin (Gen 42:38). In this clause, the parallel is again made.

[78] On the usual form of the verb יָחְנְךָ, see Gesenius, *Grammar,* §67n.

Table of Discourse Constellations for Genesis 43

		Present Ch.	Prev. Chs.	Total in JN
ND	*QATAL*	2	13	15
	QATAL, WAYYIQTOL	1	3	4
	QATAL, (Ptc./Vbl.)		8	8
	QATAL, WAYYIQTOL, (Ptc./Vbl.)	1	2	3
	QATAL, WAYYIQTOL, (Ptc./Vbl.), *YIQTOL*		2	2
	QATAL, YIQTOL (w/ past adverb)		0	0
	WAYYIQTOL, (Ptc./Vbl.)		0	0
	Vbl/Ptc/Inc (Dream Report)		1	1
PD	*YIQTOL*	2	8	10
	YIQTOL, WeQATAL		3	3
	YIQTOL, WeQATAL, (Ptc./Vbl../Inc.)		1	1
	YIQTOL, (Ptc./Vbl../Inc.)		1	1
	WeQATAL		1	1
	WeYIQTOL		0	0
ED	Ptc./Vbl.	3	13	16
	Ptc./ Vbl., Inc.		0	0
	Inc.		5	5
	Ptc./Vbl., *QATAL/YIQTOL* of היה		2	2
	Ptc./Vbl., *QATAL/YIQTOL* of היה, Front. Obj.+ *QATAL/YIQTOL*		2	2
	QATAL/YIQTOL of היה		0	0
HD	Impv./Coh./Juss.	5	10	15
	Impv./Coh./Juss., *WeYIQTOL/YIQTOL*	2	6	8
	Impv./Coh./Juss., *WeQATAL*		0	0
	Impv./Coh./Juss., *WeYIQTOL/YIQTOL, WeQATAL*	1	3	4
	Impv./Coh./Juss., *QATAL*		1	1
	Impv./Coh./Juss., *WeYIQTOL/YIQTOL*, (We)*QATAL*	1	0	1
	Impv./Coh./Juss., *ʾal-YIQTOL*		1	1
	Impv./Coh./Juss., *WeQATAL, ʾal-YIQTOL*		1	1
	ʾal-YIQTOL	1	2	3
	ʾal-YIQTOL, WeQATAL/YIQTOL		0	0
	(We)*YIQTOL-nāʾ*, (*WeQATAL/[We]YIQTOL*)		0	0
	QATAL, YIQTOL/WeQATAL		1	1

Genesis 44 – Joseph's Second Test and Judah's Speech – Clauses 658–759

Text in Syntactical/Paragraph Units

Joseph Welcomes the Brothers and Benjamin to Egypt with a Feast and Another Test (Cont.)

וַיְצַו אֶת־אֲשֶׁר עַל־בֵּיתוֹ לֵאמֹר	44.01.658
HD	
מַלֵּא אֶת־אַמְתְּחֹת הָאֲנָשִׁים אֹכֶל	44.01.659
כַּאֲשֶׁר יוּכְלוּן שְׂאֵת	44.01.660
וְשִׂים כֶּסֶף־אִישׁ בְּפִי אַמְתַּחְתּוֹ׃	44.02.661
וַיַּעַשׂ כִּדְבַר יוֹסֵף	44.02.662

The Exit of the Eleven Brothers (Comment)

הַבֹּקֶר אוֹר	44.03.663
וְהָאֲנָשִׁים שֻׁלְּחוּ הֵמָּה וַחֲמֹרֵיהֶם׃	44.03.664
הֵם יָצְאוּ אֶת־הָעִיר	44.04.665
לֹא הִרְחִיקוּ	44.04.666

Joseph Carries Out the Test of His Brothers

וְיוֹסֵף אָמַר לַאֲשֶׁר עַל־בֵּיתוֹ	44.04.667

44.06.676
44.06.677
44.07.678

HD

44.04.668
44.04.669
44.04.670
44.04.671

†ID
44.04.672

44.05.673

†ND
44.05.674

44.05.675

ID
44.07.679

ED (Oath)
44.07.680

ND

ID
44.08.681

ID (Rhetorical Question)
44.08.682

44.10.685 וְאַתֶּ֖ם

44.11.689 וַיְמַהֲר֗וּ וַיּוֹרִ֛דוּ
44.11.690 אִ֥ישׁ אֶת־אַמְתַּחְתּ֖וֹ אָֽרְצָה
44.11.691 וַֽיִּפְתְּח֖וּ אִ֥ישׁ אַמְתַּחְתּֽוֹ
44.12.692 וַיְחַפֵּ֕שׂ
44.12.693 (בַּגָּד֣וֹל הֵחֵ֔ל)
44.12.694 וּבַקָּטֹ֖ן כִּלָּ֑ה
44.12.695 וַיִּמָּצֵא֙ הַגָּבִ֔יעַ בְּאַמְתַּ֖חַת בִּנְיָמִֽן
44.13.696 וַֽיִּקְרְע֖וּ שִׂמְלֹתָ֑ם
44.13.697 וַֽיַּעֲמֹ֗ס אִ֚ישׁ עַל־חֲמֹר֔וֹ
44.13.698 וַיָּשֻׁ֖בוּ הָעִֽירָה
44.14.699 וַיָּבֹ֨א יְהוּדָ֤ה וְאֶחָיו֙ בֵּ֣יתָה יוֹסֵ֔ף
44.14.700 וְה֖וּא עוֹדֶ֣נּוּ שָׁ֑ם
44.14.701 (וַיִּפְּל֥וּ לְפָנָ֖יו) אָֽרְצָה
44.15.702 וַיֹּ֨אמֶר

44.09.683 וְגַ֨ם־אֲנַ֔חְנוּ נִֽהְיֶ֥ה לַֽאדֹנִ֖י לַעֲבָדִֽים PD
44.09.684 (מָ֣ה נְדַבֵּ֔ר) (וּמַה־נִּצְטַדָּֽק)

44.10.686 (גַּם־עַתָּ֥ה כְדִבְרֵיכֶ֖ם כֶּן־ה֑וּא) PD
44.10.687 (אֲשֶׁ֨ר יִמָּצֵ֤א אִתּוֹ֙) יִֽהְיֶה־לִּ֣י עָ֔בֶד
44.10.688 תִּֽהְי֥וּ נְקִיִּֽם

44.15.703 מָ֣ה הַֽמַּעֲשֶׂ֥ה הַזֶּ֖ה אֲשֶׁ֣ר עֲשִׂיתֶ֑ם ID

44.15.704		הֲלוֹא יְדַעְתֶּם
44.16.705		וַיֹּאמֶר יְהוּדָה
44.16.706	ID	מַה־נֹּאמַר לַאדֹנִי
44.16.707		מַה־נְּדַבֵּר
44.16.708	ID	וּמַה־נִּצְטַדָּק
44.16.709	ND / ED	הָאֱלֹהִים מָצָא אֶת־עֲוֺן עֲבָדֶיךָ
44.16.710		הִנֶּנּוּ עֲבָדִים לַאדֹנִי גַּם־אֲנַחְנוּ גַּם אֲשֶׁר־נִמְצָא הַגָּבִיעַ בְּיָדוֹ
44.17.711		וַיֹּאמֶר
44.17.712	ED (Oath) / PD	חָלִילָה לִּי מֵעֲשׂוֹת זֹאת
44.17.713	HD	הָאִישׁ אֲשֶׁר נִמְצָא הַגָּבִיעַ בְּיָדוֹ הוּא יִהְיֶה־לִּי עָבֶד
44.17.714		וְאַתֶּם עֲלוּ לְשָׁלוֹם אֶל־אֲבִיכֶם
44.18.715		וַיִּגַּשׁ אֵלָיו יְהוּדָה
44.18.716		וַיֹּאמֶר
44.18.717	HD	בִּי אֲדֹנִי
44.18.718		יְדַבֶּר־נָא עַבְדְּךָ דָבָר בְּאָזְנֵי אֲדֹנִי
44.18.719		וְאַל־יִחַר אַפְּךָ בְּעַבְדֶּךָ כִּי כָמוֹךָ כְּפַרְעֹה

ND

44.19.720 אֲדֹנִי שָׁאַל אֶל־עֲבָדָיו
44.19.721 לֵאמֹר

†ID

44.20.722 וַנֹּאמֶר אֶל־אֲדֹנִי
44.20.723 יֶשׁ־לָנוּ אָב זָקֵן וְיֶלֶד זְקֻנִים קָטָן
וְאָחִיו מֵת

†ED

44.20.724 וַיִּוָּתֵר הוּא
44.20.725 לְבַדּוֹ לְאִמּוֹ
44.20.726 וְאָבִיו אֲהֵבוֹ׃

†ND

44.21.727 וַתֹּאמֶר אֶל־עֲבָדֶיךָ
44.21.728 הוֹרִדֻהוּ אֵלָי
44.21.729 וְאָשִׂימָה עֵינִי עָלָיו׃

†HID

44.22.730 וַנֹּאמֶר אֶל־אֲדֹנִי

†PD

44.22.731 לֹא־יוּכַל הַנַּעַר
731α לַעֲזֹב אֶת־אָבִיו
732α וְעָזַב אֶת־אָבִיו
44.22.732 וָמֵת׃
44.23.733 וַתֹּאמֶר אֶל־עֲבָדֶיךָ

†PD

44.23.734 אִם־לֹא יֵרֵד אֲחִיכֶם
הַקָּטֹן אִתְּכֶם
44.24.735 לֹא תֹסִפוּן לִרְאוֹת פָּנָי׃ וַיְהִי

אֱמֹר 735α
כִּי עָלִינוּ אֶל־עַבְדְּךָ אָבִי׃ 44.24.736
וַנַּגֶּד־לוֹ אֵת דִּבְרֵי אֲדֹנִי 44.25.737
†HD
וַיֹּאמֶר† 44.25.738
אָבִינוּ שֻׁבוּ שִׁבְרוּ־לָנוּ† 44.25.739
וַנֹּאמֶר] 44.26.740

†PD
לֹא נוּכַל לָרֶדֶת† 44.26.741
אִם־יֵשׁ אָחִינוּ הַקָּטֹן אִתָּנוּ† 742α
וְיָרַדְנוּ† 44.26.742
כִּי־לֹא נוּכַל לִרְאוֹת† 742β
פְּנֵי הָאִישׁ
וְאָחִינוּ הַקָּטֹן† 742γ
אֵינֶנּוּ אִתָּנוּ׃

וַיֹּאמֶר עַבְדְּךָ אָבִי אֵלֵינוּ† 44.27.743
†ND
אַתֶּם יְדַעְתֶּם† 44.27.744
כִּי שְׁנַיִם יָלְדָה־לִּי אִשְׁתִּי† 44.28.745
וַיֵּצֵא הָאֶחָד מֵאִתִּי† 44.28.746

††ND
וָאֹמַר אַךְ טָרֹף טֹרָף†† 44.28.747
וְלֹא רְאִיתִיו עַד־הֵנָּה† 44.28.748
†PD
וּלְקַחְתֶּם גַּם־אֶת־זֶה מֵעִם פָּנַי† 44.29.749
וְקָרָהוּ אָסוֹן׃ 44.29.750

44.29.751	וְלָקַחְתֶּם גַּם־אֶת־זֶה†
	†מֵעִם פָּנַי וְקָרָהוּ
PD	אָסוֹן
	וְהוֹרַדְתֶּם
44.30.752	וְעַתָּה
44.30.753	כְּבֹאִי אֶל־עַבְדְּךָ אָבִי
44.31.754	וְהַנַּעַר אֵינֶנּוּ אִתָּנוּ
44.31.755	וְהָיָה
44.31.756	כִּרְאוֹתוֹ כִּי־אֵין הַנַּעַר
†PD	וָמֵת
757α	וְהוֹרִידוּ עֲבָדֶיךָ
44.32.757	כִּי עַבְדְּךָ עָרַב אֶת־הַנַּעַר†
HD	מֵעִם אָבִי
44.33.758	וְעַתָּה
44.33.759	יֵשֶׁב־נָא עַבְדְּךָ
[44.34]	כִּי־אֵיךְ אֶעֱלֶה אֶל־אָבִי
	וְהַנַּעַר אֵינֶנּוּ אִתִּי

Table of Independent Clause Types in Genesis 44

Clause Type	Clause Distribution	Total	Percent
QAṬAL Total Clauses: 18	Narrative: 663,664,665,666,667,693,694	7	38.9%
	ND: †675,681,709,720,†724,†726,†744,††747,†748 PD: ED: ID: †672,704 HD:	9 2	50.0% 16.7%
WeQAṬAL Total Clauses: 12	Narrative:	0	0
	ND: PD: 683,†732,†742,†749,†750,†751,754,755,756, †757 ED: ID: HD: 670,671	 10 2	 83.3% 16.7%
YIQṬOL Total Clauses: 16	Narrative:	0	0
	ND: PD: 684,687,688,713,†731,734,†741 ED: ID: †673,†674,679,682,706,707,708 HD: 661,718	 7 7 2	 43.8% 43.7% 12.5%
WeYIQṬOL Total Clauses: 0	Narrative:	0	0
	ND: PD: ED: ID: HD:	0	0
WAYYIQṬOL Total Clauses: 33	Narrative: 658,662,676,677,678,685,689,690,691, 692,695,696,697,698,699,701,702,705,711,715,716	21	63.6%
	ND: 722,†725,727,730,733,735,736,737,740,743, †745,†746 PD: ED: ID: HD:	 12	 36.4%

Participle Total Clauses: 1	Narrative:	0	0
	ND: PD: 753 ED: ID: HD:	1	100%
Verbless Total Clauses: 7	Narrative: 700	1	14.2%
	ND: PD: 686,752 ED: 710,†723 ID: 703,†721 HD:	 2 2 2	 28.6% 28.6% 28.6%
Incomplete Total Clauses: 3	Narrative:	0	0
	ND: PD: ED: 680,712 ID: HD: 717	 2 1	 66.7% 33.3%
Imperative Total Clauses: 8	Narrative:	0	0
	HD: 659,660,668,669,714,†728,†738,†739	8	100%
Cohortative Total Clauses: 1	Narrative:	0	0
	HD: 729	1	100%
Jussive Total Clauses: 2	Narrative:	0	0
	HD: 719,†758,759	3	100%

Analysis of the Narrative Structure and Discourse Text-Types in Genesis 44

Narrative Analysis

Narrative/Paragraph Structure

Genesis 44, the story of "Joseph's Second Test and Judah's Speech," is composed of the final lines of the prior paragraph from the previous chapter (clauses 658-662; see the "Narrative Analysis" of Genesis 43), and one extended paragraph.

Clauses 667-716 (763): Joseph Carries Out the Test of His Brothers[79]

The paragraph is initially marked by a *QATAL* clause, one of the few *QATAL* introductory clauses in the novella.[80] It is marked terminally by a *QATAL* clause in Genesis 45:1:

45.01.763 וְלֹא־עָמַד אִישׁ אִתּוֹ בְּהִתְוַדַּע יוֹסֵף אֶל־אֶחָיו:

This sentence provides both a conclusion to the previous chapter, by ending Joseph's reaction to Judah's emotional speech (clauses 717-759) and setting the stage for Joseph's self-revelation in the next paragraphs.

Extra-Paragraph Comments

The only extra-paragraph comment in the chapter, clauses 663-666, is composed of a series of *QATAL* clauses, broken only by the initial *waw* in clause 664:

44.03.663 הַבֹּקֶר אוֹר
44.03.664 וְהָאֲנָשִׁים שֻׁלְּחוּ הֵמָּה וַחֲמֹרֵיהֶם:
44.04.665 הֵם יָצְאוּ אֶת־הָעִיר
44.04.666 לֹא הִרְחִיקוּ

---

[79]Although the narrative portion of Genesis 44 ends with the *WAYYIQTOL* in clause 716, the paragraph continues until clause 763 in Genesis 45:1. For the non-concluding and non-commentary nature of the *QATAL* in clause 760, see discussion above.

[80]The *QATAL* in clause 667 is differentiated from the *QATAL* clauses in the preceding extra-paragraph comment (clauses 663-666; see below) by two criteria: 1) the subject matter changes from the brothers (plural verbs) to Joseph himself (singular verb); and 2) clause 667 introduces a direct speech by Joseph. Therefore, clause 667 should be seen as standing within the story line and, thus, differentiated narratively from the preceding extra-paragraph comment.

The fact that clauses 663-665 are governed by *QATAL* verb forms rather than the more usual *WAYYIQTOL* forms signals that these sentences are not to be seen as consequent actions on the main narrative story line, but rather as a digression by the narrator.[81] This aside sets the stage for the execution of the test that Joseph had planned in the final verses of the previous paragraph (clauses 659-661).

Inner-Paragraph Comments

Only three inner-paragraph comments occur in the chapter. One of these, clause 700, relates that Joseph was still at his house when the brothers were returned there:

44.14.700 וְהוּא עוֹדֶנּוּ שָׁם

Since it expresses the existence of a character in a certain place or a certain time, it is a verbless clause.

The other two comments form a merismus and occur during the search for Joseph's silver goblet in the brothers' sacks:

44.12.693 בַּגָּדוֹל הֵחֵל

44.12.694 וּבַקָּטֹן כִּלָּה

Although the clauses are governed by *QATAL* verb forms, they do not, of course, either mark the end of a paragraph, nor to they stand between coherent, discreet paragraphs as extra-paragraph commentary. The merismatic nature of the comment and its clear chiastic structure signal that it is simply an "off-line" explanation of the order of the search.[82] The significance of the order is two-fold. First, it closely parallels the order in which the brothers had sat while being served their food the previous evening by Joseph:

43.33.652 וַיֵּשְׁבוּ לְפָנָיו הַבְּכֹר כִּבְכֹרָתוֹ וְהַצָּעִיר כִּצְעִרָתוֹ

---

[81]Clause 666, of course, could not be transposed into a *WAYYIQTOL* clause since it is governed by a negated verb. The sense of the aside is clear by way of Hebrew syntax; how this sense might be translated into English is, of course, much more difficult, since English does not have a particular way of relating narrative information off the story line. My best offering is: "Now, the morning had dawned and the men, they and their donkeys, had been sent off. They had gone out of the city, but not far, when Joseph said . . . ."

[82]Other examples of *QATAL* clauses standing in parallel with either other *QATAL* clauses or with previous *WAYYIQTOL* clauses and, thus, serving as inner-paragraph commentary are found in the Court Narrative, clauses 435-436 and 1367-1368.

Second, of course, the order eldest to youngest causes a slight rise in apprehension because the reader already knows the goblet will be found in the final search of Benjamin's sack (see clause 661).

Discourse Function Analysis

Narrative Discourse

Twenty-one clauses constitute seven instances of Narrative Discourse in Genesis 44.

> Clause †675: The Messenger's Speech to the Brothers
> Clause 681: The Brothers' Report of the Returned Money
> Clause 709: Judah's Confession
> Clauses 720-743: Judah's Recounting of the Brothers' Story
> Clauses †724-†725: Judah's False Paraphrase of the Brothers'
>   Conversation with Joseph (// Clauses 450-453)
> Clauses †744-†748: Judah's False Paraphrase of the Brothers'
>   Conversation with Jacob (No Parallel)
> Clause ††747: Judah's Quotation of Jacob's Remark at Joseph's
>   Disappearance (// Clause 122)

Of these seven cases of Narrative Discourse, three are straightforward instances of a character's reporting (truly or falsely) past events. Three cases are quotations of other character's reports of past events and one case (clause 747) involves a character quoting another character who is, in turn, quoting an earlier speech. The first three cases listed above are all governed by *QATAL* verbal forms and require no comment.

This chapter contains the longest sustained speech act of any character in the Joseph Novella, encompassing in all forty-three separate clauses, covering all discourse text-types. The Speech of Judah (clauses 717-759) is primarily a narrative recounting of the events of Genesis 42–43. For this reason, the predominant verbal form used in Narrative Discourse in the chapter is the *WAYYIQTOL* form, rather than the more usual *QATAL* form. In fact, of the twenty-one clauses extant in Narrative Discourse in this chapter only two (clauses 681 and †724) are governed by *QATAL* forms. This usual nature of Judah's Speech signals that a close comparison should be made between what Judah reports has happened and what the reader knows, as a fact, has indeed occurred. Judah's Speech parallels the previous events of the narrative and by means of the similar *WAYYIQTOL* verbal forms in both the narrative prose of the narrator and the Narrative Discourse of Judah, the slightly deceptive nature of the recounted narrative is highlighted.

The initial *QAṬAL* in clause 720 and the following nine *WAYYIQṬOL* clauses which form the backbone of Judah's speech do not come directly from any single locus but are, instead, a loose conflation of clauses 450-453, 470-475, and 546-572 from the narrative prose. The two main quotations which Judah reports, clauses 724-725, the Brothers' Speech to Joseph, and clauses 744-748, the Brothers' Speech to Jacob, do not have any parallel in the narrative prose of the story. Moreover, while the original statement of Jacob's response to Joseph's disappearance is present in clause 122, Jacob never, in fact, repeated it when the Brothers returned from Egypt, demanding that Benjamin return with them. These initial discrepancies between the events of the narrative prose of the Novella and Judah's reports of them will be outlined in the other text-types below.

Predictive Discourse

Nine examples of Predictive Discourse occur in Genesis 44 encompassing nineteen complete clauses.

> Clauses 683-684: The Brothers' Plan for the Thief and Themselves
> Clauses 686-688: The Messenger's Plan for the Thief and the Brothers
> Clause 713: Joseph's Plan for the Thief
> Clauses †731-†732: Judah's False Paraphrase of the Brothers'
>   Conversation with Joseph (cf. Clauses 450-453)
> Clause †734: Judah's False Paraphrase of the Brothers' Conversation
>   with Joseph (cf. Clauses 450-453)
> Clauses †741-†742: Judah's True Paraphrase of the Brothers'
>   Conversation with Jacob (// Clauses 551-553)
> Clauses †749-†751: Judah's True Paraphrase of an Earlier Conversation
>   with Jacob (// Clauses 541-542)
> Clauses 752-756: Judah's Prediction of the Return without Benjamin
> Clause †757: Judah's Quotation of his Oath to Jacob (// Clause 572)

All the examples above with the exception of the first three and the next to last occur as inner quotation, in which Judah is providing discourse for the narrative of his speech (see Analysis of Narrative Discourse above). In every example, if the Predictive Discourse is the first text-type in a speech occurrence, the initial clause of the discourse will be a *YIQṬOL* clause; if the Predictive Discourse is continuous with a preceding text-type, the initial clause will be governed by a *WeQAṬAL*. Thus, for example, when Judah retells the story of Jacob's sending the brothers back to Egypt for grain he states:

44.26.740 וַנֹּאמֶר

†PD

44.26.741 †לֹא נוּכַל לָרֶדֶת

When, however, Judah relates Jacob's rebuff of the brothers' insistence in taking Benjamin, Jacob relates a Narrative Discourse before the Predictive Discourse, the latter headed by *WeQAȚAL* clause 749:

44.27.743 וַיֹּאמֶר עַבְדְּךָ אָבִי אֵלֵינוּ

†ND

†44.27.744 אַתֶּם יְדַעְתֶּם
כִּי שְׁנַיִם יָלְדָה־לִּי אִשְׁתִּי:
†44.28.745 וַיֵּצֵא הָאֶחָד מֵאִתִּי
†44.28.746 וָאֹמַר

††ND

††44.28.747 †† אַךְ טָרֹף טֹרָף
†44.28.748 וְלֹא רְאִיתִיו עַד־הֵנָּה:

†PD

†44.29.749 וּלְקַחְתֶּם גַּם־אֶת־זֶה מֵעִם פָּנַי
†44.29.750 וְקָרָהוּ אָסוֹן
†44.29.751 וְהוֹרַדְתֶּם אֶת־שֵׂיבָתִי בְּרָעָה שְׁאֹלָה:

The *WeQAȚAL* verbal form initiates only instances of Predictive Discourse. It, therefore, most often signals a change of text-type from Narrative or Expository Discourse (in which *WeQAȚAL* never occurs) to Predictive Discourse.

In the three cases in which punishments are proposed for the alleged thief of Joseph's goblet, the *YIQȚOL* and *WeQAȚAL* clauses feature prominently in all the clauses. Preceded by Interrogative and Expository Discourses, the brothers' original proposal is headed by a *WeQAȚAL* clause:

(אֲשֶׁר יִמָּצֵא אִתּוֹ מֵעֲבָדֶיךָ)
44.09.683 וָמֵת
44.09.684 וְגַם־אֲנַחְנוּ נִהְיֶה לַאדֹנִי לַעֲבָדִים:

Preceded only by a rhetorical introductory clause (כְּדִבְרֵיכֶם כֶּן־הוּא), the Messenger's proposal is headed by a *YIQȚOL* clause:

44.10.687 (אֲשֶׁר יִמָּצֵא אִתּוֹ) יִהְיֶה־לִּי עָבֶד
44.10.688 וְאַתֶּם תִּהְיוּ נְקִיִּם:

And finally, in Joseph's planned proposal, a *casus pendens* construction requires the *YIQȚOL* clause found here:

44.17.713 הָאִישׁ (אֲשֶׁר נִמְצָא הַגָּבִיעַ בְּיָדוֹ) הוּא יִהְיֶה־לִּי עָבֶד

In the case of the internal quotation found in clause †757, Judah repeats only the last *WeQAṬAL* clause in an original multiclause hortatory speech:

757α אִם־לֹא אֲבִיאֶנּוּ אֵלֶיךָ

44.32.757 וְחָטָאתִי לְאָבִי כָּל־הַיָּמִים:

The original speech (clauses 565-572) was defined above as a Hortatory Discourse by the initial unambiguous volitive clausal forms, imperative (565) and cohortative (566 and 567). Its repetition in the speech of Judah, however, stripped of these hortatory features, takes on a simple predictive meaning ("I will be guilty") rather than the original hortatory meaning ("Let me become guilty").

Expository Discourse

The four cases of Expository Discourse in Genesis 44 are composed of a single clause each.

    Clause 680: The Brothers' Oath of Innocence
    Clause 710: Judah's Admission
    Clause 712: Joseph's Oath of Innocence
    Clause †723: Judah's False Paraphrase of the Brothers'
        Conversation with Joseph (cf. Clauses 450-453)

Two of the examples are incomplete clauses, serving as oaths taken by a character (680, 712). The remaining examples (clauses 710 and 723) are both verbless clauses, the former introduced by הִנֵּה, and the latter serving as a false recollection by Judah in his speech (see above under Narrative Discourse).

Interrogative Discourse

Twelve clauses make up the six examples of Interrogative Discourse in Genesis 44.

    Clauses †672-†674: The Messenger's Speech to the Brothers
    Clause 679: The Brothers' Rhetorical Answer to the Messenger
    Clause 682: The Brothers' Rhetorical Denial to the Messenger
    Clauses 703-704: Joseph's Rhetorical Accusation of the Brothers
    Clauses 706-708: Judah's Rhetorical Denial to Joseph
    Clause †721: Judah's False Paraphrase of the Brothers' Conversation
        with Joseph (cf. Clauses 450-453)

The particles used to designate the clauses as interrogative include those used by true questions (לָמָּה, clauses †672 and 679; הֲ, clauses 673 and †721; מָה, clauses

703, 706, 707, and 708), as well as those used in rhetorical questions (וְאֵיךְ,
clause 682; הֲלוֹא, clause 704).

In the first example above, there is also a case of a clause standing
unmarked as interrogative yet, because it is closely semantically tied with the
preceding clause, performing an interrogative function:

44.04.672 לָמָּה שִׁלַּמְתֶּם רָעָה תַּחַת טוֹבָה:
44.05.673 הֲלוֹא זֶה אֲשֶׁר יִשְׁתֶּה אֲדֹנִי בּוֹ
44.05.674 וְהוּא נַחֵשׁ יְנַחֵשׁ בּוֹ

Although clause 674 syntactically stands as independent and has no interrogative particle, its close syntactic and semantic tie with the relative clause in clause
673 (אֲשֶׁר יִשְׁתֶּה אֲדֹנִי בּוֹ) causes the interrogative function to include it within
the discourse.

Hortatory Discourse

There are seven examples of Hortatory Discourse in Genesis 44, consisting
of seventeen total clauses.

> Clauses 659-661: Joseph's Orders concerning the Second Test
> Clauses 668-671: Joseph's Execution of the Second Test
> Clauses 714: Joseph's Orders concerning the Brothers
> Clauses 717-719: Judah's Entreaty for a Hearing
> Clauses †728-†729: Judah's False Paraphrase of the Brothers'
> Conversation with Joseph (cf. Clauses 450-453)
> Clauses †738-†739: Judah's True Quotation of the Brothers'
> Conversation with Jacob (// Clauses 659-661)
> Clauses 758-759: Judah's Request from Joseph

In all cases, an unambiguous volitive form occurs in the first or second clause of
each discourse (clauses 659, 668, 714, †719, †728, †738, 758); this volitive
form, therefore, defines the hortatory nature of non-volitional forms (*YIQTOL* or
WeQATAL) and clauses in their respective discourses.

Table of Discourse Constellations for Genesis 44

		Present Ch.	Prev. Chs.	Total in JN
	QATAL	3	15	18
	QATAL, WAYYIQTOL	3	4	7
	QATAL, (Ptc./Vbl.)		8	8
ND	*QATAL, WAYYIQTOL*, (Ptc./Vbl.)		3	3
	QATAL, WAYYIQTOL, (Ptc./Vbl.), *YIQTOL*		2	2
	QATAL, YIQTOL (w/ past adverb)		0	0
	WAYYIQTOL, (Ptc./Vbl.)		0	0
	Vbl/Ptc/Inc (Dream Report)		1	1
	YIQTOL	2	10	12
	YIQTOL, WeQATAL	3	3	6
PD	*YIQTOL, WeQATAL*, (Ptc./Vbl../Inc.)		1	1
	YIQTOL, (Ptc./Vbl../Inc.)	1	1	2
	WeQATAL	3	1	4
	WeYIQTOL		0	0
	Ptc./Vbl.	2	16	18
	Ptc./ Vbl., Inc.		0	0
	Inc.		5	5
ED	Ptc./Vbl., *QATAL/YIQTOL* of היה		2	2
	Ptc./Vbl., *QATAL/YIQTOL* of היה, Front. Obj.+ *QATAL/YIQTOL*		2	2
	QATAL/YIQTOL of היה		0	0
	Impv./Coh./Juss.	3	15	18
	Impv./Coh./Juss., *WeYIQTOL/YIQTOL*	1	8	9
	Impv./Coh./Juss., *WeQATAL*	1	0	1
	Impv./Coh./Juss., *WeYIQTOL/YIQTOL, WeQATAL*		4	4
	Impv./Coh./Juss., *QATAL*		1	1
HD	Impv./Coh./Juss., *WeYIQTOL/YIQTOL*, (*We)QATAL*		1	1
	Impv./Coh./Juss., *ʾal-YIQTOL*		1	1
	Impv./Coh./Juss., *WeQATAL, ʾal-YIQTOL*		1	1
	ʾal-YIQTOL	1	3	4
	ʾal-YIQTOL, WeQATAL/YIQTOL		0	0
	(*We)YIQTOL-nāʾ*, (*WeQATAL/[We]YIQTOL*)		0	0
	QATAL, YIQTOL/WeQATAL		1	1

Genesis 45 – Joseph Reveals Himself and Sends for His Father – Clauses 760-843

Text in Syntactical/Paragraph Units

Joseph Carries Out the Test of the Eleven Brothers (Cont.)

וַיְמַהֵר יוֹסֵף לְהָבִיא אֶת־פֶּלֶךְ הַכְּבָרִים עָלָיו		45.01.760
וַיִּבְךְּ		45.01.761
HD וַיִּצְעַק כָּל־אִישׁ מֵעָלָי		45.01.762
וַיִּקְרָא אִישׁ לֹא עָמַד הַנִּצָּבִים אֶל־יוֹסֵף		45.01.763

Joseph Reveals Himself to His Eleven Brothers

וַיֹּאמֶר יוֹסֵף אֶל־אֶחָיו		45.02.764
אֲנִי יוֹסֵף		45.02.765
הַעוֹד אָבִי חָי		45.02.766
וְלֹא־יָכְלוּ אֶחָיו לַעֲנוֹת אֹתוֹ		45.03.767
	ED וַיֹּאמֶר יוֹסֵף	45.03.768
	ID גְּשׁוּ־נָא אֵלַי	45.03.769
וַיִּגַּשׁוּ		45.03.770
וַיֹּאמֶר אֲנִי יוֹסֵף אֲחִיכֶם		45.04.771
	HD אֲשֶׁר־מְכַרְתֶּם אֹתִי	45.04.772
וְעַתָּה		45.04.773
וְאַל־יֵרַע		45.04.774

ED

45.04.775 אֹמֶר יוֹסֵף אֶל־אֶחָיו

HD

45.05.776 אֲנִי יוֹסֵף אֲחִיכֶם אֲשֶׁר־מְכַרְתֶּם אֹתִי מִצְרָיְמָה:

45.05.777 וְעַתָּה אַל־תֵּעָצְבוּ
| וְאַל־יִחַר

[45.06] כִּי מְכַרְתֶּם אֹתִי הֵנָּה
כִּי לְמִחְיָה שְׁלָחַנִי אֱלֹהִים לִפְנֵיכֶם:

ND

45.07.778 וַיִּשְׁלָחֵנִי אֱלֹהִים לִפְנֵיכֶם:
לָשׂוּם לָכֶם שְׁאֵרִית בָּאָרֶץ
וּלְהַחֲיוֹת לָכֶם לִפְלֵיטָה גְּדֹלָה:

45.08.779 וְעַתָּה לֹא־אַתֶּם שְׁלַחְתֶּם אֹתִי הֵנָּה
כִּי הָאֱלֹהִים
וַיְשִׂימֵנִי לְאָב לְפַרְעֹה

45.08.780 וּלְאָדוֹן לְכָל־בֵּיתוֹ
וּמֹשֵׁל בְּכָל־אֶרֶץ מִצְרָיִם:

HD

45.09.781 מַהֲרוּ וַעֲלוּ אֶל־אָבִי
45.09.782 וַאֲמַרְתֶּם אֵלָיו
45.09.783 כֹּה אָמַר בִּנְךָ יוֹסֵף

†ND

וַיֹּ֤סֶף עֹוד֙ אַבְרָהָ֔ם וַיִּקַּ֥ח אִשָּׁ֖ה 45.09.784

††ND

45.09.785 וּשְׁמָ֖הּ קְטוּרָ֑ה

††ND

45.09.786 וַתֵּ֣לֶד ל֗וֹ

45.09.787 אֶת־זִמְרָן֙

††HD

45.10.788 וְאֶת־יָקְשָׁ֔ן

45.10.789 וְאֶת־מְדָ֖ן וְאֶת־מִדְיָ֑ן

45.11.790 וְאֶת־יִשְׁבָּ֖ק וְאֶת־שֽׁוּחַ׃

ED

PD

45.12.791 וְיָקְשָׁ֣ן יָלַ֔ד אֶת־שְׁבָ֖א וְאֶת־דְּדָ֑ן

45.13.792 וּבְנֵ֣י דְדָ֔ן הָי֛וּ אַשּׁוּרִ֥ם וּלְטוּשִׁ֖ים וּלְאֻמִּֽים׃

45.13.793 וּבְנֵ֣י מִדְיָ֗ן

45.13.794 עֵיפָ֤ה וָעֵ֙פֶר֙ וַחֲנֹ֔ךְ וַאֲבִידָ֖ע וְאֶלְדָּעָ֑ה

45.14.795 כָּל־אֵ֖לֶּה בְּנֵ֥י קְטוּרָֽה׃

וַיַּ֣רְא 45.14.796

וּבִנְיָמִ֔ן בָּכָ֖ה עַל־צַוָּארָ֑יו׃ 45.14.797

Joseph's Reunion with the Eleven Brothers (Comment)

—————

וַיְנַשֵּׁ֥ק לְכָל־אֶחָ֖יו 45.15.798

וַיֵּ֣בְךְּ עֲלֵיהֶ֑ם 45.15.799

וְאַחֲרֵי כֵ֔ן דִּבְּר֥וּ אֶחָ֖יו אִתּֽוֹ׃ 45.15.800

—————

Pharaoh Gives Commands about the Eleven Brothers

וְהַקֹּ֣ל נִשְׁמַ֗ע בֵּ֤ית פַּרְעֹה֙ לֵאמֹ֔ר 45.16.801

בָּ֖אוּ אֲחֵ֣י יוֹסֵ֑ף 45.16.802   ND

וַיִּיטַ֤ב בְּעֵינֵ֣י פַרְעֹ֔ה וּבְעֵינֵ֖י עֲבָדָֽיו׃ 45.16.803

וַיֹּ֤אמֶר פַּרְעֹה֙ אֶל־יוֹסֵ֔ף 45.17.804

אֱמֹ֥ר אֶל־אַחֶ֖יךָ 45.17.805   HD

†HD

זֹ֣את עֲשׂ֑וּ 45.17.806 †

טַֽעֲנוּ֙ אֶת־בְּעִ֣ירְכֶ֔ם 45.17.807 †

וּלְכוּ־ 45.17.808 †

בֹ֖אוּ אַ֥רְצָה כְּנָֽעַן׃ 45.17.809 †

וּקְח֧וּ אֶת־אֲבִיכֶ֛ם וְאֶת־בָּתֵּיכֶ֖ם 45.18.810

וּבֹ֣אוּ אֵלָ֑י 45.18.811

וְאֶתְּנָ֣ה לָכֶ֗ם אֶת־טוּב֙ אֶ֣רֶץ מִצְרַ֔יִם 45.18.812

45.21.820   וַיִּתֵּן לָהֶם יוֹסֵף עֲגָלוֹת עַל־פִּי פַרְעֹה

45.21.821   וַיִּתֵּן לָהֶם צֵדָה לַדָּרֶךְ׃

45.21.822   לְכֻלָּם נָתַן לָאִישׁ חֲלִפוֹת שְׂמָלֹת

Joseph's Gifts to His Ten Brothers, Benjamin, and Jacob
(Comment)

45.22.823   וּלְבִנְיָמִן נָתַן שְׁלֹשׁ מֵאוֹת כֶּסֶף וְחָמֵשׁ חֲלִפֹת שְׂמָלֹת׃

45.22.824   וּלְאָבִיו שָׁלַח כְּזֹאת עֲשָׂרָה חֲמֹרִים נֹשְׂאִים מִטּוּב מִצְרָיִם

45.23.825   וְעֶשֶׂר אֲתֹנֹת נֹשְׂאֹת בָּר וָלֶחֶם וּמָזוֹן לְאָבִיו לַדָּרֶךְ׃

45.18.813   וְאִכְלוּ אֶת־חֵלֶב הָאָרֶץ׃ †
(HD)

45.19.814   וְאַתָּה צֻוֵּיתָה

†HD

45.19.815   זֹאת עֲשׂוּ †

45.19.816   קְחוּ־לָכֶם מֵאֶרֶץ מִצְרַיִם עֲגָלוֹת לְטַפְּכֶם וְלִנְשֵׁיכֶם †

45.19.817   וּנְשָׂאתֶם אֶת־אֲבִיכֶם †

45.19.818   וּבָאתֶם׃ †

45.20.819   וְעֵינְכֶם אַל־תָּחֹס עַל־כְּלֵיכֶם כִּי־טוּב כָּל־אֶרֶץ מִצְרַיִם לָכֶם הוּא׃

The Eleven Brothers Bring Jacob to Egypt

וַיְשַׁלַּח אֶת־אֶחָיו	45.24.826
וַיֵּלֵכוּ	45.24.827
וַיֹּאמֶר אֲלֵהֶם	45.24.828

HD
| אַל־תִּרְגְּזוּ בַּדָּרֶךְ: | 45.24.829 |

וַיַּעֲלוּ מִמִּצְרָיִם	45.25.830
וַיָּבֹאוּ אֶרֶץ כְּנַעַן	45.25.831
אֶל־יַעֲקֹב אֲבִיהֶם	45.26.832

ED
| וַיַּגִּדוּ לוֹ לֵאמֹר | 45.26.833 |
| עוֹד יוֹסֵף חַי וְכִי־הוּא מֹשֵׁל בְּכָל־אֶרֶץ מִצְרָיִם | 45.26.834 |

וַיָּפָג לִבּוֹ	45.26.835
כִּי לֹא־הֶאֱמִין לָהֶם:	45.27.836
וַיְדַבְּרוּ אֵלָיו אֵת כָּל־דִּבְרֵי יוֹסֵף אֲשֶׁר דִּבֶּר אֲלֵהֶם	45.27.837
וַיַּרְא אֶת־הָעֲגָלוֹת אֲשֶׁר־שָׁלַח יוֹסֵף לָשֵׂאת אֹתוֹ	45.27.838
וַתְּחִי רוּחַ יַעֲקֹב אֲבִיהֶם:	45.28.839

ED
| וַיֹּאמֶר יִשְׂרָאֵל | 45.28.840 |
| רַב | 45.28.841 |

HD
| עוֹד־יוֹסֵף בְּנִי חָי | 45.28.842 |
| אֵלְכָה וְאֶרְאֶנּוּ בְּטֶרֶם אָמוּת: | 45.28.843 |

Table of Independent Clause Types in Genesis 45

Clause Type	Clause Distribution	Total	Percent
QAṬAL Total Clauses: 14	Narrative: 760,763,770,797,800,801,823,824,825	9	64.3%
	ND: 779,†784,††785,802 PD: ED: ID: HD: 814	4 1	28.6% 7.1%
WeQAṬAL Total Clauses: 9	Narrative:	0	0
	ND: PD: 792,793,794 ED: ID: HD: 783,††788,††789,††790,817,818	 3 6	 33.3% 66.7%
YIQṬOL Total Clauses: 3	Narrative:	0	0
	ND: PD: ED: ID: HD: 776,787,829	 3	 100%
WeYIQṬOL Total Clauses: 1	Narrative:	0	0
	ND: PD: ED: ID: HD: 843	 1	 100%
WAYYIQṬOL Total Clauses: 30	Narrative: 761,764,765,766,767,771,773,774,795, 796,798,799,803,804,820,821,822,826,827,828,830, 831,835,837,838,839	28	93.3%
	ND: 778,780 PD: ED: ID: HD:	2	6.7%

	Narrative:	0	0
Participle	ND:		
	PD:		
Total Clauses: 2	ED: 791,834	2	100%
	ID:		
	HD:		
	Narrative:		
Verbless	ND:		
	PD:		
Total Clauses: 5	ED: 768,775,833,841	4	80.0%
	ID: 769	1	20.0%
	HD:		
	Narrative:	0	0
Incomplete	ND:		
	PD:		
Total Clauses: 1	ED: 840	1	100%
	ID:		
	HD:		
Imperative	Narrative:	0	0
Total Clauses: 15	HD: 762,772,781,782,††786,805,†806,†807,†808, †809,†810,†811,†813,†815,†816	15	100%
Cohortative	Narrative:	0	0
Total Clauses: 2	HD: †812,842	2	100%
Jussive	Narrative:	0	0
Total Clauses: 2	HD: 777,†819	2	100%

Analysis of the Narrative Structure and Discourse Text-Types in Genesis 45

Narrative Structural Analysis

Narrative/Paragraph Structure

Genesis 45, the story of "Joseph Reveals Himself and Sends for His Father," is composed of three main paragraphs.

> Clauses 764-797: Joseph Reveals Himself to His Eleven Brothers,
> Clauses 801-822: Pharaoh Gives Commands about the Eleven Brothers
> Clauses 826-839 (862): The Eleven Brothers Bring Jacob to Egypt[83]

The only paragraph that has an explicitly marked beginning is the second:

45.16.801 וְהַקֹּל נִשְׁמַע בֵּית פַּרְעֹה
לֵאמֹר

ND

45.16.802 בָּאוּ אֲחֵי יוֹסֵף

The initial *QAṬAL* clause 801 defines the third paragraph by differentiating its subject from that of the previous paragraph (Joseph's conversation with his brothers). This change of subject matter, without the more usual וַיְהִי temporal clause, is marked by a clause governed by *QAṬAL*.[84]

The chapter begins with the concluding lines of a paragraph that began at clause 667 in the previous chapter. This paragraph, "Joseph Carries Out the Test of the Eleven Brothers," is terminally marked by the negated *QAṬAL* clause 763.[85] The first and third complete paragraphs in the chapter are both terminally

---

[83]The narrative portion of Gen 45 ends with a *WAYYIQṬOL* clause (839). The *WAYYIQṬOL* chain of the paragraph continues until clause 861 in Gen 46:6 and the paragraph itself ends with the following *QAṬAL* clause (862) in verse 7.

[84]The narrator could have, of course, chosen to begin the paragraph with a *WAYYIQṬOL*, as is done elsewhere in this chapter (clauses 761,771,826). These instances, however, usually occur when either the previous narrative locus is the same (the *WAYYIQṬOL*, therefore, merely changing scenes within the setting) or after an extended extra-paragraph comment (further differentiation—temporal clauses, *QAṬAL* clauses—being unnecessary).

[85]Clauses 760 and 770 are both negated QATAL clauses and stand within the surrounding WAYYIQTOL chain as instances of momentous negation, in which the negation of the verb implies a type of activity and thus serves to cause the narrative to progress. In both cases the negation of the verb, יכל, implies a resistance or struggle of the subject. This inability of a character to perform some desired action (to control oneself, to

marked by concluding *QAṬAL* clauses (797, 862). The end of the second paragraph is marked by the extended extra-paragraph comment of clauses 823-825
(see below).

Extra-Paragraph Comments

The two extra-paragraph comments in the chapter provide information not
directly related to the narrative sequence of the paragraphs surrounding them. In
the first case, the scene of the reunion of Joseph and his brothers is provided.

45.15.798 וַיְנַשֵּׁק לְכָל־אֶחָיו
45.15.799 וַיֵּבְךְּ עֲלֵיהֶם
45.15.800 וְאַחֲרֵי כֵן דִּבְּרוּ אֶחָיו אִתּוֹ:

The three clauses are bounded before and after by the concluding and initial
markers of the paragraphs surrounding it. The WAYYIQTOL clauses within it
(798-799) do not form a true narrative chain but relate information outside the
sequence of the larger narrative prose story line. While the scene fits between
the paragraphs on either side of it, the general actions within it are not sequential
but are, rather, ongoing and random ("kissing", "crying").

The second case provides a listing of the various gifts that Joseph gives to
his ten brothers, to his brother Benjamin, and to his father Jacob:

45.22.823 לְכֻלָּם נָתַן לָאִישׁ חֲלִפוֹת שְׂמָלֹת
45.22.824 וּלְבִנְיָמִן נָתַן שְׁלֹשׁ מֵאוֹת כֶּסֶף וְחָמֵשׁ חֲלִפֹת שְׂמָלֹת:
45.23.825 וּלְאָבִיו שָׁלַח כְּזֹאת עֲשָׂרָה חֲמֹרִים נֹשְׂאִים מִטּוּב מִצְרָיִם
וְעֶשֶׂר אֲתֹנֹת נֹשְׂאֹת בָּר וָלֶחֶם וּמָזוֹן לְאָבִיו לַדָּרֶךְ:

The clauses are all governed by *QAṬAL* verbal forms and should not, therefore, be thought of as telling about sequentially given gifts (i.e., Joseph gave A
to B, then he gave C to D, then he gave E to F) but these clauses stand simply as
a digression of the narrator off the story line.

Inner-Paragraph Comments

No inner-paragraph comments occur in Genesis 45.

---

respond to a situation) actually causes the narrative to move forward in a way very similar to *WAYYIQTOL* clauses. Note, however, the static nature of usual negated *QAṬAL*
clauses that serve as paragraph boundary markers: e.g., clause 763, "No one stood with
Joseph when he revealed himself to his brothers."

Discourse Function Analysis

Narrative Discourse

Five clauses make up the three cases of Narrative Discourse which occur in Genesis 45.

> Clauses 778-780: Joseph's Recounting His Descent to Egypt
> Clause †784: A Formal Introduction to Joseph's Speech to Jacob
> Clause ††785: Joseph's Recounting His Station in Egypt
> Clause 802: The Report to Pharaoh concerning the Brothers

Clauses †784, ††785 and 802 are governed by expected *QATAL* verbal forms, and thus need no comment.[86] In clauses 778-780, Joseph provides the structuring theological perspective of the Novella:

45.07.778 וַיִּשְׁלָחֵנִי אֱלֹהִים לִפְנֵיכֶם לָשׂוּם לָכֶם שְׁאֵרִית בָּאָרֶץ
וּלְהַחֲיוֹת לָכֶם לִפְלֵיטָה גְּדֹלָה:

(וְעַתָּה

45.08.779 לֹא־אַתֶּם שְׁלַחְתֶּם אֹתִי הֵנָּה
כִּי הָאֱלֹהִים)

45.08.780 וַיְשִׂימֵנִי
לְאָב לְפַרְעֹה
וּלְאָדוֹן לְכָל־בֵּיתוֹ
וּמֹשֵׁל בְּכָל־אֶרֶץ מִצְרָיִם:

The basic structure of this small report is built upon the two *WAYYIQTOL* clauses found in 778 and 780 with an intervening *QATAL* clause serving as a parenthetical comparative statement, introduced by the disjunctive particle וְעַתָּה. This is the only example of Narrative Discourse in the Joseph Novella in which the initial sentence is a *WAYYIQTOL* clause. The *WAYYIQTOL* clauses that are used here provide no substantial narrative because only two actions are related: God brought Joseph to Egypt and God set Joseph over Egypt.

Predictive Discourse

One example of Predictive Discourse occurs in Genesis 45.

---

[86]The case of clause †784, however, does require further study. The concretized messenger formula, *kōh 'āmar X*, has received several treatments. The general scholarly consensus is that the form represents the beginning of a quotation of an earlier speech by the sender. As such, the form implies that the subsequent message represents the original *past* message (thus, the *QATAL* verb in the clause), spoken to the messenger, either literally or as a paraphrase. The form is very common in prophetic literature (see, e.g., Hans Walter Wolff, *Joel and Amos*, [Hermeneia; Philadelphia: Fortress, 1977], 135-37).

Clauses 792-794: Joseph's Plan for the Brothers to Bring Jacob

As has been seen in numerous previous examples, when a case of Predictive Discourse is juxtaposed to another type of discourse, the initial (and often subsequent) clauses are governed by *WeQATAL* verbs. Here, after relating his message to his father via his brothers (clauses 784-790) and stating the fact that they could see him with their own eyes (clause 791), Joseph goes on to plan how the brothers are to bring Jacob down to Egypt:

(Embedded Direct Discourse, Clauses †784-††790)

ED

וְהִנֵּה

45.12.791 עֵינֵיכֶם רֹאוֹת וְעֵינֵי אָחִי בִנְיָמִין
כִּי־פִי הַמְדַבֵּר אֲלֵיכֶם:

45.13.792 וְהִגַּדְתֶּם לְאָבִי אֶת־כָּל־כְּבוֹדִי בְּמִצְרַיִם וְאֵת כָּל־אֲשֶׁר רְאִיתֶם

45.13.793 וּמִהַרְתֶּם

45.13.794 וְהוֹרַדְתֶּם אֶת־אָבִי הֵנָּה:

PD

45.13.792 וְהִגַּדְתֶּם לְאָבִי אֶת־כָּל־כְּבוֹדִי בְּמִצְרַיִם וְאֵת כָּל־אֲשֶׁר רְאִיתֶם

45.13.793 וּמִהַרְתֶּם

45.13.794 וְהוֹרַדְתֶּם אֶת־אָבִי הֵנָּה:

Clauses 792-794, being attached to an earlier discourse, are consistently governed by *WeQATAL* clauses and are predictive in their meaning.

Expository Discourse

The six examples of Expository Discourse found in Genesis 45 are composed of eight clauses.

> Clause 768: Joseph's Revelation of Himself
> Clause 775: Joseph's Second Revelation of Himself
> Clause 791: Joseph's Remark concerning the Brothers as Eyewitnesses
> Clauses 833-834: The Brothers' Report of Joseph's Survival
> Clauses 840-841: Jacob's Response to the News

Of these examples, four clauses (768, 775, 833, 841) are verbless, explaining a present state of affairs. Moreover, two clauses (791 and 834) are participial, explaining a present activity. The remaining two clauses consist of an interjectory particle introducing the final example above (840) and a *QATAL* clause (784) which has a fronted object, serving as a formal introduction to a further speech.

Interrogative Discourse

There is only a single clause in Genesis 45 that is included as an example of Interrogative Discourse:

Clause 769: Joseph's Question about Jacob

The question occurs immediately after Joseph reveals himself to his brothers the first time and concerns Jacob:

45.03.769 הַעוֹד אָבִי חָי

The pointing of the interrogative הֲ is regular in this instance, occurring as it does before a guttural.[87]

Hortatory Discourse

The twelve examples of Hortatory Discourse in Genesis 45 consist of thirty-three separate clauses.

Clause 762: Joseph's Orders to His Servants
Clause 772: Joseph's Order to His Brothers
Clauses 776-777: Joseph's Plea to His Brothers
Clauses 781-783: Joseph's Orders for His Brothers to Return to Jacob
Clauses 786-790: Joseph's Orders for Jacob to Come to Egypt
Clause 805: Pharaoh's Order to Joseph
Clauses †806-†813: Pharaoh's Orders to the Brothers
Clause 814: Pharaoh's Further Order to Joseph
Clauses †815-†819: Pharaoh's Further Orders to the Brothers
Clause 829: Joseph's Order to the Brothers
Clauses 842-843: Jacob's Desire to See Joseph

In most of the cases, an unambiguous volitive clause either heads the clause or appears immediately after the initial clause of the speech (clauses 762, 772, 777, 781, 786, 805, †806, †815 and 842). In two cases, the initial *YIQTOL* clause of a discourse also has the volitive negation אַל־ (clauses 776 and 829).

Clause 814 (וְאַתָּה צֻוֵּיתָה) also retains a hortatory function because of the preceding imperative clause 805, even though it is separated by an imbedded direct discourse (clauses †806-†813). Even though clause 814 is governed by a

---

[87]Gesenius, §100m.

QAṬAL verbal form, the hortatory force is retained, צֻוֵּיתָה being, a "performative utterance," having the sense of "You are hereby commanded."[88]

---

[88]Thus, Hillers, "Performative Utterances," 763-64. The speech by Pharaoh is obviously directed to Joseph, being a second person singular verbal form with a fronted personal pronoun. The imbedded speech that is commanded (clauses †815-†819), however, is consistently governed by plural imperative and *WeQAṬAL* verbal forms. The addresses of the imbedded speech are, therefore, Joseph and his brothers, as opposed to the brothers alone (clauses †806-†813).

Table of Discourse Constellations for Genesis 45

		Present Ch.	Prev. Chs.	Total in JN
ND	*QATAL*	3	18	21
	QATAL, WAYYIQTOL	1	7	8
	QATAL, (Ptc./Vbl.)		8	8
	QATAL, WAYYIQTOL, (Ptc./Vbl.)		3	3
	QATAL, WAYYIQTOL, (Ptc./Vbl.), *YIQTOL*		2	2
	QATAL, YIQTOL (w/ past adverb)		0	0
	WAYYIQTOL, (Ptc./Vbl.)		0	0
	Vbl/Ptc/Inc (Dream Report)		1	1
PD	*YIQTOL*		12	12
	YIQTOL, WeQATAL		6	6
	YIQTOL, WeQATAL, (Ptc./Vbl../Inc.)		1	1
	YIQTOL, (Ptc./Vbl../Inc.)		2	0
	WeQATAL	1	4	5
	WeYIQTOL		0	0
ED	Ptc./Vbl.	4	18	22
	Ptc./ Vbl., Inc.	1	0	1
	Inc.		5	5
	Ptc./Vbl., *QATAL/YIQTOL* of היה		2	2
	Ptc./Vbl., *QATAL/YIQTOL* of היה, Front. Obj.+ *QATAL/YIQTOL*		2	2
	QATAL/YIQTOL of היה		0	0
HD	Impv./Coh./Juss.	3	18	21
	Impv./Coh./Juss., *WeYIQTOL/YIQTOL*	1	9	10
	Impv./Coh./Juss., *WeQATAL*	2	1	3
	Impv./Coh./Juss., *WeYIQTOL/YIQTOL, WeQATAL*		4	4
	Impv./Coh./Juss., *QATAL*	1	1	1
	Impv./Coh./Juss., *WeYIQTOL/YIQTOL*, (We)*QATAL*		1	1
	Impv./Coh./Juss., *ʾal-YIQTOL*	1	1	2
	Impv./Coh./Juss., *WeQATAL, ʾal-YIQTOL*	1	1	2
	ʾal-YIQTOL	1	4	5
	ʾal-YIQTOL, WeQATAL/YIQTOL		0	0
	(We)*YIQTOL-nāʾ*, (*WeQATAL/[We]YIQTOL*)		0	0
	QATAL, YIQTOL/WeQATAL		1	1

Genesis 46 – Jacob's Migration and Reunion with Joseph – Clauses 844-887

Text in Syntactical/Paragraph Units

The Eleven Brothers Bring Jacob to Egypt (Cont.)

46.01.844	וַיֵּשֶׁב יוֹסֵף אֶת־יִשְׂרָאֵל
46.01.845	בְּאֶרֶץ מִצְרַיִם
46.01.846	וְאֶת־אֶחָיו וְאֵת כָּל־בֵּית אָבִיו
46.02.847	וַיִּתֵּן לָהֶם אֲחֻזָּה בְּאֶרֶץ מִצְרַיִם
46.02.848	וַיֹּאמֶר

| 46.02.849 | יַעֲקֹב־ | ED (Vocative) |
| 46.02.850 | יַעֲקֹב־ | |

| 46.02.851 | וַיֹּאמֶר |

| 46.03.852 | וַיֹּאמֶר |
| 46.03.853 | הִנֵּנִי | ED |

46.03.854	וְאֶת־בְּנֵי יִשְׂרָאֵל הַבָּאִים מִצְרָיְמָה	HD
46.04.855		PD
46.04.856	
46.04.857	

| 46.05.858 | |
| 46.05.859 | |

46.06.860 [וְאֶת־דִּינָה בִתּוֹ]
כָּל־נֶפֶשׁ בָּנָיו וּבְנוֹתָיו שְׁלֹשִׁים וְשָׁלֹשׁ׃

46.06.861 וּבְנֵי גָד צִפְיוֹן וְחַגִּי שׁוּנִי וְאֶצְבֹּן
עֵרִי וַאֲרוֹדִי וְאַרְאֵלִי׃

46.07.862 וּבְנֵי אָשֵׁר יִמְנָה וְיִשְׁוָה וְיִשְׁוִי וּבְרִיעָה
וְשֶׂרַח אֲחֹתָם וּבְנֵי בְרִיעָה חֶבֶר וּמַלְכִּיאֵל׃

The Name List of the Children of Israel (Comment)

46.08.863 וְאֵלֶּה שְׁמוֹת בְּנֵי־יִשְׂרָאֵל הַבָּאִים מִצְרַיְמָה יַעֲקֹב וּבָנָיו

The Name List of the Children of Israel – Genesis 46:8a–25 (Deleted)

46.26.864 כָּל־הַנֶּפֶשׁ הַבָּאָה לְיַעֲקֹב מִצְרַיְמָה
יֹצְאֵי יְרֵכוֹ

46.27.865 מִלְּבַד נְשֵׁי בְנֵי־יַעֲקֹב (אֱלֹהִים) כָּל־נֶפֶשׁ
שִׁשִּׁים וָשֵׁשׁ׃

46.27.866 וּבְנֵי יוֹסֵף אֲשֶׁר־יֻלַּד־לוֹ בְמִצְרַיִם נֶפֶשׁ שְׁנָיִם
כָּל־הַנֶּפֶשׁ לְבֵית־יַעֲקֹב הַבָּאָה מִצְרַיְמָה שִׁבְעִים׃

Joseph Meets Israel/Jacob and Plans for His Settlement

46.28.867 וְאֶת־יְהוּדָה שָׁלַח לְפָנָיו אֶל־יוֹסֵף לְהוֹרֹת לְפָנָיו גֹּשְׁנָה

46.28.868 וַיָּבֹאוּ אַרְצָה גֹּשֶׁן׃

46.29.869 וַיֶּאְסֹר יוֹסֵף מֶרְכַּבְתּוֹ

46.29.870 וַיַּעַל לִקְרַאת־יִשְׂרָאֵל אָבִיו גֹּשְׁנָה

46.29.871 וַיֵּרָא אֵלָיו

46.29.872 וַיִּפֹּל עַל־צַוָּארָיו

46.29.873 וַיֵּבְךְּ עַל־צַוָּארָיו עוֹד׃

46.30.874 וַיֹּאמֶר יִשְׂרָאֵל אֶל־יוֹסֵף

46.31.876 וַיֹּאמֶר יוֹסֵף אֶל־אֶחָיו וְאֶל־בֵּית אָבִיו

HD

46.30.875 אָמוּתָה הַפָּעַם אַחֲרֵי רְאוֹתִי אֶת־פָּנֶיךָ כִּי עוֹדְךָ חָי

HD
46.31.877 אֶעֱלֶה
46.31.878 וְאַגִּידָה לְפַרְעֹה
46.31.879 וְאֹמְרָה אֵלָיו

†ND
46.31.880 אַחַי וּבֵית־אָבִי אֲשֶׁר בְּאֶרֶץ־כְּנַעַן בָּאוּ אֵלָי

46.32.881 וְהָאֲנָשִׁים רֹעֵי צֹאן
46.32.882 כִּי־אַנְשֵׁי מִקְנֶה הָיוּ

PD
46.33.883 וְהָיָה

46.33.884 כִּי־יִקְרָא לָכֶם פַּרְעֹה

ID
46.33.885 וְאָמַר מַה־מַּעֲשֵׂיכֶם

46.34.886 וַאֲמַרְתֶּם

†ED
46.34.887 אַנְשֵׁי מִקְנֶה הָיוּ עֲבָדֶיךָ מִנְּעוּרֵינוּ וְעַד־עַתָּה גַּם־אֲנַחְנוּ גַּם־אֲבֹתֵינוּ

886α בַּעֲבוּר תֵּשְׁבוּ בְּאֶרֶץ גֹּשֶׁן

כִּי־תוֹעֲבַת מִצְרַיִם כָּל־רֹעֵה צֹאן

Table of Independent Clause Types in Genesis 46

Clause Type	Clause Distribution	Total	Percent
QAṬAL Total Clauses: 5	Narrative: 862,867	2	40.0%
	ND: †880,†882	2	40.0%
	PD:		
	ED: 887	1	20.0%
	ID:		
	HD:		
WeQAṬAL Total Clauses: 3	Narrative:	0	0
	ND: PD: 883,884,886	3	100%
	ED:		
	ID:		
	HD:		
YIQṬOL Total Clauses: 5	Narrative:	0	0
	ND: PD: 855,856,857	3	60.0%
	ED:		
	ID:		
	HD: 854,877	2	40.0%
WeYIQṬOL Total Clauses: 0	Narrative:	0	0
	ND:		
	PD:		
	ED:	0	0
	ID:		
	HD:		
WAYYIQṬOL Total Clauses: 19	Narrative: 844,845,851,852,856,857,858,859,860, 861,868,869,870,871,872,873,874,876	19	100%
	ND:		
	PD:		
	ED:	0	0
	ID:		
	HD:		

	Narrative:	0	0
Participle	ND:		
	PD:		
Total Clauses: 0	ED:	0	0
	ID:		
	HD:		
	Narrative: 863,864,865,866	4	57.1%
Verbless	ND: †881	1	
	PD:		
Total Clauses: 7	ED: 853		
	ID: †885	1	
	HD:	1	
	Narrative:	0	0
Incomplete	ND:		
	PD:		
Total Clauses: 2	ED: 849,850	2	100%
	ID:		
	HD:		
Imperative	Narrative:	0	0
Total Clauses: 0	HD:	0	0
Cohortative	Narrative:		
Total Clauses: 3	HD: 875,878,879	3	100%
Jussive	Narrative:	0	0
Total Clauses: 0	HD:	0	0

Analysis of the Narrative Structure and Discourse Text-Types in Genesis 46

Narrative Structural Analysis

Narrative/Paragraph Structure

Genesis 46, the story of "Jacob's Migration and Reunion with Joseph," begins with a continued paragraph from the previous chapter (see analysis of Genesis 45), which concludes with the *QATAL* clause in Genesis 46:7 (clause 862). In addition to this partial paragraph, Genesis 46 also contains a genealogical list of the names of the descendents of Jacob who accompany him on his trip to Egypt (vs. 8-27). For reasons discussed in this study's introduction to the Joseph Novella, the Name List has largely been ignored in this examination. The introduction and conclusion of the name list (clauses 863, 864-866) have, however, been retained as a representative inclusion of the list and will be treated as an extra-paragraph comment. The remainder of Genesis 46 comprises only one main paragraph, which, itself, continues into the next chapter.

Clauses 867-876 (890): Joseph Meets Israel/Jacob and Plans for His Settlement.

The paragraph is initially marked by a *QATAL* clause:

46.28.867 וְאֶת־יְהוּדָה שָׁלַח לְפָנָיו אֶל־יוֹסֵף לְהוֹרֹת לְפָנָיו גֹּשְׁנָה

The final clause of the paragraph is governed by a *WAYYIQTOL* verbal form (clause 890). The end of the paragraph is marked, therefore, externally by the introductory *QATAL* clause of the next paragraph (clause 893; see Narrative Analysis of Genesis 47 below).

Extra-Paragraph Comments

The long genealogical "Name List of the Children of Israel" serves, narratively, as an extended extra-paragraph comment. Formally, however, the genre of the list is clearly not narrative, but rather genealogy. It has, therefore, largely been omitted in this study of narrative in biblical Hebrew prose. The introductory and concluding statements of the list have been retained and serve, by metonymy, for the whole. The Name List primarily serves as an explication of the extant familial relations between the various descendants of Jacob. The primary clause types are, therefore, verbless clauses, which relate the existence of people or things.[89]

Inner-Paragraph Comments

No inner-paragraph comments occur in Genesis 46.

Discourse Function Analysis

Narrative Discourse

The single case of Narrative Discourse in Genesis 46 employs a *QATAL* clause as its only verbal feature.

Clause †880: Joseph's Planned Speech Before Pharaoh

In this case, Joseph proleptically reports his brothers' arrival, which he will present before Pharaoh in the next chapter (clause 891).

Predictive Discourse

Two examples of Predictive Discourse occur in Genesis 46, the first employing only *YIQTOL* clauses; the second, only *WeQATAL* clauses.

Clauses 855-857: God's Promise of Divine Protection
Clauses 883-886: Joseph's Plan for his Brothers

In the first case, clauses 855-857, fronted pleonastic pronouns make the *YIQTOL* verbal forms necessary:

46.04.855 אָנֹכִי אֵרֵד עִמְּךָ מִצְרַיְמָה
46.04.856 וְאָנֹכִי אַעַלְךָ גַם־עָלֹה
46.04.857 וְיוֹסֵף יָשִׁית יָדוֹ עַל־עֵינֶיךָ:

The second case, clauses 883-886, is initially marked with a predictive temporal introduction, using the *WeQATAL* verbal form וְהָיָה:

46.33.883 וְהָיָה
כִּי־יִקְרָא לָכֶם פַּרְעֹה
46.33.884 וְאָמַר

---

[89]The few clauses found within the Name List that are not verbless clauses in no way can be construed as narrative. Their placement does not provide enough context to form a coherent narrative.

ID

46.33.885 †מַה־מַּעֲשֵׂיכֶם:

46.33.886 וַאֲמַרְתֶּם

The subsequent *WeQAṬAL* clauses 884 and 886 follow from the introduction, uninterrupted by the inserted quotation of Interrogative Discourse in clause 885.

Expository Discourse

The six clauses of Expository Discourse are set into four separate speeches.

Clauses 849-850: God's Calling of Jacob
Clause 853: God's Self-Identification
Clauses †881-†882: Joseph's Planned Speech Before Pharaoh
Clause †887: The Brothers' Planned Answer to Pharaoh's Question

Of the six clauses, two are verbless (853 and 881) and two employ *QAṬAL* clauses, either with a fronted object (882) or using היה as a substitute for a verb-less clause (887). The remaining two, clauses 849 and 850, are incomplete and serve as vocative interjections, consisting of Jacob's name twice in succession as God calls to him:

46.02.849 יַעֲקֹב
46.02.850 יַעֲקֹב

Interrogative Discourse

Only one example of Interrogative Discourse occurs in Genesis 46, com-posed of a single two word clause.

Clause †885: Pharaoh's Planned Question of the Brothers

While Joseph premeditates on how he can manage getting his newly recovered family land for their flocks and herds, he tells his brothers that he will bring them before Pharaoh and that Pharaoh will, in turn, ask them a question:

46.33.885 †מַה־מַּעֲשֵׂיכֶם

Joseph's predictions, even here, prove to be correct for when, in the next chap-ter, the brothers are brought before the king, Pharaoh does indeed ask them pre-cisely the question Joseph foresaw that he would (clause 896).

Hortatory Discourse

There are only three examples of Hortatory Discourse in Genesis 46, encompassing five clauses.

> Clause 854: God's Plea for Jacob not to Fear
> Clause 875: Jacob's Desire to Die after Seeing Joseph
> Clauses 877-879: Joseph's Desire to Go to Pharaoh

In the first example, God encourages Jacob concerning his descent to Egypt to meet Joseph:

46.03.854 אַל־תִּירָא מֵרְדָה מִצְרַיְמָה
כִּי־לְגוֹי גָּדוֹל אֲשִׂימְךָ שָׁם:

The use of the negative hortatory particle אַל־, of course, unambiguously distinguishes this discourse from Predictive Discourse.

In the second example, an explicit cohortative clause signals Jacob's desire to die after seeing Joseph:

46.30.875 אָמוּתָה הַפָּעַם אַחֲרֵי רְאוֹתִי אֶת־פָּנֶיךָ
כִּי עוֹדְךָ חָי:

In the third example above, while an ambiguous *YIQTOL* clause heads the discourse (877), subsequent explicit cohortative clauses define the discourse as hortatory:[90]

46.31.877 אֶעֱלֶה
46.31.878 וְאַגִּידָה לְפַרְעֹה
46.31.879 וְאֹמְרָה אֵלָיו

---

[90]The initial verb in clause 877, עלה, being a III-ה weak form, cannot have a distinctive cohortative form. See also Waltke and O'Connor, *Syntax,* 565; and E. J. Revell, "First Person Imperfect Forms with *Waw* Consecutive," *VT* 38 (1988), 419-26.

Table of Discourse Constellations for Genesis 46

		Present Ch.	Prev. Chs.	Total in JN
ND	*QAṬAL*			21	21
	QAṬAL, WAYYIQṬOL			8	8
	QAṬAL, (Ptc./Vbl.)			8	8
	QAṬAL, WAYYIQṬOL, (Ptc./Vbl.)	1	3	4
	QAṬAL, WAYYIQṬOL, (Ptc./Vbl.), *YIQṬOL*		2	2
	QAṬAL, YIQṬOL (w/ past adverb)		0	0
	WAYYIQṬOL, (Ptc./Vbl.)		0	0
	Vbl/Ptc/Inc (Dream Report)		1	1
PD	*YIQṬOL*	1	12	13
	YIQṬOL, WeQAṬAL		6	6
	YIQṬOL, WeQAṬAL, (Ptc./Vbl../Inc.)		1	1
	YIQṬOL, (Ptc./Vbl../Inc.)		0	0
	WeQAṬAL		5	5
	WeYIQṬOL		0	0
ED	Ptc./Vbl.	1	22	23
	Ptc./ Vbl., Inc.		1	1
	Inc.	1	5	6
	Ptc./Vbl., *QAṬAL/YIQṬOL* of היה		2	2
	Ptc./Vbl., *QAṬAL/YIQṬOL* of היה, Front. Obj.+ *QAṬAL/YIQṬOL*		2	2
	QAṬAL/YIQṬOL of היה	1	0	1
HD	Impv./Coh./Juss.	2	21	23
	Impv./Coh./Juss., *WeYIQṬOL/YIQṬOL*		10	10
	Impv./Coh./Juss., *WeQAṬAL*		3	3
	Impv./Coh./Juss., *WeYIQṬOL/YIQṬOL, WeQAṬAL*		4	4
	Impv./Coh./Juss., *QAṬAL*		1	1
	Impv./Coh./Juss., *WeYIQṬOL/YIQṬOL*, (We)*QAṬAL*		1	1
	Impv./Coh./Juss., *ʾal-YIQṬOL*		2	2
	Impv./Coh./Juss., *WeQAṬAL, ʾal-YIQṬOL*		2	2
	ʾal-YIQṬOL	1	5	6
	ʾal-YIQṬOL, WeQAṬAL/YIQṬOL		0	0
	(We)*YIQṬOL-nāʾ*, (We*QAṬAL/[We]YIQṬOL*)		0	0
	QAṬAL, YIQṬOL/WeQAṬAL		1	1

Genesis 47 – Joseph Settles Israel in Goshen and Buys Egypt for Pharaoh – Clauses 888-971

Text in Syntactical/Paragraph Units

Joseph Meets Israel/Jacob and Plans for his Settlement (Cont.)

	וַיֹּשֵׁב יוֹסֵף	47.01.888
	אֶת־אָבִיו	47.01.889
	וְאֶחָיו	47.01.890
ND	וַיִּתֵּן לָהֶם אֲחֻזָּה בְּאֶרֶץ מִצְרַיִם בְּמֵיטַב הָאָרֶץ בְּאֶרֶץ רַעְמְסֵס	47.01.891
ED	כַּאֲשֶׁר צִוָּה פַרְעֹה:	47.01.892

Joseph Acquires Goshen for his Family and Egypt for Pharaoh

	וַיְכַלְכֵּל יוֹסֵף אֶת־אָבִיו וְאֶת־אֶחָיו	47.02.893
	וְאֵת כָּל־בֵּית אָבִיו לֶחֶם לְפִי הַטָּף:	47.02.894
	וְלֶחֶם אֵין בְּכָל־הָאָרֶץ	47.03.895
ID	כִּי־כָבֵד הָרָעָב מְאֹד	47.03.896
	וַתֵּלַהּ אֶרֶץ מִצְרַיִם	47.03.897
ED	וְאֶרֶץ כְּנַעַן מִפְּנֵי הָרָעָב:	47.03.898
	וַיְלַקֵּט יוֹסֵף אֶת־כָּל־הַכֶּסֶף	47.04.899

47.04.900   ND
47.04.901   HD
47.05.902
47.05.903   ND
47.06.904   ED
47.06.905   HD
47.06.906
907α
907β
47.06.907
47.07.908
47.07.909
47.07.910
47.08.911
47.08.912   ID
47.09.913

47.10.917

47.10.918

47.11.919

47.11.920

47.12.921

47.13.922

47.13.923

47.14.924

47.14.925

47.15.926

47.15.927

HD   47.15.928

ID   47.15.929

ED   47.09.914

47.09.915

47.09.916

47.16.930	וַיֹּאמֶר יוֹסֵף
	47.16.931
	47.16.932
	HD
47.17.933	
47.17.934	
47.18.936	
47.18.937	
47.18.938	
	47.18.939
	PD
	47.18.940
	ND
47.17.935	
	47.19.941
	ID
	HD
	47.19.942
	47.19.943
	47.19.944
	47.19.945
	47.19.946
	47.19.947

וַיִּ֣קֶן יוֹסֵ֞ף אֶת־כָּל־אַדְמַ֤ת מִצְרַ֙יִם֙ לְפַרְעֹ֔ה 47.20.948

כִּֽי־מָכְר֤וּ מִצְרַ֙יִם֙ אִ֣ישׁ שָׂדֵ֔הוּ 47.20.949

כִּֽי־חָזַ֥ק עֲלֵהֶ֖ם הָרָעָ֑ב 47.21.950

וַתְּהִ֥י הָאָ֖רֶץ לְפַרְעֹֽה׃

וְאֶ֨ת־הָעָ֔ם הֶעֱבִ֥יר אֹת֖וֹ לֶעָרִ֑ים

מִקְצֵ֥ה גְבוּל־מִצְרַ֖יִם וְעַד־קָצֵֽהוּ׃

The Egyptian Priests' Land (Comment)

רַ֛ק אַדְמַ֥ת הַכֹּהֲנִ֖ים לֹ֣א קָנָ֑ה 47.22.951

כִּי֩ חֹ֨ק לַכֹּהֲנִ֜ים מֵאֵ֣ת פַּרְעֹ֗ה 47.22.952

וְאָֽכְל֤וּ אֶת־חֻקָּם֙ אֲשֶׁ֨ר נָתַ֤ן לָהֶם֙ פַּרְעֹ֔ה 47.22.953

עַל־כֵּ֕ן לֹ֥א מָכְר֖וּ אֶת־אַדְמָתָֽם׃

Joseph Taxes Egypt and Israel Increases in Goshen

וַיֹּ֤אמֶר יוֹסֵף֙ אֶל־הָעָ֔ם 47.23.954

הֵן֩ קָנִ֨יתִי אֶתְכֶ֥ם הַיּ֛וֹם וְאֶת־אַדְמַתְכֶ֖ם לְפַרְעֹ֑ה 47.23.955

ND

הֵֽא־לָכֶ֣ם זֶ֔רַע 47.23.956
ED

וּזְרַעְתֶּ֖ם אֶת־הָאֲדָמָֽה׃ 47.23.957
PD

וְהָיָה֙ בַּתְּבוּאֹ֔ת 47.24.958

וּנְתַתֶּ֥ם חֲמִישִׁ֖ית לְפַרְעֹ֑ה וְאַרְבַּ֣ע הַיָּדֹ֡ת יִהְיֶ֣ה לָכֶם֩ לְזֶ֨רַע הַשָּׂדֶ֧ה וּֽלְאָכְלְכֶ֛ם וְלַאֲשֶׁ֥ר בְּבָתֵּיכֶ֖ם וְלֶאֱכֹ֥ל לְטַפְּכֶֽם׃ 47.24.959

47.25.961   וַיֹּאמְרוּ

47.26.965   וְיֹשֵׁב מִזֶּה פֹּה לִרְאוֹת אֶת־פְּנֵי הַמֶּלֶךְ

47.26.966   (וְיֵלֶךְ אֹתוֹ נְתַתִּיו חֶלְקוֹ בֶּן־יִשַׁי וַיֵּלֶךְ לְפָנֶיךָ:)

47.27.967   וַיֹּאמֶר וַיֹּאמְרוּ אֵלָיו עֲבָדָיו אֲשֶׁר מָה

47.27.968   וַיַּעֲנוּ כֵן

47.27.969   וַיֵּלְכוּ

47.27.970   וַיֹּאמְרוּ אֵלָיו:

47.24.960   וְכַאֲשֶׁר יַרְאֶה אֶבֶן הַיּוֹם בְּעֵינֶיךָ לְפָנֶיךָ:
וַיֵּלֶךְ הַנֹּעַר וַיֵּלֶךְ בְּקֶרֶב גַּיְא הַנָּחַל:

ND   47.25.962   הַמְדֻבָּר

PD   47.25.963   וַיֹּאמֶר אָבִי יָשִׁיב אֵלֶיךָ

47.25.964   וַיֹּאמֶר אֶת־פְּנֵי לְפָנֶיךָ:

Table of Independent Clause Types in Genesis 47

Clause Type	Clause Distribution	Total	Percent
QAṬAL Total Clauses: 13	Narrative: 893,950,951,953,966	5	38.5%
	ND: 891,900,903,940,955,962	6	46.1%
	PD:		
	ED: 915,916	2	15.4%
	ID:		
	HD:		
WeQAṬAL Total Clauses: 6	Narrative: 952	1	16.7%
	ND:		
	PD: 957,958,959,964	4	66.6%
	ED:		
	ID:		
	HD: 907	1	16.7%
YIQṬOL Total Clauses: 9	Narrative:	0	0
	ND:		
	PD: 939,960,963	3	33.3%
	ED:		
	ID: 929,941	2	22.2%
	HD: 901,906,946,947	4	44.5%
WeYIQṬOL Total Clauses: 2	Narrative:	0	0
	ND:		
	PD:		
	ED:		
	ID:		
	HD: 943,945	2	100%
WAYYIQṬOL Total Clauses: 39	Narrative: 888,889,890,894,895,897,899,902,908, 909,910,911,913,917,918,919,920,921,923,924,925, 926,927,930,933,934,935,936,937,938,948,949,954, 961,965,967,968,969,970	39	100%
	ND:		
	PD:		
	ED:	0	0
	ID:		
	HD:		

	Narrative:	0	0
Participle Total Clauses: 0	ND: PD: ED: ID: HD:	0	0
	Narrative: 922	1	12.5%
Verbless Total Clauses: 8	ND: PD: ED: 892,898,904,914,956 ID: 896,912 HD:	 5 2	 62.5% 25.0%
	Narrative:	0	0
Incomplete Total Clauses: 0	ND: PD: ED: ID: HD:	0	0
Imperative	Narrative:	0	0
Total Clauses: 5	HD: 905,928,931,942,944	5	100%
Cohortative	Narrative:	0	0
Total Clauses: 1	HD: 932	1	100%
Jussive	Narrative:	0	0
Total Clauses: 0	HD:	0	0

Analysis of the Narrative Structure and Discourse Text-Types in Genesis 47

Narrative Structural Analysis

Narrative/Paragraph Structure

Genesis 47:1-27, the story of "Joseph Settles Israel in Goshen and Buys Egypt for Pharaoh," begins with three clauses (47:1; clauses 888-890) from the final paragraph of Genesis 46 (see analysis of Genesis 46). In addition to this initial paragraph fragment, Genesis 47:2-27 is composed of two main paragraphs, both explicitly marked.

Clauses 893-950: Joseph Acquires Goshen for His Family and Egypt
for Pharaoh
Clauses 954-970: Joseph Taxes Egypt and Israel Increases in Goshen

Only the first paragraph is initially marked. The *QATAL* clause

47.02.893 וּמִקְצֵה אֶחָיו לָקַח חֲמִשָּׁה אֲנָשִׁים

serves as the introduction for the plan of Joseph to settle his brothers in the most fertile land in Egypt, where, supposedly, the harsh famine that afflicts the majority of Egyptians is absent. The second paragraph has an initial *WAYYIQTOL* clause and is, therefore, externally marked by the preceding extra-paragraph comment (clauses 951-953). The first paragraph is terminally marked by *QATAL* clause 950.

The final *WAYYIQTOL* clause of the last paragraph stands before another *WAYYIQTOL* clause in Genesis 47:28. However, because of the narratological parallels pointed out in this study's introduction to the Joseph Novella, and because the nature of the verb in following clause performs a much more commentary (rather than sequential-active) role, the end of the Novella stands at clause 970 in Genesis 47:27.

Extra-Paragraph Comments

Only one extra-paragraph comment occurs in Genesis 47:1-27. The narrator explicitly states that Joseph did not purchase the land of the Egyptian priests for Pharaoh. The note about the priests' land occurs in an extra-paragraph comment:

47.22.951 רַק אַדְמַת הַכֹּהֲנִים לֹא קָנָה
כִּי חֹק לַכֹּהֲנִים מֵאֵת פַּרְעֹה
47.22.952 וְאָכְלוּ אֶת־חֻקָּם

אֲשֶׁר נָתַן לָהֶם פַּרְעֹה
47.22.953 עַל־כֵּן לֹא מָכְרוּ אֶת־אַדְמָתָם:

In the comment, the *WeQATAL* verbal form (וְאָכְלוּ) has caused much confusion.[91] Looked at from a text-linguistic perspective, however, it is clear that the function of the form is to provide information about a known character's actions off the narrative story line.[92]

Inner-Paragraph Comments

Three inner-paragraph comments occur in Genesis 47:1-27. The first expresses the nonexistence of its subject and, therefore, employs a verbless clause containing the particle אֵין:

47.13.922 וְלֶחֶם אֵין בְּכָל־הָאָרֶץ כִּי־כָבֵד הָרָעָב מְאֹד

The second inner-paragraph comment tells of the ownership of something by someone. In this case, the idiom for acquisition of ownership ($\text{X} \ldots \text{לְ Y}$ וַיְהִי) is used in a היה verbal clause:

47.20.949 וַתְּהִי הָאָרֶץ לְפַרְעֹה:

Thus, the land of Egypt itself becomes the property of Pharaoh. The third inner-paragraph comment expresses the nonpossession of the priests' land by Pharaoh and, therefore, has a negated היה verbal clause:

47.26.966 רַק אַדְמַת הַכֹּהֲנִים לְבַדָּם לֹא הָיְתָה לְפַרְעֹה:

Discourse Function Analysis

Narrative Discourse

Six cases of Narrative Discourse occur in Genesis 47, one composed of a three-clause speech and the rest composed of single clauses.

---

[91]See the Narrative Analysis of Genesis 37 above for references to the view of *WeQATAL* as a "past progressive tense" in the history of scholarship.

[92]Both in clause 952 and in clause 007 (וְעָשָׂה לוֹ כְּתֹנֶת פַּסִּים 37.03.007), the subject of the verb is explicitly named beforehand. If, in a comment, the subject of the verb is ambiguous, the narrator most usually heads the sentence with the subject and provides the *QATAL* verb alone. There is no necessarily inherent "progressive" or "incomplete" sense in either instance of the *WeQATAL* in the Novella.

Clause 891: Joseph's Report to Pharaoh concerning His Father's and
           Brothers' Arrival
Clause 900: The Brothers' Report to Pharaoh concerning Their Arrival
Clause 903: Pharaoh's Report to Joseph concerning Jacob's and the
           Brothers' Arrival
Clauses 914-916: Jacob's Answer to Pharaoh's Question
Clause 940: The Egyptians' Confession of Their Loss
Clause 955: Joseph's Recounting the Purchase of Egypt for Pharaoh
Clause 962: The Egyptians' Report of Joseph's Saving Them

In the cases of single clause speeches, a *QATAL* provides the governing verbal
form for each clause. These clauses are, therefore, highly regular and expected.
In the case of Jacob's answer to Pharaoh's question concerning his life, the patriarch begins the response with a verbless clause, but quickly reverts to *QATAL*
clauses to describe the misery and brevity of his life:

ED

47.09.914 יְמֵי שְׁנֵי מְגוּרַי שְׁלֹשִׁים וּמְאַת שָׁנָה

47.09.915 מְעַט וְרָעִים הָיוּ יְמֵי שְׁנֵי חַיַּי

47.09.916 וְלֹא הִשִּׂיגוּ אֶת־יְמֵי שְׁנֵי חַיֵּי אֲבֹתַי בִּימֵי מְגוּרֵיהֶם:

Predictive Discourse

Three examples of Predictive Discourse occur in Genesis 47, one expressing despair and two expressing hope for the future, one from the mouth of
Joseph and one from the mouths of the Egyptians.

Clause 939: The Egyptians' Despair over Their Loss
Clauses 957-960: Joseph's Hope for Egyptian Taxation
Clauses 963-964: The Egyptians' Hope for the Future

At the conclusion of the drought, Joseph provides grain to the Egyptians, here
not for food, but rather for seed. His plan, however, has consequences:

47.23.957 וּזְרַעְתֶּם אֶת־הָאֲדָמָה:

47.24.958 וְהָיָה בַּתְּבוּאֹת

47.24.959 וּנְתַתֶּם חֲמִישִׁית לְפַרְעֹה

47.24.960 וְאַרְבַּע הַיָּדֹת יִהְיֶה לָכֶם לְזֶרַע הַשָּׂדֶה
וּלְאָכְלְכֶם וְלַאֲשֶׁר בְּבָתֵּיכֶם וְלֶאֱכֹל לְטַפְּכֶם:

The accumulation of a twenty-percent tax on the produce in the future (clause 958) secures Egypt against further calamity. The *WeYIQTOL* clauses and the final *YIQTOL* clause distinguish this speech as a Predictive Discourse.[93]

The final discourse of the Novella is given to the Egyptians and consists of a simple narrative statement set as a *QATAL* clause (see the Analysis above) and, based upon the historical fact of that statement, a hope for the future:

ND
47.25.962   הֶחֱיִתָנוּ
PD
47.25.963   נִמְצָא־חֵן בְּעֵינֵי אֲדֹנִי
47.25.964   וְהָיִינוּ עֲבָדִים לְפַרְעֹה:

Based upon the fact that Joseph has rescued them in the past (clause 962), the Egyptians hope that they continue to "find grace" in Joseph's eyes and be servants of Pharaoh (thus, under his protection). The change from the narrative *QATAL* to the Predictive *YIQTOL* and *WeQATAL* here is unambiguous and shows clearly how text-types are juxtaposed and related.

Expository Discourse

The five examples of Expository Discourse in Genesis 47 are comprised of seven clauses.

> Clause 892: Joseph's Report to Pharaoh concerning His Father's and
>   Brothers' Presence in Goshen
> Clause 898: The Brothers' Answer to Pharaoh's Question
> Clause 904: Pharaoh's Statement concerning the Land of Egypt
> Clause 956: Joseph's Explanation that the Egyptians Have Seed

Of the nine clauses, five (892, 898, 904, 914, 956) are verbless clauses, explaining a present state of affairs. The remaining clauses are comprised of two *QATAL* clauses, of which one is negated with לֹא (916), and one uses היה as a substitute for a verbless clause (915).

---

[93]Spurrel (*Notes*, 220) suggests that a *WeQATAL* standing alone is "used as a precative or mild imperative," and notes Gen 47:23 as an example. This hortatory nature of the verbs is, however, not present if the discourse is seen in its entirety. Clauses 958 and 960 cannot be seen as hortatory in any sense. In the cases of clauses 957 and 959, unambiguous means are available to express the hortatory nature of "sowing" and "giving" if it were intended. The discourse here is, through and through, one of prediction and lays out Joseph's planned taxation of the land.

Interrogative Discourse

Four examples of Interrogative Discourse occur in Genesis 47, all unambiguously marked with prefixed interrogative particles.

> Clause 896: Pharaoh's Question to the Brothers
> Clause 912: Pharaoh's Question to Jacob
> Clause 929: The Egyptians' Question concerning Their Death I
> Clause 941: The Egyptians' Question concerning Their Death II

The clauses are all marked with adverbs or particles indicating the true nature of the questions asked: מָה, clause 896; כַּמָּה, clause 912; and לָמָּה , both with *waw*, clause 929, and without *waw*, clause 941. Because the final two examples are immediately juxtaposed to examples of Hortatory Discourse (clauses 928 and 942-947), the questions, while still standing as true questions, also take on rhetorical significance.

Hortatory Discourse

There are five examples of Hortatory Discourse in Genesis 47, consisting of thirteen total clauses.

> Clause 901: The Brothers' Request of Pharaoh
> Clauses 905-907: Pharaoh's Orders to Joseph concerning His Brothers
> Clause 928: The Egyptians' Demand of Food
> Clauses 931-932: Joseph's Demand of the Egyptians' Cattle
> Clauses 942-947: Joseph's Demand of the Egyptians' Land

The first example, clause 901, is differentiated from the preceding Narrative Discourse (clause 900) by the metasyntactic marker וְעַתָּה and is defined as hortatory by the particle of entreaty, ־נָא , attached to the *YIQTOL* verb form:

וְעַתָּה
47.04.901 יֵשְׁבוּ־נָא עֲבָדֶיךָ בְּאֶרֶץ גֹּשֶׁן:

In the remaining four examples found in Genesis 47, an initial imperative clause defines the discourse as hortatory and causes the volitive force of the speech to be extended unto verb forms and clauses not explicitly marked as volitive, *YIQTOL* clauses (906, 946, and 947) and *WeQATAL* clauses (907, 943, and 945).

Table of Discourse Constellations for Genesis 47

		Present Ch.	Prev. Chs.	Total in JN
	QAṬAL	6	21	27
	QAṬAL, WAYYIQṬOL		8	8
	QAṬAL, (Ptc./Vbl.)		8	8
ND	*QAṬAL, WAYYIQṬOL*, (Ptc./Vbl.)		4	4
	QAṬAL, WAYYIQṬOL, (Ptc./Vbl.), *YIQṬOL*		2	2
	QAṬAL, YIQṬOL (w/ past adverb)		0	0
	WAYYIQṬOL, (Ptc./Vbl.)		0	0
	Vbl/Ptc/Inc (Dream Report)		1	1
	YIQṬOL		13	13
	YIQṬOL, WeQAṬAL	2	6	8
PD	*YIQṬOL, WeQAṬAL*, (Ptc./Vbl../Inc.)		1	1
	YIQṬOL, (Ptc./Vbl../Inc.)		0	0
	WeQAṬAL		5	5
	WeYIQṬOL		0	0
	Ptc./Vbl.	4	23	27
	Ptc./ Vbl., Inc.		1	1
	Inc.		6	6
ED	Ptc./Vbl., *QAṬAL/YIQṬOL* of היה	1	2	3
	Ptc./Vbl., *QAṬAL/YIQṬOL* of היה, Front. Obj.+ *QAṬAL/YIQṬOL*		2	2
	QAṬAL/YIQṬOL of היה		1	1
	Impv./Coh./Juss.	3	23	26
	Impv./Coh./Juss., *WeYIQṬOL/YIQṬOL*	1	10	11
	Impv./Coh./Juss., *WeQAṬAL*		3	3
	Impv./Coh./Juss., *WeYIQṬOL/YIQṬOL, WeQAṬAL*	1	4	5
	Impv./Coh./Juss., *QAṬAL*		1	1
HD	Impv./Coh./Juss., *WeYIQṬOL/YIQṬOL*, (We)*QAṬAL*		1	1
	Impv./Coh./Juss., ʾal-*YIQṬOL*		2	2
	Impv./Coh./Juss., *WeQAṬAL*, ʾal-*YIQṬOL*		2	2
	ʾal-*YIQṬOL*		6	6
	ʾal-*YIQṬOL, WeQAṬAL/YIQṬOL*		0	0
	(We)*YIQṬOL*-nāʾ, (*WeQAṬAL*/[*We*]*YIQṬOL*)		0	0
	QAṬAL, YIQṬOL/WeQAṬAL		1	1

Chapter Three
The Narrative of David's Court:
A Discourse-Linguistic Analysis

Formal Considerations:
Limits of the Narrative of David's Court

The History of Scholarship

For the past century and a half, the traditions which surround the events of David's court (2 Sam 9–20; 1 Kings 1–2) have been interpreted by many scholars as having a narrative integrity that distinguishes them from the surrounding account. While the Narrative of David's Court as a whole contains evidence that it was compiled of several smaller units, the overall structural integrity of the narrative lends support to the view that it may be interpreted as a whole.

Leonhard Rost's pivotal book, *Die Überlieferung von der Thronnachfolge Davids*, published in 1926, propelled the study of the "Throne Succession Document" or, more recently, "Court History" into the prominence it still receives today.[1] Prior to Rost's study, most scholars assumed that the sources of

---

[1] The question of the nomenclature of the work is, of course, the question of the intent and purpose of it. The name given to the story in scholarly circles remains one of the prime areas of controversy in the interpretation of the narrative as a whole. The two major contenders that have been suggested, the "Throne Succession Document/ Narrative" and the "Court History," each have basic flaws representing the nature of the story. Most scholars no longer hold to the view that the basic purpose of the story is a legitimation of the succession of Solomon to the throne of his father David. On the other hand, the question of whether the genre of the narrative can rightly be called "history" (as von Rad, among others, thought) is doubtful. In this study the generic names "The Narrative of David's Court" and "The Court Narrative" avoid, I hope, either of these pitfalls. For further discussion concerning the genre of the work, see Leonhard Rost, *Die Überlieferung von der Thronnachfolge Davids* (BWANT 42; Stuttgart: Kohlhammer, 1926); P. R. Ackroyd, "The Succession Narrative (so-called)," *Interpretation* 35 (1981), 383-96; Joseph

the Pentateuch extended into the stories of 1 and 2 Samuel and believed that the traditions of the latter half of Samuel derive from the J (Yahwistic) source found in Genesis, Exodus, and Numbers.[2] In 1912, Claus Steuernagel noted that two sources were indeed present up to 2 Samuel 8, but the traditions of 2 Samuel 9–20 were, on the contrary, "a distinct and well constructed history emanating from Jerusalem, a history which he could describe as one of the most magnificent pieces of Israelite literature."[3]

Other scholars, however, did not agree with Steuernagel's view of the unified nature of the traditions surrounding the activities within David's court. Gressmann, for example, saw much of the latter half of 2 Samuel as made of smaller, individual "Novellen." The story of the rivalry between Amnon and Absalom (2 Sam 13:1-14:33) and the story of the rebellions of Absalom and Sheba (2 Sam 15:1-20:22) were seen as independent traditions with very little connection with each other.[4]

With the publication of Rost's volume, however, the modern scholarly view that these traditions have a unified scope and purpose was established. Rost delineated the materials found in 2 Samuel 6:16, 20-23; 7:11b, 16; 9:1-10:5; (perhaps 10:6-11:1); 11:2-12:7a; 12:13-25 (perhaps 26-31); 13:1-14:24;

Blenkinsopp, "Theme and Motif in the Succession History (2 Sam. XI 2ff) and the Yahwist Corpus," in *Volume du Congrès, Genève, 1965* (VTSupp 15; Leiden: Brill, 1966), 44-57; W. Caspari, "Literarische Art und historischer Wert von 2 Sam. 15–20," *TSK* 82 (1909), 317-48; G. W. Coats, "Parable, Fable and Anecdote: Story-telling in the Succession Narrative," *Interpretation* 35 (1981), 368-82; J. W. Flanagan, "Court History or Succession Document? A Study of 2 Samuel 9–20 and 1 Kings 1–2," *JBL* 91 (1972), 172-81; E. Würthwein, *Die Erzählung von der Thronfolge Davids—theologische oder politische Geschichtsschreibung?* (Theologische Studien 115; Zurich: Theologische Verlag, 1974).

[2]Among the many who constructed evidence for the J source in Samuel were the renowned scholars Karl Budde (*Die Bücher Samuel* [KHCAT 8; Tübingen: J. C. B. Mohr, 1902]) and Otto Eissfeldt (*Hexateuch-Synopse* [Leipzig: J. C. Hinrich, 1922]; *Die Quellen des Richterbuches* [Leipzig: J. C. Hinrich, 1925]).

[3]C. Steuernagel, *Lehrbuch der Einleitung in das Alte Testament* (Tübingen: J. C.B. Mohr, 1912), 334-35. It is unclear whether Steuernagel saw 1 Kings 1–2 as a part of the "history." The quotation is from the overview of the history of scholarship concerning the "Court History" by Harold Forshey, "Court Narrative (2 Samuel 9–1 Kings 2)," *ABD* (ed. David N. Freedman; New York: Doubleday, 1992), 1:1172-79.

[4]The novelistic nature of the two cycles was emphasized by the depth of characterization used by the author. H. Gressmann, *Die älteste Geschichtsschreibung und Prophetie Israels* (2d ed.; Göttingen: Vanderhoeck & Ruprecht, 1921), xiv, 181. This "atomistic" view of the narrative also has its modern supporters who do not recognize any overarching unity to 2 Sam 9–20 and 1 Kings 1–2 (see below).

14:28-18:17; 18:19-20:22; 1 Kings 1:1-2:1, 5-10, 12-27a, 28-46 as constituting a continuous narrative whose purpose was to exemplify the glory of Solomon.

Rost's view was quickly accepted by Albrecht Alt, Martin Noth, and Gerhard von Rad and, through the influence of those scholars, was widely accepted throughout the mid-twentieth century as the standard scholarly view for the traditions found in the last half of 2 Samuel. Von Rad, in particular, saw the "Succession Document" as expressing one of the finest theological views in the whole Hebrew Bible:

> Unlike the great literary works which have concerned us up to now, and which are well known to be compilations of a large number of originally independent traditions, this work . . . is a unity from beginning to end. Thus, even from a literary viewpoint we are dealing with an account of exceptional quality and title. Its almost entirely flawless literary unity leads us to expect from the start a much greater spiritual and theological unity than could have been the case with those literary compositions whose component parts each had already their own specific stamp.[5]

This "spiritual and theological unity" has, however, come under fire recently among scholars. These recent reconsiderations of the work have approached the work from two distinct perspectives.

First, some scholars have questioned Rost's view of the purpose for the narrative. L. Delekat, in his essay "Tendenz und Theologie der David-Salomo-Erzählung," soundly criticized the perspective that saw the *Tendenz* of the narrative as legitimizing the reign of Solomon and whose goal was the greater glory of Solomon, "in majorem gloriam Solomonis." If, in fact, the central issue of the story is the succession to the throne of David, the story is basically unfavorable to Solomon, not supportive.

> If it was correct that Bethsheba was an adulteress, that Adonijah was generally and with David's approbation regarded as the crown prince, and that there was no divine oracle granting the throne to Solomon, the narrative is implicitly critical of Solomon and the process by which he came to the throne. Clearly then, the concern of the narrative is more generally the reign of David until the consolidation of the kingship in the hand of Solomon. The affirmation that the kingdom

---

[5]Gerhard von Rad, *Old Testament Theology*, Vol. 1 (New York: Harper & Row, 1962), 312.

was secure in Solomon's hands (1 Kgs 2:46) begs the question, How did this come about?[6]

While Delekat's critique was not immediately accepted, it has, in fact, become one of the standard interpretations for the work, his criticisms overpowering Rost's original viewpoint propounded by von Rad and Noth.[7]

The second front on which scholars are reexamining Rost's original work questions the historicity of the narrative. Rost originally saw the text as one of the most historically well-supported traditions found within the Hebrew Bible, a view taken up, again, by von Rad.[8] In recent decades, however, studies investigating the literary structure and organization of the work have called into question the inherent unity of the narrative and, furthermore, the designation of the work as "history." The first foray into the literary artistry of the work, in 1965, was J. J. Jackson's article, "David's Throne: Patterns in the Succession Story."[9] Jackson noted several elements of oral narrative technique that were present in the "Succession Story" including the opposite characterizations of David and Joab and the use of suspense and climax. C. Conroy called into question the basic unified nature of the work by going back to some of the work by pre-Rost scholars and investigating the story of Absalom's revolt, which he views as a self-contained narrative.[10] Furthermore, Joseph Blenkinsopp and David Gunn have noted folkloristic qualities found within the story.[11] Taken together, these treatments have seriously damaged the unqualified designation of the narrative as history.

On the other hand, the discussion concerning the overall unity or disunity of the narrative has not reached a consensus. It seems clear that the author(s) of the Court Narrative used and incorporated (sometimes wholecloth) earlier narratives

---

[6]Forshey, "Court Narrative," 1176

[7]Note, among many treatments, those taken up by T. Veijola ("Salomo—der erstgeborene Bathsebas," In *Congress Volume, 1978* [VTSupp 30; Leiden: Brill, 1979], 230-50), F. Langlamet ("Pour ou contre Salomon? La Rédaction prosalomonienne de I Rois," *Revue Biblique* 83 [1976], 321-79, 481-529), and P. Kyle McCarter (*II Samuel* [AB; Garden City, NY: Doubleday, 1984], 15-16).

[8]Rost, *Thronnachfolge*, 115; Von Rad, *Theology*, 312-318.

[9]J. J. Jackson, "David's Throne: Patterns in the Succession Story," *CJT* 11 (1965), 183-95.

[10]C. Conroy, *Absalom Absalom! Narrative and Language in 2 Samuel 13–20* (Analecta Biblica 81; Rome: Pontifical Biblical Institute, 1978).

[11]Blenkinsopp, "Theme," 44-57; David M. Gunn, *The Story of King David* (JSOTSupp 6; Sheffield: JSOT, 1978).

into their final product.[12] This does not, however, deny the possible scenario that much of 2 Samuel 9–1 Kings 2 was composed during a single period.[13] The incorporation of earlier material would, of course, lead to a complex view of the "final form" or "purpose" for the narrative, as has been noted by McCarter.[14] This does not necessarily imply, however, that the narrative cannot be interpreted as a whole, with consistent, although multivalent, motifs. While these motifs probably can no longer be seen as consistently legitimizing Solomon's reign, as Rost originally believed, the themes of political enmity and alliance and the general atmosphere of intrigue pervade the narrative.

Forshey, in his article on the "Court Narrative," questions the inclusion of 2 Samuel 9 within the overall framework of the text. Interpreting the references to Bathsheba/Nathan/Solomon in both 2 Samuel 11 and in 1 Kings 1–2 as an inclusio, Forshey argues that "there is little reason to try to include 2 Samuel 9 as part of the larger composition."[15] On the other hand, the main characters in 2 Samuel 9–the servant of Saul, Ziba, and the son of Jonathan, Mephibosheth–do, nevertheless, appear at a major crux within the midst of the story, the return of David to the city in 2 Samuel 19:24-30. If chapter 9 is separated from the larger work, the narrative context for the presence of these two characters within the story (with no re-introduction of their prior history) is lacking. For this reason, in this investigation, 2 Samuel 9 will be included within the scope of the "Narrative of David's Court."[16]

---

[12]K. K. Sacon, "A Study of the Literary Structure of 'The Succession Narrative'" in *Studies in the Period of David and Solomon and Other Essays* (ed. T. Ishida; Winona Lake: Eisenbrauns, 1982), 27-57.

[13]The original date of the composition argued by Rost was set in the "early Solomonic period" (mid-tenth century BCE). This, like most of Rost's other views, has come into serious question. Both Forshey ("Court Narrative," 1178) and Gunn (*Story*, 32-33) note several clues in the text that the work possibly comes from a much later time than the events it relates, such as the reference to the attire of royal daughters (2 Sam 13:18) and the question of whether Absalom did or did not have sons (2 Sam 14:27 and 18:18). Note also the recent work of Serge Frolov, "Succession Narrative: A 'Document' or a Phantom?" *JBL* 121 (2002), 81-104.

[14]P. Kyle McCarter, Jr., "Plots, True or False," *Interpretation* 35 (1981), 355-67.

[15]Forshey, "Court Narrative," 1178.

[16]As, in the previous chapter, the answer to the question of the inclusion or exclusion of Gen 38 from the Joseph Novella is, in fact, not absolutely essential for the conclusion argued in this study, so is the fact with 2 Sam 9–10. The thesis of this inquiry is not directly affected by differing views of the overall framework of the narrative. The question is merely a preparatory one.

Texts Used in this Study

In consideration of the formal markers of the beginning and ending of
the Narrative of David's Court, including both the inclusio formed by the Bath-
sheba/Nathan/Solomon nexus (2 Sam 10–12; 1 Kgs 1–2) and the parallel of the
Mephibosheth/Ziba stories (2 Sam 9; 19:24-30), the text of the Narrative of
David's Court which this study will use as a database for its analysis is the following: 2 Samuel 9:1-20:26 and 1 Kings 1:1-2:46.

2 Samuel 9 — David, Ziba, and Mephibosheth — Clauses 1-51

Text in Syntactical/Paragraph Units

David Finds a Descendant of Saul

09.01.001		וַיֹּאמֶר דָּוִד
09.01.002	ID	הֲכִי יֶשׁ־עוֹד
09.01.003	PD	אֲשֶׁר נוֹתַר לְבֵית שָׁאוּל וְאֶעֱשֶׂה עִמּוֹ חֶסֶד בַּעֲבוּר יְהוֹנָתָן׃
09.02.004		וַיִּקְרָא־לוֹ הַמֶּלֶךְ
09.02.005		וַיֹּאמֶר אֵלָיו הַאַתָּה צִיבָא
09.02.006		וַיֹּאמֶר עַבְדֶּךָ׃
09.02.007		וַיֹּאמֶר הַמֶּלֶךְ
09.02.008	ID	וַיֹּאמֶר צִיבָא
09.02.009		וַיֹּאמֶר
09.02.010	ED	עַבְדֶּךָ׃
09.03.011		וַיֹּאמֶר הַמֶּלֶךְ
09.03.012	ID	וַיֹּאמֶר צִיבָא אֶל־הַמֶּלֶךְ
09.03.013	PD	וַיֹּאמֶר צִיבָא אֶל־הַמֶּלֶךְ עוֹד בֵּן לִיהוֹנָתָן
09.03.014		וַיֹּאמֶר צִיבָא אֶל־הַמֶּלֶךְ
09.03.015	ED	עוֹד בֵּן לִיהוֹנָתָן נְכֵה רַגְלָיִם׃
09.04.016		וַיֹּאמֶר־לוֹ הַמֶּלֶךְ

09.04.017 ID
וַיֹּאמֶר לוֹ הִנֵּנִי

09.04.018 וַיֹּאמֶר קַח־נָא אֶת־בִּנְךָ

09.04.019 ED
וַיֹּאמֶר אֵלָיו הַמֶּלֶךְ וַיַּעֲשׂוּ כֵן וַיִּהְיוּ:

09.05.020 וַיֹּאמֶר הִנֵּה
09.06.021 וַיֹּאמֶר
09.06.022 וַיֹּאמֶר אֶל־הַנַּעַר
09.06.023 וַיֵּלֶךְ וַיָּבֹא
09.06.024 וַיֹּאמֶר
09.06.025 וַיֹּאמֶר הִנֵּה

09.06.026 ED (Vocative)
הַמֶּלֶךְ אֲדֹנִי

09.06.027 וַיֹּאמֶר

09.06.028 ED
הִנֵּה:

09.07.029 וַיֹּאמֶר כִּי הִנֵּה

09.07.030 HD
אֶל־הָעָם
כִּי אֵלָיו אֲשֶׁר

09.07.031 PD
כִּי יְדַעְתִּיךָ
וַיַּעַן וַיֹּאמֶר וַיַּעֲשׂוּ אֹתָם

09.07.032 וַיֵּלֶךְ וַיָּבֹא הַמֶּלֶךְ וַיַּעֲשׂוּ אֹתָם:
וְכָל־הָעָם הַזֶּה

09.08.033 וַיֹּאמֶר

09.13.051 וַיֹּאמֶר שֵׁנִית הֲבוֹא כִּי־עַבְדֶּךָ׃)

09.13.050 בְּעֵינֵי אֲדֹנִי הַמֶּלֶךְ כַּאֲשֶׁר צִוָּה אֶת־

09.12.049 לְכֹל אֲשֶׁר יְצַוֶּה אֲדֹנִי הַמֶּלֶךְ אֶת־עַבְדּוֹ

09.12.048 וַיֹּאמֶר צִיבָא

09.12.047 כַּאֲשֶׁר צִוָּה הַמֶּלֶךְ

09.11.046 (וּמְפִיבֹשֶׁת אֹכֵל עַל־שֻׁלְחָנִי כְּאַחַד בְּנֵי הַמֶּלֶךְ׃)

09.11.044 וַיֹּאמֶר צִיבָא אֶל־הַמֶּלֶךְ

09.10.043 (וְלִמְפִיבֹשֶׁת בֶּן־אֲדֹנֶיךָ אַרְבָּעָה עָשָׂר וַעֲבָדָיו עֶשְׂרִים׃)

09.11.045 צִיבָא (וּבָנָיו וַעֲבָדָיו וַיֹּאמֶר אֶל־הַמֶּלֶךְ)

09.10.042 וְאָכַל מְפִיבֹשֶׁת

09.10.041 לֶחֶם וְהָיָה לְבֶן־אֲדֹנֶיךָ לֶחֶם וַאֲכָלוֹ

09.10.040 וְעָבַדְתָּ לּוֹ אֶת־הָאֲדָמָה אַתָּה וּבָנֶיךָ וַעֲבָדֶיךָ

09.10.039 וְהֵבֵאתָ

09.09.038 צִיבָא (נַעַר שָׁאוּל וַיִּקְרָא אֶל־הַמֶּלֶךְ)

ND

09.09.037 וַיֹּאמֶר אֵלָיו

09.09.036 וַיֹּאמֶר הִנֵּה עַבְדְּךָ

ID

09.08.034 וַיִּשְׁתַּחוּ

09.08.035 וַיֹּאמֶר מֶה עַבְדֶּךָ כִּי פָנִיתָ אֶל־הַכֶּלֶב הַמֵּת

PD

Table of Independent Clause Types in 2 Samuel 9

Clause Type	Clause Distribution	Total	Percent
QAṬAL Total Clauses: 1	Narrative:	0	0
	ND: 038 PD: ED: ID: HD:	1	100%
WeQAṬAL Total Clauses: 4	Narrative:	0	0
	ND: PD: 031,038,039,041 ED: ID: HD:	4	100%
YIQṬOL Total Clauses: 4	Narrative:	0	0
	ND: PD: 032,042,045 ED: ID:	3	75.0%
	HD: 030	1	25.0%
WeYIQṬOL Total Clauses: 2	Narrative:	0	0
	ND: PD: 003,013 ED: ID: HD:	2	100%
WAYYIQṬOL Total Clauses: 21	Narrative: 001,006,007,009,011,014,016,018,020, 021,022,023,024,025,027,029,033,034,036,037,044	21	100%
	ND: PD: ED: ID: HD:	0	0

	Narrative: 046,049,050	3	100%
Participle	ND:		
	PD:		
Total Clauses: 3	ED:	0	0
	ID:		
	HD:		
	Narrative: 004,005,043,047,048,051	6	46.1%
Verbless	ND:		
	PD:		
Total Clauses:	ED: 015,019	2	15.4%
13	ID: 002,008,012,017,035	5	38.5%
	HD:		
	Narrative:	0	0
Incomplete	ND:		
	PD:		
Total Clauses: 3	ED: 010,026,028	3	100%
	ID:		
	HD:		
Imperative	Narrative:	0	0
Total Clauses: 0	HD:	0	0
Cohortative	Narrative:	0	0
Total Clauses: 0	HD:	0	0
Jussive	Narrative:	0	0
Total Clauses: 0	HD:	0	0

Analysis of the Narrative Structure and
Discourse Text-Types in 2 Samuel 9

Narrative Structural Analysis

Narrative/Paragraph Structure

The basic backbone of the narrative of 2 Samuel 9 is constructed of twenty-one *WAYYIQTOL* clauses, with no major disruptions in the *WAYYIQTOL* chain. The whole of chapter 9 is a single continuous paragraph. The beginning of the paragraph is marked externally by the concluding *QATAL* clause of the previous chapter (2 Sam 8:18):

וּבְנָיָהוּ בֶּן־יְהוֹיָדָע וְהַכְּרֵתִי וְהַפְּלֵתִי וּבְנֵי דָוִד כֹּהֲנִים הָיוּ:

The end of the paragraph is, likewise, externally marked by the initial וַיְהִי temporal clause in 2 Samuel 10:1 (וַיְהִי אַחֲרֵי־כֵן). The whole of the chapter is, therefore, a single unified paragraph with no disjunctive narrative markers within it.

Extra-Paragraph Comments

Because the whole of 2 Samuel 9 is a sustained paragraph, there are no extra-paragraph comments within the chapter.

Inner-Paragraph Comments

Three inner-paragraph comments occur within the narrative of 2 Samuel 9, all of which consist of combinations of verbless and participial clauses. The first introduces the character of Ziba, the servant of Saul:

09.02.004 (וּלְבֵית שָׁאוּל עֶבֶד

09.02.005 וּשְׁמוֹ צִיבָא)

The second, occurring near the end of the paragraph and consisting of a single off-line clause, enumerates the sons and slaves which Ziba, in turn, had:

09.10.043 (וּלְצִיבָא חֲמִשָּׁה עָשָׂר בָּנִים וְעֶשְׂרִים עֲבָדִים:)

The final inner-paragraph comment actually occurs at the end of the paragraph and provides the station and status of the characters of Mephiboshet and Ziba at the conclusion of the narrative:[17]

09.11.046 (וּמְפִיבֹשֶׁת אֹכֵל עַל־שֻׁלְחָנִי כְּאַחַד מִבְּנֵי הַמֶּלֶךְ:

09.12.047 וְלִמְפִיבֹשֶׁת בֵּן־קָטָן

09.12.048 וּשְׁמוֹ מִיכָא

09.12.049 וְכֹל מוֹשַׁב בֵּית־צִיבָא עֲבָדִים לִמְפִיבֹשֶׁת:

09.13.050 וּמְפִיבֹשֶׁת יֹשֵׁב בִּירוּשָׁלַם

כִּי עַל־שֻׁלְחַן הַמֶּלֶךְ תָּמִיד הוּא אֹכֵל

09.13.051 וְהוּא פִּסֵּחַ שְׁתֵּי רַגְלָיו:)

In all these cases, the comments do not in any way cause the action of the narrative to progress but rather simply provide information to the reader. Even the long final comment contains no finite verbal form (e.g., *QATAL*, *WeQATAL WeQATAL WeYIQTOL*, *YIQTOL*) but simply informs the reader concerning the narrative outcome of the paragraph.

Discourse Function Analysis

Narrative Discourse

The only instance of Narrative Discourse in 2 Samuel 9 occurs in clause 038, and is governed by a *QATAL* verbal form. It is, therefore, completely consistent with Narrative Discourse in general and requires no comment.[18]

Predictive Discourse

Most instances of Predictive Discourse in 2 Samuel 9 are consistent with other examples of Predictive Discourse in biblical prose, being governed by either *WeQATAL* clauses, the usual form found in Predictive Discourse (clauses 031, 039-041), or *YIQTOL* clauses, if the clause either concludes the example of

---

[17]The status of clause 046 is complex. The first person suffix on עַל־שֻׁלְחָנִי would place this statement within direct discourse. Yet the words are completely out of place within the speech of Ziba immediately preceding it. The LXX witness for the phrase, ἐπὶ τῆς τραπέζης Δαυιδ, suggests the original reading of עַל־שֻׁלְחָנוֹ, which has generally been adopted by most commentators and modern translations. The clause is, therefore, a part of the narrative instead of direct discourse.

[18]In consideration of space, the various exemplars of each type of discourse will not be explicitly listed in the analysis of the Court History. Each example is, however, explicitly marked with its abbreviation (ND, PD, ED, ID, HD) in the text of the formatted Hebrew database.

Predictive Discourse (clauses 032, 042) or initiates the speech in which it stands (clause 045).

The two cases of *WeYIQTOL* clauses found in Predictive Discourse in chapter 9 (clauses 003, 013) are the only two examples of this type of clause outside Hortatory Discourse in the Court Narrative.[19] In both cases, the Predictive Discourse follows an Interrogative Discourse and may provide the motivation behind the question. That is, in the initial discourse in the narrative,

ID

09.01.002 הֲכִי יֶשׁ־עוֹד

אֲשֶׁר נוֹתַר לְבֵית שָׁאוּל

PD

09.01.003 וְאֶעֱשֶׂה עִמּוֹ חֶסֶד בַּעֲבוּר יְהוֹנָתָן:

The Predictive Discourse may provide the motivation for David's question: "Is there still someone remaining from the House of Saul, so that I can/may/shall extend fidelity to him because of Jonathan?"[20] While in English the second clause is incorporated into the question, in Hebrew it stands separate, being an independent clause to itself.[21]

Expository Discourse

All examples of Expository Discourse in 2 Samuel 9 are consistent with other examples of this text-type in biblical prose. The specific examples are governed either by verbless (015, 019) or incomplete clauses (010, 026, 028).

---

[19]Since *WeYIQTOL* clauses normally occur in Hortatory Discourse, they may be markers for Hortatory Discourse rather than Predictive Discourse, which usually employs *WeQATAL* clauses. The hortatory nature of clause 003 (as well as its designation as a cohortative) is entirely possible and the first person verb would, therefore, take on volitive force: "I *will* extend fidelity!" Unfortunately, the morphology of this particular case is ambiguous. I, therefore, conservatively designate it as a *WeYIQTOL* clause.

[20]Lambdin (*Introduction*, §107.c) notes that *WeYIQTOL* clauses which follow imperatives, cohortatives, or jussives often express the purpose or result of the hortatory clause. Such a function, while here occurring after an Interrogative Discourse, seems to apply in this case as well.

[21]The connection between the two clauses is, however, not one of explicit subordination. The juxtaposition of the Interrogative and Predictive Discourses in this case *implies* that clause 003 provides the motivation for the asking of the question in clause 002, but this is by no means explicitly obvious in the syntax of the clauses. Note Gesenius, *Grammar*, §165.1, who seems to see a closer, subordinate connection between the two clauses. Note also H. G. T. Mitchell, *Final Constructions of Biblical Hebrew* (Leipzig: J. C. Hinrichs, 1879).

These three instances of incomplete clauses used in Expository Discourse are consistently examples of vocative phrases, used when one character addresses another character in the immediate vicinity.

Interrogative Discourse

As with Interrogative Discourse in general, the specific clauses of this text-type in 2 Samuel 9 are consistently marked as questions by prefixed interrogative particles, הַ/הֲ (clauses 002, 008, 012), אֵיפֹה (clause 017), and מֶה/מָה (clause 035).[22]

Hortatory Discourse

The only instance of Hortatory Discourse within 2 Samuel 9 occurs as an independent *YIQṬOL* clause:

אַל־תִּירָא   09.07.030

The designation of the speech as hortatory is not dependent upon the form of the verb as is usually the case, since independent *YIQṬOL* clauses generally occur in Predictive Discourse. In clause 030, however, the negative particle אַל marks the clause as a hortatory speech, much in the same way that interrogative particles mark Interrogative Discourse, regardless of the verbal or clausal type.

---

[22]The designation of clause 026 as interrogative as in some English translations has no basis, since it does not occur within any clearly marked interrogative context, as is the case with other examples of unmarked interrogative clauses.

Table of Discourse Constellations for 2 Samuel 9

		Present Ch.	Total in JN	Total
	QATAL	1	27	28
	QATAL, WAYYIQTOL		8	8
	QATAL, (Ptc./Vbl.)		8	8
ND	*QATAL, WAYYIQTOL*, (Ptc./Vbl.)		4	4
	QATAL, WAYYIQTOL, (Ptc./Vbl.), *YIQTOL*		2	2
	QATAL, YIQTOL (w/ past adverb)		0	0
	WAYYIQTOL, (Ptc./Vbl.)		0	0
	Vbl/Ptc/Inc (Dream Report)		1	1
	YIQTOL	1	13	14
	YIQTOL, WeQATAL	2	8	10
PD	*YIQTOL, WeQATAL*, (Ptc./Vbl../Inc.)		1	1
	YIQTOL, (Ptc./Vbl../Inc.)		0	0
	WeQATAL		5	5
	WeYIQTOL	2	0	2
	Ptc./Vbl.	2	27	29
	Ptc./ Vbl., Inc.		1	1
	Inc.	3	6	9
ED	Ptc./Vbl., *QATAL/YIQTOL* of היה		3	3
	Ptc./Vbl., *QATAL/YIQTOL* of היה, Front. Obj.+ *QATAL/YIQTOL*		2	2
	QATAL/YIQTOL of היה		1	1
	Impv./Coh./Juss.		26	26
	Impv./Coh./Juss., *WeYIQTOL/YIQTOL*		11	11
	Impv./Coh./Juss., *WeQATAL*		3	3
	Impv./Coh./Juss., *WeYIQTOL/YIQTOL, WeQATAL*		5	5
	Impv./Coh./Juss., *QATAL*		1	1
HD	Impv./Coh./Juss., *WeYIQTOL/YIQTOL*, (*We*)*QATAL*		1	1
	Impv./Coh./Juss., *ʾal-YIQTOL*		2	2
	Impv./Coh./Juss., *WeQATAL, ʾal-YIQTOL*		2	2
	ʾal-YIQTOL	1	6	7
	ʾal-YIQTOL, WeQATAL/YIQTOL		0	0
	(*We*)*YIQTOL-nāʾ*, (*WeQATAL*/[*We*]*YIQTOL*)		0	0
	QATAL, YIQTOL/WeQATAL		1	1

2 Samuel 10 — Joab and David Defeat Ammon and Syria — Clauses 52-116

Text in Syntactical/Paragraph Units

Ammon Disgraces the Emissaries of David

10.01.052	וַיְהִי אַחֲרֵי־כֵן
10.01.053	וַיָּמָת מֶלֶךְ בְּנֵי עַמּוֹן
10.01.054	וַיִּמְלֹךְ חָנוּן בְּנוֹ תַּחְתָּיו׃
10.02.055	וַיֹּאמֶר דָּוִד
10.02.056 (PD)	אֶעֱשֶׂה־חֶסֶד עִם־חָנוּן בֶּן־נָחָשׁ כַּאֲשֶׁר עָשָׂה אָבִיו עִמָּדִי חֶסֶד
10.02.057	וַיִּשְׁלַח דָּוִד לְנַחֲמוֹ בְּיַד־עֲבָדָיו אֶל־אָבִיו
10.02.058	וַיָּבֹאוּ עַבְדֵי דָוִד אֶרֶץ בְּנֵי עַמּוֹן׃
10.03.059	וַיֹּאמְרוּ שָׂרֵי בְנֵי־עַמּוֹן אֶל־חָנוּן אֲדֹנֵיהֶם
10.03.060 (ID)	הַמְכַבֵּד דָּוִד אֶת־אָבִיךָ בְּעֵינֶיךָ כִּי־שָׁלַח לְךָ מְנַחֲמִים
10.03.061	הֲלוֹא בַּעֲבוּר חֲקוֹר אֶת־הָעִיר וּלְרַגְּלָהּ וּלְהָפְכָהּ שָׁלַח דָּוִד אֶת־עֲבָדָיו אֵלֶיךָ׃
10.04.062	וַיִּקַּח חָנוּן אֶת־עַבְדֵי דָוִד
10.04.063	וַיְגַלַּח אֶת־חֲצִי זְקָנָם
10.04.064	וַיִּכְרֹת אֶת־מַדְוֵיהֶם בַּחֵצִי עַד שְׁתוֹתֵיהֶם
10.04.065	וַיְשַׁלְּחֵם׃
10.05.066	וַיַּגִּדוּ לְדָוִד

Joab Prepares for War Against Ammon at Rabbah

10.05.067	וַיֵּלְכוּ וַיַּגִּדוּ
10.05.068	לְדָוִד עַל־הָאֲנָשִׁים וַיִּשְׁלַח לִקְרָאתָם
10.05.069	וַיֹּאמֶר:
10.05.070	שְׁבוּ בִירֵחוֹ עַד־יְצַמַּח זְקַנְכֶם וְשַׁבְתֶּם

HD

10.06.071	וַיִּרְאוּ בְּנֵי עַמּוֹן
10.06.072	כִּי נִבְאֲשׁוּ בְּדָוִד
10.06.073	וַיִּשְׁלְחוּ בְנֵי־עַמּוֹן וַיִּשְׂכְּרוּ אֶת־אֲרַם בֵּית־רְחוֹב וְאֶת־אֲרַם צוֹבָא עֶשְׂרִים אֶלֶף רַגְלִי
10.07.074	וַיִּשְׁמַע דָּוִד
10.07.075	וַיִּשְׁלַח אֶת־יוֹאָב וְאֵת כָּל־הַצָּבָא הַגִּבֹּרִים
10.08.076	וַיֵּצְאוּ בְּנֵי עַמּוֹן
10.08.077	וַיַּעַרְכוּ מִלְחָמָה פֶּתַח הַשָּׁעַר
10.08.078	(וַאֲרַם צוֹבָא וּרְחוֹב וְאִישׁ־טוֹב וּמַעֲכָה לְבַדָּם בַּשָּׂדֶה)
10.09.079	וַיַּרְא יוֹאָב
10.09.080	כִּי־הָיְתָה אֵלָיו פְּנֵי הַמִּלְחָמָה מִפָּנִים וּמֵאָחוֹר [ס. וַיַּרְא]
10.09.081	וַיִּבְחַר מִכֹּל בְּחוּרֵי [בְיִשְׂרָאֵל]
10.10.082	וְאֵת יֶתֶר הָעָם נָתַן בְּיַד אַבְשַׁי אָחִיו
10.10.083	וַיַּעֲרֹךְ לִקְרַאת בְּנֵי עַמּוֹן
10.11.084	וַיֹּאמֶר:

10.16.101 וַיָּנָס אֲרָם

10.16.100 מִפְּנֵי יִשְׂרָאֵל

10.16.099 וַיַּהֲרֹג דָּוִד מֵאֲרָם

10.15.098 וַיֹּאמֶר יוֹאָב:

10.15.097 כִּי רָאָה אֲרָם

10.14.096 וַיֹּאמֶר אֲבִישַׁי:

10.14.095 וַיַּהֲרֹג אֲרָם שֶׁבַע מֵאוֹת רֶכֶב

10.14.094 וַיָּנָס אֲרָם

10.14.093 וַיָּנָס אֲרָם מִפְּנֵי יִשְׂרָאֵל

10.14.092 וַיֶּאֱסֹף אֲרָם יָד

David Fights a War against Syria at Helam

10.13.091 וַיָּבֹאוּ חֵילָמָה:

10.13.090 וַיַּעֲבֹר אֶת־הַיַּרְדֵּן (מֵאֲבֹר אֶת־הַיַּרְדֵּן) אֲשֶׁר (בְּעֵבֶר) וַיֵּצְאוּ הֲדַדְעֶזֶר אֶת־הַמְּלָכִים

PD

085α וַיַּשְׁלַח וַיֵּצֵא (הֲדַדְעֶזֶר) אֶת־אֲרָם

10.11.085 [וַיֹּא]מֶר לָהֶם

086α וַיַּהֲרֹג מֵהֶם דָּוִד

10.11.086 וַיֵּצְאוּ לִקְרָאתָם

HD

10.12.087 חֲזַק

10.12.088 וְנִתְחַזַּק בְּעַד עַמֵּנוּ:

10.12.089 וַיהוָה יַעֲשֶׂה הַטּוֹב בְּעֵינָיו:

10.19.116	ס וַיֹּאמֶר שְׁלֹשֶׁת הַיָּמִים הָאֵלֶּה לֶחֶם וָמָיִם:
10.19.115	וַיֹּאכְלוּ
10.19.114	וַיָּכְרֹת אִתָּם בְּרִית
10.19.114	פֶּן יַעֲזֹב מַלְאָךְ
10.19.113	וַיֹּאמֶר הֵן שִׁמַעְתִּים מַלְכֵי יִשְׂרָאֵל
10.19.113	וַיַּעַן מֶלֶךְ:
10.18.111	וַיֵּצְאוּ הָעִיר מַלְכֵי יִשְׂרָאֵל וַיֵּלְכוּ
10.18.112	
10.18.110	וַיַּחְגְּרוּ הֶחָגוּר מָתְנֵיהֶם וַחֲבָלִים וַיֵּלְכוּ אֶל מֶלֶךְ יִשְׂרָאֵל וַיֹּאמְרוּ
10.18.109	וַיֹּאמֶר הַחַי עוֹדֶנּוּ:
10.17.108	הֲשָׁלוֹם בֶּן:
10.17.107	וַיְמַהֲרוּ שְׁלוֹם לְבֶן הֲדַד חַי
10.17.106	אֶל בֶּן הֲדָד
10.17.105	וַיֹּאמְרוּ
10.17.104	וְהֵמָּה נַחֲשׁוּ
10.17.103	וְהָאֲנָשִׁים
10.16.102	(וַיֹּאמֶר מֶלֶךְ יִשְׂרָאֵל הוֹרִדוּ לְכֶם:)

Syria's Vassals Make Peace with Israel

Table of Independent Clause Types in 2 Samuel 10

Clause Type	Clause Distribution	Total	Percent
QAṬAL Total Clauses: 4	Narrative: 082,092,111	3	75.0%
	ND: PD: ED: ID: 061 HD:	 1	 25.0%
WeQAṬAL Total Clauses: 3	Narrative:	0	0
	ND: PD: 085,086 ED: ID: HD: 070	 2 1	 66.7% 33.3%
YIQṬOL Total Clauses: 2	Narrative:	0	0
	ND: PD: 056 ED: ID: HD: 089	 1 1	 50.0% 50.0%
WeYIQṬOL Total Clauses: 1	Narrative:	0	0
	ND: PD: ED: ID: HD: 088	 1	 100%
WAYYIQṬOL Total Clauses: 50	Narrative: 052,053,054,055,057,058,059,062,063, 064,065,066,067,068,071,072,073,074,075,076,077, 079,080,081,083,084,090,091,093,094,095,096,097, 098,099,100,101,103,104,105,106,107,108,109,110, 112,113,114,115,116	50	100%
	ND: PD: ED: ID: HD:		

Participle	Narrative:	0	0
Total Clauses: 1	ND: PD: ED: ID: 060 HD:	1	100%
Verbless	Narrative: 078,102	2	100%
Total Clauses: 2	ND: PD: ED: ID: HD:	0	0
Incomplete	Narrative:	0	0
Total Clauses: 0	ND: PD: ED: ID: HD:	0	0
Imperative	Narrative:	0	0
Total Clauses: 2	HD: 069,087	2	100%
Cohortative	Narrative:	0	0
Total Clauses: 0	HD:	0	0
Jussive	Narrative:	0	0
Total Clauses: 0	HD:	0	0

Analysis of the Narrative Structure and Discourse Text-Types in 2 Samuel 10

Narrative Structural Analysis

Narrative/Paragraph Structure

The narrative of 2 Samuel 10 consists of a basic backbone of *WAYYIQTOL* clauses which is divided into four independent paragraphs, each initially marked either with an initial וַיְהִי temporal clause (052), or with a *QATAL* clause (082, 092, 111). In each of these cases, the paragraphs are terminally marked externally by the initial clause of the following paragraph. The final paragraph is terminally marked by the initial וַיְהִי temporal clause of 2 Samuel 11:1:

11.01.117 וַיְהִי לִתְשׁוּבַת הַשָּׁנָה לְעֵת צֵאת הַמַּלְאָכִים

Extra-Paragraph Comments

No extra-paragraph comments occur in 2 Samuel 10.

Inner-Paragraph Comments

Two inner-paragraph comments occur in 2 Samuel 10, each consisting of a single verbless clause. The first provides the information of the placement of the Ammonite forces before the battle (clause 078):

10.08.078 (וַאֲרַם צוֹבָא וּרְחוֹב וְאִישׁ־טוֹב וּמַעֲכָה לְבַדָּם בַּשָּׂדֶה:)

The second tells of the presence of Shobak, the Ammonite commander (clause 102):

10.16.102 (וְשׁוֹבַךְ שַׂר־צְבָא הֲדַרְעֶזֶר לִפְנֵיהֶם:)

In both cases, the comment does not cause the narrative to progress but does provide important information for the understanding of the narrative at hand.

Discourse Function Analysis

Narrative Discourse

No instances of Narrative Discourse occur in 2 Samuel 10.

Predictive Discourse

The two cases of Predictive Discourse that occur in 2 Samuel 10 are consistent with other examples of this text-type in biblical prose. In the first case, the *YIQTOL* clause 056 (אֶעֱשֶׂה־חֶסֶד עִם־חָנוּן בֶּן־נָחָשׁ) is completely consistent with what one expects in Predictive Discourse. In the case of clauses 085-086, the discourse consists of two *WeQATAL* clauses:

PD

085α אִם־תֶּחֱזַק אֲרָם מִמֶּנִּי
10.11.085 וְהָיְתָה לִּי לִישׁוּעָה
086α וְאִם־בְּנֵי עַמּוֹן יֶחֶזְקוּ מִמְּךָ
10.11.086 וְהָלַכְתִּי לְהוֹשִׁיעַ לָךְ:

The initial *WeQATAL* clause is slightly unusual since the speech is not immediately preceded by a speech of another text-type.[23] The *WeQATAL* clause 085 may initiate the speech because of the prefixed conditional phrase in clause 085α. In this case, nevertheless, the clausal form is consistent with other examples of *WeQATAL* clauses in Predictive Discourse.

Expository Discourse

No instances of Expository Discourse occur in 2 Samuel 10.

Interrogative Discourse

The only instance of Interrogative Discourse present in 2 Samuel 10 consists of two joined independent clauses, each explicitly marked as interrogative by the prefixed particle הַ (clauses 060-061).

Hortatory Discourse

The two cases of Hortatory Discourse in 2 Samuel 10 are both initially marked with imperative verbs (clauses 069, 087). In both cases the speech continues with verbal forms that are not explicitly hortatory; the hortatory nature of their meaning, however, is provided by the explicit imperative verbs within the speech. In one case, the hortatory speech is continued by a *WeQATAL* clause:

---

[23]As in the previous chapter, the *WeQATAL* clauses generally occur either within a predictive speech or, if they occur initially, there is another speech immediately preceding the Predictive Discourse. Note clauses 031 and 039 above.

10.05.069 שְׁבוּ בִירֵחוֹ עַד־יְצַמַּח זְקַנְכֶם
10.05.070 וְשַׁבְתֶּם:

In the other case, the hortatory speech is continued by a *WeQATAL* clause and a simple, non-jussive *YIQTOL* clause:

10.12.087 חֲזַק
10.12.088 וְנִתְחַזַּק בְּעַד־עַמֵּנוּ וּבְעַד עָרֵי אֱלֹהֵינוּ
10.12.089 וַיהוָה יַעֲשֶׂה הַטּוֹב בְּעֵינָיו:

Although the subject of clause 089 differs from that of clauses 087–088, because the clause is not set apart from the preceding hortatory speech by any disjunction (e.g., וְעַתָּה, הִנֵּה), it is included within the Hortatory Discourse. Because of this junction, the sense of the verb, although explicitly not hortatory, takes on hortatory functions: "May YHWH do what is right in his eyes."

Table of Discourse Constellations for 2 Samuel 10

		Present Ch.	Prev. Chs.	Total
ND	QATAL		28	28
	QATAL, WAYYIQTOL		8	8
	QATAL, (Ptc./Vbl.)		8	8
	QATAL, WAYYIQTOL, (Ptc./Vbl.)		4	4
	QATAL, WAYYIQTOL, (Ptc./Vbl.), YIQTOL		2	2
	QATAL, YIQTOL (w/ past adverb)		0	0
	WAYYIQTOL, (Ptc./Vbl.)		0	0
	Vbl/Ptc/Inc (Dream Report)		1	1
PD	YIQTOL	1	14	15
	YIQTOL, WeQATAL		10	10
	YIQTOL, WeQATAL, (Ptc./Vbl../Inc.)		1	1
	YIQTOL, (Ptc./Vbl../Inc.)		0	0
	WeQATAL	1	5	6
	WeYIQTOL		2	2
ED	Ptc./Vbl.		29	29
	Ptc./ Vbl., Inc.		1	1
	Inc.		9	9
	Ptc./Vbl., QATAL/YIQTOL of היה		3	3
	Ptc./Vbl., QATAL/YIQTOL of היה, Front. Obj.+ QATAL/YIQTOL		2	2
	QATAL/YIQTOL of היה		1	1
HD	Impv./Coh./Juss.		26	26
	Impv./Coh./Juss., WeYIQTOL/YIQTOL		11	11
	Impv./Coh./Juss., WeQATAL	1	3	4
	Impv./Coh./Juss., WeYIQTOL/YIQTOL, WeQATAL	1	5	6
	Impv./Coh./Juss., QATAL		1	1
	Impv./Coh./Juss., WeYIQTOL/YIQTOL, (We)QATAL		1	1
	Impv./Coh./Juss., ʾal-YIQTOL		2	2
	Impv./Coh./Juss., WeQATAL, ʾal-YIQTOL		2	2
	ʾal-YIQTOL		7	7
	ʾal-YIQTOL, WeQATAL/YIQTOL		0	0
	(We)YIQTOL-nāʾ, (WeQATAL/[We]YIQTOL)		0	0
	QATAL, YIQTOL/WeQATAL		1	1

2 Samuel 11 — David, Bathsheba, Joab, and Uriah — Clauses 117-224

Text in Syntactical/Paragraph Units

David Stays in Jerusalem during the Ammonite War

וַיְהִי לִתְשׁוּבַת הַשָּׁנָה ׀ לְעֵת צֵאת הַמַּלְאֿכִים	11.01.117
וַיִּשְׁלַח דָּוִד אֶת־יוֹאָב וְאֶת־עֲבָדָיו עִמּוֹ וְאֶת־כָּל־יִשְׂרָאֵל	11.01.118
וַיַּשְׁחִתוּ אֶת־בְּנֵי עַמּוֹן וַיָּצֻרוּ עַל־רַבָּה	11.01.119
וְדָוִד יוֹשֵׁב בִּירוּשָׁלָ͏ִם	11.01.120
(וַיְהִי) לְעֵת הָעֶרֶב	11.01.121

David Sends for Bathsheba and Sends for Uriah

וַיָּקָם דָּוִד מֵעַל מִשְׁכָּבוֹ	11.02.122
וַיִּתְהַלֵּךְ עַל־גַּג בֵּית־הַמֶּלֶךְ	11.02.123
וַיַּרְא אִשָּׁה רֹחֶצֶת מֵעַל הַגָּג	11.02.124
וְהָאִשָּׁה טוֹבַת מַרְאֶה מְאֹד	11.02.125
(וַיִּשְׁלַח דָּוִד וַיִּדְרֹשׁ לָאִשָּׁה:)	11.02.126
וַיֹּאמֶר	11.03.127
הֲלוֹא־זֹאת בַּת־שֶׁבַע	11.03.128
בַּת־אֱלִיעָם אֵשֶׁת אוּרִיָּה הַחִתִּי	11.03.129

וַיִּשְׁלַח דָּוִד מַלְאָכִים וַיִּקָּחֶהָ וַתָּבוֹא אֵלָיו	11.03.130
ID	

וַתָּבוֹא אֵלָיו	11.04.131
וַיִּשְׁכַּב עִמָּהּ	11.04.132
וַתִּתְקַדָּשׁ	11.04.133
מִטֻּמְאָתָהּ וַתָּשָׁב אֶל־בֵּיתָהּ	11.04.134

11.04.135 (וַיְהִי בָעֶרֶב וַיֵּצֵא אוּרִיָּה)

11.04.136 וְאֶל־בֵּיתוֹ לֹא יָרָד:

11.05.137 וַיָּשֶׁב

11.05.138 וַיֹּאמְרוּ

11.05.139 לֵאמֹר

11.05.140 וַיֹּאמֶר

ED 11.05.141 הִנֵּה אוּרִיָּה:

11.06.142 וַיִּקְרָא־לוֹ דָוִד

HD 11.06.143 וַיֹּאכַל לְפָנָיו וַיֵּשְׁתְּ וַיְשַׁכְּרֵהוּ

11.06.144 וַיִּשְׁלַח אֹתוֹ אֶל־אֲבֵנֵר:

11.07.145 וַיֵּצֵא אוּרִיָּה

11.07.146 לִשְׁכַּב בְּמִשְׁכָּבוֹ עִם־עַבְדֵי אֲדֹנָיו

11.08.147 וַיֹּאמְרוּ לְדָוִד לֵאמֹר

HD 11.08.148 לֹא יָרַד

HD 11.08.149 אוּרִיָּה אֶל־בֵּיתוֹ

11.08.150 וַיֹּאמֶר דָּוִד אֶל־אוּרִיָּה

11.08.151 הֲלוֹא מִדֶּרֶךְ אַתָּה בָא

11.09.152 מַדּוּעַ לֹא־יָרַדְתָּ אֶל־בֵּיתֶךָ:

11.09.153 וַיֹּאמֶר אוּרִיָּה אֶל־דָּוִד

הָאָרוֹן וְיִשְׂרָאֵל וִיהוּדָה יֹשְׁבִים בַּסֻּכּוֹת וַאדֹנִי יוֹאָב וְעַבְדֵי אֲדֹנִי עַל־פְּנֵי

Uriah Refuses to Go to His House and Wife Twice More

11.10.154 וַיֹּאמֶר דָּוִד אֶל־אוּרִיָּה

11.13.173   וַיֹּאמֶר אֶל דָּוִד

11.13.172   וַיֵּצֵא גַם יָצֹא לִקְרַאת הַיֹּצְאִים מִן הָעִיר אֵלֵינוּ

11.13.171   וַיֵּצְאוּ

11.13.170   וַיֹּרוּ

11.13.169   אַנְשֵׁי הָעִיר

11.13.168   וַיִּלָּחֲמוּ אִתּוֹ

11.12.167   וַיֹּאמֶר הַמַּלְאָךְ אֶל דָּוִד כִּי גָבְרוּ עָלֵינוּ הָאֲנָשִׁים וַיֵּצְאוּ אֵלֵינוּ הַשָּׂדֶה

11.12.164   וַיֹּאמֶר דָּוִד אֶל הַמַּלְאָךְ

11.11.159   וַיֹּאמֶר אוּרִיָּה אֶל דָּוִד

11.10.156   וַיֹּאמֶר דָּוִד אֶל אוּרִיָּה

HD   11.12.166   וַיְמֻתוּ מֵעַבְדֵי הַמֶּלֶךְ

    11.12.165   וַגַּם עַבְדְּךָ אוּרִיָּה הַחִתִּי מֵת

ED   11.11.163   חַי נַפְשְׁךָ

ED (Oath)   וְחֵי נַפְשֶׁךָ

PD   11.11.162   אִם אֶעֱשֶׂה אֶת הַדָּבָר הַזֶּה

    11.11.161   וַאֲנִי אָבוֹא אֶל בֵּיתִי

ED   11.11.160   לֶאֱכֹל וְלִשְׁתּוֹת וְלִשְׁכַּב עִם אִשְׁתִּי

ID   11.10.158   מַדּוּעַ לֹא יָרַדְתָּ אֶל בֵּיתֶךָ

    11.10.157   הֲלוֹא מִדֶּרֶךְ אַתָּה בָא

ND   11.10.155   וַיַּגִּדוּ לְדָוִד לֵאמֹר לֹא יָרַד אוּרִיָּה אֶל בֵּיתוֹ

David Orders Joab to Kill Uriah

11.14.174	וַיְהִי בַבֹּקֶר
11.14.175	וַיִּכְתֹּב דָּוִד סֵפֶר אֶל־יוֹאָב
11.14.176	וַיִּשְׁלַח בְּיַד אוּרִיָּה
11.15.177	וַיִּכְתֹּב בַּסֵּפֶר לֵאמֹר

HD

11.15.178	הָבוּ אֶת־אוּרִיָּה אֶל־מוּל פְּנֵי הַמִּלְחָמָה הַחֲזָקָה
11.15.179	וְשַׁבְתֶּם מֵאַחֲרָיו
11.15.180	וְנִכָּה
11.15.181	וָמֵת

Joab Kills Uriah and God Punishes David

11.16.182	וַיְהִי בִּשְׁמוֹר יוֹאָב אֶל־הָעִיר
11.16.183	וַיִּתֵּן אֶת־אוּרִיָּה אֶל־הַמָּקוֹם
11.17.184	וַיֵּצְאוּ אַנְשֵׁי הָעִיר
11.17.185	וַיִּלָּחֲמוּ אֶת־יוֹאָב
11.17.186	וַיִּפֹּל מִן־הָעָם מֵעַבְדֵי דָוִד
11.17.187	וַיָּמָת גַּם אוּרִיָּה הַחִתִּי
11.18.188	וַיִּשְׁלַח יוֹאָב
11.18.189	וַיַּגֵּד לְדָוִד אֶת־כָּל־דִּבְרֵי הַמִּלְחָמָה
11.19.190	וַיְצַו אֶת־הַמַּלְאָךְ לֵאמֹר

11.22.201   וַיֵּלֶךְ הַמַּלְאָךְ אֶל־דָּוִד

11.22.202   אֵת כָּל־אֲשֶׁר יְשָׁלָחוֹ:

11.22.203   וַיָּבֹא

11.23.204   וַיֵּלֶךְ הַמַּלְאָךְ

PD

191α   [בְּשׁוּבְכֶם] אֵת כָּל־דִּבְרֵי הַמִּלְחָמָה

11.20.191   וְהָיָה

[אֵל־הַמֶּלֶךְ] אִם־תַּעֲלֶה חֲמַת הַמֶּלֶךְ

192α   [וְאָמַר לְךָ]

11.20.192   וְאָמַר לָךְ

†ID

11.20.193   מַדּוּעַ נִגַּשְׁתֶּם†

11.20.194   אֶל־הָעִיר לְהִלָּחֵם†

       הֲלוֹא יְדַעְתֶּם

11.21.195   אֵת אֲשֶׁר־יָרוּ†

11.21.196   מֵעַל הַחוֹמָה†

11.21.197   מִי־הִכָּה אֶת־אֲבִימֶלֶךְ†

11.21.198   בֶּן־יְרֻבֶּשֶׁת†

11.21.199   הֲלוֹא־אִשָּׁה

†ND

11.21.200   הִשְׁלִיכָה עָלָיו†

11.25.211   וַיֹּאמֶר דָּוִד אֶל־הַצְּרֻיָה

11.26.217   וַתֵּלֶד הֵרֹדָה (שֵׁם־לִ׳) בְּנֹ׳ ׳׳׳
11.26.218   וַתֹּסֶף עֹד־
11.27.219   וַתֹּסֶף עֹד
11.27.220   וַיֹּאמֶר אֶל־הָעָם
11.27.221   וַיָּשֻׁב
11.27.222   (וְ׳׳׳ וְ׳ לְ׳׳׳)
11.27.223   כֵּן
11.27.224   כִּי־אֹמֵר אֲנִי־לֹ׳׳

ND
11.23.205   כִּי־בֵרֵךְ יְבָרֶךְ לִשְׁמֹ׳׳
11.23.206   וַיֹּאמֶר לָהֶם
11.23.207   וַיֹּאמֶר אֶל־
11.24.208   וַיֹּאמֶר [וְ׳׳׳׳] אֲשֶׁר ׳׳
11.24.209   וַיֹּאמֶר אֵלָיו
11.24.210   וַיֹּאמֶר

PD
11.25.212   וַיֹּאמֶר אֶל־הָעָם
†HD
11.25.213   וַיֹּאמֶר אֶל־דָּוִד†
11.25.214   הֲלֹא אֲנִי †
11.25.215   וַיֹּאמֶר†
11.25.216   :וַיֹּאמֶר†

Table of Independent Clause Types in 2 Samuel 11

Clause Type	Clause Distribution	Total	Percent
QAṬAL Total Clauses: 13	Narrative: 153,173	2	15.4%
	ND: 155,200,205,210 PD: ED: ID: 157,158,193,194,195,196,198 HD:	4 7	30.8% 53.8%
WeQAṬAL Total Clauses: 6	Narrative:	0	0
	ND: PD: 191,192,199 ED: ID: HD: 179,180,181	 3 3	 50.0% 50.0%
YIQṬOL Total Clauses: 4	Narrative:	0	0
	ND: PD: 212 ED: 162 ID: HD: 166,213	 1 1 2	 25.0% 25.0% 50.0%
WeYIQṬOL Total Clauses: 0	Narrative:	0	0
	ND: PD: ED: ID: HD:	0	0
WAYYIQṬOL Total Clauses: 69	Narrative: 117,118,119,120,122,123,124,125,127, 128,129,131,132,133,134,136,137,138,139,140,142, 144,145,146,147,150,151,152,154,156,159,164,167, 168,169,170,171,172,174,175,176,177,182,183,184, 185,186,187,188,189,190,201,202,203,204,211,217, 218,219,220,221,222,223,224	64	92.8%
	ND: 206,207,208,209 PD: ED: ID: 197 HD:	4 1	5.8% 1.4%

Participle	Narrative: 121,135	2	50.0%
Total Clauses: 4	ND: PD: ED: 160,161,200 ID: HD:	2	50.0%
Verbless	Narrative: 126	1	25.0%
Total Clauses: 4	ND: PD: ED: 141,163 ID: 130 HD:	2 1	50.0% 25.0%
Incomplete	Narrative:	0	0
Total Clauses: 0	ND: PD: ED: ID: HD:	0	0
Imperative	Narrative:	0	0
Total Clauses: 8	HD: 143,148,149,165,178,214,215,216	8	100%
Cohortative	Narrative:	0	0
Total Clauses: 0	HD:	0	0
Jussive	Narrative:	0	0
Total Clauses: 0	HD:	0	0

Analysis of the Narrative Structure and
Discourse Text-Types in 2 Samuel 11

Narrative Structural Analysis

Narrative/Paragraph Structure

The narrative of 2 Samuel 11 is composed of a backbone of sixty-four *WAYYIQTOL* clauses. This basic foundation is broken into five paragraph blocks marked either by initial וַיְהִי temporal clauses (clauses 117, 122, 174, 182) or by terminal *QATAL* clauses (clauses 153, 173). The final paragraph of this chapter continues into the next chapter, the chain of *WAYYIQTOL* clauses being unbroken from the beginning of the paragraph in clause 182 unto the chain of *WeQATAL* and *QATAL* clauses explaining David's intercessory ritual for his infant son in 2 Samuel 12:16-17 (clauses 276-282). This extra-paragraph comment finally breaks the *WAYYIQTOL* chain and provides an external marker for the end of the paragraph.

Extra-Paragraph Comments

No extra-paragraph comments occur within 2 Samuel 11.

Inner-Paragraph Comments

Only three inner-paragraph comments occur within 2 Samuel 11, one composed of a single verbless clause (126) and two others composed of single participial clauses each (121, 135).[24] While much of the narrative is simply told and such comments are minimal, they are extremely necessary for the understanding of the meaning of the story as a whole.[25]

---

[24]S. R. Driver (*A Treatise on the Use of the Tenses in Hebrew* [2d ed.; Oxford: Clarendon, 1881] 238-40; hereafter as *Tenses*) describes clause 135 as a circumstantial clause "defining the state of Bath-sheba at the time of וישכב עמה = '*as she* purified herself from her uncleanness.'" This, however, is not true since in the narrative, her bathing in clauses 125-126 happens before she does, in fact, have sex with David, not co-incident with it. The clause is not circumstantial but, rather, provides a subsequent comment about the previous scene and, thus, causes a deepening of the interpretive options for the narrative (see next footnote).

[25]Note, for example, Meir Sternberg's understanding of the importance of clause 135: וְהִיא מִתְקַדֶּשֶׁת מִטֻּמְאָתָהּ / "she was purifying herself from her uncleanness": "This unit, whose location and grammar signify not an action but a description of Bathsheba's state, breaks the otherwise chronological line of development. What is more, not only

Discourse Function Analysis

Narrative Discourse

Three examples of Narrative Discourse occur in 2 Samuel 11, all entirely regular for this text-type. Two of the examples are single sentences composed of a *QAṬAL* clause (155, †200). The third example, the report of the messenger to David concerning the war and the death of Uriah (clauses 205-210), is a combination of an initial *QAṬAL* clause followed by *WAYYIQṬOL* clauses:[26]

11.23.205 כִּי־נָבְרוּ עָלֵינוּ הָאֲנָשִׁים
11.23.206 וַיֵּצְאוּ אֵלֵינוּ הַשָּׂדֶה
11.23.207 וַנִּהְיֶה עֲלֵיהֶם עַד־פֶּתַח הַשָּׁעַר:
11.24.208 וַיֹּרְאוּ [Q וַיֹּרוּ] הַמּוֹרְאִים [Q הַמּוֹרִים] אֶל־עֲבָדֶךָ מֵעַל הַחוֹמָה
11.24.209 וַיָּמוּתוּ מֵעַבְדֵי הַמֶּלֶךְ
11.24.210 וְגַם עַבְדְּךָ אוּרִיָּה הַחִתִּי מֵת:

The final, climactic clause 210, providing the information concerning Uriah, is marked with the prefixed וְגַם and a governing *QAṬAL* verbal form.

Predictive Discourse

Three examples of Predictive Discourse occur within 2 Samuel 11, all entirely consistent with the verbal combinations that have been outlined thus far. Two examples consist of single *YIQṬOL* clauses. The first is Uriah's contrary-to-fact, theoretical contemplation of his going to his house in spite of the discomfort of his commander and fellow-soldiers on the field of battle outlined in the Expository Discourse immediately preceding it:[27]

---

does it seem out of place in terms of dramatic logic, but the reference to 'purification' (and as an ongoing process at that) after 'he lay with her' is simply absurd. So the reader must wonder: Why is this information necessary? And why here of all places?" *The Poetics of Biblical Narrative: Ideological Literature and the Drama of Reading* (Bloomington: Indiana University Press, 1987), 198. Sternberg sees the narrator's delay in providing the reader with the information about Bathsheba's menses as adding to the suspense of the story.

[26]The initial כִּי in clause 205 is taken here as an emphatic, or asseverative, כִּי (See the discussion in Waltke and O'Connor, *Syntax*, 665, especially the bibliographical references in note 81.) For the differences between the *Ketiv* and *Qere* in clause 208, see Driver, *Notes*, 291 and Gesenius, *Grammar*, §75rr.

[27]S. R. Driver (*Notes on the Hebrew Text and the Topography of the Books of Samuel* [2d ed. Oxford: Clarendon, 1960], 289) analyses clause 162 as an instance of (unmarked) Interrogative Discourse: "וַאֲנִי אָבוֹא אֶל בֵּיתִי = 'and shall *I* enter into my house?' etc., the juxtaposition of two incongruous ideas, aided by the tone in which the

ED
11.11.160 הָאָרוֹן וְיִשְׂרָאֵל וִיהוּדָה יֹשְׁבִים בַּסֻּכּוֹת
11.11.161 וַאדֹנִי יוֹאָב וְעַבְדֵי אֲדֹנִי־עַל־פְּנֵי הַשָּׂדֶה חֹנִים
PD
11.11.162 וַאֲנִי אָבוֹא אֶל־בֵּיתִי לֶאֱכֹל וְלִשְׁתּוֹת וְלִשְׁכַּב עִם־אִשְׁתִּי

The second is simply the instruction for the messenger to provide the following encouraging message to Joab, and consists of a single *YIQTOL* clause:

11.25.212 כֹּה־תֹאמַר אֶל־יוֹאָב

The remaining example consists of a string of *WeQATAL* clauses (191, 192, 199). In it, Joab outlines the message that the courier will later repeat (somewhat) to David. The series is completely expected and consistent with Predictive Discourse elsewhere.

Expository Discourse

The three examples of Expository Discourse in 2 Samuel 11 consist of either a single instance of a verbless clause (141), a collection of two participial clauses (160-161), or an incomplete clause (163), used as an oath. All three cases are consistent with Expository Discourse in general.

Interrogative Discourse

There are three examples of Interrogative Discourse in 2 Samuel 11. In the first two cases, the clauses within the speeches are marked explicitly with interrogative particles, either הֲלוֹא (130,157) or מַדּוּעַ (158). The third example of Interrogative Discourse is a long string of rhetorical questions, consisting of Joab's supposed response by David to the news of Uriah's death:

---

words are pronounced, betokening surprise, and so suggesting a question." The tone of the speaker, of course, has been lost and is nowhere designated by the text. The simple syntax of the verb defines the clause as predictive, while, perhaps, incongruous with the preceding Expository Discourse. The incongruity, however, is not explicitly present either in the syntax or the "tone of the speaker" but by the immediately following oath formula in the speech. The clause in its present form and context probably implies Uriah's use of irony, a rhetorical device rarely acknowledged by biblical scholars.

†ID

11.20.193 מַדּוּעַ נִגַּשְׁתֶּם אֶל־הָעִיר לְהִלָּחֵם

11.20.194 הֲלוֹא יְדַעְתֶּם אֵת אֲשֶׁר־יֹרוּ מֵעַל הַחוֹמָה:

11.21.195 מִי־הִכָּה אֶת־אֲבִימֶלֶךְ בֶּן־יְרֻבֶּשֶׁת

11.21.196 הֲלוֹא־אִשָּׁה הִשְׁלִיכָה עָלָיו פֶּלַח רֶכֶב מֵעַל הַחוֹמָה

11.21.197 וַיָּמָת בְּתֵבֵץ

11.21.198 לָמָּה נִגַּשְׁתֶּם אֶל־הַחוֹמָה

All clauses are explicitly marked as interrogative with prefixed interrogative particles, with the single exception of clause 197. The *WAYYIQTOL* clause here remains interrogative in spite of the absence of any particle. The verb וַיָּמָת is paralleled with the preceding *QATAL* verb הִשְׁלִיכָה, thus tying the two clauses together. The particle הֲלוֹא initiating clause 196, therefore, governs the text-type of clause 197, making it interrogative also. The sense of the two clauses is, "Didn't a woman throw...? And (didn't) he die...?"

Hortatory Discourse

Five examples of Hortatory Discourse occur within 2 Samuel 11. Four of the five examples have imperative clauses as the first clause in the discourse. The fifth example, clauses 213-216, begins with an אַל־ negative particle pre-fixed to a *YIQTOL* verbal form (יֵרַע). The hortatory nature of clause 213 is, therefore, dependent upon the prefixed hortatory particle and upon the following three imperative clauses following it (214-216).

Table of Discourse Constellations for 2 Samuel 11

		Present Ch.	Prev. Chs.	Total
ND	*QATAL*	2	28	30
	QATAL, WAYYIQTOL	1	8	9
	QATAL, (Ptc./Vbl.)		8	8
	QATAL, WAYYIQTOL, (Ptc./Vbl.)		4	4
	QATAL, WAYYIQTOL, (Ptc./Vbl.), *YIQTOL*		2	2
	QATAL, YIQTOL (w/ past adverb)		0	0
	WAYYIQTOL, (Ptc./Vbl.)		0	0
	Vbl/Ptc/Inc (Dream Report)		1	1
PD	*YIQTOL*	2	15	17
	YIQTOL, WeQATAL		10	10
	YIQTOL, WeQATAL, (Ptc./Vbl../Inc.)		1	1
	YIQTOL, (Ptc./Vbl../Inc.)		0	0
	WeQATAL	1	6	7
	WeYIQTOL		2	2
ED	Ptc./Vbl.	2	29	31
	Ptc./ Vbl., Inc.		1	1
	Inc.	1	9	10
	Ptc./Vbl., *QATAL/YIQTOL* of היה		3	3
	Ptc./Vbl., *QATAL/YIQTOL* of היה, Front. Obj.+ *QATAL/YIQTOL*		2	2
	QATAL/YIQTOL of היה		1	1
HD	Impv./Coh./Juss.	2	26	28
	Impv./Coh./Juss., *WeYIQTOL/YIQTOL*	1	11	12
	Impv./Coh./Juss., *WeQATAL*	1	4	5
	Impv./Coh./Juss., *WeYIQTOL/YIQTOL, WeQATAL*		6	6
	Impv./Coh./Juss., *QATAL*		1	1
	Impv./Coh./Juss., *WeYIQTOL/YIQTOL*, (*We*)*QATAL*		1	1
	Impv./Coh./Juss., ʾal-*YIQTOL*	1	2	3
	Impv./Coh./Juss., *WeQATAL*, ʾal-*YIQTOL*		2	2
	ʾal-*YIQTOL*		7	7
	ʾal-*YIQTOL, WeQATAL/YIQTOL*		0	0
	(*We*)*YIQTOL-nāʾ*, (*WeQATAL/*[*We*]*YIQTOL*)		0	0
	QATAL, YIQTOL/WeQATAL		1	1

2 Samuel 12 — Nathan's Judgment: Internal Violence and Violation— Clauses 225-354

Text in Syntactical/Paragraph Units

Joab Kills Uriah and God Punishes David (Cont.)

12.01.225	וַיְצַ֤ו אֶת־הַמַּלְאָךְ֙ לֵאמֹ֔ר
12.01.226	כְּכַלּוֹתְךָ֗
12.01.227	וַיֹּ֣אמֶר לֹ֔ו
12.01.228	ND
12.01.228	אֵ֣ת כָּל־אֲשֶׁ֣ר יַעֲנֶ֣ה אֹתְךָ֗ הַמֶּ֙לֶךְ֙ וְהָיָ֗ה
12.01.229	אַ֚ף עָלֹ֔ו
12.01.230	וַיֵּ֖לֶךְ הַמַּלְאָ֑ךְ
12.02.231	וַיָּבֹ֖א
12.03.232	וַיַּגֵּ֣ד לְדָוִ֔ד אֵ֛ת כָּל־אֲשֶׁ֥ר שְׁלָחֹ֖ו יוֹאָ֑ב
12.03.233	וַיֹּ֤אמֶר
12.03.234	כִּֽי־גָבְר֤וּ עָלֵ֙ינוּ֙ הָֽאֲנָשִׁ֔ים
12.03.235	וַיֵּצְא֥וּ אֵלֵ֖ינוּ הַשָּׂדֶ֑ה
12.03.236	וַנִּהְיֶ֥ה עֲלֵיהֶ֖ם
12.03.237	עַד־פֶּ֥תַח הַשָּֽׁעַר׃
12.03.238	וַיֹּר֣וּ הַמּוֹרִ֗ים
12.04.239	אֶל־עֲבָדֶ֙ךָ֙ מֵעַ֣ל הַחֹומָ֔ה
12.04.240	וַיָּמ֖וּתוּ מֵעַבְדֵ֣י הַמֶּ֑לֶךְ
12.04.241	וְגַ֗ם עַבְדְּךָ֛ אוּרִיָּ֥ה הַחִתִּ֖י מֵֽת׃
12.04.242	וַיֹּ֨אמֶר הַמֶּ֜לֶךְ אֶל־הַמַּלְאָ֗ךְ

12.05.243 וַיִּחַר־אַף דָּוִד
12.05.244 בָּאִישׁ מְאֹד וַיֹּאמֶר אֶל־נָתָן

12.07.247 וַיֹּאמֶר נָתָן אֶל־דָּוִד

ED (Oath)
12.05.245 חַי־יְהוָה
PD
12.06.246 כִּי בֶן־מָוֶת הָאִישׁ הָעֹשֶׂה זֹאת׃ וְאֶת־הַכִּבְשָׂה יְשַׁלֵּם אַרְבַּעְתָּיִם

ED
12.07.248 אַתָּה הָאִישׁ
ND
12.07.249 כֹּה־אָמַר יְהוָה אֱלֹהֵי יִשְׂרָאֵל

12.07.250 אָנֹכִי מְשַׁחְתִּיךָ לְמֶלֶךְ עַל־יִשְׂרָאֵל
12.07.251 וְאָנֹכִי הִצַּלְתִּיךָ מִיַּד שָׁאוּל׃
12.08.252 וָאֶתְּנָה לְךָ אֶת־בֵּית אֲדֹנֶיךָ
†HD
12.08.253 וְאֶת־נְשֵׁי אֲדֹנֶיךָ בְּחֵיקֶךָ
254α
ID
12.08.254 וָאֶתְּנָה לְךָ אֶת־בֵּית יִשְׂרָאֵל וִיהוּדָה

12.09.255 מַדּוּעַ בָּזִיתָ אֶת־דְּבַר יְהוָה
ND
12.09.256 אֵת אוּרִיָּה הַחִתִּי הִכִּיתָ בַחֶרֶב
12.09.257 וְאֶת־אִשְׁתּוֹ לָקַחְתָּ לְּךָ לְאִשָּׁה

12.09.258 וְאֹתוֹ הָרַגְתָּ בְּחֶרֶב בְּנֵי עַמּוֹן:
PD

וְעַתָּה

12.10.259 לֹא־תָסוּר חֶרֶב מִבֵּיתְךָ עַד־עוֹלָם
ND

260α עֵקֶב כִּי בְזִתָנִי

260β |וַתִּקַּח אֶת־אֵשֶׁת אוּרִיָּה הַחִתִּי
|לִהְיוֹת לְךָ לְאִשָּׁה:

12.11.260 כֹּה ׀ אָמַר יְהוָה
†PD

†הִנְנִי

12.11.261 †מֵקִים עָלֶיךָ רָעָה מִבֵּיתֶךָ

12.11.262 †וְלָקַחְתִּי אֶת־נָשֶׁיךָ לְעֵינֶיךָ

12.11.263 †וְנָתַתִּי לְרֵעֶיךָ

12.11.264 †וְשָׁכַב עִם־נָשֶׁיךָ לְעֵינֵי
†|הַשֶּׁמֶשׁ הַזֹּאת:

265α †|כִּי אַתָּה עָשִׂיתָ בַסָּתֶר

12.12.265 †|וַאֲנִי אֶעֱשֶׂה אֶת־הַדָּבָר הַזֶּה
†|נֶגֶד כָּל־יִשְׂרָאֵל וְנֶגֶד הַשָּׁמֶשׁ:

12.13.266 וַיֹּאמֶר דָּוִד אֶל־נָתָן

ND

12.13.267 חָטָאתִי לַיהוָה

12.13.268 וַיֹּאמֶר נָתָן אֶל־דָּוִד

ND

12.13.269 גַּם־יְהוָה הֶעֱבִיר חַטָּאתְךָ
PD

12.13.270 לֹא תָמוּת:

271α |אֶפֶס

271β |כִּי־נִאֵץ נִאַצְתָּ אֶת־אֹיְבֵי יְהוָה

וַיֵּלֶךְ נָתָן אֶל־בֵּיתוֹ 12.15.272
וַיִּגֹּף יְהוָה אֶת־הַיֶּלֶד 12.15.273

אֲשֶׁר 12.15.274
יָלְדָה אֵשֶׁת־אוּרִיָּה לְדָוִד 12.16.275
וַיֵּאָנַשׁ: 12.16.276

וַיְבַקֵּשׁ דָּוִד 12.16.277

David's Intercessory Ritual (Comment)

וַיָּצֶם 12.16.277
צוֹם 12.16.278
[וּ] 12.16.279
[וּבָא] 12.17.280
וְלָן 12.17.281
וְשָׁכַב אָרְצָה: 12.17.282

The Son Dies and David Does Not Mourn

וַיָּקֻמוּ זִקְנֵי בֵיתוֹ עָלָיו 12.18.283
לַהֲקִימוֹ 12.18.284
וְלֹא אָבָה 12.18.285

וַיֹּאמֶר

ND

וַיְהִי בַּיּוֹם הַשְּׁבִיעִי וַיָּמָת הַיָּלֶד: 12.14.271

12.19.291

12.19.292

12.19.293

12.19.295

12.20.297
12.20.298
12.20.299
12.20.300
12.20.301
12.20.302
12.20.303
12.20.304
12.20.305

286α

12.18.286
12.18.287
ID
12.18.288
†ND
12.18.289
12.18.290

ID
12.19.294

ND
12.19.296

וַיֵּלֶךְ דָּוִד אֶל־בֵּיתוֹ 12.20.306
וַיֹּאמְרוּ 12.21.307

וַיֹּאמֶר 12.22.313

ID
וְעַתָּה מֵת 12.21.308
ND
אֵלָיו עֲבָדָיו
[הַדָּבָר הַזֶּה] 309α
אֲשֶׁר 12.21.309
עָשִׂיתָ 12.21.310
311α
בַּעֲבוּר הַיֶּלֶד חַי 12.21.311
צַמְתָּ 12.21.312
וַתֵּבְךְּ לָמָּה:

ND
[וּבְעוֹד הַיֶּלֶד חַי] 314α
צַמְתִּי 12.22.314
וָאֶבְכֶּה 12.22.315

בְּעוֹד הַיֶּלֶד חַי 12.22.316 †ID
†PD
מִי יוֹדֵעַ [וַחֲנַנִי Q] יְהֹוָה 12.22.317
וְחַי הַיָּלֶד: 12.22.318

וְעַתָּה מֵת 12.23.319 ID
לָמָּה זֶּה אֲנִי צָם 12.23.320
הַאוּכַל לַהֲשִׁיבוֹ עוֹד 12.23.321

וַיְנַחֵם דָּוִד אֵת בַּת־שֶׁבַע אִשְׁתּוֹ	12.24.324
וַיָּבֹא אֵלֶיהָ	12.24.325
וַיִּשְׁכַּב עִמָּהּ	12.24.326
וַתֵּלֶד בֵּן	12.24.327
וַיִּקְרָא אֶת־שְׁמוֹ [שְׁלֹמֹה Q] שׁלמה	12.24.328

A Son is Named and a City is Taken

וַיהוָה אֲהֵבוֹ:	12.24.329
וַיִּשְׁלַח בְּיַד נָתָן הַנָּבִיא	12.25.330
וַיִּקְרָא אֶת־שְׁמוֹ יְדִידְיָהּ בַּעֲבוּר יְהוָה:	12.25.331
וַיִּלָּחֶם יוֹאָב בְּרַבַּת בְּנֵי עַמּוֹן	12.26.332
וַיִּלְכֹּד אֶת־עִיר הַמְּלוּכָה:	12.26.333
וַיִּשְׁלַח יוֹאָב מַלְאָכִים אֶל־דָּוִד	12.27.334
וַיֹּאמֶר	12.27.335

PD

אֲנִי הֹלֵךְ אֵלָיו	12.23.322
וְהוּא לֹא־יָשׁוּב אֵלָי:	12.23.323

ND

נִלְחַמְתִּי בְרַבָּה	12.27.336
גַּם־לָכַדְתִּי אֶת־עִיר הַמָּיִם:	12.27.337

HD

וְעַתָּה אֱסֹף אֶת־יֶתֶר הָעָם	12.28.338
וַחֲנֵה עַל־הָעִיר	12.28.339
וְלָכְדָהּ פֶּן־אֶלְכֹּד אֲנִי אֶת־הָעִיר וְנִקְרָא שְׁמִי עָלֶיהָ:	12.28.340

David's Policy with the Ammonites (Comment)

12.29.341	וַיֶּאֱסֹף דָּוִד אֶת־כָּל־הָעָם
12.29.342	וַיֵּלֶךְ רַבָּתָה
12.29.343	וַיִּלָּחֶם בָּהּ
12.29.344	וַיִּלְכְּדָהּ
12.30.345	וַיִּקַּח אֶת־עֲטֶרֶת־מַלְכָּם מֵעַל רֹאשׁוֹ
12.30.346	וּמִשְׁקָלָהּ כִּכַּר זָהָב וְאֶבֶן יְקָרָה
12.30.347	(וַתְּהִי עַל־רֹאשׁ דָּוִד)
12.30.348	וּשְׁלַל הָעִיר
12.30.349	הוֹצִיא הַרְבֵּה מְאֹד
—	—
12.31.350	וְאֶת־הָעָם אֲשֶׁר־בָּהּ הוֹצִיא
12.31.351	וַיָּשֶׂם בַּמְּגֵרָה וּבַחֲרִצֵי הַבַּרְזֶל וּבְמַגְזְרֹת הַבַּרְזֶל
12.31.352	וְהֶעֱבִיר אוֹתָם בַּמַּלְכֵּן [בַּמַּלְבֵּן Q]
12.31.353	וְכֵן יַעֲשֶׂה לְכֹל עָרֵי בְנֵי־עַמּוֹן
12.31.354	וַיָּשָׁב דָּוִד וְכָל־הָעָם יְרוּשָׁלָ͏ִם

Table of Independent Clause Types in 2 Samuel 12

Clause Type	Clause Distribution	Total	Percent
QAṬAL Total Clauses: 28	Narrative: 281,282,329,349,350	5	17.9%
	ND: 228,231,249,†250,†251,256,257,258,260,267, 269,286,287,†289,296,309,311,314,319,336,337	21	75.0%
	PD:		
	ED:		
	ID: 255,294	2	7.1%
	HD:		
WeQAṬAL Total Clauses: 8	Narrative: 277,278,279,352	4	50.0%
	ND:		
	PD: 262,263,264	3	37.5%
	ED:		
	ID: 290	1	12.5%
	HD:		
YIQṬOL Total Clauses: 12	Narrative: 353	1	8.3%
	ND: 235,236,237	3	25.0%
	PD: 246,259,265,270,271,321	6	50.0%
	ED:		
	ID: 288,317	2	16.7%
	HD:		
WeYIQṬOL Total Clauses: 0	Narrative:	0	0
	ND:		
	PD:		
	ED:	0	0
	ID:		
	HD:		
WAYYIQṬOL Total Clauses: 64	Narrative: 225,226,227,243,244,247,266,268,272, 273,274,275,276,280,283,284,285,291,292,293,295, 297,298,299,300,301,302,303,304,305,306,307,313, 324,325,326,327,328,330,331,332,333,334,335,341, 342,343,344,345,348,351,354	52	81.3%
	ND: 233,234,238,239,240,241,242,252,253,310, 312,315	12	18.7%
	PD:		
	ED:		
	ID:		
	HD:		

Participle	Narrative:	0	0
	ND:		
	PD: 261,320,322,323	4	80.0%
Total Clauses: 5	ED:		
	ID: 316	1	20.0%
	HD:		
Verbless	Narrative: 346,347	2	25.0%
	ND: 229,230,232	3	37.5%
	PD:		
Total Clauses: 8	ED: 248	1	12.5%
	ID: 308,318	2	25.0%
	HD:		
Incomplete	Narrative:	0	0
	ND:		
	PD:		
Total Clauses: 1	ED: 245	1	100%
	ID:		
	HD:		
Imperative	Narrative:	0	0
Total Clauses: 3	HD: 338,339,340	3	100%
Cohortative	Narrative:	0	0
Total Clauses: 1	HD: 254	1	100%
Jussive	Narrative:	0	0
Total Clauses: 0	HD:	0	0

Analysis of the Narrative Structure and
Discourse Text-Types in 2 Samuel 12

Narrative Structural Analysis

Narrative/Paragraph Structure

The narrative contained within 2 Samuel 12 is composed of three paragraphs, the first of which is a continuation of the final paragraph of the previous
chapter, "Joab Kills Uriah and God Punishes David." The *WAYYIQTOL* clause
that introduces the chapter, וַיִּשְׁלַח יְהוָה אֶת־נָתָן אֶל־דָּוִד, continues the narrative
syntactic progression from the previous sentence without any disjunction. The
beginning of the paragraph stands, therefore, back in 2 Samuel 11 at clause 182.
The end of this continued paragraph is marked externally by the chain of non-
WAYYIQTOL clauses which comprise an extra-paragraph comment about
David's intercessory ritual in clauses 277-282. The beginning of the second
paragraph is marked by the initial וַיְהִי temporal clause 283, and is terminally
marked by the initial *QATAL* clause of the next paragraph, clause 329, אָהֲבוּ
וַיהוָה. The third paragraph is terminally marked by a final *QATAL* clause (349).
The chapter ends with an extra-paragraph comment concerning David's social
policies with the defeated Ammonites (clauses 350-354).

Extra-Paragraph Comments

The two extra-paragraph comments within 2 Samuel 12 are both explicitly
marked by the absence of any *WAYYIQTOL* chain, the usual sequential form
found within the larger narrative. The first comment concerns David's actions
while interceding for his ill son.

12.16.277	וּבָא
12.16.278	וְלָן
12.16.279	וְשָׁכַב אָרְצָה:
12.17.280	וַיָּקֻמוּ זִקְנֵי בֵיתוֹ עָלָיו לַהֲקִימוֹ מִן־הָאָרֶץ
12.17.281	וְלֹא אָבָה
12.17.282	וְלֹא־בָרָא אִתָּם לָחֶם:

While one *WAYYIQTOL* clause does appear within the comment (280), it is
bounded on either side by multiple non-*WAYYIQTOL* clauses, either *WeQATAL*
clauses (277-279) or *QATAL* clauses (281-282). In either case, the two *QATAL*
clauses which follow the *WAYYIQTOL* clause clearly do not imply a noncon-
tinuous "perfected" action that is not accounted for in the *WeQATAL* clauses

which precede the single *WAYYIQTOL* clause. The comment, taken as a whole, describes an ongoing, repetitious, nonlinear series of actions that occur between the narrative of the first paragraph and the narrative of the second paragraph, during the seven days noted in clause 283.[28] While it is difficult in this particular passage to ascertain, it seems as if the *WAYYIQTOL* verbal form may be seen as a single occurrence within this general repetitive description. *WAYYIQTOL* verbal forms in extra-paragraph comments, therefore, share the characteristic of *WAYYIQTOL* verbal forms in narrative, in that they relate the happening of a single action. Within extra-paragraph comments, however, the isolated *WAYYIQTOL* verbal form simply relates this single active occurrence rather than having the more fluid, sequential aspect that it conveys in narrative.

The second extra-paragraph comment concerns the tasks to which David placed the defeated Ammonites. Here, the two instances of *WAYYIQTOL* verbal forms in this comment, likewise, relate single instances of actions within a description of more general, nonsequential, ongoing activities:

12.31.350 וְאֶת־הָעָם אֲשֶׁר־בָּהּ הוֹצִיא

12.31.351 וַיָּשֶׂם בַּמְּגֵרָה וּבַחֲרִצֵי הַבַּרְזֶל וּבְמַגְזְרֹת הַבַּרְזֶל

12.31.352 וְהֶעֱבִיר אוֹתָם בַּמַּלְכֵּן [Q בַּמַּלְבֵּן]

12.31.353 וְכֵן יַעֲשֶׂה לְכֹל עָרֵי בְנֵי־עַמּוֹן

12.31.354 וַיָּשָׁב דָּוִד וְכָל־הָעָם יְרוּשָׁלָ͏ם:

Within the general activities of bringing the Ammonites out of their cities and transplanting them to Malken (or Malben or brickkilns),[29] David assigns them to certain manual labors and returns to Jerusalem. The comment does not provide a sequential statement of David's activities. Instead, the piling up of *QATAL*, *WeQATAL*, and *YIQTOL* clauses within the narrative implies a static description of activities rather than an ongoing narrative. The two *WAYYIQTOL* clauses relate specific actions which David performed within this general description.

---

[28]Driver (*Notes*, 292) remarks that, in v. 16, "the series of perfects with *waw* conv., indicate that David acted as here described repeatedly." Driver, however, does not address the double *QATAL* sequence in the following verse following the *WAYYIQTOL* clause 280. The whole of clauses 277-282 appear to be ongoing and not sequential in the narrative, with the single occurrence of the action in clause 280 happening within the general description. Moreover, Gesenius (*Grammar*, §107e), cites 12:3 as an example of the "imperfect" being used "to express actions, etc., which were *repeated* in the past, either at fixed intervals or occasionally (the *modus rei repetitae*)." He does not, however, note the instance in 12:31 (clause 353) and the example he does cite from 13:18 occurs in a dependent clause and, therefore, does not exactly parallel most of his other examples.

[29]For an extended discussion of the etymology of this place name, see Driver, *Notes*, 294-97. H. W. Hertzberg (*1 & 2 Samuel* [OTL; Philadelphia: Westminster, 1964], 318-20) seems to assume the reading "brickkilns", argued for by Driver.

Inner-Paragraph Comments

Only one inner-paragraph comment occurs within 2 Samuel 12 and is composed of verbless clauses and an instance of היה used as a true verbal form:

12.30.346 וּמִשְׁקָלָהּ כִּכַּר זָהָב
12.30.347 וְאֶבֶן יְקָרָה
12.30.348 וַתְּהִי עַל־רֹאשׁ דָּוִד

As such, the comment stands within the last paragraph of the chapter and relates information off-line from the surrounding narrative but dealing with information directly related to the paragraph.

Discourse Function Analysis

Narrative Discourse

Within 2 Samuel 12, thirteen instances of Narrative Discourse occur. Of these thirteen examples in which a character relates events that occurred in the past, twelve are entirely regular for this text-type, employing either *QATAL* clauses alone or in conjunction with *WAYYIQTOL* clauses. In one case, Nathan's "Case of the Little Ewe Lamb," the usual *QATAL* and *WAYYIQTOL* clauses are supplemented by three verbless clauses (229-230,232) and a series of three *YIQTOL* clauses (235-237):

12.01.228 שְׁנֵי אֲנָשִׁים הָיוּ בְּעִיר אֶחָת
12.01.229 אֶחָד עָשִׁיר
12.01.230 וְאֶחָד רָאשׁ:
12.02.231 לְעָשִׁיר הָיָה צֹאן וּבָקָר הַרְבֵּה מְאֹד:
12.03.232 וְלָרָשׁ אֵין־כֹּל
כִּי אִם־כִּבְשָׂה אַחַת קְטַנָּה
אֲשֶׁר קָנָה
12.03.233 וַיְחַיֶּהָ
12.03.234 וַתִּגְדַּל עִמּוֹ וְעִם־בָּנָיו יַחְדָּו
12.03.235 מִפִּתּוֹ תֹאכַל
12.03.236 וּמִכֹּסוֹ תִשְׁתֶּה
12.03.237 וּבְחֵיקוֹ תִשְׁכָּב
12.03.238 וַתְּהִי־לוֹ כְּבַת:
12.04.239 וַיָּבֹא הֵלֶךְ לְאִישׁ הֶעָשִׁיר
12.04.240 וַיַּחְמֹל לָקַחַת מִצֹּאנוֹ וּמִבְּקָרוֹ לַעֲשׂוֹת לָאֹרֵחַ הַבָּא־לוֹ
12.04.241 וַיִּקַּח אֶת־כִּבְשַׂת הָאִישׁ הָרָאשׁ
12.04.242 וַיַּעֲשֶׂהָ לָאִישׁ הַבָּא אֵלָיו:

The verbless clauses in this discourse (229, 230, 232) clearly function in the same way that inner-paragraph clauses function within narrative in general. They provide off-line information about the status of characters or settings within the narrative sequence of the story. The three-fold chain of *YIQTOL* clauses (235-237), on the other hand, function similar to extra-paragraph comments within narrative—they report repetitive, nonsequential (and, therefore, nonnarrative) actions or states of characters further removed from the larger story.[30] The three *YIQTOL* clauses above outline the usual daily activities which the poor man performs with the ewe lamb. The final clause (238) following the sequence, וַתְּהִי־לוֹ כְּבַת, is governed by the verb היה, and, therefore, serves the same purpose as inner-paragraph comments in narrative, providing static information off-line of the larger story.

Predictive Discourse

Within 2 Samuel 12, six cases of Predictive Discourse occur. All six cases are completely regular, employing *YIQTOL* and *WeQATAL* clauses as the backbone of the discourse. Among these six cases, two examples (clauses 261-265, 322-333) also employ single participial clauses within the speech. These cases of participial usage within Predictive Discourse are similar to the function of participles within Narrative Discourse, that is, to provide information alongside the report but not temporally set within the sequential frame of the report.

Expository Discourse

The two cases of Expository Discourse within 2 Samuel 12 are entirely regular for this text-type. One case, Nathan's accusation of David (clause 248), אַתָּה הָאִישׁ, is a verbless clause, and the other, David's oath of condemnation following Nathan's parable (clause 245), חַי־יְהוָה כִּי בֶן־מָוֶת הָאִישׁ הָעֹשֶׂה זֹאת, is an incomplete clause.

Interrogative Discourse

Most of the clauses comprising the five cases of Interrogative Discourse within 2 Samuel 12 are explicitly marked with interrogative particles: מַדּוּעַ (255), אֵיךְ (288), הֲ (294, 321), מָה (308), מִי (†316), לָמָּה (320). The case of clauses 288-290 includes an unmarked question:

12.18.288 וְאֵיךְ נֹאמַר אֵלָיו

---

[30]Thus Driver, *Notes*, 291: "The impff. expressing significantly its *habit*."

†ND

12.18.289 ‏תֵּמֶת הַיֶּלֶד†‏

12.18.290 ‏וְעָשָׂה רָעָה:‏

The sense of clause 290 parallels that in clause 288; the particle ‏וְאֵיךְ‏ governs both clauses, although the change in subject in the second clause makes any literal translation difficult.[31] Apart from this clear and unambiguous exception, all other cases are entirely regular for the text-type of Interrogative Discourse.

Hortatory Discourse

Both cases of Hortatory Discourse in 2 Samuel 12 are entirely regular for this text-type. The first example, clause 254, employs a cohortative clause; the second example, clauses 338-340, employs a three-fold series of imperative clauses. Note should also be made in this final example that the Hortatory Discourse is explicitly separated from the Narrative Discourse immediately preceding it by the disjunctive particle ‏וְעַתָּה‏.

---

[31]Driver, *Tenses*, 156.

Table of Discourse Constellations for 2 Samuel 12

		Present Ch.	Prev. Chs.	Total
ND	*QATAL*	9	30	39
	QATAL, WAYYIQTOL	3	9	12
	QATAL, (Ptc./Vbl.)		8	8
	QATAL, WAYYIQTOL, (Ptc./Vbl.)		4	4
	QATAL, WAYYIQTOL, (Ptc./Vbl.), *YIQTOL*	1	2	3
	QATAL, YIQTOL (w/ past adverb)		0	0
	WAYYIQTOL, (Ptc./Vbl.)		0	0
	Vbl/Ptc/Inc (Dream Report)		1	1
PD	*YIQTOL*	3	17	20
	YIQTOL, WeQATAL		10	10
	YIQTOL, WeQATAL, (Ptc./Vbl../Inc.)	1	1	2
	YIQTOL, (Ptc./Vbl../Inc.)	2	0	2
	WeQATAL		7	7
	WeYIQTOL		2	2
ED	Ptc./Vbl.	1	31	32
	Ptc./ Vbl., Inc.		1	1
	Inc.	1	10	11
	Ptc./Vbl., *QATAL/YIQTOL* of היה		3	3
	Ptc./Vbl., *QATAL/YIQTOL* of היה, Front. Obj.+ *QATAL/YIQTOL*		2	2
	QATAL/YIQTOL of היה		1	1
HD	Impv./Coh./Juss.	1	28	29
	Impv./Coh./Juss., *WeYIQTOL/YIQTOL*		12	12
	Impv./Coh./Juss., *WeQATAL*		5	5
	Impv./Coh./Juss., *WeYIQTOL/YIQTOL, WeQATAL*		6	6
	Impv./Coh./Juss., *QATAL*		1	1
	Impv./Coh./Juss., *WeYIQTOL/YIQTOL*, (We)QATAL		1	1
	Impv./Coh./Juss., *ʾal-YIQTOL*		3	3
	Impv./Coh./Juss., *WeQATAL, ʾal-YIQTOL*		2	2
	ʾal-YIQTOL		7	7
	ʾal-YIQTOL, WeQATAL/YIQTOL		0	0
	(We)*YIQTOL-nāʾ*, (*WeQATAL*/[*We*]*YIQTOL*)		0	0
	QATAL, YIQTOL/WeQATAL		1	1

2 Samuel 13 — Amnon's Rape of Tamar and Its Consequences — Clauses 355–516

Text in Syntactical/Paragraph Units

Amnon Rapes His Half-sister Tamar

13.01.355		וַיַּחֲזֶק־בָּהּ
13.01.356		וַיֹּאמֶר לָהּ אֲחוֹתִי (בּוֹאִי שִׁכְבִי עִמִּי)
13.01.357		(בּוֹאִי) שִׁכְבִי
13.01.358		וַתֹּאמֶר לוֹ
13.02.359		אַל־אָחִי
13.02.360		אַל־תְּעַנֵּנִי כִּי לֹא־יֵעָשֶׂה כֵן בְּיִשְׂרָאֵל
13.03.361		אַל־תַּעֲשֵׂה אֶת־הַנְּבָלָה הַזֹּאת׃
13.03.362		וַאֲנִי אָנָה אוֹלִיךְ אֶת־חֶרְפָּתִי
13.03.363		(וְאַתָּה תִּהְיֶה כְּאַחַד הַנְּבָלִים בְּיִשְׂרָאֵל)
13.04.364		וְעַתָּה דַּבֶּר־נָא אֶל־הַמֶּלֶךְ׃
13.04.365	ID	כִּי לֹא יִמְנָעֵנִי מִמֶּךָּ ... וְאַתָּה תִּהְיֶה כְּאַחַד הַנְּבָלִים
13.04.366	ID	(וְעַתָּה דַּבֶּר־נָא) אֶל־הַמֶּלֶךְ
13.03.367		וַיֹּאמֶר לָהּ אֲחוֹתִי
13.03.368	ED	וְלֹא אָבָה לִשְׁמֹעַ בְּקוֹלָהּ ... אֶל־הַמֶּלֶךְ
13.05.369		וַיֶּחֱזַק מִמֶּנָּה
13.05.370	HD	וַיְעַנֶּהָ
13.05.371	HD	וַיִּשְׁכַּב אֹתָהּ׃

13.08.388	וַתֹּאמֶר לוֹ אֲחוֹתוֹ תָמָר
13.08.389	אַל־אָחִי אַל־תְּעַנֵּנִי
13.08.390	כִּי לֹא־יֵעָשֶׂה כֵן בְּיִשְׂרָאֵל
13.08.391	אַל־תַּעֲשֵׂה אֶת־הַנְּבָלָה הַזֹּאת
13.08.392	וַאֲנִי אָנָה אוֹלִיךְ אֶת־חֶרְפָּתִי
13.08.393	וְאַתָּה תִּהְיֶה כְּאַחַד הַנְּבָלִים בְּיִשְׂרָאֵל

13.07.385	וְעַתָּה דַּבֶּר־נָא אֶל־הַמֶּלֶךְ

13.06.378	וַיֹּאמֶר לָהּ אַמְנוֹן
13.06.379	בּוֹאִי שִׁכְבִי עִמִּי
13.06.380	אֲחוֹתִי
13.06.381	וַתֹּאמֶר לוֹ

PD

13.05.372	וַיֹּאמֶר לְאַמְנוֹן
13.05.373	וַיֹּאמֶר אֵלָיו

tHD

13.05.374	מַדּוּעַ אַתָּה כָּכָה
13.05.375	דַּל בֶּן־הַמֶּלֶךְ
13.05.376	בַּבֹּקֶר בַּבֹּקֶר
13.05.377	הֲלוֹא תַּגִּיד לִי

HD

13.06.382	וַיֹּאמֶר לוֹ אַמְנוֹן
13.06.383	אֶת־תָּמָר אֲחוֹת אַבְשָׁלֹם
13.06.384	אֲנִי אֹהֵב

HD

13.07.386	כִּי לֹא יִמְנָעֵנִי מִמֶּךָּ
13.07.387	וַיֹּאמֶר אֵלָיו יְהוֹנָדָב

13.09.394 וַיֹּאמֶר אֵלָיו אֲדֹנָי
13.09.395 וַיֹּאמֶר אֵלָיו
13.09.396 וַיֹּאמֶר אֵלָיו
13.09.397 וַיֹּאמֶר אֵלָיו

13.09.398 HD

13.09.399 וַיֹּאמֶר אֵלָיו
13.10.400 וַיֹּאמֶר אֵלָיו

13.10.401
13.10.402 HD

13.10.403 וַיֹּאמֶר אֵלָיו
13.10.404 וַיֹּאמֶר אֵלָיו

13.11.405
13.11.406
13.11.407

13.11.408
13.11.409 HD

13.12.410 וַיֹּאמֶר

13.12.411
13.12.412 HD

13.12.413

13.13.414 ID

13.13.415		PD
	אֶל־אָנָה אוֹלִיךְ אֶת־חֶרְפָּתִי וְאַתָּה תִּהְיֶה כְּאַחַד הַנְּבָלִים בְּיִשְׂרָאֵל	
13.13.416		HD
	וְעַתָּה דַּבֶּר־נָא אֶל־הַמֶּלֶךְ כִּי לֹא יִמְנָעֵנִי מִמֶּךָּ	
13.14.417	וְלֹא אָבָה	
13.14.418	לִשְׁמֹעַ בְּקוֹלָהּ	
13.14.419	וַיֶּחֱזַק מִמֶּנָּה	
13.14.420	וַיְעַנֶּהָ	
13.14.421	וַיִּשְׁכַּב אֹתָהּ	
13.15.422	וַיִּשְׂנָאֶהָ אַמְנוֹן (שִׂנְאָה גְּדוֹלָה מְאֹד כִּי גְדוֹלָה הַשִּׂנְאָה אֲשֶׁר שְׂנֵאָהּ מֵאַהֲבָה אֲשֶׁר אֲהֵבָהּ)	
13.15.423		HD
	קוּמִי	
13.15.424	לֵכִי:	
13.16.425	וַתֹּאמֶר לוֹ	
13.16.426		ED (?)
	אַל־אוֹדֹת הָרָעָה הַגְּדוֹלָה הַזֹּאת מֵאַחֶרֶת אֲשֶׁר־עָשִׂיתָ עִמִּי לְשַׁלְּחֵנִי	
13.16.427	וְלֹא אָבָה לִשְׁמֹעַ לָהּ:	
13.17.428	וַיִּקְרָא אֶת־נַעֲרוֹ מְשָׁרְתוֹ	
13.17.429	וַיֹּאמֶר	
13.17.430		HD
	שִׁלְחוּ־נָא אֶת־זֹאת מֵעָלַי הַחוּצָה	
13.17.431	וּנְעֹל הַדֶּלֶת אַחֲרֶיהָ:	
13.18.432	(וְעָלֶיהָ כְּתֹנֶת פַּסִּים) כִּי כֵן תִּלְבַּשְׁןָ בְנוֹת־הַמֶּלֶךְ הַבְּתוּלֹת מְעִילִים	

וַיֹּצֵא אוֹתָהּ מְשָׁרְתוֹ הַחוּץ   13.18.433
וְנָעַל הַדֶּלֶת אַחֲרֶיהָ׃   13.18.434

Tamar Mourns and Absalom Advises

וַתִּקַּח תָּמָר אֵפֶר עַל־רֹאשָׁהּ   13.19.435
וּכְתֹנֶת הַפַּסִּים אֲשֶׁר עָלֶיהָ קָרָעָה (קָרָעָה)   13.19.436
וַתָּשֶׂם יָדָהּ עַל־רֹאשָׁהּ   13.19.437
וַתֵּלֶךְ הָלוֹךְ וְזָעָקָה   13.19.438
וַיֹּאמֶר אֵלֶיהָ אַבְשָׁלוֹם אָחִיהָ   13.20.439

הַאֲמִינוֹן אָחִיךְ הָיָה עִמָּךְ   13.20.440   ID
וְעַתָּה אֲחוֹתִי הַחֲרִישִׁי   13.20.441   HD
אָחִיךְ הוּא   13.20.442   ED
אַל־תָּשִׁיתִי אֶת־לִבֵּךְ לַדָּבָר הַזֶּה   13.20.443   HD
וַתֵּשֶׁב תָּמָר וְשֹׁמֵמָה   13.20.444
(בֵּית אַבְשָׁלוֹם אָחִיהָ׃)   13.20.445

David's and Absalom's Responses to the Rape (Comment)

וְהַמֶּלֶךְ דָּוִד שָׁמַע אֵת כָּל־הַדְּבָרִים הָאֵלֶּה   13.21.446
וַיִּחַר לוֹ מְאֹד׃   13.21.447
וְלֹא־דִבֶּר אַבְשָׁלוֹם עִם־אַמְנוֹן לְמֵרָע וְעַד־טוֹב
כִּי־שָׂנֵא אַבְשָׁלוֹם אֶת־אַמְנוֹן
עַל־דְּבַר אֲשֶׁר עִנָּה אֵת תָּמָר אֲחֹתוֹ   13.22.448

Absalom Plots the Revenge upon His Half-brother Amnon

13.23.449 וַיְהִי לִשְׁנָתַיִם יָמִים
13.23.450 (וַיִּהְיוּ גֹזְזִים לְאַבְשָׁלוֹם בְּבַעַל חָצוֹר
אֲשֶׁר עִם־אֶפְרָיִם)
13.23.451 וַיִּקְרָא אַבְשָׁלוֹם לְכָל־בְּנֵי הַמֶּלֶךְ׃
13.24.452 וַיָּבֹא אַבְשָׁלוֹם אֶל־הַמֶּלֶךְ
13.24.453 וַיֹּאמֶר

HD

13.24.454 הִנֵּה־נָא
13.24.455 (גֹזְזִים לְעַבְדֶּךָ)
13.24.456 יֵלֶךְ־נָא הַמֶּלֶךְ וַעֲבָדָיו עִם־עַבְדֶּךָ׃

13.25.457 וַיֹּאמֶר הַמֶּלֶךְ אֶל־אַבְשָׁלוֹם

HD

13.25.458 אַל־בְּנִי
13.25.459 אַל־נָא נֵלֵךְ כֻּלָּנוּ
13.25.460 וְלֹא נִכְבַּד עָלֶיךָ

13.25.461 וַיִּפְרָץ־בּוֹ
13.25.462 וְלֹא־אָבָה לָלֶכֶת
13.25.463 וַיְבָרְכֵהוּ׃
13.26.464 וַיֹּאמֶר אַבְשָׁלוֹם

HD

13.26.465 וָלֹא
13.26.466 יֵלֶךְ־נָא אִתָּנוּ אַמְנוֹן אָחִי

13.26.467 וַיֹּאמֶר לוֹ הַמֶּלֶךְ

ID

13.26.468 לָמָּה יֵלֵךְ עִמָּךְ׃

13.27.469 וַיִּפְרָץ־בּוֹ אַבְשָׁלוֹם

13.27.470 וַיֹּאמֶר אַבְשָׁלוֹם אֶל־אֲמָנוֹן וְאֶת־כָּל־בְּנֵי הַמֶּלֶךְ׃
13.28.471 וַיְצַו אַבְשָׁלוֹם אֶת־נְעָרָיו
לֵאמֹר׃

HD
13.28.472 וּרְאוּ נָא
473α כְּטוֹב לֵב־אַמְנוֹן בַּיַּיִן
13.28.473 וְאָמַרְתִּי אֲלֵיכֶם
†HD
13.28.474 הַכּוּ אֶת־אַמְנוֹן
13.28.475 וַהֲמִתֶּם אֹתוֹ
13.28.476 אַל־תִּירָאוּ
ID
13.28.477 הֲלוֹא כִּי אָנֹכִי צִוִּיתִי אֶתְכֶם
HD
13.28.478 חִזְקוּ
13.28.479 וִהְיוּ לִבְנֵי־חָיִל׃

David Hears Conflicting Reports about the Murder

13.29.480 וַיַּעֲשׂוּ נַעֲרֵי אַבְשָׁלוֹם לְאַמְנוֹן
כַּאֲשֶׁר צִוָּה אַבְשָׁלוֹם
13.29.481 וַיָּקֻמוּ כָּל־בְּנֵי הַמֶּלֶךְ
13.29.482 וַיִּרְכְּבוּ אִישׁ עַל־פִּרְדּוֹ
13.29.483 וַיָּנֻסוּ׃

13.30.484 וַיְהִי הֵמָּה בַדֶּרֶךְ
13.30.485 וְהַשְּׁמֻעָה בָאָה אֶל־דָּוִד לֵאמֹר

ND
13.30.486 הִכָּה אַבְשָׁלוֹם אֶת־כָּל־בְּנֵי הַמֶּלֶךְ
13.30.487 וְלֹא־נוֹתַר מֵהֶם אֶחָד׃

13.31.488	וַיָּקָם הַמֶּלֶךְ	
13.31.489	וַיִּקְרַע אֶת־בְּגָדָיו	
13.31.490	וַיִּשְׁכַּב אָרְצָה	
13.31.491	וְכָל־עֲבָדָיו נִצָּבִים (קְרֻעֵי בְגָדִים׃)	
13.32.492	וַיַּעַן יוֹנָדָב ׀ בֶּן־שִׁמְעָה אֲחִי־דָוִד	
13.32.493	וַיֹּאמֶר	

HD
| 13.32.494 | אַל־יֹאמַר אֲדֹנִי אֵת כָּל־הַנְּעָרִים בְּנֵי־הַמֶּלֶךְ |
†ND
| 13.32.495 | הֵמִיתוּ כִּי־אַמְנוֹן לְבַדּוֹ מֵת |

†ND
13.33.496	כִּי עַל־פִּי אַבְשָׁלוֹם הָיְתָה שׂוּמָה מִיּוֹם
	עַנֹּתוֹ
13.33.497	וְעַתָּה אַל־יָשֵׂם אֲדֹנִי הַמֶּלֶךְ אֶל־לִבּוֹ
	לֵאמֹר

13.34.498	וַיִּבְרַח אַבְשָׁלוֹם	
13.34.499	וַיִּשָּׂא	
13.34.500	וַיַּעַן הַנַּעַר הַצֹּפֶה אֶת־עֵינָו [וַיַּרְא Q וְהִנֵּה]	
13.34.501	וַיַּעַן יוֹנָדָב אֶל־הַמֶּלֶךְ הָלְכוּ בְנֵי הַמֶּלֶךְ הֵמָּה	
13.35.502	וַיֹּאמֶר	

ND
| 13.35.503 | אֵת בְּנֵי־הַמֶּלֶךְ בָּאוּ |

13.35.504   בְּנֵי־הַמֶּלֶךְ בָּאוּ כִּדְבַר עַבְדְּךָ כֵּן הָיָה׃

David, His Servants, and His Sons Mourn

13.36.505   וַיְהִי כְּכַלֹּתוֹ | לְדַבֵּר וְהִנֵּה

13.36.506   בְנֵי־הַמֶּלֶךְ בָּאוּ (וַ)

13.36.507   וַיִּשְׂאוּ קוֹלָם

13.36.508   וַיִּבְכּוּ

13.36.509   וְגַם־הַמֶּלֶךְ וְכָל־עֲבָדָיו בָּכוּ בְּכִי גָּדוֹל מְאֹד׃

Absalom's Escape and David's Response (Comment)

13.37.510   וְאַבְשָׁלוֹם בָּרַח

13.37.511   וַיֵּלֶךְ אֶל־תַּלְמַי בֶּן־[עַמִּיהוּד] [עַמִּיחוּר]

13.37.512   מֶלֶךְ גְּשׁוּר וַיִּתְאַבֵּל עַל־בְּנוֹ כָּל־הַיָּמִים׃

Joab Attempts to Get Absalom Back to Jerusalem

13.38.513   וְאַבְשָׁלוֹם בָּרַח

13.38.514   וַיֵּלֶךְ גְּשׁוּר

13.38.515   וַיְהִי־שָׁם שָׁלֹשׁ שָׁנִים׃

13.39.516   וַתְּכַל דָּוִד הַמֶּלֶךְ לָצֵאת אֶל־אַבְשָׁלוֹם כִּי־נִחַם עַל־אַמְנוֹן כִּי־מֵת׃

Table of Independent Clause Types in 2 Samuel 13

Clause Type	Clause Distribution	Total	Percent
QATAL Total Clauses: 16	Narrative: 417,427,436,446,448,462,506,509,510, 513	10	62.5%
	ND: 486,487,†495,†497,503,504 PD: ED: ID: HD:	6	37.5%
WeQATAL Total Clauses: 7	Narrative: 434	1	14.3%
	ND: PD: 372,373 ED: ID: HD: †376,†377,473,475	2 4	28.6% 57.1%
YIQTOL Total Clauses: 12	Narrative:	0	0
	ND: PD: 415 ED: ID: HD: †374,382,412,413,443,456,459,460,466,476, 494	 12	 100%
WeYIQTOL Total Clauses: 4	Narrative:	0	0
	ND: PD: ED: ID: HD: †375,383,384,402	 4	 100%
WAYYIQTOL Total Clauses: 79	Narrative: 355,358,359,360,364,367,369,378,379,380, 381,385,388,390,391,392,393,394,395,396,397,399, 400,403,404,405,406,407,410,418,419,420,421,422, 425,428,429,433,435,437,438,439,444,447,449,450, 451,452,453,457,461,463,464,467,469,470,471,480, 481,482,483,484,488,489,490,492,493,498,499,500, 502,505,507,508,511,512,514,515,516	79	100%
	ND: PD: ED: ID: HD:		

Participle Total Clauses: 5	Narrative: 389,485,491,501	4	80.0%
	ND: PD: ED: 368 ID: HD:	1	20.0%
Verbless Total Clauses: 8	Narrative: 356,357,361,362,363,432,445	7	87.5%
	ND: PD: ED: 442 ID: HD:	1	12.5%
Incomplete Total Clauses: 6	Narrative:	0	0
	ND: PD: ED: 426 ID: HD: 411,454,455,458,465	1 5	16.7% 83.3%
Imperative Total Clauses: 18	Narrative:	0	0
	HD: 370,371,386,387,398,401,408,409,416,423, 424,430,431,441,472,†474,478,479	18	100%
Cohortative Total Clauses: 0	Narrative:	0	0
	HD:	0	0
Jussive Total Clauses: 1	Narrative:	0	0
	HD: 496	1	100%

Analysis of the Narrative Structure and Discourse Text-Types in 2 Samuel 13

Narrative Structural Analysis

Narrative/Paragraph Structure

The structure of 2 Samuel 13 is very complex, paralleling the complexity of the narrative story line presented in the chapter. The account of the Rape of Tamar and its subsequent consequences is built upon a basic backbone of seventy-nine *WAYYIQTOL* clauses which are, in turn, broken into six discreet paragraphs. A final, seventh paragraph of the chapter, beginning with the *QATAL* clause 513, continues into 2 Samuel 14 and finally reaches its conclusion with clause 610.

Of the six complete paragraphs found within the chapter, four are initiated by וַיְהִי temporal clauses (355, 449, 484, 505).[32] One of the two remaining paragraphs (clauses 435-445) is initially marked by the immediately preceding *WeQATAL* clause (434) that concludes the paragraph before it. The final complete paragraph of the chapter is initially marked by *QATAL* clause 510.[33]

All the paragraphs of the chapter, with the exception of the first (which is terminally marked with the *WeQATAL* clause 434) and the fifth (which is terminally marked by the *QATAL* clause 509), have their conclusions marked only externally by either the initial וַיְהִי temporal clauses or the initial *QATAL* clauses of the paragraphs which follow them.[34]

---

[32]The temporal nature of clause 484 is not as readily apparent as in most other cases of this type of paragraph initiation. The usual form of the וַיְהִי temporal clause contains either some form of an infinitive construct (e.g., clause 505: וַיְהִי כְּכַלֹּתוֹ לְדַבֵּר) or a preposition (e.g., clause 355: וַיְהִי אַחֲרֵי־כֵן). The fact that the subject and verb of clause 484 do not agree in number provides evidence that this clause is to be understood temporally and may be translated as "While they were in the road . . ." as opposed to the awkward "And they were/was in the road . . . ." Understood temporally, therefore, the clause begins the paragraph that follows it.

[33]The case of clause 438 (וַתֵּלֶךְ הָלוֹךְ וְזָעֲקָה) is unusual. The presence of the *WeQATAL* here is unexpected; the usual construction would require an infinitive absolute in parallel to הָלֹךְ in order to produce an adverbial phrase ("She kept on going and crying"). The text should probably be emended here, in agreement with most commentators, to וַתֵּלֶךְ הָלוֹךְ וְזָעֹק. See the extended discussion of this case, along with Josh 6:13a, in Gesenius, *Grammar,* §§112h-i; 113t-u.

[34]Note should be made of the three examples of *QATAL* clauses in the chapter that *do not* conclude or begin paragraphs: clauses 417, 427 and 462. These clauses all have the negation of the verb אבה. The negation of אבה within a clause is an example of

Extra-Paragraph Comments

Only one extra-paragraph comment occurs within 2 Samuel 13. The comment notes the different responses of David and Absalom to Amnon's rape of Tamar:

13.21.446 וְהַמֶּלֶךְ דָּוִד שָׁמַע אֵת כָּל־הַדְּבָרִים הָאֵלֶּה
13.21.447 וַיִּחַר לוֹ מְאֹד:
13.22.448 וְלֹא־דִבֶּר אַבְשָׁלוֹם עִם־אַמְנוֹן לְמֵרָע וְעַד־טוֹב
כִּי־שָׂנֵא אַבְשָׁלוֹם אֶת־אַמְנוֹן עַל־דְּבַר
אֲשֶׁר עִנָּה אֵת תָּמָר אֲחֹתוֹ:

The comment is bounded on either side by explicit paragraph markers. These three clauses, therefore, stand independent of their context. Although the comment contains two *QATAL* clauses and one *WAYYIQTOL*, no real progression of the story line occurs here. The notice explains that, while David was visibly angry with Amnon, Absalom remained silent, ironically, because of the same reason why David was angry.

Inner-Paragraph Comments

A remarkably large number of inner-paragraph comments occur within 2 Samuel 13. Of the ten comments made off the line of the narrative of the chapter, most are entirely regular syntactically for this type of comment. The comments employ either verbless clauses (356, 357, 361, 362, 363, 432, 445), participial clauses (389, 485, 491, 501), or clauses that are based upon היה as a true verb (450, 515).[35] In one unusual case, a *QATAL* clause introduced by וְהִנֵּה, occurs immediately after an initial וַיְהִי temporal clause.

13.36.505 וַיְהִי כְּכַלֹּתוֹ לְדַבֵּר
וְהִנֵּה
13.36.506 בְנֵי־הַמֶּלֶךְ בָּאוּ
13.36.507 וַיִּשְׂאוּ קוֹלָם

"momentous negation," in which the negation of the verb should be seen as having an active role in propelling the narrative forward and not as simply stating a fact about what was not done. A similar example occurs in Gen 39:10 when Joseph's not listening to Potiphar's wife's advances actually propels the narrative forward. Note the discussion in footnote 11 in the analysis of Gen 37.

[35]While the word וְשֹׁמֵמָה in clause 445 is a participial form, it is most probably standing in for a substantive ("a devastated woman") and the clause as a whole is verbless rather than participial. See Driver, *Notes,* 301; Gesenius, *Grammar,* §154a note (b). With either option, the clause remains an inner-paragraph comment.

13.36.508 וַיִּבְכּוּ

13.36.509 וְגַם־הַמֶּלֶךְ וְכָל־עֲבָדָיו בָּכוּ בְּכִי גָּדוֹל מְאֹד:

Because it stands immediately after an initial וַיְהִי temporal clause, *QATAL* clause 506 functions as an inner-paragraph comment between the temporal clause and the subsequent *WAYYIQTOL* clause.[36]

A case of a *QATAL* clause closely related, semantically and syntactically, to an immediately preceding *WAYYIQTOL* clause stands in this chapter:

13.19.435 וַתִּקַּח תָּמָר אֵפֶר עַל־רֹאשָׁהּ

13.19.436 (וּכְתֹנֶת הַפַּסִּים אֲשֶׁר עָלֶיהָ קָרָעָה)

The close parallel of syntactical and semantic elements in these two clauses is clear:

(1)And-she-took Tamar (2)ashes (3)upon-her-head
(2)And-the-*passim* coat (3)that was upon-her (1)she-tore

In cases such as this, the *QATAL* clause functions as an inner-paragraph comment, providing information about an action that is to be seen as simultaneous with the paralleled preceding clause.[37]

Discourse Function Analysis

Narrative Discourse

Of the four examples of Narrative Discourse in 2 Samuel 13, all employ simple *QATAL* clauses (486, 487, †495, †497, 503, 504) and are, therefore, entirely regular for this text-type.

Predictive Discourse

The two examples of Predictive Discourse in 2 Samuel 13 employ either *WeQATAL* clauses (372, 373) or simple *YIQTOL* clauses (415) and are, therefore, entirely regular for this text-type.

---

[36]The cases of *QATAL* clauses standing immediately after וַיְהִי temporal clauses and, therefore, functioning as an inner-paragraph comment, have been discussed extensively in the analyses of Gen 39 and 40 in the previous chapter of this study.

[37]Such cases have been seen in the Joseph Novella (clauses 693-694; Gen 44:12) and will be seen again in the Court Narrative (clauses 1367-1368; 1 Kgs 1:9-10). Consistently, cases of paralleled *QATAL* clauses provide information that is not subordinate nor subsequent to the preceding clause, but seen as a part of the preceding action.

Expository Discourse

Two of the three examples of Expository Discourse employ either participial clauses (368) or verbless clauses (442).[38] The case of clause 426 is unusual.

13.16.426   אַל־אוֹדֹת הָרָעָה הַגְּדוֹלָה הַזֹּאת מֵאַחֶרֶת אֲשֶׁר־עָשִׂיתָ עִמִּי לְשַׁלְּחֵנִי

In spite of the initial אַל־, the speech does not seem hortatory but rather explanatory.[39] Tamar explains that Amnon's refusal to have any dealings with her is
worse than his rape of her. The speech is incomplete and, for this reason, should
be seen as expository.

Interrogative Discourse

The clauses composing the five examples of Interrogative Discourse in 2
Samuel 13 are all explicitly marked with interrogative particles: מַדּוּעַ (365), הֲלֹא
(366, 477), אָנָה (414), הֲ (440), לָמָּה (468).

Hortatory Discourse

Nineteen examples of Hortatory Discourse occur within 2 Samuel 13. Of
these, ten cases employ imperative, cohortative, or jussive clauses and are,
therefore, entirely regular. One case uses a *WeYIQTOL* clause along with an
imperative (401-402); one case uses an *ʾal-YIQTOL* clause along with a jussive
(494-496). And one case uses a *WeQATAL* clause and an *ʾal-YIQTOL* clause
along with an initial imperative clause (472-476).

The hortatory character of three cases is determined solely by the negative
particle *ʾal* prefixed to *YIQTOL* verbal forms: two cases have *ʾal-YIQTOL*
clauses standing alone (411-413,443) and one case also employs a simple
YIQTOL clause in addition to the *ʾal-YIQTOL* clause (458-460).

In four cases, the hortatory character of the speech is determined by the
negative particle *-nāʾ* appended to initial *YIQTOL* clauses. In two of these cases,
the clause basically stands alone (454-456, 465-466). In the other two cases, the
hortatory discourse is continued after the initial *YIQTOL-nāʾ* clause by
WeYIQTOL clauses (382-384), or by a combination of a *WeYIQTOL* clause and

---

[38]The inverted word order of clause 368 is not unusual for clauses in direct discourse. The OSV sequence occurs regularly in participial clauses and interrogative
clauses. See Gesenius, *Grammar,* §142fd note; Driver, *Tenses*, §208.

[39]There seems to be some textual evidence that the initial word should not be אַל־
but rather עַל־. Driver attempts to argue for an extended textual emendation of the sentence based upon Lucian's recension of LXX and upon the Old Latin, but the argument is
too hypothetical (*Notes,* 298-99).

WeQAṬAL clauses (374-377). These cases show that, although *WeYIQṬOL* clauses occasionally serve as a purpose clause to a previous explicit command, there often does not seem to be any clearly defined differentiation between the usage of *WeYIQṬOL* clauses and *WeQAṬAL* clauses in continuing a hortatory speech.

Table of Discourse Constellations for 2 Samuel 13

		Present Ch.	Prev. Chs.	Total
ND	QAṬAL	4	39	43
	QAṬAL, WAYYIQṬOL		12	12
	QAṬAL, (Ptc./Vbl.)		8	8
	QAṬAL, WAYYIQṬOL, (Ptc./Vbl.)		4	4
	QAṬAL, WAYYIQṬOL, (Ptc./Vbl.), YIQṬOL		3	3
	QAṬAL, YIQṬOL (w/ past adverb)		0	0
	WAYYIQṬOL, (Ptc./Vbl.)		0	0
	Vbl/Ptc/Inc (Dream Report)		1	1
PD	YIQṬOL	1	20	21
	YIQṬOL, WeQAṬAL		10	10
	YIQṬOL, WeQAṬAL, (Ptc./Vbl../Inc.)		2	2
	YIQṬOL, (Ptc./Vbl../Inc.)		2	2
	WeQAṬAL	1	7	8
	WeYIQṬOL		2	2
ED	Ptc./Vbl.	2	32	34
	Ptc./ Vbl., Inc.		1	1
	Inc.	1	11	12
	Ptc./Vbl., QAṬAL/YIQṬOL of היה		3	3
	Ptc./Vbl., QAṬAL/YIQṬOL of היה, Front. Obj.+ QAṬAL/YIQṬOL		2	2
	QAṬAL/YIQṬOL of היה		1	1
HD	Impv./Coh./Juss.	10	29	39
	Impv./Coh./Juss., WeYIQṬOL/YIQṬOL	1	12	13
	Impv./Coh./Juss., WeQAṬAL		5	5
	Impv./Coh./Juss., WeYIQṬOL/YIQṬOL, WeQAṬAL		6	6
	Impv./Coh./Juss., QAṬAL		1	1
	Impv./Coh./Juss., WeYIQṬOL/YIQṬOL, (We)QAṬAL		1	1
	Impv./Coh./Juss., ʾal-YIQṬOL		3	3
	Impv./Coh./Juss., WeQAṬAL, ʾal-YIQṬOL	1	2	3
	ʾal-YIQṬOL	2	7	9
	ʾal-YIQṬOL, WeQAṬAL/YIQṬOL	1	0	1
	(We)YIQṬOL-nāʾ, (WeQAṬAL/[We]YIQṬOL)	4	0	4
	QAṬAL, YIQṬOL/WeQAṬAL		1	1

2 Samuel 14 — David, Joab, and the Wise Woman from Tekoa — Clauses 517–650

Text in Syntactical/Paragraph Units

Joab Attempts to Get Absalom Back to Jerusalem (Cont.)

14.01.517	וַיֹּאמֶר הַמֶּלֶךְ אֶל־יוֹאָב
14.02.518	הִנֵּה־נָא עָשִׂיתִי אֶת־הַדָּבָר הַזֶּה
14.02.519	וְלֵךְ הָשֵׁב אֶת־הַנַּעַר
14.02.520	אֶת־אַבְשָׁלוֹם׃
14.02.521	וַיִּפֹּל יוֹאָב אֶל־פָּנָיו אַרְצָה
14.02.522	וַיִּשְׁתַּחוּ
14.02.523	וַיְבָרֶךְ אֶת־הַמֶּלֶךְ
14.02.524	וַיֹּאמֶר יוֹאָב הַיּוֹם יָדַע עַבְדְּךָ
HD 14.03.525	כִּי־מָצָאתִי חֵן בְּעֵינֶיךָ אֲדֹנִי הַמֶּלֶךְ
14.03.526	אֲשֶׁר־עָשָׂה הַמֶּלֶךְ אֶת־דְּבַר עַבְדּוֹ׃
14.03.527	וַיָּקָם יוֹאָב
14.04.528	וַיֵּלֶךְ גְּשׁוּרָה
14.04.529	וַיָּבֵא אֶת־אַבְשָׁלוֹם יְרוּשָׁלִָם׃
14.04.530	וַיֹּאמֶר הַמֶּלֶךְ
14.04.531	יִסֹּב אֶל־בֵּיתוֹ
HD 14.04.532	וּפָנַי לֹא יִרְאֶה׃
14.05.533	וַיִּסֹּב אַבְשָׁלוֹם אֶל־בֵּיתוֹ
ID 14.05.534	וּפְנֵי הַמֶּלֶךְ לֹא רָאָה׃

14.05.535   וַיֹּאמֶר

14.05.536   ED   אַל־תִּקְרֶבָֽה הֲלֹם שַׁל־נְעָלֶיךָ

14.05.537   ND   מֵעַל

14.06.538   רַגְלֶיךָ כִּי

14.06.539   הַמָּקוֹם אֲשֶׁר

14.06.540   אַתָּה עוֹמֵד עָלָיו (וַיֹּאמֶר)

14.06.541   אַדְמַת־קֹדֶשׁ הוּא (אָנֹכִי אֱלֹהֵי

14.06.542   אָבִיךָ אֱלֹהֵי אַבְרָהָם, אֱלֹהֵי)

14.07.543   יִצְחָק וֵאלֹהֵי יַעֲקֹב וַיַּסְתֵּר מֹשֶׁה פָּנָיו

14.07.544   וַיֹּאמֶר

14.07.545   †HD   רָאֹה רָאִיתִי אֶת־עֳנִי

14.07.546   עַמִּי אֲשֶׁר בְּמִצְרָיִם וְאֶת־צַעֲקָתָם

14.07.547   PD   שָׁמַעְתִּי מִפְּנֵי נֹגְשָׂיו כִּי

14.07.548   יָדַעְתִּי אֶת־מַכְאֹבָיו

14.08.549   וָאֵרֵד לְהַצִּילוֹ מִיַּד מִצְרַיִם וּלְהַעֲלֹתוֹ מִן־הָאָרֶץ הַהִוא אֶל־אֶרֶץ טוֹבָה וּרְחָבָה

14.08.550   HD   אֶל־אֶרֶץ זָבַת חָלָב וּדְבָשׁ

14.08.551   אֶל־מְקוֹם הַכְּנַעֲנִי וְהַחִתִּי

ותאמר האשׁה התקועית אל־המלך	14.09.552	
		ED
כי־יֹאמַר הַמֶּלֶךְ עַל־אֲשֶׁר	14.09.553	
וַיַּגֵּד הַדָּבָר אֵלָיו:	14.09.554	
וַיֹּאמֶר הַמֶּלֶךְ	14.10.555	
		PD
הַמְדַבֵּר אֵלַיִךְ	556α	
וַהֲבֵאתוֹ אֵלַי	14.10.556	
וְלֹא־יֹסִיף עוֹד לָגַעַת בָּךְ:	14.10.557	
וַתֹּאמֶר	14.11.558	
		HD
יִזְכָּר־נָא הַמֶּלֶךְ אֶת־יְהוָה אֱלֹהֶיךָ	14.11.559	
מֵהַרְבִּית גֹּאֵל הַדָּם לְשַׁחֵת וְלֹא יַשְׁמִידוּ אֶת־בְּנִי	14.11.560	
וַיֹּאמֶר	14.11.561	
		ED (Oath)
חַי־יְהוָה	14.11.562	
וַתֹּאמֶר הָאִשָּׁה	14.12.563	
		HD
תְּדַבֶּר־נָא שִׁפְחָתְךָ אֶל־אֲדֹנִי הַמֶּלֶךְ דָּבָר	14.12.564	
וַיֹּאמֶר	14.12.565	
		HD
דַּבֵּרִי:	14.12.566	
וַתֹּאמֶר הָאִשָּׁה	14.13.567	
		ID
וְלָמָּה חָשַׁבְתָּה כָּזֹאת עַל־עַם אֱלֹהִים	14.13.568	

ED

14.13.569
וַיֹּאמֶר מֹשֶׁה אֶל־הָעָם
אַל־תִּירָאוּ
הִתְיַצְבוּ וּרְאוּ אֶת־יְשׁוּעַת יְהוָה
אֲשֶׁר־יַעֲשֶׂה לָכֶם הַיּוֹם׃

PD

14.14.570
כִּי אֲשֶׁר רְאִיתֶם אֶת־מִצְרַיִם הַיּוֹם

14.14.571
לֹא תֹסִפוּ לִרְאֹתָם עוֹד עַד־עוֹלָם׃

14.14.572
יְהוָה יִלָּחֵם לָכֶם

14.14.573
וְאַתֶּם תַּחֲרִישׁוּן׃

ND

14.15.574
וַיֹּאמֶר יְהוָה אֶל־מֹשֶׁה
מַה־תִּצְעַק אֵלָי

14.15.575
דַּבֵּר אֶל־בְּנֵי־יִשְׂרָאֵל
וְיִסָּעוּ׃

†HD   14.15.576
וְאַתָּה הָרֵם אֶת־מַטְּךָ

†PD   14.15.577
וּנְטֵה אֶת־יָדְךָ עַל־הַיָּם

[14.16]
וּבְקָעֵהוּ
וְיָבֹאוּ בְנֵי־יִשְׂרָאֵל בְּתוֹךְ הַיָּם בַּיַּבָּשָׁה׃

14.17.578
וַאֲנִי הִנְנִי מְחַזֵּק אֶת־לֵב מִצְרַיִם
וְיָבֹאוּ אַחֲרֵיהֶם

†HD   14.17.579
וְאִכָּבְדָה בְּפַרְעֹה וּבְכָל־חֵילוֹ
בְּרִכְבּוֹ וּבְפָרָשָׁיו׃

14.17.580 HD וַתֹּאמֶר שִׁפְחָתְךָ יִֽהְיֶה־נָּא דְבַר־אֲדֹנִי הַמֶּלֶךְ לִמְנוּחָה כִּי כְּמַלְאַךְ הָאֱלֹהִים כֵּן אֲדֹנִי הַמֶּלֶךְ

14.18.581 וַיַּעַן הַמֶּלֶךְ וַיֹּאמֶר
14.18.582 אֶל־הָאִשָּׁה

14.18.583 HD אַל־נָא תְכַחֲדִי מִמֶּנִּי דָּבָר אֲשֶׁר אָנֹכִי שֹׁאֵל אֹתָךְ

14.18.584 וַתֹּאמֶר הָאִשָּׁה

14.18.585 HD יְדַבֶּר־נָא אֲדֹנִי הַמֶּלֶךְ

14.19.586 וַיֹּאמֶר הַמֶּלֶךְ

14.19.587 ID הֲיַד יוֹאָב אִתָּךְ בְּכָל־זֹאת

14.19.588 וַתַּעַן הָאִשָּׁה וַתֹּאמֶר
14.19.589 וַתֹּאמֶר

14.19.590 ED (Oath) חֵי־נַפְשְׁךָ אֲדֹנִי הַמֶּלֶךְ אִם־אִשׁ לְהֵמִין וּלְהַשְׂמִיל מִכֹּל אֲשֶׁר־דִּבֶּר אֲדֹנִי הַמֶּלֶךְ

14.19.591 ND כִּי־עַבְדְּךָ יוֹאָב הוּא צִוָּנִי וְהוּא שָׂם בְּפִי שִׁפְחָתְךָ אֵת כָּל־הַדְּבָרִים הָאֵלֶּה

592α

14.20.592 לְבַעֲבוּר סַבֵּב אֶת־פְּנֵי הַדָּבָר עָשָׂה עַבְדְּךָ יוֹאָב אֶת־הַדָּבָר הַזֶּה
14.20.593 וַאדֹנִי חָכָם כְּחָכְמַת מַלְאַךְ הָאֱלֹהִים לָדַעַת אֶת־כָּל־אֲשֶׁר בָּאָרֶץ

14.21.594	וַיַּעַן הַמֶּלֶךְ אֶל־יוֹאָב

14.22.598	וַיַּעַן יוֹאָב
14.22.599	וַיִּקֹּד אֶל־אַרְצָה
14.22.600	וַיִּשְׁתָּחוּ
14.22.601	וַיְבָרֶךְ אֶת־הַמֶּלֶךְ

14.23.603	וַיַּעַן הַמֶּלֶךְ
14.23.604	וַיֹּאמֶר אֶל־אַבְשָׁלוֹם הַנַּעַר
14.23.605	וַיֵּלֶךְ
14.24.606	אֶל־יְרוּשָׁלָ‍ִם

14.24.609	וַיֹּאמֶר הַמֶּלֶךְ יִסֹּב אֶל־בֵּיתוֹ
14.24.610	וּפָנַי לֹא יִרְאֶה

HD

14.21.595	וַיֹּאמֶר הַמֶּלֶךְ אֶל־יוֹאָב
14.21.596	הִנֵּה
14.21.597	עָשִׂיתִי אֶת־הַדָּבָר הַזֶּה

ND

14.22.602	וַיִּפֹּל עַל־פָּנָיו אַרְצָה

PD

14.24.607	וְאֶת־פָּנַי לֹא יִרְאֶה
14.24.608	וַיִּסֹּב אֶל־בֵּיתוֹ

The Handsomeness of Absalom and His Hair (Comment)

וּכְאַבְשָׁלוֹם לֹא־הָיָה אִישׁ־יָפֶה בְּכָל־יִשְׂרָאֵל לְהַלֵּל מְאֹד	14.25.611
מִכַּף רַגְלוֹ וְעַד קָדְקֳדוֹ לֹא־הָיָה בוֹ מוּם:	14.25.612
וּבְגַלְּחוֹ אֶת־רֹאשׁוֹ וְהָיָה מִקֵּץ יָמִים לַיָּמִים	14.26.613
אֲשֶׁר יְגַלֵּחַ כִּי־כָבֵד עָלָיו וְגִלְּחוֹ	14.26.614
וְשָׁקַל אֶת־שְׂעַר רֹאשׁוֹ	14.26.615
מָאתַיִם שְׁקָלִים בְּאֶבֶן הַמֶּלֶךְ:	14.26.616

Absalom's Children (Comment)

וַיִּוָּלְדוּ לְאַבְשָׁלוֹם שְׁלוֹשָׁה בָנִים וּבַת אַחַת	14.27.617
וּשְׁמָהּ תָּמָר	14.27.618
הִיא הָיְתָה אִשָּׁה יְפַת מַרְאֶה:	14.27.619

Absalom's Banishment in Jerusalem (Comment)

וַיֵּשֶׁב אַבְשָׁלוֹם בִּירוּשָׁלִַם שְׁנָתַיִם יָמִים	14.28.620
וּפְנֵי הַמֶּלֶךְ לֹא רָאָה:	14.28.621

Absalom Is Brought before David and Is Welcomed

וַיִּשְׁלַח אַבְשָׁלוֹם אֶל־יוֹאָב לִשְׁלֹחַ אֹתוֹ אֶל־הַמֶּלֶךְ	14.29.622

14.29.623	וַיֹּאמֶר אֵלָיו בָּלָק
14.29.624	לְךָ־נָּא אִתִּי
14.29.625	אֶל־מָקוֹם אַחֵר
14.30.626	אֲשֶׁר תִּרְאֶנּוּ מִשָּׁם

HD	אַךְ	14.30.627
ED		14.30.628
		14.30.629
HD		14.30.630
		14.30.631

14.30.632	וַיֹּאמֶר אֵלָיו
14.31.633	לֹא אֶל־אֲבַקֶּשְׁךָ הַזֶּה
14.31.634	וְאֶל־יוֹם
14.31.635	וַיִּקַּח בָּלָק אֲשֶׁר אֶת־בִּלְעָם רֹאשׁ הַפְּעוֹר:

ID	14.31.636

14.32.637	וַיֹּאמֶר אֶל־בָּלָק בְּנֵה־לִי

ND	14.32.638 וַיַּעַשׂ בָּלָק כַּאֲשֶׁר

†HD	14.32.639 וַיֹּאמֶר בָּלָק
	14.32.640 וַיֵּלֶךְ בִּלְעָם אֶל־

14.33.645 וַיָּקָם יוֹאָב וַיָּבֹא אֶל־הַמֶּלֶךְ

14.33.646 וַיַּגֶּד־לוֹ

14.33.647 וַיִּקְרָא אֶל־אַבְשָׁלוֹם

14.33.648 וַיָּבֹא אֶל־הַמֶּלֶךְ

14.33.649 וַיִּשְׁתַּחוּ לוֹ עַל־אַפָּיו אַרְצָה לִפְנֵי הַמֶּלֶךְ

14.33.650 וַיִּשַּׁק הַמֶּלֶךְ לְאַבְשָׁלוֹם:

†† ID
14.32.641 וַיֹּאמֶר אַבְשָׁלֹם אֶל־יוֹאָב

†† ED
14.32.642 הִנֵּה שָׁלַחְתִּי אֵלֶיךָ

PD
וַיֹּאמֶר
14.32.643 לֵךְ־נָא אֶל־הַמֶּלֶךְ
644α [וְאִם־יֶשׁ־בִּי עָוֺן]
14.32.644 וֶהֱמִיתָנִי:

Table of Independent Clause Types in 2 Samuel 14

Clause Type	Clause Distribution	Total	Percent
QAṬAL Total Clauses: 17	Narrative: 610,611,612,619,621,623,625	7	41.2%
	ND: 543,574,591,592,602,638 PD: ED: ID: 568,636,††641 HD: 595	6 3 1	35.3% 17.6% 5.9%
WeQAṬAL Total Clauses: 10	Narrative: 614,615,616	3	30.0%
	ND: PD: 548,556,573,644 ED: ID: HD: 524,525,526	 4 3	 40.0% 30.0%
YIQṬOL Total Clauses: 15	Narrative:	0	0
	ND: PD: 557,570,572,†577,607,608,643 ED: ID: HD: 523,551,559,560,564,†579,583,585	 7 8	 46.7% 53.3%
WeYIQṬOL Total Clauses: 2	Narrative:	0	0
	ND: PD: ED: ID: HD: 546,547	 2	 100%
WAYYIQṬOL Total Clauses: 52	Narrative: 517,518,519,520,527,528,529,530,531, 533,535,549,552,555,558,561,563,565,567,594,598, 599,600,601,603,604,605,606,609,617,620,622,624, 626,632,633,634,635,637,645,646,647,648,649,650	45	86.5%
	ND: 537,539,541,542,544,575,578 PD: ED: ID: HD:	7	13.5%

	Narrative:	0	0
Participle	ND:		
	PD:		
Total Clauses: 1	ED: 569	1	100%
	ID:		
	HD:		
	Narrative: 618		
Verbless	ND: 538,540,593		
	PD:		
Total Clauses:	ED: 536,553,554,628,629		
12	ID: 534,587,††642		
	HD:		
	Narrative: 613	0	0
Incomplete	ND:		
	PD: 571		
Total Clauses: 4	ED: 562	0	0
	ID: 590		
	HD:		
Imperative	Narrative:	0	0
Total Clauses:	HD: 521,522,532,545,550,566,596,597,627,630,	12	100%
12	631,639		
Cohortative	Narrative:	0	0
Total Clauses: 2	HD: †576,†640	2	100%
Jussive	Narrative:	0	0
Total Clauses: 1	HD: 580	1	100%

Analysis of the Narrative Structure and
Discourse Text-Types in 2 Samuel 14

Narrative Structural Analysis

Narrative/Paragraph Structure

The story of 2 Samuel 14 is built upon a narrative backbone of forty-five *WAYYIQTOL* clauses which are grouped into two main paragraphs (clauses 513-610, 622-650), the first of which begins in the previous chapter. These two paragraphs are separated by a long series of non-*WAYYIQTOL* clauses (clauses 611-621) which form a central extra-paragraph comment. The first paragraph concludes with the *QATAL* clause 610: וּפְנֵי הַמֶּלֶךְ לֹא רָאָה. The second paragraph begins with the simple *WAYYIQTOL* clause 622 and is terminally marked externally by the temporal clause beginning the comment following it in 2 Samuel 15:1 at clause 651.[40]

Extra-Paragraph Comments

The long complex of non-*WAYYIQTOL* clauses in the central portion of the chapter (611-621) form a long description of Absalom; this commentary is off-line from the surrounding narrative. For ease of reading, the comment is divided into three sections in the text layout. This division is, however, purely based upon the content of the comment; syntactically, the entire comment is a single block of information about Absalom, his appearance, his children, and his status in Jerusalem. The comment as a whole is set apart from the surrounding narrative by the echoing effect of the final clause of the previous paragraph, clause 610, וּפְנֵי הַמֶּלֶךְ לֹא רָאָה, with the final clause of the comment, clause 621, רָאָה וּפְנֵי הַמֶּלֶךְ לֹא. This parallel brings the comment to a close and the narrative, in a sense, begins where it left off previously in clause 610.

Inner-Paragraph Comments

No inner-paragraph comments occur within 2 Samuel 14.

---

[40]As in the previous chapter, the negated verb אבה in clauses 623 and 625 does not mark the end of the paragraph, but is, rather, an instance of "momentous negation." See footnote 34 in the analysis of 2 Samuel 13 above.

Discourse Function Analysis

Narrative Discourse

The five examples of Narrative Discourse within 2 Samuel 14 are consistent with other examples of this text-type within the data samples investigated thus far in this study. All examples are explicitly marked as Narrative Discourse by the presence of *QAṬAL* and *WAYYIQṬOL* clauses within them. The narrative speeches in the chapter have either exclusively *QAṬAL* clauses (602,638), or a combination of *QAṬAL* clauses and other types: *WAYYIQṬOL* clauses (574-578), verbless clauses (591-593), or with both *WAYYIQṬOL* and verbless clauses (537-544).

Predictive Discourse

Of the six examples of Predictive Discourse found within 2 Samuel 14, five are explicitly marked by the presence of *YIQṬOL* clauses found within them (clauses 556-557; 570-573; 577; 607-608; 643-644).[41] The sixth example, the eventual outcome of the plight of the woman of Tekoa, occurs immediately after other text-types in her speech and contains a single, predictive *WeQAṬAL* clause (548):

וְכִבּוּ אֶת־גַּחַלְתִּי אֲשֶׁר נִשְׁאָרָה / "and they will quench my remaining coal."

Expository Discourse

The five examples of Expository Discourse include three cases of participial or verbless clauses (clauses 536; 553-554; 628-629) and two cases of incomplete clauses, each of which is an oath formula (clauses 562; 590).

Interrogative Discourse

The five examples of Interrogative Discourse contain a total of six clauses. Five of these clauses are explicitly marked as interrogative by interrogative particles: מַה־ (534); וְלָמָּה (568; 636; †641); and הֲ (587). The case of two clauses appearing in an interrogative speech contains one clause explicitly marked as interrogative and one clause as unmarked:

---

[41]The use of the participle in the *casus pendens* introductory phrase in clauses 556-557 has received much commentary. See Driver, *Tenses*, §123a; *Notes*, 306-7; Gesenius, *Grammar*, §116w; Waltke and O'Connor, *Syntax*, 536, 621.

14.13.568 וְלָמָּה חָשַׁבְתָּה כָּזֹאת עַל־עַם אֱלֹהִים
14.13.569 וּמִדַּבֵּר הַמֶּלֶךְ הַדָּבָר הַזֶּה כְּאָשֵׁם לְבִלְתִּי הָשִׁיב הַמֶּלֶךְ אֶת־נִדְּחוֹ׃

The second clause in this speech continues the rhetorical questioning of the previous clause, so that the original interrogative pronoun וְלָמָּה questions the entire
situation of David's not returning Absalom to Jerusalem; the interrogative, therefore, governs both clauses.[42]

Hortatory Discourse

Of the fifteen examples of Hortatory Discourse found within 2 Samuel 14,
ten cases are clearly marked as hortatory by the presence of imperative, cohortative, or (unambiguous) jussive clauses within the speech. Six cases employ only
imperative, cohortative, or (unambiguous) jussive clauses within the speech; two
cases also use *YIQTOL* clauses (clauses 550-551; 559-560) and one case also
contains *WeQATAL* clauses and an *ʾal-YIQTOL* clause (clauses 521-526).

One case (clauses 595-597) employs a *QATAL* clause within the hortatory
speech:

הִנֵּה־נָא
14.21.595 עָשִׂיתִי אֶת־הַדָּבָר הַזֶּה
14.21.596 וְלֵךְ
14.21.597 הָשֵׁב אֶת־הַנַּעַר אֶת־אַבְשָׁלוֹם׃

The hortatory nature of the speech is signaled by the initial phrase הִנֵּה־נָא. The
QATAL clause 595 is, therefore, an example of a performative utterance and has
the sense of "I hereby do this thing."[43]

Additionally, there are five cases in which the sole marker of a speech as
being hortatory is presence of the particle נָא following the verb in the initial
clause of a speech (clauses 559-560; 564; †579; 583; 585). Clause †579 is especially interesting because the verbal form is explicitly not a jussive, but rather a
simple *YIQTOL*:

---

[42]Note the discussion on p. 268 above of the Interrogative Discourse contained in
clauses 288-290, in which a similar construction occurs.

[43]Both Driver (*Notes,* 309) and Gesenius (*Grammar,* §106m) interpret the *QATAL* in
this way, in order "to express *future* actions, when the speaker intends by an express as-
surance to represent them as finished, or as equivalent to accomplished facts." More
contemporary views of the function of "perfomative utterances" see the action as either
coincident with the speech or, more accurately, performed by the act of pronouncing the
speech itself.

14.17.579 יְהִי־נָא דְּבַר־אֲדֹנִי הַמֶּלֶךְ לִמְנוּחָה

In spite of the fact of the non-jussive, *YIQTOL* verbal form of the clause, the discourse is unambiguously marked as hortatory by the particle נָא.

Table of Discourse Constellations for 2 Samuel 14

		Present Ch.	Prev. Chs.	Total
ND	*QATAL*	2	43	45
	QATAL, WAYYIQTOL	1	12	13
	QATAL, (Ptc./Vbl.)	1	8	9
	QATAL, WAYYIQTOL, (Ptc./Vbl.)	1	4	5
	QATAL, WAYYIQTOL, (Ptc./Vbl.), *YIQTOL*		3	3
	QATAL, YIQTOL (w/ past adverb)		0	0
	WAYYIQTOL, (Ptc./Vbl.)		0	0
	Vbl/Ptc/Inc (Dream Report)		1	1
PD	*YIQTOL*	2	21	23
	YIQTOL, WeQATAL	1	10	11
	YIQTOL, WeQATAL, (Ptc./Vbl../Inc.)	2	2	4
	YIQTOL, (Ptc./Vbl../Inc.)		2	2
	WeQATAL	1	8	9
	WeYIQTOL		2	2
ED	Ptc./Vbl.	3	34	37
	Ptc./ Vbl., Inc.		1	1
	Inc.	2	12	14
	Ptc./Vbl., *QATAL/YIQTOL* of היה		3	3
	Ptc./Vbl., *QATAL/YIQTOL* of היה, Front. Obj.+ *QATAL/YIQTOL*		2	2
	QATAL/YIQTOL of היה		1	1
HD	Impv./Coh./Juss.	6	39	45
	Impv./Coh./Juss., *WeYIQTOL/YIQTOL*	2	13	15
	Impv./Coh./Juss., *WeQATAL*		5	5
	Impv./Coh./Juss., *WeYIQTOL/YIQTOL, WeQATAL*		6	6
	Impv./Coh./Juss., *QATAL*	1	1	2
	Impv./Coh./Juss., *WeYIQTOL/YIQTOL*, (We)*QATAL*		1	1
	Impv./Coh./Juss., *ʾal-YIQTOL*		3	3
	Impv./Coh./Juss., *WeQATAL, ʾal-YIQTOL*	1	3	4
	ʾal-YIQTOL		9	9
	ʾal-YIQTOL, WeQATAL/YIQTOL		1	1
	(We)*YIQTOL-nāʾ*, (We*QATAL*/[We]*YIQTOL*)	5	4	9
	QATAL, YIQTOL/WeQATAL		1	1

2 Samuel 15 — Absalom Leads a Rebellion against David — Clauses 651-774

Text in Syntactical/Paragraph Units

Absalom's Elevating of Himself (Comment)

וֽיְהִי֙ מֵאַחֲרֵי כֵ֔ן	15.01.651
וַיַּ֤עַשׂ לוֹ֙ אַבְשָׁל֔וֹם	15.01.652
מֶרְכָּבָ֖ה וְסֻסִ֑ים וַחֲמִשִּׁ֥ים אִ֖ישׁ רָצִ֥ים לְפָנָֽיו׃	
וְהִשְׁכִּים֙ אַבְשָׁל֔וֹם	15.02.653
וְעָמַ֕ד עַל־יַ֖ד דֶּ֥רֶךְ הַשָּֽׁעַר	15.02.654

Absalom Converses with Plaintiffs

וַיְהִ֡י	15.02.655
כָּל־הָאִ֣ישׁ אֲשֶֽׁר־יִהְיֶה־לּוֹ־רִיב֩ לָב֨וֹא אֶל־הַמֶּ֜לֶךְ לַמִּשְׁפָּ֗ט	656α
וַיִּקְרָ֨א אַבְשָׁל֤וֹם אֵלָיו֙	15.02.656
וַיֹּ֔אמֶר	15.02.657
	אֵֽי־מִזֶּ֥ה עִ֖יר אַ֑תָּה ID 15.02.658
וַיֹּ֕אמֶר	15.02.659
	עַבְדְּךָ֛ מֵאַחַ֥ד שִׁבְטֵֽי־יִשְׂרָאֵֽל׃ ED 15.02.660
וַיֹּ֤אמֶר אֵלָיו֙ אַבְשָׁל֔וֹם	15.03.661
	רְאֵ֥ה דְבָרֶ֖ךָ HD 15.03.662
	טוֹבִ֣ים וּנְכֹחִ֑ים ED 15.03.663
	וְשֹׁמֵ֥עַ אֵֽין־לְךָ֖ מֵאֵ֥ת הַמֶּֽלֶךְ׃ 15.03.664

וַיֹּאמֶר אֲבְשָׁלוֹם 15.04.665

ID
אַךְ טוֹב דְּבָרֶיךָ וְנָכֹחַ 15.04.666
PD
וְשֹׁמֵעַ אֵין לְךָ מֵאֵת הַמֶּלֶךְ 15.04.667
וַיֹּאמֶר אַבְשָׁלוֹם 15.04.668

Absalom's Actions to the Plaintiffs (Comment)

וַיְהִי בְּכָל יִשְׂרָאֵל מִי יְשִׂמֵנִי לְ 15.05.669
וְעָלַי יָבוֹא 15.05.670
הָיָה לֹּו 15.05.671
וַהֲצִדַּקְתִּיו 15.05.672

וְהָיָה בִּקְרָב אִישׁ לְהִשְׁתַּחֲוֹת לֹו 15.06.673
וְשָׁלַח אֶת יָדוֹ וְהֶחֱזִיק לֹו וְנָשַׁק לֹו 15.06.674

Absalom Begins the Rebellion against David

וַיַּעַשׂ אַבְשָׁלוֹם כַּדָּבָר הַזֶּה לְכָל יִשְׂרָאֵל 15.07.675
וַיֹּאמֶר אַבְשָׁלוֹם אֶל הַמֶּלֶךְ 15.07.676

HD
אֵלְכָה נָּא 15.07.677
[15.08]
וַאֲשַׁלֵּם אֶת נִדְרִי 15.07.678

וַיֵּלֶךְ

		15.09.680 וַיִּשְׁתַּחוּ־לוֹ הַמֶּלֶךְ

לְאֹמַר

†PD
[הֵנָּה, Q] הַ־שֹׁבְ־אֹמֶר]† 679α
וַיֹּאמֶר אֶל־אִתַּי
מַדּוּעַ תֵּלֵךְ גַּם־אַתָּה אִתָּנוּ:

15.08.679 וַיֹּאמֶר הַמֶּלֶךְ

15.09.682 וַיֹּאמֶר
15.09.683 וַיֵּלֶךְ
15.10.684 וַיֵּלֶךְ הַמֶּלֶךְ

HD
שׁוּב וָשֵׁב עִם־הַמֶּלֶךְ 15.09.681

לָכֵן

וְהָיוּ אֲשֶׁר־תִּמְצָא בַלֶּחֶם בְּבֵית אֲבִי שְׁאוּל, וַיֹּאמֶר
שׁוּב

15.11.687 וַיֹּאמֶר אֶל־הַמֶּלֶךְ:
[חַי־יְהוָה וְחֵי הַמֶּלֶךְ] 15.11.688
בַּמָּקוֹם אֲשֶׁר יִהְיֶה־שָּׁם

PD
[וַיַּעֲבֹר 685α
וַיֹּאמֶר לְאִתַּי הַגִּתִּי 15.10.685

וַיֹּאמֶר אֶל־הַמֶּלֶךְ וְאֶת־כָּל־אֲנָשָׁיו אֲשֶׁר־אִתּוֹ 15.11.687
כִּי־אִם בַּמָּקוֹם אֲשֶׁר יִהְיֶה־שָּׁם

†ND
הַמֶּלֶךְ אֲדֹנִי בָּמָּוֶת: 15.10.686

David and His Servants Leave Jerusalem

דָּוִד יָצָא וְכָל־בֵּיתוֹ בְּרַגְלָיו וַיַּעֲזֹב הַמֶּלֶךְ

15.12.689 וְאֵת־עֶשֶׂר־נָשִׁים פִּלַגְשִׁים לִשְׁמֹר הַבָּיִת

15.12.690 (וְלַנֵּעָר יִתֵּן)
15.12.691 וַיֵּצֵא הַמֶּלֶךְ
(אֲשֶׁר בְּרַגְלָיו:)

15.13.692 וַיֵּלֶךְ הַמֶּלֶךְ וְכָל־הָעָם אֲשֶׁר־בְּרַגְלָיו

15.13.693   ED

15.14.694

15.14.695

15.14.696   HD

15.14.697   PD

15.14.698

15.14.699

15.14.700

15.15.701

702α   ED

15.15.702

15.16.703

15.16.704

15.17.705

15.17.706

15.18.707

708α

15.18.708

15.19.709

15.

ID
וַיֹּאמֶר דָּוִד אֶל־אִתַּי 15.19.710
HD לָלֶכֶת גַּם־אַתָּה אִתָּנוּ 15.19.711
שׁוּב 15.19.712
וְשֵׁב עִם־הַמֶּלֶךְ 15.19.713
כִּי־נָכְרִי אַתָּה 15.20.714
וְגַם־גֹּלֶה אַתָּה לִמְקוֹמֶךָ 15.20.715

PD
תְּמוֹל בּוֹאֶךָ 15.20.716
וְהַיּוֹם אֲנִיעֲךָ עִמָּנוּ לָלֶכֶת 15.20.717
HD שׁוּב 15.20.718
ED וְהָשֵׁב אֶת־אַחֶיךָ עִמָּךְ 15.20.719
חֶסֶד וֶאֱמֶת׃ 15.21.720

וַיַּעַן אִתַּי אֶת־הַמֶּלֶךְ 15.21.721
וַיֹּאמַר 15.21.722

ED (Oath)
חַי־יְהוָה 15.21.722
וְחֵי אֲדֹנִי הַמֶּלֶךְ 15.21.723
כִּי אִם־בִּמְקוֹם אֲשֶׁר יִהְיֶה־שָּׁם אֲדֹנִי הַמֶּלֶךְ 15.21.723
(אִם־לְמָוֶת אִם־לְחַיִּים)
כִּי־שָׁם יִהְיֶה עַבְדֶּךָ׃

HD
וַיֹּאמֶר דָּוִד אֶל־אִתַּי 15.22.724
לֵךְ 15.22.725
וַעֲבֹר 15.22.726

15.22.727 וַיֹּאמֶר אֵלָיו נָתָן לֵךְ אֲשֶׁר בִּלְבָבְךָ

15.23.728 וַיֹּאמֶר נָתָן אֶל־הַמֶּלֶךְ

15.23.729 כֹּל אֲשֶׁר בִּלְבָבְךָ לֵךְ עֲשֵׂה

15.23.730 כִּי יְהוָה עִמָּךְ

15.23.731 וַיְהִי בַּלַּיְלָה הַהוּא

15.24.732 וַיְהִי דְּבַר־יְהוָה אֶל־נָתָן לֵאמֹר

15.24.733 לֵךְ וְאָמַרְתָּ אֶל־עַבְדִּי אֶל־דָּוִד

15.24.734 כֹּה אָמַר יְהוָה

15.25.735 הַאַתָּה תִּבְנֶה־לִּי בַיִת לְשִׁבְתִּי

HD 15.25.736 כִּי לֹא יָשַׁבְתִּי בְּבַיִת לְמִיּוֹם הַעֲלֹתִי אֶת־בְּנֵי יִשְׂרָאֵל מִמִּצְרַיִם

PD 737α
15.25.737 וָאֶהְיֶה מִתְהַלֵּךְ בְּאֹהֶל וּבְמִשְׁכָּן

15.25.738 בְּכֹל אֲשֶׁר הִתְהַלַּכְתִּי בְּכָל־בְּנֵי יִשְׂרָאֵל

†ND 15.26.739 הֲדָבָר דִּבַּרְתִּי אֶת־אַחַד שִׁבְטֵי יִשְׂרָאֵל

740α

ID 15.26.740 אֲשֶׁר צִוִּיתִי לִרְעוֹת אֶת־עַמִּי אֶת־יִשְׂרָאֵל לֵאמֹר

15.27.741 וַיֹּאמֶר הַמֶּלֶךְ אֶל־נָתָן הַנָּבִיא

HD 15.27.742 וְעַתָּה כֹּה תֹאמַר לְעַבְדִּי לְדָוִד

HD 15.27.743 כֹּה אָמַר יְהוָה צְבָאוֹת

15.27.744 וַיֹּאמֶר הַמֶּלֶךְ אֶל־צָדוֹק הַכֹּהֵן הֲרוֹאֶה אַתָּה ED

15.28.745 שֻׁבָה הָעִיר בְּשָׁלוֹם וַאֲחִימַעַץ בִּנְךָ וִיהוֹנָתָן בֶּן־אֶבְיָתָר HD

15.28.746 אָנֹכִי ED

15.29.747 מִתְמַהְמֵהַּ בְּעַרְבוֹת הַמִּדְבָּר עַד בּוֹא דָבָר מֵעִמָּכֶם לְהַגִּיד לִי

15.29.748 וַיָּשֶׁב צָדוֹק וְאֶבְיָתָר אֶת־אֲרוֹן הָאֱלֹהִים יְרוּשָׁלִָם וַיֵּשְׁבוּ שָׁם

15.30.749 [וְדָוִד] עֹלֶה בְמַעֲלֵה הַזֵּיתִים

15.30.750 עֹלֶה וּבוֹכֶה

15.30.751 וְרֹאשׁ לוֹ חָפוּי

15.30.752 וְהוּא הֹלֵךְ יָחֵף (אֹתוֹ) אֲשֶׁר־אִתּוֹ

15.30.753 חָפוּ אִישׁ רֹאשׁוֹ

David Plans to Undermine Ahitophel's Counsel by Hushai

15.31.754 וְדָוִד הִגִּיד לֵאמֹר

15.31.755 אֲחִיתֹפֶל בַּקֹּשְׁרִים עִם־אַבְשָׁלוֹם ED

15.31.756 וַיֹּאמֶר דָּוִד

15.31.757 סַכֶּל־נָא אֶת־עֲצַת אֲחִיתֹפֶל יְהוָה׃ HD

15.32.758 (וַיְהִי) דָוִד בָּא עַד־הָרֹאשׁ אֲשֶׁר־יִשְׁתַּחֲוֶה שָׁם לֵאלֹהִים

759α   וַיֹּאמְר֖וּ
15.32.759   וַיַּעַשׂ יֵה֔וּא לְכָל־
15.32.760   וְאֵ֣ת כָּל־
15.33.761   וְאֵ֖ת כָּל־נְבִיאָֽיו׃

15.37.773   וַיִּשְׁמֹ֣ר יֵה֔וּא לָלֶ֖כֶת
15.37.774   וַיֹּ֤אמֶר יְהוָֽה־אֱלֹהֵ֣י יִשְׂרָאֵ֔ל

PD   762α   וַיֹּ֣אמֶר אֵלָ֑יו
15.33.762   וַיַּשְׁלִ֖יךְ אַרְצָ֑ה
763α   וַיֹּ֣אמֶר
15.34.763   וַיִּקְרָ֣א אֶל־

†ED
15.34.764   וַיֵּ֨לֶךְ יְהוֹרָ֜ם אֵ֣ת יֵהוּא
15.34.765   וְאֵ֤ת אֲשֶׁ֣ר בֵּ֔ית
15.34.766   וַיֹּ֣אמֶר אֵלָ֑יו

ID   15.34.767   וְכָל־אֲשֶׁ֣ר עַ֖ל לִ֥י יֵהוּא׃
15.35.768   כִּֽי־הֵבִ֣יאוּ אֶת־שֵׁ֣ם אוֹתָ֑ם

PD
15.35.769   וַיֵּ֑עַשׂ
770α   (וַיֵּ֣לֶךְ וַיָּבֹ֣א מֵֽחֲדָרַ֣ר)
15.35.770   וַיֶּֽהֶרֶס מַצֶּ֣בֶת
וַיֵּ֑שֶׁב

15.36.771   וַֽיַּעֲשׂ֣וּ בֵ֣ית הַבַּ֣עַל

15.36.772   וַיִּתְּצ֞וּ לְכֶ֣פֶר אֲשֶׁ֣ר לֹא־יִרְד֔וּ עַ֖ד הַיּ֥וֹם הַזֶּֽה׃

Table of Independent Clause Types in 2 Samuel 15

Clause Type	Clause Distribution	Total	Percent
QAṬAL Total Clauses: 7	Narrative: 687,688,752,754	4	57.1%
	ND: †686,†739	2	28.6%
	PD:		
	ED: 693	1	14.3%
	ID:		
	HD:		
WeQAṬAL Total Clauses: 20	Narrative: 653,654,669,670,671,672,753	7	35.0%
	ND:		
	PD: 668,†679,685,698,699,700,737,738,762,763, 767,769,772	13	65.0%
	ED:		
	ID:		
	HD:		
YIQṬOL Total Clauses: 8	Narrative: 774	1	12.5%
	ND:		
	PD: 667,715,740,770	4	50.0%
	ED: †764	1	12.5%
	ID: 666,710	2	25.0%
	HD:		
WeYIQṬOL Total Clauses: 1	Narrative:	0	0
	ND:		
	PD:		
	ED:		
	ID:		
	HD: 678	1	100%
WAYYIQṬOL Total Clauses: 40	Narrative: 651,652,655,656,657,659,661,665,673, 674,675,676,680,682,683,684,689,690,692,694,701, 703,704,705,706,709,720,721,724,727,733,734,735, 741,747,748,756,758,761,773	40	100%
	ND:		
	PD:		
	ED:		
	ID:		
	HD:		

Participle Total Clauses: 12	Narrative: 691,707,708,728,729,730,731,732,749, 751	10	83.4%
	ND: PD: 716 ED: 746 ID: HD:	 1 1	 8.3% 8.3%
Verbless Total Clauses: 16	Narrative: 750,759,760	3	18.8%
	ND: PD: 771 ED: 660,663,664,713,714,744,755,†765,†766 ID: 658,742,768 HD:	 1 9 3	 6.2% 56.2% 18.8%
Incomplete Total Clauses: 4	Narrative:	0	0
	ND: PD: ED: 702,719,722,723 ID: HD:	 4	 100%
Imperative Total Clauses: 14	Narrative:	0	0
	HD: 662,681,695,697,711,712,717,718,725,726, 736,743,745,757	14	100%
Cohortative Total Clauses: 2	Narrative:	0	0
	HD: 677,696	2	100%
Jussive Total Clauses: 0	Narrative:	0	0
	HD:	0	0

Analysis of the Narrative Structure and
Discourse Text-Types in 2 Samuel 15

Narrative Structural Analysis

Narrative/Paragraph Structure

The story of the initiation of Absalom's rebellion against the house of David in 2 Samuel 15 is constructed of a backbone of 40 *WAYYIQTOL* clauses which are grouped into four main paragraphs. In addition, two strings of non-*WAYYIQTOL* chains form two extra-paragraph comments, one occurring before the first paragraph of the chapter and one occurring after it. The first and second paragraphs of the chapter are each marked initially by וַיְהִי temporal clauses (655; 675). The third paragraph is initially marked externally by the *QATAL* clause marking the end of the preceding paragraph (clause 688). The fourth paragraph is marked initially by the *QATAL* clause at its head (clause 754). The paragraph is terminally marked by an unusual *YIQTOL* clause (774): וְאַבְשָׁלוֹם יָבֹא יְרוּשָׁלָיִם.[44]

---

[44] S. R. Driver, in his *Tenses* (§26βγ), after noting the few cases of an "imperfect" following the temporal adverbs אָז and טֶרֶם, records the rare examples of the form standing alone in prose: Gen 37:7; Ex 8:20; Deut 32:35; 2 Sam 15:37; 23:10; 1 Kgs 7:8b; 20:33; 21:6; 2 Kgs 8:29; 13:20; Job 6:17; Ps 56:4a; Jer 52:7; Ezr 9:4. The majority of these cases, however, occur either in direct discourse (usually, Narrative Discourse) or in contexts with other, non-*WAYYIQTOL* clauses, and, as defined in this study, they stand in extra-paragraph comments. The case of 2 Sam 15:37 is rare, not because of its *YIQTOL* governing verbal form, but because this *YIQTOL* clause occurs in isolation, outside of any extra-paragraph comment. In his *Notes*, Driver translates the clause as "[And Absalom] went on to enter [Jerusalem]" (318). However, the ongoing nature of the "imperfect" verbal form here is, by no means, obvious. Davidson (*Syntax*, §45, R2) notes that the use of the "imperfect" in this context is "elevated style": "The speaker does not bring the past into his own present, he transports himself back into the past, with the events in which he is thus face to face. . . . So perhaps 2 S. 15.37 יָבֹא *proceeded.*" Almost all of Davidson's other examples of this phenomenon are, however, drawn from poetic contexts rather than prose. Its presence here is unusual and parallels the general usage of *WeQATAL* clauses elsewhere in narrative prose. When used in contexts with other non-*WAYYIQTOL* clauses, both *WeQATAL* and *YIQTOL* clauses are part of extra-paragraph comments and provide information on actions which occur outside the narrative sequence of the storyline (e.g., clauses 350-354 in chapter 12, where both *WeQATAL* and *YIQTOL* clauses occur in a comment). When, however, they occur in isolation within narrative *WAYYIQTOL* chains they mark boundaries of narrative blocks, or paragraphs (e.g., clause 434 in chapter 13 and clause 753 in chapter 15). The question of why a *YIQTOL* clause is used in 15:37 as opposed to a *QATAL* or *WeQATAL* clause is still open to argument. The

Extra-Paragraph Comments

As in all the preceding examples, the two extra-paragraph comments in this chapter record events that are seen as repetitive and nonsequential to the actions described within the paragraphs of the wider story. In the first comment, Absalom elevates himself by supplying himself with a chariot, horses, and fifty messengers and by standing at the gate of the city:

15.01.651 וַיְהִי מֵאַחֲרֵי כֵן
15.01.652 וַיַּעַשׂ לוֹ אַבְשָׁלוֹם מֶרְכָּבָה וְסֻסִים וַחֲמִשִּׁים אִישׁ רָצִים לְפָנָיו:
15.02.653 וְהִשְׁכִּים אַבְשָׁלוֹם
15.02.654 וְעָמַד עַל־יַד דֶּרֶךְ הַשָּׁעַר

While the *WAYYIQTOL* clause 652 resolves the temporal clause heading the chapter, it is further linked, not to a following *WAYYIQTOL* clause as it would in a narrative paragraph, but rather to two *WeQATAL* clauses. These two clauses signal that the clauses in general should not be seen as narrative but as off-line comment, perhaps as repetitive and fluid in their actions.

The second extra-paragraph comment, likewise, is mostly composed of *WeQATAL* clauses and has a similar, nonsequential nature with respect to the surrounding narrative:

15.05.669 וְהָיָה בִּקְרָב־אִישׁ לְהִשְׁתַּחֲוֹת לוֹ
15.05.670 וְשָׁלַח אֶת־יָדוֹ
15.05.671 וְהֶחֱזִיק לוֹ
15.05.672 וְנָשַׁק לוֹ:
15.06.673 וַיַּעַשׂ אַבְשָׁלוֹם כַּדָּבָר הַזֶּה לְכָל־יִשְׂרָאֵל
         אֲשֶׁר־יָבֹאוּ לַמִּשְׁפָּט אֶל־הַמֶּלֶךְ
15.06.674 וַיְגַנֵּב אַבְשָׁלוֹם אֶת־לֵב אַנְשֵׁי יִשְׂרָאֵל:

Here, the four *WeQATAL* clauses which head the comment are resolved by the final two *WAYYIQTOL* clauses which provide the specific outcome of the general actions practiced by Absalom.

---

form may be influenced by the *WAYYIQTOL* of the same verb in the immediately preceding clause. As such, the two actions are, perhaps, to be seen as contemporary, as opposed to sequential: "Hushai . . . entered the city, and [at the same time] Absalom entered/was entering Jerusalem." The second clause could not be an inner-paragraph comment employing a participial clause in this case, because such clauses do not generally indicate specific, punctilliar action, which is needed if specific, contemporaneous events are related in the narrative. An inflected form is, therefore, necessary. The use of *QATAL* and *WeQATAL* clauses imply a narrative sequentiality; in such a case, the verb of clause 774 would be seen as occurring *after* the verb of clause 773, not contemporaneous with it.

Inner-Paragraph Comments

The five inner-paragraph comments within 2 Samuel 15 are composed of participial clauses alone (707-708, 728-732, 749-751), a participial clause in conjunction with a היה verbal clause (690-691), or a participial clause in conjunction with a היה verbal clause and a verbless clause (758-760).

Discourse Function Analysis

Narrative Discourse

The two cases of Narrative Discourse within 2 Samuel 15 (clauses †686, †739) consist of single clause speeches, both governed by *QATAL* verbal forms. In this respect, both examples of Narrative Discourse are completely regular and require no extensive comment.[45]

Predictive Discourse

The eight examples of Predictive Discourse within 2 Samuel 15 are regular with regard to this text-type. Four of the cases have *YIQTOL* clauses as the predominant clause type in the discourse, accompanied either by *WeQATAL* clauses alone (667-668; 737-740) or *WeQATAL* clauses with a verbless clause (769-772), or participial clauses (715-716). In four cases, the Predictive Discourse is immediately preceded by either another type of discourse or a subordinate clause and the primary clause type in the speech is *WeQATAL* (†679, 685, 698-700, 762-767).

Expository Discourse

The twelve examples of Expository Discourse within 2 Samuel 15 are all regular for this text type. Seven of the cases are composed of either participial (746) or verbless clauses (660, 713, 714, 744, 755) or both (663-664). The three cases of incomplete clauses occur as an oath (722-723), as a direct response to an earlier speech (702), or as a formulaic conclusion to a speech (719). In one case the verbless clauses are accompanied by a היה clause (764-766) and, in the final example, a היה clause stands alone (693).

---

[45]The *QATAL* form of מלך used in 2 Sam. 15:10 has the sense "to be made king," as it functions elsewhere in biblical Hebrew (cf. 1 Kgs 15:25; 16:29; 2 Kgs 3:1; etc.). When the verb has the definition "to reign," its form is usually *WAYYIQTOL*.

Interrogative Discourse

The four examples of Interrogative Discourse present within 2 Samuel 15 are all explicitly marked with initial interrogative particles: אֵי (658); מִי (666); לָמָה (710); and הֲלֹא (768).

Hortatory Discourse

Of the eleven cases of Hortatory Discourse within 2 Samuel 15, ten are composed solely of imperative clauses (662[46], 681, 711-712, 717-718, 725-726, 736, 743, 745, 757) or a combination of imperative and cohortative clauses (695-697). The remaining example has an initial cohortative clause accompanied by a *WeYIQTOL* clause (677-678). All cases are, therefore, explicitly marked as hortatory by the presence of imperative and/or cohortative clauses within the discourse.

---

[46]The function of clauses 662 and 745 (both רְאוּ) in 2 Sam 15:3 is simply to intro-duce the following Expository Discourses (clauses 663-664, 746), much in the same way as הִנֵּה is used throughout the Hebrew Bible. Its verbal form, however, as an imperative, causes it to be accounted in this analysis as a separate instance of Hortatory Discourse.

Table of Discourse Constellations for 2 Samuel 15

		Present Ch.	Prev. Chs.	Total
ND	*QATAL*	2	45	47
	QATAL, WAYYIQTOL		13	13
	QATAL, (Ptc./Vbl.)		9	9
	QATAL, WAYYIQTOL, (Ptc./Vbl.)		5	5
	QATAL, WAYYIQTOL, (Ptc./Vbl.), *YIQTOL*		3	3
	QATAL, YIQTOL (w/ past adverb)		0	0
	WAYYIQTOL, (Ptc./Vbl.)		0	0
	Vbl/Ptc/Inc (Dream Report)		1	1
PD	*YIQTOL*		23	23
	YIQTOL, WeQATAL	2	11	13
	YIQTOL, WeQATAL, (Ptc./Vbl../Inc.)	1	4	5
	YIQTOL, (Ptc./Vbl../Inc.)	1	2	3
	WeQATAL	4	9	13
	WeYIQTOL		2	2
ED	Ptc./Vbl.	7	37	44
	Ptc./ Vbl., Inc.		1	1
	Inc.	3	14	17
	Ptc./Vbl., *QATAL/YIQTOL* of היה	1	3	4
	Ptc./Vbl., *QATAL/YIQTOL* of היה, Front. Obj.+ *QATAL/YIQTOL*		2	2
	QATAL/YIQTOL of היה	1	1	2
HD	Impv./Coh./Juss.	10	45	55
	Impv./Coh./Juss., *WeYIQTOL/YIQTOL*	1	15	16
	Impv./Coh./Juss., *WeQATAL*		5	5
	Impv./Coh./Juss., *WeYIQTOL/YIQTOL, WeQATAL*		6	6
	Impv./Coh./Juss., *QATAL*		2	2
	Impv./Coh./Juss., *WeYIQTOL/YIQTOL*, (We)*QATAL*		1	1
	Impv./Coh./Juss., *ʾal-YIQTOL*		3	3
	Impv./Coh./Juss., *WeQATAL, ʾal-YIQTOL*		4	4
	ʾal-YIQTOL		9	9
	ʾal-YIQTOL, WeQATAL/YIQTOL		1	1
	(We)*YIQTOL-nāʾ*, (We*QATAL*/[We]*YIQTOL*)		9	9
	QATAL, YIQTOL/WeQATAL		1	1

2 Samuel 16 — David Retreats and Absalom Settles in Jerusalem — Clauses 775-854

Text in Syntactical/Paragraph Units

Ziba Receives All the Inheritance of Saul

16.01.775	וְדָוִד עָבַר מְעַט מֵהָרֹאשׁ (וְהִנֵּה)
16.01.776	צִיבָא נַעַר מְפִי־בֹשֶׁת לִקְרָאתוֹ
16.01.777	וְצֶמֶד חֲמֹרִים חֲבֻשִׁים
16.01.778	וַעֲלֵיהֶם מָאתַיִם לֶחֶם וּמֵאָה צִמּוּקִים וּמֵאָה קַיִץ וְנֵבֶל יָיִן׃

16.02.779   וַיֹּאמֶר הַמֶּלֶךְ אֶל־צִיבָא

ID
16.02.780   מָה־אֵלֶּה לָּךְ

16.02.781   וַיֹּאמֶר צִיבָא

ED
16.02.782   הַחֲמוֹרִים לְבֵית־הַמֶּלֶךְ לִרְכֹּב
16.02.783   וְהַלֶּחֶם וְהַקַּיִץ לֶאֱכוֹל הַנְּעָרִים
16.02.784   וְהַיַּיִן לִשְׁתּוֹת הַיָּעֵף בַּמִּדְבָּר׃

16.03.785   וַיֹּאמֶר הַמֶּלֶךְ

ID
16.03.786   וְאַיֵּה בֶּן־אֲדֹנֶיךָ

16.03.787   וַיֹּאמֶר צִיבָא אֶל־הַמֶּלֶךְ

ED
16.03.788   הִנֵּה יוֹשֵׁב בִּירוּשָׁלִַם כִּי אָמַר

16.07.800   וַיֵּצֵא אֲבִישַׁי בֶּן־צְרוּיָה

16.06.799   וַיֹּאמֶר אֲבִישַׁי בֶּן־צְרוּיָה אֶל־הַמֶּלֶךְ

16.05.798   אֶל־חַי יְהוָה

16.05.797   וַיֹּאמֶר אֲבִישַׁי

16.05.796   וַיֵּצֵא אִישׁ־מֵבֵית שָׁאוּל מִשְׁפַּחַת בֵּית־שָׁאוּל

16.05.795   כֹּה אָמַר יְהוָה בֶּן־אֲבִישַׁי

Shimei's Curse of David (Comment)

16.07.801   אֵשׁ

16.07.802   אֵשׁ אֲשֶׁר

ND

16.08.803   וַיַּעַן

HD

HD

16.04.793

16.04.794

HD

16.04.791

ED

16.03.789 †PD

16.04.792   וַיֹּאמֶר אֵלָיו

16.04.790   וַיֹּאמֶר הַמֶּלֶךְ אֲבִישַׁי

David and His Servants Respond to Shimei's Curse

וַיֹּאמֶר אֲבִישַׁי בֶּן־צְרוּיָה אֶל־הַמֶּלֶךְ	16.09.806
לָמָּה יְקַלֵּל הַכֶּלֶב הַמֵּת הַזֶּה אֶת־אֲדֹנִי הַמֶּלֶךְ	16.09.807
אֶעְבְּרָה־נָּא	16.09.808
וְאָסִירָה אֶת־רֹאשׁוֹ׃	16.09.809
וַיֹּאמֶר הַמֶּלֶךְ	16.10.810
מַה־לִּי וְלָכֶם בְּנֵי צְרֻיָה	16.10.811
כִּי [Q יְקַלֵּל] [וְכִי]	813α
יִקַּלֵּל	813β
וַיהוָה אָמַר לוֹ	16.10.812
קַלֵּל אֶת־דָּוִד	16.10.813
וּמִי יֹאמַר	16.10.814
מַדּוּעַ עָשִׂיתָה כֵּן׃	
וַיֹּאמֶר דָּוִד אֶל־אֲבִישַׁי וְאֶל־כָּל־עֲבָדָיו	16.11.815

ED

ID

HD

ID

†HD

†ID

ED

16.13.821	וַיֵּלֶךְ דָּוִד
16.13.822	וַאֲנָשָׁיו בַּדָּרֶךְ:
16.13.823	וְשִׁמְעִי
16.13.824	הֹלֵךְ בְּצֵלַע הָהָר לְעֻמָּתוֹ
16.13.825	הָלוֹךְ וַיְקַלֵּל וַיְסַקֵּל בָּאֲבָנִים לְעֻמָּתוֹ וְעִפַּר בֶּעָפָר:

The Goings of David and Absalom (Comment)

16.14.826	וַיָּבֹא הַמֶּלֶךְ
16.14.827	וְכָל־הָעָם אֲשֶׁר־אִתּוֹ עֲיֵפִים
16.14.828	וַיִּנָּפֵשׁ שָׁם:
16.15.829	וְאַבְשָׁלוֹם וְכָל־הָעָם אִישׁ יִשְׂרָאֵל בָּאוּ יְרוּשָׁלִָם
16.15.830	וַאֲחִיתֹפֶל אִתּוֹ:

16.11.816	כִּי (אֱלֹהִים אָמַר) לוֹ HD
16.11.	קַלֵּל אֶת־
817α	דָּוִד:
16.11.817	וּמִי
16.11.818	יֹאמַר
	מַדּוּעַ עָשִׂיתָה כֵּן:
16.12.819	אוּלַי יִרְאֶה יְהוָה בְּעֵנִי [וְ בְּעֵינִי] PD
16.12.820	וְהֵשִׁיב יְהוָה לִי טוֹבָה תַּחַת קִלְלָתוֹ הַיּוֹם הַזֶּה:

The Advice of Ahitophel and the Advice of Hushai

וַיֹּאמֶר דָּוִד אֶל־חוּשַׁי רֵעֵהוּ לָמָּה לֹא־הָלַכְתָּ אֶת־רֵעֶךָ	16.16.831	
וַיֹּאמֶר חוּשַׁי אֶל־אַבְשָׁלֹם	16.16.832	
וַיֹּאמֶר אַבְשָׁלֹם אֶל־חוּשַׁי	16.17.835	
וַיֹּאמֶר חוּשַׁי אֶל־אַבְשָׁלֹם	16.18.838	
וַיֹּאמֶר אַבְשָׁלֹם אֶל־אֲחִיתֹפֶל	16.20.844	

HD		
לַמֶּלֶךְ יְחִי	16.16.833
לַמֶּלֶךְ יְחִי׃	16.16.834
ID	
זֶה חַסְדְּךָ אֶת־רֵעֶךָ	16.17.836
לָמָּה לֹא־הָלַכְתָּ אֶת־רֵעֶךָ׃	16.17.837
ED	
לֹא	16.18.839
כִּי אֲשֶׁר בָּחַר יְהוָה	
לֹא אֵלֵהוּ אֶהְיֶה	16.18.840
PD	
וְאִתּוֹ אֵשֵׁב	
ID	
וְהַשֵּׁנִית	
לְמִי אֲנִי אֶעֱבֹד	16.19.841
הֲלוֹא לִפְנֵי בְנוֹ	16.19.842
PD	
כַּאֲשֶׁר עָבַדְתִּי לִפְנֵי אָבִיךָ	843α
כֵּן אֶהְיֶה לְפָנֶיךָ׃	16.19.843
HD	
הָבוּ לָכֶם עֵצָה	16.20.845
מַה־נַּעֲשֶׂה׃	16.20.846
ID	

16.21.847

16.23.854

16.22.851

16.22.852

16.23.853

16.21.848

16.21.849

16.21.850

HD

PD

Table of Independent Clause Types in 2 Samuel 16

Clause Type	Clause Distribution	Total	Percent
QAṬAL Total Clauses: 7	Narrative: 775,800,829	3	42.9%
	ND: 803 PD: ED: ID: †814,837 HD: 793	1 2 1	14.3% 28.5% 14.3%
WeQAṬAL Total Clauses: 5	Narrative: 795,825	2	40.0%
	ND: PD: 820,849,850 ED: ID: HD:	 3	 60.0%
YIQṬOL Total Clauses: 9	Narrative:	0	0
	ND: PD: †789,819,840,843 ED: ID: 807,813,841,846 HD: 794	 4 4 1	 44.4% 44.4% 11.2%
WeYIQṬOL Total Clauses: 1	Narrative:	0	0
	ND: PD: ED: ID: HD: 818	 1	 100%
WAYYIQṬOL Total Clauses: 24	Narrative: 779,781,785,787,790,792,799,806,810, 815,821,823,824,826,828,831,832,835,838,844,847, 851,852	23	95.8%
	ND: 804 PD: ED: ID: HD:		4.2%

Participle Total Clauses: 6	Narrative: 777,796,798,822	4	66.7%
	ND: PD: ED: 788,816 ID: HD:	2	33.3%
Verbless Total Clauses: 14	Narrative: 778,797,827,830,853,854	6	42.8%
	ND: PD: ED: 782,783,784,791 ID: 780,786,811,836 HD:	4 4	28.6% 28.6%
Incomplete Total Clauses: 4	Narrative: 776	1	25.0%
	ND: PD: ED: 805,839 ID: 842 HD:	2 1	50.0% 25.0%
Imperative Total Clauses: 6	Narrative:	0	0
	HD: 801,802,†812,817,845,848	6	100%
Cohortative Total Clauses: 2	Narrative:	0	0
	HD: 808,809	2	100%
Jussive Total Clauses: 2	Narrative:	0	0
	HD: 833,834	2	100%

Analysis of the Narrative Structure and Discourse Text-Types in 2 Samuel 16

Narrative Structural Analysis

Narrative/Paragraph Structure

The narrative of 2 Samuel 16 is built upon the twenty-three *WAYYIQTOL* clauses that comprise the backbone of the story. These clauses are combined into three major paragraph groupings (clauses 775-792, 795-825, 831-854), all initially marked either by a *QATAL* clause (775), a *WeQATAL* clause (795) or a וַיְהִי temporal clause (831).[47] In addition, the second paragraph is also terminally marked by a *WeQATAL* clause (825) which separates it from a following extra-paragraph comment (826-830).[48] The final paragraph in the chapter continues into the next chapter, coming to a conclusion at the *QATAL* clause 900 in 2 Samuel 17:14.

Extra-Paragraph Comments

The only extra-paragraph comment within 2 Samuel 16 concerns the actions of David and Absalom:

16.14.826 וַיָּבֹא הַמֶּלֶךְ

16.14.827 וְכָל־הָעָם אֲשֶׁר־אִתּוֹ עֲיֵפִים

16.14.828 וַיִּנָּפֵשׁ שָׁם:

16.15.829 וְאַבְשָׁלוֹם וְכָל־הָעָם אִישׁ יִשְׂרָאֵל בָּאוּ יְרוּשָׁלָם

16.15.830 וַאֲחִיתֹפֶל אִתּוֹ:

Although the comment contains two *WAYYIQTOL* clauses (826,828), they are unconnected and, therefore, the comment as a whole does not provide any progression in the story line.

---

[47]Gesenius (*Grammar,* §112tt) believes that the *WeQATAL* in clause 795 is due to "errors in the text or incorrect modes of expression."

[48]The traditional view that instances of *WeQATAL* are "frequentive" (Driver, *Tenses,* §133) does not account at all for its presence in clause 825. The sense of the clause is clearly that Shimei "threw dust," in a similar way that he "cursed and threw stones near [David]" (clauses 823-824), rather than he "used to throw dust" or "regularly threw dust" or even "and cast dust continually" (thus Gesenius, *Grammar,* §112f).

Inner-Paragraph Comments

Five inner-paragraph comments occur within the narrative of 2 Samuel 16. Four of these are composed either of verbless clauses (830, 853-854), participial clauses (822), or a combination of both (796-798). The first inner-paragraph comment in the chapter contains two verbless clauses preceded by an unusual incomplete clause introduced by וְהִנֵּה:

(וְהִנֵּה)

16.01.776 צִיבָא נַעַר מְפִי־בֹשֶׁת לִקְרָאתוֹ

16.01.777 וְצֶמֶד חֲמֹרִים חֲבֻשִׁים

16.01.778 וַעֲלֵיהֶם מָאתַיִם לֶחֶם וּמֵאָה צִמּוּקִים וּמֵאָה קַיִץ וְנֵבֶל יָיִן׃)

The incomplete clause appears to be elliptical by the exclusion of the verb, perhaps a deleted participial verbal form.

Discourse Function Analysis

Narrative Discourse

The single case of Narrative Discourse in 2 Samuel 16 contains two clauses, one governed by a *QATAL* verb and the other governed by a *WAYYIQTOL* verb:

16.08.803 הֵשִׁיב עָלֶיךָ יְהוָה כֹּל דְּמֵי בֵית־שָׁאוּל

אֲשֶׁר מָלַכְתָּ תַּחְתּוֹ [Q תַּחְתָּיו

16.08.804 וַיִּתֵּן יְהוָה אֶת־הַמְּלוּכָה בְּיַד אַבְשָׁלוֹם בְּנֶךָ

This case is completely regular for this text-type and requires no additional comment.

Predictive Discourse

The five examples of Predictive Discourse found in 2 Samuel 16 are completely regular for this text-type. Three cases contain only *YIQTOL* clauses (†789, 840, 843); the remaining cases contain either *YIQTOL* and *WeQATAL* clauses (819-820) or *WeQATAL* clauses alone (849-850). All four cases are, therefore, completely consistent with Predictive Discourse elsewhere in biblical Hebrew prose.

Expository Discourse

The six examples of Expository Discourse in 2 Samuel 16 conform to the verbal groups of other cases of Expository Discourse found elsewhere in speeches. The cases are made of verbless clauses (782-784, 791), participial clauses (788, 816), or incomplete clauses (805, 839).

Interrogative Discourse

Of the eight instances of Interrogative Discourse in 2 Samuel 16, seven are clearly marked as questions by the use of interrogative particles prefixed to them. The particles employed in this chapter are: מָה (780, 811, 846); אַיֵּה (786); לָמָה (807, 837); מַדּוּעַ (814); לְמִי (841); הֲלוֹא (842).

The case of the interrogative nature of clause 836 is ambiguous. Absalom makes the speech after hearing Hushai, the friend of David, wishing him well in his newly usurped role as king. Absalom's speech consists of two short clauses:

16.17.836   זֶה חַסְדְּךָ אֶת־רֵעֶךָ
16.17.837   לָמָה לֹא־הָלַכְתָּ אֶת־רֵעֶךָ׃

Clause 836 appears, on first sight, as a case of Expository Discourse, being a simple verbless clause. The nature of the comment and the fact that it is closely connected with the following, clearly marked interrogative clause cause a question of whether it is expository or an example of an unmarked, rhetorical question. In either case, the statement cannot but be seen as sarcastic and an accusation of Hushai's supposed capricious betrayal of David.

Hortatory Discourse

The seven cases of Hortatory Discourse in 2 Samuel 16 are generally well marked and require little comment. Five of the cases are speeches containing only imperative (801-802, †812, 845, 848), cohortative (808-809), or explicitly jussive clauses (833-834). One case involves a two clause discourse, one an imperative and one a *WeYIQTOL* (817-818).

The remaining example is an unusual juxtaposition of a *QATAL* clause and a *YIQTOL* clause.[49] The speech comes from the mouth of Ziba, the servant of

---

[49]Only one other example of this type of juxtaposition of *QATAL* and *YIQTOL* clauses occurs in the Court History (clauses 1187-1188). Coincidentally, it occurs in the reprisal of the Ziba/Mephibosheth conflict in 2 Sam 19 and is another illustration of a performative utterance and an ambiguous *YIQTOL* clause. Note the discussion in the analysis of Hortatory Discourse at 2 Sam 19.

Mephibosheth, in response to David's granting him the sum total of the assets belonging to his master (clause 791). Ziba's reply is short, comprising two clauses:

16.04.793 הִשְׁתַּחֲוֵיתִי

16.04.794 אֶמְצָא־חֵן בְּעֵינֶיךָ אֲדֹנִי הַמֶּלֶךְ:

While the syntax of the clauses might require that the first be seen as an example of Narrative Discourse and the second as an example of Predictive Discourse, their close juxtaposition and the formulaic content of the speech leads one to suspect the hortatory nature of this short speech. As such, clause 793 should be read as an instance of a performative utterance and clause 794, thus appearing in a hortatory context, takes on the sense of a cohortative: "I, hereby, prostrate myself! May I find grace in your eyes, my lord, the king!"[50]

---

[50]Thus, Waltke and O'Connor (*Syntax*, 488) translate clause 793 as "I *humbly* bow" (italics theirs); they do not, however, provide any criterion by which this "perfective form" should be translated in this way.

Table of Discourse Constellations for 2 Samuel 16

		Present Ch.	Prev. Chs.	Total
ND	*QATAL*		47	47
	QATAL, WAYYIQTOL	1	13	14
	QATAL, (Ptc./Vbl.)		9	9
	QATAL, WAYYIQTOL, (Ptc./Vbl.)		5	5
	QATAL, WAYYIQTOL, (Ptc./Vbl.), *YIQTOL*		3	3
	QATAL, YIQTOL (w/ past adverb)		0	0
	WAYYIQTOL, (Ptc./Vbl.)		0	0
	Vbl/Ptc/Inc (Dream Report)		1	1
PD	*YIQTOL*	3	23	26
	YIQTOL, WeQATAL	1	13	14
	YIQTOL, WeQATAL, (Ptc./Vbl../Inc.)		5	5
	YIQTOL, (Ptc./Vbl../Inc.)		3	3
	WeQATAL		13	13
	WeYIQTOL		2	2
ED	Ptc./Vbl.	4	44	48
	Ptc./ Vbl., Inc.		1	1
	Inc.	2	17	19
	Ptc./Vbl., *QATAL/YIQTOL* of היה		4	4
	Ptc./Vbl., *QATAL/YIQTOL* of היה, Front. Obj.+ *QATAL/YIQTOL*		2	2
	QATAL/YIQTOL of היה		2	2
HD	Impv./Coh./Juss.	5	55	60
	Impv./Coh./Juss., *WeYIQTOL/YIQTOL*		16	16
	Impv./Coh./Juss., *WeQATAL*	1	5	6
	Impv./Coh./Juss., *WeYIQTOL/YIQTOL, WeQATAL*		6	6
	Impv./Coh./Juss., *QATAL*		2	2
	Impv./Coh./Juss., *WeYIQTOL/YIQTOL*, (We)*QATAL*		1	1
	Impv./Coh./Juss., *ʾal-YIQTOL*		3	3
	Impv./Coh./Juss., *WeQATAL, ʾal-YIQTOL*		4	4
	ʾal-YIQTOL		9	9
	ʾal-YIQTOL, WeQATAL/YIQTOL		1	1
	(We)*YIQTOL-nāʾ*, (*WeQATAL*/[*We]YIQTOL*)		9	9
	QATAL, YIQTOL/WeQATAL	1	1	2

2 Samuel 17 — Hushai Advises Absalom and David — Clauses 855-956

Text in Syntactical/Paragraph Units

The Advice of Ahitophel and the Advice of Hushai (Cont.)

17.01.855 וַיֹּאמֶר אַבְשָׁלוֹם אֶל־אֲחִיתֹפֶל

HD
17.01.856 אֵת מַה־נַּעֲשֶׂה לָנוּ הָאִישׁ
17.01.857 אֲשֶׁר דִּבֵּר
17.01.858 אֲשֶׁר־אָמַר אֲחִיתֹפֶל
17.02.859 ED אִם־לֹא זֹאת תַּעֲשֶׂה
17.02.860 וַיֹּאמֶר חוּשַׁי
17.02.861 PD אַתָּה יָדַעְתָּ
17.02.862 כִּי־אָבִיךָ וַאֲנָשָׁיו גִּבֹּרִים
17.02.863 וּמָרֵי נֶפֶשׁ הֵמָּה
17.02.864 וְאָבִיךָ אִישׁ מִלְחָמָה

HD ED
17.03.865 וְלֹא יָלִין אֶת־הָעָם:
17.03.866 ED הִנֵּה עַתָּה הוּא נֶחְבָּא

17.03.867 בְּאַחַת הַפְּחָתִים אוֹ בְאַחַד הַמְּקוֹמֹת:

17.04.868 וְהָיָה כִּנְפֹל בָּהֶם
17.05.869 וְשָׁמַע הַשֹּׁמֵעַ וְאָמַר הָיְתָה מַגֵּפָה בָעָם אֲשֶׁר אַחֲרֵי אַבְשָׁלֹם:

HD
17.05.870 וְגַם בֶּן־חַיִל אֲשֶׁר לִבּוֹ כְּלֵב הָאַרְיֵה

	17.06.872	וַיָּבֹא חוּשַׁי אֶל־אַבְשָׁלוֹם
	17.06.873	וַיֹּאמֶר אַבְשָׁלוֹם אֵלָיו
		לֵאמֹר

17.05.871	וְנִשְׁמְעָה מַה־בְּפִיו גַּם־הוּא:	

		ND
	17.06.874	כַּדָּבָר הַזֶּה דִּבֶּר אֲחִיתֹפֶל
		ID
	17.06.875	הַנַעֲשֶׂה אֶת־דְּבָרוֹ
		HD
806α	וְאִם־אַיִן	
	17.06.876	אַתָּה דַבֵּר:

17.07.877	וַיֹּאמֶר חוּשַׁי אֶל־אַבְשָׁלֹם	

		ED
	17.07.878	לֹא־טוֹבָה הָעֵצָה
		אֲשֶׁר־יָעַץ אֲחִיתֹפֶל בַּפַּעַם הַזֹּאת:

17.08.879	וַיֹּאמֶר חוּשַׁי	

		ND
	17.08.880	אַתָּה יָדַעְתָּ אֶת־אָבִיךָ וְאֶת־אֲנָשָׁיו
		כִּי גִבֹּרִים הֵמָּה
		ED
	17.08.881	וּמָרֵי נֶפֶשׁ הֵמָּה כְּדֹב שַׁכּוּל בַּשָּׂדֶה
	17.08.882	וְאָבִיךָ אִישׁ מִלְחָמָה
		PD
	17.08.883	וְלֹא יָלִין אֶת־הָעָם:
		הִנֵּה
		עַתָּה
	17.09.884	הוּא־נֶחְבָּא בְּאַחַת הַפְּחָתִים
		אוֹ בְּאַחַד הַמְּקוֹמֹת
	17.09.885	וְהָיָה כִּנְפֹל בָּהֶם בַּתְּחִלָּה

17.14.898 וַיֹּאמֶר אַבְשָׁלוֹם וְכָל־אִישׁ יִשְׂרָאֵל

17.13.897 וְאִם־אֶל־עִיר יֵאָסֵף וְהִשִּׂיאוּ כָל־יִשְׂרָאֵל אֶל־הָעִיר הַהִיא חֲבָלִים

17.13.896 וְסָחַבְנֻהוּ עַד־הַנַּחַל עַד אֲשֶׁר־לֹא־נִמְצָא שָׁם גַּם־צְרוֹר׃

896α

17.12.895 וּבָאנוּ אֵלָיו בְּאַחַת הַמְּקוֹמֹת אֲשֶׁר נִמְצָא שָׁם וְנַחְנוּ עָלָיו כַּאֲשֶׁר יִפֹּל הַטַּל עַל־הָאֲדָמָה

17.12.894 וְלֹא־נוֹתַר בּוֹ וּבְכָל־הָאֲנָשִׁים אֲשֶׁר־אִתּוֹ גַּם־אֶחָד׃

17.11.892 כִּי יָעַצְתִּי הֵאָסֹף יֵאָסֵף עָלֶיךָ כָל־יִשְׂרָאֵל מִדָּן וְעַד־בְּאֵר שֶׁבַע כַּחוֹל אֲשֶׁר־עַל־הַיָּם לָרֹב

17.11.891

17.11.890

PD
ND

17.10.889 וְהוּא גַם־בֶּן־חַיִל אֲשֶׁר לִבּוֹ כְּלֵב הָאַרְיֵה הִמֵּס יִמָּס

†ED 17.09.888 כִּי־יֹדֵעַ כָּל־יִשְׂרָאֵל כִּי־גִבּוֹר אָבִיךָ וּבְנֵי־חַיִל אֲשֶׁר אִתּוֹ׃

17.09.887 לֵאמֹר

17.09.886 הָיְתָה מַגֵּפָה בָעָם

17.14.900   וַיְהִי הָעָם רַבִּים ... וַיְחַזְּקוּ אֶת־הָעִיר ...
|אֶת־הָרֹכְבִים אֶל־בֵּית־אַחִיתֹפֶל וְיֹנָתָן|

Hushai's Advice and Its Transmission to David (Comment)

17.15.901   וַיֹּאמֶר חוּשַׁי אֶל־צָדוֹק וְאֶל־אֶבְיָתָר הַכֹּהֲנִים

17.17.908
17.17.909
17.17.910
17.17.911
17.17.912

ED   17.14.899

ND   17.15.902
  17.15.903

HD   17.16.904
  17.16.905

†HD   17.16.906
  17.16.907

Ahimaaz and Jehonathan Are Almost Captured

וַיֵּ֣רֶא אֹתָ֔ם נַ֖עַר	17.18.913
וַיַּגֵּ֥ד לְאַבְשָׁלֹֽם	17.18.914
וַיֵּלְכ֤וּ שְׁנֵיהֶם֙ מְהֵרָ֔ה	17.18.915
וַיָּבֹ֣אוּ אֶל־בֵּֽית־אִ֣ישׁ בְּבַחֻרִ֗ים	17.18.916
(וְל֖וֹ בְאֵ֣ר בַּחֲצֵר֑וֹ)	17.18.917
וַיֵּ֥רְדוּ שָֽׁם׃	17.18.918
וַתִּקַּ֣ח הָאִשָּׁ֗ה	17.19.919
וַתִּפְרֹ֤שׂ אֶת־הַמָּסָךְ֙ עַל־פְּנֵ֣י הַבְּאֵ֔ר	17.19.920
וַתִּשְׁטַ֥ח עָלָ֖יו הָֽרִפ֑וֹת	17.19.921
וְלֹ֥א נוֹדַ֖ע דָּבָֽר׃	17.19.922

The Servants of Absalom Cannot Find Ahimaaz and Jehonathan

וַיָּבֹ֣אוּ עַבְדֵ֣י אַבְשָׁל֣וֹם אֶל־הָאִשָּׁ֣ה הַבַּ֗יְתָה	17.20.923
וַיֹּֽאמְרוּ֙	17.20.924

אַיֵּ֗ה אֲחִימַ֙עַץ֙ וִיה֣וֹנָתָ֔ן	17.20.925 ID
וַתֹּ֤אמֶר לָהֶם֙ הָֽאִשָּׁ֔ה	17.20.926
עָבְר֥וּ מִיכַ֖ל הַמָּ֑יִם	17.20.927 ND
וַיְבַקְשׁ֖וּ	17.20.928
וְלֹ֣א מָצָ֔אוּ	17.20.929
וַיָּשֻׁ֖בוּ יְרוּשָׁלָֽ͏ִם׃	17.20.930

David Obeys the Advice of Hushai

וַיְהִ֣י ׀ אַחֲרֵ֣י לֶכְתָּ֗ם	17.21.931
וַיַּעֲל֣וּ מֵֽהַבְּאֵ֔ר	17.21.932

וַיְלַ֥	17.21.933
וַיַּ֖עַל מֵעָלָ֑יו	17.21.934
וַיֵּ֧לֶךְ אֶל־בֵּית֛וֹ	17.21.935

וְאֶת־בֵּית֛וֹ וַיְצַ֖ו אֶל־בֵּית֑וֹ	17.22.938
וַיֵּחָנַ֖ק וַיָּמֹ֑ת	17.22.939

Ahitophel Commits Suicide

וְאֶת־אֲחִיתֹ֖פֶל	17.23.940
כִּ֣י	17.23.941
וַיָּ֖קׇם	17.23.942
וַיֵּ֥לֶךְ אֶל־בֵּית֖וֹ אֶל־עִיר֑וֹ	17.23.943
וַיְצַ֖ו אֶל־בֵּית֑וֹ	17.23.944
וַיֵּחָנַ֖ק	17.23.945
וַיָּמֹ֑ת	17.23.946
וַיִּקָּבֵ֖ר בְּקֶ֥בֶר אָבִֽיו׃	17.23.947

David's and Absalom's Preparations for War (Comment)

וְדָוִ֖ד בָּ֣א מַחֲנָ֑יְמָה	17.24.948
וְאַבְשָׁלֹ֗ם עָבַר֙ אֶת־הַיַּרְדֵּ֔ן ה֖וּא וְכׇל־אִ֥ישׁ יִשְׂרָאֵ֖ל עִמּֽוֹ׃	17.24.949
וְאֶת־עֲמָשָׂ֗א שָׂ֤ם אַבְשָׁלֹם֙ תַּ֣חַת יוֹאָ֔ב עַל־הַצָּבָ֑א	17.25.950

HD

וַיָּ֖קׇם	17.21.936
וַיָּ֥שׇׁב לִפְנֵ֖י אַבְשָׁלֽוֹם	17.21.937

17.25.951

17.25.952

17.26.953

———

17.27.954

David Remains in Mahanaim During the War

17.29.955

ED

17.29.956

Table of Independent Clause Types in 2 Samuel 17

Clause Type	Clause Distribution	Total	Percent
QAṬAL Total Clauses: 14	Narrative: 900,922,929,940,948,949,950,955	8	57.1%
	ND: 874,880,890,902,903,927	5	35.7%
	PD: ED: †888 ID: HD:	1	7.2%
WeQAṬAL Total Clauses: 13	Narrative: 909,910,912	3	23.1%
	ND: PD: 862,863,864,885,886,887,893,894,896,897 ED: ID: HD:	10	76.9%
YIQṬOL Total Clauses: 9	Narrative: 911	1	11.1%
	ND: PD: 883,889,891,895	4	44.5%
	ED: 867	1	11.1%
	ID: 875	1	11.1%
	HD: †906,†907	2	22.2%
WeYIQṬOL Total Clauses: 1	Narrative:	0	0
	ND: PD: ED: ID: HD: 859	1	100%
WAYYIQṬOL Total Clauses: 38	Narrative: 855,868,869,872,873,877,879,898,901, 913,914,915,916,918,919,920,921,923,924,926,928, 930,931,932,933,934,935,938,939,941,942,943,944, 945,946,947,953,954	38	100%
	ND: PD: ED: ID: HD:	0	0

Participle Total Clauses: 3	Narrative: 908	1	33.3%
	ND: PD: 884,892 ED: ID: HD:	2	66.7%
Verbless Total Clauses: 12	Narrative: 917,951,952	3	25.0%
	ND: PD: ED: 860,861,866,878,881,882,899,956 ID: 925 HD:	8 1	66.6% 8.4%
Incomplete Total Clauses: 0	Narrative:	0	0
	ND: PD: ED: ID: HD:	0	0
Imperative Total Clauses: 6	Narrative:	0	0
	HD: 870,876,904,905,936,937	6	100%
Cohortative Total Clauses: 5	Narrative:	0	0
	HD: 856,857,858,865,871	5	100%
Jussive Total Clauses: 0	Narrative:	0	0
	HD:	0	0

Analysis of the Narrative Structure and
Discourse Text-Types in 2 Samuel 17

Narrative Structural Analysis

Narrative/Paragraph Structure

The story of the thwarting of the advice of Ahitophel in 2 Samuel 17 is built upon a backbone of thirty-eight *WAYYIQTOL* clauses. These clauses are divided into six paragraph blocks. The first paragraph of the chapter is, in fact, a continuation of the final paragraph of the previous chapter, separated from it only by the final inner-paragraph comment concerning the trustworthiness of the advice of Ahitophel (clauses 853-854). This first paragraph is terminally marked by the *QATAL* clause 900, one of the few explicitly theological statements in the Court History. The second paragraph occurs after an extra-paragraph comment composed of a string of non-*WAYYIQTOL* clauses. It is terminally marked by a *QATAL* clause (922).

The third paragraph is terminally marked by the initial וַיְהִי temporal clause of the fourth paragraph (clause 931). The *QATAL* verbal form in clause 940 marks the beginning of the fifth paragraph of the chapter. The string of non-*WAYYIQTOL* clauses near the conclusion of the chapter (most of which are *QATAL* clauses) form a long comment concerning the setting before the subsequent battle between David's small army and Absalom in 2 Samuel 18.

The final paragraph of the chapter is initially marked by clause 954, a וַיְהִי temporal clause. This long introductory clause of the beginning of the paragraph is resolved by the first *WAYYIQTOL* clause of the following chapter (957). The final *QATAL* clause of 2 Samuel 17, occurring immediately after the introductory temporal clause before it, serves as an extended inner-paragraph comment before the true resumption of the narrative in the following *WAYYIQTOL* clause.

Extra-Paragraph Comments

The two extra-paragraph comments within the chapter are both extensive and explicitly marked. In both cases the chain of *WAYYIQTOL* clauses that precedes them are decisively broken by a chain of non-*WAYYIQTOL* clauses and the information given in the comment, while necessary for an understanding of the story line, does not propel the narrative forward in any real sense.

The first extra-paragraph comment of the chapter is introduced by the fateful advice of Hushai, given to the priests Zadok and Abiathar (clauses 901-907). This initial *WAYYIQTOL* clause, however, is not continued with another but rather by a long string of participial, *WeQATAL*, and *YIQTOL* clauses:

17.17.908 יְהוֹנָתָן וַאֲחִימַעַץ עֹמְדִים בְּעֵין־רֹגֵל
17.17.909 וְהָלְכָה הַשִּׁפְחָה
17.17.910 וְהִגִּידָה לָהֶם
17.17.911 וְהֵם יֵלְכוּ
17.17.912 וְהִגִּידוּ לַמֶּלֶךְ דָּוִד
כִּי לֹא יוּכְלוּ לְהֵרָאוֹת לָבוֹא הָעִירָה:

The fate of the advice of Hushai is, therefore, held at bay while the narrator provides this explanation about the general transmission of news from Hushai in the
city of Jerusalem to David by means of a female servant and Jehonathan and
Ahimaaz. These comments, not being *WAYYIQTOL* clauses, do not cause the
story line itself to progress, but rather provide background information so that
the reader is better able to appreciate the sequestering of Jehonathan and Ahimaaz in clauses 913-922 and their near capture in clauses 923-930.

The final extra-paragraph comment of the chapter provides additional information about the setting of the narrative scene before the fateful conflict in
the next chapter. It is marked by a string of *QATAL* and verbless clauses and
ends with an independent *WAYYIQTOL* clause:

17.24.948 וְדָוִד בָּא מַחֲנָיְמָה
17.24.949 וְאַבְשָׁלֹם עָבַר אֶת־הַיַּרְדֵּן הוּא וְכָל־אִישׁ יִשְׂרָאֵל עִמּוֹ:
17.25.950 וְאֶת־עֲמָשָׂא שָׂם אַבְשָׁלֹם תַּחַת יוֹאָב עַל־הַצָּבָא
17.25.951 וַעֲמָשָׂא בֶן־אִישׁ
17.25.952 וּשְׁמוֹ יִתְרָא הַיִּשְׂרְאֵלִי
אֲשֶׁר־בָּא אֶל־אֲבִיגַל בַּת־נָחָשׁ אֲחוֹת צְרוּיָה אֵם יוֹאָב:
17.26.953 וַיִּחַן יִשְׂרָאֵל וְאַבְשָׁלֹם אֶרֶץ הַגִּלְעָד:

Inner-Paragraph Comments

The two inner-paragraph comments in this chapter are clearly marked. One,
a verbless clause (917), provides the information about the possession of a well
by a man living at Bahurim:

17.18.917 (וְלוֹ בְאֵר בַּחֲצֵרוֹ)

The final inner-paragraph comment occurs immediately after the temporal
clause introducing the last paragraph in the chapter. It is governed by a *QATAL*
verbal form, an unusual clause for an inner-paragraph comment but one that may
occur immediately after an initial וַיְהִי temporal clause in a paragraph.[51] The

---

[51]For the case of a *QATAL* clause occurring immediately after initial וַיְהִי temporal
clause, note the discussion under the analysis of inner-paragraph comments for Gen 39 on

comment explains that three men, Shobi ben Nahash, Makir ben Amiel, and Barzillai the Gileadite gave David and his men many, many commodities, including foodstuffs and furniture before their battle with Absalom:

17.27.954 וַיְהִי כְּבוֹא דָוִד מַחֲנָיְמָה
(וְשֹׁבִי בֶן־נָחָשׁ מֵרַבַּת בְּנֵי־עַמּוֹן
וּמָכִיר בֶּן־עַמִּיאֵל מִלֹּא דְבָר
וּבַרְזִלַּי הַגִּלְעָדִי מֵרֹגְלִים:
17.28 וּמִשְׁכָּב וְסַפּוֹת וּכְלִי יוֹצֵר וְחִטִּים וּשְׂעֹרִים וְקֶמַח וְקָלִי
וּפוֹל וַעֲדָשִׁים וְקָלִי:
17.29 וּדְבַשׁ וְחֶמְאָה וְצֹאן וּשְׁפוֹת בָּקָר
17.29.955 הִגִּישׁוּ לְדָוִד וְלָעָם אֲשֶׁר־אִתּוֹ לֶאֱכוֹל
כִּי אָמְרוּ

ED

17.29.956 הָעָם רָעֵב וְעָיֵף וְצָמֵא בַּמִּדְבָּר:)

The reader thus knows that when David prepares for war at the beginning of 2 Samuel 18, his army has been well supplied.

Discourse Function Analysis

Narrative Discourse

The five instances of Narrative Discourse in 2 Samuel 17 (clauses 874, 890, 902-903, 927) are all composed of only *QATAL* clauses.[52] This is paradigmatic for this text-type in biblical Hebrew prose and requires no additional comment.

---

pp. 79-81. The case of Gen 39:5 (clauses 142-144) found there is similar to the syntax of 2 Sam 17:27-29. Note also the treatments under clause 202 in the Joseph Novella (Gen 40:1), and clause 506 in the Court Narrative (2 Sam 13:36).

[52]The question of whether clause 890 (כִּי יָצְתִי) is, in fact, Narrative or Hortatory Discourse is ambiguous. (See Driver, *Notes,* 322; Davidson, *Syntax,* §40b; Waltke and O'Connor, *Syntax,* 464, 488.) It is true that Hushai has not, at this point in the narrative provided any advice about David to Absalom; therefore, the narrative nature of the statement may be doubted. However, there is no hortatory clause nearby to cause the reader to see clause 890 as a performative utterance. The introductory כִּי, which seems out of place in the clause (Driver, *Notes,* 322), perhaps sets the clause off as hortatory, but parallel examples of this phenomenon are lacking. Therefore, in spite of the lack of narrative precedent for Hushai's advising Absalom in this matter, I have conservatively assigned the clause as Narrative Discourse.

Predictive Discourse

The two examples of Predictive Discourse contain *YIQTOL* clauses, *WeQATAL* clauses and either participial clauses (883-887) or participial and verbless clauses (891-897). The text-type of the former speech resolves the meaning of an ambiguous form in clause 884:

17.08.883 וְלֹא יָלִין אֶת־הָעָם:
הִנֵּה
עַתָּה
17.09.884 הוּא־נֶחְבָּא בְּאַחַת הַפְּחָתִים אוֹ בְּאַחַד הַמְּקוֹמֹת
17.09.885 וְהָיָה כִּנְפֹל בָּהֶם בַּתְּחִלָּה
17.09.886 וְשָׁמַע הַשֹּׁמֵעַ
17.09.887 וְאָמַר...

The verbal form governing clause 884, נֶחְבָּא, may be either a *QATAL* or a participle.[53] Standing within a clearly defined Predictive Discourse, with unambiguous predictive forms before and after in clauses 883 and 885, the possibility that the form is a *QATAL* is less likely, since *QATAL* verbal forms without a prefixed *waw* never occur in Predictive Discourse.

Expository Discourse

The seven cases of Expository Discourse in 2 Samuel 17 are regular for this text type. Five of the instances are constructed of verbless clauses (860-861, 878, 881-882, 899, 956). In addition, the chapter also contains an instance of clause governed by the verb היה (†888) and an instance of a speech having both a verbless clause and a היה clause (866-867). All of these examples are regular for Expository Discourse and require little comment.

Interrogative Discourse

The two cases of Interrogative Discourse both involve single clauses and are clearly marked with initial interrogative particles, הֲ (875) and אַיֵּה (925).

---

[53] BDB records the Niphal verb נֶחְבָּא as a "perfect" but notes that the verbs here in 2 Sam 17 and in 1 Sam 10:22 "both may be [participles]." The case of the verb in Jdg 9:5 seems clearly to be a *QATAL* form. The accounting in the *Concordance* of Evan-Shoshan recognizes both instances in 1 and 2 Samuel as participles and the instance in Judges as a *QATAL* .

Hortatory Discourse

The seven examples of Hortatory Discourse in 2 Samuel 17 are all regular and consistent with this text-type. Five of the examples have only imperative (876, 904-905, 936-937) or cohortative clauses (865) or a combination of both (870-871).[54] In addition, the first speech of the chapter consists of a string of unambiguous cohortative clauses followed by a *WeYIQTOL* clause:

17.01.856 אֶבְחֲרָה נָּא שְׁנֵים־עָשָׂר אֶלֶף אִישׁ

17.01.857 וְאָקוּמָה

17.01.858 וְאֶרְדְּפָה אַחֲרֵי־דָוִד הַלָּיְלָה:

17.02.859 וְאָבוֹא עָלָיו

There does not appear to be any difference in meaning between the cohortative clauses and the *WeYIQTOL* clause in this speech.[55] There is finally a case of a clause defined as hortatory by an *ʾal-YIQTOL* clause. This is followed by a *YIQTOL* clause with an infinitive absolute:

17.16.906 ‡אַל־תָּלֶן הַלַּיְלָה בְּעַרְבוֹת הַמִּדְבָּר

17.16.907 ‡וְגַם עָבוֹר תַּעֲבוֹר

פֶּן יְבֻלַּע לַמֶּלֶךְ וּלְכָל־הָעָם אֲשֶׁר אִתּוֹ:

Clause 907 carries the hortatory sense of the preceding clause, the *YIQTOL* verb taking on the sense of an imperative.

---

[54]The general method of treating clauses separately instead of seeing them as part of a larger discourse can easily lead to misreadings of individual clauses as, for example, the translation of the clearly hortatory clause 905 (וְהִגִּידוּ לְדָוִד / "and tell David!") by Waltke and O'Connor as "'they told to David' > 'David was told'" (*Syntax*, 207, note 71).

[55]Examples of unambiguous cohortative forms of בוא occur in Gen 29:21; Jdg 15:1; 2 Kgs 19:23; Ps 43:4; and 2 Chr 1:10.

Table of Discourse Constellations for 2 Samuel 17

		Present Ch.	Prev. Chs.	Total
ND	QAṬAL	5	47	52
	QAṬAL, WAYYIQṬOL		14	14
	QAṬAL, (Ptc./Vbl.)		9	9
	QAṬAL, WAYYIQṬOL, (Ptc./Vbl.)		5	5
	QAṬAL, WAYYIQṬOL, (Ptc./Vbl.), YIQṬOL		3	3
	QAṬAL, YIQṬOL (w/ past adverb)		0	0
	WAYYIQṬOL, (Ptc./Vbl.)		0	0
	Vbl/Ptc/Inc (Dream Report)		1	1
PD	YIQṬOL		26	26
	YIQṬOL, WeQAṬAL		14	14
	YIQṬOL, WeQAṬAL, (Ptc./Vbl../Inc.)	2	5	7
	YIQṬOL, (Ptc./Vbl../Inc.)		3	3
	WeQAṬAL		13	13
	WeYIQṬOL		2	2
ED	Ptc./Vbl.	5	48	53
	Ptc./ Vbl., Inc.		1	1
	Inc.		19	19
	Ptc./Vbl., QAṬAL/YIQṬOL of היה	1	4	5
	Ptc./Vbl., QAṬAL/YIQṬOL of היה, Front. Obj.+ QAṬAL/YIQṬOL		2	2
	QAṬAL/YIQṬOL of היה	1	2	3
HD	Impv./Coh./Juss.	5	60	65
	Impv./Coh./Juss., WeYIQṬOL/YIQṬOL	1	16	17
	Impv./Coh./Juss., WeQAṬAL		6	6
	Impv./Coh./Juss., WeYIQṬOL/YIQṬOL, WeQAṬAL		6	6
	Impv./Coh./Juss., QAṬAL		2	2
	Impv./Coh./Juss., WeYIQṬOL/YIQṬOL, (We)QAṬAL		1	1
	Impv./Coh./Juss., ʾal-YIQṬOL		3	3
	Impv./Coh./Juss., WeQAṬAL, ʾal-YIQṬOL		4	4
	ʾal-YIQṬOL		9	9
	ʾal-YIQṬOL, WeQAṬAL/YIQṬOL	1	1	2
	(We)YIQṬOL-nāʾ, (WeQAṬAL/[We]YIQṬOL)		9	9
	QAṬAL, YIQṬOL/WeQAṬAL		2	2

2 Samuel 18 — Joab Has Absalom Killed — Clauses 957-1085

Text in Syntactical/Paragraph Units

David Remains in Mahanaim during the War (Cont.)

18.01.957	וַיִּצְבַּר יָאָב אֶת־הָעָם וַיִּפְקֹד אֹתָם
18.01.958	וַיָּשֶׂם עֲלֵיהֶם שָׂרֵי אֲלָפִים וְשָׂרֵי מֵאוֹת
18.02.959	וַיְשַׁלַּח דָּוִד אֶת־הָעָם הַשְּׁלִשִׁית בְּיַד־יוֹאָב
18.02.960	וְהַשְּׁלִשִׁית בְּיַד אֲבִישַׁי בֶּן־צְרוּיָה אֲחִי יוֹאָב
18.03.962	וַיֹּאמֶר הַמֶּלֶךְ

Clause	Note	Hebrew
18.02.961		וְהַשְּׁלִשִׁת בְּיַד אִתַּי הַגִּתִּי
18.03.963	PD	
964α		לֹא תֵצֵא
18.03.964	PD	כִּי
965α		אִם־נֹס נָנוּס
18.03.965	ED	לֹא־יָשִׂימוּ אֵלֵינוּ לֵב
18.03.966		וְאִם־יָמֻתוּ חֶצְיֵנוּ
18.03.967		כִּי־עַתָּה כָמֹנוּ עֲשָׂרָה אֲלָפִים

18.04.968	וַיֹּאמֶר אֲלֵיהֶם הַמֶּלֶךְ

PD	
969α　אֲשֶׁ[רְ...]ֹם לַנַּ֫עַר לְאַבְשָׁלֹ֑ום	18.04.969

וַיְצַ֣ו הַמֶּ֡לֶךְ אֶת־יֹואָ֣ב וְאֶת־אֲבִישַׁ֨י 18.04.970

וְאֶת־אִתַּ֜י לֵאמֹ֗ר לְאַט־לִ֥י לַנַּ֖עַר 18.04.971

David's Order concerning Absalom (Comment)

וְכָל־הָעָ֣ם שָׁמְע֔וּ בְּצַוֹּ֥ת הַמֶּ֛לֶךְ אֶת־כָּל־הַשָּׂרִ֖ים 18.05.972

לְאַבְשָׁלֹֽום

ED	
עַל־דְּבַ֖ר אַבְשָׁלֹֽום:	18.05.973

וַיֵּצֵ֥א הָעָ֛ם הַשָּׂדֶ֖ה לִקְרַ֣את יִשְׂרָאֵ֑ל 18.05.974

Absalom is Caught in a Thicket

וַתְּהִ֧י הַמִּלְחָמָ֛ה בְּיַ֥עַר אֶפְרָֽיִם: 18.06.975

וַיִּנָּ֤גְפוּ שָׁם֙ עַ֣ם יִשְׂרָאֵ֔ל 18.06.976

(לִפְנֵ֖י עַבְדֵ֣י דָוִ֑ד) 18.07.977

וַתְּהִי־שָׁ֞ם הַמַּגֵּפָ֧ה גְדֹולָ֛ה 18.07.978

בַּיֹּ֥ום הַה֖וּא עֶשְׂרִ֥ים אָֽלֶף: 18.08.979

וַתְּהִי־שָׁ֣ם הַמִּלְחָמָ֗ה נָפֹ֨צֶת עַל־פְּנֵ֣י כָל־הָאָ֑רֶץ 18.08.980

וַיֶּ֤רֶב הַיַּ֨עַר֙ לֶאֱכֹ֣ל בָּעָ֔ם 18.09.981

מֵאֲשֶׁ֥ר אָכְלָ֖ה הַחֶ֥רֶב בַּיֹּ֥ום הַהֽוּא: 18.09.982

וַיִּקָּרֵא֙ אַבְשָׁלֹ֔ום לִפְנֵ֖י עַבְדֵ֣י דָוִ֑ד 18.09.983

(וְאַבְשָׁלֹ֗ום רֹכֵב֮ עַל־הַפֶּ֒רֶד֒) 18.09.984

וַיָּבֹ֣א הַפֶּ֡רֶד תַּ֩חַת שֹׂ֨ובֶךְ הָאֵלָ֤ה הַגְּדֹולָה֙ 18.09.985

Joab Has Absalom Killed and Rallies David's Servants

18.09.986	וַיִּקָּרֵא֙ אַבְשָׁל֔וֹם לִפְנֵ֖י עַבְדֵ֣י דָוִ֑ד	
18.10.987	וַיַּ֖רְא אִ֣ישׁ אֶחָ֑ד	
18.10.988	וַיַּגֵּ֣ד לְיוֹאָ֔ב	
18.10.989	וַיֹּ֕אמֶר	

| 18.11.991 | וַיֹּ֤אמֶר יוֹאָ֙ב לָאִ֣ישׁ הַמַּגִּ֣יד ל֔וֹ | |

| 18.12.995 | וַיֹּ֥אמֶר הָאִ֖ישׁ אֶל־יוֹאָ֑ב | |

ND	18.10.990	וַיֹּ֕אמֶר הִנֵּ֥ה רָאִ֛יתִי אֶת־אַבְשָׁלֹ֖ם תָּל֥וּי בָּאֵלָֽה׃
ND	18.11.992	וְהִנֵּ֣ה רָאִ֔יתָ
ID	18.11.993	וּמַדּ֛וּעַ לֹא־הִכִּית֥וֹ שָׁ֖ם אָֽרְצָה
ED	18.11.994	וְעָלַ֗י לָֽתֶת־לְךָ֙ עֲשָׂ֣רָה כֶ֔סֶף וַחֲגֹרָ֖ה אֶחָֽת׃
PD	18.12.996	לֽוּ־אָנֹכִי֩ שֹׁקֵ֨ל עַל־כַּפַּ֜י אֶ֣לֶף כֶּ֗סֶף
	996α	[לֹ֣א אֶשְׁלַ֣ח]
†HD	18.13.998	אֽוֹ־עָשִׂ֤יתִי בְנַפְשׁוֹ֙ [בְנַפְשִׁי] שֶׁ֔קֶר
	18.12.997	וְכָל־הַדָּבָ֖ר לֹ֥א יִכָּחֵ֥ד מִן־הַמֶּֽלֶךְ׃
	999α	[וְאַתָּ֖ה תִּתְיַצֵּ֥ב מִנֶּֽגֶד׃]
	996α	לֹֽא־אֶשְׁלַ֤ח יָדִי֙ אֶל־בֶּן־הַמֶּ֔לֶךְ

18.13.999 וַאֲנִי עָשִׂיתִי בְנַפְשִׁי שֶׁקֶר:

18.14.1000 וַיֹּאמֶר יוֹאָב

18.14.1001 לֹא־כֵן אֹחִילָה לְפָנֶיךָ   HD

18.14.1002 וַיִּקַּח שְׁלֹשָׁה שְׁבָטִים בְּכַפּוֹ

18.14.1003 וַיִּתְקָעֵם בְּלֵב אַבְשָׁלוֹם

18.15.1004 עוֹדֶנּוּ חַי בְּלֵב הָאֵלָה:

18.15.1005 וַיָּסֹבּוּ עֲשָׂרָה נְעָרִים

18.15.1006 נֹשְׂאֵי כְּלֵי יוֹאָב

18.16.1007 וַיַּכּוּ אֶת־אַבְשָׁלוֹם

18.16.1008 וַיְמִיתֻהוּ:

18.16.1008 וַיִּתְקַע יוֹאָב בַּשֹּׁפָר

18.16.1008 וַיָּשָׁב הָעָם מִרְדֹף אַחֲרֵי יִשְׂרָאֵל

18.17.1009 כִּי־חָשַׂךְ יוֹאָב אֶת־הָעָם:

18.17.1010 וַיִּקְחוּ אֶת־אַבְשָׁלוֹם

18.17.1011 וַיַּשְׁלִיכוּ אֹתוֹ בַיַּעַר אֶל־הַפַּחַת הַגָּדוֹל

18.17.1012 וַיַּצִּבוּ עָלָיו גַּל־אֲבָנִים גָּדוֹל מְאֹד

18.17.1012 וְכָל־יִשְׂרָאֵל נָסוּ אִישׁ לְאֹהָלָיו:

Absalom's Massebah (Retrospective Comment)

18.18.1013 וְאַבְשָׁלֹם לָקַח וַיַּצֶּב־לוֹ בְחַיָּו

18.18.1014 אֶת־מַצֶּבֶת אֲשֶׁר בְּעֵמֶק־הַמֶּלֶךְ

18.18.1015 כִּי אָמַר אֵין־לִי בֵן   ED

18.18.1016 וַיִּקְרָא לַמַּצֶּבֶת עַל־שְׁמוֹ

18.18.1017 וַיִּקָּרֵא לָהּ יַד אַבְשָׁלֹם עַד הַיּוֹם הַזֶּה:

The News of Absalom's Death Reaches David

Ref.	Text	Label	Ref.	Text
18.19.1018	וַיֹּאמֶר אֲחִימַעַץ בֶּן־צָדוֹק אָרֻצָה נָּא	HD	18.19.1019	אֵלָיו יוֹאָב
			18.19.1020	לֹא־אִישׁ בְּשֹׂרָה אַתָּה הַיּוֹם הַזֶּה
18.20.1021	וַיֹּאמֶר לוֹ יוֹאָב	ED	18.20.1022	וַיֹּאמֶר אֲחִימַעַץ עוֹד מָה־יְהִי וְאָרֻצָה־נָּא אֲנִי
			18.20.1023	וַיֹּאמֶר לוֹ רוּץ
		PD	18.20.1024	וַיָּרָץ אֲחִימַעַץ
18.21.1025	וַיֹּאמֶר יוֹאָב לַכּוּשִׁי	HD	18.21.1026	וַיֹּאמֶר הַצֹּפֶה
18.21.1028	וַיֹּאמֶר אֶל־יוֹאָב		18.21.1027	לֵךְ
18.21.1029	וּמַה־יֵּשׁ־אֵפוֹא לִרְצֹךְ בְּנִי			
18.22.1030	וַיֹּאמֶר			
18.22.1031	וַיֹּסֶף עוֹד אֲחִימַעַץ בֶּן־צָדוֹק	HD	18.22.1032	וַיֹּאמֶר יוֹאָב
			18.22.1033	לָמָּה־זֶּה
18.22.1034	וַיֹּאמֶר	ID	18.22.1035	וַיֹּאמֶר הַמֶּלֶךְ סֹבּ הִתְיַצֵּב כֹּה

18.23.1038　וַיֹּאמֶר לוֹ

18.23.1040　וַיֹּאמֶר הַמֶּלֶךְ
18.23.1041　סֹב הִתְיַצֵּב כֹּה
18.24.1042　וַיִּסֹּב וַיַּעֲמֹד׃
18.24.1043　וְדָוִד יוֹשֵׁב בֵּין־שְׁנֵי הַשְּׁעָרִים
18.24.1044　וַיֵּלֶךְ הַצֹּפֶה אֶל־גַּג הַשַּׁעַר
18.24.1045　אֶל־הַחוֹמָה
18.24.1046　וַיִּשָּׂא אֶת־עֵינָיו
(1046)　וַיַּרְא

18.25.1047　וְהִנֵּה־אִישׁ רָץ לְבַדּוֹ׃
18.25.1048　וַיִּקְרָא הַצֹּפֶה
18.25.1049　וַיַּגֵּד לַמֶּלֶךְ

18.25.1051　וַיֹּאמֶר
18.26.1052　וַיֹּאמֶר הַמֶּלֶךְ גַּם־זֶה מְבַשֵּׂר׃
18.26.1053　וַיֹּאמֶר הַצֹּפֶה אֲנִי רֹאֶה אֶת־הָרִאשׁוֹן
18.26.1054　כְּמִרֻצַת אֲחִימַעַץ בֶּן־צָדוֹק׃

ED
18.22.1036　וַיֹּאמֶר אֲחִימַעַץ בֶּן־צָדוֹק׃
HD
18.23.1037　וִיהִי־מָה אָרוּצָה

HD
18.23.1039　רוּץ

ED
1050α
18.25.1050　אִם־לְבַדּוֹ
בְּשׂוֹרָה בְּפִיו׃

ED
וַיֵּלֶךְ

18.26.1055

18.26.1056

18.26.1057 ED

18.27.1058

18.27.1059 ED

18.27.1060

18.27.1061 ED

18.27.1062 ED PD

18.28.1063

18.28.1064

18.28.1065 ED

18.28.1066

18.28.1067

18.28.1068 ED

18.29.1069

18.29.1070 ED

18.29.1071

18.29.1072 ND

18.29.1073		וַיֹּאמֶר הַמֶּלֶךְ שָׁלוֹם לַנַּעַר לְאַבְשָׁלוֹם
18.30.1074	וַיֹּאמֶר הַמֶּלֶךְ	
18.30.1075	HD　סֹב	
18.30.1076	הִתְיַצֵּב כֹּה	
18.30.1077	וַיִּסֹּב	
18.30.1078	וַיַּעֲמֹד	
18.31.1079	וְהִנֵּה הַכּוּשִׁי	
18.31.1080	בָּא	
18.31.1081	PD　וַיֹּאמֶר הַכּוּשִׁי יִתְבַּשֵּׂר אֲדֹנִי הַמֶּלֶךְ	
18.32.1082	וַיֹּאמֶר הַמֶּלֶךְ אֶל הַכּוּשִׁי	
18.32.1083	ID　הֲשָׁלוֹם לַנַּעַר לְאַבְשָׁלוֹם	
18.32.1084	וַיֹּאמֶר הַכּוּשִׁי	
18.32.1085	PD　יִהְיוּ כַנַּעַר אֹיְבֵי אֲדֹנִי הַמֶּלֶךְ	

Table of Independent Clause Types in 2 Samuel 18

Clause Type	Clause Distribution	Total	Percent
QAṬAL Total Clauses: 11	Narrative: 971,974,986,1012,1013,1018	6	54.5%
	ND: 990,992,1072,1073	4	36.4%
	PD:		
	ED:		
	ID: 993	1	9.1%
	HD:		
WeQAṬAL Total Clauses: 1	Narrative:	0	0
	ND:		
	PD: 1023	1	100%
	ED:		
	ID:		
	HD:		
YIQṬOL Total Clauses: 12	Narrative:	0	0
	ND: PD: 961,963,964,965,969,996,998,999,1024,1062, 1081,1085	12	100%
	ED:		
	ID:		
	HD:		
WeYIQṬOL Total Clauses: 0	Narrative:	0	0
	ND:		
	PD:		
	ED:	0	0
	ID:		
	HD:		
WAYYIQṬOL Total Clauses: 72	Narrative: 957,958,959,961,962,968,970,972,975, 976,977,978,979,980,981,982,984,985,987,988,989, 991,995,1000,1002,1003,1004,1005,1006,1007, 1008,1009,1010,1011,1014,1016,1017,1021,1025, 1028,1029,1030,1031,1034,1038,1040,1041,1043, 1044,1045,1047,1048,1049,1051,1052,1053,1054, 1056,1058,1060,1063,1064,1066,1067,1069,1071, 1074,1077, 1078,1080,1082,1084	72	100%

WAYYIQṬOL (cont.) Total Clauses: 72	ND: PD: ED: ID: HD:	0	0
	Narrative: 983,1042,1046,1079	4	50.0%
Participle Total Clauses: 8	ND: PD: ED: 1055,1059,1068 ID: 1035 HD:	 3 1	 37.5% 12.5%
	Narrative:	0	0
Verbless Total Clauses: 9	ND: PD: ED: 966,967,1015,1022,1036,1050,1061,1070 ID: 1083 HD:	 8 1	 88.9% 11.1%
	Narrative:	0	0
Incomplete Total Clauses: 3	ND: PD: ED: 973,994,1065 ID: HD:	 3	 100%
Imperative	Narrative:	0	0
Total Clauses: 6	HD: †997,1026,1027,1039,1075,1076	6	100%
Cohortative	Narrative:	0	0
Total Clauses: 4	HD: 1001,1019,1020,1033	4	100%
Jussive	Narrative:	0	0
Total Clauses: 2	HD: 1032,1037	2	100%

Analysis of the Narrative Structure and Discourse Text-Types in 2 Samuel 18

Narrative Structural Analysis

Narrative/Paragraph Structure

The story of the death of Absalom in 2 Samuel 18 is built upon a narrative backbone of seventy-two *WAYYIQTOL* clauses. These clauses are compiled into five paragraph blocks; the first (clauses 948-971) is a continuation of the last paragraph of chapter 17 and the last (clauses 1018-1098) continues into chapter 19. The first paragraph of the chapter is terminally marked by the *QATAL* clause 971. After a short extra-paragraph comment (clauses 972-974), the second paragraph is initially marked externally by the final *QATAL* clause of the comment. The *QATAL* clause 986 marks the boundary between the second and third paragraphs; likewise, the *QATAL* clauses 1012 and 1013 mark the boundary between the third and fourth paragraphs.

The fourth paragraph, initially marked by *QATAL* clause 1013 and terminally marked by the initial *QATAL* clause of the following paragraph, is, syntactically, an independent narrative unit.

18.18.1013 וְאַבְשָׁלֹם לָקַח

18.18.1014 וַיַּצֶּב־לוֹ בְחַיָּו [Q וַחַיָּיו] אֶת־מַצֶּבֶת
אֲשֶׁר בְּעֵמֶק־הַמֶּלֶךְ
כִּי אָמַר

ED
18.18.1015 אֵין־לִי בֵן בַּעֲבוּר הַזְכִּיר שְׁמִי

18.18.1016 וַיִּקְרָא לַמַּצֶּבֶת עַל־שְׁמוֹ

18.18.1017 וַיִּקָּרֵא לָהּ יַד אַבְשָׁלֹם עַד הַיּוֹם הַזֶּה:

The setting up of the *maṣṣebah* by Absalom, however, occurred before his death (clause 1014), which is recorded in 2 Samuel 18:15 (clause 1006), seven clauses before this paragraph. Its content, therefore, requires that it be interpreted narratively in the same vein as an extra-paragraph comment, even though its syntax parallels that of a simple paragraph.[56]

The final paragraph of the chapter begins with *QATAL* clause 1018 and ends with David's lament over Absalom in 2 Samuel 19:1 (clause 1089/1098).

---

[56]The reason why the narrator did not employ the usual clause types used in extra-paragraph comments in this paragraph is unclear. It may be that the comment here originally stood somewhere in the previous narrative, and for narratological reasons was transferred here, with the insertion of the prepositional phrase "in his life" / בְּחַיָּו.

Extra-Paragraph Comments

The one syntactically marked extra-paragraph comment in 2 Samuel 18 occurs immediately after the final *QAṬAL* clause of the first paragraph of the
chapter and consists of three clauses, an independent *WAYYIQṬOL* clause, a line
of Expository Discourse and a *QAṬAL* clause:

18.05.972 וַיְצַו הַמֶּלֶךְ אֶת־יוֹאָב וְאֶת־אֲבִישַׁי וְאֶת־אִתַּי
לֵאמֹר

ED
18.05.973 לְאַט־לִי לַנַּעַר לְאַבְשָׁלוֹם

18.05.974 וְכָל־הָעָם שָׁמְעוּ בְּצַוֺּת הַמֶּלֶךְ
וְאֶת־כָּל־הַשָּׂרִים עַל־דְּבַר אַבְשָׁלוֹם:

Narratively, the comment is bounded by an inclusio notice of Israel's going out
to war in clauses 971 and 975.

Inner-Paragraph Comments

The six inner-paragraph comments that occur in 2 Samuel 18 are all entirely
regular, consisting of היה verbal clauses (976, 978-979) and participial clauses
(983, 1042, 1046, 1079).

Discourse Function Analysis

Narrative Discourse

The three examples of Narrative Discourse in 2 Samuel 18 all consist of
only *QAṬAL* clauses (990, 992, 1072-1073). As such, they are completely regular for this text-type and require no additional comment.

Predictive Discourse

The eight cases of Predictive Discourse in 2 Samuel 18 are completely
regular for this type of discourse. Five cases consist of *YIQṬOL* clauses alone
(961, 963-965, 969, 996-999, 1062, 1081, 1085); the sixth case is a combination
of a *WeQAṬAL* and a *YIQṬOL* clause (1023-1024).

Expository Discourse

Eleven of the cases of Expository Discourse in 2 Samuel 18 consist of participial (1055, 1059, 1068) or verbless clauses (966, 994, 1015, 1022, 1050, 1057, 1061, 1070).[57] Additionally, there are two incomplete clauses in this chapter. One of these, clause 1065, consists of a formulaic word of greeting, שָׁלוֹם. The other incomplete clause occurs within the inner-paragraph comment mentioned above, as David provides instructions concerning the treatment of Absalom if he is captured:

18.05.972 וַיְצַו הַמֶּלֶךְ אֶת־יוֹאָב וְאֶת־אֲבִישַׁי וְאֶת־אִתַּי לֵאמֹר

ED
18.05.973 לְאַט־לִי לַנַּעַר לְאַבְשָׁלוֹם

18.05.974 וְכָל־הָעָם שָׁמְעוּ בְּצַוֹּת הַמֶּלֶךְ
וְאֶת־כָּל־הַשָּׂרִים עַל־דְּבַר אַבְשָׁלוֹם:

This case is unusual because, in light of the use of צוה in clause 972, one expects the speech to be hortatory. Instead, the clause is without a verb at all, consisting simply of an adverb, לְאַט, and three prepositional phrases governed by ל.[58]

Interrogative Discourse

The two examples of Interrogative Discourse are both clearly marked with interrogative particles. The second interrogative speech in the chapter, spoken by David, consists of a single clause, defined by הֲ:

18.32.1083 הֲשָׁלוֹם לַנַּעַר לְאַבְשָׁלוֹם

---

[57]The Massorah (*Minḥat Shai,* ad loc.) has a note at 18:29, concerned with clause 1070 (שָׁלוֹם לַנַּעַר לְאַבְשָׁלוֹם): ג׳ סבירין הֲשָׁלוֹם. The clause is almost exactly paralleled in the Interrogative Discourse of clause 1083 (below). Clause 1070 here, however, need not necessarily be a question. David is simply stating a supposed fact that Absalom has indeed come through the battle safe, in line with his earlier command to protect him (in 18:5; clause 973). When Ahimaaz casts doubt on the survival of Absalom (clauses 1072-1073), David then *asks* the Cushite, in clause 1083, הֲשָׁלוֹם לַנַּעַר לְאַבְשָׁלוֹם.

[58]The use of the verb אטט with the prefixed ל here is unusual. In every other case of the adverbial use of this phrase, the verb is explicitly stated (Gen 33:14; 1 Kings 21:27; Is 8:6; Jb 15:11). The word could actually represent an imperative from the root לוט "to wrap closely, to do something secretly" but its sense here would be curious. Note, however, its use in the next chapter at 2 Sam 19:5 (clause 1105). See BDB 31, 532 for additional examples.

The other case of Interrogative Discourse in chapter 18 is a two clause speech, the first clause marked by לְמָה־זֶּה and the second clause left unmarked:

18.22.1035 לְמָה־זֶּה אַתָּה רָץ בְּנִי
18.22.1036 וּלְכָה אֵין־בְּשׂוֹרָה מֹצֵאת:

The initial לְמָה־זֶּה governs both clauses, questioning both the running of Ahimaaz (clause 1035) and the lack of any reward for his running (clause 1036).

Hortatory Discourse

The clauses in all eight examples of Hortatory Discourse in 2 Samuel 18 are governed by either imperative (†997, 1026-1027, 1039, 1075-1076), cohortative (1001, 1019-1020), or jussive clauses (1037) or a combination of jussive and cohortative clauses (1032-1033). All cases of Hortatory Discourse are, therefore, completely regular and require no additional comment.

Table of Discourse Constellations for 2 Samuel 18

		Present Ch.	Prev. Chs.	Total
ND	*QATAL*	3	52	55
	QATAL, WAYYIQTOL		14	14
	QATAL, (Ptc./Vbl.)		9	9
	QATAL, WAYYIQTOL, (Ptc./Vbl.)		5	5
	QATAL, WAYYIQTOL, (Ptc./Vbl.), *YIQTOL*		3	3
	QATAL, YIQTOL (w/ past adverb)		0	0
	WAYYIQTOL, (Ptc./Vbl.)		0	0
	Vbl/Ptc/Inc (Dream Report)		1	1
PD	*YIQTOL*	7	26	33
	YIQTOL, WeQATAL	1	14	15
	YIQTOL, WeQATAL, (Ptc./Vbl../Inc.)		7	7
	YIQTOL, (Ptc./Vbl../Inc.)		3	3
	WeQATAL		13	13
	WeYIQTOL		2	2
ED	Ptc./Vbl.	11	53	64
	Ptc./ Vbl., Inc.		1	1
	Inc.	2	19	21
	Ptc./Vbl., *QATAL/YIQTOL* of היה		5	5
	Ptc./Vbl., *QATAL/YIQTOL* of היה, Front. Obj.+ *QATAL/YIQTOL*		2	2
	QATAL/YIQTOL of היה		3	3
HD	Impv./Coh./Juss.	8	65	73
	Impv./Coh./Juss., *WeYIQTOL/YIQTOL*		17	17
	Impv./Coh./Juss., *WeQATAL*		6	6
	Impv./Coh./Juss., *WeYIQTOL/YIQTOL, WeQATAL*		6	6
	Impv./Coh./Juss., *QATAL*		2	2
	Impv./Coh./Juss., *WeYIQTOL/YIQTOL,* (We)*QATAL*		1	1
	Impv./Coh./Juss., *ʾal-YIQTOL*		3	3
	Impv./Coh./Juss., *WeQATAL, ʾal-YIQTOL*		4	4
	ʾal-YIQTOL		9	9
	ʾal-YIQTOL, WeQATAL/YIQTOL		2	2
	(We)*YIQTOL-nāʾ,* (*WeQATAL/[We]YIQTOL*)		9	9
	QATAL, YIQTOL/WeQATAL		2	2

2 Samuel 19 — David Begins His Return to Jerusalem — Clauses 1086-1238

Text in Syntactical/Paragraph Units

The News of Absalom's Death Reaches David (Cont.)

וַיִּרְגַּז הַמֶּלֶךְ	19.01.1086
וַיַּעַל עַל־עֲלִיַּת הַשַּׁעַר	19.01.1087
וַיֵּבְךְּ	19.01.1088
וְכֹה אָמַר בְּלֶכְתּוֹ	19.01.1089

ED (Vocative)

בְּנִי	19.01.1090
אַבְשָׁלוֹם	19.01.1091
בְּנִי	19.01.1092
בְּנִי	19.01.1093
אַבְשָׁלוֹם	19.01.1094
מִי־יִתֵּן מוּתִי אֲנִי תַחְתֶּיךָ	19.01.1095
אַבְשָׁלוֹם	19.01.1096
בְּנִי	19.01.1097
בְנִי׃	19.01.1098

The People Respond to David's Lament

וַיֻּגַּד לְיוֹאָב	19.02.1099

ND

הִנֵּה הַמֶּלֶךְ בֹּכֶה	19.02.1100
וַיִּתְאַבֵּל עַל־אַבְשָׁלֹם׃	19.02.1101

וַתְּהִי הַתְּשֻׁעָה בַּיּוֹם הַהוּא לְאֵבֶל לְכָל־הָעָם	19.03.1102

ND

19.03.1103   וַיָּבֹא הַמֶּלֶךְ עַד־בֵּיתוֹ

19.04.1104   וְהַמֶּלֶךְ לָאַט אֶת־פָּנָיו וַיִּזְעַק הַמֶּלֶךְ קוֹל גָּדוֹל בְּנִי אַבְשָׁלוֹם אַבְשָׁלוֹם בְּנִי בְנִי׃

Joab Gives Advice to David concerning His Mourning

19.05.1105   וַיֻּגַּד לְיוֹאָב
19.05.1106   הִנֵּה הַמֶּלֶךְ בֹּכֶה וַיִּתְאַבֵּל עַל־אַבְשָׁלֹם

ED (Vocative)

19.05.1107   בְּנִי
19.05.1108   אַבְשָׁלוֹם
19.05.1109   אַבְשָׁלוֹם
19.05.1110   בְּנִי
19.05.1111   בְנִי׃

19.06.1112   וַיֹּאמֶר
19.06.1113   וַתְּהִי הַתְּשֻׁעָה לְאֵבֶל הַיּוֹם

19.06.1114   וַיֵּדַע הָעָם בַּיּוֹם הַהוּא לֵאמֹר

ND

[19.07]

19.07.1115   כִּי נֶעֱצַב הַמֶּלֶךְ עַל־בְּנוֹ׃

[11]

19.09.1120   וַיַּ֥בֶא הַמֶּ֖לֶךְ

19.09.1121   וַיֵּ֖שֶׁב הַמֶּ֑לֶךְ

Israel's Decision to Bring David Back (Comment)

19.09.1122   וַיְהִ֤י כָל־הָעָם֙ נָד֔וֹן

19.09.1124   בְּכָל־שִׁבְטֵ֣י יִשְׂרָאֵ֔ל לֵאמֹ֑ר

19.09.1125   הַמֶּ֨לֶךְ הִצִּילָ֜נוּ מִכַּ֣ף אֹיְבֵ֗ינוּ

19.10.1126   וְה֤וּא מִלְּטָ֙נוּ֙ מִכַּ֣ף פְּלִשְׁתִּ֔ים

19.09.1123   וְעַתָּ֛ה בָּרַ֥ח מִן־הָאָ֖רֶץ

ED

PD
19.08.1119   וְאַבְשָׁל֗וֹם אֲשֶׁ֤ר מָשַׁ֙חְנוּ֙ עָלֵ֔ינוּ
             מֵ֖ת בַּמִּלְחָמָֽה

19.08.1116   וַיְהִ֤י כָל־הָעָם֙ נָד֔וֹן
19.08.1117   בְּכָל־שִׁבְטֵ֣י
19.08.1118   וְעַתָּ֕ה לָ֥מָּה

HD
לֵאמֹ֑ר
וְהַמֶּ֖לֶךְ אֵינֶ֥נּוּ
מַחֲרִשִׁ֖ים לְהָשִׁ֥יב אֶת־הַמֶּֽלֶךְ

Judah Responds to David's Encouragement to Bring Him Back

לֵאמֹר

ND	19.10.1127	וַיְהִי כָל־הָעָם נָדוֹן בְּכָל־שִׁבְטֵי יִשְׂרָאֵל
	19.10.1128	לֵאמֹר
	19.10.1129	הַמֶּלֶךְ הִצִּילָנוּ מִכַּף אֹיְבֵינוּ
ID	19.11.1130	וְהוּא מִלְּטָנוּ מִכַּף פְּלִשְׁתִּים
	19.11.1131	וְעַתָּה בָּרַח מִן־הָאָרֶץ מֵעַל אַבְשָׁלוֹם׃

19.12.1132 — וְהַמֶּלֶךְ דָּוִד שָׁלַח אֶל־צָדוֹק וְאֶל־אֶבְיָתָר הַכֹּהֲנִים לֵאמֹר

לֵאמֹר

HD	19.12.1133	דַּבְּרוּ אֶל־זִקְנֵי יְהוּדָה לֵאמֹר
†ID	19.12.1134	לָמָּה תִהְיוּ אַחֲרֹנִים לְהָשִׁיב אֶת־הַמֶּלֶךְ אֶל־בֵּיתוֹ
†ND	19.12.1135	וּדְבַר כָּל־יִשְׂרָאֵל בָּא אֶל־הַמֶּלֶךְ אֶל־בֵּיתוֹ׃
†ED	19.13.1136	אַחַי אַתֶּם עַצְמִי וּבְשָׂרִי אַתֶּם
	19.13.1137	וְלָמָּה תִהְיוּ אַחֲרֹנִים לְהָשִׁיב אֶת־הַמֶּלֶךְ׃

Background Information concerning Shimei (Comment)

19.13.1138 †ID

19.14.1139 (HD)

19.14.1140 †ID

19.14.1141 †PD (Oath)

19.15.1142

19.15.1143

19.15.1144 HD

19.16.1145

19.16.1146

19.16.1147

19.17.1148

19.17.1149

19.18.1150

19.18.1151

19.18.1152

19.19.1153

19.19.1154

19.20.1155

David's Converses with Shimei and Abishai

19.20.1156

19.20.1157

HD

19.21.1158

ND

[19.21]

19.22.1159

19.22.1160

19.22.1161

ID

19.23.1162 וַיֹּ֥אמֶר דָּוִ֖ד

19.23.1163 ID מַה־לִּ֥י וְלָכֶ֖ם בְּנֵ֣י צְרוּיָ֑ה

19.23.1164 כִּֽי־תִהְיוּ־לִ֥י הַיּ֖וֹם לְשָׂטָ֑ן הַיּ֗וֹם י֤וּמַת אִישׁ֙ בְּיִשְׂרָאֵ֔ל כִּ֚י הֲל֣וֹא יָדַ֔עְתִּי כִּ֥י הַיּ֖וֹם אֲנִי־מֶ֥לֶךְ עַל־יִשְׂרָאֵֽל׃

19.24.1165 וַיֹּ֧אמֶר הַמֶּ֛לֶךְ אֶל־שִׁמְעִ֖י

19.24.1166 PD לֹ֣א תָמ֑וּת

19.24.1167 וַיִּשָּֽׁבַֽע־ל֖וֹ הַמֶּֽלֶךְ׃

Background Information concerning Mephibosheth (Comment)

19.25.1168 וּמְפִבֹ֙שֶׁת֙ בֶּן־שָׁא֔וּל יָרַ֖ד לִקְרַ֣את הַמֶּ֑לֶךְ

19.25.1169 וְלֹא־עָשָׂ֤ה רַגְלָיו֙

19.25.1170 וְלֹא־עָשָׂ֣ה שְׂפָמ֔וֹ

19.25.1171 וְאֶת־בְּגָדָיו֙ לֹ֣א כִבֵּ֔ס לְמִן־הַיּוֹם֙ לֶ֣כֶת הַמֶּ֔לֶךְ עַד־הַיּ֖וֹם אֲשֶׁר־בָּ֥א בְשָׁלֽוֹם׃

David Converses with Mephibosheth

19.26.1172 וַֽיְהִ֛י

19.26.1173 כִּי־בָ֥א יְרוּשָׁלַ֖͏ִם לִקְרַ֣את הַמֶּ֑לֶךְ וַיֹּ֤אמֶר לוֹ֙ הַמֶּ֔לֶךְ

19.26.1174 ID לָ֛מָּה לֹא־הָלַ֥כְתָּ עִמִּ֖י מְפִיבֹֽשֶׁת׃

19.27.1175 וַיֹּאמַ֑ר

ND

19.27.1176 אֲדֹנִ֥י הַמֶּ֖לֶךְ עַבְדִּ֣י רִמָּ֑נִי

כִּֽי־אָמַ֨ר עַבְדְּךָ֜

†HD

19.27.1177 †אֶחְבְּשָׁה־לִּ֨י הַחֲמ֜וֹר

19.27.1178 †וְאֶרְכַּ֤ב עָלֶ֙יהָ֙

19.27.1179 †וְאֵלֵ֣ךְ אֶת־הַמֶּ֔לֶךְ

כִּ֥י פִסֵּ֖חַ עַבְדֶּֽךָ׃

19.28.1180 וַיְרַגֵּ֣ל בְּעַבְדְּךָ֔ אֶל־אֲדֹנִ֖י הַמֶּ֑לֶךְ

19.28.1181 וַאדֹנִ֤י הַמֶּ֙לֶךְ֙ כְּמַלְאַ֣ךְ הָאֱלֹהִ֔ים

HD

19.28.1182 וַעֲשֵׂ֥ה הַטּ֖וֹב בְּעֵינֶֽיךָ׃

ND

1183α כִּ֡י לֹא֩ הָיָ֨ה כָּל־בֵּ֜ית אָבִ֗י

כִּ֣י אִם־אַנְשֵׁי־מָ֜וֶת לַאדֹנִ֤י הַמֶּ֙לֶךְ֙

19.29.1183 וַתָּ֙שֶׁת֙ אֶֽת־עַבְדְּךָ֔ בְּאֹכְלֵ֖י שֻׁלְחָנֶ֑ךָ

ID

19.29.1184 וּמַה־יֶּשׁ־לִ֥י עוֹד֙ צְדָקָ֔ה וְלִזְעֹ֥ק ע֖וֹד אֶל־הַמֶּֽלֶךְ׃

19.30.1185 וַיֹּ֤אמֶר לוֹ֙ הַמֶּ֔לֶךְ

ID

19.30.1186 לָ֛מָּה תְּדַבֵּ֥ר ע֖וֹד דְּבָרֶ֑יךָ

HD

19.30.1187 אָמַ֕רְתִּי

19.30.1188 אַתָּ֣ה וְצִיבָ֔א תַּחְלְק֖וּ אֶת־הַשָּׂדֶֽה׃

19.31.1189 וַיֹּ֤אמֶר מְפִיבֹ֙שֶׁת֙ אֶל־הַמֶּ֔לֶךְ

PD

19.31.1190 גַּ֥ם אֶת־הַכֹּ֖ל יִקָּ֑ח

Background Information Concerning Barzillai (Comment)

-----	19.32.1191
	19.32.1192
	19.33.1193
	19.33.1194

וּבַרְזִלַּי הַגִּלְעָדִי יָרַד מֵרֹגְלִים
וַיַּעֲבֹר אֶת־הַיַּרְדֵּן אֶת־הַמֶּלֶךְ לְשַׁלְּחוֹ אֶת־בַּיַּרְדֵּן
וּבַרְזִלַּי זָקֵן מְאֹד בֶּן־שְׁמֹנִים שָׁנָה
וְהוּא־כִלְכַּל אֶת־הַמֶּלֶךְ בְשִׁיבָתוֹ בְמַחֲנַיִם כִּי־אִישׁ גָּדוֹל הוּא מְאֹד׃

David Converses with Barzillai

19.34.1195 וַיֹּאמֶר הַמֶּלֶךְ אֶל־בַּרְזִלָּי

19.35.1198 וַיֹּאמֶר בַּרְזִלַּי אֶל־הַמֶּלֶךְ

HD		
אַתָּה עֲבֹר אִתִּי	19.34.1196	
וְכִלְכַּלְתִּי אֹתְךָ עִמָּדִי בִּירוּשָׁלִָם׃	19.34.1197	

ID
19.35.1199 כַּמָּה יְמֵי שְׁנֵי חַיַּי

ED
19.36.1200 כִּי־אֶעֱבֹר אֶת־הַמֶּלֶךְ יְרוּשָׁלִָם׃

ID
19.36.1201 לֹא־יֵדַע עַבְדְּךָ אֵת אֲשֶׁר־אֹכַל
19.36.1202 וְאֶת־אֲשֶׁר אֶשְׁתֶּה אִם־אֶשְׁמַע עוֹד בְּקוֹל שָׁרִים וְשָׁרוֹת

שָׁלֹשִׁים אֹתְךָ הַמֶּלֶךְ׃

David Leaves Barzillai and Goes to Gilgal

19.36.1203	בֶּן־שְׁמֹנִים שָׁנָה אָנֹכִי הַיּוֹם
19.36.1204	הַאֵדַע בֵּין־טוֹב לְרָע אִם־יִטְעַם עַבְדְּךָ אֶת־אֲשֶׁר אֹכַל וְאֶת־אֲשֶׁר אֶשְׁתֶּה
PD	
19.37.1205	כִּמְעַט יַעֲבֹר עַבְדְּךָ אֶת־הַיַּרְדֵּן אֶת־הַמֶּלֶךְ
ID	
19.37.1206	וְלָמָּה יִגְמְלֵנִי הַמֶּלֶךְ הַגְּמוּלָה הַזֹּאת
HD	
19.38.1207	יָשָׁב־נָא עַבְדְּךָ
19.38.1208	וְאָמֻת בְּעִירִי עִם קֶבֶר אָבִי וְאִמִּי
19.38.1209	וְהִנֵּה עַבְדְּךָ כִמְהָם
19.38.1210	יַעֲבֹר עִם־אֲדֹנִי הַמֶּלֶךְ וַעֲשֵׂה־לוֹ אֵת אֲשֶׁר־טוֹב בְּעֵינֶיךָ
PD	
19.39.1211	וַיֹּאמֶר הַמֶּלֶךְ
19.39.1212	אִתִּי יַעֲבֹר כִּמְהָם
19.39.1213	וַאֲנִי אֶעֱשֶׂה־לּוֹ אֶת־הַטּוֹב בְּעֵינֶיךָ
19.39.1214	וְכֹל אֲשֶׁר־תִּבְחַר עָלַי אֶעֱשֶׂה־לָּךְ
19.40.1215	וַיַּעֲבֹר כָּל־הָעָם אֶת־הַיַּרְדֵּן
19.40.1216	וְהַמֶּלֶךְ עָבָר
19.40.1217	וַיִּשַּׁק הַמֶּלֶךְ לְבַרְזִלַּי
19.40.1218	וַיְבָרֲכֵהוּ
19.40.1219	וַיָּשָׁב לִמְקֹמוֹ
19.41.1220	וַיַּעֲבֹר הַמֶּלֶךְ הַגִּלְגָּלָה
19.41.1221	וְכִמְהָן עָבַר עִמּוֹ

Judah and Israel Argue about Their Rights to the King

19.41.1222

19.42.1223

19.42.1224

19.42.1225

19.42.1226

ID

19.43.1227

19.43.1228

ED

19.43.1229

19.43.1230

ID

19.43.1231

19.44.1232

19.44.1233

19.44.1234

ED

19.44.1235

19.44.1236

ID

19.44.1237

19.44.1238

Table of Independent Clause Types in 2 Samuel 19

Clause Type	Clause Distribution	Total	Percent
QAṬAL Total Clauses: 32	Narrative: 1089,1105,1122,1125,1132,1147,1154, 1168,1169,1170,1171,1191,1194,1216,1221,1222	16	50.0%
	ND: 1103,1127,1128,1129,1130,†1135,1158,1176	8	25.0%
	PD:		
	ED:		
	ID: 1174,1225,1229,1230,1231,1236,1237	7	21.9%
	HD: 1187	1	3.1%
WeQAṬAL Total Clauses: 4	Narrative: 1152,1153	2	50.0%
	ND:		
	PD: 1119	1	25.0%
	ED:		
	ID:		
	HD: 1197	1	25.0%
YIQṬOL Total Clauses: 22	Narrative:	0	0
	ND:		
	PD: †1141,1166,1190,1205,1212,1213,1214	7	31.8%
	ED:		
	ID: †1134,†1138,1161,1164,1186,1201,1202,1203, 1204,1206	10	45.5%
	HD: 1139,1156,1157,1207,1209	5	22.7%
WeYIQṬOL Total Clauses: 4	Narrative:	0	0
	ND:		
	PD:		
	ED:		
	ID:		
	HD: †1178,†1179,1188,1208	4	100%
WAYYIQṬOL Total Clauses: 50	Narrative: 1086,1087,1088,1099,1102,1104,1106, 1112,1113,1120,1121,1124,1126,1142,1143,1145, 1146,1148,1149,1155,1159,1160,1162,1165,1167, 1172,1173,1175,1185,1189,1192,1195,1198,1211, 1215,1217,1218,1219,1220,1224,1227,1232,1233, 1238	44	88.0%
	ND: 1101,1114,1115,1180,1183	5	10.0%
	PD:		
	ED:		
	ID: 1226	1	2.0%
	HD:		

	Narrative: 1223	1	25.0%
Participle	ND: 1100	1	25.0%
	PD:		
Total Clauses: 4	ED: 1123	1	25.0%
	ID: 1131	1	25.0%
	HD:		
	Narrative: 1150,1151,1193	3	21.4%
Verbless	ND: 1181	1	7.1%
	PD:		
Total Clauses:	ED: †1136,†1137,1200,1228,1234,1235	6	42.9%
14	ID: †1140,1163,1184,1199	4	28.6%
	HD:		
	Narrative:	0	0
Incomplete	ND:		
	PD:		
Total Clauses:	ED:	14	100%
14	1090,1091,1092,1093,1094,1095,1096,1097,1098,		
	1107,1108,1109,1110,1111		
	ID:		
	HD:		
Imperative	Narrative:	0	0
Total Clauses: 8	HD: 1116,1117,1118,1133,1144,1182,1196,1210	8	100%
Cohortative	Narrative:	0	0
Total Clauses: 1	HD: †1177	1	100%
Jussive	Narrative:	0	0
Total Clauses: 0	HD:	0	0

Analysis of the Narrative Structure and Discourse Text-Types in 2 Samuel 19

Narrative Structural Analysis

Narrative/Paragraph Structure

The story of David's return to Jerusalem after the death of Absalom is built upon a backbone of forty-four *WAYYIQTOL* clauses. These clauses are grouped into nine paragraph blocks. The predominant marker for the boundaries between paragraphs in this chapter is the *QATAL* clause which, in this chapter marks the beginning (clauses 1105, 1132, 1154, 1222) or the ending (clauses 1089, 1147, 1126, 1221) of most of the paragraphs. The use of *QATAL* clauses in the extra-paragraph comments scattered throughout the chapter (clauses 1122, 1125, 1168-1171, 1191, 1194) also define paragraph beginnings and ends. In addition to the use of *QATAL* clauses as defining elements in this chapter, the וַיְהִי temporal clause 1172 also delimits the beginning of the sixth paragraph of the chapter.

Extra-Paragraph Comments

Four extra-paragraph comments occur within 2 Samuel 19. The first, an explanation of Israel's decision to bring David back to Jerusalem, is composed of two *QATAL* clauses, and two *WAYYIQTOL* clauses, the second of which contains the verb היה:

19.09.1122 וּלְכָל־הָעָם הִגִּידוּ
לֵאמֹר

ED

הִנֵּה
19.09.1123 הַמֶּלֶךְ יוֹשֵׁב בַּשַּׁעַר

19.09.1124 וַיָּבֹא כָל־הָעָם לִפְנֵי הַמֶּלֶךְ
19.09.1125 וְיִשְׂרָאֵל נָס אִישׁ לְאֹהָלָיו:
19.09.1126 וַיְהִי כָל־הָעָם נָדוֹן בְּכָל־שִׁבְטֵי יִשְׂרָאֵל

The remaining three extra-paragraph comments in the chapter report information about certain characters before a narrative paragraph tells of their respective encounters with David. The comment concerning Shimei (clauses 1148-1153), composed of *WeQATAL*, verbless, and *WAYYIQTOL* clauses, occurs immediately before David converses with him (clauses 1154-1167).[59] Likewise, the comment concerning Mephibosheth (1168-1171), composed of four *QATAL* clauses, occurs before David's encounter with him (clauses 1172-1190) and the comment concerning Barzillai (clauses 1191-1194), composed of two *QATAL* clauses, a verbless clause and a *WAYYIQTOL* clause, occurs immediately before David's conversation with him (clauses 1195-1216). In all these cases, the use of non-*WAYYIQTOL* clauses, especially *QATAL* clauses, signals the extensive report of information that is off-line of the narrative and does not cause the story to progress.

Inner-Paragraph Comments

Only two inner-paragraph comments occur in 2 Samuel 19, one a היה verbal clause (1102) and one a participial clause (1223). In both cases, the inner-paragraph comment reports information that does not cause the narrative to proceed, but is not as extensive as that reported in the extra-paragraph comments above.

Discourse Function Analysis

Narrative Discourse

The eight cases of Narrative Discourse in 2 Samuel 19 are entirely regular for this text-type. Five of the cases (1103, 1114-1115, 1127-1130, 1135, 1158) contain only *QATAL* clauses. A single narrative speech contains *QATAL* and

---

[59]On this comment, Waltke and O'Connor see clause 1152 as having the sense of a pluperfect: "The *weqatalti* form may indicate a disjunction, *signaling a situation out of chronological sequence.* As Johnson notes, 'In several instances a parenthetical remark— a parenthetically inserted particular or preliminary remark—is designated by *we* + perfect. If this occurs in a narration of past time, *we* + perfect corresponds ordinarily to our pluperfect.'" In their examples, Waltke and O'Connor translate 2 Sam 19:17-18 as: "And Shimei . . . hurried and went down with the men of Judah. . . . Now there were with him one thousand Benjaminites . . . *and* they *had rushed* to the Jordan before the king" (*Syntax,* 542). While the clause is, indeed, a "parenthetical remark," the *entire passage* is marked as off the narrative line by the concluding clause of the previous paragraph (clause 1147). Moreover, they do not continue and translate the following *WeQATAL* clause (1153), "And they crossed the fords to bring over the retinue of the king," as a pluperfect because the crossing is clearly happening as the comment is being told, not before it.

WAYYIQTOL clauses, as in narrative prose, as well as a verbless clause (1176-1181):[60]

19.27.1176 אֲדֹנִי הַמֶּלֶךְ עֲבְדִּי רִמָּנִי
כִּי־אָמַר עַבְדְּךָ

. . . .

19.28.1180 וַיְרַגֵּל בְּעַבְדְּךָ אֶל־אֲדֹנִי הַמֶּלֶךְ
19.28.1181 וַאדֹנִי הַמֶּלֶךְ כְּמַלְאַךְ הָאֱלֹהִים

There are also two cases of narrative speeches that have no QATAL clauses and are defined solely by the WAYYIQTOL clauses within them (1100-1101, 1183).[61]

Predictive Discourse

The six examples of Predictive Discourse in 2 Samuel 19 exactly conform to their text-type. Five of the cases (†1141, 1166, 1190, 1205, 1212-1214) contain only YIQTOL clauses.[62] An additional case, occurring parallel to a

---

[60]In this example, clause 1181, being verbless, could be considered a single clause of Expository Discourse. The sense of the fact of David's being "like the messenger of God," however, seems to be Mephibosheth's explanatory reason why he came to David for him to redress his problem. As such, I have included it within the Narrative Discourse. If clause 1181 is considered to be a separate case of Expository Discourse, of course, it would be entirely regular for that text-type also.

[61]Waltke and O'Connor (Syntax, 561-62) believe that in such cases as clause 1100-1101, in which a "participle used as a predicate in present time" is followed by a "subordinate wayyqtl," the WAYYIQTOL clause "may have a stative present sense or a persistent perfective sense." In this, they follow Driver (Tenses, §80), Davidson (Syntax, §49a), and Gesenius (Grammar, §111u). In all four explications of this phenomenon, however, the only case from prose narrative comes from 2 Sam 19:2; all other cases come from poetic or prophetic contexts. Moreover, the classic grammarians all state that this sense is expressive "of a general truth" (Driver) or "expresses a general truth" (Davidson). They, furthermore, do not treat other cases of a WAYYIQTOL clause following a participial clause in narrative in this way (e.g., Gen 41:18; or even in poetry, Jb 12:4). Since temporally Joab's being told of David's actions occurs after the narrator's report of his mourning, it is probable that the report is temporally set in the past tense. The participial clause standing before the WAYYIQTOL clause may, perhaps, lend an "on-going" sense to the action, but the action itself, being reported by a WAYYIQTOL clause, is firmly set in the past: "The king was weeping and mourning over Absalom."

[62]Clause 1212 is not explicitly marked as a jussive, contrary to the translation of Waltke and O'Connor, Syntax, 569.

subordinate clause after a preceding Hortatory Discourse, contains a single
WeQATAL clause:

19.08.1116 קוּם
19.08.1117 צֵא
19.08.1118 וְדַבֵּר עַל־לֵב עֲבָדֶיךָ
כִּי בַיהוָה נִשְׁבַּעְתִּי
PD
1119α כִּי־אֵינְךָ יוֹצֵא
1119β אִם־יָלִין אִישׁ אִתְּךָ הַלָּיְלָה
19.08.1119 וְרָעָה לְךָ זֹאת מִכָּל־הָרָעָה
אֲשֶׁר־בָּאָה עָלֶיךָ מִנְּעֻרֶיךָ עַד־עָתָּה:

Joab's prediction that the people's abandonment of David (זֹאת) would turn out
worse for him than anything else in David's life is part of Joab's oath, stated as a
dependent clause (כִּי בַיהוָה נִשְׁבַּעְתִּי) to Joab's original imperative וְדַבֵּר. As such,
the *WeQATAL* clause is not parallel to the preceding Hortatory Discourse and
must be considered separately. If clause 1119 had been parallel with the
preceding discourse, of course, the *WeQATAL* clause would have taken on
hortatory force, as elsewhere.[63]

Expository Discourse

The eight examples of Expository Discourse in this chapter are entirely
regular for this text-type. One case contains a single participial clause (1123)
and four cases involve verbless clauses (†1136-1137, 1200, 1228, 1234-1235).
In addition, two extended cases of incomplete clauses (1090-1098, 1107-1111)
are accounted here, both instances of David's vocative lament over Absalom's
death.

Interrogative Discourse

Fifteen examples of Interrogative Discourse occur in 2 Samuel 19. Of these,
the majority of the clauses are marked by interrogative particles: (וְ)לָמָה/לָמָה
(1131, 1134, 1138, 1174, 1186, 1204, 1206, 1229); הֲלוֹא (1140); הֲ (1161,
1164[64], 1201, 1230); מָה (1163, 1184); כַּמָּה (1199); (וּ)מַדּוּעַ (1225, 1236). In

---

[63]Note, in this chapter, clauses 1196-1197, in which an imperative clause is
followed by a first person *WeQATAL* clause which takes on cohortative force.

[64]The presence of the interrogative particle in this clause most probably dropped out
because of the definite article. Note LXX: εἰ σήμερον. The first word of the clause
should read הַהַיּוֹם. See Driver, *Notes*, 336.

addition, there are two cases (clauses 1202-1203, 1231) of polar questions in this chapter, the leading clause introduced by הֲ and the second (and, in one case, third) introduced by אִם:[65]

19.36.1201   הַאֵדַע בֵּין־טוֹב לְרָע

19.36.1202   אִם־יִטְעַם עַבְדְּךָ אֶת־אֲשֶׁר אֹכַל וְאֶת־אֲשֶׁר אֶשְׁתֶּה

19.36.1203   אִם־אֶשְׁמַע עוֹד בְּקוֹל שָׁרִים וְשָׁרוֹת

19.43.1230   הֶאָכוֹל אָכַלְנוּ מִן־הַמֶּלֶךְ

19.43.1231   אִם־נִשֵּׂאת נִשָּׂא לָנוּ:

In addition, there are two cases of unmarked questions, one governed by a *WAYYIQTOL* verb (clause 1226) and one governed by a *QATAL* verb (clause 1237). In both examples, the preceding clause is defined as interrogative by (וּ)מַדּוּעַ and the question of "why" extends to the second clause as well.

Hortatory Discourse

Nine examples of Hortatory Discourse occur in 2 Samuel 19. Of these, seven cases are marked as hortatory by the presence of imperative or, in one instance, cohortative clauses. In three cases (1116-1118, 1144, 1182), the speech consists solely of imperative clauses. In each of three additional cases, the imperative (1133-1139, 1207-1210) or cohortative (†1177-1179) clause is joined by *WeYIQTOL* or *YIQTOL* clauses which also have hortatory force. In one case the original imperative clause is continued by a *WeQATAL* clause which also has hortatory force (clauses 1196-1197).

In addition to these cases defined by explicit hortatory verbal forms, there is also a two-clause speech defined as hortatory by the presence of the negative particle אַל־ prefixed to the governing *YIQTOL* forms (clauses 1156-1157). Finally, there is a case of a *QATAL* clause being juxtaposed to a *YIQTOL* clause in a two-clause speech by David:

19.30.1187   אָמַרְתִּי

19.30.1188   אַתָּה וְצִיבָא תַּחְלְקוּ אֶת־הַשָּׂדֶה:

Under most circumstances, these two clauses would be considered separate examples of Narrative and Predictive Discourse. In this specific case, however, the narrative context involves David's pronouncing a judgment concerning the paternal inheritance of Mephibosheth. Ziba, Mephibosheth's servant, has

---

[65]For the characteristics of polar questions in general, see Waltke and O'Connor, *Syntax*, 684-85.

claimed that his master has committed treason against David and that he himself should receive the inheritance. Mephibosheth himself claims that his servant tricked him and should, rightly, receive nothing. David pronounces his judgment in this speech. The narrative context, therefore, allows the reader to interpret the text-type of the speech contrary to the simple syntax of its clausal forms.[66] The speech, being hortatory, involves an example of a *QATAL* performative utterance and a *YIQTOL* clause having hortatory force: "I hereby say: You and Ziba divide the field!"

---

[66]In his discussion of the "performative sentence," Eep Talstra ("Text Grammar and Hebrew Bible II: Syntax and Semantics," *Bibliotheca Orientalis* 39 [1982] 26-38, quotation below from 27-28) provides this short discussion, with a list of supposed general characteristics of the syntax of the construction:

> Modern European languages always use a first person present tense for performative speech: "I name this ship . . ."; "I give you . . ."; "Ich taufe dich . . ."; "Ik beloof . . ."; "Ik verklaar hierbij . . .", etc. In classical Hebrew the perfect tense form is used for it:
>
> *ntty*: "I give" (Jud. 1,2; I Ki. 3,11; Jer. 1,9)
>
> *nšbᶜty*: "I swear" (Gen. 22,16)
>
> *ʾmrty*: "I command" (II Sam. 19,30)
>
> *hᶜdty*: "I affirm" (Dtn. 8,19)

A similar use of the perfect in Akkadian is mentioned by A. Ungnad-Matoush (*Grammatik des Akkadischen* [1969]) §57.a: *innana aṭṭardakkum*— "I hereby send to you." G. Leech (*Semantics* [Harmondsworth: Peregrine, 1974], 345) lists five syntactic markers of a performative sentence (presupposing, of course, that act and utterance coincide):

    1. The subject is in first person. . . .

    2. The verb is in simple present tense. In Hebrew: perfect tense.

    3. The indirect object, if present, is "you". In Hebrew: the pronominal suffix.

    4. It is possible to insert the adverb "hereby". In Hebrew: *hnh, hywm, wᶜth*.

    5. The sentence is not negative. In that case the Hebrew has an imperfect or a participle.

Unfortunately, the five "syntactic markers" listed by Talstra can apply to many, many cases of first person *QATAL* verbal forms besides performative utterances. The presupposition that act and utterance coincide (that is, whether a particular case is an instance of a performative utterance) is exactly what must be proven syntactically. In this study, the argument is made that a performative utterance must be a *QATAL* clause that stands in parallel with other explicit hortatory forms (imperative, cohortative, or jussive clauses) or immediately preceding a *YIQTOL* clause, as is the case in 2 Sam 19:30.

Table of Discourse Constellations for 2 Samuel 19

		Present Ch.	Prev. Chs.	Total
ND	QAṬAL	4	55	59
	QAṬAL, WAYYIQṬOL		14	14
	QAṬAL, (Ptc./Vbl.)		9	9
	QAṬAL, WAYYIQṬOL, (Ptc./Vbl.)	1	5	6
	QAṬAL, WAYYIQṬOL, (Ptc./Vbl.), YIQṬOL		3	3
	QAṬAL, YIQṬOL (w/ past adverb)		0	0
	WAYYIQṬOL, (Ptc./Vbl.)	2	0	2
	Vbl/Ptc/Inc (Dream Report)		1	1
PD	YIQṬOL	5	33	38
	YIQṬOL, WeQAṬAL		15	15
	YIQṬOL, WeQAṬAL, (Ptc./Vbl../Inc.)		7	7
	YIQṬOL, (Ptc./Vbl../Inc.)		3	3
	WeQAṬAL	1	13	14
	WeYIQṬOL		2	2
ED	Ptc./Vbl.	5	64	69
	Ptc./ Vbl., Inc.		1	1
	Inc.	2	21	23
	Ptc./Vbl., QAṬAL/YIQṬOL of היה		5	5
	Ptc./Vbl., QAṬAL/YIQṬOL of היה, Front. Obj.+ QAṬAL/YIQṬOL		2	2
	QAṬAL/YIQṬOL of היה		3	3
HD	Impv./Coh./Juss.	3	73	76
	Impv./Coh./Juss., WeYIQṬOL/YIQṬOL	3	17	20
	Impv./Coh./Juss., WeQAṬAL	1	6	7
	Impv./Coh./Juss., WeYIQṬOL/YIQṬOL, WeQAṬAL		6	6
	Impv./Coh./Juss., QAṬAL		2	2
	Impv./Coh./Juss., WeYIQṬOL/YIQṬOL, (We)QAṬAL		1	1
	Impv./Coh./Juss., ʾal-YIQṬOL		3	3
	Impv./Coh./Juss., WeQAṬAL, ʾal-YIQṬOL		4	4
	ʾal-YIQṬOL	1	9	10
	ʾal-YIQṬOL, WeQAṬAL/YIQṬOL		2	2
	(We)YIQṬOL-nāʾ, (WeQAṬAL/[We]YIQṬOL)		9	9
	QAṬAL, YIQṬOL/WeQAṬAL	1	2	3

2 Samuel 20 — The Rebellion of Sheba is Stopped — Clauses 1239-1339

Text in Syntactical/Paragraph Units

Sheba Leads the Rebellion of Israel against David

20.01.1239	וְשָׁם נִקְרָא אִישׁ בְּלִיַּעַל
20.01.1240	וּשְׁמוֹ שֶׁבַע בֶּן־בִּכְרִי אִישׁ יְמִינִי
20.01.1241	וַיִּתְקַע בַּשֹּׁפָר
20.01.1242	וַיֹּאמֶר

ED		
20.01.1243	אֵין־לָנוּ חֵלֶק בְּדָוִד
20.01.1244	וְלֹא נַחֲלָה־לָנוּ בְּבֶן־יִשַׁי
20.01.1245	אִישׁ לְאֹהָלָיו יִשְׂרָאֵל:

20.02.1246	וַיַּעַל כָּל־אִישׁ יִשְׂרָאֵל מֵאַחֲרֵי דָוִד אַחֲרֵי שֶׁבַע בֶּן־בִּכְרִי
20.02.1247	וְאִישׁ יְהוּדָה דָּבְקוּ בְמַלְכָּם מִן־הַיַּרְדֵּן וְעַד־יְרוּשָׁלִָם:

David Sequesters His Harem

20.03.1248	וַיָּבֹא דָוִד אֶל־בֵּיתוֹ יְרוּשָׁלִַם
20.03.1249	וַיִּקַּח הַמֶּלֶךְ אֵת עֶשֶׂר־נָשִׁים פִּלַגְשִׁים
20.03.1250	אֲשֶׁר הִנִּיחַ לִשְׁמֹר הַבַּיִת
20.03.1251	וַיִּתְּנֵם בֵּית־מִשְׁמֶרֶת
20.03.1252	וַיְכַלְכְּלֵם
20.03.1253	וַאֲלֵיהֶם לֹא־בָא וַתִּהְיֶינָה צְרֻרוֹת עַד־יוֹם מֻתָן אַלְמְנוּת חַיּוּת:

David Sends Joab after Sheba

20.04.1254	וַיֹּאמֶר הַמֶּלֶךְ אֶל־עֲמָשָׂא

Joab Kills Amasa

20.08.1270		וַיֹּאמֶר יוֹאָב
20.08.1271		הֲשָׁלוֹם:
20.07.1264		וְיוֹאָב [Q וְיֹאב] הָלַךְ לֹרָה בְחֶרֶב וַיִּקְרָא (מְעִיל
20.07.1265		וְעָלֶיהָ חֲגֹר	חֶרֶב לֹדָה
20.08.1266		וַתִּלָּבֵשׁ אֶת יָדוֹ לֹ
20.08.1267		יֹצֵא וַתִּפֹּל
20.08.1268		וַיֹּאמֶר יוֹאָב לַעֲמָשָׂא
20.08.1269		וְיוֹאָב אָחַז בִּזְקַן עֲמָשָׂא בְּיָדוֹ הַיְמָנִית לִנְשָׁק
20.05.1257		וַיֹּאמֶר יוֹאָב אֶל־עֲמָשָׂא
20.05.1258		הֲשָׁלוֹם [Q הֲשָׁלוֹם] אַתָּה אָחִי
20.06.1259		וַיַּךְ בְּחֹמֶשׁ הַחֲמֵשׁ אֶל־הַחֹמֶשׁ

20.04.1255	HD	וַיְהִי הֵמָּה עִם־הָאֶבֶן אֲשֶׁר בְּגִבְעוֹן
1256a		וַעֲמָשָׂא בָּא לִפְנֵיהֶם
20.04.1256		וְעֲמָשָׂא לֹא נִשְׁמַר:
20.06.1260	PD	וַיֹּפֵךְ
20.06.1261	HD	וְלֹא־שָׁנָה לוֹ וַיָּמֹת
20.06.1262	PD	וַיֹּאמֶר עָמַד עַל הָאִישׁ
20.06.1263	PD	וַיֹּמֶת [Q וַיָּמֹת]:

20.09.1272	וַיֹּאמֶר יוֹאָב לַעֲמָשָׂא

ID

20.09.1273	הֲשָׁלוֹם אַתָּה אָחִי

20.09.1274	וַתֹּחֶז יַד־יְמִין יוֹאָב בִּזְקַן עֲמָשָׂא
20.10.1275	לִנְשָׁק־לוֹ:
20.10.1276	וַעֲמָשָׂא לֹא־נִשְׁמַר בַּחֶרֶב אֲשֶׁר בְּיַד־יוֹאָב
20.10.1277	וַיַּכֵּהוּ בָהּ אֶל־הַחֹמֶשׁ
20.10.1278	וַיִּשְׁפֹּךְ מֵעָיו אַרְצָה
20.10.1279	וְלֹא־שָׁנָה לוֹ
20.10.1280	וַיָּמֹת:

Amasa's Corpse Causes a Delay

20.11.1281	וְיוֹאָב וַאֲבִישַׁי אָחִיו רָדַף אַחֲרֵי שֶׁבַע בֶּן־בִּכְרִי:
20.11.1282	וְאִישׁ עָמַד עָלָיו מִנַּעֲרֵי יוֹאָב

ED

20.11.1283	וַיֹּאמֶר מִי אֲשֶׁר חָפֵץ בְּיוֹאָב וּמִי אֲשֶׁר לְדָוִד אַחֲרֵי יוֹאָב:

20.12.1284	וַעֲמָשָׂא מִתְגֹּלֵל בַּדָּם בְּתוֹךְ הַמְסִלָּה
20.12.1285	וַיַּרְא הָאִישׁ כִּי־עָמַד כָּל־הָעָם
20.12.1286	וַיַּסֵּב אֶת־עֲמָשָׂא מִן־הַמְסִלָּה הַשָּׂדֶה וַיַּשְׁלֵךְ עָלָיו בֶּגֶד
20.12.1287	כַּאֲשֶׁר רָאָה כָּל־הַבָּא עָלָיו וְעָמָד
1288α	
20.13.1288	כַּאֲשֶׁר הֹגָה מִן־הַמְסִלָּה עָבַר כָּל־אִישׁ אַחֲרֵי יוֹאָב לִרְדֹּף אַחֲרֵי שֶׁבַע בֶּן־בִּכְרִי:

The Wise Woman of Abel Hands Over the Head of Sheba

וַיַּעֲבֹר בְּכָל־שִׁבְטֵי יִשְׂרָאֵל אָבֵלָה וּבֵית מַעֲכָה וְכָל־הַבֵּרִים	20.14.1289
[וַיִּקָּלֻהוּ ס] [וַיִּקָּהֲלוּ]	20.14.1290
וַיָּבֹאוּ אַף־אַחֲרָיו׃	20.14.1291
וַיָּבֹאוּ	20.15.1292
וַיָּצֻרוּ עָלָיו בְּאָבֵלָה בֵּית הַמַּעֲכָה	20.15.1293
וַיִּשְׁפְּכוּ סֹלְלָה אֶל־הָעִיר	20.15.1294
וַתַּעֲמֹד בַּחֵל	20.15.1295
וְכָל־הָעָם אֲשֶׁר אֶת־יוֹאָב מַשְׁחִתִם לְהַפִּיל הַחוֹמָה׃	20.15.1296
וַתִּקְרָא אִשָּׁה חֲכָמָה מִן־הָעִיר	20.16.1297

HD	שִׁמְעוּ שִׁמְעוּ	20.16.1298
	אִמְרוּ־נָא	20.16.1299
	אֶל־יוֹאָב קְרַב עַד־הֵנָּה †	20.16.1300
†HD	וַאֲדַבְּרָה אֵלֶיךָ ‡	20.16.1301
	וַיִּשְׁמַע אֵלֶיהָ׃	20.16.1302

	וַיִּקְרַב אֵלֶיהָ	20.17.1303
	וַתֹּאמֶר הָאִשָּׁה	20.17.1304
ID	הַאַתָּה יוֹאָב	20.17.1305
	וַיֹּאמֶר	20.17.1306
ED	אָנִי	20.17.1307
	וַתֹּאמֶר לוֹ	20.17.1308
HD	שְׁמַע דִּבְרֵי אֲמָתֶךָ	20.17.1309
	וַיֹּאמֶר	20.17.1310

20.18.1312 וֶאָמַרְתָּ
לֵאמֹר

20.20.1319 וַיַּעַן
20.20.1320 יוֹאָב וַיֹּאמַר

20.17.1311 שֹׁמֵעַ אָנֹכִי: ED

ND
20.18.1313 וַתֹּאמֶר לֵאמֹר דַּבֵּר יְדַבְּרוּ

†PD
20.18.1314 בָרִאשֹׁנָה לֵאמֹר שָׁאֹל יְשָׁאֲלוּ בְאָבֵל

20.18.1315 וְכֵן הֵתַמּוּ: ED

20.19.1316 אָנֹכִי שְׁלֻמֵי אֱמוּנֵי יִשְׂרָאֵל
20.19.1317 אַתָּה מְבַקֵּשׁ לְהָמִית עִיר וְאֵם בְּיִשְׂרָאֵל ID

20.19.1318 לָמָּה תְבַלַּע נַחֲלַת יְהוָה:

ED (Oath)
20.20.1321 חָלִילָה חָלִילָה לִּי אִם־אֲבַלַּע וְאִם־אַשְׁחִית: ED

20.21.1322 לֹא־כֵן הַדָּבָר ED

20.21.1323 כִּי אִישׁ מֵהַר אֶפְרַיִם שֶׁבַע בֶּן־בִּכְרִי שְׁמוֹ נָשָׂא יָדוֹ בַּמֶּלֶךְ בְּדָוִד HD
20.21.1324 תְּנוּ־אֹתוֹ לְבַדּוֹ וְאֵלְכָה מֵעַל הָעִיר

20.21.1325 וַיֹּאמֶר יְהוָה אֶל־מֹשֶׁה

20.22.1327
20.22.1328
20.22.1329
20.22.1330
20.22.1331
20.22.1332
20.23.1333
20.23.1334
20.24.1335
20.24.1336
20.25.1337
20.25.1338
20.26.1339

ED

20.21.1326 וַיֹּאמֶר יְהוָה אֶל־מֹשֶׁה
רקע

Table of Independent Clause Types in 2 Samuel 20

Clause Type	Clause Distribution	Total	Percent
QAṬAL Total Clauses: 12	Narrative: 1239,1247,1252,1270,1275,1278,1280, 1281,1288,1332,1339	11	91.7%
	ND: 1315 PD: ED: ID: HD:	1	8.3%
WeQAṬAL Total Clauses: 1	Narrative:	0	0
	ND: PD: 1263 ED: ID: HD:	1	100%
YIQṬOL Total Clauses: 4	Narrative:	0	0
	ND: 1313	1	25.0%
	PD: 1260,1424	2	50.0%
	ED:		
	ID: 1318	1	25.0%
	HD:		
WeYIQṬOL Total Clauses: 0	Narrative:	0	0
	ND: PD: ED: ID: HD:	0	0
WAYYIQṬOL Total Clauses: 46	Narrative: 1241,1242,1246,1248,1249,1250,1251, 1253,1254,1257,1258,1259,1264,1265,1271,1272, 1274,1276,1277,1279,1282,1285,1286,1287,1289, 1290,1291,1292,1293,1294,1295,1297,1303,1304, 1306,1308,1310,1312,1319,1320,1325,1327,1328, 1329,1330,1331	46	100%
	ND: PD: ED: ID: HD:		

Participle Total Clauses: 7	Narrative: 1267,1268,1284,1296	4	57.1%
	ND: PD: ED: 1311,1317,1326 ID: HD:	3	42.9%
Verbless Total Clauses: 16	Narrative: 1240,1266,1269,1333,1334,1335,1336, 1337,1338	9	56.3%
	ND: PD: ED: 1243,1244,1283,1316,1322 ID: 1273,1305 HD:	5 2	31.2% 12.5%
Incomplete Total Clauses: 3	Narrative:	0	0
	ND: PD: ED: 1245,1307,1321 ID: HD:	3	100%
Imperative Total Clauses: 10	Narrative:	0	0
	HD: 1255,1256,1261,1262,1298,1299,1300,†1300, 1209,1323	10	100%
Cohortative Total Clauses: 2	Narrative:	0	0
	HD: †1302,1324	2	100%
Jussive Total Clauses: 0	Narrative:	0	0
	HD:	0	0

Analysis of the Narrative Structure and
Discourse Text-Types in 2 Samuel 20

Narrative Structural Analysis

Narrative/Paragraph Structure

The narrative of the thwarting of Sheba's rebellion in 2 Samuel 20 is built upon a backbone of forty-six *WAYYIQTOL* clauses. These clauses are grouped into six paragraphs, marked either initially or terminally with *QATAL* clauses. *QATAL* clauses signal the beginning of the first (clause 1239), fourth (clause 1270), and fifth (clause 1281) paragraphs and the end of the first (clause 1247), second (clause 1252), fourth (clause 1280), fifth (clause 1288), and sixth (clause 1332) paragraphs.[67] The remaining beginnings and ends of paragraphs are marked externally by the *QATAL* clauses in the immediately preceding or following paragraphs.

Extra-Paragraph Comments

No examples of extra-paragraph comments stand within 2 Samuel 20.

Inner-Paragraph Comments

The four inner-paragraph comments in 2 Samuel 20 are composed of verbless (1240, 1266, 1269) and participial (1267, 1268, 1284, 1296) clauses as well as a single case of a היה verbal clause (1253).

The inner-paragraph comment that concludes the chapter is comprised of a final היה clause, preceded by a string of verbless clauses:

20.23.1333 וְיוֹאָב אֶל כָּל־הַצָּבָא יִשְׂרָאֵל
20.23.1334 וּבְנָיָה בֶּן־יְהוֹיָדָע עַל־הַכְּרִי Q] הַכְּרֵתִי וְעַל־הַפְּלֵתִי:
20.24.1335 וַאֲדֹרָם עַל־הַמַּס
20.24.1336 וִיהוֹשָׁפָט בֶּן־אֲחִילוּד הַמַּזְכִּיר
20.25.1337 וְשֵׁיָא Q] וּשְׁוָא סֹפֵר
20.25.1338 וְצָדוֹק וְאֶבְיָתָר כֹּהֲנִים:
20.26.1339 וְגַם עִירָא הַיָּאִרִי הָיָה כֹהֵן לְדָוִד:

---

[67]The *QATAL* clauses 1275 and 1278, negated by the particle לֹא, are both instances of "momentous negation" and cause the narrative to progress and are not, therefore, accounted as paragraph markers.

The comment is initially marked by the final *QATAL* clause of the sixth paragraph (clause 1332).[68] The list, of course, does not cause the narrative to progress in any way.

Discourse Function Analysis

Narrative Discourse

The single instance of Narrative Discourse in 2 Samuel 20 is extremely unusual. It comes from the mouth of the Wise Woman of Abel and consists of an initial *YIQTOL* clause, an internal quoted instance of Predictive Discourse, and a *QATAL* clause:

ND

20.18.1313 דַּבֵּר יְדַבְּרוּ בָרִאשֹׁנָה
לֵאמֹר

†PD

20.18.1314 †שָׁאֹל יְשָׁאֲלוּ בְּאָבֵל

20.18.1315 וְכֵן הֵתַמּוּ׃

While both the Narrative and Predictive Discourses here contain a *YIQTOL* clause with an infinitive absolute paralleling the verb, clause 1313 clearly refers to an (ongoing?) action in the past ("they formerly used to say . . . "), while clause †1314 refers to a planned future activity ("they will/should ask at Abel").[69] Clause 1313, therefore, is defined as Narrative Discourse by two characteristics. First, the presence of the adverbial phrase בָרִאשֹׁנָה places the activity of "saying" decisively in the past. Because of the adverb, the speech is already defined as narrative, since no other text-type, with the possible exception of Interrogative Discourse, could contain the adverbial phrase בָרִאשֹׁנָה.[70] Second, clause 1313 is defined as narrative because it is temporally parallel with clause

---

[68]As has been seen before (e.g., 2 Sam 16:15; clause 830), an inner-paragraph comment may stand after the terminal boundary clause of a paragraph. Since the comment neither causes the narrative to progress nor relates any activity outside the narrative story line, an inner-paragraph comment may stand in such a position.

[69]Here, Driver's designation of the *YIQTOL* verbal form as portraying a repetitive action in past time seems correct (*Notes*, 346-47), but only because of the adverbial phrase בָרִאשֹׁנָה.

[70]Since, however, no interrogative particle begins the clause and it is not parallel to a preceding interrogative clause, clause 1313 cannot be an instance of Interrogative Discourse. For other prose examples of the adverbial use of בָרִאשֹׁנָה, see Gen 13:4; Josh 8:5-6; 2 Sam 7:10 and Jer 7:12. Note also its use in Isa 52:4.

1315, a clearly defined *QAṬAL* clause. Because of these two characteristics, the discourse contained in clauses 1313-1315 is narrative.[71]

Predictive Discourse

The three cases of Predictive Discourse in 2 Samuel 20 all conform to the general characteristics of this particular text-type. Two cases employ *YIQṬOL* clauses (1260, 1424); the remaining case employs a single *WeQAṬAL* clause (1263).

Expository Discourse

The seven instances of Expository Discourse in 2 Samuel 20 all adhere to the clausal combinations seen thus far. Four of the examples employ either participial (1311, 1326) or verbless clauses (1283, 1322) or a combination of both (1316-1317). Two cases use incomplete clauses, one an oath (1321) and one an answer to a question (1307). The remaining case is composed of two verbless clauses and an incomplete clause:[72]

20.01.1243 אֵין־לָנוּ חֵלֶק בְּדָוִד
20.01.1244 וְלֹא נַחֲלָה־לָנוּ בְּבֶן־יִשַׁי
20.01.1245 אִישׁ לְאֹהָלָיו יִשְׂרָאֵל׃

Interrogative Discourse

The three examples of Interrogative Discourse in 2 Samuel 20 are all composed of single clause utterances and are all explicitly marked with interrogative particles: הֲ (1273, 1305) and לָמָה (1318).[73]

---

[71]A major variant reading of this verse in the LXX could point to a scribal error in clause 1313 (see Driver, *Notes,* 346-347 for a critical reading of the LXX and the supposed *Vorlage* of the MT). The insertion of the *yod* between the infinitive absolute and the main verb can be explained by proximity of the parallel construction (infinitive absolute + Piel *YIQṬOL* verb) in the next clause. The form is difficult nonetheless.

[72]The elliptical nature of clause 1245 seems to be tied to its "slogan-like" character. The missing verb could clarify its true text-type as either Expository ("each one [has] his own tents, O Israel!"), Predictive ("each one [will go] to his own tents, O Israel.") or Hortatory ("[Let] each one [go] to his tents, O Israel!"). Standing, as it does, parallel to two verbless clauses, clause 1245 should be interpreted as expository.

[73]The use of מִי in clause 1283 (מִי אֲשֶׁר־לְדָוִד אַחֲרֵי יוֹאָב׃) is as (מִי אֲשֶׁר חָפֵץ בְּיוֹאָב וּמִי אֲשֶׁר־לְדָוִד אַחֲרֵי יוֹאָב) an indefinite pronoun rather than an interrogative particle. The clause is, therefore, an example of Expository Discourse. See Waltke and O'Connor, *Syntax,* 320-21.

Hortatory Discourse

All six examples of Hortatory Discourse in 2 Samuel 20 are composed of imperative clauses (1255-1256, 1261-1262, 1298-1300, 1309) or a combination of imperative and cohortative clauses (†1301-1302, 1323-1324). As such, all cases in this chapter conform explicitly to the clausal characteristics of Hortatory Discourse.

Table of Discourse Constellations for 2 Samuel 20

		Present Ch.	Prev. Chs.	Total
ND	QAṬAL		59	59
	QAṬAL, WAYYIQṬOL		14	14
	QAṬAL, (Ptc./Vbl.)		9	9
	QAṬAL, WAYYIQṬOL, (Ptc./Vbl.)		6	6
	QAṬAL, WAYYIQṬOL, (Ptc./Vbl.), YIQṬOL		3	3
	QAṬAL, YIQṬOL (w/ past adverb)	1	0	1
	WAYYIQṬOL, (Ptc./Vbl.)		2	2
	Vbl/Ptc/Inc (Dream Report)		1	1
PD	YIQṬOL	2	38	40
	YIQṬOL, WeQAṬAL		15	15
	YIQṬOL, WeQAṬAL, (Ptc./Vbl../Inc.)		7	7
	YIQṬOL, (Ptc./Vbl../Inc.)		3	3
	WeQAṬAL	1	14	15
	WeYIQṬOL		2	2
ED	Ptc./Vbl.	4	69	73
	Ptc./ Vbl., Inc.	1	1	2
	Inc.	2	23	26
	Ptc./Vbl., QAṬAL/YIQṬOL of היה		5	5
	Ptc./Vbl., QAṬAL/YIQṬOL of היה, Front. Obj.+ QAṬAL/YIQṬOL		2	2
	QAṬAL/YIQṬOL of היה		3	3
HD	Impv./Coh./Juss.	6	76	82
	Impv./Coh./Juss., WeYIQṬOL/YIQṬOL		20	20
	Impv./Coh./Juss., WeQAṬAL		7	7
	Impv./Coh./Juss., WeYIQṬOL/YIQṬOL, WeQAṬAL		6	6
	Impv./Coh./Juss., QAṬAL		2	2
	Impv./Coh./Juss., WeYIQṬOL/YIQṬOL, (We)QAṬAL		1	1
	Impv./Coh./Juss., ᵓal-YIQṬOL		3	3
	Impv./Coh./Juss., WeQAṬAL, ᵓal-YIQṬOL		4	4
	ᵓal-YIQṬOL		10	10
	ᵓal-YIQṬOL, WeQAṬAL/YIQṬOL		2	2
	(We)YIQṬOL-nāᵓ, (WeQAṬAL/[We]YIQṬOL)		9	9
	QAṬAL, YIQṬOL/WeQAṬAL		3	3

1 Kings 1 — Solomon Becomes King Instead of Adonijah— Clauses 1340-1516

Text in Syntactical/Paragraph Units

The Feebleness of David (Comment)

וְהַמֶּלֶךְ דָּוִד זָקֵן בָּא בַּיָּמִים	1.01.1340
וַיְכַסֻּהוּ בַּבְּגָדִים	1.01.1341
וְלֹא יִחַם לוֹ׃	1.01.1342

Abishag Becomes David's Nurse

וַיֹּאמְרוּ לוֹ עֲבָדָיו	1.02.1343

HD

יְבַקְשׁוּ לַאדֹנִי הַמֶּלֶךְ נַעֲרָה בְתוּלָה	1.02.1344
וְעָמְדָה לִפְנֵי הַמֶּלֶךְ	1.02.1345
וּתְהִי־לוֹ סֹכֶנֶת	1.02.1346
וְשָׁכְבָה בְחֵיקֶךָ	1.02.1347
וְחַם לַאדֹנִי הַמֶּלֶךְ׃	1.02.1348

וַיְבַקְשׁוּ נַעֲרָה יָפָה	1.03.1349
וַיִּמְצְאוּ	1.03.1350
וַיָּבִאוּ אֹתָהּ לַמֶּלֶךְ׃	1.03.1351
וְהַנַּעֲרָה יָפָה עַד־מְאֹד	1.04.1352
(וַתְּהִי לַמֶּלֶךְ סֹכֶנֶת)	1.04.1353
וַתְּשָׁרְתֵהוּ	1.04.1354
וְהַמֶּלֶךְ לֹא יְדָעָהּ׃	1.04.1355

Adonijah's Assumption of Power (Comment)

—— 1.05.1356 לֵאמֹר

אֲנִי אֶמְלֹךְ

PD 1.05.1357 אֲנִי אֶמְלֹךְ

1.05.1358 לֵאמֹר
1.06.1359 וַיַּעַשׂ לוֹ רֶכֶב וּפָרָשִׁים וַחֲמִשִּׁים אִישׁ רָצִים לְפָנָיו:

ID 1.06.1360 וְלֹא עֲצָבוֹ אָבִיו

1.06.1361
1.06.1362 וְגַם הוּא טוֹב תֹּאַר מְאֹד
1.07.1363 וְאֹתוֹ יָלְדָה אַחֲרֵי אַבְשָׁלוֹם:
1.07.1364 וַיִּהְיוּ דְבָרָיו עִם יוֹאָב

1365α וַיַּעְזְרוּ אַחֲרֵי אֲדֹנִיָּה:

1.08.1365 וְצָדוֹק הַכֹּהֵן וּבְנָיָהוּ בֶן יְהוֹיָדָע
וְנָתָן הַנָּבִיא וְשִׁמְעִי וְרֵעִי וְהַגִּבּוֹרִים אֲשֶׁר לְדָוִד לֹא הָיוּ עִם אֲדֹנִיָּהוּ:

——

Nathan and Bathsheba Conspire to Have Solomon Appointed as Heir Apparent

וַיִּזְבַּח אֲדֹנִיָּהוּ צֹאן וּבָקָר וּמְרִיא עִם אֶבֶן הַזֹּחֶלֶת

1.09.1366 אֲשֶׁר אֵצֶל עֵין רֹגֵל

1.09.1367 וַיִּקְרָא אֶת כָּל אֶחָיו בְּנֵי הַמֶּלֶךְ
1.10.1368 (וּלְכָל אַנְשֵׁי יְהוּדָה עַבְדֵי הַמֶּלֶךְ:)
1.11.1369 וְאֶת נָתָן הַנָּבִיא וּבְנָיָהוּ וְאֶת הַגִּבּוֹרִים וְאֶת שְׁלֹמֹה אָחִיו לֹא קָרָא:

ID

וַיִּקְרָא אֶתְכֶם 1.11.1370

1.11.1371

HD

לָהֶם

לֵךְ 1.12.1372

אֱלֹהֵי אָבִיךָ 1.12.1373

אֲשֶׁר 1.12.1374

לֵךְ 1.13.1375

וַיֹּאמֶר 1.13.1376

1.13.1377

ttID

לֹא־אֶת־אֲנָשִׁים הָיָה 1.13.1378

ttPD

וַיֹּאמֶר אֲלֵיהֶם 1.13.1379

(tID) 1.13.1380

PD

וַיְהִי 1.13.1381

הֵנָּה

1.14.1382

1.14.1383

1.14.1384

וַיֹּאמֶר אֲלֵיהֶם 1.15.1385

1.17.1392 לֹא יָדַע

1.16.1390 וַיֹּאמֶר הַמֶּלֶךְ

1.16.1389 וַתִּשְׁתַּחוּ לַמֶּלֶךְ

1.16.1388 וַתִּקֹּד בַּת־שֶׁבַע

1.15.1387 וַתָּבֹא בַת־שֶׁבֶו אֶל־הַמֶּלֶךְ הַחַדְרָה אֲבִישַׁג הַשּׁוּנַמִּית:)

1.15.1386 (וַתְּשָׁרֶת אֶת הַמֶּלֶךְ

1.21.1402 וְהָיָה כִּשְׁכַב אֲדֹנִי־הַמֶּלֶךְ עִם־אֲבֹתָיו

PD
וְהָיִיתִי אֲנִי וּבְנִי שְׁלֹמֹה חַטָּאִים:

1.20.1401 וְאַתָּה אֲדֹנִי הַמֶּלֶךְ עֵינֵי כָל־יִשְׂרָאֵל עָלֶיךָ לְהַגִּיד לָהֶם מִי יֵשֵׁב עַל־כִּסֵּא אֲדֹנִי־הַמֶּלֶךְ אַחֲרָיו

ED
1.19.1400 וַיִּזְבַּח שׁוֹר וּמְרִיא־וְצֹאן לָרֹב

1.19.1399 וַיִּקְרָא לְכָל־בְּנֵי הַמֶּלֶךְ

1.19.1398 וּלְאֶבְיָתָר הַכֹּהֵן וּלְיֹאָב שַׂר־הַצָּבָא

1.18.1397 וַעַתָּה אֲדֹנִי הַמֶּלֶךְ לֹא יָדָעְתָּ:

1.18.1396 וְעַתָּה הִנֵּה אֲדֹנִיָּה מָלָךְ

(ND)

ND
1.17.1393 וְהִיא אָמְרָה לוֹ אֲדֹנִי אַתָּה נִשְׁבַּעְתָּ בַּיהוָה אֱלֹהֶיךָ לַאֲמָתֶךָ

†PD 1.17.1394 כִּי־שְׁלֹמֹה בְנֵךְ

1.17.1395 יִמְלֹךְ אַחֲרָי וְהוּא יֵשֵׁב עַל־כִּסְאִי:

ID
1.16.1391 מַה־לָּךְ:

Nathan's Confirmation Causes David to Appoint Solomon as King

וַיַּעַן

(וְלִבְנֵי יֹם הַזֶּה מֵ) 1.22.1404
וַיֹּאמֶר אֲבִישָׁג הַשֻּׁנַמִּית 1.22.1405

וַיְבָרֶךְ 1.23.1406
לֵאמֹר

וַיֹּאמֶר יִשְׂרָאֵל לֵאמֹר 1.23.1408
הָאָרֶץ 1.23.1409
וַיֹּאמֶר הַמֶּלֶךְ 1.24.1410

וַיֹּאמֶר אֵלַי אֹמֵר לִבְנֵי 1.21.1403

ED (Vocative)
הַמֶּלֶךְ
וַיַּעַן הַמֶּלֶךְ 1.23.1407

ND
וַיָּבֵן אַבְנֵר הַמֶּלֶךְ וַיֹּאמֶר 1.24.1411
†PD
וַיֹּאמֶר הַמֶּלֶךְ וַיֹּאמֶר† 1.24.1412
וַיֹּאמֶר בֶּן־עַם אֲדֹנָי† 1.24.1413
כִּי יִהְיֶה הַיּוֹם
(ND)
כִּי הֵם אֲדֹנָי וַיֹּאמֶר 1.25.1414
וַיֹּאמֶר לִבְנֵי־כֵן 1.25.1415
וַיֹּאמֶר אֲבִישַׁי וַיֹּאמֶר 1.25.1416
(וַיֹּאמֶר יָדַע אֲדֹנָי) 1.25.1417
וַיֹּאמֶר

1.31.1431 וַיִּשְׁתַּחוּ לַמֶּלֶךְ

1.31.1432 וַתֹּאמֶר יְחִי אֲדֹנִי הַמֶּלֶךְ דָּוִד לְעֹלָם:

1.28.1421 וַיֹּאמֶר

1.28.1422 קִרְאוּ־לִי לְבַת־שָׁבַע

1.28.1424 וַתָּבֹא לִפְנֵי הַמֶּלֶךְ

1.28.1425 וַתַּעֲמֹד לִפְנֵי הַמֶּלֶךְ:

1.29.1426 וַיִּשָּׁבַע הַמֶּלֶךְ

1.29.1427 וַיֹּאמַר חַי־יְהוָה

ED (Oath)

1.29.1428 אֲשֶׁר־פָּדָה אֶת־נַפְשִׁי מִכָּל־צָרָה:

†PD

1.30.1429 כִּי כַּאֲשֶׁר נִשְׁבַּעְתִּי לָךְ בַּיהוָה אֱלֹהֵי יִשְׂרָאֵל לֵאמֹר

1.30.1430 כִּי־שְׁלֹמֹה בְנֵךְ יִמְלֹךְ אַחֲרַי וְהוּא יֵשֵׁב עַל־כִּסְאִי תַּחְתָּי כִּי כֵּן אֶעֱשֶׂה הַיּוֹם הַזֶּה:

HD

1.28.1423 וַתָּבֹא לִפְנֵי־הַמֶּלֶךְ

1.25.1418 כִּי יָרַד הַיּוֹם †

1.26.1419 וְלִי אֲנִי־עַבְדֶּךָ וּלְצָדֹק הַכֹּהֵן וְלִבְנָיָהוּ בֶן־יְהוֹיָדָע וְלִשְׁלֹמֹה עַבְדְּךָ לֹא קָרָא:

1.27.1420 אִם מֵאֵת אֲדֹנִי הַמֶּלֶךְ נִהְיָה הַדָּבָר הַזֶּה

1420α וְלֹא הוֹדַעְתָּ אֶת־עֲבָדֶיךָ מִי יֵשֵׁב עַל־כִּסֵּא אֲדֹנִי־הַמֶּלֶךְ אַחֲרָיו:

†HD

1.31.1433

1.32.1435

1.32.1437
1.33.1438

1.36.1452
1.36.1453

1.31.1434   HD

1.32.1436   HD

1.33.1439   HD
1.33.1440
1.33.1441
1.34.1442
1.34.1443
1.34.1444

1.35.1447
1.35.1448
1.35.1449
1.35.1450
1.35.1451

1.34.1556   †HD

ED

HD

1.36.1454 וַיֹּאמֶר

1.36.1455 בְּנָיָהוּ בֶן־יְהוֹיָדָע אֶת־הַמֶּלֶךְ וַיֹּאמֶר

1456α אָמֵן

1.37.1456 כֵּן יֹאמַר יְהוָה אֱלֹהֵי אֲדֹנִי הַמֶּלֶךְ

1.37.1457 כַּאֲשֶׁר הָיָה יְהוָה עִם־אֲדֹנִי הַמֶּלֶךְ כֵּן יִהְיֶה עִם־שְׁלֹמֹה

1.38.1458 וַיֵּרֶד צָדוֹק הַכֹּהֵן

1.38.1459 וְנָתָן הַנָּבִיא

1.38.1460 וּבְנָיָהוּ בֶן־יְהוֹיָדָע

1.39.1461 וְהַכְּרֵתִי וְהַפְּלֵתִי

1.39.1462 וַיַּרְכִּבוּ אֶת־שְׁלֹמֹה

1.39.1463 עַל־פִּרְדַּת הַמֶּלֶךְ דָּוִד

1.39.1464 וַיֹּלִכוּ אֹתוֹ עַל־גִּחוֹן

HD

1.39.1465 וַיִּקַּח צָדוֹק הַכֹּהֵן אֶת־קֶרֶן הַשֶּׁמֶן מִן־הָאֹהֶל וַיִּמְשַׁח אֶת־שְׁלֹמֹה

1.40.1466 וַיִּתְקְעוּ בַּשּׁוֹפָר

1.40.1467 וַיֹּאמְרוּ כָּל־הָעָם

1.40.1468 יְחִי הַמֶּלֶךְ שְׁלֹמֹה

1.41.1469 וַיַּעֲלוּ כָל־הָעָם אַחֲרָיו

1.41.1470 וְהָעָם מְחַלְּלִים בַּחֲלִלִים

1.41.1471 וַיִּשְׁמַע אֲדֹנִיָּהוּ

וְכָל־הַקְּרֻאִים אֲשֶׁר אִתּוֹ

Joab Hears the Sound of the Anointing of Solomon

1.41.1472 וַיִּשְׁמַע יוֹאָב אֶת־קוֹל הַשּׁוֹפָר

1.41.1473 וַיֹּאמֶר

The Anointing of Solomon is Reported to Adonijah and His Supporters

ID
1.41.1474 וַיִּשְׁמַע אֲדֹנִיָּהוּ

1.42.1475 (וְכָל־הַקְּרֻאִים אֲשֶׁר)
1.42.1476 וַיֹּאמֶר לְיוֹנָתָן בֶּן־אֶבְיָתָר הַכֹּהֵן בֹּא
1.42.1477 (וְהֵם אֹכְלִים וַיִּשְׁמָעוּ)

HD
1.42.1478 בֹּא

1.42.1479 כִּי אִישׁ חַיִל אָתָּה וְטוֹב תְּבַשֵּׂר:
PD

1.43.1480 וַיַּעַן יוֹנָתָן
1.43.1481 וַיֹּאמֶר לַאֲדֹנִיָּהוּ

ND
1.43.1482 אֲבָל אֲדֹנֵינוּ הַמֶּלֶךְ־דָּוִד הִמְלִיךְ אֶת־שְׁלֹמֹה:
1.44.1483 וַיִּשְׁלַח אִתּוֹ הַמֶּלֶךְ אֶת־צָדוֹק הַכֹּהֵן
1.44.1484 וְאֶת־נָתָן הַנָּבִיא וּבְנָיָהוּ בֶּן־יְהוֹיָדָע
1.45.1485 וְהַכְּרֵתִי וְהַפְּלֵתִי וַיַּרְכִּבוּ אֹתוֹ עַל פִּרְדַּת הַמֶּלֶךְ:
1.45.1486 וַיִּמְשְׁחוּ אֹתוֹ צָדוֹק הַכֹּהֵן
1.45.1487 וְנָתָן הַנָּבִיא לְמֶלֶךְ
1.45.1488 בְּגִחוֹן וַיַּעֲלוּ מִשָּׁם שְׂמֵחִים

1.49.1497   וַיִּתֵּן

1.49.1498   וַיִּשְׁתַּחוּ

1.49.1499   וַיָּקֻמוּ כָל־הַקְּרֻאִים

אֲשֶׁר לַאֲדֹנִיָּהוּ:

וַיֵּלְכוּ אִישׁ לְדַרְכּוֹ׃

Solomon Subdues Adonijah and Receives Instruction from David

1.50.1500   וַאֲדֹנִיָּהוּ יָרֵא מִפְּנֵי שְׁלֹמֹה

1.50.1501   וַיָּקָם

1.50.1502   וַיֵּלֶךְ

1.50.1503   וַיַּחֲזֵק בְּקַרְנוֹת הַמִּזְבֵּחַ׃

1.51.1504   וַיֻּגַּד לִשְׁלֹמֹה לֵאמֹר

1.46.1489   וְגַם יָשַׁב שְׁלֹמֹה עַל כִּסֵּא הַמְּלוּכָה׃

1.47.1490   וְגַם בָּאוּ עַבְדֵי הַמֶּלֶךְ לְבָרֵךְ אֶת־אֲדֹנֵינוּ הַמֶּלֶךְ דָּוִד לֵאמֹר

1.47.1491   יֵיטֵב אֱלֹהִים [אֱלֹהֶיךָ Q] אֶת־שֵׁם שְׁלֹמֹה† †HD

1.47.1492   מִשְּׁמֶךָ וִיגַדֵּל אֶת־כִּסְאוֹ מִכִּסְאֶךָ׃

1.47.1493   וַיִּשְׁתַּחוּ הַמֶּלֶךְ עַל־הַמִּשְׁכָּב׃

1.48.1494   וְגַם־כָּכָה אָמַר הַמֶּלֶךְ† †ED

1.48.1495   בָּרוּךְ יְהוָה אֱלֹהֵי יִשְׂרָאֵל

1.48.1496   אֲשֶׁר נָתַן הַיּוֹם יֹשֵׁב עַל־כִּסְאִי וְעֵינַי רֹאוֹת׃

לֵאמֹר

1.52.1508 וַיֹּאמֶר פַּרְעֹה

1.53.1511 וַיֹּאמֶר אֶל־פַּרְעֹה
1.53.1512 וַיֹּאמֶר לֹא בִלְעָדָי
1.53.1513 אֱלֹהִים
1.53.1514 יַעֲנֶה אֶת־שְׁלוֹם פַּרְעֹה
1.53.1515 וַיְדַבֵּר פַּרְעֹה אֶל־יוֹסֵף

ND

1.51.1505 וַיִּגְדַּל הַיֶּלֶד הַזֶּה
1.51.1506 וַיֹּאמֶר

†PD

1.51.1507 וַיִּקְרָא שֵׁם הַיֶּלֶד

PD

1.52.1509 וְאֵת נַפְשְׁכֶם
1.52.1510 וַיֹּאמֶר

HD

1.53.1516 כִּי לְפָנֶיךָ

Table of Independent Clause Types in 1 Kings 1

Clause Type	Clause Distribution	Total	Percent
QAṬAL Total Clauses: 25	Narrative: 1355,1359,1362,1365,1368,1405,1471, 1476,1500	9	36.0%
	ND: 1393,1396,1397,1400,1411,1420,1482,1489, 1490,1505,1506	11	44.0%
	PD:		
	ED:		
	ID: 1360,1370,1371,1381	4	16.0%
	HD: 1451	1	4.0%
WeQAṬAL Total Clauses: 16	Narrative:	0	0
	ND: PD: 1402,1403,1510	3	18.8%
	ED:		
	ID:		
	HD: 1345,1347,1348,1377,1384,1440,1441,1442, 1443,1444,1447,1448,1449	13	81.2%
YIQṬOL Total Clauses: 18	Narrative: 1342	1	5.6%
	ND: PD: 1357,††1379,††1380,1383,†1394,†1395, †1412,†1413,†1429,†1430,1479,†1507,1509	13	72.2%
	ED:		
	ID:		
	HD: 1344,1373,1450,1455	4	22.2%
WeYIQṬOL Total Clauses: 2	Narrative:	0	0
	ND: PD:		
	ED:		
	ID:		
	HD: 1457,†1492	2	100%
WAYYIQṬOL Total Clauses: 77	Narrative: 1341,1343,1349,1350,1351,1353,1354, 1358,1363,1364,1366,1367,1369,1385,1388,1389, 1390,1392,1406,1408,1409,1410,1421,1422,1424, 1425,1426,1427,1431,1432,1433,1435,1437,1438, 1452,1453,1458,1459,1460,1461,1462,1463,1464, 1466,1469,1470,1472,1473,1477,1480,1481,1497, 1498,1499,1501,1502,1503,1504,1508,1511,1512, 1513,1514,1515	64	83.1%

WAYYIQTOL (cont.) Total Clauses: 77	ND: 1398,1399,1414,1415,1417,1419,1483,1484, 1485,1486,1487,1493,1494 PD: ED: ID: HD:	13	16.9%
Participle Total Clauses: 10	Narrative: 1356,1387,1404,1467,1468,1475	6	60.0%
	ND: 1416	1	10.0%
	PD: 1382	1	10.0%
	ED: †1495,†1496	2	20.0%
	ID: HD:		
Verbless Total Clauses: 9	Narrative: 1340,1352,1361,1386	4	44.5%
	ND: 1488	1	11.1%
	PD:		
	ED: 1401	1	11.1%
	ID: †1378,1391,1474	3	33.3%
	HD:		
Incomplete Total Clauses: 3	Narrative:	0	0
	ND: PD: ED: 1407,1428,1454 ID: HD:	3	100%
Imperative Total Clauses: 9	Narrative:	0	0
	HD: 1372,1374,1375,1376,1423,1436,1439,1478, 1516	9	100%
Cohortative Total Clauses: 0	Narrative:	0	0
	HD:	0	0
Jussive Total Clauses: 7	Narrative:	0	0
	HD: 1346,†1418,1434,1446,1456,1465,†1491	7	100%

Analysis of the Narrative Structure and
Discourse Text-Types in 1 Kings 1

Narrative Structural Analysis

Narrative/Paragraph Structure

The narrative of the accession of Solomon to the throne of his aged father David is built upon a backbone of sixty-four WAYYIQTOL clauses. The story line is broken into five paragraph blocks and two strings of non-WAYYIQTOL clauses that comprise extra-paragraph comments (clauses 1340-1342, 1356-1365). The paragraphs are defined either by, in one case, an initial QATAL clause (1500) or, externally, by the final QATAL clause of the previous paragraph (1405, 1471) or by a preceding string of non-WAYYIQTOL clauses that comprise an extra-paragraph comment (clauses 1340-1342, 1356-1365).[74] The final paragraph does not conclude at the end of the chapter but, by a continued WAYYIQTOL chain, finally reaches its conclusion in 1 Kings 2:10 (clause 1541), defined there by the insertion of a following extra-paragraph comment (clauses 1542-1544).

Extra-Paragraph Comments

The two extra-paragraph comments in the chapter, dealing with David's advancing age and frailty and with Adonijah's gaining of power and assumption of the kingship, decisively break the WAYYIQTOL chain established throughout the narrative. The first comment, composed of a verbless clause, an independent WAYYIQTOL clause and a YIQTOL clause, describes the state of the elderly King David:[75]

01.01.1340 וְהַמֶּלֶךְ דָּוִד זָקֵן בָּא בַּיָּמִים
01.01.1341 וַיְכַסֻּהוּ בַּבְּגָדִים
01.01.1342 וְלֹא יִחַם לוֹ:

---

[74]Clause 1368 is an instance of a QATAL clause standing in explicit syntactical parallel with a preceding clause. As such, the QATAL clause stands as an off-line comment rather than as paragraph boundary marker.

[75]Driver (Tenses, §42) seems to be unsure of the meaning and purpose of the YIQTOL verbal form in 1 Kgs 1:1, clause 1342. C. F. Burney, in his Notes on the Hebrew Text of the Books of Kings (Oxford: Clarendon, 1903), proposes that "the imperfect expresses the habitual character of the king's condition: 'he was not' or 'used not to be warm'" (p. 1). While such a reading makes sense, it is important to note that the clause, being a part of a comment, simply expresses actions off the line of the main narrative.

In the second comment, the narrative chain is broken by means of *QATAL*, verbless, participial, and independent *WAYYIQTOL* clauses:

01.05.1356 וַאֲדֹנִיָּה בֶן־חַגִּית מִתְנַשֵּׂא
לֵאמֹר

PD

01.05.1357 אֲנִי אֶמְלֹךְ

01.05.1358 וַיַּעַשׂ לוֹ רֶכֶב וּפָרָשִׁים וַחֲמִשִּׁים אִישׁ רָצִים לְפָנָיו:
01.06.1359 וְלֹא־עֲצָבוֹ אָבִיו מִיָּמָיו
לֵאמֹר

ID

01.06.1360 מַדּוּעַ כָּכָה עָשִׂיתָ

01.06.1361 וְגַם־הוּא טוֹב־תֹּאַר מְאֹד
01.06.1362 וְאֹתוֹ יָלְדָה אַחֲרֵי אַבְשָׁלוֹם:
01.07.1363 וַיִּהְיוּ דְבָרָיו עִם יוֹאָב בֶּן־צְרוּיָה וְעִם אֶבְיָתָר הַכֹּהֵן
01.07.1364 וַיַּעְזְרוּ אַחֲרֵי אֲדֹנִיָּה:
01.08 וְצָדוֹק הַכֹּהֵן וּבְנָיָהוּ בֶן־יְהוֹיָדָע וְנָתָן הַנָּבִיא וְשִׁמְעִי וְרֵעִי
וְהַגִּבּוֹרִים אֲשֶׁר לְדָוִד
01.08.1365 לֹא הָיוּ עִם־אֲדֹנִיָּהוּ:

Although *WAYYIQTOL* clauses appear in the comment (1358, 1363, 1364), they do not comprise a narrative chain and, therefore, do not resume the narrative. The comment as a whole does not further the sequential character of the larger narrative but rather provides information about Adonijah's general activities, including how he gained his power (clauses 1356-1359), his appearance (clauses 1361-1362), and his political alliances (clauses 1363-1365).

Inner-Paragraph Comments

The inner-paragraph comments in the chapter are composed of either participial clauses (1404, 1467-1468, 1475), verbless clauses (1340), or a combination of verbless and היה verbal clauses (1352-1353) or verbless and participial clauses (1386-1387). In a single case, a *QATAL* clause stands in explicit syntactical parallel with a preceding clause and functions, therefore, as an off-line comment rather than a paragraph boundary marker:

01.09.1367 וַיִּקְרָא אֶת־כָּל־אֶחָיו בְּנֵי הַמֶּלֶךְ וּלְכָל־אַנְשֵׁי יְהוּדָה עַבְדֵי הַמֶּלֶךְ:
01.10.1368 (וְאֶת־נָתָן הַנָּבִיא וּבְנָיָהוּ וְאֶת־הַגִּבּוֹרִים וְאֶת־שְׁלֹמֹה אָחִיו לֹא קָרָא:)

In all cases, the comments provide off-line information within the narrative but do not progress the sequence of the narrative but are not as expansive as an extra-paragraph comment.

Discourse Function Analysis

Narrative Discourse

Of the five cases of Narrative Discourse in 1 Kings 1, three cases are composed of either *QATAL* clauses alone (1411-1420, 1505-1506) or a combination of *QATAL* and *WAYYIQTOL* clauses (1393-1400). In two cases (1414-1419, 1482-1494), the discourse also contains a verbless clause (1488), which gives information contemporaneous with the report, or a participial clause (1416), which tells of an ongoing action within the time frame of the report. In all cases, the Narrative Discourses are regular for this text-type.

Predictive Discourse

The ten examples of Predictive Discourse present in this chapter are varied but are consistent with patterns established for this text-type. Seven cases are composed of only *YIQTOL* clauses (1357, †1379-1380, †1394-1395, †1412-1413, †1429-1430, 1479, †1507). Furthermore, two cases are defined by a combination of *YIQTOL* and *WeQATAL* clauses either alone (1509-1510) or with an inserted participial clause (1382-1384) portraying an on-going action within a specific future plan. There is, finally, a case of Predictive Discourse that is defined simply by the *WeQATAL* clauses within it (1402-1403).

Expository Discourse

Of the five cases of Expository Discourse within 1 Kings 1, two are composed of either participial clauses alone (†1495-1496) or a single verbless clause (1401). In addition, the three cases of independent incomplete clauses standing in the chapter comprise a vocative statement (1407), an oath (1428), and a response to a previous statement (1454).

Interrogative Discourse

The five cases of Interrogative Discourse in this chapter are all explicitly marked as questions by the prefixed interrogative particles attached to the clauses: (וּ)מַדּוּעַ (1360;1381;1474); הֲלוֹא (1370;1378); מַה (1391). The clauses in a double clause question (1378-1381) are both explicitly marked.

Hortatory Discourse

The twelve examples of Hortatory Discourse in 1 Kings 1 are all explicitly marked by the presence of imperative or jussive clauses within them. In eight cases, the hortatory clauses stand alone (†1418, 1423, 1434, 1436, †1556, 1465,

1478, 1516). In two cases the hortatory speech involves a combination of hortatory, *YIQTOL* and *WeYIQTOL* clauses (1455-1457, 1491-1492). More-over, in
two cases *WeQATAL* clauses supplement the speech along with the defining
hortatory and *YIQTOL* clauses (1344-1348, 1372-1377).[76] Finally, in David's
command to Nathan and Bathsheba to have Solomon crowned as king (clauses
1439-1451), an initial imperative clause leads into a long string of *WeQATAL*
clauses and concludes with a *YIQTOL* clause and an example of a performative
utterance *QATAL* clause:

01.33.1439 קְחוּ עִמָּכֶם אֶת־עַבְדֵי אֲדֹנֵיכֶם
01.33.1440 וְהִרְכַּבְתֶּם אֶת־שְׁלֹמֹה בְנִי עַל־הַפִּרְדָּה אֲשֶׁר־לִי
01.33.1441 וְהוֹרַדְתֶּם אֹתוֹ אֶל־גִּחוֹן:
01.34.1442 וּמָשַׁח אֹתוֹ שָׁם צָדוֹק הַכֹּהֵן וְנָתָן הַנָּבִיא לְמֶלֶךְ עַל־יִשְׂרָאֵל
01.34.1443 וּתְקַעְתֶּם בַּשׁוֹפָר
01.34.1444 וַאֲמַרְתֶּם

†HD
01.34.1446 †יְחִי הַמֶּלֶךְ שְׁלֹמֹה:

01.35.1447 וַעֲלִיתֶם אַחֲרָיו
01.35.1448 וּבָא
01.35.1449 וְיָשַׁב עַל־כִּסְאִי
01.35.1450 וְהוּא יִמְלֹךְ תַּחְתָּי
01.35.1451 וְאֹתוֹ צִוִּיתִי לִהְיוֹת נָגִיד עַל־יִשְׂרָאֵל וְעַל־יְהוּדָה:

The juxtaposition of different clausal types in this speech does not, however,
obscure the sense that the entire speech is hortatory and that each of the clauses,
whatever its governing verbal form, is interpreted as hortatory.

---

[76]In 1:2, Burney is correct in his reading of וְעָמְדָה as "And let her stand." His explanation is, however, confusing in that he explains that the "Imperf. with ן *consec.*
[performs] the continuation of the cohortative יְבַקְשׁוּ." The initial verb of the speech,
יְבַקְשׁוּ, is clearly not cohortative nor is it unambiguously hortatory (i.e., jussive). The hortatory nature of the speech is defined by the third clause of the discourse, clause 1346,
whose governing verbal form is an unambiguous jussive (וּתְהִי־).

Table of Discourse Constellations for 1 Kings 1

		Present Ch.	Prev. Chs.	Total
ND	*QATAL*	2	59	61
	QATAL, WAYYIQTOL	1	14	15
	QATAL, (Ptc./Vbl.)		9	9
	QATAL, WAYYIQTOL, (Ptc./Vbl.)	2	6	8
	QATAL, WAYYIQTOL, (Ptc./Vbl.), *YIQTOL*		3	3
	QATAL, YIQTOL (w/ past adverb)		1	1
	WAYYIQTOL, (Ptc./Vbl.)		2	2
	Vbl/Ptc/Inc (Dream Report)		1	1
PD	*YIQTOL*	7	40	47
	YIQTOL, WeQATAL	1	15	16
	YIQTOL, WeQATAL, (Ptc./Vbl../Inc.)	1	7	8
	YIQTOL, (Ptc./Vbl../Inc.)		3	3
	WeQATAL	1	15	16
	WeYIQTOL		2	2
ED	Ptc./Vbl.	2	73	75
	Ptc./ Vbl., Inc.		2	2
	Inc.	3	26	29
	Ptc./Vbl., *QATAL/YIQTOL* of היה		5	5
	Ptc./Vbl., *QATAL/YIQTOL* of היה, Front. Obj.+ *QATAL/YIQTOL*		2	2
	QATAL/YIQTOL of היה		3	3
HD	Impv./Coh./Juss.	8	82	90
	Impv./Coh./Juss., *WeYIQTOL/YIQTOL*	2	20	22
	Impv./Coh./Juss., *WeQATAL*		7	7
	Impv./Coh./Juss., *WeYIQTOL/YIQTOL, WeQATAL*	2	6	8
	Impv./Coh./Juss., *QATAL*		2	2
	Impv./Coh./Juss., *WeYIQTOL/YIQTOL*, (We)*QATAL*	1	1	2
	Impv./Coh./Juss., *ʾal-YIQTOL*		3	3
	Impv./Coh./Juss., *WeQATAL, ʾal-YIQTOL*		4	4
	ʾal-YIQTOL		10	10
	ʾal-YIQTOL, WeQATAL/YIQTOL		2	2
	(We)*YIQTOL-nāʾ*, (*WeQATAL/[We]YIQTOL*)		9	9
	QATAL, YIQTOL/WeQATAL		3	3

1 Kings 2 — David Dies and Solomon Secures His Kingship — Clauses 1517-1679

Text in Syntactical/Paragraph Units

Solomon Subdues Adonijah and Receives Instruction from David (Cont.)

וַיַּקְרֵב יְהוָֽה׃ יִשְׂרָאֵל	2.01.1517
וַיֹּ֥אמֶר אֲלֵהֶֽם דָּוִ֖ד הַמֶּ֥לֶךְ	2.01.1518
לֵאמֹֽר׃	

ED
| אָנֹכִ֤י הֹלֵךְ֙ בְּדֶ֣רֶךְ כָּל־הָאָ֔רֶץ | 2.02.1519 |

PD
וְחָזַקְתָּ֖	2.02.1520
וְהָיִ֥יתָֽ לְאִֽישׁ׃	2.02.1521
וְשָׁמַרְתָּ֞ אֶת־מִשְׁמֶ֣רֶת ׀ יְהוָ֣ה אֱלֹהֶ֗יךָ	2.03.1522
לָלֶ֤כֶת בִּדְרָכָיו֙ לִשְׁמֹ֨ר חֻקֹּתָ֤יו מִצְוֺתָיו֙	
וּמִשְׁפָּטָ֣יו וְעֵדְוֺתָ֔יו כַּכָּת֖וּב בְּתוֹרַ֣ת מֹשֶׁ֑ה	
לְמַ֣עַן תַּשְׂכִּ֗יל אֵ֚ת כָּל־אֲשֶׁ֣ר תַּֽעֲשֶׂ֔ה	
וְאֵ֛ת כָּל־אֲשֶׁ֥ר תִּפְנֶ֖ה שָֽׁם׃	
לְמַעַן֩ יָקִ֨ים יְהוָ֜ה אֶת־דְּבָר֗וֹ [2.04]	
אֲשֶׁ֨ר דִּבֶּ֣ר עָלַי֮	
לֵאמֹר֒	

†PD
אִם־יִשְׁמְר֤וּ בָנֶ֨יךָ֙ אֶת־דַּרְכָּ֔ם† 1523α	
לָלֶ֤כֶת לְפָנַי֙ בֶּאֱמֶ֔ת†	
בְּכָל־לְבָבָ֖ם וּבְכָל־נַפְשָֽׁם†	

| לֵאמֹ֔ר | |
| לֹֽא־יִכָּרֵ֤ת לְךָ֙ אִ֔ישׁ מֵעַ֖ל כִּסֵּ֥א יִשְׂרָאֵֽל׃† | 2.04.1523 |

2.05.1524	ND
2.05.1525	ND
2.05.1526	
2.05.1527	ND
2.06.1528	HD
2.06.1529	ED
2.07.1530	
2.07.1531	
2.08.1532	ND
2.08.1533	ED
2.08.1534	
2.08.1535	
2.08.1536	†ED (Oath) HD

וַיִּשְׁכַּב דָּוִד עִם־אֲבֹתָיו 2.09.1537
וַיִּקָּבֵר בְּעִיר דָּוִד׃ 2.09.1538
וְהַיָּמִים אֲשֶׁר מָלַךְ דָּוִד עַל־יִשְׂרָאֵל 2.09.1539
אַרְבָּעִים שָׁנָה

וַיֵּשֶׁב שְׁלֹמֹה עַל־כִּסֵּא דָּוִד אָבִיו 2.10.1540
וַתִּכֹּן מַלְכֻתוֹ מְאֹד׃ 2.10.1541

The Regnal Notice of David (Comment)

בְּחֶבְרוֹן מָלַךְ עַל־יְהוּדָה 2.11.1542
שֶׁבַע שָׁנִים

וּבִירוּשָׁלִַם מָלַךְ שְׁלֹשִׁים 2.11.1543
וְשָׁלֹשׁ שָׁנִים׃
[אַרְבָּעִים שָׁנָה] 2.11.1544

Adonijah Asks for Abishag and Is Killed

וַיָּבֹא אֲדֹנִיָּהוּ בֶן־חַגֵּית אֶל־בַּת־שֶׁבַע 2.12.1545
אֵם־שְׁלֹמֹה

וַתֹּאמֶר הֲשָׁלוֹם בֹּאֶךָ 2.12.1546

ID
וַיֹּאמֶר שָׁלוֹם 2.13.1549

וַיֹּאמֶר דָּבָר לִי אֵלַיִךְ 2.13.1547

ED (Answer)
וַתֹּאמֶר דַּבֵּר׃ 2.13.1551

וַתֹּאמֶר׃ 2.13.1548

וַתֹּאמֶר 2.13.1550

ED
וַיֹּאמֶר אִמְרִי־נָא לִשְׁלֹמֹה הַמֶּלֶךְ 2.14.1553

וַיֹּאמֶר׃ 2.14.1552

וַתֹּאמֶר 2.14.1554

וַתֹּאמֶר 2.15.1556

וַתֹּאמֶר לוֹ אֲדֹנִי 2.16.1563

וַיֹּאמֶר 2.17.1565

וַתֹּאמֶר בַּת־שֶׁבַע 2.18.1568

HD שָׁלוֹם: 2.14.1555

ND אַתְּ יָדַעַתְּ 2.15.1557

כִּי־לִי הָיְתָה הַמְּלוּכָה 2.15.1558

וְעָלַי שָׂמוּ כָל־יִשְׂרָאֵל פְּנֵיהֶם לִמְלֹךְ 2.15.1559

וַתִּסֹּב הַמְּלוּכָה 2.15.1560

ED וַתְּהִי לְאָחִי כִּי מֵיְהוָה הָיְתָה לּוֹ: 2.15.1560

HD וְעַתָּה שְׁאֵלָה אַחַת אָנֹכִי שֹׁאֵל מֵאִתָּךְ 2.16.1561

HD אַל־תָּשִׁבִי אֶת־פָּנָי 2.16.1562

HD וַתֹּאמֶר לוֹ: 2.16.1564

HD אִמְרִי־נָא לִשְׁלֹמֹה הַמֶּלֶךְ כִּי לֹא־יָשִׁיב אֶת־פָּנָיִךְ 2.17.1566

וְיִתֶּן־לִי אֶת־אֲבִישַׁג הַשֻּׁנַמִּית לְאִשָּׁה: 2.17.1567

ED טוֹב 2.18.1569

PD אָנֹכִי אֲדַבֵּר עָלֶיךָ אֶל־הַמֶּלֶךְ: 2.18.1570

2.19.1571   וַיֹּאמֶר יְהוָה אֶל־מֹשֶׁה בְּמִדְיָן לֵךְ שֻׁב מִצְרַיִם כִּי־מֵתוּ כָּל־הָאֲנָשִׁים הַֽמְבַקְשִׁים אֶת־נַפְשֶֽׁךָ׃

2.19.1572   וַיִּקַּח מֹשֶׁה אֶת־אִשְׁתּוֹ וְאֶת־בָּנָיו

2.19.1573   וַיַּרְכִּבֵם עַל־הַחֲמֹר

2.19.1574   וַיָּשָׁב אַרְצָה מִצְרָיִם

2.19.1575   וַיִּקַּח מֹשֶׁה אֶת־מַטֵּה הָאֱלֹהִים בְּיָדֽוֹ׃

2.19.1576   וַיֹּאמֶר יְהוָה אֶל־מֹשֶׁה

2.20.1577   בְּלֶכְתְּךָ

2.20.1580   וַיֹּאמֶר יְהוָה אֶל־מֹשֶׁה

2.21.1582   וַיְהִי

2.22.1584   וַיֹּאמֶר יְהוָה אֶל־אַהֲרֹן

2.22.1585   וַיֵּלֶךְ

2.23.1588   וַיֵּלֶךְ מֹשֶׁה וְאַהֲרֹן

ED   2.20.1578

HD   2.20.1579

HD   2.20.1581

PD   2.21.1583

ID   2.22.1586

HD   2.22.1587

לֵאמֹר

2.23.1589 PD רַם־אֱלֹהִים וְיֹסִף כִּי בְנַפְשׁוֹ דִּבֶּר אֲדֹנִיָּהוּ אֶת־הַדָּבָר הַזֶּה׃

2.24.1590 ED (Oath) וְעַתָּה חַי־יְהוָה אֲשֶׁר הֱכִינַנִי

2.24.1591 ND וַיּוֹשִׁיבַנִי עַל־כִּסֵּא דָּוִד אָבִי
וַאֲשֶׁר עָשָׂה־לִי בַּיִת כַּאֲשֶׁר דִּבֵּר
כִּי הַיּוֹם יוּמַת אֲדֹנִיָּהוּ׃

2.25.1592 וַיִּשְׁלַח הַמֶּלֶךְ שְׁלֹמֹה בְּיַד בְּנָיָהוּ בֶן־יְהוֹיָדָע
2.25.1593 וַיִּפְגַּע־בּוֹ
2.25.1594 וַיָּמֹת׃

Solomon Has Abiathar Exiled and Joab Killed

2.26.1595 וּלְאֶבְיָתָר הַכֹּהֵן אָמַר הַמֶּלֶךְ

2.26.1596 HD עֲנָתֹת לֵךְ עַל־שָׂדֶךָ
כִּי אִישׁ מָוֶת אָתָּה
וּבַיּוֹם הַזֶּה לֹא אֲמִיתֶךָ

2.26.1597 כִּי־נָשָׂאתָ אֶת־אֲרוֹן אֲדֹנָי יְהוִֹה לִפְנֵי דָּוִד אָבִי
וְכִי הִתְעַנִּיתָ בְּכֹל אֲשֶׁר־הִתְעַנָּה אָבִי׃

2.27.1598 וַיְגָרֶשׁ שְׁלֹמֹה אֶת־אֶבְיָתָר מִהְיוֹת כֹּהֵן לַיהוָה לְמַלֵּא אֶת־דְּבַר יְהוָה

וַיֵּרָא אֵלָיו יְהוָה

2.28.1599 וַיַּעַקֹב הַנִּצָּב עָלָיו (וַיֹּאמַר)
1600α אֲנִי יְהוָה אֱלֹהֵי אַבְרָהָם אָבִיךָ
1600β וֵאלֹהֵי יִצְחָק
2.28.1600 הָאָרֶץ אֲשֶׁר אַתָּה שֹׁכֵב עָלֶיהָ
2.28.1601 לְךָ אֶתְּנֶנָּה וּלְזַרְעֶךָ׃
2.29.1602 וְהָיָה זַרְעֲךָ כַּעֲפַר הָאָרֶץ

ND 2.29.1603 וְהָיָה זַרְעֲךָ אֶל־אֲבָרֶךָ גַּם
ED 2.29.1604 וְהָיָה
וַיִּיקַץ יַעֲקֹב

2.29.1605 וַיֹּאמַר

HD 2.29.1606 לוֹ
2.29.1607 מִשְּׁנָתוֹ׃

2.30.1608 וַיִּירָא וַיֹּאמַר מַה־נּוֹרָא
2.30.1609 וַיֹּאמַר אֵלָיו

ND 2.30.1610 זֶה כִּי אִם־בֵּית אֱלֹהִים
†HD 2.30.1611 וְזֶה׃

2.30.1612 וַיֹּאמַר ׀

ED (Particle)
2.30.1613 כִּי זֶה אֲשֶׁר

2.34.1627 וַיֹּאמֶר לוֹ הַמֶּלֶךְ
2.34.1628 וַיִּפְגַּע־בּוֹ
2.34.1629 וַיָּמֹת
2.34.1630 וּשְׁלֹמֹה
2.35.1631 נָתַן הַמֶּלֶךְ אֶת־בְּנָיָהוּ בֶּן־יְהוֹיָדָע עַל־הַצָּבָא

2.33.1625 וְהֵשִׁיבוּ דָמוֹ עַל־רֹאשׁוֹ
2.33.1626 אֲשֶׁר פָּגַע בִּשְׁנֵי־אֲנָשִׁים צַדִּקִים וְטֹבִים (HD)

ND
2.32.1623
2.32.1624 וַיָּשֵׁב יְהוָה אֶת־דָּמוֹ
1623α וַיַּהֲרֹג אֹתָם בַּחֶרֶב (HD)
1623β וְאָבִי דָוִד לֹא יָדָע

2.32.1622 וַיֹּאמֶר־לוֹ הַמֶּלֶךְ

HD
2.31.1618
2.31.1619
2.31.1620
2.31.1621

ND
2.30.1615
2.30.1616

2.30.1614 וַיָּבֹא בְנָיָהוּ אֶל־אֹהֶל יְהוָה
2.31.1617 וַיֹּאמֶר לוֹ הַמֶּלֶךְ

וַיְצַו הַמֶּלֶךְ אֶת־בְּנָיָהוּ בֶּן־יְהוֹיָדָע וַיֵּצֵא וַיִּפְגַּע־בּוֹ וַיָּמֹת׃ 2.35.1632

Solomon Puts Shimei under House Arrest in Jerusalem

וַיִּשְׁלַח הַמֶּלֶךְ 2.36.1633
וַיִּקְרָא לְשִׁמְעִי 2.36.1634
וַיֹּאמֶר לוֹ 2.36.1635

בְּנֵה־לְךָ בַיִת בִּירוּשָׁלִַם 2.36.1636   HD
וְיָשַׁבְתָּ שָּׁם 2.36.1637
וְלֹא־תֵצֵא מִשָּׁם אָנֶה וָאָנָה׃ 2.36.1638   PD
וְהָיָה בְּיוֹם צֵאתְךָ 2.37.1639
וְעָבַרְתָּ אֶת־נַחַל קִדְרוֹן 2.37.1640
יָדֹעַ תֵּדַע 2.37.1641
כִּי מוֹת תָּמוּת 2.37.1642   PD
דָּמְךָ יִהְיֶה בְרֹאשֶׁךָ׃ 2.37.1642

וַיֹּאמֶר שִׁמְעִי לַמֶּלֶךְ 2.38.1643

טוֹב הַדָּבָר 2.38.1644   ED
כַּאֲשֶׁר דִּבֶּר אֲדֹנִי הַמֶּלֶךְ 1645α   PD
כֵּן יַעֲשֶׂה עַבְדֶּךָ 2.38.1645
וַיֵּשֶׁב שִׁמְעִי בִּירוּשָׁלִַם יָמִים רַבִּים׃ 2.38.1646

Solomon Has Shimei Killed and Secures His Reign

וַיְהִי לְקֵץ 2.39.1647
וַיִּשְׁלַח שְׁלֹמֹה וַיִּקְרָא לְשִׁמְעִי וַיֹּאמֶר אֵלָיו 2.39.1648
וַיְצַו הַמֶּלֶךְ אֶת־בְּנָיָהוּ 2.39.1649

לאמר־

2.40.1651 וַיֹּאמֶר הַמֶּלֶךְ
2.40.1652 וַיֵּלֶךְ לְבִנְיָהוּ
2.40.1653 וַיַּעַן אֲדֹנִיָּהוּ וַיֹּאמֶר
2.40.1654 וַיֵּלֶךְ שְׁלֹמֹה
2.40.1655 וַיֹּאמֶר בֶּן־שֶׁלֶם נָכְרִיָּה אֶל־אֲדֹנִיָּהוּ
2.41.1656 בִּדְבַר שְׁלֹמֹה

כִּי־

2.42.1659 וַיֹּאמֶר אֵלָיו
2.42.1660 וַיֵּאֶל לַאֲדֹנִיָּהוּ
2.42.1661 וַיַּעַן הַמֶּלֶךְ

ED הִנֵּה
2.39.1650 בִּדְבַר בֵּיתוֹ:

ND
2.41.1657 וַיֵּלֶךְ שְׁלֹמֹה וַיַּעֲשֶׂה אֶת
2.41.1658 לֵאמֹר:

ID
2.42.1662 כִּי אוֹדֶה וַתָּאֲבֵל בְּיוֹם
2.42.1663 וַיֹּאמֶר אֵלָיו
לֵאמֹר־

†PD
יוֹם צֵאתְךָ [וְיָצָאתָ]† 1664α
2.42.1664 וְאָמַרְתָּ לֹא אֹמֵר
2.42.1665 דָּמְךָ עָלַי:
חַטָּאתְךָ כִּי־

(ID)
2.42.1666 אֵל יֹאמַר וַיֹּאמֶר

2.44.1670 וְאֹמַר חֲדַל נָא אֲדֹנָי׃

2.46.1675 וַיִּתֵּן יְהוָה אֶת־
2.46.1676 וַיֵּצֵא
2.46.1677 וַיַּעֲבֹר
2.46.1678 וַיֹּאמֶר
2.46.1679 וַיֵּלֶךְ

†ED
2.42.1667 וַיַּרְא נֹחַ
†ND
2.42.1668 וַיָּבֹא אֶל תּוֹךְ
2.43.1669 וַיֹּאמֶר

ND
PD
2.44.1671 וַיֹּאמֶר אֶל

2.44.1672 וְכֹל אֲשֶׁר
2.45.1673 וַיַּעַשׂ
2.45.1374 וַיֵּלֶךְ

Table of Independent Clause Types in 1 Kings 2

Clause Type	Clause Distribution	Total	Percent
QAṬAL Total Clauses: 21	Narrative: 1543,1544,1545,1595,1632,1679	6	28.6%
	ND: 1524,1533,1534,1557,1558,1603,1610,1615, 1616,1624,1657,†1668,1669,1671	14	66.7%
	PD:		
	ED:		
	ID: 1662	1	4.7%
	HD:		
WeQAṬAL Total Clauses: 16	Narrative:	0	0
	ND:		
	PD: 1520,1521,1522,1528,1531,†1664,1672	7	43.7%
	ED:		
	ID:		
	HD: 1538,1539,1620,1621,1622,1625,1637,1639, 1640	9	56.3%
YIQṬOL Total Clauses: 16	Narrative:	0	0
	ND:		
	PD: †1523,1530,1570,1583,1589,1645,†1665,1674	8	50.0%
	ED:		
	ID:		
	HD: 1537,1562,1579,1626,1638,1641,1642	8	50.0%
WeYIQṬOL Total Clauses: 1	Narrative:		
	ND:		
	PD:		
	ED:		
	ID:		
	HD: 1567	1	100%
WAYYIQṬOL Total Clauses: 77	Narrative: 1517,1518,1540,1541,1546,1547,1548, 1550,1552,1554,1556,1563,1565,1568,1571,1572, 1573,1574,1575,1576,1577,1580,1582,1584,1585, 4588,1592,1593,1594,1598,1600,1601,1602,1605, 1608,1609,1612,1614,1617,1627,1628,1629,1630, 1631,1633,1634,1635,1643,1646,1647,1648,1649, 1651,1652,1653,1654,1655,1656,1659,1660,1661, 1670,1675,1676,1677,1678	66	85.7%

WAYYIQTOL (cont.) Total Clauses: 77	ND: 1525,1526,1527,1535,1559,1560,1591,1623, 1658	9	11.7%
	PD:		
	ED:		
	ID: 1663,1666	2	2.6%
	HD:		
Participle Total Clauses: 6	Narrative: 1599	1	16.7%
	ND:		
	PD: 1673	1	16.7%
	ED: 1519,1561,1578	3	50.0%
	ID: 1586	1	16.7%
	HD:		
Verbless Total Clauses: 6	Narrative: 1542	1	16.7%
	ND:		
	PD:		
	ED: 1532,1553,1644,1650		66.6%
	ID: 1549		16.7%
	HD:		
Incomplete Total Clauses: 7	Narrative:	0	0
	ND:		
	PD:		
	ED: †1536,1551,1569,1590,1604,1613,†1667	7	100%
	ID:		
	HD:		
Imperative Total Clauses: 12	Narrative:	0	0
	HD: 1555,1564,1566,1581,1587,1596,1606,1607, †1611,1618,1619,1636	12	100%
Cohortative Total Clauses: 0	Narrative:	0	0
	HD:	0	0
Jussive Total Clauses: 1	Narrative:	0	0
	HD: 1529	1	100%

Analysis of the Narrative Structure and
Discourse Text-Types in 1 Kings 2

Narrative Structural Analysis

Narrative/Paragraph Structure

The story of Solomon's securing of his kingdom after the death of David is built upon a narrative backbone of sixty-six *WAYYIQTOL* clauses. After the initial continued paragraph from chapter 1, the narrative backbone is segmented into four paragraphs and one extra-paragraph comment about the reign of David (clauses 1542-1544). The paragraphs in this chapter are initially marked either by *QATAL* clauses (1545, 1595), by a וַיְהִי temporal clause (1647), or by the final *QATAL* clause of a previous paragraph (1632). The first, continued paragraph is terminally marked by the insertion of the extra-paragraph comment (composed of *QATAL* and verbless clauses) and the final paragraph of the chapter and of the Court Narrative as a whole is defined by a final *QATAL* clause (1679).

Extra-Paragraph Comments

The one example of an extra-paragraph comment in 1 Kings 2 consists of three clauses, an initial verbless clause followed by two *QATAL* clauses:

02.11.1542 וְהַיָּמִים אֲשֶׁר מָלַךְ דָּוִד עַל־יִשְׂרָאֵל אַרְבָּעִים שָׁנָה

02.11.1543 בְּחֶבְרוֹן מָלַךְ שֶׁבַע שָׁנִים

02.11.1544 וּבִירוּשָׁלַםִ מָלַךְ שְׁלֹשִׁים וְשָׁלֹשׁ שָׁנִים:

The comment breaks the *WAYYIQTOL* chain established in the first paragraph. The comment serves a wider purpose in the books of Kings by providing a precedent structural form that, throughout the books, divides individual reigns of Israelite and Judahite monarchs from each other.[77]

---

[77]See, among other works, Helga Weippert, "Die 'deuteronomistischen' Beurteilungen der Könige von Israel und Juda und das Problem der Redaktion der Königsbücher," *Biblica* 53 (1972), 301-39.

Inner-Paragraph Comments

The only example of an inner-paragraph comment in this chapter is the participial clause that divides the exile of Abiathar from the assassination of Joab in the second paragraph of the chapter:[78]

02.28.1599 וְהַשְּׁמֻעָה בָּאָה עַד־יוֹאָב

Discourse Function Analysis

Narrative Discourse

The thirteen examples of Narrative Discourse in 1 Kings 2 are all consistent with this text-type. Eleven of the cases are defined by the *QATAL* clauses within them, either exclusively (1524, 1557, 1603, 1610, 1615-1616, †1668, 1671) or in combination with *WAYYIQTOL* clauses (1533-1535, 1558-1560, 1623-1624, 1657-1658). In addition, there are two cases in which *WAYYIQTOL* clauses alone define the speech as Narrative Discourse (1525-1527, 1591).

Predictive Discourse

The ten cases of Predictive Discourse in this chapter all conform to the other examples of this text-type seen throughout the Court Narrative. Ten of the cases are defined as predictive by the governing *YIQTOL* clauses within them. Five of these cases are composed of *YIQTOL* clauses exclusively (†1523, 1570, 1583, 1589, 1645); three cases also have *WeQATAL* clauses (1528-1531, 1639-1642, †1664-1665) and one case has a *YIQTOL*, a *WeQATAL*, and a participial clause (1672-1674). A single case of a predictive speech defined solely by the string of *WeQATAL* clauses that comprise it stands in clauses 1520-1522.[79]

---

[78]Although the Masoretic accenting of the first syllable of the middle-weak verb, בָּאָה, might be interpreted as a *QATAL*, it seems much more likely, in light of the single *WAYYIQTOL* clause that precedes it in the paragraph, that it should be interpreted as a participle; the paragraph, therefore, does not end at clause 1598 but continues after the participial clause 1599.

[79]Burney (*Notes*, 13), Driver (*Tenses*, §119d), and Gesenius (*Grammar*, §112aa) all agree that the speech of 2:2-3 is hortatory: "the perf. with ו *consec.* is used as a mild imperative; cf.v. 6 וְעָשִׂיתָ" (Burney). The speech of verse 6, however, is clearly defined as hortatory by the presence of the jussive clause within it (1529). Moreover, the speech of verses 2-3 is easily interpreted as predictive, in that a distinction is being made by David between himself ("I am going the way of all the earth") and his surviving son Solomon ("*But* you will be strong and be a man and you will keep").

Expository Discourse

Eight of the thirteen cases of Expository Discourse found in this chapter are composed of participial clauses (1519, 1569, 1578) or verbless clauses (1532, 1553, 1644, 1650, †1667). Additionally, there are six cases of incomplete clauses which occur as an oath (clauses †1536, 1590), as a response to a preceding question or statement (clauses 1551, 1569, 1613), or as a logical consequence of an immediately preceding statement in which the subject is, therefore, not defined (clause 1604).

Interrogative Discourse

Two of the three examples of Interrogative Discourse present in this chapter consist of single clauses, each explicitly marked as a question by the prefixed interrogative particles הַ (clause 1549) and וְלָמָה (clause 1586). In the third case, an initial הֲלוֹא governs the string of two *WAYYIQTOL* clauses which follow, causing the entire retrospective to be a part of the rhetorical question. The final clause of the discourse is marked as interrogative by וּמַדּוּעַ:

ID
02.42.1662 הֲלוֹא הִשְׁבַּעְתִּיךָ בַיהוָה
02.42.1663 וָאָעַד בְּךָ
לֵאמֹר

†PD
1664α וּבְיוֹם צֵאתְךָ
02.42.1664 וְהָלַכְתָּ אָנֶה וָאָנָה
02.42.1665 יָדֹעַ תֵּדַע
כִּי מוֹת תָּמוּת

(ID)
02.42.1666 וַתֹּאמֶר אֵלַי

†ED
02.42.1667 טוֹב הַדָּבָר
†ND
02.42.1668 שָׁמָעְתִּי׃

(ID)
02.43.1669 וּמַדּוּעַ לֹא שָׁמַרְתָּ אֵת שְׁבֻעַת יְהוָה וְאֶת־הַמִּצְוָה
אֲשֶׁר־צִוִּיתִי עָלֶיךָ׃

While only two of the four clauses that make up the speech are explicitly marked as interrogative, the whole of the discourse is clearly an extended rhetorical question.

Hortatory Discourse

Ten of the thirteen cases of Hortatory Discourse in 1 Kings 2 are marked as hortatory by the presence of imperative clauses within them. Six of these cases have imperative clauses exclusively (1555, 1564, 1581, 1587, 1606-1607, †1611). In addition, two speeches contain imperative clauses and either a *YIQTOL* clause (1596-1597) or a *WeYIQTOL* clause (1566-1567). Two cases contain a combination of imperative, *YIQTOL*, and *WeQATAL* clauses (1618-1626, 1636-1638).

One speech is defined as hortatory by the jussive clause within it and also contains *YIQTOL* and *WeQATAL* clauses (1528-1531).[80] Finally, there are three cases of Hortatory Discourse that are defined by the negated *ʾal-YIQTOL* clauses within them, either alone (1562, 1579) or with *WeQATAL* clauses (1537-1539). In all cases, the *YIQTOL*, *WeYIQTOL*, and *WeQATAL* clauses consistently continue the hortatory character of the speech established by the imperative and *ʾal-YIQTOL* clauses.

---

[80]Waltke and O'Connor (*Syntax*, 567) are correct in their assessment of the speech as hortatory in spite of the negative particle לֹא (instead of the more regular אַל) before the jussive verb תּוֹרֵד. (The *YIQTOL* would be תּוֹרִיד.) Other cases of לֹא with the jussive include Gen 4:12; 24:8; Deut 13:1; 1 Sam 14:36; 2 Sam 17:12; Ezek 48:14 and Joel 2:2.

Table of Discourse Constellations for 1 Kings 2

		Present Ch.	Prev. Chs.	Total JN+CN
ND	*QATAL*	7	61	68
	QATAL, WAYYIQTOL	4	15	19
	QATAL, (Ptc./Vbl.)		9	9
	QATAL, WAYYIQTOL, (Ptc./Vbl.)		8	8
	QATAL, WAYYIQTOL, (Ptc./Vbl.), *YIQTOL*		3	3
	QATAL, YIQTOL (w/ past adverb)		1	1
	WAYYIQTOL, (Ptc./Vbl.)	2	2	4
	Vbl/Ptc/Inc (Dream Report)		1	1
PD	*YIQTOL*	5	47	52
	YIQTOL, WeQATAL	2	16	18
	YIQTOL, WeQATAL, (Ptc./Vbl../Inc.)	1	8	9
	YIQTOL, (Ptc./Vbl../Inc.)		3	3
	WeQATAL	1	16	17
	WeYIQTOL		2	2
ED	Ptc./Vbl.	8	75	83
	Ptc./ Vbl., Inc.		2	2
	Inc.	6	29	35
	Ptc./Vbl., *QATAL/YIQTOL* of היה		5	5
	Ptc./Vbl., *QATAL/YIQTOL* of היה, Front. Obj.+ *QATAL/YIQTOL*		2	2
	QATAL/YIQTOL of היה		3	3
HD	Impv./Coh./Juss.	6	90	96
	Impv./Coh./Juss., *WeYIQTOL/YIQTOL*	2	22	24
	Impv./Coh./Juss., *WeQATAL*		7	7
	Impv./Coh./Juss., *WeYIQTOL/YIQTOL, WeQATAL*	3	8	11
	Impv./Coh./Juss., *QATAL*		2	2
	Impv./Coh./Juss., *WeYIQTOL/YIQTOL*, (We)*QATAL*		2	2
	Impv./Coh./Juss., *ʾal-YIQTOL*		3	3
	Impv./Coh./Juss., *WeQATAL, ʾal-YIQTOL*		4	4
	ʾal-YIQTOL	2	10	12
	ʾal-YIQTOL, WeQATAL/YIQTOL	1	2	3
	(We)*YIQTOL-nāʾ*, (*WeQATAL*/[We]*YIQTOL*)		9	9
	QATAL, YIQTOL/WeQATAL		3	3
Total Number of Discourse Examples in JN and CN				520

Chapter Four
Toward a Functional Approach to the
Arrangement of Clauses in Biblical Hebrew Narrative

While much work has been done recently on the various types of clauses in biblical Hebrew from the perspective of discourse-linguistics or text-grammar, most studies continue to deal with the problem in one of two ways. On the one hand, some studies highlight only one particular conjugation or clause type and analyze the various contexts in which the conjugation or clause type occurs.[1] On the other hand, some studies look at several conjugations or clause types in biblical Hebrew, but only sporadically refer to common uses of verbal forms or clause types and, very often, spend most of their time highlighting unusual or rare occurrences in their analysis.[2] This study, on the contrary, has attempted to analyze two extended prose texts comprehensively from a discourse perspective, accounting for *every* independent clause whether verbal or non-verbal, noting especially the different syntactical patterns which occur with verbal and clausal combinations in different contexts, whether in narrative or in direct discourse.

In addition to the normal aspectual connotations that the various Hebrew verbal forms imply, this study has also attempted to show that, in narrative, the

---

[1]Examples of this approach include F. C. Fensham, "The Use of the Suffix Conjugation and the Prefix Conjugation in a Few Old Poems," *JNSL* 6 (1978), 9-18; Edward Greenstein, "On the Prefixed Preterite in Biblical Hebrew," *Hebrew Studies* 29 (1988), 7-17; Delbert Hillers, "Some Performative Utterances in the Bible," in *Pomegranates and Golden Bells* (ed. D. Wright, D. N. Freedman, and A. Hurwitz; Winona Lake: Eisenbrauns, 1995), 757-66; Bo Johnson, *Hebräisches Perfekt und Imperfekt mit vorangehendem wᵉ* (Lund: CWK Gleerup, 1979); Leslie McFall, *The Enigma of the Hebrew Verbal System* (Sheffield: Almond, 1982); Mark S. Smith, *Origins and Development of the* Waw-Consecutive (HSS 39; Atlanta: Scholars, 1991).

[2]Examples of this approach include Francis I. Andersen, *The Sentence in Biblical Hebrew* (The Hague: Mouton, 1974); S. R. Driver, *A Treatise on the Use of the Tenses in Hebrew and Some Other Syntactical Questions* (2d ed., Oxford: Clarendon, 1881); Yoshinobu Endo, *The Verbal System of Classical Hebrew in the Joseph Story: An Approach from Discourse Analysis* (SSN 32; Assen: Van Gorcum, 1996); Mats Eskhult, *Studies in Verbal Aspect and Narrative Technique in Biblical Hebrew Prose* (SSU 12; Uppsala: Uppsala University Press, 1990); J. A. Hughes, "Another Look at the Hebrew Tenses," *JNES* 29 (1970), 12-24; Diethelm Michel, *Tempora und Satzstellung in den Psalmen* (Bonn: Bouvier, 1960); Alviero Niccacci, *The Syntax of the Verb in Classical Hebrew Prose* (JSOTSupp 86; Sheffield: JSOT, 1990); R. J. Williams, *Hebrew Syntax: An Outline* (2d ed.; Toronto: University of Toronto Press, 1976); Beat Zuber, *Das Tempussystem des biblischen Hebräisch: Eine Untersuchung am Text* (BZAW 164; Berlin: Walter de Gruyter, 1986).

differing verbal forms also play functional roles with respect to the organization and structure of the story told. The work of Thomas Lambdin was foundational to this type of approach of narrative organization. Lambdin, in his *Introduction to Biblical Hebrew,* argues that non-*WAYYIQTOL* verbal clauses may often provide contrastive, circumstantial, or explanatory information within a narrative or may indicate the initiation or termination of a narrative block.[3]

While Lambdin's explication of this phenomenon and other previous studies' investigations of it have recognized that various syntactical patterns occasionally begin or end narrative blocks or provide off-line, backgrounded information, this analysis attempts to investigate the criteria by which any *particular* disjunctive clause in narrative may be classified as either contrastive, circumstantial, explanatory, or initial/terminative. The goal of this study is to take the question of the function or meaning of these clauses out of the realm of intuition and to base their meanings and functions upon objective criteria.

This inquiry further refines these insights for narrative in two main areas. First, this study delimits and illustrates the specific verbal syntactical patterns that introduce or conclude paragraph blocks. By noting how the text itself *syntactically* defines paragraphs, the interpreter can better know what elements of the narrative are to be read together or separately. Second, this examination shows that "off-line" commentary in narrative is of two sorts: extra-paragraph comments and inner-paragraph comments. These two types of off-line, nonsequential comments within the larger narrative differ in their syntactical organization and in their narratological purpose. Whereas inner-paragraph comments provide information about some particular element within the narrative at hand, extra-paragraph comments always provide information of a much wider scope, explaining either backgrounded circumstances, repeated and complex activities within the narrative, or the consequences of or the eventual outcome of a narrative block.

In its treatment of direct discourse within biblical Hebrew narrative prose, this study has also noted that specific combinations of verbal forms found in speeches consistently have delimited functional purposes. Four of the five major types of direct discourse, Narrative, Predictive, Expository, and Hortatory Discourses, all differ from each other in the verbal/clausal patterns that they employ and, further, in the basic pragmatic or, in the case of Hortatory Discourse, volitional meaning that they all have. The fifth type of direct discourse, Interrogative Discourse, is not defined by the verbal/clausal patterns that occur in it but by (usually prefixed) interrogative particles or adverbs. The set of verbal or clausal options, which in the other speech types define the purpose of the speech, in Interrogative Discourse explicitly defines the temporal setting of the question.

---

[3]Thomas O. Lambdin, *Introduction to Biblical Hebrew* (New York: Charles Scribner's Sons, 1971), §132.

This final chapter provides a summary analysis of the verbal and clausal forms found in narrative and direct discourse within the texts used as a database for this study.

Clause Function in Narrative Contexts

While in some societies or literary contexts narrative as a genre may consistently employ present tense verbal forms as the foundational grammatical framework of a story, the verbal forms found in narrative texts in the Hebrew Bible are generally acknowledged consistently to report events that happened in the past.[4] The use of differing verbal forms in narrative does not, therefore, mark changes in tense (which is consistently past), but rather changes in aspect and changes in narrative organization (initiation or conclusion of narrative blocks or the providing of off-line commentary).

WAYYIQṬOL Chains and non-WAYYIQṬOL Clauses

By far the most predominant verbal form in biblical Hebrew narrative prose is WAYYIQṬOL. In the texts chosen as a database for this study, WAYYIQṬOL clauses constitute 41.6% of the total clauses in the texts and 79.2% of the total clauses in the narrative portion of the texts.[5] The use of WAYYIQṬOL clauses in uninterrupted syntactical chains consistently implies sequentiality of action in the narrative—the syntactical sequentiality of the WAYYIQṬOL clauses in the chain parallels the temporal sequentiality of the actions described by them.[6]

---

[4]For various treatments of the verbal tense of narrative genres in other languages, see Ilham Nayef Abu-Ghazaleh, "Theme and Function of the Verb in Palestinian Arabic Narrative Discourse" (Ph.D. dissertation; University of Florida, 1983); H. G. Bartelt, "Mode and Aspect Transfer in Navajo and Western Apache English Narrative Technique," *International Review of Applied Linguistics in Language Teaching* 21 (1983), 105-24; Clyde Thogmartin, "Tense, Aspect, and Context in French Narrative," *The French Review* 57 (1984), 344-49.

[5]In the Joseph Novella, there are 970 total independent clauses. Of these, 480 occur in narrative and 490 occur in direct discourse. Of those that occur in narrative, 397 are WAYYIQṬOL clauses. In the Narrative of David's Court, there are 1679 total independent clauses. Of these, 910 occur in narrative and 769 occur in direct discourse. Of those that occur in narrative, 704 are WAYYIQṬOL clauses.

[6]In their treatment of the WAYYIQṬOL clause, Waltke and O'Connor note that clauses governed by a "*Waw* + Prefix Conjugation" (their designation for WAYYIQṬOL) do not always imply sequentiality of action (*Syntax*, 543-62). Consistently, however, their examples of nonsequential WAYYIQṬOL clauses occur in one of three contexts: 1) poetic material, 2) direct discourse, or 3) in conjunction with multiple non-WAYYIQṬOL clauses. In the first case, poetry is constrained by facets (both temporal and formal) not present in narrative. In direct discourse, multiple types of discourse (e.g., Hortatory,

In narrative, all other clauses that occur within the backbone of the basic *WAYYIQTOL* chain and are governed by anything except *WAYYIQTOL* verbal forms provide two different types of information for the reader. On one hand, *independent* non-*WAYYIQTOL* verbal clauses often mark boundaries of paragraphs—that is, they mark the beginning and/or end of blocks of narrative that, because of consistency of focus, should be read and understood as a whole.[7] On the other hand, nonfinite clauses (i.e., participial, verbless, or incomplete clauses), *multiple* non-*WAYYIQTOL* verbal clauses, and unchained, independent *WAYYIQTOL* clauses provide background or off-line information, which does not occur within the sequentiality of the main narrative. These off-line comments may occur either within a paragraph or between paragraph blocks. The former are called in this study "inner-paragraph comments"; the latter, "extra-paragraph comments".[8]

These two basic functions of non-*WAYYIQTOL* clauses, marking paragraph boundaries and providing the two separate types of off-line commentary, are the defining characteristics of the shape and structure of Hebrew narrative in general. By means of the interplay between the consecutive, consequential *WAYYIQTOL* chains which bind the story line together in paragraphs and the disjunctive non-*WAYYIQTOL* clauses which cause the story line either to begin

---

Predictive, Expository, Interrogative) may be juxtaposed in a single speech. In such cases, the temporal setting of the *WAYYIQTOL* clause would, of course, not necessarily be consistent with preceding clauses if they were not also Narrative Discourse. In the final case, in contexts with multiple non-*WAYYIQTOL* clauses, the off-line comment is neither consistent nor consequent with the temporal setting of the prevailing narrative. In these cases of extra-paragraph comments, however, the *WAYYIQTOL* clauses do not appear in chains but rather individually and are grouped with multiple non-*WAYYIQTOL* forms.

[7]Among the paragraph markers are ויהי temporal clauses, which are technically *WAYYIQTOL* verbal clauses. In both their sense and function, however, they do not parallel usual *WAYYIQTOL* clauses. They are, therefore, here listed among the other *independent* non-*WAYYIQTOL* verbal clauses that consistently mark paragraph boundaries.

[8]It is important to note that the term "paragraph" in this study refers only to a narrative block of material organized by a coherent *WAYYIQTOL* chain. These paragraph blocks are what move the narrative forward. Off-line comments may occur either inside a narrative block (paragraph) or outside a narrative block (paragraph). Comments made within a paragraph do not break the "flow" of the narrative and, thus, the *WAYYIQTOL* chain before and after them has integrity. It is also important to note that, while an extended offline description of activity—an "extra-paragraph comment"—may be told to the reader and, *in an English translation*, may be formatted as a separate paragraph (complete with a new initial line and indentation), in the structure of the Hebrew narrative itself, such a description should be seen as outside or between "paragraph blocks" of narrative material.

or end, or which provide off-line, but essential, information for the understanding of the significance of the story, the rich texture and complexity which define biblical storytelling are possible. These two basic functions of non-*WAYYIQTOL* clauses and their literary significance for biblical narrative will be illustrated in the following sections.

Paragraph Boundary Clausal Markers

I. Initial Markers of Paragraphs

In the Joseph Novella and in the Narrative of David's Court, the insertion of solitary non-*WAYYIQTOL* clauses into the basic narrative backbone of *WAYYIQTOL* clauses breaks the foundational story line into discrete sections; the inserted independent non-*WAYYIQTOL* verbal clauses consistently mark the beginning and ending of paragraphs.[9] The beginnings of paragraphs are explicitly marked by one of two types of independent clauses: ויהי temporal clauses and independent *QATAL* clauses.[10] The occurrences of these clauses in the textual databases are provided in the chart below.

---

[9]Two items must be mentioned in connection with these paragraph boundary clauses. First, they are *solitary* non-*WAYYIQTOL* clauses (i.e., usually *QATAL* clauses and ויהי temporal clauses, but occasionally *WeQATAL* and *YIQTOL* clauses, and, in this study's text database, single cases each of a clause governed by *We* + infinitive construct, an independent prepositional clause, or an incomplete clause). The fact that these clauses are independent (i.e., bounded on at least one side—and often on both sides—by a *WAYYIQTOL* chain) marks them as paragraph boundary markers. If they were multiple, they would instead stand within extra-paragraph comments. Second, in a few cases, the paragraph boundary marker concludes a paragraph juxtaposed to an extra-paragraph comment. In these cases, the non-*WAYYIQTOL* clause may either be the final clause of the paragraph or the initial clause of the comment and the information provided by the paragraph and by the comment will determine which function the non-*WAYYIQTOL* clause has.

[10]A third means of marking the initiation of a paragraph block is the use of *YIQTOL* immediately after the prepositions אָז, טֶרֶם, or בְּטֶרֶם, although no case of any of these constructions appears in either of the textual databases used in this study. See footnote 13 below for a fuller explanation.

Table of Paragraph Initial Boundary Clauses

ויהי Temporal Clauses	Joseph Novella: 079,142,149,163,171,188,201,254, 262, 278,524,544
	Court Narrative: 052,117,122,174,182,283,355, 449,505, 655,675,831,931,954,1172,1595,1647
QAṬAL Clauses	Joseph Novella: 132,408,419,667,801,867,893
	Court Narrative: 082,092,111,329,513,754,775,940, 1018, 1105,1132,1154,1195,1222Q,1239,1270,1281, 1500,1545

1) The use of a ויהי temporal clause to mark the beginning of paragraphs has already been thoroughly examined in several previous works.[11] The first examples of this phenomenon in the Joseph Novella and in the Court Narrative will illustrate how the initiation of paragraphs is marked by the ויהי temporal clause:

37.21.071 וַיֹּאמֶר אֲלֵהֶם רְאוּבֵן
"(inserted quotation)"
075α לְמַעַן הַצִּיל אֹתוֹ מִיָּדָם לַהֲשִׁיבוֹ אֶל־אָבִיו:
(Paragraph break)
37.23.079 וַיְהִי כַּאֲשֶׁר־בָּא יוֹסֵף אֶל־אֶחָיו
37.23.080 וַיַּפְשִׁיטוּ אֶת־יוֹסֵף אֶת־כֻּתָּנְתּוֹ אֶת־כְּתֹנֶת הַפַּסִּים אֲשֶׁר עָלָיו:

Reuben said to them,
"(inserted quotation)"
in order to rescue [Joseph] from their hand, to return him to his father.
¶ As soon as Joseph came to his brothers, they stripped Joseph of his coat, the *passim* coat that was on him . . .

09.13.050 וּמְפִיבֹשֶׁת יֹשֵׁב בִּירוּשָׁלַםִ
כִּי עַל־שֻׁלְחַן הַמֶּלֶךְ תָּמִיד הוּא אֹכֵל
09.13.051 וְהוּא פִּסֵּחַ שְׁתֵּי רַגְלָיו:
(Paragraph break)

---

[11]Genesius noted this function of ויהי long ago: "The introduction of independent narratives, *or of a new section of the narrative,* [is often accomplished] by means of an imperfect consecutive. Such a connexion (*sic*) is especially often established by means of וַיְהִי" (*Grammar,* §111 f-h, emphasis mine). Recently, note the work of Wolfgang Schneider, *Grammatik des biblischen Hebräisch* (Munich: Claudius, 1974), and Wolfgang Richter, *Grundlagen einer althebräischen Grammatik* (St. Ottilien: EOS, 1978-1980) 3.205-6.

10.01.052 וַיְהִי אַחֲרֵי־כֵן
10.01.053 וַיָּמָת מֶלֶךְ בְּנֵי עַמּוֹן
10.01.054 וַיִּמְלֹךְ חָנוּן בְּנוֹ תַּחְתָּיו:

. . . (and Mephiboshet was staying in Jerusalem because he always ate at the royal table. And he was lame in both of his feet.)

¶ After this, the king of the Ammonites died, and Hanun his son was made king in his place . . .

In all cases a וִיהי temporal clause is a metasyntactical marker for the beginning of a paragraph. This phenomenon is almost a universal marker of paragraph initiation in biblical Hebrew prose.

2) The use of independent *QAṬAL* clauses as boundary markers of paragraphs has also been noted by some scholars.[12] While independent *QAṬAL* clauses more often mark the end of paragraphs (see below), occasionally they initiate paragraphs. The decision of whether an independent *QAṬAL* clause marks the beginning or end of a paragraph is solely dependent upon the narrative context and whether the focus of the *QAṬAL* clause is the same as the *WAYYIQṬOL* clause immediately before it (in which case it ends the preceding paragraph) or the *WAYYIQṬOL* clause immediately after it (in which case it begins the subsequent paragraph). The two cases below illustrate this function of the independent *QAṬAL* clause as a paragraph initiator.

Previous story of Judah and Tamar (Gen. 38)
(Paragraph break)
39.01.132 וְיוֹסֵף הוּרַד מִצְרָיְמָה
39.01.133 וַיִּקְנֵהוּ פּוֹטִיפַר סְרִיס פַּרְעֹה שַׂר הַטַּבָּחִים

¶ Joseph was brought down to Egypt and Potiphar, the officer of Pharaoh, chief of the guards, purchased him. . . .

10.09.080 וַיִּבְחַר מִכֹּל בְּחוּרֵי בְיִשְׂרָאֵל [Q1 יִשְׂרָאֵל]
10.09.081 וַיַּעֲרֹךְ לִקְרַאת אֲרָם:
(Paragraph break)
10.10.082 וְאֵת יֶתֶר הָעָם נָתַן בְּיַד אַבְשַׁי אָחִיו
10.10.083 וַיַּעֲרֹךְ לִקְרַאת בְּנֵי עַמּוֹן:
10.00.084 וַיֹּאמֶר אִם־תֶּחֱזַק

---

[12]In particular note the recent work of Longacre (*Joseph*, 76-77) and the notes by Lambdin (*Introduction*, §132).

. . . he chose some of the best men of Israel and crossed over to meet the Syrians.

¶ The rest of the people he placed under the authority of Abishai his brother, and he crossed over to meet the Ammonites. He said . . .

In both cases the insertion of *QATAL* clauses between the *WAYYIQTOL* chains on either side of them signals a topic shift within the larger narrative. In the first example, the focus changes from the previous story of Judah and Tamar to the narrative of Joseph in Egypt; in the other, from the initial war with Syria to a wider scope war with Ammon.[13]

II. Terminal Markers of Paragraphs

In the Joseph Novella and in the Court Narrative of David, the conclusion of paragraphs is explicitly marked by one of five types of independent non-*WAYYIQTOL* clauses: *QATAL* clauses, *WeQATAL* clauses, *YIQTOL* clauses, clauses governed by We + infinitive absolute, and incomplete clauses. In all cases, the boundary clause stands independent of any other non-*WAYYIQTOL* clause and is, therefore, usually found between *WAYYIQTOL* chains. Their presence, therefore, breaks the continuity of the story and effectively provides a boundary between discrete sections of narrative. The instances of these clauses within the textual databases of this study are provided in the chart below.

---

[13]In addition to these two clausal types, a paragraph block may also be initiated the prepositions אָז, טֶרֶם, or בְּטֶרֶם, followed by a *YIQTOL* verbal form, although this particular construction does not appear anywhere in the Joseph Novella or the Court Narrative. Waltke and O'Connor (*Syntax*, 513-14) follow the argument of Isaac Rabinowitz ("'āz Followed by Imperfect Verb-Form in Preterite Contexts: A Redactional Device in Biblical Hebrew," *VT* 34 [1984], 53-62) who sees such *YIQTOL* clauses as marking a "consecution in an uninterrupted narration of past actions or events" (54). On the contrary, every instance of this phenomenon in *independent clauses within narrative prose* always marks an initiation to events in a following paragraph block that are logically separate from the events of the previous narrative block. Note, in particular the cases in Exod 15:1; Num 21:17; Deut 4:41; Josh 3:1; 8:30; 22:1; 1 Kgs 3:16; 8:1; 9:11; 11:7; 16:21.

Table of Paragraph Terminal Boundary Clauses

QAṬAL Clauses	Joseph Novella: 036,131,141,147,259,435, 486,587,770, 797,862,950
	Court Narrative: 153,173,349,484,509,687-688, 752,900,922,971,986,1012,1089,1147, 1216,1221,1247,1252,1280, 1288,1332, 1355,1405,1471,1476,1632,1679
WeQAṬAL Clauses	Joseph Novella: Ø
	Court Narrative: 434,753,825
YIQṬOL Clauses	Joseph Novella: Ø
	Court Narrative: 774
We + Infinitive Absolute	Joseph Novella: 375
	Court Narrative: Ø
Incomplete Clause	Joseph Novella: 277
	Court Narrative: Ø

1) The use of *QAṬAL* as a paragraph initial marker parallels its use here as a paragraph terminal marker. In both cases the independent *QAṬAL* clause provides either an introduction or conclusion to a segment of narrative that can be interpreted as a whole. The simple function of a *QAṬAL* clause as a paragraph terminator can most easily be seen in two examples taken from the Joseph Novella and the Narrative of David's Court.

37.11.035 וַיְקַנְאוּ־בוֹ אֶחָיו
37.11.036 וְאָבִיו שָׁמַר אֶת־הַדָּבָר:
(Paragraph break)
37.12.037 וַיֵּלְכוּ אֶחָיו לִרְעוֹת אֶת־צֹאן אֲבִיהֶם בִּשְׁכֶם:
37.13.038 וַיֹּאמֶר יִשְׂרָאֵל אֶל־יוֹסֵף

His brothers were jealous of him, but his father kept the matter.
¶ His brothers went to shepherd the flock of their father in Shechem. Israel said to Joseph . . .

18.09.984 וַיֶּחֱזַק רֹאשׁוֹ בָאֵלָה
18.09.985 וַיֻּתַּן בֵּין הַשָּׁמַיִם וּבֵין הָאָרֶץ
18.09.986 וְהַפֶּרֶד אֲשֶׁר־תַּחְתָּיו עָבָר:
(Paragraph break)
18.10.987 וַיַּרְא אִישׁ אֶחָד
18.10.988 וַיַּגֵּד לְיוֹאָב
18.10.989 וַיֹּאמֶר

He (Absalom) caught his head in the oak tree and he was put
between heaven and earth and the mule under him went on by.
¶ A certain man saw (it) and told (it) to Joab. He said . . .

In both cases the inserted *QATAL* clause shifts the reader's attention to a
new focus within the larger narrative (i.e., from the emotional reactions within
Joseph's family to his brothers' shepherding journey; from the entanglement of
Absalom in the tree to the report of an eyewitness).

In addition to this simple function, independent *QATAL* clauses may also
function as terminal markers in two different ways. First, a concluding *QATAL*
clause with a prefixed לֹא has a common rhetorical function of highlighting what
might have occurred but did not occur in the preceding paragraph.[14] The following two examples from 2 Samuel 11 show how the narrative story line is divided
into three basic blocks. The initial ploy of David to arrange for Uriah to go down
to his own house and sleep with Bathsheba his wife concludes with the following sequence:

11.08.150 וַיֵּצֵא אוּרִיָּה מִבֵּית הַמֶּלֶךְ
11.08.151 וַתֵּצֵא אַחֲרָיו מַשְׂאַת הַמֶּלֶךְ:
11.09.152 וַיִּשְׁכַּב אוּרִיָּה פֶּתַח בֵּית הַמֶּלֶךְ אֵת כָּל־עַבְדֵי אֲדֹנָיו
11.09.153 וְלֹא יָרַד אֶל־בֵּיתוֹ:

Uriah went out from the king's house and the king's gift went
out after him. Uriah lay down at the entrance of the king's
house with all the servants of his lord, and he did not go down
to his house.

The next paragraph reveals how David attempts to inebriate Uriah in order
to achieve his plan. This paragraph, likewise, concludes with the sequence:

11.13.168 וַיִּקְרָא־לוֹ דָוִד
11.13.169 וַיֹּאכַל לְפָנָיו
11.13.170 וַיֵּשְׁתְּ

---

[14]It is often difficult to differentiate between לֹא + *QATAL* being used as a paragraph boundary marker, in which the negation simply sums up the preceding action (e.g.,
2 Sam 11:9,13), and לֹא + *QATAL* being used as an instance of "momentous negation,"
in which the negation actually propels the narrative forward in a way similar to a positive
WAYYIQTOL clause (e.g., 2 Sam 13:14, 16). In most cases, the negation of the verbs אָבָה
and יָכֹל signal an instance of momentous negation, since the semantic meaning of those
verbs, when they are negated, implies a type of action: "not to be willing" ≈ "to resist,
refuse"; "not to be able" ≈ "to fail". It is also clear that, in some instances, other verbs
may also be employed for momentous negation (e.g., clauses 1275 and 1278).

11.13.171 וַיְשַׁכְּרֵהוּ
11.13.172 וַיֵּצֵא בָעֶרֶב לִשְׁכַּב בְּמִשְׁכָּבוֹ עִם־עַבְדֵי אֲדֹנָיו
11.13.173 וְאֶל־בֵּיתוֹ לֹא יָרָד:

David called him and he ate before him and drank and he
made him drunk. He went out at in the evening to lie down in
his bed with the servants of his lord, and did not go down to
his house.

In both cases, the narrator concludes the paragraph by explicitly expressing
what might have occurred but did *not* occur in the preceding paragraph. By
means of this negative conclusion, the narrator builds suspense by two means.
First, by breaking the narrative into subsections, the narrator delays the eventual
climax of the story. Second, by consistently reminding the reader of what did *not*
occur, the narrator creates and overturns the expectations of his audience.[15]

Second, in addition to providing a concluding negative statement, final
QAṬAL clauses also often provide a syntactical break between a narrative
WAYYIQṬOL chain and an extended extra-paragraph comment. A single exam-
ple of this phenomenon will suffice to show how this phenomenon functions:

18.17.1009 וַיִּקְחוּ אֶת־אַבְשָׁלוֹם
18.17.1010 וַיַּשְׁלִיכוּ אֹתוֹ בַיַּעַר אֶל־הַפַּחַת הַגָּדוֹל
10.17.1011 וַיַּצִּבוּ עָלָיו גַּל־אֲבָנִים גָּדוֹל מְאֹד
18.17.1012 וְכָל־יִשְׂרָאֵל נָסוּ אִישׁ לְאֹהֱלוֹ ‏[Q לְאֹהָלָיו]:

Absalom's Massebah (Retrospective Comment)

- - - - -

18.18.1013 וְאַבְשָׁלֹם לָקַח
18.18.1014 וַיַּצֶּב־לוֹ בְחַיָּו ‏[Q בְחַיָּיו] אֶת־מַצֶּבֶת
אֲשֶׁר בְּעֵמֶק־הַמֶּלֶךְ

They took Absalom and threw him in the thicket into a large
pit and set up over him a very large heap of stones. All Israel
fled, each to his own tent.
---Now Absalom, while he was alive, had taken and had set up
a *maṣṣebah* in the King's Valley. . . .

---

[15]The difference of word order between the two concluding QATAL clauses is significant for the building of suspense in this passage. In clause 153, וְלֹא יָרַד אֶל בֵּיתוֹ,
the clause is simply negated, stating what Uriah did not do ("go down to his house"). In
clause 173, וְאֶל בֵּיתוֹ לֹא יָרָד, the fronting of the prepositional phrase causes a slight
rise in suspense: "And to his house . . . he finally *did* go down??" The resolution of the
clause, however, resolves the suspense of the scene—Uriah again does not go to Bathsheba—but heightens it within the larger story—how will David cover his adulterous sin?

The narrative of Absalom's execution is decisively broken by the concluding *QATAL* clause (1012) which, in turn, provides the introduction to the off-line information about the past actions of Absalom.[16]

2) The uses of independent *WeQATAL* and independent *YIQTOL* clauses in narrative as paragraph terminal markers are absent in the Joseph Novella but occur four times in the Court Narrative (clauses 434, 753, 774, 825). The terminal clauses function to break the narrative flow of the preceding *WAYYIQTOL* verbal chain in a way identical to the *QATAL* terminal paragraph marker.[17]

3) Additionally, in the Joseph Novella, a single case of an independent clause governed by *We* + infinitive absolute (clause 375) and a single case of an independent incomplete clause (277) in narrative each *seem* to function as paragraph terminal markers.[18] Their unique status, however, makes any further analysis uncertain since no comparison with other contexts is possible.

III. Default Paragraph Boundary Markers

In rare cases, juxtaposed paragraphs may have both a terminal and an initial boundary marker. For example, in 2 Samuel 20:8–13, after Joab kills Amasa, the

---

[16]In this extra-paragraph comment, the verbs are understood in English as past perfects, not simply because of the use of the *QATAL* and *WAYYIQTOL* verbal forms (which would normally indicate a new paragraph) but because of the sense of the larger narrative. Since Absalom has previously died in clause 1006 in verse 15, he could not subsequently perform the actions outlined in clauses 1013–1017. These clauses, therefore, function as an extra-paragraph comment and relate actions that occurred before the immediate narrative.

[17]The narratological reason why these clauses were used instead of the more usual *QATAL* terminal clause is related to their inherent semantic and aspectual meanings, since discourse pragmatics and the semantic fields of the verbs work together to provide the sense of the clauses. In all cases, however, their introduction into the narrative consistently and explicitly delimits boundaries of narrative blocks.

[18]In the case of the independent incomplete clause (Gen 41:7; clause 277), the following sentence is a ויהי temporal clause—an explicit paragraph initial marker. Clause 277, therefore, must indeed conclude the preceding paragraph. Whether, however, it is itself a terminal paragraph marker is unclear. In the case of the independent clause governed by *We* + infinitive absolute (Gen 41:43; clause 375), the narrative context seems to be the guide. The preceding paragraph (clauses 278–375) deals with Joseph's interpretation of Pharaoh's dream and his appointment within the Egyptian hierarchy. The following paragraph (clauses 376–387) is specifically concerned with Joseph's actions of gathering grain during the years of plenty. If the *We* + infinitive absolute clause is *not* seen as a paragraph break, its significance is completely unclear (note the use of the concluding word "thus" used here by Longacre, *Joseph*, 253: "Thus he set him over all the land of Egypt.").

troops with Joab stop marching and watch as Amasa's corpse rolls about in the midst of the footpath. The break between these two discrete sections of narrative is marked by both a terminal paragraph marker (*QATAL* clause 1280) and an initial paragraph marker (*QATAL* clause 1281):

20.10.1279 וַיָּמֹת

20.10.1280 וְיוֹאָב וַאֲבִישַׁי אָחִיו רָדַף אַחֲרֵי שֶׁבַע בֶּן־בִּכְרִי:

(Paragraph break)

20.11.1281 וְאִישׁ עָמַד עָלָיו מִנַּעֲרֵי יוֹאָב

20.11.1282 וַיֹּאמֶר

He (Amasa) died and Joab and Abishai his brother chased after Sheba ben-Bichri.

¶ A man from the servants of Joab stood over him, and said...

In the large majority of cases, however, when two discrete paragraphs are juxtaposed, the boundary between the two is marked by either a concluding paragraph marker *or* an initial paragraph marker. A corresponding initial *WAYYIQTOL* clause tied to a *WAYYIQTOL* chain, therefore, usually stands at the beginning of paragraphs whose preceding paragraph is terminally explicitly marked; likewise, a terminal *WAYYIQTOL* clause tied to a preceding *WAYYIQTOL* chain, stands at the end of paragraphs whose following paragraph is initially explicitly marked. These cases of default *WAYYIQTOL* paragraph boundaries are noted in the following chart.

Table of *WAYYIQTOL* Clauses That Head or Close Paragraphs Marked Externally

Initial *WAYYIQTOL* Clauses in Chain	Joseph Novella: 011,037,376,395,409,421, 436,487,588, 764,771,826,954
	Court Narrative: 001,154,435,622,689,806, 913,923,975, 987,1099,1217,1248,1254, 1289,1343,1366,1406,1477,1633
Terminal *WAYYIQTOL* Clauses in Chain	Joseph Novella: 075,154,170,183,197,248, 387,538,662, 702,822,890,970
	Court Narrative: 044,081,091,110,116,120, 177,276,444, 483,502,610,650,665,792,939, 947,1104,1121,1167,1189, 1238,1265,1541, 1594

These externally marked paragraphs are bounded by the final clauses of preceding paragraphs or the initial clauses of following paragraphs. The corresponding

WAYYIQṬOL clauses either begin or conclude the *WAYYIQṬOL* chains which comprise the paragraph in which they are found.

Inner-Paragraph Comment Clause Types

In addition to the list of independent non-WAYYIQTOL clauses noted above as paragraph boundary markers, the basic narrative backbone of WAYY-IQTOL chains may incorporate four types of clauses which, by their nature, do not propel the narrative forward. They provide information about a particular element in the narrative but do so apart from the sequentiality of the foundational narrative and do not break that sequentiality. Participial and verbless clauses, clauses governed by the verb היה, and incomplete clauses do not cause the narrative to progress but rather provide static information off the line of the narrative. In addition to these four types of clauses, individual *QAṬAL* clauses may also function as comment clauses when they appear in a clause that is semantically parallel with a preceding *QAṬAL* or *WAYYIQṬOL* clause or when they appear *immediately* after an initial ויהי temporal clause. These six types of clauses consistently appear *within* paragraphs, comment upon specific characters or actions within the paragraph, and, in the cases of participial, verbless, and היה clauses, may appear as both single and multiple clauses. The instances of these "inner-paragraph comments" are listed in the table below.

Table of Inner-Paragraph Comment Clauses

Verbless Clauses	Joseph Novella: 083,084,103,165,199,283, 382,422,423, 499,700,922
	Court Narrative: 004,005,043,047,048,051, 078,102,126, 346,347;356,357,361,362,363, 432,760,778,853,854,917, 1240,1266,1269, 1333,1334,1335,1336,1337,1338,1352,1368
Participial Clauses	Joseph Novella: 050,088,089,090,200,211, 543
	Court Narrative: 046,049,050,121,135,389, 445,485,491, 501,691,707,708,728,729,730, 731,732,749,750,751,759, 777,822,983, 1042,1046,1079,1223,1267,1268,1284, 1296,1387,1404,1467,1468,1475,1599
היה Verbal Clauses	Joseph Novella: 134,135,136,145,193,194, 198,207,397, 398,404,948,966
	Court Narrative: 222,348,450,515,690,758, 976,978,979, 1102,1253,1339,1353

Incomplete Clause	Joseph Novella: Ø
	Court Narrative: 776
QATAL Clauses in Parallel	Joseph Novella: 693-694
	Court Narrative: 436,1368
QATAL Clauses after ויהי Temporal Clauses	Joseph Novella: 143,202
	Court Narrative: 506

1) Verbless clauses consistently appear within paragraphs in order to explain some *thing* within the paragraph. The thing that is explained by the verbless clause, may be the identity, status, or significance of a character or place. A few examples taken from the Joseph Novella will be sufficient to reveal their function within Hebrew narrative.

37.23.079 וַיְהִי כַּאֲשֶׁר־בָּא יוֹסֵף אֶל־אֶחָיו

37.23.080 וַיַּפְשִׁיטוּ אֶת־יוֹסֵף אֶת־כֻּתָּנְתּוֹ אֶת־כְּתֹנֶת הַפַּסִּים אֲשֶׁר עָלָיו:

37.24.081 וַיִּקָּחֻהוּ

37.24.082 וַיַּשְׁלִכוּ אֹתוֹ הַבֹּרָה

37.24.083 (וְהַבּוֹר רֵק

37.24.084 אֵין בּוֹ מָיִם:)

37.25.085 וַיֵּשְׁבוּ לֶאֱכָל־לֶחֶם

37.25.086 וַיִּשְׂאוּ עֵינֵיהֶם

37.25.087 וַיִּרְאוּ

¶ As soon as Joseph came to his brothers, they stripped Joseph of his coat, the *passim* coat that was on him. They took him and threw him into a cistern. (Now, the cistern was empty; there was no water in it!) And they sat down to eat food and they lifted their eyes and looked . . .

In this case, the status of the well as "empty" and "without water" (clauses 083-084) is important for the narrative; yet the information provided is not a part of the sequentiality of the narrative.

39.11.163 וַיְהִי כְּהַיּוֹם הַזֶּה

39.11.164 וַיָּבֹא הַבַּיְתָה לַעֲשׂוֹת מְלַאכְתּוֹ

39.11.165 וְאֵין אִישׁ מֵאַנְשֵׁי הַבַּיִת שָׁם בַּבָּיִת:

39.12.166 וַתִּתְפְּשֵׂהוּ בְּבִגְדוֹ

¶ It happened about that day, he came into the house to do his work. (Now, there were none of the men of the house there in the house.) She grasped him by his cloak . . .

Here, likewise, the fact that none of the servants were "in the house" is important for the narrative to progress; yet the reader does not witness their egress. Only the fact of the servants' absence is provided.

42.05.421 וַיָּבֹאוּ בְּנֵי יִשְׂרָאֵל לִשְׁבֹּר בְּתוֹךְ הַבָּאִים
כִּי־הָיָה הָרָעָב בְּאֶרֶץ כְּנָעַן:
42.06.422 וְיוֹסֵף הוּא הַשַּׁלִּיט עַל־הָאָרֶץ
42.06.423 (הוּא הַמַּשְׁבִּיר לְכָל־עַם הָאָרֶץ
42.06.424 וַיָּבֹאוּ אֲחֵי יוֹסֵף)
42.06.425 וַיִּשְׁתַּחֲווּ־לוֹ אַפַּיִם אָרְצָה:

The sons of Israel came to buy grain along with the travelers, because there was a famine in the land of Canaan. (Now, Joseph himself was the ruler over the land; it was he who was the grain distributor for all the people of the land!) The brothers of Joseph came and prostrated themselves before him . . .

Here, the identity of Joseph as the "ruler" and "grain distributor" in Egypt is explicitly noted immediately before the advent of Joseph's brothers. Joseph's identity is, again, important for the reader's understanding of the narrative; yet his identity is simply given as a fact. All cases of verbless clauses in inner-paragraph comments function in this same identical manner.

2) Participial clauses consistently appear within paragraphs in order to explain some *action* within the paragraph. The action explained within the inner-paragraph comment does not, however, reside within the sequentiality of the larger narrative. The participial clause, instead, tells of some action that is done either throughout the narrative or prior to its placement in the narrative. Note the following examples from the Court Narrative.

11.01.117 וַיְהִי לִתְשׁוּבַת הַשָּׁנָה לְעֵת צֵאת הַמַּלְאָכִים
11.01.118 וַיִּשְׁלַח דָּוִד אֶת־יוֹאָב וְאֶת־עֲבָדָיו עִמּוֹ וְאֶת־כָּל־יִשְׂרָאֵל
11.01.119 וַיַּשְׁחִתוּ אֶת־בְּנֵי עַמּוֹן
11.01.120 וַיָּצֻרוּ עַל־רַבָּה
11.01.121 (וְדָוִד יוֹשֵׁב בִּירוּשָׁלָ͏ִם:)

¶ At the turn of the year, the time when kings go out to battle, David sent Joab and his servants with him and all Israel and they wiped out the Ammonites and laid siege to Rabbah. (Now, David had been staying in Jerusalem!)

In this example, the "residing" of David does not occur sequentially after the destruction of the Ammonites and the siege of Rabbah (clauses 119–120). Instead, David's remaining in Jerusalem occurs during all the preceding clauses. While the information is important for the reader to know, the participial nature of the clause removes it from the sequential backbone of the paragraph and the clause functions essentially as an aside from the narrator about an action ("staying") outside the scope of the paragraph: "(Now, David had been staying in Jerusalem!)".

13.08.388 וַתֵּלֶךְ תָּמָר בֵּית אַמְנוֹן אָחִיהָ
13.08.389 וְהוּא שֹׁכֵב
13.08.390 וַתִּקַּח אֶת־הַבָּצֵק
13.08.391 וַתָּלוֹשׁ [ק וַתָּלָשׁ]
13.08.392 וַתְּלַבֵּב לְעֵינָיו
13.08.393 וַתְּבַשֵּׁל אֶת־הַלְּבִבוֹת:

Tamar came to the house of Amnon, her brother.
(Now, he had been lying down.) She took the dough,
and kneaded, and made cakes before his eyes, and
cooked the cakes . . .

In this example, the "lying down" of Amnon does not occur after Tamar enters his house. In fact, Amnon originally "lies down" in verse 6, and in that context it is directly joined with his pretense of being sick:

13.06.378 וַיִּשְׁכַּב אַמְנוֹן
13.06.379 וַיִּתְחָל

. . . and Amnon lay down and pretended to be sick . . .

Therefore, when Tamar enters his house, the narrator reminds the reader that Amnon is still "lying down," pretending to be sick—a pretense which will continue until clause 406 in verse 11. The action of "lying" related in clause 389, therefore, is not sequentially related to the actions in the paragraph expressed by WAYYIQTOL, but is rather an off-line inner-paragraph comment.

3) Because of the semantic nature of the verb itself, clauses governed by היה do not cause the action of the narrative to progress.[19] The verb היה is usually used as a copula in order to provide a description of the state of a noun. As such, the force of היה clauses is almost identical to that of verbless clauses.[20] Two examples of this type of inner-paragraph comment are provided here.

---

[19]The ויהי temporal clause is, of course, excluded from this category. True verbal clauses governed by היה (including the WAYYIQTOL form, ויהי) are, however, consistently present in narrative as extra-paragraph comments.

[20]Note Gesenius, *Grammar*, §141 g-i. Gesenius notes here that in instances in which היה conveys the meaning "*to become, to fare, to exist*, [the verb] retains its full force as a verb." Consistently, however, the verbal force in these cases is syntactically similar to that of a verbless clause.

39.01.132 וְיוֹסֵף הוּרַד מִצְרָיְמָה
39.01.133 וַיִּקְנֵהוּ פּוֹטִיפַר סְרִיס פַּרְעֹה שַׂר הַטַּבָּחִים
[אִישׁ מִצְרִי מִיַּד הַיִּשְׁמְעֵאלִים
אֲשֶׁר הוֹרִדֻהוּ שָׁמָּה:
39.02.134 (וַיְהִי יְהֹוָה אֶת־יוֹסֵף
39.02.135 וַיְהִי אִישׁ מַצְלִיחַ
39.02.136 וַיְהִי בְּבֵית אֲדֹנָיו הַמִּצְרִי:)
39.03.137 וַיַּרְא אֲדֹנָיו

¶ Joseph was brought down to Egypt and Potiphar, the officer
of Pharaoh, chief of the guards, an Egyptian, purchased him
from the Ishmaelites who had brought him there. (Now,
YHWH was with Joseph and he was a successful man and was
in the house of his lord, the Egyptian.) His lord saw. . . .

In this case, the three היה clauses that reveal that YHWH was with Joseph, that
Joseph was a successful man, and that he was in his Egyptian master's house do
not cause the narrative itself to progress. The information is simply provided in a
means similar to the verbless clauses noted above.

In the following example, three inner-paragraph comment clauses (clauses
976, 978-979) are broken into two parts by an intervening *WAYYIQTOL* clause
(977).

18.06.975 וַיֵּצֵא הָעָם הַשָּׂדֶה לִקְרַאת יִשְׂרָאֵל
18.06.976 (וַתְּהִי הַמִּלְחָמָה בִּיַעַר אֶפְרָיִם:)
18.07.977 וַיִּנָּגְפוּ שָׁם עַם יִשְׂרָאֵל לִפְנֵי עַבְדֵי דָוִד
18.07.978 (וַתְּהִי־שָׁם הַמַּגֵּפָה גְדוֹלָה בַּיּוֹם הַהוּא עֶשְׂרִים אָלֶף:
08.08.979 וַתְּהִי־שָׁם הַמִּלְחָמָה נָפֹצֵית [Q נָפֹצֶת] עַל־פְּנֵי כָל־הָאָרֶץ)
08.08.980 וַיֶּרֶב הַיַּעַר לֶאֱכֹל בָּעָם מֵאֲשֶׁר אָכְלָה הַחֶרֶב בַּיּוֹם הַהוּא:

The people went out on the field to meet Israel. (Now, the war
was in the forest of Ephraim.) The people of Israel were
crushed there before the servants of David. (The defeat there
was great on that day: about 20,000 [casualties]. The war was
spreading out everywhere!) The forest killed more people than
the sword on that day.

Here, likewise, the היה verbal clauses are semantically and syntactically similar
to the verbless clauses noted above.

4) The single case of an incomplete clause in an inner-paragraph comment
is found at the beginning of 2 Samuel 16. Here, it is combined with a participial
(777) and a verbless clause (778) to form the comment.

16.01.775 וְדָוִד עָבַר מְעַט מֵהָרֹאשׁ

16.01.776 (וְהִנֵּה צִיבָא נַעַר מְפִי־בֹשֶׁת לִקְרָאתוֹ

16.01.777 וְצֶמֶד חֲמֹרִים חֲבֻשִׁים

16.01.778 וַעֲלֵיהֶם מָאתַיִם לֶחֶם וּמֵאָה צִמּוּקִים וּמֵאָה קַיִץ וְנֵבֶל יָיִן:)

16.02.779 וַיֹּאמֶר הַמֶּלֶךְ אֶל־צִיבָא

¶ David crossed over a little way from the top. (And there was
Ziba the servant of Mephiboshet to meet him! A couple of
donkeys were saddled and upon them were two hundred
pieces of bread, a hundred bunches of raisins, a hundred summer fruits and a skin of wine!) The king said to Ziba . . .

The reason why clause 776 appears as an incomplete clause rather than, for example, a participial clause (וְהִנֵּה צִיבָא נַעַר מְפִי־בֹשֶׁת בָּא לִקְרָאתוֹ*) is unclear. Its
presence here, however, is clearly a part of the off-line comment continued by
clauses 777-778.[21]

5) When a *QATAL* clause stands in semantic and/or syntactical parallel with
an immediately preceding *QATAL* or *WAYYIQTOL* clause, the *QATAL* clause
takes on the function of an inner-paragraph comment. Three examples of this
phenomenon stand within the textual databases used in this study: one (clauses
693-694) stands in the Joseph Novella; two (clauses 436, 1368), in the Court
Narrative.

After Joseph has hidden his silver goblet in Benjamin's grain-sack and has
sent messengers to accuse the brothers of stealing the cup, a pair of parallel
QATAL clauses (693-694) provide an off-line comment about the order of the
search:

44.11.689 וַיְמַהֲרוּ

44.11.690 וַיּוֹרִדוּ אִישׁ אֶת־אַמְתַּחְתּוֹ אָרְצָה

44.11.691 וַיִּפְתְּחוּ אִישׁ אַמְתַּחְתּוֹ:

44.12.692 וַיְחַפֵּשׂ

44.12.693 (בַּגָּדוֹל הֵחֵל

44.12.694 וּבַקָּטֹן כִּלָּה)

44.12.695 וַיִּמָּצֵא הַגָּבִיעַ בְּאַמְתַּחַת בִּנְיָמִן:

They (the brothers) hurried and each brought down his sack to
the ground and each opened his sack. He searched–(he began

---

[21]The presence of the incomplete clause here is clearly of a different nature than the
paragraph terminal boundary marker noted above. In the case of its paragraph boundary
function in clause 277 of the Joseph Novella, the verbless clause stands independently
between two *WAYYIQTOL* chains and immediately before a paragraph initial marker.
Here, clause 776, on the other hand, appears in conjunction with other non-*WAYYIQTOL*
clauses which make up the inner-paragraph comment.

with the oldest and finished with the youngest)—and the goblet
was found in the sack of Benjamin. . . .

The syntactically parallel construction בַּנָּדוֹל הֵחֵל // וּבַקָּטֹן כִּלָּה causes the
pair of clauses to be seen as joined together in an off-line comment, rather than
the more usual paragraph initial and terminal boundary markers which they
would otherwise be.

A similar construction occurs with the recounting of the immediate consequences of the rape of Tamar. When she leaves Amnon's house she performs
three actions: 1) she puts dust upon her head; 2) she tears her garment; and 3)
she places her hand upon her head. The second of these actions is provided as an
extra-paragraph off-line comment.

13.19.435 וַתִּקַּח תָּמָר אֵפֶר עַל־רֹאשָׁהּ

13.19.436 (וּכְתֹנֶת הַפַּסִּים אֲשֶׁר עָלֶיהָ קָרָעָה)

13.19.437 וַתָּשֶׂם יָדָהּ עַל־רֹאשָׁהּ

13.19.438 וַתֵּלֶךְ הָלוֹךְ וְזָעָקָה:

Tamar took ashes upon her head. (Now, she also tore the *pas-*
sim coat that was upon her.) She then placed her hand upon
her head and walked, screaming as she went . . .

Contrary to what the reader might expect, the narrator does not have Tamar sequentially tear her garment (וַתִּקְרַע כְּתֹנֶת הַפַּסִּים אֲשֶׁר עָלֶיהָ*) in clause 436 after
she takes ashes upon her head. Because of the close cultural connection between
throwing dust on one's head and tearing one's garment, the governing *QATAL* in
clause 436 relates that this clause is a natural and concomitant element of her
mourning.[22]

In the final example of this phenomenon, when Adonijah attempts to establish himself as the rightful heir to the throne of David, he garners support from
several of David's servants but does not call on others whom he, possibly, sees
as more hostile. The refusal to call Nathan, Benaiah, the soldiers, and Solomon
(clause 1368) is provided in the narrative as an off-line inner-paragraph comment:

10.09.1366 וַיִּזְבַּח אֲדֹנִיָּהוּ צֹאן וּבָקָר וּמְרִיא עִם אֶבֶן הַזֹּחֶלֶת
אֲשֶׁר־אֵצֶל עֵין רֹגֵל

10.09.1367 וַיִּקְרָא אֶת־כָּל־אֶחָיו בְּנֵי הַמֶּלֶךְ וּלְכָל־אַנְשֵׁי יְהוּדָה עַבְדֵי הַמֶּלֶךְ:

10.10.1368 (וְאֶת־נָתָן הַנָּבִיא וּבְנָיָהוּ וְאֶת־הַגִּבּוֹרִים וְאֶת־שְׁלֹמֹה אָחִיו לֹא קָרָא:)

10.11.1369 וַיֹּאמֶר נָתָן אֶל־בַּת־שֶׁבַע אֵם־שְׁלֹמֹה

---

[22]For "dust/ashes on the head" and "tearing of garments" as signs of mourning, see
Josh 7:6 and Job 2:12; note also the terms in Amos 2:7 and Lam 2:10.

Adonijah sacrificed flocks and herds and lambs at the Serpent's Stone, which is beside Ein-rogel, and he called all his brothers the princes and all the men of Judah, servants of the king. (Now he did not call Nathan the prophet, nor Benaiah, nor the warriors, nor Solomon his brother!) And Nathan said to Bathsheba, Solomon's mother . . .

The semantic and syntactical parallel of clause 1368 with the immediately preceding clause (1367) is unmistakable (Verb [קרא]—Objects//Objects—Negated Verb [קרא]). The close tie between these two, therefore, causes the *QATAL* clause to be seen as a natural (and off-line) parallel with the preceding *WAYYIQTOL* clause.[23]

6) In three cases within the textual databases used by this study, *QATAL* clauses stand immediately after initial ויהי temporal clauses (Joseph Novella: clauses 143, 202; Court Narrative: clause 506).[24] In all other cases of initial ויהי temporal clauses, the narrative progression introduced by the initial clause ("When X occurred . . .") is taken up by an immediately following *WAYYIQTOL* clause ("Y did so and so . . . ."). In these three cases however, an intervening *QATAL* clause stands between the ויהי temporal clause and the complementary *WAYYIQTOL* clause.

39.05.142 וַיְהִי מֵאָז

39.05.143 (הִפְקִיד אֹתוֹ בְּבֵיתוֹ וְעַל כָּל־אֲשֶׁר יֶשׁ־לוֹ)

39.05.144 וַיְבָרֶךְ יְהוָה אֶת־בֵּית הַמִּצְרִי בִּגְלַל יוֹסֵף

---

[23]In this case, the negated clause *could* perhaps be a paragraph terminal marker, as outlined above. One element which may argue for this reading is the shift in focus before (Adonijah) and after (Nathan) the *QATAL* clause. Two characteristics, however, argue against this reading. First, the beginning of the paragraph is headed in clause 1366. If clause 1368 concludes the paragraph, only three clauses would constitute the paragraph—a very short paragraph indeed! Second, the close, unambiguous parallel with the preceding clause does not usually occur with negated *QATAL* clauses functioning as paragraph terminal markers.

Also noteworthy in this regard is the syntactical significance of Gen 1:5a: וַיִּקְרָא אֱלֹהִים לָאוֹר יוֹם וְלַחֹשֶׁךְ קָרָא לָיְלָה. In this case, the main on-line *WAYYIQTOL* clause (וַיִּקְרָא אֱלֹהִים לָאוֹר יוֹם) is paralleled syntactically by an immediately following *QATAL* clause (וְלַחֹשֶׁךְ קָרָא לָיְלָה) which appears as an off-line comment. The naming of the "Day" has a natural counterpart, which is provided here as an inner-paragraph comment: "He (also) named the darkness 'Night'".

[24]Clause 485 in the Court Narrative could be a similar construction. The Masoretic accenting of בָּאָה, however, marks the clause as participial.

From that time, ([Potiphar] having appointed him within his
house and over everything which he had), YHWH blessed the
house of the Egyptian because of Joseph. . . .

In this example from the Joseph Novella, the *QATAL* clause 143 interrupts the
usual construction of the initial ויהי temporal clause (142) and the following
WAYYIQTOL clause (144): "From that time . . . YHWH blessed the house of the
Egyptian because of Joseph." The appointment of Joseph over Potiphar's house
and possessions does *not* occur sequentially between clauses 142 and 144; his
appointment occurred immediately before this paragraph and is the temporal
point of reference for the introductory ויהי temporal clause 142:

39.04.138 וַיִּמְצָא יוֹסֵף חֵן בְּעֵינָיו
39.04.139 וַיְשָׁרֶת אֹתוֹ
39.04.140 וַיַּפְקִדֵהוּ עַל־בֵּיתוֹ
39.04.141 וְכָל־יֶשׁ־לוֹ נָתַן בְּיָדוֹ:
(Paragraph break)
39.05.142 וַיְהִי מֵאָז
39.05.143 (הִפְקִיד אֹתוֹ בְּבֵיתוֹ וְעַל כָּל־אֲשֶׁר יֶשׁ־לוֹ)
39.05.144 וַיְבָרֶךְ יְהוָה אֶת־בֵּית הַמִּצְרִי בִּגְלַל יוֹסֵף

The intervening *QATAL* clause, therefore, functions as an inner-paragraph off-
line comment, reminding the reader of the appointment of Joseph and, furthermore, intimating that the appointment is, in fact, the reason for the blessing of
YHWH: "From that time, ([Potiphar] having appointed him within his house and
over everything which he had), YHWH blessed the house of the Egyptian
because of Joseph. . . ."

In the second example from the Joseph Novella, the information provided
by the intervening *QATAL* clause is not given in any previous *WAYYIQTOL*
clause as in the previous example. Yet the *QATAL* clause performs the same
function as an off-line inner-paragraph comment.

40.01.201 וַיְהִי אַחַר הַדְּבָרִים הָאֵלֶּה
40.01.202 (חָטְאוּ מַשְׁקֵה מֶלֶךְ־מִצְרַיִם וְהָאֹפֶה לַאֲדֹנֵיהֶם לְמֶלֶךְ מִצְרָיִם:)
40.02.403 וַיִּקְצֹף פַּרְעֹה עַל שְׁנֵי סָרִיסָיו
After these things, (the butler of the king of Egypt and the
baker having committed a crime against the king of Egypt),
Pharaoh was angry with his two officers.

The intervening *QATAL* clause 202 here provides the reader (again, in an off-
line comment) with the detail that the royal butler and baker had previously

committed a crime against Pharaoh and, for that reason, Pharaoh was enraged against the butler and baker (clause 203).

In the final example, from the Court Narrative, David and his servants react to the news that Amnon had been killed by Absalom. The lifting of their voices (clause 507) and weeping (clauses 508-509) occur immediately after the announcement that the sons of David had arrived (ויהי temporal clause 505, referencing Jonadab's preceding speech, clauses 503-504):

13.35.502 וַיֹּאמֶר יוֹנָדָב אֶל־הַמֶּלֶךְ
הִנֵּה

13.35.503 בְנֵי־הַמֶּלֶךְ בָּאוּ
13.35.504 כִּדְבַר עַבְדְּךָ כֵּן הָיָה:

(Paragraph break)

13.36.505 וַיְהִי כְּכַלֹּתוֹ לְדַבֵּר
(וְהִנֵּה)

13.36.506 (בְנֵי־הַמֶּלֶךְ בָּאוּ)
13.36.507 וַיִּשְׂאוּ קוֹלָם
13.36.508 וַיִּבְכּוּ

Jonadab said to the king, "Look! The sons of the king have arrived! It has been just as the word of your servant!"

¶ As soon as he finished speaking, (the sons of the king having arrived), they lifted up their voice and wept . . .

The arrival of the royal princes referenced in *QATAL* clause 506 had already occurred, since in the announcement (Narrative Discourse clauses 503-504), their arrival was already an accomplished fact.[25] The intervening *QATAL* clause, therefore, reminds the reader—by means of an inner-paragraph comment—of the presence of the sons of David in the mourning activities outlined in the paragraph: "As soon as [Jonadab] had finished speaking, (the princes having arrived), they lifted up their voice and wept and both the king and his servants wept very greatly."

Summary: Inner-Paragraph Comments

Inner-paragraph comments occur within paragraphs and provide information to the reader about items or actions *connected directly to elements within the narrative*. The information provided, however, is never a part of the sequential nature of the basic story but is, rather, off-line from the narrative. Inner-

---

[25]Note the discussion of *QATAL* clauses in Narrative Discourse below for the temporal significance of the announcement of clauses 503-504.

paragraph comments are composed of six types of non-*WAYYIQTOL* clauses. Their types and combinations are listed here.

Type A: Independent or multiple, singly or in combination with each other:
1) Verbless Clauses
2) Participial Clauses
3) היה Verbal Clauses
Only in combination with Type A clauses above:
4) Incomplete Clauses
Independent or in combination with Type A clauses above:
5) *QATAL* Clauses in Parallel
Only Independent:
6) *QATAL* Clauses after ויהי Temporal Clauses

Extra-Paragraph Comment Clause Types

In addition to the off-line comments that occur within paragraphs, biblical Hebrew narrative prose also regularly provides extended off-line commentary between paragraphs. In general, the type of information provided by these "extra-paragraph comments" is of a more extended nature and is further removed from the basic narrative backbone. The information provided by extra-paragraph comments often concerns actions which are regularly performed over an extended length of time, multiple actions which occurred before the larger narrative framework of the preceding and following paragraphs, or the long term outcome of actions related in previous paragraphs.

Extra-paragraph comments are based upon the foundation of *multiple QATAL, WeQATAL,* and/or *YIQTOL* clauses. In addition to these three clause types, non-chained single *WAYYIQTOL* clauses may also appear with any of the basic, foundational clause types. Individual or multiple participial or verbless clauses may also appear within extra-paragraph comments, provided they are joined to any of the three foundational types.[26] The clause types found in these "extra-paragraph comments" are listed in the table below.

---

[26]If, of course, participial or verbless clauses are not joined to *QATAL, WeQATAL,* or *YIQTOL* clauses, they perform the role of inner-paragraph commentary and the information they provide is more closely tied to the narrative backbone of the surrounding paragraph.

Table of Extra-Paragraph Comment Clauses

QATAL Clauses	Joseph Novella: 006,010,162,260,388,390, 393,663,664, 665,666,760,763,800,823,824, 825,951,953
	Court Narrative: 281,282,350,446,448,510, 621,800,829, 948,949,950,974,1013,1122, 1125,1168,1169,1170,1171, 1191,1194,1359, 1362,1543,1544
WeQATAL Clauses	Joseph Novella: 007,952
	Court Narrative: 277,278,279,352,354,615, 616,653,654, 670,671,672,795,909,910,912, 1152,1153
YIQTOL Clauses	Joseph Novella: Ø
	Court Narrative: 353,911,1342
Independent *WAYYIQTOL* Clauses	Joseph Novella: 005,008,009,261,389,391, 761,798,799
	Court Narrative: 280,351,447,511,512,617, 620,652,673, 674,799,826,828,901,953,972, 1014,1016,1017,1124,1148, 1149,1192, 1341,1358,1364
Participial Clauses	Joseph Novella: Ø
	Court Narrative: 796,798,908,1356,1361
Verbless Clause	Joseph Novella: 004,863,864,865,866
	Court Narrative: 618,797,827,830,951,952, 1150,1151, 1193,1340,1542

Multiple *QATAL*, *WeQATAL*, and/or *YIQTOL* clauses, by their nature, break the *WAYYIQTOL* chain of the narrative preceding them. Furthermore, the off-line nature of participial and verbless clauses, already shown in simple inner-paragraph comments, may be added to these multiple verbal clauses to express on-going actions or states within an extra-paragraph comment. The extra-paragraph comment composed of the multiplicity of all these clauses, moreover, provides extended information about actions or relationships that are removed from the sequentiality of the larger story. Examples of extra-paragraph commentary from the Joseph Novella and the Court Narrative will serve to illustrate the verbal and clausal combinations that comprise them and the specific type of information they provide within the larger narrative.

In the final paragraph of 2 Samuel 12, David conquers the Ammonite city of Rabbah and plunders it.

. . .

12.30.345 וַיִּקַּח אֶת־עֲטֶרֶת־מַלְכָּם מֵעַל רֹאשׁו
12.30.346 (וּמִשְׁקָלָהּ כִּכַּר זָהָב)
12.30.347 וְאֶבֶן יְקָרָה
12.30.348 (וַתְּהִי עַל־רֹאשׁ דָּוִד)
12.30.349 וּשְׁלַל הָעִיר הוֹצִיא הַרְבֵּה מְאֹד:

(Comment)

12.31.350 וְאֶת־הָעָם אֲשֶׁר־בָּהּ הוֹצִיא
12.31.351 וַיָּשֶׂם בַּמְּגֵרָה וּבַחֲרִצֵי הַבַּרְזֶל וּבְמַגְזְרֹת הַבַּרְזֶל
12.31.352 וְהֶעֱבִיר אוֹתָם בַּמַּלְכֵּן [Q בַּמַּלְבֵּן]
12.31.353 וְכֵן יַעֲשֶׂה לְכֹל עָרֵי בְנֵי־עַמּוֹן
12.31.354 וַיָּשָׁב דָּוִד וְכָל־הָעָם יְרוּשָׁלָם:

...and he (David) took the crown of their king from off his head. (Its weight was a talent of gold and its stone was precious. It was on David's head.) And he brought out the great spoil of the city.
—Now, he brought out the people that were in it and set them with saws and iron picks and iron axes. He brought them over to Malken (?). This is what he used to do to all the Ammonite cities. And David and all the people returned to Jerusalem.—

In the final sentences of the paragraph, the narrator records, in particular, David's taking the crown of their king (clause 345), which is described in detail (clauses 346-348), as well as other types of spoil (clause 349). After this paragraph, the narrator further explains David's ongoing political policy with the conquered Ammonites. By means of *QATAL* (clause 350), *WeQATAL* (clause 352), *YIQTOL* (clause 353), and unchained *WAYYIQTOL* clauses (clauses 351 and 354), the off-line extra-paragraph comment provides the long-term eventual outcome of the above paragraph.[27]

In 2 Samuel 17, David is exiled while Absalom takes up residence in the royal city. An elaborate system of transferring messages from the high priests in Jerusalem to David is established, Ahimaaz and Jehonathan, the sons of the high priests, serving as the main intercessors. The plan involves a female servant who regularly goes to draw water at the well, gives messages to the two sons, who in

---

[27]The final *WAYYIQTOL* clause does not resume the narrative because of the immediately following ויהי temporal clause (355) that begins the following narrative paragraph.

turn go to David and report the messages. This complex repeated system is related in the story by means of an off-line extra-paragraph comment:

17.17.908 וִיהוֹנָתָן וַאֲחִימַעַץ עֹמְדִים בְּעֵין־רֹגֵל
17.17.909 וְהָלְכָה הַשִּׁפְחָה
17.17.910 וְהִגִּידָה לָהֶם
17.17.911 וְהֵם יֵלְכוּ
17.17.912 וְהִגִּידוּ לַמֶּלֶךְ דָּוִד
כִּי לֹא יוּכְלוּ לְהֵרָאוֹת לָבוֹא הָעִירָה:

Jehonathan and Ahimaaz would stand at Ein-rogel and a servant-girl would come and tell them (the message). And they
used to go and tell (it) to the king, David, because they could
not be seen entering into the city.

The fact that this information occurs in an extra-paragraph comment implies that
the actions involved occur numerous times in the course of the story, although
only a single instance of the transmission of the messages of David is actually
reported in the narrative portion of the story line.[28]

Near the end of David's life, the king begins to grow feeble. The narrator
provides this ongoing information by means of an extra-paragraph comment at
the beginning of 1 Kings 1:

01.01.1340 וְהַמֶּלֶךְ דָּוִד זָקֵן בָּא בַּיָּמִים
01.01.1342 וַיְכַסֻּהוּ בַּבְּגָדִים
01.01.1343 וְלֹא יִחַם לוֹ:

The king David was old, full of years. They would cover him
with cloaks but it wouldn't warm him.

In this case, the presence of the final YIQTOL clause signals the nature of the
extra-paragraph comment as removed from the wider narrative and as preparatory for the following story, whose basic premise is based upon this background
information. While the verbless clause and WAYYIQTOL clause both may appear in other contexts (i.e., in inner-paragraph comments and in narrative,
respectively), their juxtaposition with the YIQTOL clause here signals for the
reader that David's inability to be warm (virile?) has been occurring for awhile.

---

[28]Note that the participial clause 908 is considered a part of the extra-paragraph
comment because of its close connection with the foundational extra-paragraph markers,
namely the WeQATAL (909,910,912) and YIQTOL (911) clauses. If clause 908 had stood
alone, it would, of course, be an *inner*-paragraph comment and would simply imply that
in this one instance the two sons were standing while the wider narrative occurred.

The clearest example of an extra-paragraph comment is found in Genesis 37. The narratological basis of the entire Joseph Novella is provided at the very beginning of the story in an extended off-line commentary:

37.02.003 יוֹסֵף בֶּן־שְׁבַע־עֶשְׂרֵה שָׁנָה הָיָה רֹעֶה אֶת־אֶחָיו בַּצֹּאן

37.02.004 וְהוּא נַעַר אֶת־בְּנֵי בִלְהָה וְאֶת־בְּנֵי זִלְפָּה נְשֵׁי אָבִיו

37.02.005 וַיָּבֵא יוֹסֵף אֶת־דִּבָּתָם רָעָה אֶל־אֲבִיהֶם:

37.03.006 וְיִשְׂרָאֵל אָהַב אֶת־יוֹסֵף מִכָּל־בָּנָיו
כִּי־בֶן־זְקֻנִים הוּא לוֹ

37.03.007 וְעָשָׂה לוֹ כְּתֹנֶת פַּסִּים:

37.04.008 וַיִּרְאוּ אֶחָיו
כִּי־אֹתוֹ אָהַב אֲבִיהֶם מִכָּל־אֶחָיו

37.04.009 וַיִּשְׂנְאוּ אֹתוֹ

37.04.010 וְלֹא יָכְלוּ דַּבְּרוֹ לְשָׁלֹם:

Joseph, a seventeen year old boy, was a shepherd of the flock with his brothers. He was a youngster with the sons of Bilhah and the sons of Zilpah, wives of his father. Joseph once brought an evil report about them to their father, but Israel loved Joseph more than all his sons because he was his "son of old age" and he made him a *passim* coat. His brothers saw that their father loved him more than all his brothers and they hated him and could not speak to him peacefully.

In this example, the presence of *QAṬAL*, *WeQAṬAL*, unchained *WAYYIQṬOL*, and verbless clauses combine to portray, in this extended extra-paragraph comment, the set of ongoing relationships and actions against which the following ten chapters will be played out. The shepherd who is dressed like a prince, the rightful son who is compared to the children of concubines, the favored child who is the most hated, the one who brings evil reports is, in turn, not spoken to—all of these ongoing perennial tensions are given to the reader in this extra-paragraph comment.

Summary: Extra-Paragraph Comments

Extra-paragraph comments occur between paragraphs and provide information to the reader about items or actions *removed from the immediate narrative sequence of the story line*. The information provided in extra-paragraph comments relates to longstanding and ongoing relationships or actions that either form the basis of a following story, occur throughout a story but are not tied to the sequentiality of the narrative, or are the eventual outcome of a preceding story. Extra-paragraph comments are composed of six types of clauses. The types and combinations are listed here.

Type B: Only multiple:
1) *QATAL* Clauses
2) *WeQATAL* Clauses
3) *YIQTOL* Clauses
Only singly and in combination with multiple Type B clauses above:
4) Non-Chained *WAYYIQTOL* Clauses
Independent or multiple, in combination with multiple Type B clauses above:
5) Participial Clauses
6) Verbless Clauses

Summary: Narrative Structure in Biblical Hebrew Prose

The basic building block of biblical storytelling is the sequence of clauses which propel a narrative forward, the *WAYYIQTOL* chain. This chain causes the narrative to move forward and drives the story from a beginning, through a middle, to an end.

Using various combinations of non-*WAYYIQTOL* clauses, the biblical narrator organizes and structures this narrative sequence in two ways. First, by means of independent paragraph boundary markers, the narrative backbone of the basic *WAYYIQTOL* chain is broken into smaller units: paragraphs. These discrete paragraph blocks, each have a coherent focus and a consistent sequential momentum and should be read and interpreted in their own integrity. Second, by means of various types of multiple non-*WAYYIQTOL* clauses and unchained *WAYYIQTOL* clauses, the narrator provides information to the reader about characters, settings, or actions not directly situated within the sequentiality of the main narrative. These types of comments may either occur within paragraphs or between paragraphs. When they occur within paragraphs, they relate information about immediate, specific elements in the story. When they occur between paragraphs, they relate information generally removed from any specific element in the story. It is by means of these foundational combinations of syntactical patterns that the intricate complexity of biblical Hebrew narrative is shaped, read, and understood.

Clause Function in Discourse Contexts

The structure of direct discourse in biblical Hebrew prose differs from that of narrative proper in several respects. Because they are marked otherwise, no predominant verbal or clausal type characterizes the beginning or ending of speeches of characters.[29] Moreover, whereas narrative is marked throughout by chains of *WAYYIQTOL* clauses, no consistent clause type occurs regularly throughout speeches. Likewise, in general, there is no consistent syntactically marked means of expressing points on or off the main line of the discourse. Furthermore, whereas the predominant purpose of narrative proper is to relate events in the past, only rarely is this the purpose of direct discourse. Finally, whereas narrative generally has the single predominant function of relating sequential events in the past, direct discourse has multiple functions: occasionally to relate past events, in other cases to predict or plan the future, in still other cases to explain universal truths or to declare immediate relationships or actions. Moreover, direct discourse, unlike narrative, can occasionally directly motivate action in its hearers, either as a response to a stated question or as a reaction (or rebellion) to a command or request.[30] For this reason, the structure of direct discourse is more complex than that found in narrative. Although it is more complex, however, its structure is still consistent and regular.

The use of differing verbal forms or clausal varieties in direct discourse in most cases defines the type and function of the speech. A speech by a character may contain a single word or a multitude of clauses.[31] Yet the verbal or clausal form used in the single word or the combinations of verbal forms present in

---

[29]In general, speeches in narrative are introduced by "quotative frames" in narrative. These discourse introductions often are verbs of direct speech (e.g., ענה, דבר, אמר) with or without לאמר. In her analysis, Cynthia Miller defines three categories of direct speech and four categories of indirect speech depending upon the quotative frame introduction to various speeches by characters in 2 Samuel. See her "Discourse Functions of Quotative Frames in Biblical Hebrew Narrative," in *Discourse Analysis of Biblical Literature* (ed. Walter R. Bodine; Atlanta: Scholars, 1995), 155-182.

[30]The predominant weakness of the work of A. Niccacci (in particular, *The Syntax of the Verb in Classical Hebrew Prose,* [JSOTSupp 86; Sheffield: JSOT, 1990]) is that, in contrasting the syntax of narrative and discourse, he attempts to treat all direct discourse as the same and does not recognize the multivalent and complex nature of direct discourse. His analysis, therefore, does not account for the multitude of differences found in direct discourse. Note the lucid review in David A. Dawson, *Text-Linguistics and Biblical Hebrew* (Sheffield: JSOT, 1994), particularly 28-39.

[31]The shortest speech in the textual databases used in this study is clause 1039 in the Court Narrative (2 Sam 18:23), spoken by Joab to Ahimaaz and contains a single word having a single syllable: "רוּץ". The longest sustained speech by a single character is the example encompassing clauses 717-759 in the Joseph Novella (Gen 44:18-34), spoken by Judah to Joseph and contains 218 words arranged into 43 independent and 11 dependent clauses.

multiple clauses determine the various types and functions of the speech. In general, any speech by a character will be one of five types of discourse:[32]

1) Narrative Discourse, in which a character relates a real or imagined sequence of events that occurred prior to the report;
2) Predictive Discourse, in which a character proposes, plans or predicts a sequence of events that will occur after the speech
3) Expository Discourse, in which a character explains a state or activity that is occurring at the time of the speech or that is perpetually true.
4) Interrogative Discourse, in which a character attempts to elicit a verbal response from a hearer of the speech;[33] and
5) Hortatory Discourse, in which a character attempts to elicit an active response form a hearer of the speech.

Each of these discourse text-types is composed of a finite and delimited number of verbal or clausal possibilities. These various possible combinations, or "constellations," define the text-type and, therefore, the purpose and function of the speech.

Narrative Discourse (ND)

Discourse Constellations

Among those speeches or parts of speeches in the textual database used in this study whose primary purpose is to relate the sequential occurrence of events before the speech-event, the set of verbal or clausal possibilities present in the discourses are restricted to eight sets, or constellations. These are listed below, along with the total number of instances in the Joseph Novella (JN), in the Narrative of David's Court (CN), and the combined total of both.

---

[32]The five categories listed here cannot, of course, encompass all the various purposes or nuances conveyed by direct discourse, either in real life conversations or in stylized textual reproductions. The categories set forth here serve, rather, as a broadly based heuristic device to aid in the analysis of verbal constellations in direct discourse on a surface level. Further analysis is necessary into the uses of, for example, modality, irony, inference, or rhetorical questions (see the next footnote) in biblical representations of direct discourse.

[33]Also included in Interrogative Discourse are rhetorical questions, which generally have the form of questions but have the function of persuasive commands (Hortatory Discourse). For example, when Mephiboshet is brought before David, he performs an act of obeisance and asks, "מֶה עַבְדְּךָ"/"What is your servant?" His question is not intended to incite a verbal reaction from David (which it indeed does not), but rather an active one, i.e., to have mercy upon him (which it does in clauses 038-042). The syntactical form, however, is that of an interrogative discourse, under which it is accounted in this study.

		JN	CN	Total	%
	QATAL	27	34	61	59.2%
	QATAL, WAYYIQTOL	8	11	19	18.4%
	QATAL, (Ptc./Vbl.)	6	1	7	6.8%
	QATAL, WAYYIQTOL, (Ptc./Vbl.)	4	4	8	7.8%
ND	*QATAL, WAYYIQTOL*, (Ptc./Vbl.), *YIQTOL*	1	1	2	1.9%
	QATAL, YIQTOL (w/ past adverb)		1	1	1.0%
	WAYYIQTOL, (Ptc./Vbl.)		4	4	3.9%
	Vbl/Ptc/Inc (Dream Report)	1		1	1.0%
	Total cases	47	56	103	100%

Function of the Discourse

The overwhelming presence of *QATAL* in all except five cases of Narrative Discourse marks it as the foundational verbal form upon which this discursive functional type is built. In 61 cases (59.2% of the total), *QATAL* is the sole verbal form employed in the speech; in 29 cases (28.2%), it is combined with *WAYYIQTOL*. In only four cases (3.9%), *WAYYIQTOL* is the sole form in speeches of Narrative Discourse.[34]

This basic function of *QATAL*, with or without *WAYYIQTOL*, in direct discourse is so compelling, in fact, that even when it is combined with *YIQTOL*, a form usually found in Predictive Discourse, the function of the discourse (including the *YIQTOL* clause itself) is to relate the occurrence of events that have happened in the past. Note, for instance, an example of this combination, found in Nathan's Parable of the Ewe Lamb in 2 Samuel 12:

12.01.228 שְׁנֵי אֲנָשִׁים הָיוּ בְּעִיר אֶחָת

12.01.229 אֶחָד עָשִׁיר

12.01.230 וְאֶחָד רָאשׁ׃

12.02.231 לְעָשִׁיר הָיָה צֹאן וּבָקָר הַרְבֵּה מְאֹד׃

---

[34]Note this major difference between Narrative Discourse and narrative proper. Examples of Narrative Discourse most often contain only *QATAL* clauses, and very often have a combination of *QATAL* and *WAYYIQTOL* clauses. It rarely consists of only *WAYYIQTOL* clauses. Narrative proper usually consists of *WAYYIQTOL* clauses, and rarely with a combination of both *WAYYIQTOL* and *QATAL* clauses (with *QATAL* clauses functioning only as paragraph boundary markers), and *never* with only *QATAL* clauses.

12.03.232 וְלָרָשׁ אֵין־כֹּל
כִּי אִם־כִּבְשָׂה אַחַת קְטַנָּה
אֲשֶׁר קָנָה
12.03.233 וַיְחַיֶּהָ
12.03.234 וַתִּגְדַּל עִמּוֹ וְעִם־בָּנָיו יַחְדָּו
12.03.235 מִפִּתּוֹ תֹאכַל
12.03.236 וּמִכֹּסוֹ תִשְׁתֶּה
12.03.237 וּבְחֵיקוֹ תִשְׁכָּב
12.03.238 וַתְּהִי־לוֹ כְּבַת:
12.04.239 וַיָּבֹא הֵלֶךְ לְאִישׁ הֶעָשִׁיר
12.04.240 וַיַּחְמֹל לָקַחַת מִצֹּאנוֹ וּמִבְּקָרוֹ לַעֲשׂוֹת לָאֹרֵחַ הַבָּא־לוֹ
12.04.241 וַיִּקַּח אֶת־כִּבְשַׂת הָאִישׁ הָרָאשׁ
12.04.242 וַיַּעֲשֶׂהָ לָאִישׁ הַבָּא אֵלָיו:

In this example, the narrative story line, like that of narrative proper, is built upon *WAYYIQTOL* (233,234,239-242) and *QATAL* (228) clauses, with verbless (229,230,232) and היה verbal clauses (231,238) performing roles similar to off-line inner-paragraph commentary within the story. Into the basic story line, however, three *YIQTOL* clauses (235,236,237) appear whose purpose seems to be similar to that of inner-paragraph commentary in narrative proper– they relate actions that occur outside the strict sequentiality of the narrative:

235 מִפִּתּוֹ תֹאכַל From his mouth she used to eat
236 וּמִכֹּסוֹ תִשְׁתֶּה And from his cup she used to drink
237 וּבְחֵיקוֹ תִשְׁכָּב And on his chest she used to lie

In this example, the presence of *YIQTOL* forms, while appearing in Narrative Discourse and translated as past tense, designate a specific type of action— ongoing, habitual actions.[35]

This particular function of *YIQTOL* clauses in Narrative Discourse is also present in the short speech of the wise woman of Abel-maacah in 2 Samuel 20:

20.18.1313 דַּבֵּר יְדַבְּרוּ בָרִאשֹׁנָה
לֵאמֹר
†PD
20.18.1314 שָׁאֹל יְשָׁאֲלוּ בְּאָבֵל
20.18.1315 וְכֵן הֵתַמּוּ:

---

[35]This specific type of action is also usually implied when *YIQTOL* clauses appear in extra-paragraph comments within narrative proper. In direct discourse, however, *YIQTOL* clauses generally function as inner-paragraph commentary along with participial, verbless, and היה clauses, as opposed to between paragraph blocks.

They truly used to say in earlier times,
> "They will certainly ask in Abel."
And this is how they finished [a matter].

This example is unusual because, although the speech begins with a *YIQTOL* form, the temporal adverb בְּרִאשֹׁנָה along with the following *QATAL* clause 1315 marks her speech as Narrative Discourse. As in other examples, the *YIQTOL* clause here also denotes ongoing, habitual actions in past time.

The sole case of an instance of Narrative Discourse being composed of participial, verbless, and incomplete clauses occurs in the dream report of the baker in Genesis 40:16-17:

40.16.243 אַף־אֲנִי בַּחֲלוֹמִי
וְהִנֵּה
40.16.244 שְׁלֹשָׁה סַלֵּי חֹרִי עַל־רֹאשִׁי:
40.17.245 וּבַסַּל הָעֶלְיוֹן מִכֹּל מַאֲכַל פַּרְעֹה מַעֲשֵׂה אֹפֶה
40.17.246 וְהָעוֹף אֹכֵל אֹתָם מִן־הַסַּל מֵעַל רֹאשִׁי:

I, also, in my dream: There were three woven baskets upon my head. In the highest basket were some of all the foods of Pharaoh, baked goods! The birds were eating them from the basket upon my head.

While the narrative context demands that this speech is Narrative Discourse, the verbal constellation of incomplete (243), participial (246), and verbless (244, 245) clauses would lead one to view the report as Expository Discourse. The high number of expository clausal forms, however, is due to the specific nature of the speech as a "dream report." In both narrative accounts of dreams (clauses 262-277) and in their narrative discourse reports (clauses 016-020; 028-029; 222-230; 243-246; 313-327), a higher percentage of nonnarrative forms occurs than in other types of narrative or discourse. This is perhaps tied to the character of dreams as either unreal and ephemeral or ongoing in their significance.

Excluding this exception, however, Narrative Discourse is regular throughout Hebrew prose in its delimited set of verbal and clausal options. The discourse is based upon *QATAL* clauses with *WAYYIQTOL* clauses functioning as a continuing form. In addition to these two, verbless, participial, and *YIQTOL* clauses perform roles of providing off-line commentary within narrative speeches.

Discourse Constellation of Narrative Discourse

Primary Verbal/Clausal	*QATAL*	Basic past
Forms	*WAYYIQTOL*	Continuative Past
Secondary Verbal/Clausal Forms	Verbless	Off-line status
	היה Verbal	Off-line status
	Participial	Off-line action
	YIQTOL	Off-line ongoing action

Predictive Discourse (PD)

Discourse Constellations

Among those speeches or parts of speeches in the textual database used in this study whose primary purpose is to relate the sequential occurrence of events after the speech-event (functioning as either a proposal, a wish, or a prophecy), the set of verbal or clausal possibilities present in the discourses are restricted to six constellations. These are listed in the following chart.

		JN	CN	Total	%
	YIQTOL	13	42	55	51.9%
	YIQTOL, WeQATAL	8	10	18	17.0%
PD	*YIQTOL, WeQATAL*, (Ptc./Vbl../Inc.)	1	8	9	8.5%
	YIQTOL, (Ptc./Vbl../Inc.)	2	3	5	4.7%
	WeQATAL	5	12	17	16.0%
	WeYIQTOL		2	2	1.9%
	Total cases	29	77	106	100%

Function of the Discourse

Even as *QATAL* and *WAYYIQTOL* are the basic and continuative forms for Narrative Discourse, the basic and continuative verbal forms for Predictive Discourse are *YIQTOL* and *WeQATAL* respectively. In 55 cases (51.9%), *YIQTOL* is the sole form of the discourse; in 5 cases (4.7%), it is combined with off-line commentary composed of participial or verbless clauses. Furthermore, in 27 cases (25.5%), the basic *YIQTOL* clauses are combined and continued within the speech with *WeQATAL* clauses (with or without off-line commentary).

In 17 cases (16.0%), the Predictive Discourse immediately follows some other type of discourse within a speech. Note this paradigmatic example from the extended speech by Judah, in which he relates the trials of the brothers up to this point:

ND

44.27.743 וַיֹּאמֶר עַבְדְּךָ אָבִי אֵלֵינוּ

†ND

44.27.744 אַתֶּם יְדַעְתֶּם

כִּי שְׁנַיִם יָלְדָה־לִּי אִשְׁתִּי:

44.28.745 וַיֵּצֵא הָאֶחָד מֵאִתִּי

44.28.746 וָאֹמַר

††ND

44.28.747 אַךְ טָרֹף טֹרָף

44.28.748 וְלֹא רְאִיתִיו עַד־הֵנָּה:

†PD

44.29.749 וּלְקַחְתֶּם גַּם־אֶת־זֶה מֵעִם פָּנַי

44.29.750 וְקָרָהוּ אָסוֹן

44.29.751 וְהוֹרַדְתֶּם אֶת־שֵׂיבָתִי בְּרָעָה שְׁאֹלָה:

Your servant, my father, said to us: "You yourselves knew that
my wife bore me two [boys]. Then the one left me and I said,
'Surely, he is completely torn apart!' And I have not seen him
until now.

　　　And you will take this one from me and something evil
will befall him and you will bring down my gray hairs to
Sheol in misery!"

The presence of the governing *WeQAṬAL* in clause 749 signals a change in
discourse tense from past to future ("I have not seen him until now. And you will
take this one from me."). Because *WeQAṬAL* never occurs in either Narrative or
Expository Discourses, when it is present it signals the change to Predictive Discourse in the speech.

　　In two cases (1.9%), *WeYIQṬOL* is present within a speech and stands as
the sole form. Both of these instances occur at the beginning of the Court Narrative and immediately follow David's two questions about any remaining heirs to
Saul. These two cases appear below:

ID

09.01.002 הֲכִי יֶשׁ־עוֹד

אֲשֶׁר נוֹתַר לְבֵית שָׁאוּל

PD

09.01.003 וְאֶעֱשֶׂה עִמּוֹ חֶסֶד בַּעֲבוּר יְהוֹנָתָן:

Is there still someone left from the house of Saul?
I shall/want to show fidelity with him because of Jonathan.

ID

09.03.12 הָאֶפֶס עוֹד אִישׁ לְבֵית שָׁאוּל

PD

09.03.13 וְאֶעֱשֶׂה עִמּוֹ חֶסֶד אֱלֹהִים

Isn't there still a man from the house of Saul?
I shall/want to show the fidelity of God to him.

In both cases, it is clear that the *WeYIQTOL* clauses do not continue the original Interrogative Discourses (e.g., "Is there anyone remaining of the house of Saul and shall I perform the *ḥesed* of God for him?"). The clauses are often translated as dependent clauses in most English translations, yet their syntactical structure in Hebrew sets them distinctly apart as independent clauses in both cases.[36]

While these examples *may* be Predictive Discourse ("I shall show"), the usual form governing the clauses of such speeches would be *WeQATAL*. *WeYIQTOL* clauses, however, do occur within Hortatory Discourse as a continuative form (see below), and may perform a weak hortatory function here ("I will/want to show"). The forms as they stand here are, nevertheless, ambiguous.

With these two minor exceptions, however, Predictive Discourse is regular throughout Hebrew prose in its delimited set of verbal and clausal options. The discourse is based upon *YIQTOL* clauses with *WeQATAL* clauses serving as the continuing form. In addition to these, verbless and participial clauses perform roles of providing off-line commentary within predictive speeches.

Discourse Constellation of Predictive Discourse

Primary Verbal/Clausal Forms	*YIQTOL*	Basic future
	WeQATAL	Continuative Future
Secondary Verbal/Clausal Forms	Verbless	Off-line status
	היה Verbal	Off-line status
	Incomplete	Off-line status
	Participial	Off-line action

Expository Discourse (ED)

Discourse Constellations

Among those speeches or parts of speeches in the textual database used in this study whose primary purpose is to explain a state or activity that is occurring at the time of the speech or that is perpetually true, the set of verbal or clausal possibilities present in the discourses are restricted to six constellations. These are listed in the following chart.

---

[36]The clauses appear as dependent clauses in RSV, NRSV, NIV, JB, and the Tanakh.

		JN	CN	Total	%
	Ptc./Vbl.	29	56	85	64.4%
	Ptc./ Vbl., Inc.	1	1	2	1.5%
ED	Inc.	7	28	35	26.5%
	Ptc./Vbl., *QATAL/YIQTOL* of היה	3	2	5	3.8%
	Ptc./Vbl., *QATAL/YIQTOL* of היה, Front. Obj.+ *QATAL/YIQTOL*	2		2	1.5%
	QATAL/YIQTOL of היה	1	2	3	2.3%
	Total cases	43	89	132	100%

Function of the Discourse

The predominant verbal and clausal forms for Expository Discourse are verbless, participial, incomplete, and היה clauses, which combined account for 130 of the 132 instances of Expository Discourse within the textual database. Within this constellation, the overwhelming combinations are participial and verbless clauses, present separately or in combination (85 cases; 64.4%), and incomplete clauses, present solely in a speech (35 cases; 26.5%). When speeches contain only participial or verbless clauses, the tense of the speech is always set in the present tense, as in these examples from the Joseph Novella:

42.13.450 שְׁנֵים עָשָׂר עֲבָדֶיךָ אַחִים
42.13.451 אֲנַחְנוּ בְּנֵי אִישׁ־אֶחָד בְּאֶרֶץ כְּנָעַן
וְהִנֵּה
42.13.452 הַקָּטֹן אֶת־אָבִינוּ הַיּוֹם
42.13.453 וְהָאֶחָד אֵינֶנּוּ:

Your twelve servants are brothers. We are sons of a certain
man in the land of Canaan. Look, today the young one is with
our father and one is no more.

45.26.833 עוֹד יוֹסֵף חַי
45.26.834 וְכִי־הוּא מֹשֵׁל בְּכָל־אֶרֶץ מִצְרָיִם

Joseph is still alive! And he really is ruling over all the land of
Egypt!

This also holds true for instances which also incorporate היה as a verb:

47.09.914 יְמֵי שְׁנֵי מְגוּרַי שְׁלֹשִׁים וּמְאַת שָׁנָה
47.09.915 מְעַט וְרָעִים הָיוּ יְמֵי שְׁנֵי חַיַּי

> The length of the years of my sojourn is 130 years. The length
> of the years of my living is small and evil.

When a speech is composed only of incomplete clauses, the discourse relates the immediate character of the narrative context either through an interjection, an oath, a vocative call, or an answer to a previously asked question.[37] In the last case, when an Expository Discourse is a reply to a preceding Interrogative Discourse, the Expository Discourse will often stand as a single or multiple incomplete clauses.[38]

In two cases, an Expository Discourse incorporates *QATAL* or *YIQTOL* clauses within its speech boundary. In both cases, the discourse is established by an initial verbless clause and the *QATAL* or *YIQTOL* clause stands as a secondary form along with regular expository verbal/clausal forms. Furthermore, the object of the *QATAL* or *YIQTOL* clause is consistently fronted, thus emphasizing the present character of the clause rather than its past occurrence. Note this case in particular:

41.25.331 חֲלוֹם פַּרְעֹה אֶחָד הוּא

41.25.332 אֵת אֲשֶׁר הָאֱלֹהִים עֹשֶׂה הִגִּיד לְפַרְעֹה:

41.26.333 שֶׁבַע פָּרֹת הַטֹּבֹת שֶׁבַע שָׁנִים הֵנָּה

41.26.334 וְשֶׁבַע הַשִּׁבֳּלִים הַטֹּבֹת שֶׁבַע שָׁנִים הֵנָּה

41.26.335 חֲלוֹם אֶחָד הוּא:

41.27.336 וְשֶׁבַע הַפָּרוֹת הָרַקּוֹת וְהָרָעֹת
הָעֹלֹת אַחֲרֵיהֶן שֶׁבַע שָׁנִים הֵנָּה

41.27.337 וְשֶׁבַע הַשִּׁבֳּלִים הָרֵקוֹת שְׁדֻפוֹת הַקָּדִים
יִהְיוּ שֶׁבַע שְׁנֵי רָעָב:

41.28.338 הוּא הַדָּבָר
אֲשֶׁר דִּבַּרְתִּי אֶל־פַּרְעֹה

41.28.339 אֲשֶׁר הָאֱלֹהִים עֹשֶׂה הֶרְאָה אֶת־פַּרְעֹה:

> The dream of Pharaoh is one. That which God is doing he has
> told to Pharaoh!

---

[37]In all of these cases, of course, the lack of a predicate in the clause does not allow for *any* indication of tense. The subject of all of the clauses, however, is present and the force of the statement pertains to some contemporary setting: The interjection responds to a present situation (e.g., clause 374 in the Joseph Novella; Gen 41:43), the oath responds to a present accusation (clause 163 in the Court Narrative; 2 Sam 11:11), the vocative calls to a character present in the setting (e.g., clause 026 in the Court Narrative; 2 Sam 9:6), and the answer responds to an immediately asked question (e.g., clause 120 in the Joseph Novella; Gen 37:33). For these reasons, incomplete clauses, when they occur alone, are accounted as Expository Discourse in this study.

[38]Note, for instance, clause 433 in the Joseph Novella (Gen 42:7).

The seven good cows are seven years. And the seven good
ears are seven years. It is one dream!

The seven thin and bad cows who were coming after them
are seven years. And the seven thin ears blasted from the east,
they are seven years of famine.

This is the matter that I speak to Pharaoh. What God is doing he has shown Pharaoh!

In Joseph's explication of Pharaoh's dream, verbless, participial and היה
clauses abound. Clauses 332 and 339, both governed by *QATAL* clauses, stand
within the Expository Discourse and function within the present tense nature of
the speech as explanations about the origin of the dream (which is fronted in
both cases), rather than past tense accounts of the dreaming of Pharaoh: "What
God is doing he has told/has shown to Pharaoh!"

Note also Jacob's reaction when his sons return from Egypt and require that
their youngest brother, Benjamin, return with them:

42.36.530 יוֹסֵף אֵינֶנּוּ
42.36.531 וְשִׁמְעוֹן אֵינֶנּוּ
42.36.532 וְאֶת־בִּנְיָמִן תִּקָּחוּ
42.36.533 עָלַי הָיוּ כֻלָּנָה:

Joseph is no more! And Simeon is no more! And you are taking Benjamin! All of this [burden] is on me!

Here, the discourse is established by the verbless and היה verbal clauses within
it. Clause 532, a *YIQTOL* clause with a fronted object, stands within the discourse as a present tense realization of the incipient exit of the brothers with
Benjamin: "And now you are taking *Benjamin*!"

With this exception, however, Expository Discourse is regular throughout
Hebrew prose in its delimited set of verbal and clausal options. The discourse is
based upon verbless, participial, incomplete, and היה clauses. In addition to
these, *QATAL* and *YIQTOL* clauses with fronted objects may also stand within
examples of Expository Discourse, providing notices of secondary actions
whose object or completion is emphasized within the present tense nature of the
larger discourse.

Discourse Constellation of Expository Discourse

Primary Verbal/Clausal Forms	Verbless	Primary Present status
	היה Verbal	Primary Present status
	Incomplete	Interj./Oath/Voc./Answer
	Participial	Primary Present action
Secondary Verbal/ Clausal Form	Obj. + *QATAL/ YIQTOL*	Secondary Present action

Hortatory Discourse (HD)

Discourse Constellations

For a number of reasons, those verbal forms which express degrees of voli-tion (i.e., imperative, cohortative, and jussive, along with other attendant forms), comprise a set of functional clausal types separate from the declarative classes considered above. While in most languages such forms are associated with a separate mood, in Hebrew the volitives do not make up a mood but rather form a "functional class."[39] In the development of the language, many archaic voli-tional forms were unified and set within the truncated volitive class. For this reason, Hortatory Discourse is more complex from a morphological point of view than the three declarative discourse types above. Yet, even here, the possi-ble verbal combinations are finite and delimited. Those volitional clauses that appear in hortatory speeches in the textual databases used in this study are ac-counted in the following table of verbal constellations.

		JN	CN	Total	%
HD	Impv./Coh./Juss.	26	62	88	51.8%
	Impv./Coh./Juss., *WeYIQTOL/YIQTOL*	11	14	25	14.7%
	Impv./Coh./Juss., *WeQATAL*	3	4	7	4.1%
	Impv./Coh./Juss., *WeYIQTOL/YIQTOL*, *WeQATAL*	5	6	11	6.5%
	Impv./Coh./Juss., *QATAL*	2	1	3	1.8%
	Impv./Coh./Juss., *WeYIQTOL/YIQTOL*, *WeQATAL*, *QATAL*	1	1	2	1.2%

---

[39]See Waltke and O'Connor, *Syntax*, 564-79, for a lucid discussion of the volitional forms. There is some diachronic evidence that the jussive and cohortative originally formed distinct conjugations in all persons. By the time of the writing of the biblical text, however, imperative, jussive, and cohortative forms did not overlap extensively in their uses. See W. L. Moran, "Early Canaanite *yaqtula*," *Or* 29 (1960), 1-19; P. Joüon, *Grammaire de l'hébreu biblique* (Rome: Pontifical Biblical Institute, 1923), §114.

HD cont.	Impv./Coh./Juss., *ʾal-YIQTOL*	2	1	3	1.8%
	Impv./Coh./Juss., *WeQATAL, ʾal-YIQTOL*	2	2	4	2.4%
	ʾal-YIQTOL	6	6	12	7.1%
	ʾal-YIQTOL, WeQATAL/YIQTOL		3	3	1.8%
	(We)*YIQTOL-nāʾ, (WeQATAL/WeYIQTOL/YIQTOL)*		9	9	5.3%
	QATAL, YIQTOL/WeQATAL	1	2	3	1.8%
	Total cases	59	111	170	100%

Function of the Discourse

The foundational verbal forms that express volition are imperative, cohortative, and jussive.[40] As they appear within the present state of the biblical text, these three are functionally equal and their use is dependent only upon the subject of the volitional action: first person (cohortative), second person (imperative), or third person (jussive). When any of these forms appear in a speech, the associated discourse is, by default, hortatory. In 88 cases (51.8%), these forms comprise the entire discourse, with no other attendant forms. In 55 cases (32.4%) these foundational forms are accompanied by other verbal forms. Therefore, in the large majority of cases (143 cases; 84.1%), the three foundational volitional forms identify and define a discourse as hortatory.

Among the clauses that accompany the foundational hortatory clauses, the usual governing verbal forms are *YIQTOL* (with or without a prefixed *We*) and *WeQATAL*. In both cases, the inherent aspectual sense of the two forms as non-punctilliar and their parallel usage in Predictive Discourse cause them to be natural continuative forms for Hortatory Discourse also. While their sense in Predictive Discourse is simply declarative future, in Hortatory Discourse the foundational forms lend their volitional force to their accompanying *(We)YIQTOL* and *WeQATAL* clauses. In all cases, the accompanying forms also take on hortatory force very similar, if not identical, to their imperative, cohortative, and jussive counterparts. Note the following examples.

---

[40]Note Joüon, *Grammaire,* 307-12; Gesenius, *Grammar,* 319-26. In this discussion, only unambiguous jussive forms are treated as such. While many third person *YIQTOL* forms undoubtedly function as jussives, the similarity of such forms makes it usually impossible to distinguish on morphological grounds. It should also be noted that the presence of second person *YIQTOL* forms often function as parallel constructions with imperative clauses. In rare circumstances, an unambiguous *YIQTOL* may stand within a Hortatory Discourse and function as a jussive (note Gen 41:34; clause 349).

Impv./Coh./Juss. with *(We)YIQTOL*:[41]

37.13.040 לְכָה

37.13.041 וְאֶשְׁלָחֲךָ אֲלֵיהֶם

Come, so that I can send you to them!

42.02.414 רְדוּ־שָׁמָּה

42.02.415 וְשִׁבְרוּ־לָנוּ מִשָּׁם

42.02.416 וְנִחְיֶה

42.02.417 וְלֹא נָמוּת:

Go down there and buy grain for us from there, so
that we can live and not die!

44.01.659 מַלֵּא אֶת־אַמְתְּחֹת הָאֲנָשִׁים אֹכֶל כַּאֲשֶׁר יוּכְלוּן שְׂאֵת

44.01.660 וְשִׂים כֶּסֶף־אִישׁ בְּפִי אַמְתַּחְתּוֹ:

44.02.661 וְאֶת־גְּבִיעִי גְּבִיעַ הַכֶּסֶף תָּשִׂים בְּפִי אַמְתַּחַת הַקָּטֹן וְאֵת כֶּסֶף שִׁבְרוֹ

Fill the sacks of the men with food--as much as they
are able to carry! And place each one's silver in the
mouth of his sack! But place my silver goblet and the
money for his grain in the mouth of the sack of the
young one!

Impv./Coh./Juss. with *WeQATAL*:

45.09.781 מַהֲרוּ

45.09.782 וַעֲלוּ אֶל־אָבִי

45.09.783 וַאֲמַרְתֶּם אֵלָיו

Hurry! Go up to my father and say to him . . . !

---

[41]Clauses governed by *WeYIQTOL* and *YIQTOL* in Hortatory Discourse differ in
their basic functions. While *YIQTOL* clauses *continue* the hortatory force of the foundational imperative, cohortative, or jussive clause, *WeYIQTOL* clauses most often provide a
consequential force to the speech. Thus, the *WeYIQTOL* clauses in the first and second
examples under this heading both provide the purpose for the preceding volitional forms:
"Come, so that I will/may/can send you to them!" and "Go down there and buy grain for
us from there, so that we will/may/can live and not die!" See Waltke and O'Connor, *Syntax*, 562-63, and Lambdin, *Introduction*, §107, for a general overview of this usage. Also
see the discussion in Johnson, *Perfekt und Imperfekt*, 59-62. Note, however, that this
consequential force of *WeYIQTOL* is not universal, as can be seen below.

11.15.178 הָבוּ אֶת־אוּרִיָּה אֶל־מוּל פְּנֵי הַמִּלְחָמָה הַחֲזָקָה
11.15.179 וְשַׁבְתֶּם מֵאַחֲרָיו
11.15.180 וְנִכָּה
11.15.181 וָמֵת:

Set Uriah in the front of the harsh fighting and turn away from him! Let him be stuck and let him die!

Impv./Coh./Juss. with (We)*YIQTOL* and *WeQATAL*:[42]

37.20.065 לְכוּ
37.20.066 וְנַהַרְגֵהוּ
37.20.067 וְנַשְׁלִכֵהוּ בְּאַחַד הַבֹּרוֹת
37.20.068 וְאָמַרְנוּ

Come! Let's kill him and toss him into one of the cisterns and let's say . . . .

01.02.1344 יְבַקְשׁוּ לַאדֹנִי הַמֶּלֶךְ נַעֲרָה בְתוּלָה
01.02.1345 וְעָמְדָה לִפְנֵי הַמֶּלֶךְ
01.02.1346 וּתְהִי־לוֹ סֹכֶנֶת
01.02.1347 וְשָׁכְבָה בְחֵיקֶךָ
01.02.1348 וְחַם לַאדֹנִי הַמֶּלֶךְ:

Let them seek out a virgin servant-girl for my lord the king! Let her wait upon the king and become his nurse and lie upon his chest! Let it be warm (?) to my lord the king!

In this final example, the hortatory nature of the entire discourse is based upon the jussive clause 1346. The accompanying *YIQTOL* and *WeQATAL* clauses all take their jussive force from their juxtaposition alongside the jussive וּתְהִי in the discourse.

The presence of *QATAL* in Hortatory Discourse most often signals the usage of a "perfomative utterance," in which the action described by the *QATAL* is actually performed by the speech itself.[43] *QATAL* performative utterances usually occur as first person singular forms, as in these examples:

---

[42]In this example, the *WeYIQTOL* clauses (066,067) do *not* provide consequential force to the discourse but rather continue the volitional force of the original imperative and are thus interpreted as cohortatives, although their morphology is ambiguous.

[43]For a full discussion of this note Werner Meyer, *Untersuchungen zur Formensprache der babylonischen "Gebetsbeschwörungen"* (Studia Pohl: Series Maior 5; Rome: Pontifical Biblical Institute, 1976); Dennis Pardee and Robert M. Whiting, "Aspects of Epistolary Verbal Usage in Ugaritic and Akkadian," *BSO(A)S* 50 (1987), 1-31;

41.41.366 רְאֵה

41.41.367 נָתַתִּי אֹתְךָ עַל כָּל־אֶרֶץ מִצְרָיִם:

See, I (hereby) place you over all the land of Egypt!

הִנֵּה־נָא

14.21.595 עָשִׂיתִי אֶת־הַדָּבָר הַזֶּה

14.21.596 וְלֵךְ

14.21.597 הָשֵׁב אֶת־הַנַּעַר אֶת־אַבְשָׁלוֹם:

See, I (hereby) do this! Go, bring back the young man Absa-lom!

Yet, they may also appear in other persons or numbers, as in this example:

45.17.805 אֱמֹר אֶל־אַחֶיךָ

†45.17.806 זֹאת עֲשׂוּ . . .

(An extended series of commands follows.)

45.19.814 וְאַתָּה צֻוֵּיתָה

†45.19.815 זֹאת עֲשׂוּ

†45.19.816 קְחוּ־לָכֶם מֵאֶרֶץ מִצְרַיִם . . .

Say to your brothers:
    "Do this . . ."
And you are (hereby) commanded:
    "Do this: Take for yourselves from the land
    of Egypt . . . ."

The usage of *QATAL* as performative utterance without the accompanying foundational volitional forms is rare. In the textual databases used in this study, when the narrative context demands that *QATAL* be understood as a performative utterance even though no imperative, cohortative, or jussive clauses appear in the surrounding discourse, the volitional force of the *QATAL* is always signaled by accompanying *YIQTOL* or *WeQATAL* clauses. The verbal constellation *QATAL* with *YIQTOL* or *WeQATAL* occurs only within Hortatory Discourse and the volitional force of *QATAL* is, therefore, unambiguous from a wider syntactical perspective. Note the following cases:

19.30.1187 אָמַרְתִּי

19.30.1188 אַתָּה וְצִיבָא תַּחְלְקוּ אֶת־הַשָּׂדֶה:

I (hereby) speak: you and Ziba must divide the field!

Waltke and O'Connor, *Syntax,* 488–89; and Dilbert Hillers, "Performative Utterances," 757–66.

16.04.793 הִשְׁתַּחֲוֵיתִי

16.04.794 אֶמְצָא־חֵן בְּעֵינֶיךָ אֲדֹנִי הַמֶּלֶךְ:

I (hereby) bow down! May I find favor in your eyes, O my
lord, the king!

In the following case, a *QATAL* clause clearly functions with hortatory
force, both from contextual considerations and from the fact that it stands within
a Hortatory Discourse. Yet the exact purpose of the clause is unclear. In the narrative context, Joseph has just finished interpreting the dream of the royal butler
(Gen 40:12-13; clauses 232-236) and changes his discourse into a request that,
when the butler is restored to his position as foreseen by Joseph, the butler
should remember Joseph and mention him to Pharaoh:

40.14.237 כִּי אִם־זְכַרְתַּנִי אִתְּךָ
כַּאֲשֶׁר יִיטַב לָךְ

40.14.238 וְעָשִׂיתָ־נָּא עִמָּדִי חָסֶד

40.14.239 וְהִזְכַּרְתַּנִי אֶל־פַּרְעֹה

40.14.240 וְהוֹצֵאתַנִי מִן־הַבַּיִת הַזֶּה:

However, you must certainly remember me
whenever it goes well for you
And act faithfully with me!
And remind Pharaoh about me,
And bring me out form this prisonhouse!

The hortatory nature of clause 237 is undisputed among the major translations of
this passage. The fact that a *QATAL* performative utterance appears in a second
person singular form is unusual. Seen from the perspective of the verbal constellations set for Hortatory Discourse, however, it is entirely regular.

The negation of hortatory clauses in narrative prose is usually accomplished
by a prefixed *ʾal-* on *YIQTOL* verbal forms. These occasionally accompany one
of the foundational volitional forms:

37.22.076 אַל־תִּשְׁפְּכוּ־דָם

37.22.077 הַשְׁלִיכוּ אֹתוֹ אֶל־הַבּוֹר הַזֶּה
אֲשֶׁר בַּמִּדְבָּר

37.22.078 וְיָד אַל־תִּשְׁלְחוּ־בוֹ

Do not shed blood! Throw him into this cistern in the desert!
But may a hand not stretch out against him!

45.09.786 רְדָה אֵלַי

45.09.787 אַל־תַּעֲמֹד:

45.10.788 וְיָשַׁבְתָּ בְאֶרֶץ־גֹּשֶׁן

45.10.789 וְהָיִיתָ קָרוֹב אֵלַי

> Come down to me! Don't stay! Dwell in the land of Goshen
> and be near to me!

Most often, the entire discourse is negative and, therefore, ʾal-YIQṬOL clauses either stand alone in the discourse, for example:

42.22.483 אַל־תֶּחֶטְאוּ בַיֶּלֶד

> Do not sin because of the boy!

and

וְעַתָּה
45.05.776 אַל־תֵּעָצְבוּ
45.05.777 וְאַל־יִחַר בְּעֵינֵיכֶם
כִּי־מְכַרְתֶּם אֹתִי הֵנָּה

> So now, don't be upset and don't be angry with yourselves be-
> cause you sold me here!

Rarely, however, ʾal-YIQṬOL clauses may introduce YIQṬOL or WeQAṬAL clauses, as in this example:

וְעַתָּה
02.09.1537 אַל־תְּנַקֵּהוּ
כִּי אִישׁ חָכָם אָתָּה
02.09.1538 וְיָדַעְתָּ אֵת אֲשֶׁר תַּעֲשֶׂה־לּוֹ
02.09.1539 וְהוֹרַדְתָּ אֶת־שֵׂיבָתוֹ בְּדָם שְׁאוֹל׃

> So now, don't forgive, since you are a wise man! Know what
> you will do to him! Bring down his gray hairs to Sheol with
> blood!

In nine cases in the textual database, the hortatory nature of a discourse is solely defined by the precative particle נָא/-nāʾ suffixed to a YIQṬOL verbal form within the discourse. The YIQṬOL clause may either stand alone or, like the foundational volitional clauses, be accompanied by YIQṬOL or WeQAṬAL clauses:[44]

וְעַתָּה
47.04.901 יֵשְׁבוּ־נָא עֲבָדֶיךָ בְּאֶרֶץ גֹּשֶׁן׃

> So now, may your servants dwell in the land of Goshen!

---

[44]In addition to these examples, note also the example under the discussion of the QAṬAL performative utterance above, Gen 40:14-15; clauses 237-240.

13.05.374 תָּבֹא נָא תָמָר אֲחוֹתִי
13.05.375 וּתְבָרֵנִי לָחֶם
13.05.376 וְעָשְׂתָה לְעֵינַי אֶת־הַבִּרְיָה
לְמַעַן אֲשֶׁר אֶרְאֶה
13.05.377 וְאָכַלְתִּי מִיָּדָהּ:

Let Tamar, my sister come and cook me food! Let her make
the meal in front of me so that I can watch! I want to eat from
her hand!

14.11.559 יִזְכָּר־נָא הַמֶּלֶךְ אֶת־יְהוָה אֱלֹהֶיךָ מֵהַרְבִית [Q מֵהַרְבַּת] גֹּאֵל הַדָּם לְשַׁחֵת
14.11.560 וְלֹא יַשְׁמִידוּ אֶת־בְּנִי

Let the king remember the LORD your God, that the redeemer
of blood not continue slaying! Don't let him destroy my son!

The volitional nature of a discourse is defined by the combination of verbal
clauses that appear within it. While the number or type of clauses which appear
in Hortatory Discourses are more complex than those found in declarative
speeches, the constellation of verbal possibilities are delimited and the pragmatic force of any single clause is defined by its presence within the larger
complex of verbal possibilities. These possibilities are listed in the following
chart.

Verbal Constellation of Hortatory Discourse

	Imperative	Second Person Volitional
Primary Verbal/Clausal Forms	Cohortative	First Person Volitional
	Jussive	Third Person Volitional
	'al-YIQTOL	Negative Volitional
	(We)YIQTOL-naʾ	Precatory Volitional
Secondary Verbal/ Clausal Forms	QATAL	Performative Utterance
	WeQATAL	Continuative Volitional
	YIQTOL	Continuative Volitional
	WeYIQTOL	Consequential/Purpose

Interrogative Discourse (ID)

Throughout Hebrew narrative prose, Interrogative Discourse is marked by
the use of interrogative adverbs or particles. While several studies have defined
questions in Hebrew under several different headings, the consistent presence of

fronted interrogative adverbs or particles marks this type of discourse as sepa-rate from the four discourse types considered before.[45] The interrogative particle הֲ, in general, marks alternative or polar questions, in which "the entire proposi-tion is questioned rather than just one feature of it."[46] Interrogative adverbs, on the other hand, mark circumstantial questions, in which some single element is questioned: a person (who?), a thing (what?), a place (where?), a time (when?), a manner (how?), or a motive (why?). The presence of these particles and ad-verbs in Interrogative Discourses is noted in the following two charts. In each chart, the left-hand column notes the interrogative particle or adverb, the second column provides the clauses governed by the particle, the third column notes its verbal or clausal type, the fourth column notes whether the question is rhetorical (*) or true (†), and the final column notes the tense of the question.

Interrogative Clauses in the Joseph Novella

Particle					Particle				
POLAR הֲ	022	YIQTOL	*	Future	מָה	033		*	Present
	034	YIQTOL	*	Future		052		†	Present
	359	YIQTOL	*	Future		092	Verbless	*	Present
	559	Verbless	†	Present		505	Verbless	*	Present
	560	Verbless	†	Present		703	Verbless	*	Present
	562	YIQTOL	*	Past		706	YIQTOL	*	Future
	629	Verbless	†	Present		707	YIQTOL	*	Future
	630	Verbless	†	Present		708	YIQTOL	*	Future
	639	Verbless	†	Present		896	Verbless	†	Present
	721	Verbless	†	Present	לָמָה	411	YIQTOL	*	Future
	769	Verbless	†	Present		556	QATAL`	†	Past
	218	Verbless	*	Present		672	QATAL	†	Past
	482	QATAL	*	Past		679	YIQTOL	†	Present
הֲלֹא	673	Verbless	*	Present		929	YIQTOL	*	Future
	704	QATAL	*	Past		941	Verbless	*	Future
	039	Participle	*	Present	כָּמָה	912	YIQTOL	†	Present

---

[45]See the discussion in C. Brockelmann, *Grundriss der vergleichenden Grammatik der semitischen Sprachen* (Berlin: Reuter & Reichard, 1913), 2.192-93; Gesenius, *Gram-mar,* §150; Waltke and O'Connor, *Syntax,* 315-29. Also note that Hortatory Discourse is occasionally marked only by the hortatory particle -nā' suffixed to a *YIQTOL* verbal form; in this case, Horatory Discourse, like Interrogative Discourse, is not marked by verbal constellations but by "hortatory particles." In Hortatory Discourse, however, it is not necessary for the suffixed -nā' to appear in the first clause of the discourse; in Inter-rogative Discourse, the fronted interrogative adverb or particle will always appear as the first element in the discourse.

[46]Waltke and O'Connor, *Syntax,* 684.

POLAR אם	023	YIQTOL	*	Future
ALTERNA-TIVE אם	117	Verbless	†	Present
	463	Verbless	†	Present

מַדּוּעַ	213	Participle	†	Present
אַיֵּה	431	QATAL	†	Past
אִי	159	YIQTOL	*	Future
	682	YIQTOL	*	Present
אָנָה	108	Participle	*	Present
Unmarked	160	WeQATAL	*	Future

Interrogative Clauses in the Court History of David

	002	Verbless	†	Present
	008	Verbless	†	Present
	012	Verbless	†	Present
	060	Participle	*	Present
	294	QATAL	†	Past
	321	YIQTOL	*	Future
	440	QATAL	†	Past
	587	Verbless	†	Present
POLAR	742	Verbless	*	Present
הֲ	875	YIQTOL	†	Future
	1083	Verbless	†	Present
	1161	YIQTOL	†	Future
	1201	YIQTOL	*	Future
	1230	QATAL	*	Past
	1273	Verbless	†	Present
	1305	Verbless	†	Present
	1549	Verbless	†	Present
	195	QATAL	*	Past
מִי	316	YIQTOL ידע	*	Present
	666	YIQTOL שים	*	Present
	841	YIQTOL	*	Future
	035	Verbless	*	Present
	308	Verbless	*	Present
	780	Verbless	*	Present
מָה	811	Verbless	*	Present
	846	YIQTOL	†	Future
	1163	Verbless	*	Present
	1184	Verbless	*	Present
	1391	Verbless	†	Present
אֵיפֹה	017	Verbless	†	Present

אֵי	658	Verbless	†	Present
	061	QATAL	*	Past
	002	Verbless	†	Present
	130	Verbless	†	Present
	157	Participle	*	Present
	194	QATAL	*	Past
	196	QATAL	*	Past
הֲלֹא	366	YIQTOL	†	Future
	842	Incomplete	*	Present
	477	QATAL	*	Past
	768	Verbless	*	Present
	1140	Verbless	*	Present
	1370	QATAL	*	Past
	1378	QATAL	*	Past
	1662	QATAL	*	Past
	198	QATAL	†	Past
	320	Participle	*	Present
	468	YIQTOL	†	Future
	568	QATAL	*	Past
	636	QATAL	†	Past
	641	QATAL	†	Past
	710	YIQTOL	*	Future
	807	YIQTOL	*	Future
	837	QATAL	†	Past
לָמָה	1035	Participle	†	Present
	1131	Participle	†	Present
	1134	YIQTOL	†	Future
	1138	YIQTOL	†	Future
	1186	YIQTOL	*	Future
	1204	YIQTOL	*	Future
	1206	YIQTOL	*	Future

לָמָה Cont.	1229	QATAL	*	Past
	1318	YIQTOL	†	Future
	1586	Participle	*	Present
מַדּוּעַ	158	QATAL	†	Past
	193	QATAL	†	Past
	365	Verbless	†	Present
	814	QATAL	†	Past
	993	QATAL	†	Past
	1225	QATAL	†	Past
	1236	QATAL	†	Past
	1360	QATAL	·†	Past
	1381	QATAL	†	Past
	1474	Participle	†	Present

כָּמָה	1199	Verbless	†	Present
אַיֵּה	786	Verbless	†	Present
	925	Verbless	†	Present
אֵיךְ	288	YIQTOL	*	Future
Unmarked	290	WeQATAL	*	Future
	836	Verbless	*	Present
	1164	YIQTOL	*	Future
	1226	WAYYIQTOL	†	Past
	1237	QATAL	*	Past
	1663	WAYYIQTOL	*	Past
	1666	WAYYIQTOL	*	Past

Because Interrogative Discourse is marked, in a sense, externally by these adverbs or particles, verbal constellations are not the defining factor in determining the boundaries of the discourse. As can be seen in the above charts, however, in almost all cases, the governing verbal or clausal type determines the tense of an interrogative. The basic tense of each verbal form or clausal type is determined by those discourses that employ the verbal form of clausal type as a foundational base.

Verbal Form/Clausal Type	Foundational Discourse	Primary Tense
QATAL	Narrative Discourse	Past
WeQATAL	Predictive Discourse	Future
YIQTOL	Predictive Discourse	Future
WAYYIQTOL	Narrative Discourse	Past
Participle	Expository Discourse	Present
Verbless	Expository Discourse	Present
Incomplete	Expository Discourse	Present

Exceptions to this basic paradigm for tense in Interrogative Discourse are rare.

In conclusion, two remaining aspects of Interrogative Discourse should be noted. First, in the textual databases used in this study, eight clauses stand in Interrogative Discourses without any interrogative particle or adverb. In all cases, the unmarked interrogative clause is always juxtaposed to an unambiguously marked interrogative clause. These unmarked interrogative clauses function in two ways. In five of the cases, the clause temporally continues an immediately juxtaposed, marked interrogative clause and the governing interrogative adverb governs both clauses:

39.09.159 וְאֵיךְ אֶעֱשֶׂה הָרָעָה הַגְּדֹלָה הַזֹּאת

39.09.160 וְחָטָאתִי לֵאלֹהִים:

How can I do this great evil?

(How) can I sin against God?

12.18.288 וְאֵיךְ נֹאמַר אֵלָיו

†12.18.289 מֵת הַיֶּלֶד

12.18.290 וְעָשָׂה רָעָה:

How can we say to him, "The child died"?

(How) can we perform evil?

19.42.1225 מַדּוּעַ גְּנָבוּךָ אַחֵינוּ אִישׁ יְהוּדָה

19.42.1226 וַיַּעֲבִרוּ אֶת־הַמֶּלֶךְ וְאֶת־בֵּיתוֹ אֶת־הַיַּרְדֵּן וְכָל־אַנְשֵׁי דָוִד עִמּוֹ:

Why did our brethren, the men of Judah, take you?

(Why) did they bring the king and his house across the Jordan,

and all the men of David with him?

02.42.1662 הֲלוֹא הִשְׁבַּעְתִּיךָ בַיהוָה

02.42.1663 וָאָעִד בָּךְ

. . .

02.42.1666 וַתֹּאמֶר אֵלַי

. . .

02.42.1669 וּמַדּוּעַ לֹא שָׁמַרְתָּ אֵת שְׁבֻעַת יְהוָה וְאֶת־הַמִּצְוָה אֲשֶׁר־צִוִּיתִי עָלֶיךָ:

Didn't I swear to you by the LORD?

(Didn't) I testify to you, saying,

"(intervening quote)"?

(Didn't) you say to me,

"(intervening quote)"?

Why didn't you keep the oath of the LORD and the order that

I commanded you?

In three cases, the sense of the clause is contradictory to facts given in the narrative or in the immediately preceding discourse and, therefore, has an ironic sense:

(Absalom to Hushai, who has supposedly deserted his friend David.)

16.17.836 זֶה חַסְדְּךָ אֶת־רֵעֶךָ

16.17.837 לָמָּה לֹא־הָלַכְתָּ אֶת־רֵעֶךָ:

This is your faithfulness for your friend?!

Why didn't you go with your friend?

(David to Abishai, who suggested that Shimei, whom David forgave, be put to death.)

19.23.1163 מַה־לִּי וְלָכֶם בְּנֵי צְרוּיָה
כִּי־תִהְיוּ־לִי הַיּוֹם לְשָׂטָן
19.23.1164 הַיּוֹם יוּמַת אִישׁ בְּיִשְׂרָאֵל
כִּי הֲלוֹא יָדַעְתִּי
כִּי הַיּוֹם אֲנִי־מֶלֶךְ עַל־יִשְׂרָאֵל:

What is that to me and to you, sons of Zeruiah, that you become my adversary today? Shall a man from Israel be put to
death today, since I know (don't I?) that today I am king over
Israel?!

(A group of Israelites, who first suggested the reinstatement of David to the
royal throne, to a group of Judahites.)

19.44.1236 וּמַדּוּעַ הֱקִלֹּתַנִי
19.44.1237 וְלֹא־הָיָה דְבָרִי רִאשׁוֹן לִי לְהָשִׁיב אֶת־מַלְכִּי
Why did you belittle us? Wasn't my word the first one (to
suggest) bringing back my king?!

In these cases, the interrogative nature of the clause is determined by the
juxtaposed, marked interrogative clause and the contradictory nature of the
clause itself. Such cases of contrary, unmarked interrogative clauses consistently
function as rhetorical questions.

The final characteristic of Interrogative Discourse to be noted from the
above charts involves the nature of marked rhetorical questions, to which an
answer is neither given or expected, and marked true questions, which seek answers. While the function of these two types of questions differ radically, there
is no consistent morphological or syntactical marker to distinguish either. The
most consistent marker of rhetorical questions is the particle הֲלֹא, which marks a
clause as rhetorical in the majority of cases. An unusual example of this is from
a discourse from the Court Narrative, in which Jonadab asks Amnon about his
heartsickness. Joanadab's questions function as a semi-hortatory enticement to
share information; the הֲלֹא clause here functions as a rhetorical question, causing the speech to border on Hortatory Discourse, rather than simple Interrogative
Discourse:

13.04.365 מַדּוּעַ אַתָּה כָּכָה דַּל בֶּן־הַמֶּלֶךְ בַּבֹּקֶר בַּבֹּקֶר
13.04.366 הֲלוֹא תַּגִּיד לִי
Why are you, O prince, so weak every morning?
Won't you tell me?

In all cases the rhetorical or true nature of a question is entirely dependent upon the narrative context, not upon the verbal or clausal form or the interrogative particle or adverb employed.

Concluding Comments

This study has investigated the role and function that the nine verbal forms (*QATAL, WeQATAL, YIQTOL, WeYIQTOL, WAYYIQTOL*, participles, Imperatives, Cohortatives, and Jussives) and two clausal types (verbless and incomplete) play within biblical Hebrew prose narrative. It has been shown that within the narrative portion of Hebrew prose, *WAYYIQTOL* clauses form the backbone of the story line and all divergent verbal and clausal forms either organize and structure the story line backbone into major narrative blocks, or provide one of two types of off-line commentary. In general, information given by the divergent verbal and clausal types is organized into "inner-paragraph comments," which refer to things or actions directly related to the story line of the paragraph in which they occur, or "extra-paragraph comments," which provide information further removed from the larger narrative story line of the surrounding paragraphs. By means of these four syntactically marked structuring elements (narrative backbone, paragraph blocks, extra- and inner-paragraph commentary), all Hebrew narrative prose is organized and through this organization the various shades and levels of meaning unfold.

In direct discourse, this study has shown that the various verbal and clausal types appear in regular and limited combinations, depending upon the purpose and function of the speech in which they appear. Each of four basic functions of speech, Narrative Discourse, Predictive Discourse, Expository Discourse, and Hortatory Discourse, has its own specific and finite set, or constellation, of possible verbal and/or clausal types that make it up. A fifth function of speech, Interrogative Discourse, is defined by the use of interrogative particles and adverbs, rather than a set of verbal or clausal constellations. In Interrogative Discourse, nonetheless, the use of verbal and clausal types is a consistent marker of the tense of the clauses. Throughout Hebrew prose, therefore, the various verbal and clausal combinations organize and delimit the multitude of hermeneutical possibilities that lie before the interpreter of biblical stories.

All interpretations of biblical narratives are based upon how one reads the text. All readings, furthermore, are based upon a knowledge of the grammar and syntax of the language read. Without a firm grasp of the grammar and syntax of the language, therefore, all readings are faulty, all interpretations are weak, and all understandings and views based upon them are uncertain. Armed with an understanding of how the grammar and syntax of clauses in biblical Hebrew organize and define the narrative and direct discourse of the biblical material, the reader may more fully appreciate the wonderful complexity of the world that the Hebrew Bible portrays. This study has attempted to provide a thorough study of some of the contextual functions of the verbal and verbless clauses that comprise biblical Hebrew narrative. It is hoped that it may furnish a rough framework by means of which those further readings, interpretations, and understandings could be more firmly secured.

Bibliography

Abu-Ghazaleh, Ilham Nayef. "Theme and Function of the Verb in Palestinian Arabic Narrative Discourse." Ph.D. diss., University of Florida, 1983.

Ackroyd, Peter R. "The Succession Narrative (so-called)." *Interpretation* 35 (1981): 383-96.

Alter, Robert. *The Art of Biblical Narrative.* New York: Basic Books, 1981.

Andersen, Francis I. *The Hebrew Verbless Clause in the Pentateuch.* JBLMS 14. Nashville: Abingdon, 1970.

_____. *The Sentence in Biblical Hebrew.* The Hague: Mouton, 1974.

_____. Review of Mats Eskhult, *Studies in Verbal Aspect and Narrative Technique in Biblical Hebrew Prose. Biblica* 72 (1991): 575-80.

Aro, Jussi. "Parallels to the Akkadian Stative in West Semitic Languages." In *Studies in Honor of Benno Landsberger on His Seventy-fifth Birthday, April 21, 1965,* 407-15. Edited by H. Güterbock and T. Jacobsen. Chicago: University of Chicago Press, 1965.

Bar-Efrat, S. "Some Observations on the Analysis of Structure in Biblical Narrative." Vetus Testamentum 30 (1980): 154-73.

Bartelt, H. G. "Mode and Aspect Transfer in Navajo and Western Apache English Narrative Technique." *International Review of Applied Linguistics in Language Teaching* 21 (1983): 105-24.

Barth, J. "Das semitische Perfect im Assyrischen." *Zeitschrift für Assyriologie* 2 (1887): 375-86.

Bauer, H. "Die Tempora im Semitischen." *Beiträge zur Assyriologie und semitischen Sprachwissenschaft* 8 (1910): 1-53.

Bauer, H., and P. Leander. *Historische Grammatik der hebräischen Sprache des Alten Testaments.* Halle: Niemeyer, 1922.

Bayley, Cornelius. *An Entrance into the Sacred Language Containing the Necessary Rules of Hebrew Grammar in English.* London: n.p., 1782.

Bergen, Robert D., ed. *Biblical Hebrew and Discourse Linguistics.* Dallas: Summer Institute of Linguistics, 1994.

Bergsträsser, G. *Hebräische Grammatik.* Vol. 2. Leipzig: J. C. Hinrichs, 1929.

Berlin, Adele. *Poetics and Interpretations of Biblical Narrative.* Bible and Literature Series 9. Sheffield: Almond, 1983.

Blenkinsopp, Joseph. "Theme and Motif in the Succession History (2 Sam. XI 2ff) and the Yahwist Corpus." In *Volume du Congrès, Genève, 1965,* 44-57. VTSupp 15. Leiden: Brill, 1966.

_____. *The Pentateuch: An Introduction to the First Five Books of the Bible.* New York: Doubleday, 1992.

Bloomfield, Leonard. *Language.* New York: Henry Holt, 1933.

Bodine, Walter R. "Linguistics and Philology in the Study of Ancient Near Eastern Languages." In *Working with No Data: Semitic and Egyptian Studies Presented to Thomas O. Lambdin*, 39-54. Edited by D. M. Golomb. Winona Lake: Eisenbrauns, 1987.

_____. "Discourse Analysis of Biblical Literature: What It Is and What It Offers." In *Discourse Analysis of Biblical Literature*, 1-18. Edited by Walter R. Bodine. Atlanta: Scholars, 1995.

Brockelmann, C. *Grundriss der vergleichenden Grammatik der semitischen Sprachen*. Berlin: Reuter & Reichard, 1913.

_____. "Die 'Tempora' des Semitischen." *Zeitschrift für Phonetik* 5 (1951): 133-54.

_____. *Hebräische Syntax*. Neukirchen: Neukirchener, 1956.

Brown, F., S. R. Driver, and C. A. Briggs. *A Hebrew and English Lexicon of the Old Testament*. Oxford: Clarendon, 1907.

Brown, M. L. "'Is It Not?' or 'Indeed!': HL in Northwest Semitic." *Maarav* 4 (1987): 201-19.

Brueggemann, Walter. *Genesis*. Atlanta: John Knox, 1982.

Buccellati, Giorgio. "An Interpretation of the Akkadian Stative as a Nominal Sentence." *Journal of Near Eastern Studies* 27 (1968): 1-12.

_____. "The State of the 'Stative'." In *Fucus: A Semitic/Afrasian Gathering in Remembrance of Albert Ehrman*, 153-89. Edited by Y. L. Arbeitman. CILT 58. New York: Benjamins, 1988.

Budde, Karl. *Die Bücher Samuel*. Tübingen: J. C. B. Mohr, 1902.

_____. "Ellä Toledoth." *Zeitschrift fur die alttestamentliche Wissenschaft* 34 (1914): 241-53.

_____. "Noch einmal 'Ellä Toledoth'." *Zeitschrift fur die alttestament-liche Wissenschaft* 36 (1916): 1-7.

Burney, C. F. *Notes on the Hebrew Text of the Books of Kings*. Oxford: Clarendon, 1903.

Caspari, W. "Literarische Art und historischer Wert von 2 Sam. 15–20." *Theologische Studien und Kritiken* 82 (1909): 317-48.

Childs, Brevard S. *Introduction to the Old Testament as Scripture*. Philadelphia: Fortress, 1979.

Coats, George W. *From Canaan to Egypt: Structural and Theological Context for the Joseph Story*. CBQMS 4. Washington, D.C.: The Catholic Biblical Association of America, 1976.

_____. "The Joseph Story and Ancient Wisdom: A Reappraisal." *Catholic Biblical Quarterly* 35 (1973): 285-97.

_____. "Parable, Fable and Anecdote: Storytelling in the Succession Narrative." *Interpretation* 35 (1981): 368-82.

_____. *Genesis with an Introduction to Narrative Literature*. FOTL 1. Grand Rapids: Eerdmans, 1983.

Collins, C. J. "The *WAYYIQTOL* as 'Pluperfect': When and Why." *Tyndale Bulletin* 46.1 (1995): 117-40.

Conroy, C. *Absalom! Absalom! Narrative and Language in 2 Samuel 13–20.* Analecta Biblica 81. Rome: Pontifical Biblical Institute, 1978.

Dawson, David A. *Text-Linguistics and Biblical Hebrew.* Sheffield: Sheffield Academic, 1994.

Davidson, A. B. *Introductory Hebrew Grammar: Syntax,* 3d ed. Vol. 2. Edinburgh: T. & T. Clark, 1901.

Davidson, Robert. *Genesis 12–50.* Cambridge Bible Commentary. New York: Cambridge University Press, 1979.

Dillmann, A. *Genesis: Critically and Exegetically Expounded.* Vol. 2. Edinburgh: T. & T. Clark, 1897.

Driver, G. R. *Problems of the Hebrew Verbal System.* Edinburgh: T. & T. Clark, 1936.

Driver, Samuel R. *A Treatise on the Use of the Tenses in Hebrew and Some Other Syntactical Questions.* 2d ed. (3d ed., 1892.) Oxford: Clarendon, 1881.

_____. *Notes on the Hebrew Text and the Topography of the Books of Samuel.* 2d ed. Oxford: Clarendon, 1960.

Eissfeldt, Otto. *Hexateuch-Synopse.* Leipzig: J. C. Hinrichs, 1922.

_____. *Die Quellen des Richterbuches.* Leipzig: J. C. Hinrichs, 1925.

_____. "Toledoth." *Texte und Untersuchungen* 77 (1961): 1-8.

Endo, Yoshinobu. *The Verbal System of Classical Hebrew in the Joseph Story: An Approach from Discourse Analysis.* Studia Semitica Neerlandica 32. Assen: Van Gorcum, 1996.

Eskhult, Mats. *Studies in Verbal Aspect and Narrative Technique in Biblical Hebrew Prose.* SSU 12. Uppsala: Uppsala University Press, 1990.

Evan-Shoshan, A., ed. *A New Concordance of the Old Testament.* Jerusalem: Kiryat Sepher, 1983.

Ewald, G. H. A. von. *Kritische Grammatik der hebräischen Sprache.* Leipzig: J. C. Hinrichs, 1827.

_____. *Ausführliches Lehrbuch der hebräischen Sprache des alten Bundes.* Leipzig: J. C. Hinrichs, 1870.

_____. *The Syntax of the Hebrew Language.* Translated by J. Kennedy. Edinburgh: T. & T. Clark, 1879.

Fensham, F. C. "The Use of the Suffix Conjugation and the Prefix Conjugation in a Few Old Poems." *Journal of Near Eastern Studies* 6 (1978): 9-18.

Flanagan, J. W. "Court History or Succession Narrative? A Study of 2 Samuel 9–20 and 1 Kings 1–2." *Journal of Biblical Literature* 91 (1972): 172-81.

Forbes, A. D. "Syntactic Sequences in the Hebrew Bible." In *Perspectives on Language and Text: Essays and Poems in Honor of Francis I. Andersen,* 59-70. Edited by E. W. Conrad and E. G. Newing. Winona Lake: Eisenbrauns, 1987.

Forshey, Harold. "Court Narrative (2 Samuel 9–1 Kings 2)." *Anchor Bible Dictionary,* 1:1172-79. Edited by David Noel Freedman. New York: Doubleday, 1992.

Gell, Philip. *Observations on the Idiom of the Hebrew Language, Respecting the Powers Peculiar to the Different Tenses.* 2d ed. London: Richard Watts, 1821.

Goldin, Judah. "The Youngest Son or Where does Genesis 38 Belong." *Journal of Biblical Literature* 96 (1977): 27-44.

Gottwald, Norman K. *The Hebrew Bible—A Socio-Literary Introduction.* Philadelphia: Fortress, 1985.

Greenstein, Edward. "On the Prefixed Preterite in Biblical Hebrew." *Hebrew Studies* 29 (1988): 7-17.

Gressmann, Hugo. *Die älteste Geschichtsschreibung und Prophetie Israels.* 2d ed. Göttingen: Vanderhoeck & Ruprecht, 1921.

_____. "Ursprung und Entwicklung der Joseph-Sage." *Forschungen zur Religion und Literatur des Alten und Neuen Testaments* 36 (1923): 1-55.

Grimes, J. E. *The Thread of Discourse.* The Hague: Mouton, 1975.

Gropp, Douglas M. "Progress and Cohesion in Biblical Hebrew Narrative: The Function of kĕ/bĕ + the Infinitive Construct." In *Discourse Analysis of Biblical Literature,* 183-212. Edited by Walter R. Bodine. Atlanta: Scholars, 1995.

Gross, Walter. *Verbform und Funktion:* wayyiqtol *für die Gegenwart?* St. Ottilien: EOS, 1976.

Gunkel, Hermann. "Die Komposition der Joseph-Geschichten." *Zeitschrift der deutschen morgenländischen Gesellschaft* 76 (1922): 55-71.

_____. *The Legends of Genesis: The Biblical Saga and History.* New York: Schocken, 1964.

_____. *The Stories of Genesis.* Edited by William R. Scott. Vallejo, CA: BIBAL, 1994.

Gunn, David M. *The Story of King David.* JSOTSup 6. Sheffield: Sheffield Academic, 1978.

Harris, Zellig. "Discourse Analysis." *Language* 28 (1952): 1-30.

Held, Moshe. "Rhetorical Questions in Ugaritic and Biblical Hebrew." *Eretz-Israel* 9 (1969): 71-79.

Hertzberg, H. W. *1 & 2 Samuel.* Philadelphia: Westminster, 1964.

Hillers, Delbert. "Some Performative Utterances in the Bible." In *Pomegranates and Golden Bells: Studies in Biblical, Jewish, and Near Eastern Ritual, Law, and Literature in Honor of Jacob Milgrom,* 757-69. Edited by David P. Wright, David Noel Freedman, and Avi Hurwitz. Winona Lake: Eisenbrauns, 1995.

Holzinger, H. *Genesis.* Freiburg: J. C. B. Mohr, 1898.

Hopper, P. J. "Aspect and Foregrounding in Discourse." In *Discourse and Syntax.* Edited by T. Givón. SS 12. New York: Academic, 1979.

Huehnergard, John. "'Stative,' Predicative Form, Pseudo-Verb." *Journal of Near Eastern Studies* 46 (1987): 215-32.

_____. "The Early Hebrew Prefix-Conjugations." *Hebrew Studies* 29 (1988): 19-23.

Hughes, J. A. "Another Look at the Hebrew Tenses." *Journal of Near Eastern Studies* 29 (1970): 12-24.

Humphreys, W. Lee. *Joseph and His Family*. Studies on Personalities of the Old Testament. Columbia, SC: University of South Carolina Press, 1988.

Isaksson, Bo. *Studies in the Language of Qoheleth: With Special Emphasis on the Verbal System*. SSU 10. Uppsala: Uppsala University Press, 1987.

Jackson, J. J. "David's Throne: Patterns in the Succession Story." *Canadian Journal of Theology* 11 (1965): 183-95.

Jakobson, R. "On Linguistic Aspects of Translation." In *On Translation*, 232-39. Edited by R. A. Brower. Cambridge: Harvard University Press, 1959.

_____. *Russian and Slavic Grammar: Studies, 1931-1981*. Edited by L. R. Waugh and M. Halle. Berlin: Mouton, 1984.

Janssens, G. "The Present-Imperfect in Semitic." *Bibliotheca Orientalis* 29 (1972): 3-7.

Johnson, Bo. *Hebräisches Perfekt und Imperfekt mit vorangehendem wᵉ*. Lund: CWK Gleerup, 1979.

Joüon, P. *Grammaire de l'hébreu biblique*. Rome: Pontifical Biblical Institute, 1923.

_____. *A Grammar of Biblical Hebrew*. Translated and revised by T. Muraoka. Rome: Pontifical Biblical Institute, 1991.

Kautzsch, E. *Gesenius' Hebrew Grammar*. Translated and revised by A. E. Cowley. Oxford: Clarendon, 1910.

Keil, Carl F. *Genesis und Exodus*. Basel: Brunnen, 1983.

Kienast, Burkhart. "Der sogenannte 'Stativ' des Akkadischen." *Zeitschrift der deutschen morgenländischen Gesellschaft* Supplementband 4 (1980): 84-86.

Koehler, L. and W. Baumgartner. *Hebräisches und aramäisches Lexikon zum Alten Testament*. Leiden: E. J. Brill, 1974.

Kogut, S. "On the Meaning and Syntactical Status of *hinneh* in Biblical Hebrew." *Scripta Hierosolymitana* 31 (1986): 133-54.

Korchin, Paul Dmytro. *Markedness and Semitic Morphology*. Ph.D. diss., Harvard University, 2001.

Kouwenberg, N. J. C. "Nouns as Verbs: The Verbal Nature of the Akkadian Stative." *Orientalia* 69 (2000): 21-71.

Kraus, F. R. *Nominalsätze in Altbabylonische Briefen und der Stativ*. Amsterdam: Noordhollandsche Uitgevers Maatschappij, 1984.

Kurylowicz, J. "Verbal Aspect in Semitic." *Orientalia* 42 (1973): 114-20.

Kustár, Péter. *Aspekt im Hebräischen*. Basel: Reinhardt, 1972.

Lambdin, T. O. *Introduction to Biblical Hebrew*. New York: Charles Scribner's Sons, 1971.

_____. Review of Bo Johnson, *Hebräisches Perfekt und Imperfekt mit vorangehendem wᵉ*. *Catholic Biblical Quarterly* 42 (1980): 388-89.

Langlamet, F. "Pour ou contre Salomon? La Rédaction prosalomonienne de I Rois." *Revue Biblique* 83 (1976): 321-79, 481-529.

Longacre, Robert E. "The Discourse Structure of the Flood Narrative." *Journal of the American Academy of Religion* 47, Suppl. B (1979): 89-133.

_____. *The Grammar of Discourse*. New York: Plenum, 1983.

_____. "Who Sold Joseph into Egypt?" In *Interpretation and History: Essays in Honour of Allan A. MacRae*, 75-92. Edited by R. L. Harris, S.-H. Quek and J. R. Vannoy. Singapore: Christian Life, 1986.

_____. *Joseph–A Story of Divine Providence: A Text Theoretical and Textlinguistic Analysis of Genesis 37 and 39–48*. Winona Lake: Eisenbrauns, 1989.

_____. "Discourse Perspective on the Hebrew Verb: Affirmation and Restatement." In *Linguistics and Biblical Hebrew*, 177-89. Edited by Walter R. Bodine. Winona Lake: Eisenbrauns, 1992.

_____. "*Weqatal* Forms in Biblical Hebrew Prose." In *Biblical Hebrew and Discourse Linguistics*, 50-98. Edited by Robert D. Bergen. Winona Lake: Eisenbrauns, 1994.

Lowery, Kirk E. "The Theoretical Foundations of Hebrew Discourse Grammar." In *Discourse Analysis of Biblical Literature*, 103-30. Edited by Walter R. Bodine. Atlanta: Scholars, 1990.

Lyons, J. *Introduction to Theoretical Linguistics*. Cambridge: Cambridge University Press, 1968.

Merwe, C. H. J. van der. "Discourse Linguistics and Biblical Hebrew Grammar." In *Biblical Hebrew and Discourse Linguistics*, 13-49. Edited by Robert D. Bergen. Winona Lake: Eisenbrauns, 1994.

McCarter, P. Kyle, Jr. "Plots, True or False." *Interpretation* 35 (1981): 355-67.

_____. *II Samuel*. AB 8. Garden City: Doubleday, 1984.

McCarthy, D. J. "The Uses of *wᵉhinneh* in Biblical Hebrew." *Biblica* 61 (1980): 330-42.

McFall, Leslie. The Enigma of the Hebrew Verbal System: Solutions from Ewald to the Present Day. Sheffield: Almond, 1982.

Meyer, Werner. *Untersuchungen zur Formensprache der babylonischen "Gebets-beschwörungen."* Studia Pohl: Series Maior 5. Rome: Pontifical Biblical Institute, 1976.

Michel, Diethelm. *Tempora und Satzstellung in den Psalmen*. Bonn: Bouvier, 1960.

Miller, Cynthia. "Discourse Functions of Quotative Frames in Biblical Hebrew Narrative." In *Discourse Analysis of Biblical Literature*, 155-182. Edited by Walter R. Bodine. Atlanta: Scholars, 1995.

Mitchell, H. G. T. *Final Constructions of Biblical Hebrew*. Leipzig: J. C. Hinrichs, 1879.

_____. "The Omission of the Interrogative Particle." In *Old Testament and Semitic Studies in Memory of William Rainey Harper*. Edited by Robert Francis Harper, Francis Brown, and George Foot Moore. Chicago: University of Chicago Press, 1908.

Moberly. R. W. L. *Genesis 12-50*. Old Testament Guides. Sheffield: Sheffield Academic, 1992.

Moran, William L. "A Syntactical Study of the Dialect of Byblos as Reflected in the Amarna Tablets." Ph.D. diss., The Johns Hopkins University, 1950.

_____. "Early Canaanite *yaqtula*." *Orientalia* 29 (1960): 1-19.

_____. "The Hebrew Language in Its Northwest Semitic Background." In *The Bible and the Ancient Near East: Essays in Honor of William Foxwell Albright*, 54-66. Edited by G. E. Wright. Garden City: Doubleday, 1961.

_____. *Amarna Studies: Collected Writings*. Edited by John Huehnergard and Shlomo Isre'el. Winona Lake: Eisenbrauns, 2003.

Niccacci, Alviero. *Sintassi del verbo ebraico nella prosa biblica classica*. Jerusalem: Franciscan Printing, 1986.

_____. "Basic Principles of the Biblical Hebrew Verbal System in Prose." *Studium Biblicum Franciscanum Analecta* 38 (1988): 7-16.

_____. *The Syntax of the Verb in Classical Hebrew Prose*. JSOTSupp 86. Translated by W. G. E. Watson. Sheffield: Sheffield Academic, 1990.

_____. "On the Hebrew Verbal System," and "Analysis of Biblical Narrative." In *Biblical Hebrew and Discourse Linguistics*, 117-37, 175-98. Edited by Robert D. Bergen. Winona Lake: Eisenbrauns, 1994.

Pardee, Dennis and Robert M. Whiting. "Aspects of Epistolary Verbal Usage in Ugaritic and Akkadian." *Bulletin of the School of Oriental and African Studies* 50 (1987): 1-31.

Rabinowitz, I. "'*az* Followed by Imperfect Verb-Form in Preterite Contexts: A Redactional Device in Biblical Hebrew." *Vetus Testamentum* 34 (1984): 53-62.

Rad, Gerhard von. *Old Testament Theology*. Vol. 1. New York: Harper & Row, 1962.

_____. "The Joseph Narrative and Ancient Wisdom." In *The Problem of the Hexateuch and Other Essays*, 292-300. Translated by E. W. Trueman Dicken, New York: McGraw-Hill, 1966.

_____. *Genesis: A Commentary*. London: SCM, 1972.

Rainey, Anson F. "Reflections of the Suffix Conjugation in West Semitized Amarna Tablets." *Ugarit-Forschungen* 5 (1973): 235-62.

_____. "Morphology and the Prefix-Tenses of West Semitized El Amarna Tablets." *Ugarit-Forschungen* 7 (1975): 395-426.

_____. "The Ancient Hebrew Prefix Conjugation in the Light of Amarnah Canaanite." *Hebrew Studies* 27 (1986): 4-19.

_____. "Further Remarks on the Hebrew Verbal System." *Hebrew Studies* 29 (1988): 35-42.

_____. "The Prefix Conjugation Patterns of Early Northwest Semitic." In *Lingering over Words: Studies in Ancient Near Eastern Literature in Honor of William L. Moran*. Edited by T. Abusch, J. Huehnergard and P. Steinkeller. HSS 37. Atlanta: Scholars, 1990.

Regt, Lenart J. de. "Functions and Implications of Rhetorical Questions in the Book of Job." In *Biblical Hebrew and Discourse Linguistics*, 361-73. Edited by Robert D. Bergen. Dallas: Summer Institute of Linguistics, 1994.

Revell, E. J. "First Person Imperfect Forms with *Waw* Consecutive." *Vetus Testamentum* 38 (1988): 419-26.

Richter, Wolfgang. *Grundlagen einer althebräischen Grammatik.* St. Ottilien: EOS, 1978-1980.

Rost, Leonhard. *Die Überlieferung von der Thronnachfolge Davids.* BWANT 42. Stuttgart: Kohlhammer, 1926.

_____. *The Succession to the Throne of David.* Translated by Michael D. Rutter and David M. Gunn. Sheffield: Sheffield Academic, 1982.

Rowton, M. B. "The Use of the Permansive in Classic Babylonian." *Journal of Near Eastern Studies* 21 (1962): 233-303.

Rundgren, Frithiof. *Das althebräische Verbum: Abriss der Aspektlehre.* Stockholm: Almqvist & Wiksell, 1961.

Ruppert, Lothar. *Die Josephserzählung der Genesis: Ein Beitrag zur Theologie der Pentateuchquellen.* Munich: Kösel, 1965.

Sacon, K. K. "A Study of the Literary Structure of 'The Succession Narrative'." In *Studies in the Period of David and Solomon and Other Essays,* 27-57. Edited by T. Ishida. Winona Lake: Eisenbrauns, 1982.

Scharbert, J. "Der Sinn der Toledot-Formel in der Priesterschrift." In *Wort-Gebot-Glaube. Walther Eichrodt zum 80. Geburtstag,* 45-56. Zurich: Theologische Verlag, 1970.

Schneider, W. *Grammatik des biblischen Hebräisch.* Munich: Claudius, 1974

Seebass, Horst. *Geschichtliche Zeit und theonome Tradition in der Joseph-Erzählung.* Gütersloh: Gerd Mohn, 1978.

Skinner, John. *A Critical and Exegetical Commentary on Genesis.* ICC 1. New York: Charles Scribner's Sons, 1910.

Smith, Mark S. *The Origins and Development of the Waw-Consecutive: Northwest Semitic Evidence from Ugarit and Qumran.* HSS 39. Atlanta: Scholars, 1991.

Speiser, E. A. *Genesis: Introduction, Translation, and Notes.* AB 1. Garden City: Doubleday, 1964.

Spurrel, G. J. *Notes on the Book of Genesis.* Oxford: Clarendon, 1896.

Sternberg, Meir. *The Poetics of Biblical Narrative: Ideological Literature and the Drama of Reading.* Bloomington: Indiana University Press, 1987.

Steuernagel, C. *Lehrbuch der Einleitung in das Alte Testament.* Tübingen: J. C. Mohr, 1912.

Talstra, Eep. "Text Grammar and Hebrew Bible II: Syntax and Semantics." *Bibliotheca Orientalis* 39 (1982): 26-38.

Tengström, S. *Die Toledotformel und die literarische Struktur der priesterlichen Erweiterungsschicht im Pentateuch.* Lund: Gleerup, 1981.

Thompson, T. L. *The Origin Tradition of Ancient Israel.* Sheffield: Sheffield Academic, 1987.

Thogmartin, Clyde. "Tense, Aspect, and Context in French Narrative." *The French Review* 57 (1984): 344-49.

Veijola, T. "Salomo—der erstgeborene Bathsebas." In *Congress Volume, 1978,* 230-50. VTSupp 30. Leiden: Brill, 1979.

Walker, Dean A. *The Semitic Negative: With Special Reference to the Negative in Hebrew.* Chicago: University of Chicago Press, 1896.

Waltke, Bruce K. and M. O'Connor. *An Introduction to Biblical Hebrew Syntax.* Winona Lake: Eisenbrauns, 1990.

Watts, J. Wash. *A Survey of Syntax in the Hebrew Old Testament.* Grand Rapids: Eerdmans, 1964.

Weippert, Helga. "Die 'deuteronomischen' Beurteilungen der Könige von Israel und Juda und das Problem der Redaktion der Königsbücher." *Biblica* 53 (1972): 301-39.

Wellhausen, J. *Die Composition des Hexateuchs und der historischen Bücher des Alten Testaments.* Berlin: Walter de Gruyter, 1876-77 (reprint, 1963).

Weimar, P. "Die Toledot-Formel in der priesterschriftlichen Geschichtsdarstellung." *Biblische Zeitschrift* 18 (1974): 65-93.

Westermann, Claus. *Genesis: An Introduction.* Minneapolis: Fortress, 1992.

White, Hugh C. *Narration and Discourse in the Book of Genesis.* New York: Cambridge University Press, 1991.

Williams, Ronald J. *Hebrew Syntax: An Outline,* 2d ed. Toronto: University of Toronto Press, 1976.

Wilson, Robert R. *Genealogy and History in the Biblical World.* New Haven: Yale University Press, 1977.

Wolff, Hans Walter. *Joel and Amos.* Philadelphia: Fortress, 1977.

Würthwein, E. *Die Erzählung von der Thronfolge Davids—theologische oder politische Geschichtsschribung?* Theologische Studien 115. Zurich: Theologische Verlag, 1974.

Zevit, Ziony. "Talking Funny in Biblical Henglish and Solving a Problem of the Yaqtúl Past Tense." *Hebrew Studies* 29 (1988): 25-33.

Zuber, Beat. *Das Tempussystem des biblischen Hebräisch: Eine Untersuchung am Text.* BZAW 164. Berlin: Walter de Gruyter, 1986.

Index of Scholars